THE RIVIERA, EXPOSED

A volume in the series

Histories and Cultures of Tourism
Edited by Eric G. E. Zuelow

A list of titles in this series is available at cornellpress.cornell.edu.

THE RIVIERA, EXPOSED

AN ECOHISTORY OF POSTWAR TOURISM AND NORTH AFRICAN LABOR

STEPHEN L. HARP

FOREWORD BY
ERIC G. E. ZUELOW

CORNELL UNIVERSITY PRESS
Ithaca and London

First published 2022 by Cornell University Press

Library of Congress Cataloging-in-Publication Data

Names: Harp, Stephen L., author.
Title: The Riviera, exposed : an ecohistory of postwar tourism and North African labor / Stephen L. Harp.
Description: Ithaca [New York] : Cornell University Press, 2022. | Series: Histories and cultures of tourism | Includes bibliographical references and index.
Identifiers: LCCN 2021036794 (print) | LCCN 2021036795 (ebook) | ISBN 9781501763014 (hardcover) | ISBN 9781501763021 (pdf) | ISBN 9781501763038 (epub)
Subjects: LCSH: Tourism—France—Riviera—History—20th century. | Tourism—Environmental aspects—France—Riviera. | Foreign workers, African—France—Riviera—History—20th century. | North Africans—France—Riviera—Social conditions—20th century. | Riviera (France)—History—20th century.
Classification: LCC DC608.9 .H37 2022 (print) | LCC DC608.9 (ebook) | DDC 910.9449/4—dc23
LC record available at https://lccn.loc.gov/2021036794
LC ebook record available at https://lccn.loc.gov/2021036795

In memory of Larry Gotshall and Lloyd Bansen

CONTENTS

FOREWORD

The majority of tourists planning adventures do not spend a great deal of time thinking about the environmental history of the places they intend to visit. They don't pore over the landscape, trying to imagine what it looked like before developers got to work. If they wish to ski, they don't dream about the ecological impact of alpine resorts; they fantasize about the thrill of carving turns in fresh powder. Tropical beachgoers are more apt to consider a mai tai than an absent mangrove. And, most relevant here, visitors to the promenade des Anglais in Nice, France, almost certainly fail to wonder why it looks as it does. Too bad. It's quite a story.

Things probably aren't much different relative to labor. Tourists tip the cleaner. They give unthinking thanks for assistance at the desk. They're grateful for directions to the best authentic local food. They may even admire a particularly entertaining tour guide. But beyond this, do they think deeply about the lived experience of the service staff or those who built the hotel? Do they scratch the surface to recognize racial and class imbalances, exploitation, inexcusable mistreatment? Rarely.

As tourists, we are not meant to peel back the curtain, to explore how things look backstage.[1] We admire what is built for us and our gaze goes uninterrogated.[2] Authenticity is often found in the practice rather than in an aura inscribed by age or the tediously real.[3] Even when experiencing history is the goal and we endeavor to visit the place where *it* happened, we tend to think more about what we *think* the reality was, rather than what it *actually* was.[4] What matters is how we feel about something, not what those who were involved in constructing our experience confronted when doing so.

Tourism might be built on escape from the everyday, giving tourists an opportunity to leave behind the unpleasant realities of environmental destruction and social inequality,[5] but historians are meant to be made of sterner stuff. We must look beyond the veneers in an effort to find the rotten teeth underneath. And yet, when it comes to tourism history, we have tended to shy away. We ask questions about where our aesthetic sensibilities came from, how the construction of tourism shaped identities, what governments had in mind when they made tourism a policy objective, and what it was like to be a tourist in a given time or place. Yet, while Valene L. Smith's *Hosts and Guests: The Anthropology of Tourism* (1977) might have been among the first serious scholarly studies of tourism, there is little labor history of the industry. Although race is at the heart of tourism, it is only recently that scholars took notice.[6] Even as the environment is central to the tourist experience, environmental histories of tourism and the tourism industry are only now a growing part of the literature.

The problem is that most of us imagine our subjects can be easily compartmentalized, failing to notice that tourism is part of a much larger ecosystem. It shapes the land and is shaped by it. It has implications for the flora and fauna that are themselves part of the touristic landscape. It creates hierarchies of labor, reshapes the land, alters life for host communities, and has environmental implications ranging from the local to the global. Among the largest industries on the planet, tourism has a much larger footprint than we fully realize. To understand it, we need to think systemically and ecologically.

In this book, Stephen L. Harp offers a fascinating study of many aspects of the Mediterranean tourism ecosystem about which we previously knew little. In doing so, he causes us to think deeply. He makes us see tourism through new lenses. Here, we find interconnections between regional and national governments, the environment and environmental processes, colonial legacies and racism, labor practices, and touristic wants and desires. It pushes readers to think differently about the Côte d'Azur and, by extension, virtually every other tourist location.

In the aftermath of World War II, it was increasingly obvious that tourism was vital to the success of postwar Europe. Although historians frequently list bodies such as the Organisation for European Economic Cooperation and the European Coal and Steel Community as the institutions that led the way to European integration, this status might more aptly be attributed to the International Union of Official Travel Organisations, founded at a meeting in London in 1946, or to the European Travel Commission that grew from it in 1948 and oversaw a European advertising program as well as transnational efforts to secure easier passage across borders by easing restrictions. The United States certainly supported this push; they made tourism the third pillar of the European Recovery Program. Supporting leisure travel mattered. It was a dollar earner at a time when American currency was badly needed. Tourists spent on entry fees, meals, hotels, transportation, and souvenirs, while requiring little in the way of raw materials. As the Cold War took shape, tourism promised to promote greater international understanding. Optimistic advocates imagined it might even facilitate peace.[7]

Tourists did demand infrastructure, however: hotels, restaurants, airports, train stations, beaches, roads, and sites to visit—not to mention clean water (for drinking, swimming, bathing, etc.), efficient sewerage, effective trash disposal, and other backstage services we do not tend to think about. France was particularly keen to invest, and it is here that Harp's narrative begins.

The Riviera had attracted visitors for some time before World War II— elites who enjoyed the culture of grand hotels during stays of several weeks to six months—but postwar tourists were different. They wanted to enjoy the beach, dine in different restaurants (rather than staying in the hotel), and stick around for only a few days. Places such as Nice needed more beds, waste management that could handle a rapidly growing population, and easy access by air and road while managing noise, safety, and aesthetics. It was even necessary to provide large, sandy beaches when they did not already exist. Making the Riviera suitable for tourists was no small task.

Such a large effort demanded a substantial and affordable labor force. Much of it arrived from the other side of the Mediterranean: North African colonial subjects keen to work for cash that they could send to their families. Scant attention was paid to their welfare. There were no benefits, assistance with accommodations, or even adequate sanitation facilities. Landlords frequently refused to rent apartments to Maghrebian workers on racist grounds, while at the same time the reality of gentrification and rising rents priced them out of the market. Workers were forced to build their own shantytowns, best referred to as *bidonvilles*, a term with imperialist implications because it created an inherent contrast between "French superiority, medical advances, and cleanliness" and "backwardness, disease, and dirt." These communities were quickly deemed dangerous, unhygienic, and unsightly by residents and city governments alike. Politicians, the press, and many residents accused the workers of supporting Algerian nationalist organizations seeking to end French colonial rule, while at the same time declaring them to be oversexed and violent. Workers who simply wanted to support their families found themselves facing physical and verbal attacks, political pressure, and job insecurity. The mayor of Nice, Jacques Médecin, made his treatment of North Africans a political virtue, declaring that if he had not acted to keep them out of Vieux Nice, "the people of Nice would have been afraid to set foot on certain streets."[8]

The places that tourists would visit, that politicians and developers sought to create, and that a largely North African workforce labored away to construct had myriad implications. Beyond rising rents and an influx of short-term visitors came increasing traffic and noise—especially from the growing airport. It was so bad that walls shook. Children and their parents found it difficult to sleep. Some even experienced debilitating noise-related illnesses, not to mention infertility.

The impact was not limited to people; the seaside itself was utterly recast. For many visitors, it was the blue skies, warm weather, and azure-colored sea that lured them to the Riviera. They wanted wide, clean, sandy beaches. For Nice, this posed a problem. During the nineteenth century, right into the interwar years, tourists had wanted to ramble along the seashore on the promenade des Anglais. It started as a small walkway and was then widened to allow for pedestrians and carriages. In 1930 the city extended it fifteen meters over what had been beach. Not only did this reduce the size of the beach immediately, but the promenade altered the way that winter storms battered the shore. Unaltered, the waves would build up the strand. Now, they further reduced its size. Indeed, erosion was so much a problem that the waves threatened to eat up the promenade itself. Authorities started to dump fill, as much as 10,000 metric tons of it a year, which the ocean just as quickly started to wash away.

The city attempted various mitigation efforts. In the early 1950s Nice constructed groynes, little walls extending into the sea designed to block erosion. It did not work. By the 1960s it seemed that the only solution was more fill, available as a consequence of other construction projects that had altered the flow of two area rivers. More dump trucks, more fill. Winter storms washed it away. The simple reality was that the land dropped off too quickly into deep water at Nice. There was no easy resolution, only to dump lots of construction waste.

It was not necessarily clean fill, but at least bulldozers made spreading it around efficient. As a consequence, when developers struggled to provide adequate beach, their efforts had an impact on the environment. Bits of metal and wood started to show up in fishing nets. Perhaps it did not matter as the fish weren't keen on the changes and had apparently gone elsewhere.

Scientists found that the construction of groynes altered the ocean floor with profound implications. Marinas, buildings, and beaches introduced pollutants that were not friendly to the flora and fauna. Swimmers might find areas protected by jetties to be good for swimming, but the water was stagnant and anything but good for biodiversity.

It did not end there. The beaches themselves were petri dishes, polluted by waste and chemicals in the water, not to mention by tourists and their pets. As the area's population increased, dealing with wastewater emerged as a growing challenge. The arrival of flush toilets in the nineteenth century shot night soil into nearby waterways. Cities such as Cannes pumped their sewage into the sea, assuring that neither tourist nor local "now wanted to spend significant time in the water and on the beach during the summer months." Human and animal waste, as well as attendant germs, were not conducive to happy beachgoing. So authorities beefed up sewerage, directing outflows farther and farther out to sea. At the same time, they disinfected the beaches nightly with scented solutions to cover up unpleasant odors. In the early 1970s, municipal staff sprayed 600 liters of disinfectant twice a week across six kilometers of beach, at a cost of 650,000 francs.[9] Of course, it ended up in the sea, killing fish.

Every action had a variety of reactions. Getting tourists to the Riviera demanded expanding the airport. Limited space meant building into the Mediterranean, which impacted flora and fauna, while it also altered the interaction of land and sea. The larger airport meant more flights and greater noise. The deafening sound made people sick. And, always, the expanding building projects demanded more workers, which generated more shanty-towns and increased tensions. One thing leads to another.

Harp's narrative covers all of this and more. It takes us through the construction of hotels and into the bidonvilles of those who built them. It recounts the challenge of providing enough potable water in the face of ever-expanding demand. It takes us into the sewers tasked with removing the unspeakable. It follows the construction of roadways and airports, while recounting the relentless struggle against the ocean. The connections that he makes leave the reader incapable of seeing tourist destinations in the same way as before. Once the curtain is pulled back, the area behind the stage made visible, we are left wondering about what else we've missed when engaging in a bit of leisured recreation. Everything seems that much more complicated.

All of this is for the good. It is the connections that Harp makes (that we all need to make), this uncovering of a complicated ecology, that makes this narrative so intellectually stimulating. Harp's elegant prose and expert story-telling make it a difficult book to put down.

Even if nothing else seems simple after poring over these pages, it should be abundantly clear that we cannot stop our studies of tourism history with policy makers or tourists; we need to follow up on the implications of development. We must trace how the decision to construct a site for tourism shapes the lived experience of the people who inhabited the place before-hand and of the workers who dutifully arrived to provide the labor. We need to look deeply at how altering a beachfront, building an airport, erecting a roadway, or expanding a sewerage system irreparably alters the land and the creatures that inhabit it.

It isn't that we need, or should expect, easy binaries in which development is bad and some sort of mythical nature is good, but rather that we must understand interconnectedness. We need to see how local meets global, how guests impact hosts, and how human actions alter environments. Harp's is a brilliant exposition on interconnections that will undoubtedly inspire others, writing about all parts of the world, to detail similar tourism ecosystems.

ERIC G. E. ZUELOW

ACKNOWLEDGMENTS

The National Endowment for the Humanities (NEH) and the University of Akron made this work possible. During the tenure of an NEH University Teachers Fellowship for an earlier book, I began research on this one. In 2014 an NEH summer seminar on North African francophone cultures helped me reconsider French history, including the history of tourism, from Algerian, Moroccan, and Tunisian perspectives. I thank not only organizers Nabil Boudraa and Joseph Krause but also James Le Sueur, other presenters, and other participants for helping me think more broadly. Over the years, the University of Akron faculty research committee has generously funded research trips to France, and regular sabbatical leaves allowed me time to research and write without interruption.

Without archivists and librarians, there would be no scholarship worth writing or reading. I am indebted to archivists and staff members at the Archives départementales des Alpes-Maritimes who graciously accommodated my incessant requests for materials and permissions. I am particularly grateful to Thierry Chevalier, Véronique Pedini, Laurence Sciarri, and Simonetta Tombaccini-Villefranque. In practical terms, Georges Thaon of the prefecture was a lifesaver; he invited me to start taking the *fonctionnaires'* express bus to the center of town, shaving thirty minutes off my commute (the service had been a concession to unions when the prefecture and archives moved to western Nice; I had absolutely no right to be on it). I also need to thank archivists and librarians at the Archives départementales du Var, the Archives municipales d'Antibes, the Archives municipales de Cannes, the Archives municipales d'Hyères-les-Palmiers, the Archives municipales de Nice (especially Marion Duvigneau), the Archives municipales de Saint-Tropez, the Bibliothèque patrimoniale Roman Gary, the Bibliothèque nationale de France, the Université Côte d'Azur bibliothèques, the Centre des archives contemporaines of the Archives nationales, and the Service historique de la défense at Vincennes. At the University of Akron libraries, Don Appleby remains my hero; early in the COVID-19 pandemic, Don pulled books and delivered them to my house.

Alongside archivists and librarians, my favorite people are editors. They take manuscripts and magically transform them into books. At Cornell University Press, I have been very fortunate to have Emily Andrew, Bethany Wasik, and Eric G. E. Zuelow as my acquisition and series editors. Eric deserves special thanks for his encouragement and collegiality over many years. As the book went into production, Allegra Martschenko helped with images, while Mary Kate Murphy and Lori Rider modeled excellence in copyediting. Mike Bechthold did a fabulous job with the maps. The Press's three (originally anonymous) readers, Joseph Bohling, Catherine Dunlop, and Michael Miller, provided particularly substantive and helpful suggestions. Shelley Baranowski, Sarah Curtis, Andy Denning, and Greg Wilson also read the manuscript, pushing me to make this a better book.

At annual meetings of the Society for French Historical Studies and the Western Society for French History, comments from Annette Becker, Brett Bowles, J. P. Daughton, Sarah Griswold, Dustin Harris, Amelia Lyons, John Merriman, Tyler Stovall, and Steve Zdatny did much to improve this work. At the "Le Sens et les Sens" colloquium at Indiana University, Zac Hagins organized a session that helped me consider visual aspects of tourism I had ignored. At Eric Jennings's French seminar at the University of Toronto, Eric, Jonathan Dewald, Will Fysh, and Suzanne Langlois offered excellent feedback on parts of a couple of chapters; many thanks to Eric for such a terrific weekend.

Some of my larger intellectual debts are long-standing. I will never manage to repay Janina Traxler for teaching me good French, or Carl Caldwell and David Waas for showing me how to think and write like a historian. My dissertation advisor, Bill Cohen, was a specialist in the French empire and French cities. He would have had much to say about this book. So too would my friend Ellen Furlough, who encouraged me many years ago to take on the project.

Close to home, my colleagues Connie Bouchard, Rose Eichler, Michael Graham, Kevin Kern, Janet Klein, Mike Levin, Gina Martino, Martha Santos, Martin Wainwright, and Greg Wilson have provided consistent moral support, often in very tough times. Friends Paul Alles, George Boudreau, John Edgerton, Susan Gallagher, Lesley Gordon, Carol Harrison, John Merriman, Kira Thurman, and the whole Avon, Curtis, Levin, and Thareau families deserve thanks for their encouragement. My students have offered inspiration; what they often consider "bad" questions, that is, those most outside the box, helped me reconsider what I and other experts had learned to take for granted.

My moms Sara and Barb, dads Greg and Larry, parents-in-law Ann and Lloyd, sisters Bridget and Chris, brothers Keith and Eric, and especially daughters Sarah and Marie collectively created the wonderfully supportive bubble in which I live. Without my wife Lisa, I don't believe I would be able to write anything at all. Words cannot express the depth of my gratitude for the richness of our life together. Tusind tak; jeg elsker dig!

One last personal note—this book considers what I call the other Riviera, the one hidden under layers of tourist mythology. As you read these pages replete with shantytowns, sewers, and pollution, don't think that I too have not been under the spell of the mythical Riviera, a place I first saw in 1985. Near the end of my junior year abroad in Strasbourg, my parents and sisters came to visit. My stepdad announced on arrival that he "sure as hell" had no intention of driving. My mom will not drive a stick shift. So I took the wheel (I have always had amazingly trusting parents), and we proceeded to do a very American-style road trip to southern France. Mom opened the map on her lap, and away we went. We didn't have an itinerary, hadn't reserved rooms, hadn't even investigated our options. We happily just discovered stuff. For Bridget that was crêpes with Nutella in Saint-Raphaël. For my part, I will never forget rounding a bend on the autoroute and first seeing the stunning azure blues of the sky and the sea of the Riviera. I almost wrecked the car; I did not, but poor Chris got sick, and that rental car would never be the same. Nor can I forget the first time I swam in the Mediterranean. Warmer than the Atlantic and the Pacific, saltier and thus terrific for floating and swimming, the Mediterranean along the Riviera features mountains in one direction and that beautiful azure blue sea and sky in the other. I get why visitors and popular historians have long called the Riviera paradise. Yet there is much more to the story.

STEPHEN L. HARP

ACKNOWLEDGMENTS

NOTE ON PRIVACY

In my effort to comply with French law regarding privacy, the names of private individuals in archival files appear here as initials in both the text and the notes. However, those names already published in the French press, as well as names of officials, appear in full.

Abbreviations

BTP	Bâtiment/travaux publics
CCIN	Chambre de commerce et de l'industrie de Nice Côte d'Azur
CERBOM	Centre d'études et de recherches de biologie et d'océanographie médicale
CFDT	Confédération française démocratique du travail
CGT	Confédération générale du travail
CIESM	Commission internationale pour l'exploration scientifique de la Méditerranée
CIPALM	Cellule d'intervention contre la pollution dans les Alpes-Maritimes
CNRS	Centre national de la recherche scientifique
CRS	Compagnies républicaines de sécurité
CSHP	Conseil superieur d'hygiène publique
EDF	Électricité de France
ESCOTA	Société de l'autoroute Estérel-Côte d'Azur
FEN	Fédération de l'éducation nationale
FIANE	Fonds interministériels pour la nature et l'environnement
FIAT	Fonds interministériels pour l'aménagement du territoire
FLN	Front de libération nationale
HLM	habitation à loyer modéré
INSEE	Institut national de la statistique et des études économiques
NATO	North Atlantic Treaty Organization
PCF	Parti communiste français
PLM	Chemins de fer de Paris à Lyon et à la Méditerranée
PS	Parti socialiste
PSU	Parti socialiste unifié
RG	Renseignements généraux
RN	Route Nationale
SLEE	Société lyonnaise des eaux et de l'électricité
SNCF	Société nationale des chemins de fer français

SONACOTRA   Société nationale de construction de logements pour les travailleurs

SONACOTRAL Société nationale de construction de logement pour les travailleurs algériens

SONEXA   Société niçoise pour l'extension de l'aéroport

TCF   Touring club de France

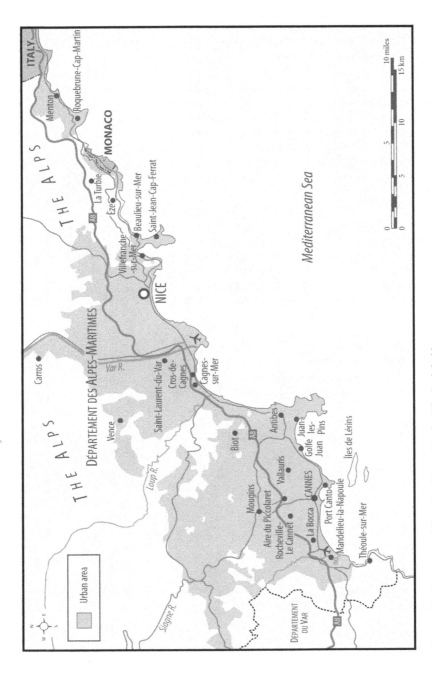

Map 1. The department of Alpes-Maritimes. Map by Mike Bechthold.

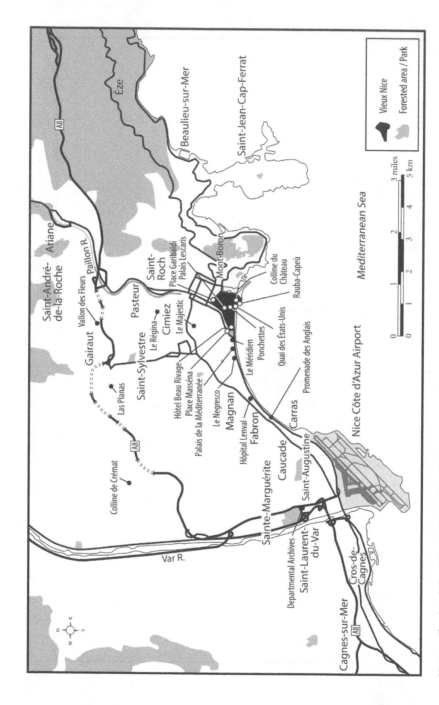

MAP 2. The city of Nice. Map by Mike Bechthold.

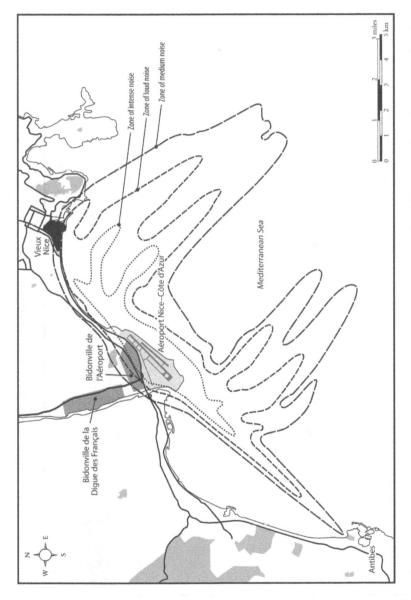

Zone of intense noise

Zone of loud noise

Zone of medium noise

Vieux Nice

Mediterranean Sea

Aéroport Nice–Côte d'Azur

Bidonville de l'Aéroport

Bidonville de la Digue des Français

Antibes

N
W · E
S

0   1   2   3 miles
0   1   2   3   4   5 km

MAP 3. The major bidonvilles in western Nice, the airport, and sound waves produced by aircraft in the early 1970s. Map by Mike Bechthold.

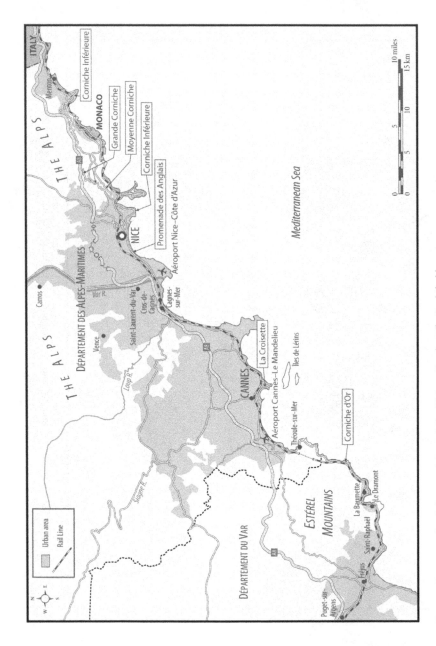

MAP 4. Transportation links to and through the Riviera. Map by Mike Bechthold.

THE RIVIERA, EXPOSED

Introduction
The Hidden Riviera

On prominent display in the Musée Chagall in Nice is a letter dated 23 April 1963 from Mayor Jean Médecin to Minister of Cultural Affairs André Malraux. In it, Médecin writes that the municipal council has authorized the acquisition of 11,650 square meters on the site named the Domaine d'Olivetto for the construction of the museum. Médecin notes that Chagall had seen the site and approved. Médecin was thus fulfilling Malraux's condition that the municipality needed to donate the land for the new museum. The Musée Chagall opened to much fanfare on Easter weekend in 1973.

The display is as interesting for what it does not say. As early as 1959, North African laborers, employed on numerous nearby construction sites and public works projects, moved into the dilapidated villa at the Domaine d'Olivetto. Shanties and moving containers soon appeared. By 1966, up to 450 single North African men lived on the property. Well-heeled neighbors complained vehemently to the police, the mayor, the prefect, and the vice president of the National Assembly, creating a written record as police, city, and departmental officials investigated.[1]

Once the city expropriated the land, authorities destroyed the shantytown. Most residents accepted their plight and left before the destruction on 12 August 1967. After a final check to ensure that shanties were empty and animal control removed a few cats, firefighters set the shantytown on fire at 6:45 a.m.[2] By noon, the controlled fire had destroyed everything. The city secured the area so that the men could not return and rebuild. Instead, the men moved on to other squats and shantytowns. Jean Chatelain, director of French museums, warmly thanked the prefect of Alpes-Maritimes for his "rapid and efficacious action in evacuating the shantytown."[3]

The Domaine d'Olivetto was typical of the remaking of the French Riviera. Postwar mass tourism transformed the area after World War II. Villas gave way to large luxury apartment blocks. The grand old hotels so much like palaces they were known in French as *palaces* were cut up into apartments, particularly if they were farther from the sea like the Hôtel Majestic, not far from Olivetto. A new airport, new roads including a new *autoroute*, new potable water lines, new sewers, newly expanded beaches, and massive new marinas all appeared in the thirty years after the war as part of dedicated efforts to increase tourism. The physical environment of the Riviera changed markedly.

The display at the Chagall museum highlights the irony of the transformation of the postwar Riviera. Tourism is above all visible; physical "sites" are also tourist "sights." Tourists visit museums, admire the mountains, and watch the sea. On the Riviera, guidebooks encourage them to appreciate the art of Chagall, Matisse, and Picasso in local museums while on vacation, or to imagine the glorious past of the rich and famous who frolicked there. What remains invisible is the infrastructure of tourism, its environmental impact, and the people whose work made that tourism possible. The technologies embedded in roads, airports, hotels, water lines, sewers, beaches, and marinas all require human intervention that tourists do not always see—and are encouraged not to see.[4] Significantly, North African workers did much of the actual work to rebuild the French Riviera for mass tourism, but they too were supposed to be invisible. They left no visible trace in the Chagall museum and rare traces in histories of the Riviera.

The Touristic Imaginary of the French Riviera

This book deepens the history of tourism, exposing the hidden Riviera so often obscured in tourist literature and popular histories alike. A thriving subfield in modern history, the history of tourism has usually been from the viewpoint of the tourists themselves. Of course, we have superb sources for that perspective. Tourists have been educated and literate, publishing individual accounts of their trips. They have used guidebooks, thus creating a market for abundant printed sources about what tourists were supposed to see and how they were supposed to see it. Diaries, letters, and memoirs often mention travels. Advocates for tourism produced tourist propaganda, as well as government paper trails, as they worked with officials. Not surprisingly, we know a great deal about tourists and tourism.[5] But what do we know about the social and environmental impacts of that tourism? For that, we need to dig deeper.

To do so, this work considers the most visited provincial destination in the world's most visited country. After World War II as before, the French Riviera, centered in the department of Alpes-Maritimes, welcomed more tourists than any French region outside Paris. Unlike Paris, which is not only the capital but has also had considerable industrial activity surrounding it, the Riviera has depended mostly on tourism as its economic lifeline. The area has the largest number of hotel rooms in the country after Paris. The airport in Nice has long been the busiest in France after those of Île-de-France. International and French visitors have flocked to the Riviera for the sunshine, the maritime air, and the temperate climate.[6]

The French Riviera is thus not a typical tourist destination so much as an emblematic one, a veritable petri dish for considering the impact of modern travel. To be sure, there is no dearth of histories of the Riviera. Every year or two a new book appears, usually in English, featuring the lives, the villas, and the parties of the rich and famous. The works are popular, designed for a mass audience. They rehash who lived where, who slept with whom, who got drunk, and who fought whom. Such histories tap into long-standing myths of the Riviera, invariably framed as a tourist paradise. In them, we repeatedly learn how foreign tourists "invented" and "made" the Riviera, a notion so widespread it figures in book titles.[7] The books repeat the accounts by famous writers, artists, musicians, and wealthy who first wintered on the coast before World War I and summered there in the interwar years. Americans inevitably appear as modern agents of change. Gerald and Sara Murphy get much of the credit for launching the summer tourist season. In their Villa America and on the Garoupe beach in Antibes, the Murphys hosted F. Scott and Zelda Fitzgerald, Ernest Hemingway, John Dos Passos, Picasso, and so many others. Inevitably, like tourist guidebooks, such histories are from the travelers' perspective. In important respects, the books read like detailed, gossipy travelogues. Thus, much of the existing historical work about the Riviera could have us believe that if we understand what tourists thought about their travels, what Rosalind Williams called the "dream worlds" of consumption, we know all we need to know.[8]

While the Riviera continues to exist as a largely mythical place for the rich in the Anglo-American imagination, in France it is also imagined much as Florida is in the United States and Canada, a place for sun, tans, beaches, and retirees. The Riviera became a summer destination for middle- and lower-middle-class French vacationers after World War II. In fact, the majority of tourists on the Riviera after 1945 were French, and they were on average much less wealthy than the North Americans. While visitors continued to come by train, they arrived increasingly by car, taking the Route Nationale (RN) 7, the north-south corridor to the Mediterranean as legendary in postwar France as Route 66 was in twentieth-century America. Immortalized by popular singer Charles Trenet's "Route Nationale 7," there is today so much nostalgia about the *route des vacances* (vacation road) that French classic car owners recreate for fun the once (in)famous traffic jams, replete with travel trailers, notably at Lapalisse in the department of Allier.[9]

Both French and American films further kept a mythical Riviera in the public eye on both sides of the Atlantic.[10] Alfred Hitchcock's *To Catch a Thief* (1955), starring Grace Kelly and Cary Grant, not only featured stunning views of the Riviera but also seemed to embody it; the place was a little risqué, a little illegal, with a lot of wealth, sun, and skin. Shot at the Victorine studio in Nice and on the beach south of Saint-Tropez, Roger Vadim's *Et Dieu créa la femme* (1956) launched his wife Brigitte Bardot's stardom and served as a veritable advertisement for local beaches. A host of other lesser-known French and American films, including *La baie des Anges, Bonjour tristesse, Du côté de la côte, Monte Carlo Story, La nuit américaine, On the Riviera,* and *La piscine,* similarly worked to keep the Riviera in the public view in the postwar years.

But the French Riviera was a real place, a fact largely obscured by the array of myths about it. It changed dramatically in the thirty years after World War II. This work examines the infrastructure of tourism during that period. As such, it reads less like the usual voyeuristic jaunt considering the lives of the rich and famous and more like an excavation, as the massive construction and public works projects on the Riviera are its subject. Along the way, we can focus on the people living and working there, particularly the North African workers who not only did much of the literal rebuilding of the Riviera but also suffered in that process. In a sense, the book offers answers to questions Geneviève Massard-Guilbaud has posed: "Development: why, for the benefit of whom, and at what price?"[11]

In short, I want to place the environment and labor at the center of the history of tourism. Whereas much of the focus of earlier work in the history of tourism has been on sights and landscapes, we also need to pay attention to what Thomas Andrews calls workscapes.[12] Who did the work, sweating as they transformed tourist infrastructure? Where did they work and sleep? What was the impact on the environment as they used dump trucks, bulldozers, and cranes to remake sites, creating sights for tourists? What might we learn about tourism by shadowing the workers who excavated for new hotels and second homes, dug trenches for water lines and sewers, dumped sand and stone to make beaches, poured cement to create marinas, asphalted runways over what had been the sea, and laid the foundations for new roads?

The Period: Thirty Glorious Years

The Riviera, Exposed concentrates on the thirty years after World War II, widely known as the *trente glorieuses*, or "Thirty Glorious Years." The expression comes from Jean Fourastié's work of that title, published in 1979. His tone is triumphant; himself an important figure in French government planning, Fourastié maintained that the *trente glorieuses* of 1946 to 1975 were an invisible revolution that unalterably changed France, as opposed to the three glorious days of 1830, a violent, if limited, revolution that changed much less.[13] Few dispute the metamorphosis of France during the years 1946–75. However, in the past few years, historians have questioned just how glorious those years were. Most notably, Céline Pessis, Sezin Topçu, and Christophe Bonneuil refer to a "counter-history" or "other history" of the *trente glorieuses*. Their coedited volume, *Une autre histoire des "trente glorieuses"* (Another History of the "Thirty Glorious Years") even goes so far as to use the expressions *les trente ravageuses* (the thirty ravaging years) and *les trente pollueuses* (the thirty polluting years) when considering the environmental impact of that period.[14] Recent work on Central Europe similarly problematizes the "economic miracle" of postwar West Germany (and implicitly Western Europe, North America, and ultimately the world); historically cheap fossil fuels made the 1960s a transitional period when the atmospheric concentration of carbon dioxide began its rapid ascent, triggering global warming.[15]

Moreover, mass tourism in pursuit of the Mediterranean sun during the *trente glorieuses* was, like construction and automobile manufacture, definitely part of what we might also call the *trente coloniales et post-coloniales* (thirty colonial and postcolonial years).[16] North African migrant laborers did a lot of the work. Except for brief mentions of "immigrants" and "foreigners," Fourastié ignores the contributions of colonial and postcolonial migrant laborers in a book on demography and economic expansion.[17] Fourastié happily describes the growth of tertiary work; *cadres* (an important term in postwar France, more or less translatable as "managers") and bureaucrats replaced peasants.[18] That presumably glorious change characterized the lives of many French and many tourists, but it was not the experience of migrant workers, who usually continued to do manual labor. In short, historians are beginning to understand that if the Thirty Glorious

Years constituted a revolution, then that revolution was *made* to seem invisible as the environmental and social effects, including the impact on North African laborers, were written out of the history by Fourastié and others.

The Place

Today the French Riviera is arguably the best-known riviera in the world. The term, meaning "seashore" in Italian, described the Ligurian coast from La Spezia to the Var River (at the western end of Nice today, near the airport). Early British travelers passed through the region on their grand tours from Paris to Florence, Rome, and Venice, appreciating the Riviera and ushering the term into English. By the mid-nineteenth century, "riviera" referred both to the Italian seashore, which included Nice until annexed by France in 1860, and the French seashore west of the Var River. In English and French, the term French Riviera today describes the coastline of the department of Alpes-Maritimes, just to the west of the Italian border. In French, the Riviera is distinct from the Côte d'Azur, which generally includes not only the historic Riviera along the coastline of the Alpes-Maritimes but also the coastline of the department of the Var (and sometimes even that of Bouches-du-Rhône) to the west.[19] Aspiring poet and National Assembly deputy Stéphane Liégeard coined the term Côte d'Azur in 1887, adapting the expression Côte d'Or from the famous grape-growing slope in Liégeard's native Burgundy.[20] The Côte d'Azur literally means "Azure coast," a description that makes perfect sense to anyone who has rounded a mountain and seen the wide expanse of azure blues of the sky and the sea.

Here the focus is on the historic Riviera, concentrated along the coastline of the department of Alpes-Maritimes. Alpes-Maritimes, one of those geographic descriptions dating from the French revolutionary naming of departments, is where the Alps meet the Mediterranean Sea. The Alps help protect the narrow seacoast from the mistral, the powerful wind that blows from north to south in France, blasting much of the rest of the French Mediterranean coast.[21] The result is a microclimate supporting subtropical plants and citrus trees. There are normally 2,694 hours of sunshine, with three hundred days of sunny weather per annum, and an average temperature of 16 degrees Celsius (71 Fahrenheit). The coastline of Alpes-Maritimes, from the Italian border at Menton in the east to the departmental border with the department of the Var in the west, is only 40 kilometers as the crow flies, 120 kilometers once one takes into account the craggy coastline.[22]

The French Riviera is distinct from the backcountry of Provence.[23] After World War II, the Riviera came to constitute a largely uninterrupted urbanized area stretching the length of the coastline of Alpes-Maritimes. The destination of international and French tourists, the Riviera relied on newcomers to maintain and increase its population. While structures hug the hillsides all along the coastline, most people lived on the narrow stretches of plain between the mountains and the sea, in and around Nice, Cannes, and Antibes.

Defined as the coastline of the department of Alpes-Maritimes, the Riviera consisted of sixteen different towns with about 800,000 inhabitants in the mid-1970s.[24] Nice, by far the largest urban center on the Riviera, appears often in these pages. Although dominated economically by tourism and construction, Nice nevertheless became the fifth largest city in France, after Paris, Marseille, Lyon, and Toulouse—which all had more diverse economies. Nice had been the fastest-growing city in Europe between 1861 and 1911 and continued to grow rapidly until the 1970s, peaking and stabilizing at just under 350,000 inhabitants. Mayors worked assiduously to diversify the economy, with mixed results. After the war, Nice got a university, managed to lure technology companies, including Texas Instruments, and became a major conference destination for business travel. Mayoral support for art exhibitions and new museums, including the Musée Matisse and the Musée Chagall, sought cultural tourism in an effort to broaden the appeal of the city. As a big city in an important regional tourist destination, Nice is not unlike Miami.[25] As in Florida, migration and immigration were important sources of population growth on the Riviera. By the early 1970s, there were about sixty thousand European residents who had once lived in former French colonies and an additional eighty thousand foreign workers who made their home in Alpes-Maritimes.[26]

While the number of residents increased, the number of tourists kept pace. The postwar population of the Riviera found itself swamped with tourists. In 1960 local officials estimated that more than one million arrived each year. Communities were saturated. Antibes received four times as many tourists as residents, Menton almost four times as many, and Cannes almost three times as many. In the summer months of July and especially August, the population tripled from Menton on the Italian border to Saint-Tropez in the Var.[27]

As a locale, the French Riviera is small enough to allow us to unearth the technologies of touristic development, but large enough to capture the environmental effects that passed beyond the limits of any given city. The Riviera is an ideal place to consider what Karl Marx and now geographers, historians, and urban planners have called urban metabolism, imagining cities as bodies. The Riviera had quite an appetite; like Rabelais's character Gargantua, the area consumed and evacuated considerable quantities. Just as the Riviera swallowed up to a hundred times more water in the late twentieth century than in the mid-nineteenth, expelling much of it as wastewater, it absorbed ever more tourists, who left behind trash and sewage. The Riviera also took in migrant workers who produced the infrastructure for tourists' planes, cars, and yachts, all of which left noise, air, and water pollution in their wake.

A look at the local qualifies the usual generalizations about the centralization of twentieth-century France. Make no mistake: Paris wielded much power. Most revenue came from Paris, hence the need for mayors to serve simultaneously in the National Assembly or the Senate, so that they might bring home the bacon. Such a *cumul des mandats* made perfect sense in a highly centralized state. Nevertheless, even before the move toward administrative decentralization in the 1980s, local interests mattered. Chambers of commerce went so far as to manage airports and seaports in provincial France. On the Riviera, associations of hotel owners were also an important force for policy. Municipalities could expedite or delay public housing projects and road building. Water and sewage projects needed state funding and state engineers of the Ponts et Chaussées oversaw their construction, but municipal governments initiated plans for development. Until the 1970s, even shantytown clearance varied by locality. Obstinate mayors could do much to alter national priorities or slow implementation, as they often had strong political machines that kept them in office for decades.

Digging Deeper

The concentration of so many people on a narrow coastline inevitably transformed the Riviera. Much of the change was redevelopment of an already developed area. After a short description of the status quo before World War II, the first chapter considers how mass tourism influenced both the hotel industry and the resulting housing options for local inhabitants. All of France faced an acute housing shortage after World War II. On the Riviera, which saw comparatively less destruction during the war, the crisis in housing was nonetheless equally dire, due to the arrival of so many tourists whose money worked, in various ways, to make housing unaffordable for many locals. Moreover, in considering the arrival of so many Europeans from the French empire, this first chapter, like the second, suggests the colonial and postcolonial nature of the postwar Riviera.

The second chapter considers squats and shantytowns. While some French families had no option besides squatting in one of the villas or apartments abandoned by owners during the war, most had alternative housing by the end of the 1950s. The situation was worse for the North African workers who had gotten jobs building the new hotels, apartments, and public housing complexes. Many had no option besides squats or shantytowns until the 1970s. This chapter tracks their housing options as well as their work. It highlights a contradiction as the men who built new housing struggled to find lodging. The chapter establishes a backdrop for the other chapters, as North African workers were equally critical in the other construction projects that transformed the postwar Riviera—even though they did not appear in the imagined Riviera of tourist accounts or tourist propaganda, let alone subsequent popular histories.[28]

The book then moves into hydro-history.[29] The third chapter considers water and waste. The postwar years saw an incredible increase in demand for potable water as tourists expected abundant fresh water for washing and flushing while working-class residents struggled to get homes with running water. All of that water had to go somewhere. Sewage systems pumped untreated waste into the sea, having been built when tourists came in winter and rarely entered the water. In the postwar rush, however, not only was there far more water waste, and far more tourists, but those tourists also expected to be able to swim and play in the Mediterranean. Given that sewage went directly into the sea, renovated sewer systems were imperative not only for residents but also for tourism, the economic lifeblood of the area. Water and sewage lines were under constant construction, providing dirty jobs often done by North African laborers. Yet in their own makeshift dwellings, those same men had limited access to potable water and rare access to WCs plumbed into sewers.

Beaches, marinas, and maritime pollution are the subjects of chapter 4. Authorities built, extended, and beautified beachfront promenades. More critical for postwar tourists were beaches. Despite constant efforts to build up and expand beaches, they nevertheless became some of the most crowded in the world. In the process, tourists themselves became a major source of illness and water pollution. At the same time, the market for touristic pleasure craft expanded quickly in the postwar years, causing developers to launch huge projects for marinas, yet another source of water pollution. Here too, North African laborers did much of the work to expand beaches and build marinas, despite obstacles they faced when they attempted to use those beaches themselves.

Chapter 5 describes the founding and frequent expansions of the airport at Nice as the local chamber of commerce worked to keep pace with postwar air travel. The airplane and especially the jet, ultimate symbols of twentieth-century modernity, revolutionized travel to the Riviera. The airport itself caused a complete refashioning of western Nice, even diverting the course of the Var River as the airport expanded out into the Var delta and the Mediterranean Sea. The airport expansions, like changes to the beachfront and the postwar sewer system, killed most of the native flora and fauna along the coast of Nice, alarming biologists. Neighbors and health specialists focused on the effect of jets' noise so close to a densely populated area. North Africans worked to build and rebuild the airport, while many lived in shantytowns just across the street, exposed to the pollution and noise of jet aircraft.

Automobiles are the subject of the final chapter. They brought relatively few tourists to Nice in 1946, and they brought most by 1975. In the process, the promenade des Anglais in Nice and the Croisette in Cannes grew wider and longer in order to accommodate ever more traffic. As tourists arrived by car, concerns about aesthetics forced moves of junkyards and dumps that suddenly seemed like eyesores for tourists' gaze. Noise and air pollution became important concerns for citizens and local governments. To facilitate access to the Riviera, the area received France's first postwar autoroute. Its extension in 1976 along the Var River bed led to the destruction of France's last large shantytown. Here North African workers had made their home for twenty years, as they worked on the airport, the autoroute, and other construction projects in western Nice.

Because the weight of the established history of the Riviera as (a white European) paradise is so heavy, I conclude each chapter by confronting that notion, attempting to render North African workers' experience visible even as it was supposed to be invisible. I am certainly not arguing that they were the only construction workers, the only immigrants, or the only people who suffered during the remaking of the Riviera for mass tourism. They made up about 40 percent of construction workers. They get attention here because, like the environmental impact of mass tourism, they are not yet part of the Anglophone historical narrative of this famous and mythical tourist place—and very marginally part of the French one.[30] Today, it is often assumed that environmental concerns are a middle-class, even wealthy preoccupation. Such a rhetorical formulation is not only an effort to discredit environmental awareness as elitist; it is also historically misleading in obscuring who often does the work and pays the price for the process of environmental change. To reuse a term that accurately describes the effects of ecological degradation near the homes of many US American minorities, North Africans in Alpes-Maritimes experienced a version of environmental racism in the presumed paradise of the Riviera.[31]

CHAPTER 1

Building Hotels and Housing for the Rich and the Rest

In 1930 Jean Vigo's *À Propos de Nice* appeared. It is a low-budget silent documentary. The film is brilliant, as Vigo manages to juxtapose the wealthy tourists who arrived on the Riviera to stroll on the promenade des Anglais, gamble, and dine with the workers who served them, cleaned up after them, and built Carnival floats for them. *À Propos de Nice* begins with an aerial view of the city, and Vigo shows the villas west of the Paillon River, often built and occupied by foreigners in Nice, as well as the huge palace hotels in which many stayed the winter. The visual record of how Nice looked from on high is reason enough to watch the film. Almost none of those villas still exists. Blocks of apartments and high rises now stand in their place. Yet, though just twenty minutes long, *À Propos de Nice* offers more. An anarchist, Vigo challenges us to go beyond the platitudes about this supposed paradise invented by well-off foreign visitors by focusing on workers as well as tourists.[1] Following in the footsteps of Vigo, this chapter explores how changes in tourism influenced housing for both tourists and residents of the Riviera.

After World War II, the arrival of unprecedented numbers of tourists did much to deepen a severe housing crisis on the Riviera, a shortage that took most of the *trente glorieuses* to resolve. Postwar expectations on the part of tourists led to two developments. On the one hand, tourists who wanted to spend some time increasingly rented apartments, avoiding hotels entirely.

On the other hand, tourists who stayed in hotels only did so for a few days. Demand from tourists simultaneously undercut the traditional hotel industry and put considerable price pressure on the housing market. Elsewhere in France, housing for locals and for tourists were normally separate issues. On the Riviera, due to the economic dominance of tourism, they were inseparable. The old palace hotels and grand hotels became apartments for the wealthy, renovated to include new bathrooms for second homeowners accustomed to amenities in their principal residences. Strong demand for these apartments and for new construction pushed up housing prices for everyone else. In a period when the Fourth Republic worked to guarantee French citizens the "right to comfort," interpreted as a right to decent housing with modern conveniences, many locals on the Riviera waited several years for that comfort, in large part because tourists and second homeowners got it first.[2] Even though most postwar tourists came in summer, their numbers and their preferences nevertheless affected the housing market for the rest of the year.

The Summer Season

After World War II, the summer tourist season, concentrated in July and August, definitively replaced the long winter season of the Belle Époque. Although popular histories like to credit Gerald and Sara Murphy or Coco Chanel with that shift, the reality is more complicated. Summertime tanning and swimming were coming into vogue generally in interwar France.[3] Hotels on the Riviera began opening for the summer season in the late 1920s and 1930s. Then in 1936, the Popular Front not only granted French employees two weeks of paid vacation but also subsidized trainloads of tourists to take their first trip to the Mediterranean. After the war, in the midst of the French postwar baby boom, increasing numbers of French salaried employees—though not most workers or even most French in the 1950s— went on vacation in the summer during the school break.[4] Factories and most shops closed for these annual vacations. July and August became the high tourist season across France.[5]

The change had long-term implications for the Riviera. Postwar tourists sought the beach. In Cannes luxury hotels already lined the Croisette and did well in the summer. In Nice some long-established hotels had excellent locations next to the sea; the Hôtel Beau-Rivage, which had hosted Henri Matisse in the 1910s and a drunken F. Scott Fitzgerald in the 1920s, sat on the quai des États-Unis just across from the beach. The Hôtel Ruhl, the Hôtel Negresco, the Palais de la Méditerranée, and a host of lesser-known hotels were on the promenade des Anglais. However, hotels far from the beach suffered, particularly during the Depression. On the Cimiez hill, 3.5 kilometers from the beach, the Hôtel Regina had already become a luxury apartment building in the late 1930s. The Hôtel Majestic, 1.3 kilometers from the beach, also closed before the war and became an upscale apartment house in the late 1940s.

After World War II, hotels had overcapacity in the winter and undercapacity in the summer. About one-half ran permanent deficits after the war, despite the summer crowds. For about 270 days per year, hotels could not cover their costs. But for about ninety days a year, there were too few rooms. In 1951 there were so many tourists in Nice during August that on any given day two to three hundred people could not find rooms, sleeping instead on park benches and the beach. There was so much demand in August 1955 that people were sleeping in bathtubs, cars, and outside, in parks and on the beach. In August 1957 there were twelve thousand hotel rooms with eighteen thousand beds in Nice, and there were no vacancies. In the 1950s and early 1960s, makeshift dormitories appeared in public spaces, a seminary and a convent rented out beds, and a private school even rented benches. The tourist office sent visitors needing rooms as far inland as Digne-les-Bains, 130 kilometers away. The few campgrounds in the region had three times the number of visitors that they were authorized to accept. Henri Tschann, the head of the Syndicat d'initiative, the association charged with promoting tourism in Nice, called the rush of tourists an "asphyxiation" of the region.[6]

The relatively short but intense summer season put pressure on the local tourist industry. How many times would visitors be willing to sleep on benches as alternative destinations emerged? As the sea, sun, and sand displaced the social scene, the Riviera increasingly faced competition from several quarters. Accessibility by train had opened the Riviera to northern Europeans in the nineteenth century when there was no other viable alternative just an overnight train ride from Paris. After the war, air travel changed everything. Nice got a civilian airport after the war, but the flight time from London to Mallorca was only five minutes longer. Costs were lower in Italy and Spain, and Mallorca became an especially popular destination with budget travelers. As British charter companies packaged airfare and hotels, they brought the cost down to half that of a trip to Nice. Since Britons long constituted the most numerous foreigners on the Riviera, the impact was considerable. In the early 1960s Syria, Lebanon, and Turkey were also competing destinations. Meanwhile, Italy, unlike France, used Marshall Plan monies for hotel renovations, giving Italian hotel owners an edge in attracting tourists to new hotels with amenities such as bathrooms.[7] Among national leaders, concern that too many French and other northern Europeans were taking the train or their cars to Spain, bypassing France, led to the massive development of the Languedocian coast.[8] Hotel owners felt the need to adapt as quickly as possible.

Hotels, Old and New

In myriad ways, hotels on the Riviera were ill suited to postwar demand. Postwar tourists did not stay long in hotels. Before World War I, visitors spent several weeks to six months in a single hotel, with the full pension (that is, taking their meals in the hotel dining room). Although the duration was already shorter in the interwar years, it got worse after the war. As the head of the hotel, café, and restaurant employees union explained in 1952, "in the day, tourists arrived from England, Paris, and beyond, with trunks for a stay of several weeks. Today they arrive with a suitcase for two or three days." In the mid-1950s receipts from the *taxe de séjour*, the room tax paid for each night for each visitor, indicated an average stay in Nice of 4.1 days. However, couples often filled out only one form, and Americans often neglected to fill it out at all. The average stay was actually two to three days. The Hôtel Beau Rivage is the sole hotel for which we still have the logs of visitors; they confirm that many tourists stayed only a night or two, balancing out those who stayed a bit longer. By contrast, when Henri Matisse avoided Paris during the last year of World War I, he stayed at the hotel from 25 December 1917 to 4 April 1918.[9]

On the axis from Paris to Rome, French and foreigners saw the Riviera en route to other places. Americans and Britons in particular opted for whirlwind European tours by the mid-1950s, and Paris and Nice were usually on the itinerary, as were Italian and German locales. By 1960, 90 percent of Americans and Britons came on organized tours, which often did eight countries in eight days. For South Americans, the Riviera was a regular stopover between important Catholic sites, notably Lourdes and Rome.[10]

Short stays had serious implications for hotels. Henri Tschann's experience as manager of the Splendid stressed just how thoroughly hotel keeping changed on the Riviera. "If, in the old days, certain hotels that I know could prosper with 600 clients per year who stayed from one to six months, [today] I am obliged to find 17,000 travelers each year. Each day we have to clean 500 sheets and 2,000–3,000 towels. We've already made commitments for next year, and we foresee 225 groups." The scale was enormous. "While just a few years prior, group size consisted of thirty to thirty-five people, now it is often fifty, and sometimes when they come by airplane, one hundred."[11]

The very architecture of the old palace hotels and grand hotels posed a problem for short-term tourists interested in quickly experiencing the city rather than being walled off with other tourists. Upstairs, floors had room for Belle Époque travelers with domestic staff. Large suites faced south, with gorgeous views of the sea. Servants had tiny rooms to the north. Of the 110 rooms of the Hôtel Luxembourg, only eighty could serve as hotel rooms by the 1950s; the others were miniscule servants' quarters. Downstairs, the grand hotels from the Belle Époque separated foreign travelers from the locals, as visitors had comprised an expatriate community closed in on itself. Iron grillwork separated the building from the street. Huge staircases, cathedral-like ceilings in dining rooms, enormous lobbies, and other common spaces took up much square footage. Postwar tourists often avoided them entirely in favor of time alone in their rooms and time outside the hotel.[12]

Postwar visitors took their meals in restaurants, rubbing shoulders with locals in pursuit of regional cuisine. Joseph Mora, vice president of the local Syndicat de l'hôtellerie, insisted in 1956 that tourists were becoming much more individualistic. With the exception of some Britons and French, postwar tourists did not want the full pension (Russians, so numerous among those taking the full pension in the Belle Époque, were rare during the Cold War).[13] Grand hotels carried the considerable expense of the kitchen and dining room without using them to capacity. There were no easy options for owners of the grand old palace hotels. Forcing tourists to eat in the hotel would drive away some customers. Closing the restaurant could hurt business by not having a restaurant, or room service, desired by customers at least some of the time. One frequent solution in new construction was to advertise the establishment as a hotel-restaurant with the dining room near the street entrance. Customers could patronize either the hotel or the restaurant and ignore the other.[14]

Hotel employees felt the pinch as existing hotels adapted to changes after the Second World War. As late as the 1920s, many hotels closed for the summer, but hotel directors sometimes moved employees to their northern hotels, as in the mountains, open for summer months and closed during the winter. Some hotel employees had year-round or nearly year-round employment. The summer openings on the Riviera theoretically promised, in the 1930s, year-round employment on the Riviera itself. However, in practice, the advent of the summer season, especially when combined with many customers' disdain for full pensions in grand hotels, led to unprecedented unemployment for hotel employees. Official unemployment figures in the hotel industry essentially doubled between February 1946 and February 1952, which was a likely undercount as it included only those employees who filed for unemployment benefits. Now hotels closed for the *winter* months. In 1950 even well-known Cannes hotels, such as the Martinez, the Carlton, and the Grand Hôtel, closed during the winter for periods ranging from two to five months. In Nice only the huge hotels, such as the Ruhl and the Splendid (buoyed by visitors to the famed Carnival in Nice), remained open all year. The head of the hotel, café, and restaurant employees' union estimated that there had been fifteen thousand employees working year-round in the hotel sector in Alpes-Maritimes before World War II, already a period of economic depression, but there were only about ten thousand in 1951, and fully 60 percent of those worked fewer than six months during the calendar year 1951. He argued that the situation was even worse than it appeared, as widespread unemployment made it possible for hotel owners to limit wage increases during the inflationary postwar years. Moreover, unemployment hit hotel employees harder than other workers, as many lived on the hotel premises when it was open and ate hotel food without having to pay.[15]

Nice in particular became a less upscale destination than it had been in the early twentieth century, welcoming more French travelers, even if foreigners were better represented here than in France as a whole. In 1958, when about two-thirds of visitors were French, Tschann bemoaned that there was "now an enormous preponderance of French clientele, which is explained by the fact that we have now become essentially a city of budget vacations [for the French]." Despite the rapid increase in the number of tourists to Nice after World War II, they spent less on hotels. To use Tschann's acute awareness of social class, "the clientele in Nice has doubled in the past ten years, but its quality declines more and more." Tschann noted that between 1927 and 1958, the number of luxury hotels declined by 60 percent, while the number of hotels of the lowest category, the equivalent of one-star hotels, grew by 10 percent. Meanwhile, mostly foreigners stayed in the remaining luxury hotels. For every two French people staying in a luxury hotel there were nine foreigners. Foreign visitors were, on average, much better heeled than French ones; in 1961 the average American tourist spent 1,300 francs during a trip to the Riviera while the average French tourist spent only 600.[16]

Hotel owners actively sought American tourists. They were less likely to be the wealthy of the Belle Époque, as the favorable exchange rate made it possible for larger numbers of middle-class Americans to see the Riviera. After World War II, the majority of Americans came in tour groups. The scale was such that a single American travel agency organized one hundred group tours to Nice in 1960. Americans moved so fast that some paid little attention to what they were seeing and where they were. One American visitor asked Tschann, "Now what exactly was the name of the city where we saw the leaning tower of Pisa?"[17]

American tourists demanded amenities, especially bathrooms. Here aging hotels had another problem. In 1958 there were 26,745 hotel rooms in Alpes-Maritimes, but only 8,239 had a bathroom in the room. Eighty percent of luxury (palace) hotels had en suite bathrooms, while 67 percent of four-star hotels did. At the lower levels, 43 percent of three-star hotels did, 20 percent of two-star hotels, and only 3 percent of one-star hotels. In 1963 *L'Espoir* sent their reporter in New York, Léo Sauvage, to ask returning Americans about their stays in France and, by implication, make an argument for the renovation of Riviera hotels. Bathrooms were a problem. The Americans asked why many French hotel owners declined to provide soap, and why there were rooms without showers or bathtubs. When the shower was down the hall, why did they need to pay 3 to 3.5 francs to use it when breakfast only cost 2.5 francs? Lighting was also an issue; "the most unlikely and stupid cost cutting concerned the wattage of electric bulbs. Will we henceforth see American tourists arriving in France carrying, along with their soap, a good [high wattage] electric bulb?"[18] Clearly, American tourists on vacation wished to consume considerable water and electricity by French standards.

New hotels with en suite bathrooms opened. By 1955, 108 had already opened in Alpes-Maritimes, including twenty-six in Nice. They continued to open. However, conversion of old hotels into apartment buildings advanced as quickly as the construction of the new hotels, as old palace hotel suites were more valuable as apartments. The underlying problem was the high cost of land on the Riviera. In 1977 *Nice Matin* again interviewed Tschann, still manager of the Splendid. The newspaper cast him as a model, and his hotel a success story. The hotel had an average occupancy rate of 72 percent. Tschann attributed his success to the fact that his was the first renovated big hotel after World War II. The Splendid was a large, beautiful hotel with modern amenities, giving him the option of establishing a clientele before the competition. Most interesting, however, he admitted that he had sold some of the land next to his hotel for development.[19] Illustrating the underlying problem for all hotels on the postwar Riviera, the property was more valuable for development than for hotel keeping.

The Building Boom

Many other tourists avoided hotels altogether, opting to rent apartments or villas. Although the Riviera witnessed an astounding building boom after

World War II, demand outpaced supply until the 1970s, in large part because tourists and second homeowners pushed up housing prices. The situation was ironic compared to many French regions, as the housing stock along the Riviera had seen comparatively less damage during the war. Most villas remained untouched by warfare itself, though many had been vacant, even abandoned, during the war. Many owners could not travel to their villas or maintain them in absentia. Italian, then German troops occupied some of them, as did squatters. Hotels had housed Jewish refugees, occupying troops, and American soldiers on leave. The situation was nothing like that of Normandy or even northern France generally. On the Riviera, houses, apartments, and hotels were mostly intact. Reconstruction focused not on rebuilding so much as ending an interwar housing shortage that became more acute in the wake of World War II.

However, residential tourists interested in vacation homes, rentals, and eventual retirement homes purchased much of the new construction, exacerbating the housing crunch for working families. After 1950 the state set up loans for builders through the Crédit Foncier, subsidies for new construction, and tax breaks, all in an effort to spur private-sector building. Already in 1952, Alpes-Maritimes ranked twenty-sixth in population but fourth in the amount of government subsidies for new construction, and almost all of that building occurred on the coast. In 1958 authorities approved the construction of 18,362 homes in the department, which had 550,000 inhabitants. By comparison, there were 43,797 authorizations to build in the department of the Seine (Paris), which had five million inhabitants; Alpes-Maritimes had four times the number of authorizations per capita. In the early 1960s, 25 percent of all apartments or houses built in France were in a single department, Alpes-Maritimes, and most of those were on the coast. Real estate agents sold apartments before builders even broke ground. In Nice historic villas with elaborate gardens sat along the promenade des Anglais, seven to ten meters back from the street. Now those properties seemed like a waste of valuable space and were worth far more as building sites. Much of the new construction consisted of luxury apartment blocks near the promenade des Anglais and featured huge windows and patio doors opening out onto balconies with views of the Mediterranean, a modernist style dubbed the *style Côte d'Azur*. In 1976 *Le Figaro* summarized the growth in the department of Alpes-Maritimes of the previous thirty years: "eighty percent of the population is crammed onto ten percent of the territory, that is to say a coastal strip four kilometers wide."[20]

Prices soared. The price of land parcels led the way. At the edge of Nice, at Saint-Sylvestre, land costing 100 francs a square meter in 1954 cost

5,000 francs a square meter in 1962. In the early 1960s land parcels in Nice increased in value by an average of 40 percent per annum. On the Croisette in Cannes in 1939, one square meter of ground cost 100 francs, and in 1965, it cost 200,000 old francs.[21] The cost of new apartments followed. One-bedroom apartments on the promenade des Anglais ran as high as 9 million francs in 1952, when the average worker earned less than 30,000 per month. Rent was also high; with monthly rents ranging from 18,000 for a studio to 50,000 francs for a one- or two-bedroom, working-class families could not afford the new apartments.[22]

After 1945 construction officially displaced the hotel industry as the most important sector of the Riviera economy, though much of the construction was for tourists and part-time residents. In 1965, of eighty thousand workers in Alpes-Maritimes, some thirty-five thousand, or 43 percent, were in construction. By contrast, only 21.3 percent of workers nationally worked in construction. In the department of Bouches-du-Rhône (which includes Marseille), with twice the population of Alpes-Maritimes, there were thirty thousand construction workers. Companies specializing in construction and public works (BTP in French, as in Bâtiment / travaux publics) were the largest employers in Alpes-Maritimes. Alongside the larger firms such as Detragiache, Martinenghi, Nicoletti, Rometti, Triverio, Spada, and Vigna were fifteen hundred smaller companies. Early twentieth-century Italian immigrants had founded many of them. There was so much building and so much demand for workers that the shortage of labor in the building trades slowed down the construction of public housing. In Nice, as the western portion of the city was remade from villas into apartment blocks, the private sector required construction workers, as did various public infrastructure projects. Monaco's building spree made things worse, as salaries there were higher than in France. Between 1950 and 1958, the building boom caused the number of masons and related skilled builders in Alpes-Maritimes to increase from sixteen thousand to twenty-five thousand. There was also much demand for semiskilled and unskilled workers. Italian immigrants filled some of the openings, but Italy too saw considerable postwar construction. North Africans filled most of the remaining positions.[23]

Residential Tourism

In the postwar years, tourism officials on the Riviera increasingly used the expression "residential tourism" to refer to those who bought apartments or villas after vacationing there. Buyers' motivations included the desire to have a principal residence in France while serving in the colonies or living abroad, to have a vacation or second home, to make an investment in a speculative building market, and to buy an eventual retirement home. Many such purchases doubled as rental property, and longer-term tenants also became residential tourists as they lived in apartments or villas rather than stayed in hotels. Of course, while the terminology was new, the practice was not. Foreigners had rented and then purchased villas on the Riviera in the eighteenth and nineteenth centuries. What changed, as pointed out in the pages of *Le Monde*, were their numbers.[24]

In theory, state subsidies for private builders were solely for the construction of apartments that would end up as principal residences. In practice, there was widespread evidence already in 1955 that builders received subsidies to construct principal residences but that the apartments ultimately became second homes and high-priced rentals. In Nice much of the new construction and renovated apartments in former grand hotels were beyond the means of even most middle-class locals. Buyers came from outside. Colonial officials and business people bought pieds-à-terre as investments. Wealthy Parisians and other northern French bought apartments for vacations and retirement. Belgians, Swiss, and Scandinavians did the same. As one builder stated in 1952, "Not one of my clients is an inhabitant of Alpes-Maritimes. They are mostly 'colonials,' civilians and military men, officers, administrators, colonizers [*colons*] coming back from Indochina. A lot of rich Belgians and Swiss, only a few English. One also finds among our clients former tourists, who finding a hotel too expensive, prefer to buy a small apartment here, where they come and stay one or two months a year."[25]

In 1976, in Alpes-Maritimes, fully 30 percent of buyers of land parcels, villas, and apartments were foreign. Although Alpes-Maritimes had more foreign buyers than France in general, the department witnessed the same rapid expansion of second home ownership that seized postwar France generally. On the Riviera, foreign buyers were overwhelmingly from northern Europe and the Middle East, including Lebanon as the civil war began. In some housing developments, 50 percent of buyers were foreign. These were usually second homes. Buyers liked prestigious locations such as the promenade des Anglais, but they also appreciated homes in the hills. There they could have gardens, garages, and swimming pools. Among the buyers who were French, many were buying eventual retirement homes. *Le Figaro* dubbed the region "the land of retirees."[26]

Many of the new apartments were short-term rentals, both legal and illegal. Nice's own tourist brochures vaunted in October 1958 that Nice had more than 1,300 studios, nearly a thousand additional apartments, and one hundred villas available for rent—and these represented only those rented out legally. In 1962 the French national statistical institute, INSEE, found that there were 214,860 dwellings in Alpes-Maritimes, of which 21,140 were vacant and 34,100 secondary residences. It was clear that many of the second homes and officially vacant apartments were secretly off-the-books rentals.[27]

Some apartments were essentially hotel-apartments, Airbnbs *avant la lettre*. More than a few owners were investors, using property managers to turn a profit on their apartments. According to hotel owners, the property managers of furnished apartments were as aggressive as representatives of hotels who approached tourists arriving by train, offering rooms. Approximately 40 percent of all tourists to Nice in the early 1950s stayed in furnished lodgings, from small apartments to villas. In 1956, 80 percent of the requests for accommodation received by the Syndicat d'initiative in Nice were for furnished apartments. Such apartments appealed both to the cost sensitive and those desiring the privacy of a small kitchen. The formula was so popular that several hotels renovated in order to add kitchenettes. For some visitors, the issue was to avoid the cost of hotel and restaurant meals. However, many postwar furnished apartments were quite luxurious, so the interest also appears to have been new expectations of individual and familial privacy. Mario Pacinotti, the general secretary of the Syndicat des loueurs de villas et appartements meublés, the association of owners who rented furnished apartments, noted that the consumption of gas in apartments was quite low, even among those with large families, indicating that they did very little cooking in the apartments. "They are not picnickers [*saucissonneurs*]" trying to save a bit on food. Rather, they get dishes "from *traiteurs* [delis] and eat in restaurants."[28]

Of course, even if rented out during the summer, many apartments remained empty the rest of the year. In 1954 officials estimated that seven thousand dwellings were empty in Nice alone. For workers stuck in horrible living conditions, the reason was clear. As "Monsieur Poudge" from Saint-Laurent-du-Var and "Monsieur R. C." of Cagnes wrote into *Le Patriote*, apartment owners could make more money renting to tourists in the summer than to locals for the entire year.[29] As both men recognized, residential tourism exacerbated the housing shortage, delaying improvements in local living conditions.

Housing Conditions

Across postwar France, there was an acute shortage of decent housing. The underlying problem was that expectations rose while neither the quantity nor the quality of housing could keep pace. In 1954 there were officially fourteen million homes in France. Fully 42 percent had no running water, while 73 percent had no WC in the apartment or house, and 90 percent had neither shower nor bathtub. On paper the Riviera was in considerably better shape. In Nice there were some ninety thousand dwellings, of which 2.5 percent had no running water, 10 percent no WC in the apartment or house, and 66 percent neither bathtub nor shower.[30] In 1955 Nice was first of the fifty-four French cities with more than fifty thousand inhabitants in the availability of "comfort" in housing, meaning amenities such as electricity, gas, hot water heaters, bathtubs, and WCs. Among departments, Alpes-Maritimes was second only to the Seine (Paris). The problem on the Riviera was inequity. Alongside comfortable apartments for the wealthy, there were intensely crowded hovels for the working poor. Despite Alpes-Maritimes's amenities in the aggregate, authorities estimated that there were at least two thousand hovels in Nice alone, mostly concentrated in the historic center, Vieux Nice. Moreover, according to INSEE, in 1962 more than 45 percent of the housing stock in Alpes-Maritimes still dated from before World War I, despite postwar construction.[31]

As elsewhere in France, rent controls dating from World War I discouraged the building of rental units during the interwar years.[32] In Alpes-Maritimes there was already a shortage of affordable housing before World War II, a problem made worse by the war. However, buildings completed after 1 September 1948 were not subject to rent control, hence real estate investors' interest in them. Former commercial buildings, such as hotels converted into apartments before 1948, were not subject to rent control either. In principle, a law of 31 December 1948 changed the situation and forbade the transformation of hotels into apartments. In fact, the owner merely needed to show that the hotel was running a deficit in order to get approval to convert the hotel into an apartment complex.[33] Investors could thus renovate a grand old palace hotel and then charge market rates. In the meantime, owners of existing housing stock had little reason to make upgrades, and they rarely did, further worsening living conditions. State subsidies for new construction were supposed to relieve the situation, but that only worked if the apartments did not end up as second homes rather than primary residences.

Workers were well aware of the gap between their living conditions and those of the buyers of the new apartments. In 1954 *Le Patriote* featured "Marcel K.," who wrote into the paper in order to describe his family's plight. As a mason in Nice, Marcel helped construct the "lodgings of paradise," those apartments featuring large windows and patio doors to balconies overlooking the sea. At the same time, he, his wife, and their four children lived in one room. In the early 1950s, the Saglia firm renovated the Hôtel Majestic at the base of the Cimiez hill in Nice, breaking it up into luxury apartments. Across the street were three basement windows, which opened at the level of tailpipes; there three families with children lived. In another example, Mme. Casagrande lived near the train station in a one-bedroom basement apartment with her husband and three children. Because the collective WC was several meters away, other residents on their way to the WC often "did their business in the basement or on the stairs, which means that most of the time, these (unknown) persons' urine passes into the room where we sleep, and where our children sleep."[34]

In many cases, working-class families lost their housing when owners tore it down in order to build luxury apartment blocks on the same parcels. In 1954 eleven families living in small buildings at 187, promenade des Anglais and 97, avenue de la Californie (they are on the same block, near what is now the Fabron Musée d'Art Naïf bus stop) received notices of eviction effective May 1954. A large apartment complex was to replace their homes. While promised apartments in the new building, residents would need to pay market rent, which was far beyond their means. On the boulevard Gorbella, four separate families squeezed into an old farmhouse without gas, electricity, or running water—until the owner sold the property to a large construction firm from Paris, which built a new apartment building on the site.[35]

The shortage of apartments made working-class people desperate for housing. Many had few options besides furnished rooms, the downscale version of the nicer furnished apartments rented to tourists. In 1966 in Nice, there were 7,869 people living in furnished rooms; 5,031 paid more than in comparable unfurnished apartments. These numbers did not include those living in dumpy hotel rooms or those renting illegally.[36] Many owners preferred to rent off the books so that they could avoid paying tax on rental income. In those cases, tenants had no rental contract, thus none of the normal legal protections. Owners often refused to give receipts for rent paid; as a result, tenants could not protest eviction, as they had no evidence that they were actually tenants.

There were by some estimates twenty thousand empty homes on the Riviera by the late 1950s, at the same time that many working-class people could not afford decent housing. In principle, they could request requisitions of vacant properties. Per the decree of 16 January 1947, French law allowed those without housing to apply for a requisition of others' second homes. The process was not easy. Young couples forming new households were not eligible. Applicants needed to have lost homes due to wartime destruction, be government employees moved to the area, or be heads of large families. After the applicant identified an empty property and did the application, the owner received a recommended letter, inviting him or her to consider the request, and laying out the conditions for an owner's refusal. As "Monsieur B" of Cagnes told *Le Patriote*, "Very few owners have a soul generous enough" to accede to the request, despite the fact that they would receive rent. Moreover, owners were sometimes well connected; as *Le Patriote* pointed out, René Laniel owned a gorgeous villa on Mont-Boron, which remained unoccupied, even as his brother Joseph Laniel, the French prime minister, worked with the abbé Pierre, famous postwar advocate for the homeless, to come up with solutions to France's housing crisis. Equally problematic, if an owner suddenly occupied or rented out the space in the meantime, an applicant needed to find yet another abandoned property and restart the process. In the end,

FIG. 1.1. Featuring steps, the rue du Malonat (1948) was typical of narrow, dark streets of Vieux Nice. There are traditional Niçois shutters on the left, including a middle section, which can be angled for control of the sunshine—even though little sunlight made it to lower floors. Archives Nice Côte d'Azur—Ville de Nice, 1064 W 25 (collection of the photographic service of the city).

most applicants were unsuccessful. Between 1946 and 1951, 5,827 applicants in Nice completed dossiers in order to requisition empty apartments. Of these, 1,272 were successful. In Cannes between 1 January 1956 and 30 April 1957, there were twenty-six requests of which four were granted.[37] Most working-class families remained in overcrowded, run-down apartments like those in Vieux Nice.

The Historic Center: Vieux Nice

Municipalities on the Riviera faced a conundrum long a challenge for tourist destinations. Should they invest in touristic infrastructure, which would increase the number of tourists, revenue, and taxes, so that the city could then spend money on local projects? Or should they fix local problems for the sake of citizens and taxpayers first, risking a decline in revenue by neglecting the tourist infrastructure? In Nice *Le Patriote* vociferously criticized the Médecin administration in the late 1950s for spending so much on the refashioning and extension of the promenade des Anglais, including streetlights the length of it (thus a considerable ongoing expense for electricity), while so many inhabitants lived without potable water, sewage, gas, and electricity in unsafe dwellings. Similarly, local communists questioned money spent on the new fountain in the place Masséna, in order to please tourists, second homeowners, and the well off, while working-class people a few meters away in Vieux Nice suffered poor living conditions.[38] Jean Médecin, whose voters were far more often builders than workers, focused more on tourism than the housing of locals. Like so many powerful French mayors, he held more than one office simultaneously, serving over the years as a deputy in the national assembly, senator, head of the departmental *conseil général*, and in leadership roles in national tourist organizations. His politics were firmly on the right, though anti-Gaullist. Frequently, communists criticized Médecin and other right-wing politicians for supporting wars in Indochina, then Algeria, which wasted precious resources that could have resolved the housing crisis and simultaneously allowed the Riviera to rebuild its tourist infrastructure. As *Le Patriote* claimed in 1954, some 263 apartments could be constructed in France for 640 million francs, the cost of eight hours of war in Indochina. Put another way, "the price of one fifty-ton tank would pay for ten apartments."[39]

Clearing slums in Vieux Nice allowed Jean Médecin and after 1966, his son and successor Jacques Médecin, the opportunity to award contracts to political supporters, foster tourism by gentrifying the city center, and improve housing conditions, albeit by removing working-class families from their neighborhoods. In Nice as in other French cities before late twentieth-century gentrification, the historic city center contained the most dilapidated housing but also the potential to attract tourists to a picturesque setting. On the left bank of the Paillon River, at the foot of the hill of the château, Vieux Nice had thrived in the seventeenth and eighteenth centuries as the site of administration, trade, and elaborate aristocratic and bourgeois homes.[40] In the nineteenth century, expansion was toward the west, on the right bank of the Paillon along the new promenade des Anglais and into the hills overlooking the city and the sea. Like the new arrivals, many well-to-do Niçois moved west of the Paillon, into new villas with gardens. Yet Vieux Nice remained the center of both retail and wholesale food and flower markets, along with varied commercial establishments with specialties often clustered by street, much like Hanoi today; in a nod to the Parisian market les Halles, immortalized by Émile Zola's novel *Le ventre de Paris*, Vieux Nice sometimes had the sobriquet "the belly of Nice."[41] The prefecture was also there.

As in other French city centers, the quality of residential offerings in Vieux Nice stagnated over the course of the eighteenth, nineteenth, and early twentieth centuries, as overcrowding led several families to live in large residences originally designed for one large aristocratic family. When potable water and sewage systems arrived in the late nineteenth and early twentieth centuries, they were concentrated in the new neighborhoods. Most residents in Vieux Nice hauled water from a public fountain. Much of Vieux Nice's infrastructure for water and waste remained little changed since the nineteenth century, despite the fact that approximately twenty-five thousand lived there. It was not unusual for six people to live in two rooms or for apartments to be bereft of any windows in the French city best known for its sunshine. At least half of Vieux Nice consisted of slums. The area had a reputation for its enormous rats. By the early 1960s, the majority of inhabitants were workers or domestic servants. The single new green space in Vieux Nice resulted from the war. Bombardments had destroyed a handful of buildings at the base of the château. The city opened up the space, establishing a basketball court, community room, public WCs and showers, and a covered public washhouse for laundering.[42]

After World War II, the Palais Lascaris—today a much-publicized city museum—symbolized the housing crisis in postwar Nice. The Lascaris had been the representatives of the counts of Savoy in Nice, and they grew rich on maritime trade across the Mediterranean. In the eighteenth century, their baroque-style home featured gorgeous rococo stucco and beautifully detailed woodwork. Since the nineteenth century, numerous families had occupied the palais. Declared a historic site worthy of preservation in 1946, the city of Nice took possession in 1947. At the time, some 268 people lived in the building, cut up into separate small apartments. As reported later by *Nice Matin*, "In the luxurious receiving rooms with high ceilings, two separate floors had been built. The vestibule, conceived to receive the sedan chairs of guests, was occupied by a grocery." In 1954 forty people in fifteen separate families still lived in the home, sharing a single WC also used by musicians of the Société musicale, who practiced in the building. The only apartment with gas belonged to the concierge. The other families lived without running water, electricity, or gas.[43]

Aware of tourists' interest in Vieux Nice, as early as 1941 Jean Médecin had overseen a competition for plans to transform the area that came to naught. In the 1950s Vieux Nice already had a fair number of tourists, and there were halting efforts to increase tourism to the area. The Cathédrale Sainte-Réparate, the Church of Saint-Martin-Saint-Augustin, the Church of le Gesù (also known as the Church of Saint-Jacques-le-Majeur), and the narrow, picturesque streets were all a draw, not to mention the well-known flower market. Tourists often viewed Vieux Nice from on high. It consti-tuted an important part of the famous panorama enjoyed by tourists and postcards. A regular tourist destination was the top of the hill that once had the château, from which tourists gazed westward, appreciating the narrow streets of Vieux Nice in the foreground and the promenade des Anglais and the sea in the background. The sight had long inspired writers and other visi-tors. Up close, however, much of Vieux Nice constituted a slum in the eyes of both tourists and politicians across the political spectrum.[44]

In 1950s, as the Médecin administration began to focus on Vieux Nice, local communists argued for the necessity of "opening up" the area. As was typical for communists, they embraced modernization; they just wanted workers as well as the middle class and the rich to share in its spoils. *Le Patriote* wanted the city to tear down existing buildings, put up big new ones, and widen streets for access, light, and air in the neighborhood. More green spaces were a priority. According to local communists, workers deserved less densely populated neighborhoods; some residents could stay in rebuilt housing while others would get apartments in public housing projects. Com-munists were particularly critical of historic preservationists who wanted to maintain the "picturesque" narrow streets at the foot of the château. In their words, "Let's send those who love our narrow streets to go and live there, with them and their children, and we'll see how long they stay!"[45]

In the early 1950s concern centered on the area near the intersection of the rue Saint-Joseph and the rue des Serruriers, where buildings were liter-ally falling down and at least one WC drained directly into the street.[46] With financing from the national government, the city oversaw the construction of a *cité de transit*, supposedly temporary housing for the families evicted from their apartments in Vieux Nice. Erected on land claimed from the Paillon, 3.5 kilometers upriver from Vieux Nice, the Cité Bon-Voyage emerged. Early buildings resembled army barracks. Begun in 1953, 150 apartments rehoused 300 inhabitants evicted from Vieux Nice. As the name indicates, these were to be transitional, not permanent apartments, and social workers were to ensure that residents lived properly before they might move into better public housing. As in other *cités de transit* in France, those transplanted would be subject to a *stage éducatif*, a period of education, during which they

FIG. 1.2. The Cité de Transit Bon-Voyage (1957), built on the left bank of the Paillon in the former riverbed. A wall protected the simple, low-rise housing from flooding. The Mediterranean is in the background. Archives Nice Côte d'Azur—Ville de Nice, 1064 W 130 (collection of the photographic service of the city).

would be "acclimated by inspectors" who would ensure that their "kitchen is clean." In the residents' defense, a reporter from *Le Patriote* had visited their light-deprived quarters in Vieux Nice and noted the "absolute cleanliness of their inhabitants" despite the horrific conditions.[47]

This early demolition was the first step in what became the gentrification of Vieux Nice. As residents departed for shelter at Bon-Voyage, they got a promise that they could later return to the new housing constructed on the site of their former apartments. By 1959 it was clear that only 103 apartments would replace the earlier 300 on the site, and that buyers would need 300,000 francs upfront for a purchase. Few could afford to return, a fact that worked to gentrify and set a precedent. Those later evicted from Vieux Nice got housing in Ariane, near the municipal dump and incinerator. Working-class residents would be forced into new quarters, farther from work and shopping, with higher rent and increased transportation costs. In the late 1960s Vieux Nice was designated a "safeguarded sector," which allowed the city to regulate the aesthetics of the area. In addition to bans on posters and lighted advertising, there were regulations requiring new roofs to use the traditional orange tiles of Provence and façades to conform to the norms of the area, as

FIG. 1.3. The Cité d'Urgence at Ariane (1956), where the original plans for the barrack-style housing were so minimalist the city had to subsidize tiling and water heaters. The city dump and incinerator were nearby. Archives Nice Côte d'Azur—Ville de Nice, 1064 W 112 (collection of the photographic service of the city).

was already the case in the place Garibaldi and the place Masséna. In becoming a pretty place for tourists, Vieux Nice would follow in the footsteps of the Marais in Paris and the Quartier Saint-Jean in Lyon.[48]

The gentrification of Vieux Nice was, in principle, simply about the elimination of a long-established slum, but behind the scenes, there was another motivation. After World War II, Vieux Nice increasingly attracted North African workers. The old, dilapidated housing kept room rates low. In 1967 there were four separate bars, where men congregated, and two of the bars served as lodging houses. Many other North Africans came to Vieux Nice in order to buy halal food. B. A. not only ran a small grocery on rue Droite but also received North Africans' mail. They frequented the Sunday morning flea market on the place Risso and caught Arab-language films at the Esplanade movie house. A. M. ran a restaurant called la Palmeraie and allowed ten North Africans to sleep in the basement.[49] Nice Matin noted that the law on "safeguarded sectors" only required the façades of buildings to remain picturesque, while the interiors could be upgraded. Renovation "in increasing the rent of certain dwellings could bring a satisfactory solution to the very acute problem currently caused by their occupation by immigrants."[50]

Later, in 1986, Mayor Jacques Médecin was more specific in taking credit for gentrifying Vieux Nice by pushing North Africans out of the now picturesque tourist area. "Ten years ago, Vieux Nice risked becoming a North African neighborhood. If I had not acted, the people of Nice would have been afraid to set foot on certain streets." Médecin and Nice Matin denied that this was a racist policy. In the words of reporter Serge Benedetti, the municipality merely tried to get a "balance of populations." Médecin's longtime deputy charged with housing policy, Raoul Bosio, explained the ostensibly not segregationist but effectively segregationist approach of the city government. "For years now, the city purchases lodgings one by one, using its right of preemption, especially the most rundown, those where it is not rare that people live five to six in a small room rented for a king's ransom. We modernize, we transform, and we re-rent. We are doing it so that Vieux Nice does not become a community where the people of Nice are afraid to walk. It would be good if other French municipalities that must tackle population problems imitated our example."[51]

Low-Income Housing: The HLM

The cités de transit, like those destined for residents from Vieux Nice, were but one of many low-income housing options in postwar France, as the French state invested heavily in efforts to resolve the housing crisis. As the right to comfort became the expectation in postwar France, the varieties of public housing illustrate the limits of that comfort for those who were not well off. In addition to subsidies for builders (known as LOGECO) and low-cost loans for would-be homeowners (usually called Plan Courant housing), in 1955 there were five categories of public housing.[52] The first, known as a *cité d'urgence type abbé-Pierre*, was "rudimentary" with "limited comfort." These apartments were so basic that at Ariane the city had to fund upgrades that included tiling and small, on-demand water heaters. A second category, *Opération million* apartments, consisted of three rooms with forty-eight square meters and included a kitchen and bathroom. In Nice a building on the rue de la Gendarmerie was in this category. A third category consisted of a slight upgrade to the *Opération million*, including better building materials, a garbage chute, and central heating. The fourth category was that of a *cité de transit*, which had the amenities of an *Opération million* but was reserved for those expelled from slums slated for destruction. Finally, the fifth category, that of the ordinary HLM (*habitations à loyer modéré*) apartments, consisted often of three rooms (52 m^2 or 560 ft^2), with a "definite comfort," notably central heat, hot water, garbage chute, bathroom with a bathtub, washtub, small balcony, and elevator. This last category would be built on a grand scale, eventually addressing the dire shortage of public housing in postwar France.[53]

In the 1950s HLMs in high-rise housing blocks (*grands ensembles*) became the norm in French public housing, but municipalities on the Riviera were particularly slow to build them. One issue was money. Immediately after the war, the French state concentrated resources in those regions most in need. Among larger cities, Nice not only saw less destruction than many French cities, but it also had a long-standing reputation as being a city of relative wealth. In the words of reporter Claude Mercadié, "metropole of tourism, battlefield of flowers, capital of Carnival, ideal site of second homes, Nice, like all of the other towns along the coast, does not receive the attention of authorities as do working-class towns (Saint-Étienne, Thionville, Merlebach), those destroyed by the war (Le Havre, Rouen, Caen, Saint-Dié) or finally the major economic centers (Paris, Bordeaux, Lyon)."[54]

The bigger issue was prestige, as wealthy property owners wanted to preserve high property values and exclusivity. Communities along the Riviera did not see themselves as locations for massive public housing projects like those sprouting up around Paris. Monaco even refused to house any of the hundreds of French construction workers employed there. In Nice, as funding became available, the Médecin administration dragged its feet, envisioning Nice like the rest of the Riviera as an upper-middle-class enclave. Radical

Lyon mayor Édouard Herriot, using the Loucheur law of 1928, had already launched building projects even before the 1950 law establishing HLMs. By 1954 municipalities controlled by communists on the outskirts of Paris, such as Aubervilliers, Ivry, Montreuil, and Saint-Denis, had already completed large apartment blocks. In 1954, before any HLM complexes had opened in Nice, Ivry, one-fifth the size of Nice, had already built six hundred HLM apartments. Nice, by contrast, had only a handful of small public housing projects in the works in the early 1950s, despite the acute crisis in housing.[55]

Only in 1954 was the first HLM launched in Nice at Saint-Roch. The new project revealed the strength of demand. Despite its distance from the center of town, when the first fifty-nine apartments opened in 1955, there were some two thousand applicants, and at least two thousand other families were eligible. In practice, there were actually fewer than fifty-nine apartments available for workers in general, as ten apartments were reserved for employees of the SNCF (the freight train station was in Saint-Roch), eight for other government employees (*fonctionnaires*), three for the family allowances agency thus destined only for larger families, and one for the concierge, leaving only thirty-seven other apartments for occupancy.[56]

As the 1950s progressed, demand for affordable housing rapidly outpaced supply. Of the 18,326 building permits issued in Alpes-Maritimes in 1958, only 948 were for HLMs. In 1958 Antibes needed a thousand HLM apartments. In 1959 there were only 1,200 completed HLM apartments and 1,250 under construction in the entire department of Alpes-Maritimes. Meanwhile, there were 11,500 applicants in Alpes-Maritimes, including 8,500 in Nice, while authorities received 1,500 additional new applicants each year. The prefecture estimated that the Alpes-Maritimes needed at least fifteen thousand HLM apartments immediately. The crisis was such that Prefect Pierre-Jean Moatti intervened, exerting pressure on Médecin and other mayors, overseeing a rapid construction of HLMs in the department in the 1960s, particularly in Nice.[57]

As it turns out, in both the 1950s and 1960s, Saint-Roch was typical in the prioritizing of applicants. As housing authorities sorted applications, they were supposed to favor those stuck in furnished rooms for at least ten years (seven hundred families in 1955), in addition to having French nationality, having lived in Alpes-Maritimes for at least ten years (not just in France, as the law stipulated), or having been born in Alpes-Maritimes. However, 20 percent of apartments were regularly reserved for government employees. In fact, government employees tended to fare even better. By late 1962, four thousand families in Alpes-Maritimes had found housing in HLMs, but of that number, five hundred were families of city employees, and fifty

FIG. 1.4. The eight-storied HLM Saint-Roch buildings (1957) with small balconies were typical of public housing developments in Nice and France generally. Archives Nice Côte d'Azur—Ville de Nice, 1064 W 119 (collection of the photographic service of the city).

families of SNCF employees. In one case, a well-constructed HLM building appeared in 1965 on the col de Villefranche, with a spectacular view of the harbor. Of the seventy-four apartments, 50 percent were occupied by residents of Villefranche, namely, employees of the mayor's office and teachers, and 20 percent by government employees working in Nice.[58]

HLM Problems

While the planners of French public housing had utopian visions of their projects, residents found their apartments wanting. It was not just that the French surveyed had wanted freestanding dwellings. HLM high-rises were also far from city centers. HLMs appeared on the outskirts of Nice, scattered in a ring not far from the current autoroute, particularly concentrated in the northeast near Ariane and Saint-Roch and in the western portions of the city north of the airport. These were, by definition, the least desirable parts of town where the property values were lower, and the commute times longer. At Ariane, residents experienced the odors of the city dump and the municipal incinerator in a valley that trapped the air. Saint-Roch had the noise of the freight station and worse air quality than near the sea. In western Nice the noise of the airport bounced off the new high-rises. Others were tucked in the valleys north of town. Far from the center of the city and from the eyes of tourists, these areas had limited public transport, even after the construction of thousands of apartments for people who in many cases could not afford a car (in 1966, 73 percent of all HLM residents earned little enough that they were subject to no income tax). Provisioning households was difficult. Groceries and other shops did not always open nearby, though sometimes vendors brought bread, fish, and other goods by truck. When shops did exist, residents complained that prices near HLMs were 20 to 30 percent higher than in markets in town centers or at supermarkets.[59]

As elsewhere in France, the poor quality of HLM construction was the most serious problem. Tenants at Saint-Roch noted that doors were so poorly hung that there were five-centimeter gaps. At Saint-Roch, kitchen sinks had no backsplash, so tenants needed to install tiles themselves or watch the wall behind the sink disintegrate. Windows would not close at the Residence Mirandoles in Cannet-Rocheville. At HLM Pasteur in Nice, bathrooms had a single faucet that swung between the sink and the tub, but it was not long enough to reach both, causing water to run over the edges. Water would not drain out of tubs and sinks, because pipes were too small. Rooms had no overhead lighting and only a single outlet. At least half of tenants had flooring that soon came loose, requiring them to replace it with new linoleum. Bad installation of wallpaper forced tenants to repaint or repaper at their own expense. At las Planas, a tenant complained, "The first time I used my bathroom sink, it fell off the wall."[60]

In 1960 *Le Patriote* reported that in the new HLM Pasteur, the gutters had been badly installed, allowing water to infiltrate fourth-floor apartments. One inhabitant noted that "in ten minutes, the suspended electric fixtures were filled with water." Another "took six buckets of water out of my bedroom." Still another "had five centimeters of water on top of my armoire." Wallpaper peeled off, water stains appeared on the walls, and furniture was covered with water-saturated plaster, as large chunks of plaster fell from ceilings. The problem was simple; builders had installed the gutters with the lower lip toward the building rather than away from it, so when gutters were obstructed, water found its way inside the building. Worse yet, this was not residents' first problem. In the previous three years, chimneys had to be rebuilt and coal gas water heaters moved from bathrooms to better-ventilated kitchens after a case of asphyxiation.[61]

The Ministry of Reconstruction and Housing dictated norms for the country as a whole, with no provision for different latitudes. As a result, at the HLM Pasteur, there were no *volets*, the shutters usually installed in French homes. In principle, volets on lower levels of buildings are for privacy and security. On the upper floors of high-rises, no one could easily see the interior of apartments, and people could install curtains. However, in the south volets are critical for temperature control. In poorly insulated high-rises without cross drafts, the summer sun was insufferable when there were no volets. Nice is known for its old-style volets with various movable parts that can be manipulated to let in air while protecting inhabitants from sunshine; even dilapidated housing usually had them. But the HLM Pasteur did not. In the words of one renter, "without volets, the apartment is not livable." At las Planas, larger apartments for bigger families also lacked volets, even after Minister of Construction Pierre Sudreau was finally persuaded on a visit to Nice that all new HLMs should have volets on the sun-drenched Riviera. The universal approach of modern building projects, disregarding regional differences, was clearly a failure.[62]

Pieds Noirs

Beginning in the late 1950s, large-scale public housing projects in the form of HLMs promised to supply enough homes, albeit with some serious deficiencies, to meet the obvious need. But soon demand on the part of Europeans from the colonies made the situation worse. By December 1962 approximately sixty thousand Europeans from the empire, mostly from Algeria, had moved to the department.[63] Known officially as *rapatriés*, or "repatriated," most had not been born in Alpes-Maritimes or even metropolitan France. Many came from Italian, Maltese, and Spanish families who had never lived in the hexagon, having migrated from elsewhere in Europe to Algeria. Initially a term of derision, *pieds noirs* came to identify as such. Of the approximately 1.5 million people who left French colonies in order to live in France, about a million were from Algeria, and about half of that number left in a mass exodus in the summer of 1962. About two-thirds arrived initially in Marseille, where they overwhelmed efforts of public assistance and where the welcome was not warm. While they ended up across France, many preferred the climate of the south, where 66.8 percent had settled by 1968. They were numerous along the coast of Alpes-Maritimes.[64] On the Riviera, tourism had already exacerbated the postwar housing crisis, which became yet worse as pieds noirs arrived.

To be sure, Europeans from the colonies were already present on the Riviera before 1962. In the eyes of locals, they tended to be reasonably well-off government officials, military officers, or businessmen. They bought many of the new apartments as investment properties, second homes, and retirement homes. They often settled permanently in Alpes-Maritimes after French colonies in Indochina, Morocco, Tunisia, and sub-Saharan Africa became independent countries. For some locals, the fact that the money had been earned in the colonies, presumably by exploiting indigenous workers, grated. As Madame L. G. wrote *Le Patriote* in 1954, "In the neighborhoods of Saint-Barthélemy and Saint-Maurice, numerous buildings with ultramodern amenities were quickly constructed and put up for sale. It is remarkable that a large part of the buyers consists of big Indochinese exploiters investing the money they acquired who knows how!" At the very least, European settlers coming from the colonies deepened the housing crisis by contributing to the rapid increase of prices and rents.[65]

In 1962, while some pieds noirs could afford to buy an apartment, many left Algeria with little more than a suitcase. When the French government organized Opération Rapatriés on their behalf in 1963, including job fairs, the prefect of Alpes-Maritimes urged local employers to give priority to pieds noirs, and the prefecture served as a clearinghouse for employers needing help and pieds noirs seeking employment. They did not always find work in the trade they had practiced in Algeria. A bank employee from Casablanca ended up as a cleaning lady in Cagnes-sur-Mer. Given the building boom after World War II, many retooled in order to take construction jobs. A guard from the port at Algiers, an interpreter at Ménerville (Thénia), a bookkeeper from Batna, and a winegrower from Mostaganem all became masons. There was eventually a serious mobilization in France on behalf of the pieds noirs in the essential domains of employment and housing. Unlike in Britain, in France even lower-level civil servants in Algeria were guaranteed employment with the French government in the metropole. In order to assist with housing, in January 1961 the French state offered a moving and lodging subsidy and low-interest loans to all construction firms reserving a certain number of new apartments for pieds noirs. The government also waived the ten-year residency requirement for HLMs. As of 1 January 1962, 10 percent of places in HLMs were reserved for pieds noirs, a figure that increased to 30 percent on 1 August. The prefect of Alpes-Maritimes even threatened to requisition vacant housing, in an effort to push owners of vacant homes to rent to pieds noirs.[66]

Pieds noirs got priority in housing over many locals already on the list. By November 1962 there were almost forty thousand households in Alpes-Maritimes seeking public housing for their families. In Antibes in 1964 there were 1,299 requests for public housing, of which 250 came from pieds noirs. In Nice, in the fall of 1962, four thousand *rapatriés* had applied for public housing, at a time when there were already some thirteen thousand outstanding requests. In 1965 Nice had 17,960 requests for housing from 13,100 "Niçois," 300 government employees, and 4,560 pieds noirs.[67]

Nice proved especially welcoming to pieds noirs, resulting from a coalescence of national and local politics. Longtime mayor Jean Médecin ran Nice much as socialist Gaston Defferre ran Marseille, as a sort of personal fief where clientelism reigned. Except for the years 1943–47, Médecin remained mayor from 1928 until his death in December 1965, succeeded by his son Jacques (who served until he fled France under indictment for corruption in 1990). Jean Médecin was fervently right wing, having flirted with fascism and served Vichy, but he opposed Charles de Gaulle. By 1962, when de Gaulle accepted the inevitability of Algerian independence, Médecin argued for a continuation of the war and preservation of *Algérie française*. When pieds noirs arrived in 1962, Médecin not only agreed with many of them that they had been sold out by de Gaulle; he also saw an opportunity to firm up his own position with new voters. He quickly worked to secure pieds noirs' votes by putting out the welcome mat. In 1962 Médecin created France's first municipal office to assist pieds noirs. He showed up at their demonstrations. He spoke out repeatedly in favor of *Algérie française*, then for the French state to grant amnesty for crimes committed during the war and indemnities for pieds noirs. In an effort to ensure that he would get pied noir votes, Médecin put three on his party's electoral list in 1965, getting them seats on the municipal council. One of them, Francis Jouhaud, became an adjunct mayor charged with *rapatriés* affairs, above all ensuring housing.[68]

Race and the Right to Comfort at Saint-Roch

Had he not died young of tuberculosis, filmmaker Jean Vigo would hardly have recognized Nice in 1975. The villas along the promenade des Anglais were gone, replaced by apartment blocks. In Vieux Nice poor children playing in the streets gave way to tourists wandering in and out of boutiques and staying in upscale apartments in picturesque buildings. Demand from tourists, second homeowners, and retirees on the Riviera had driven up real estate values, making the Riviera the least affordable French locale outside greater Paris. And at long last, locals and pieds noirs had the comfort promised by the French state in the form of public housing.

By 1975 the increased cadence of HLM construction resolved the housing crisis—for those of European descent. Given population growth, authorities estimated in 1962 that Alpes-Maritimes would need to build at least a thousand HLM apartments per year until 1975 in order to resolve the crisis in affordable housing. In fact, the population grew even more quickly, in part due to the influx of pieds noirs, but construction outpaced growth. There were ninety thousand inhabitants of Alpes-Maritimes living in HLMs in 1974, nearly one-fifth of the population of a department known worldwide as a luxurious tourist destination. Three of four children in the department lived in HLMs. In 1976 there were eighteen thousand HLM units in Alpes-Maritimes, of which ten thousand were in Nice.[69]

In the meantime, North African migrant workers had a very different experience from locals and pieds noirs. To give but one example, in the late 1950s North African men lived in northeastern Nice, in the neighborhood of Saint-Roch. They worked for the construction firms that had contracts for building Nice's first HLM. But while they built the new public housing, the North Africans lived in moving containers, abandoned rail cars, old trailers, and shanties. They stood no chance of occupying apartments in the HLM. Instead, when the first buildings were complete, complaints from the new inhabitants began. In the late 1950s residents blamed, without evidence, a case of polio in the Saint-Roch HLM on the nearby shantytown. Playing to the biases of his constituents, Jean Médecin publicly deplored the "regrettable invasion" of North Africans.[70]

When the latest section of the HLM complex opened in Saint-Roch in 1963, the new residents called for the elimination of the unsightly shanties. The HLM renters' association, representing 662 families, argued that the nearby hillside was a "full-fledged shantytown" where its inhabitants "washed themselves, cooked, [and] *relieved themselves* in full view" (emphasis in the original).[71] The head of Nice's housing bureau deplored the juxtaposition of a "modern" building entirely "devalued by primitive accommodations in the immediate vicinity." Médecin's newspaper, the *Action républicaine*, claimed that the shantytown was not only dangerous in terms of hygiene "but also unacceptable in terms of public morality."[72] For residents and the mayor, the European residents of Saint-Roch embodied hygiene as they gained access to their new homes, while they projected lack of hygiene onto working men of color. The colonial color line held fast in the postcolonial metropole.

In 1964 the one hundred or so North Africans who had lived in shanties at Saint-Roch since at least 1958 were evicted. Bulldozers flattened the space.

As *Nice Matin* reported, "The elimination of the shantytown at the bottom of the hill took place, not because a building would soon be constructed there, but for reasons of public hygiene." *L'Espoir* looked forward to the destruction of other North African dwellings on the hill that led to the touristic *grande corniche*, as they were "lodgings without hygiene, sources of possible epidemics."[73] Clearly, the right to comfort did not extend to North Africans.

CHAPTER 2

Reconstructing the Riviera, Sleeping in Squats and Shantytowns

In 1955 J. C. of Cannes wrote the mayor, "Why is there now in Cannes a swarm of Arabs? Is it to get the rich tourists to leave? I hope you will do what is necessary so that these undesirables find shelter and food elsewhere and that you will signal to [higher] authorities the mistake that they are making in letting such a population penetrate our coastline—as it is filled with venereal disease, tuberculosis, etc."[1] Meanwhile, a municipal councilor in Cannes cited "a letter from English friends, who no longer come to Cannes partly because hotels are too expensive but especially because of the number of Arabs walking around in the city." Georges Gelineau, charged with the issue of North African laborers in Cannes, proclaimed, "We need to do all we can so that our beaches and our gardens are not invaded [by North Africans] exploiting the openness of foreigners on vacation or innocent, very tempting girls in their bikinis."[2]

These comments reveal the painful irony of North African migrants' experience. Although they worked for the construction companies that rebuilt the infrastructure in order to accommodate postwar tourism, they needed to seem invisible. Their very presence raised the specter of their conquest of Europe and European women, evoking the presumed dangers of Arab men in France. Supposedly disease-ridden North Africans were "invading" and "penetrating," prowling on girls, and scaring away wealthy tourists. Police, city, and departmental officials did indeed work to keep North Africans out of public spaces. But the men, employed in construction, had to live somewhere. Unable to find housing, many moved from squat to squat, until the destruction of abandoned buildings eliminated the number of small-scale squats and pushed them into bigger *bidonvilles*, or shantytowns, at the edges of town. Yet those bidonvilles also needed to be invisible or disappear, lest they detract from the imagined paradise of the Riviera. As the superintendent of police in Antibes argued against bidonvilles, "Our community is by reputation and point of fact, one of the jewels of the touristic heritage of France and an unquestionable attraction, notably for people who desire to forget for a while the ambiance of industrial cities."[3] The Riviera never had the most or the largest bidonvilles, a distinction held by the industrial and commercial powerhouses of greater Paris, Marseille, and Lyon. However, in the eyes of both residents and tourists, the Riviera was supposed to avoid bidonvilles altogether, not for the sake of North Africans but because it had a mythic image to maintain.

In *Les trentes glorieuses*, Jean Fourastié makes much of the postwar growth of the tertiary sector, lauding the increase of white-collar, sedentary jobs to the detriment of unskilled agricultural and industrial labor. That was the experience for many French; Fourastié himself was a leading French technocrat and academic.[4] However, such was not the experience of migrant workers in France. While people of European descent increasingly got desk jobs and new apartments with appliances, North African and other migrant workers did much of the manual labor that fueled French economic expansion during the Thirty Glorious Years.

Throughout the period 1945–75, authorities cleared squat after squat, and bidonville after bidonville, arguing that they were unhygienic and unsightly, likely to spread disease and spoil the aesthetic appeal of the Riviera. The term *bidonville*, translated as "shantytown," originated in North Africa in the early twentieth century. As colonial agriculture increased rural poverty, people fled to cities in search of work.[5] With nowhere else to live, they constructed bidonvilles at the edge of cities. The term would literally translate as "container town," as a *bidon* was a container, barrel, or gas can, often cut for use as roofing. After World War II, in metropolitan France, when North African laborers could not find housing, they constructed makeshift homes on abandoned property. These groups of shanties got the name *bidonvilles*. Building materials included bidons as well as wood, tar paper, moving containers, and tin and plastic sheeting. Even more so than "shantytown" in English, the term *bidonville* connoted colonies and immigrants, in essence racial difference. Although some inhabitants of bidonvilles harkened from Europe, especially Portuguese workers at Champigny-sur-Marne in Île-de-France,

North Africans were predominant in bidonvilles. Here I use the term *bidon-ville* in order to maintain the colonial and postcolonial connotation of the word, an association that risks erasure when we use "shantytown" instead.

This chapter considers squats, bidonvilles, and some of the buildings that replaced them. The focus is on where North Africans lived in order to highlight their critical role in remaking the Riviera. The area was not unique at all in having bidonvilles; what made it distinct was the disproportionate place of construction in the local economy. In France as a whole, foreign workers (including North Africans as well as other immigrant workers) built one apartment of every two, and one automobile of every two.[6] The Riviera had no automobile plants or much other manufacturing. Instead, most North Africans worked in private construction and on public works projects (Bâtiment/travaux publics, or BTP). In 1975, for every one hundred Algerians working in France, eighty-five were semiskilled (*ouvriers spécialisés*, a category including truck drivers and operators of cranes and bulldozers) or unskilled laborers (*manoeuvres*), of whom 40 percent worked in BTP; 30 in industry, especially metallurgy, including automobile manufacture. By contrast, in the Alpes-Maritimes in 1961, fully 90 percent of North African laborers worked in BTP as unskilled or semiskilled workers. The proportion ranged between 70 and 80 percent into the early 1970s. In addition, North Africans made up a relatively large percentage of all construction workers in the region. In the Alpes-Maritimes in 1975, of the 32,000 workers employed in BTP, 16,000 to 17,000 were foreign nationals, of whom 12,000 to 13,000 were North Africans; thus about 40 percent of all construction workers in Alpes-Maritimes were North Africans.[7]

North Africans on the Riviera

The number of North Africans on the Riviera grew between the 1940s and the 1970s, particularly from the mid-1950s onward. Until the early 1970s, when sociologists assisted in the elimination of the last bidonville in Nice, numbers regularly came from the police, who attempted to count inhabitants, recording their places of birth, age, marital status, and employer. Above all, police were seeking possible Algerian Front de libération nationale (FLN) activity. Perhaps not surprisingly, I found no police counts of North Africans for the years before the outbreak of the war in Algeria in 1954. After the Évian Accords ended the war in 1962, the police and the prefecture continued to count, leaving a paper trail that gives a general sense of the size of North African communities. Data collection was not systematic, so there are inconsistencies in the reports. It was particularly difficult to track Algerians; before

1962, they were legally French citizens, able to move freely to and around metropolitan France. In the years after 1962, legally they could still move freely in France without needing to register with the local police (though both before and after 1962, police monitored their presence and sometimes charged unemployed men with vagabondage).[8]

When the Second World War ended, North African laborers, many of whom had just served in the Allied forces, found work on the Riviera. As early as 1946, North Africans lived in a bidonville across from the airport, employed in its construction. In 1954 there were about a thousand North Africans living in Nice. In 1957 the prefect of Alpes-Maritimes reported that there were 2,605 North African workers in the department. In 1959 there were 7,472 North Africans in Alpes-Maritimes, of whom 5,622 were Algerians (Français musulmans), 1,120 Tunisians, and 730 Moroccans. As of December 1968, police in Alpes-Maritimes counted 9,424 Algerians, 4,629 Tunisians, and 3,133 Moroccans. In 1970 officials estimated that there were just under twenty thousand North Africans (of whom 10,500 were Algerians, 6,000 Tunisians, and 3,000 Moroccans). About 7,000 North Africans lived in Nice, 3,000 in Cannes, and 2,000 in Antibes. In 1975 the prefecture of Alpes-Maritimes estimated that there were up to 37,000 North Africans in the department, up to 7,000 of whom were not in France legally and were not consistently part of earlier counts.[9]

Most were single or left their families in Algeria. In 1959 police also counted 388 North African children, belonging to 119 parents. In 1962 the prefecture counted some 168 "Muslim families with 498 children," of whom eighty-one were mixed North African–European couples. Almost all other families were Tunisian and Moroccan.[10] Compared with both France as a whole and with the nearby departments of the Var and Bouches-du-Rhône, Algerians in Alpes-Maritimes were more likely to be either single or to have left their families in Algeria, returning home during the summer vacation period and sending remittances the rest of the year.[11] That situation changed when Algeria banned migration in 1973 and France did so in 1974. As Algerian workers feared they might not gain reentry into France when they visited Algeria, more families joined them in Alpes-Maritimes. In 1975 France specifically exempted family reunion immigrants from the ban on immigration, further encouraging family members to move to France.[12]

Squats and Bidonvilles

There was a fine line between squats and bidonvilles. After 1945, communities along the Riviera had many vacant buildings, abandoned during the war. Given the housing shortage, squatting was frequent. In fact, until 1956 the prefecture of Alpes-Maritimes tolerated it, so police did not enforce laws against trespassing or occupying others' property.[13] Moreover, even the larger bidonvilles were usually extensions of squats. Nice in particular had a large number of abandoned villas, as well as properties in the process of expropriation and eventual redevelopment. These often became squats. As buildings filled with people, men hauled in trailers, old buses, moving containers, or materials from their worksites in order to build lean-tos and other shacks on the properties; officials called the enlarged squats bidonvilles.

North Africans were not the only squatters in the 1950s. French and European migrant families also squatted when unable to find affordable housing. With the arrival of children, young couples last on the list for public housing occasionally ended up squatting. For example, in January 1956 five families with sixteen children, including babies, occupied the Villa Mont-Roc in Nice's Cimiez neighborhood. However, these instances of squatting were widely reported as outrageous, and the families found housing.[14] In the case of North African workers, squatting drew little attention from the press. While people of European descent could find at least rudimentary and overpriced housing in the late 1950s and 1960s, the same was not always true for North Africans. They received low pay and faced discrimination, thus had fewer options. So they squatted. Interestingly, when squatters were North Africans, authorities tended to call the squats bidonvilles, even if they were small and within an existing structure, evoking racial assumptions from the colonial context. By the late 1960s, if North Africans were present, the location was seemingly by definition a bidonville rather than a squat, whether or not the men built additional shanties and no matter how small. In fact, rather than implicitly legitimize North Africans' presence by using the term "squat" for an abandoned space occupied by a couple of North African men, officials employed the term *microbidonville*.

Evictions were a constant feature of the men's experience. In September 1958 R. L. of Casablanca wrote to the prefect, asking for help in evicting North Africans living in the ruins of a building on the property he had just bought on the chemin du Malvan in Cagnes. The police investigated, finding three men, one Tunisian who worked in construction in Nice and two Algerians who worked for a construction firm in Saint-Laurent-du-Var. Although police attested that the men were "serious" with a "good reputation," they nevertheless told the men to find other housing, and the men moved on. In 1960 about thirty North Africans evicted from 80, route de Marseille in Nice moved into an abandoned veterinary clinic on the route de Grenoble, which by that time had been empty for six years. By 1961 seventy men were living there.[15] Then, in 1963, police evicted seventy-nine workers living in ruins on the chemin de la Peyregoue in Antibes. So the men split up and moved nearby. Within a few weeks, the police proceeded to evict the same men from ten different locales on nearby streets. Pushed out again, many ulti- mately settled in a former cookie factory on rue Bricka, a block away from the beach of Juan-les-Pins.[16]

As postwar redevelopment continued along the Riviera, abandoned build- ings disappeared. At the same time, the arrival of pieds noirs put contin- ued pressure on the housing stock. While the number of North Africans increased, there were even fewer places for them to live.[17] More men gath- ered in places that remained available, increasing the size of bidonvilles. The number of North Africans living in bidonvilles grew. In 1963 police counted 7,068 residents of bidonvilles and abandoned villas in Alpes-Maritimes (at a time when there were about six thousand Algerian workers total in Alpes- Maritimes; most Algerian, Moroccan, and Tunisian migrants lived in bidon- villes and squats in 1963).[18] As the prefect wrote President Charles de Gaulle's office in 1963, "It is certain that the considerable influx of North African workers to the Alpes-Maritimes has created not only a malaise but a serious problem because of the impossibility of their finding lodging in the depart- ment where the housing crisis was aggravated by the arrival of *rapatriés*. In a region dedicated to tourism, the result has been a proliferation of bidon- villes, squats, and consequently the necessity, by judicial means, of expul- sions that often affect one hundred people [at a time]." In 1974 about ten thousand people in the department still lived in bidonvilles or slums with comparably poor conditions.[19]

Until the early 1970s officials and the press often blamed the men them- selves for living in bidonvilles. They stood accused of skimping on housing in order to send more money to families in Algeria. According to one internal report in the prefecture, the men preferred bidonvilles as they were "uncon- cerned and unassimilated, held back by their ignorance of our language and their incompatibility with our practices and customs." In fact, the underlying cause had nothing to do with preference; as recognized already in 1961 by Marc Bighetti de Flogny, charged with Algerian affairs in the department, "Whether because of physical fear, or because of fear of a bad use of the lodging, landlords have systematically refused to rent to North Africans."[20]

While officials eventually understood that the shortage of housing caused the proliferation of bidonvilles, and at times even showed varying degrees of sympathy for the men, many of those residents living near bidon- villes did not. Since the men rarely occupied properties where the owner was nearby, preferring to avoid detection by taking over abandoned sites, owners normally took longer to object to the men's presence. Neighbors, however, put constant pressure on authorities, who then worked with owners to get orders of eviction and clear properties. Neighbors complained of smells, public indecency, or the very presence of the men. In Cannes in 1957 O. S. on the avenue Paul Guigou complained that the "North Africans sleep outside and make the lot look like a market in Marrakech. There is no hygiene. The odors invade the neighborhood. We have green flies as well as mosquitoes. These guys often walk around naked. No one in the world could believe that this camp is in the middle of Cannes, a city known for elegance."[21] Like many complainants, O. S. exaggerated. The property in question was two kilometers from the Croisette, up in the hills at the edge of the city, where O. S. ran a plant nursery. It was not in the middle of Cannes.

The very presence of North Africans seems to be the underlying issue. In 1958 M. L., the owner of a new house north of the Saint-Augustin train station in Nice, wrote the prefect, saying he was *absolutely alone* in the new neighborhood. But 200 meters from my home is an abandoned house, occupied by *fifty* North Africans. Their presence being both undesirable and worrisome, I would be grateful if you could remove them soon" (his emphases). Officials did not always take such bait without their own investigation; in this case, they found only fourteen North Africans and noted that there was a police post with twenty officers just one hundred meters from M. L.'s new house.[22]

Bidonvilles and Civilization

Like the term *bidonville* itself, descriptions invariably invoked the language of empire, contrasting French superiority, medical advances, and cleanliness with colonial backwardness, disease, and dirt. In the local press and in documents from both the police and the prefecture, descriptions of bidonvilles focused on their filth, ugliness, and unhealthfulness. The Riviera was imagined as an otherwise beautiful, clean cloth, while a bidonville was a "stain." "The encampments where [North Africans] live sully the landscape." Bidonvilles were "unsanitary" and "inaesthetic." They constituted "infected wounds on the flank of our department, veritable hotbeds of epidemics." A bidonville was a "canker sore." Prefect René-Georges Thomas himself declared that bidonvilles "soiled" the region, constituting a "wound." Bighetti de Flogny, the prefect's councilor for affairs regarding Algerians, referred to bidonvilles as "leprosy." The municipal councilor Georges Gelineau of Cannes mixed metaphors of insects and infections, calling North Africans at Pen Chai a "swarm" and their collective living space "an abscess."[23]

There was obvious slippage between declaring bidonvilles dirty, disease-ridden, or primitive and implying that their inhabitants, assumed to be both Arab and Muslim, were themselves dirty, diseased, and "uncivilized." Using orientalist language, when *Nice Matin* referred to bidonvilles as the "Ali Baba caves," a reader pointed out that the men in the bidonville near his residence were "wild animals." Prefect Thomas said North African migrants were "less adapted to modern material civilization, to our way of life, our conceptions; they were instead accustomed in their countries to a rudimentary way of life." In the words of *Nice Matin*, "It is a problem at once human, social, and aesthetic: public authorities have too easily accepted the bidonville cancer" that presumably required modern, surgical excision.[24] Filth could be both moral and medical, as it was widely and wrongly assumed that virtually all North Africans had venereal diseases since "syphilis and gonorrhea are endemic in Algeria."[25]

Even arguments on behalf of the integration of North Africans into the metropole sounded orientalist, essentialist, and colonial. In 1961, Bighetti de Flogny began, "What is different is not necessarily inferior." Then he proceeded to say that

> the objective is to integrate them into modern, material civilization, a group that is essentially spiritual, profoundly different in its qualities and faults: atavism of the looting nomad, traditional misery and neglect, a taste for theft and violence, a complex of humiliation and ignorance, but by contrast also a deep faith, generosity, modesty, physical courage, patience, devotion to the clan or to the family, etc. The difficulties of this work are multiplied by the very character and particular vocation of the Côte d'Azur. This department, in which all efforts tend toward embellishment, refinement, and luxury, only grudgingly accepts to serve as the stage for efforts to make a primitive group with a medieval lifestyle transition into a modern style of existence.[26]

Placing North Africans several rungs down from the French on an imagined evolutionary ladder certainly implies North African inferiority and European superiority, and of course says more about Bighetti de Flogny than about North Africans themselves.

Similarly, claims of migrants' filth and European hygiene reveal much about French notions of civilization but little about the actual cleanliness of the men. Kristen Ross has argued that "clean bodies" as well as "fast cars" helped the French forget the empire in the reordering of French culture after World War II. Cultural assumptions of French cleanliness and North African filthiness were imagined realities, with little connection to historical facts.

Such invocations served to justify the marginalization of North Africans on the Riviera, as elsewhere in France. North African workers knew that bidonvilles were muddy and filthy; personal accounts from residents of bidonvilles make that clear. Given historic norms of European Christian aversion to frequent bathing, especially since the elimination of municipal baths in the early modern period, and Muslim religious focus on cleanliness, there is no little irony in the assumption that Muslim inhabitants were essentially dirty while French and other Europeans were clean.[27]

Making Do and Pushing Back

North African workers adapted to circumstances and resisted when they could.[28] Above all, the very building of bidonvilles was an adaptation to circumstance—what Michel de Certeau would call *bricolage*, DIY, or making do.[29] The men's use of wood, tin sheets, tar paper, and other materials resulted not only from their availability on construction sites but also the transient nature of the men's living conditions. In 1958 Bighetti de Flogny noted in a report from the prefect to the Ministry of the Interior that at the early bidonville near the airport, Algerians, "reproducing the atmosphere of their village in Algeria, have constructed several small buildings of stone, of the traditional type."[30] However, as authorities eliminated one bidonville after another, and the men were pushed from one property to another, it would no longer make sense to build with stone. The widespread assumption at the time, that North Africans preferred makeshift tar paper shacks, was actually an adaptation to circumstance. The men worked in construction, and exercised more skill in building even wood, tin, and tar paper shacks than most men. Their early use of stone over wood indicates what the men could have built if they had had a bit of land; some were, after all, masons.[31]

North Africans also pushed back in various ways. In the late 1950s Algerians reminded authorities that they too were French citizens. In 1958, when the prefecture and the mayor's office worked to expel a dozen "Algerian Muslims" from a property on the avenue Gravier in Nice so that a new HLM could be built, the Algerians reminded authorities of their French nationality and refused to be evicted without due process. They threatened other workers sent to tear down the old mill and two buildings they had been occupying.[32] The situation was a double bind for the Algerians. They were to be evicted so that an HLM could be built on the site, but in 1958 the men had no chance of getting an apartment in the new HLM. The twelve Algerians whose employers could not be cajoled to provide housing were temporarily transferred to the small buildings surrounding the Château du Comté de Falicon, also property owned by the city of Nice and slated for development.[33] The pattern was familiar to them; when expelled, they sought out other abandoned properties. The difference this time was that the authorities offered assistance in locating the new shelter in return for North Africans' acceptance of the eviction.

In 1959 municipal officials in Cannes feared a mass expulsion of 250 North Africans from the grounds of the Villa Pen Chai, on the avenue Paul Guigou, because the men had threatened to demonstrate in the main streets of the city and in front of the mayor's office. The men also attempted to use their occupation of the site as leverage for some land on which they might build places to live. In the words of their spokesperson, M. A., "Give us some land and we will leave of our own accord."[34] Ultimately, they were unsuccessful in getting a building site, but the men were able to delay the eviction.

In August 1961 some fifteen North Africans were expelled from the Villa Castel Fiorentina in the ritzy enclave of Roquebrune-Cap-Martin just east of Monaco. The men worked in Monaco, but "North African workers employed by companies in Monaco were, when night fell, ruthlessly driven back into France. The principality refused to receive North Africans." The men protested the move, threatening to occupy the mayor's office, this during the high tourist season of August, unless provided with alternative lodging. For a time, the mayor let the workers camp in the woods, but the prefecture thought it likely that as winter set in the men would soon join the workers already squatting in the Villa Salambo, a mansion mostly destroyed in 1939–40 and abandoned thereafter. The men did so; seventy men lived at the Villa Salambo in late 1961.[35]

Neighbors became frustrated. P. G., the owner of a Citroën automobile dealership in Saint-Paul-lès-Dax in southwestern France, possessed a second home near the Villa Salambo. He complained to the mayor that the Villa Salambo had been "invaded by Algerian subjects" (thus both equating them with hostile military force and denying that they were French citizens as opposed to subjects) who lived in "unthinkable hygienic conditions without WC or water." E. M., who owned a Philips electronics store, also complained to the mayor. He too was horrified that the men lived without water, gas, electricity, or a WC. Evoking the fear of sexualized "Arab men," E. M. claimed that the men had propositioned his maid, and his young wife was afraid to be at home alone.[36] Under pressure from neighbors, the owner, who lived in the posh town of Vaucresson west of Paris, had already gotten an order of expulsion in 1960, but authorities delayed carrying it out.

Why the delay? Initially, police argued that these were young men who had recently arrived in France. According to the police, the men were hostile to the FLN. There was a risk that eviction would turn the men, "who have hope in us," against France.[37] Moreover, in internal memoranda in the prefecture, it is clear that authorities realized that the men had jobs in Roquebrune-Cap-Martin or in Monaco, and there was no other place for them to go. So the prefecture first contacted all of the men's employers and encouraged them to house their employees—to no avail. Efforts to remove a few of the men at a time, which had worked in the evacuation of Pen Chai in Cannes, did not work. The men had a strong sense of solidarity or, to quote the racist spin of one police officer, "these Algerians have an intellectual level lower than basic and most of them are illiterate. They adapt very badly to our norms and customs, and they cannot conceive of why some should be evicted while others not."[38]

The situation changed subtly in 1962, at the end of the war. Initially, many of the men returned to Algeria in the euphoria of independence. When they could not find jobs, they came back to the Villa Salambo. Police were no longer concerned about turning the men toward the FLN and away from France, as the war was lost. The men, including no doubt some who had threatened an occupation of the mayor's office when evicted from the Villa Fiorentina, now petitioned President de Gaulle himself. Writing in the name of eighty men, one man, the likely author, signed with a typical French signature, and another five roughly printed their names. The others do not seem to have known how to sign their names. They asked for de Gaulle's benevolence, claiming that an expulsion would be in violation of the Évian Accords. Communists in Roquebrune-Cap-Martin also asserted that French law and the Évian Accords indicated that the men deserved alternative lodging.[39]

In June 1963, to the chagrin of the Algerian consul, the police evicted the men anyway. Owners of empty villas in the community were told by the police to take measures to secure their properties, lest they be "invaded" by the men.[40] The owner of the Villa Salambo was supposed to do the same, but he obviously failed to do so, as the men found a different way to resist. Little by little, the men moved back in, so that there were at least sixty still living on the premises of the Villa Salambo in 1970. Neighbors continued to complain that the men's existence in a wooded neighborhood gave the area, "notably at night, a reputation as a dangerous zone." Yet the police found no evidence of prostitution, drug trafficking, or any other crime as they went about evicting the men once more in 1970. The men moved on, but many continued to work in Monaco. In 1974 two thousand North African laborers worked in Monaco, and still barred from staying there overnight, lived in Alpes-Maritimes.[41]

North African workers sought out abandoned buildings and empty second homes. In part, it was an incidence of opportunity, as there was no one immediately present to protest the occupation. But they were also asserting an implicit right to occupy a building otherwise unoccupied and unused. There were precedents in French law that could make workers' implicit claims seem legitimate and legal. Although underused, after World War II the French state had the right to requisition unoccupied dwellings for use by those without any housing whatsoever. Again, though little used, at the end of the Algerian War, the state also reserved the right to place pieds noirs in unoccupied dwellings. Finally, and most relevant for North Africans on the Riviera, French law stipulated that if squatters lived in an otherwise unoccupied space for two weeks without protest by the owner, that owner would need to undergo a legal process of eviction in order to remove them. Even if demolition were pending, it would need to wait until squatters had been legally evicted from the site. Not surprisingly, owners' knowledge of the law caused them to be aggressive in trying to expel squatters before the two weeks were up. Squatters, by contrast, ignored owners' entreaties to vacate as a means of asserting their right to shelter.

As owners and squatters exercised their legal rights on the ground, and quite literally to the ground, North Africans worked the system as best they could. On 25 October 1960 D. de L. wrote the prefect, demanding that North African workers be removed from the second dilapidated villa on his property behind the Lanval hospital, about ninety meters from the promenade des Anglais. A dozen North Africans had moved into the villa just two weeks prior. D. de L. approached the North Africans, whom he called "the Arabs," explained his opposition to their presence, and told them to leave. When they refused, he called the police. The police had intervened six months prior, when North Africans had earlier occupied the villa. But having expelled them once, here the workers were again. The police returned. All parties then went to the police station, where D. de L. filed a formal complaint, and the police told the man that "the Arabs [had been] ordered to leave." However, this time they refused and stayed. D. de L. complained to the prosecutor, "These Arabs cut off my gas line, flattening the pipe so that I could not repair it myself. Then they prohibited me from entering the villa they now designate as theirs, not even allowing us to move around on the grounds of the property that they occupy on their days off. They clearly consider themselves at home and are threatening." D. de L. then went after the police, claiming that a police officer told him that he was in the wrong for refusing to accept them, since "the villa is old and falling down." Nevertheless, D. de L. claimed that the police promised to expel them right after de Gaulle's visit to Nice, but they still had not left. "One of them even threatened to kill a worker who came to work for us the other day."[42]

The police explained the situation to the prefect, disregarding the villa owner's claim that the North Africans were threatening. The police officer noted that the police had begun to evict the squatters, and that they requested imprisonment, no doubt in order to gain public attention for their plight. Since de Gaulle's visit was impending, the officer admitted that he avoided arresting the North Africans. He did charge five of the twelve, those who admitted to breaking into the property. But even here there were extenuating circumstances, as one of the five was a veteran, having served as a colonial parachutist, and was honorably discharged. The officer noted that the villa had been unoccupied for six years and that he had indeed suggested that the owner "tolerate the presence of our Muslim compatriots." Interestingly, the prefect blamed D. de L. for not having secured the enclosure to his property well enough. Only further complaints by the owner led to the eventual eviction of all of the workers in November.[43]

When North Africans resisted or protested their living conditions, they do not seem to have tied their daily concerns to the broader struggle for independence in Algeria or to political developments in the Middle East. Of course, part of their approach may have been tactical; in keeping their demands limited, they were more likely to succeed in getting the shelter they needed. Yet the police intelligence service (Renseignements généraux or RG) reports also repeatedly insisted that Algerian workers were not necessarily sympathetic to the Algerian FLN, at least not enough to help it financially. When seventy North African workers squatted in a villa abandoned during its construction by a bankrupt contractor who left Nice abruptly, the RG claimed in 1959 that the workers could avoid the collections by the FLN because of strength of numbers and the family and community ties the men from the same villages had with each other. The RG, in fact, argued against eviction altogether, noting that the real problem was the lack of potable water on the property. The RG claimed that what the men really needed was thirty meters of water line, which would allow them to clean up the waste covering the villa. The RG even suggested that the men could tap into the water line of a nearby milk processing company, the Société laitière vésubienne.[44]

Other Migrant Workers

About half of all migrant workers in the Alpes-Maritimes after World War II were Italians (forty thousand of an estimated eighty thousand migrant workers in 1970), following in the footsteps of generations of Italian immigrants who arrived in Nice after French annexation in 1860.[45] While they faced considerable discrimination in the interwar years, they dealt with less after World War II, as compared to North Africans. Earlier Italian immigrants came to own many of the local construction firms, and postwar Italian immigrants were more likely to be skilled workers in construction and to work in other occupations. European immigrants, such as Italians, Spanish, and Portuguese, faced discrimination in housing, but they got access to HLMs before North Africans. They could also find housing on the private market because they were, in the words of the police in Antibes, "more easily accepted by landlords than were North Africans." North Africans got an entirely different reception. "Despite the goodwill of the [Algerian] workers, they can't find lodging with landlords, as the number of these willing to rent to them is limited; most landlords refuse to rent to them, even though those who do so say that they are pleased with the behavior of their tenants."[46]

European immigrants, who had the experience of a certain level of discrimination, were in some cases more willing to accommodate North African tenants than were well-off residents and second homeowners of the Riviera. In 1974, in part of the final push to eliminate bidonvilles throughout the region, the police began an investigation of a small bidonville just off the route Canta Galet, in the northwestern hills of Nice. Here a husband and wife from Italy rented out rooms to fifteen North African workers without having followed any administrative procedure. In the eyes of the police, the Italian couple owned a bidonville. Their interrogations and those of their tenants reveal a degree of tolerance on the part of the couple, their interest in making an extra buck, and the fluidity of North Africans' housing. The husband, who could not read or write French, told the police he had bought a hectare of property at the end of the chemin des Collettes in 1962. In the 1970s he took a job as a mason with the construction firm Cecchi, where he worked alongside North Africans looking for housing. Beginning in 1972 he and his wife rented out a room on the ground floor of their two-story house. When the workers noted that it was too small for all ten of them, they helped the husband build a barrack-like structure of rubble stone with separate doors leading to three separate rooms. The couple charged the workers ninety francs per room, a price shared by each room's occupants. There was limited electricity and an outside water spigot nearby. The WC had a porcelain bowl and at least a pit underneath, with a garden hose for flushing.[47]

Workers questioned by the police confirmed the husband's statements regarding the rent and living conditions. Each seemed resigned to the fact that he would soon have to move on; in fact, as the husband attested, the men said they would be leaving as soon as the postal strike ended and they could withdraw money for rent from their savings accounts at the post office. The men's stories give a sense of their lives on the Riviera. The men could speak some French, but none could read or write it. Each liked the place because it was quiet. A. O., who had left a wife and child in Morocco, had been in France for three years. He shared a room with his brother, B. O. Both worked as *applicateurs*, applying sealant for local construction firms. Seven other Moroccans lived in the second room. Three Tunisians shared a third room. H. G. had already left for work when the police arrived, but B. B. worked as a specialist in waterproofing for the construction firm SORECI. Tunisian A. A. also worked as an *applicateur*, in his case tarring and waterproofing terraces for the Société auréenne des bitumes. Although he had arrived first in Lyon, after a month he migrated to the coast, where he joined a cousin in the large bidonville at the Digue des Français. He then moved to the Italians' place when he learned of it, appreciating the peace and quiet.[48]

The wife, who could read and write a bit of French, confirmed the details of her husband's and the men's accounts, adding that the men had caused no trouble whatsoever. In fact, she noted that the men had often brought candy to the couple's younger daughters, aged 13 ½ and 12 ½ years. In return for the couple's tolerance when the men housed yet other workers they knew, the men would often give five or ten francs to the children.[49] Clearly, the Italian couple did not fall for the widespread cultural assumptions about the threat that North African men presumably posed to European women and girls. Although the men were being forced to move on, they and the couple had lived in harmony, despite the living conditions qualifying the area as a bidonville before the law.[50]

Employers and Housing

Both mayors and the prefecture, not to mention the press, often blamed North Africans' living conditions on their employers, who relied heavily on migrant workers. In the midst of the rapid postwar economic expansion, French employers faced a labor shortage. Algerians filled many of the openings, especially after 1958, as the Gaullist Constantine Plan encouraged employment of Algerians in the metropole as well as in Algeria in an effort to undercut Algerian sympathy for the FLN.[51] They became critical to the workforce; in 1962, when many workers returned to Algeria after the Évian Accords, construction companies on the Riviera told police that they had to close down several construction sites entirely. Once the extent of postwar unemployment in newly independent Algeria became clear, in 1963, most of those workers returned, and construction sites reopened.[52]

North Africans worked mainly in the unskilled and semiskilled categories, the latter including the operation of heavy machinery necessary for
excavation. In 1975, 53 percent of crane operators in Alpes-Maritimes were
foreign born. North Africans earned less, and they did much of the heavier
work avoided by French workers with better options. As one employer put it,
"We'd have to pay French labor twenty-five to thirty percent more."[53] While
North Africans often received blame for their higher rates of hospitalization
and thus increased health care costs, working conditions explained much of
the difference; there were 2.77 work accidents for semiskilled and unskilled
workers for every one accident for skilled workers (the numbers were much
lower yet for other professions).[54] The Muslim prohibition of alcohol was
seen as an advantage by some employers; one commentator claimed that
employers preferred Algerians because "there are never accidents due to
drinking."[55]

For those employers who violated French labor law, employment of North
Africans had even more advantages. If Moroccan or Tunisian workers came
to France without work permits, by definition, they worked illegally without benefits or protection of labor law unless employers helped them legal-
ize (régulariser) their status. Some employers required men to work off the
books, or non-déclarés.[56] By insisting that the men work illegally, employers
saved money by not contributing to postwar state-mandated benefit plans.
Of course, that also deprived the men of eligibility for family allowances, the
right to paid vacation, unemployment benefits, and reduced public transport
fare if their families were in France. In some cases, employers regularly paid
such workers for fewer hours than actually worked. In the words of reporter
Marcel Rudo, employers "treat them like beasts of burden."[57]

In the winter of 1953–54, Le Patriote did a series on North African workers on the Riviera by profiling Ali Draa, age thirty, from the village of Aim
Kercha, south of Constantine. The series was to expose the "racism pure
and simple" faced by Algerian men in France. Having worked for "rich colo-
nists" on a farm in Algeria, Ali saved, sold a sheep and a mattress, borrowed
money from family, and made his way to France in hopes of more remu-
nerative work. For his first twelve nights in Nice, he slept at the Asile de
Nuit, a homeless shelter that allowed men only twelve nights. Then he slept
alongside the Paillon until allowed to sleep on construction sites. At work,
his experience differed markedly from that of his European coworkers. He
got a job in construction as an unskilled laborer. He earned less per hour. As
significant, the employer refused to hire him legally, which precluded any
benefits, including unemployment insurance and the family allowance for
his wife back in Algeria (as Le Patriote correctly pointed out, even if he had

received the allowance, it would have been much less, as the system paid men from Algeria less). Ali had no paystub, no evidence of employment. He had no proof of residency. Once a project was done, Ali could be arrested and jailed for vagabondage, as had been Ahsene Draa (there is no mention of whether Ahsene was related to Ali), age thirty-three, and Abdellah Zebouchi, twenty-four, in November 1953.[58]

By law, only employers who recruited immigrant workers abroad had to provide housing for them, normally in condemned buildings, barracks, or shacks at building sites. Algerian employees did not become "immigrant" workers until after 1962; their legal status changed from French to Algerian citizens while they continued to live and work in France as before. Most North African workers did not arrive first on the Riviera. Rather, they had been recruited to work in large mining and manufacturing firms in northern and eastern France. When they had a bout of unemployment, workers moved to the south, finding a climate more to their liking, much as tourists did.[59] Yet other workers had arrived officially as tourists, but then got work; authorities were well aware that many Tunisians and Moroccans, alongside many European immigrants, arrived as tourists, then legalized their status with the authorities after the fact. The practice was tolerated, even normal; it became the primary way that migrant laborers entered the country in the 1960s.[60] Few firms in Alpes-Maritimes and the Var recruited abroad. They did not need to, as North African workers came to them.

If employers did not recruit the men abroad, they were under no legal obligation to provide housing. Nevertheless, before evicting residents of bidonvilles, authorities normally got in touch with the men's employers, requesting housing. For example, in 1963, seventy-one North Africans were living in four villas in Nice at 73, boulevard Carlone. The owner had begun the formal process of expulsion. But the police feared "troubling public order" if they evicted all seventy-one at once, so the prefecture contacted each of the North Africans' employers, asking that the employers house their workers. Although the eviction was not dependent on alternative housing for workers, by reducing their number it seemed less likely that remaining workers could effectively resist the process. The seventy-one men worked for fifteen different construction firms, and the police argued that sleeping at worksites would be little different than sleeping ten to a room in an abandoned villa without running water.[61]

The fifteen employers included the leading construction firms in the region and the city, firms that consistently got the contracts not only for private building but also for the public works projects. Their responses are interesting. The Société des grands travaux de Marseille assured the prefecture that an employee's salary was sufficient for him to be able to lodge himself decently at his own expense, implying that the problem was the amount of money he was sending home. Others, such as the Société Clémente, specialists in masonry, agreed to begin housing their North African workers. Vultaggio, also a specialist in masonry, noted that it could do so, but that it needed assurance from the prefecture that the work inspectors or other officials would not protest that workers were living on a worksite with only a lantern and a source of water. The Entreprise Fernand Cecchi said it was impossible to house any employees; its contracts were for road maintenance and of short duration, so it did not even have a storehouse for material. Nicoletti, a leading firm in Nice, could not house its "African workers" (given the men's names, they were clearly North African) because it was "still trying to find lodging for its European workers with much seniority in the company."[62]

When employers did provide housing, the conditions were sometimes as abysmal as at any bidonville. Employers authorized squats in buildings they owned or were working on. In 1959 the firm Déroulède-Alphonse Karr purchased the historic Hôtel Continental and slated the eastern portion of it for eventual demolition and redevelopment. In the meantime, the company authorized its Algerian workers to live there. In 1963 fifty single Algerians were living in the upstairs rooms of the former hotel, several sleeping on the floor. Two families with children lived on the third floor, with the end of the hallway serving as a toilet, as did the basement. Most of the men worked for Déroulède-Alphonse Karr, though the penury of housing had led a few working for other employers to join them. Cooking fires were on the wooden floors of the common rooms of the rez-de-chaussée.[63]

In the end, the prefecture had little luck in cajoling local employers to house their North African workers. In 1966 the prefect reported to the minister of the interior that he had "obtained a fairly considerable increase in the number of North African workers housed by [their] employers," but the results were still less than 2 percent![64] Workers were on their own.

Fires

Soon after the Évian Accords, the consulate of Algeria began pressuring the prefecture of Alpes-Maritimes on behalf of its citizens, just as the Tunisian consulate had since Tunisian independence in 1956. The consulates were consistently vigilant, but they became particularly alarmed in 1967, during the tensions before and after the Six-Day War. Tunisian citizens reported to their consulate that they had been heckled on the streets of Nice. More threatening, a series of fires in local bidonvilles seemed like a pattern of dangerous harassment of North African workers. In August 1967 the consulate of Algeria went so far as to request the police reports submitted to the prefect, clearly doubting the prefect's assurances that the causes of most fires were accidental.[65] The prefect rejected the request, but police reports now available to researchers indicate that there was good reason for the consulates to be alarmed.

Before 1967 there were occasional fires in bidonvilles. Open fires, bottled propane, and candles are simply more likely to cause fires than plumbed natural gas and electricity. In 1961 an accidental fire in the bidonville across from the airport destroyed it. A fire at the Domaine d'Olivetto was ruled accidental in 1965. In 1966 another file at Olivetto destroyed thirty-five dwellings and left 150 men without shelter, but again the cause seemed accidental.[66] Neither the police nor the local press indicated a pattern of fires. Then, in the space of a few months, repeated fires threatened both bidonvilles and the lives of their inhabitants.

In April 1967 fire broke out in the bidonville at Cagnes-sur-Mer. A month later there was a fire in the bidonville across from the airport. On June 6, there was yet another fire in the airport bidonville. The fire spread quickly, fed by four propane bottles that exploded. It destroyed two-thirds of the shanties, displacing three hundred inhabitants. While officials assumed it was accidental, *Le Patriote* suggested foul play, particularly since it occurred during the Six-Day War.[67]

Then on 8 June 1967, still during the Six-Day War, two men threw two one-liter gas cans with lit wicks made of newspaper into the bidonville housing over one hundred men in Cagnes-sur-Mer, attempting to set a fire. Though quickly extinguished, this fire was clearly an instance of arson. More disturbing, the police report indicated, "according to the opinion articulated by several North Africans, the threat of such an act has existed in a permanent manner well before the events in the Middle East."[68] It appeared that a local group opposed to the bidonville's very existence used the Six-Day War as cover, with the hope that Jews and pieds noirs would get the blame. The bidonville at Cagnes-sur-Mer had been there several years and had not caused problems, but residents of a new housing development nearby had begun to complain. Officials in the prefecture certainly wondered, on some level, if organized opposition to North Africans' squatting might be responsible for the bidonville fires. Alongside an internal prefecture report in 1967 about the fires is a rudimentary handout exhorting residents of the parc du Fournel neighborhood in Antibes to "mobilize" against squatters in their neighborhood.[69]

On June 9 yet another fire at the bidonville across from the airport destroyed the remaining shanties. Fire investigators unequivocally confirmed that the fire at Cagnes-sur-Mer was arson, but they could not say the same about the other fires. Publicly, officials attributed the likely causes to North Africans themselves. One theory was that inhabitants had an accident using propane for cooking. Police officials also theorized, without evidence, that political leaders from North African countries had the fires set in order to coerce men to return home for military service. However, in confidential reports, the police maintained that the second and third fires (those of June 6 and June 9) may have been started by "Jews or pieds noirs as a result of the events in the Middle East."[70] In Antibes officials even speculated that residents themselves had set the fire, because North Africans hoped to benefit from the goodwill of officials who would take pity on them and find them better housing. The evidence? The fact that some workers had left the bidonville in Nice, relocated in Antibes, and then left Antibes for the backcountry before they could be questioned by police. The theory seems a stretch, particularly given how frequently North Africans moved. In 1970 Bighetti de Flogny referred to the fact that the "repeated fires in the large bidonville of the airport in 1967 left some doubt as to whether they were accidental."[71]

Fires continued until the elimination of bidonvilles. There were fires at bidonvilles in le Cannet and in Ariane in 1969 and 1970. In 1972 there were two separate fires in a bidonville on the route de Turin in Nice. Residents were, according to the local Algerian consul, "unanimous in affirming the criminal origins of these acts." In 1973 a man died in a fire at the bidonville at Saint-Augustin. *Le Patriote* suspected foul play in the form of a Molotov cocktail thrown out of a car. The newspaper claimed that the police "possess precise witness accounts permitting [them] to arrest the perpetrators."[72]

If the Six-Day War was a cause of several local fires in bidonvilles, no evidence emerged that North Africans lit the fires to get others to return home in order to serve. Police claimed instead that few North Africans engaged in political activism. While the police noted that North Africans sympathized with Arab forces in 1967, they mostly wanted to have good relations with locals in France and keep their jobs. They listened to Algerian radio and read Algerian and Tunisian newspapers, but they had little visible reaction to internal political developments in Algeria or Tunisia. Officials knew of no fundraising campaigns on behalf of Arab powers.[73] Police reports both before 1967 and afterward emphasized much less political activity than police expected. In 1971 the police estimated that of the more than nine thousand

Algerians citizens confirmed to be living in Alpes-Maritimes, only a thousand belonged to the FLN, and of those only 450 had paid dues.[74]

"Be Done with the Bidonvilles Once and for All"

In the 1970s the French government became serious about eliminating bidonvilles across the country. In part, the change resulted from a longer-term shift in public opinion. In 1968 *Le Monde* claimed that the primary reason cities refused to build housing for North Africans and tolerated bidonvilles was, quite simply, "racism."[75] Then, on the night of 1 January 1970, five Malians died of asphyxiation in a fire in a squat in Aubervilliers just north of Paris. National press coverage focused on the tragedy. The incident was by no means the first bidonville fire, but it was clear that the French public was being encouraged to view it differently, as an avoidable event. Soon Prime Minister Jacques Chaban-Delmas led a renewed effort to eliminate all bidonvilles in France, announcing that France needed to "be done with the bidonvilles once and for all" ("en finir avec les bidonvilles"). At the same time, there was more happening behind the scenes, as police worried incessantly after May 1968 that left-wing "agitators" might mobilize the inhabitants of bidonvilles. The minister of the interior, in August 1970, noted that efforts to influence North Africans' views would be "particularly effective when the living conditions of these foreigners are inadequate."[76] Although relatively few North African workers appear to have become politically active on the Riviera, according to the police, that fact did not alleviate officials' concerns. In the wake of May 1968, the police and the prefecture worried about communist efforts to reach out to North Africans.[77]

In the early 1970s local sections of leftist and Catholic-leaning unions (Confédération générale du travail [CGT], Fédération de l'éducation nationale [FEN], and Confédération française démocratique du travail [CFDT]) as well as leftist and Catholic-leaning parties (Parti communiste français [PCF], Parti socialiste [PS], and Parti socialiste unifié [PSU]) called on the prefecture to build housing for North Africans housed in bidonvilles.[78] Communists in the local section of the PCF had long been at the forefront in demanding better housing for North Africans. Throughout the 1960s, local communists led by Virgile Barel were the only major political grouping that attempted to see the situation from the perspective of North Africans while simultaneously trying to tamp down racial resentment against North African workers whose presence seemed to lower everyone's wages. Barel fought to convince French workers and the population at large that North Africans suffered from the acute housing shortage—exacerbated by the strong market for second homes and short-term vacation rentals—as well as racism and substandard wages. Communists claimed these were the real causes of North Africans' abysmal living conditions. *Le Patriote* repeatedly pointed out that racism explained the treatment of North Africans.[79]

The communist union, the CGT, worked to mobilize North Africans in Alpes-Maritimes. The CGT announced a large meeting for 12 April 1970 in the bidonville at the Digue des Français along the Var River in Nice. Police informants reported that two hundred North Africans attended the meeting, where a member of the CGT secretariat from Paris addressed the crowd in Arabic.[80] In the tract announcing the meeting, communists expressed outrage at fires at le Cannet and particularly Ariane, where one "comrade was badly burned." The CGT maintained that *"THE AUTHORITIES AND THE BOSSES ARE RESPONSIBLE"* (emphases in the original). At the meeting itself, speakers called for "the relodging of victims of the fires, the construction of *foyers-hôtels* [dormitory-style housing] with modest rent so that all bidonvilles can be eliminated, and that employers make decent lodging available for their immigrant workers."[81] In 1970, as the national government was gearing up to eliminate bidonvilles and move inhabitants into other housing, the CGT's demands were not terribly radical. Local police and the prefecture were not alarmed, only irritated that the communists were attempting to use the bidonvilles politically and that they had equated the small fire at le Cannet and the accidental fire at Ariane with all of the fires in 1967, implying the government was responsible for all of them by not finding the perpetrators.[82]

Mainstream French communists of the PCF, while rhetorically embracing the overthrow of Western capitalism, did not generally advocate immediate, violent action. Maoists often did. In 1969 students from the University of Nice distributed Maoist political tracts in local bidonvilles. In the early 1970s officials were concerned about the Maoists. The police repeatedly mentioned May 1968, clearly afraid Maoists of the Gauche prolétarienne could mobilize North Africans alongside other followers. Police monitored the group closely, even noting that one member, Mlle. L., had infiltrated the CGT meeting until she realized that a police informant was also present. Maoists also called a meeting after the Ariane fire, theirs held at the Cinéma Politeama in Nice on 11 April 1970. In this case, 150 people attended, but only thirty were North Africans.[83]

In a tract, the Maoists claimed that the fires in bidonvilles served the interests of the "bosses and their friends, the city authorities, who have said that bidonvilles suffice for immigrant workers," since "the mayor's office and the bosses wanted to *flatten the shantytown. THE FIRE IS GOOD FOR THEM!* They forbid the reconstruction of shanties but don't want to pay for relodging" while the police harass "immigrant comrades" (emphases in the original). In the end, even the Maoists had practical demands, indicating that North African workers were likely more concerned with bread-and-butter issues than revolution. The Maoists advocated for free bus service, paid for by the city and employers; a free room at the new *foyer* Saint-André (near Ariane) for a month; and money for workers from the scrap metal collected after the bidonville fire. Subsequent tracts were similarly revolutionary in language but practical in specific demands, including calls for bidonvilles to get public utilities.[84]

Although left-leaning social Catholic groups did not call for violence, their efforts to mobilize Catholic public opinion on behalf of North Africans living in bidonvilles nonetheless drew attention from the police. The Association de soutien des travailleurs immigrés, an association for the support of immigrant workers, had an affiliation with the PSU. In 1971, with the support of Monseigneur Jean Mouisset, bishop of Nice, the group organized a letter-writing campaign, approaching local Catholics with a tract as they left church. It beseeched the faithful to write authorities on behalf of North Africans. The pamphlet laid out the miserable living conditions in bidonvilles. It then, like communist propaganda, made the connection between France's postwar economic growth and the North African laborers who had done much of the work. "Most of these men work in French companies. Let's open our eyes before the construction sites, the public works projects in the streets of our city, on our roads, and on our railroads. We all benefit from the economic impact of their work." To the palpable relief of the police, only 240 letters came from local Catholics to the prefecture, and six of those were "hostile to Arabs."[85] Social Catholics in Nice continued to try to raise awareness of the situation of North African laborers. In February and March 1973 (in the wake of successful Tunisian hunger strikes across France in the fall of 1972), with sanctuary from the parish council and Bishop Mouisset, ten Tunisian construction workers went on a hunger strike in the monastery at Cimiez, demanding residency cards (that is, to have their right to live and work in France legalized); they succeeded.[86]

Public attention added to the officials' sense of urgency. The Vivien Law of 10 July 1970 gave prefects new power to eliminate bidonvilles. The new law altered the public health code, making it easier for officials to tear down bidonvilles as threats to public health and facilitating funding for construction of alternative housing. The prime minister's office insisted that it was the job of prefects "personally to oversee the development of plans" for the rehousing of North Africans.[87] In a memorandum to prefects and other ministers in June 1973, there was even recognition on the part of Prime Minister

Pierre Messmer of the important role that racial discrimination had played in North African workers' inability to find adequate housing. A directive from the prime minister noted that even many Algerians who had opted for French nationality after the independence of "Algeria were still treated like foreigners," while they deserved to be treated "as any other *rapatriés*." There was also an admission that the government had systematically committed the same discrimination as the general population.[88]

Meanwhile, the plight of North Africans remained in the news in Nice, as elsewhere in France. At the bidonville near the airport, a Tunisian worker died in September 1971 when flames engulfed the old bus that served as his housing. Even though likely accidental, the event seemed a repeat of the asphyxiation of the Malians at Aubervilliers. Public discourse seemed to be shifting. In the wake of the death of the Tunisian, the local branch of the League of the Rights of Man advocated strongly and publicly for improvement of North African workers' living conditions. In December 1973 Prime Minister Messmer and President Georges Pompidou condemned racism publicly, at least in general terms.[89] François Chavaneau later claimed, "The Yom Kippur War caused an explosion of racism. North African workers were assaulted in the streets, at bus stops, and in cafés."[90] Yet attacks did not start or end with the war. In 1969 two Frenchmen and a *harki* (an Algerian who had fought against Algerian independence) split open the skull of Salah Bougrine, a sewer worker.[91] Attacks worsened after Algeria nationalized oil and natural gas in 1971. The construction union (the Union syndicale de la construction) in Alpes-Maritimes reported in June 1973, months before the Yom Kippur War, that fifteen workers had been assaulted and had their papers stolen, making them vulnerable to police raids and ID checks. Assaults continued afterward. In February 1975 an attack on the bidonville at the airport caused one scared resident to run across the railroad tracks, where a train hit him.[92]

Constructing Worker Housing

The French state had an institutional solution for housing Algerian workers as early as 1956, when the law of 4 August 1956 and accompanying decree of 30 October 1956 created the Société nationale de construction de logement pour les travailleurs algériens (SONACOTRAL), dedicated to providing housing for workers from French Algeria. SONACOTRAL was a *société d'économie mixte*, mixing private investments with state support and oversight (a bit like Fannie Mae and Freddie Mac in the US banking industry). Governmental motivations varied. Metropolitan France clearly needed migrant labor from Algeria, as industrial and construction sectors of the French economy expanded. At least 300,000 Algerian migrants worked in metropolitan France already in 1957, and numbers were on the increase. At the same time, the war in Algeria loomed in the background. Recognizing that many Algerian migrants lived in squats and bidonvilles, there was concern about the living conditions of those workers, and a hope that improved conditions would make such workers a force of moderation beholden to metropolitan France.[93] Political control was also a motivation. With Algerian workers spread out in abandoned buildings and small bidonvilles, they were difficult for police to track. In December 1957, when the minister of the interior urged prefects to oversee the building of SONACOTRAL housing for Algerian workers, he specifically noted that the new housing would allow the destruction of bidonvilles and furnished rooms in slums "where undesirable elements often live, escaping all control."[94] Initially, SONACOTRAL structures were supposed to be for both singles and families, but eventually separate regional subsidiaries took over construction of units for families. The original SONACOTRAL focused on building *foyers* for men living alone (either single men or those living alone in France with families remaining in Algeria).[95]

After the Évian Accords in 1962, Gaullist political elites and much of French public opinion reimagined the history of Algeria as if to highlight the idea that Algerian independence had always been France's objective in Algeria. "French Muslims from Algeria" now became "foreign" migrants, immigrant workers like those from Tunisia and Morocco, as well as European countries from Portugal to Yugoslavia. In 1963 SONACOTRAL, founded for Algerians, became SONACOTRA (Société nationale de construction de logements pour les travailleurs), charged with building housing for various immigrants to France, notably those from North Africa.[96] Algerians were still numerically dominant. The right to travel to and within France granted by the Évian Accords, not to mention unemployment in Algeria and strong demand for labor in France, fostered an increase in Algerian migration. Housing for migrant workers became yet more urgent as the 1960s wore on.

The longtime resistance of local mayors to SONACOTRAL housing prolonged the existence of squats and bidonvilles, as they and most of their constituents envisioned their towns as luxury tourist destinations ultimately bereft of the North African laborers. In 1961, as the prefect, following instructions from Paris, contacted mayors throughout Alpes-Maritimes urging them to accept a SONACOTRAL *foyer*, only the mayor of the village Saint-Martin-du-Var, in the hinterland nineteen kilometers from western Nice, stepped forward. Given the difficulties and cost of transport connections, that location was not realistic. The prefect and his underlings had their eye on the outskirts of Nice, hidden from tourists but closer to laborers' workplaces.[97] However, reflecting the views of their supporters, the approach of the mayors of Nice, Jean Médecin until his death in 1965, and his son Jacques Médecin thereafter, was unyielding. Like Nice, communities all along the Riviera forcefully resisted the construction of housing specifically for North African workers. Already in 1958 Jean Médecin had been concerned about encampments of North Africans at Saint-Roch, near the new HLMs constructed there in the late 1950s. In February 1959 he expressed an interest in knowing more about how SONACOTRAL would work, but then he began to drag his feet. In hopes of fostering construction of housing specifically for the Algerians, the prefecture hosted Jean Vaujour, director of SONACOTRAL, in January 1962. Jean Médecin even received him.[98] Médecin, however, refused to follow through. In 1964 his newspaper, the *Action républicaine*, blamed the prefecture and de Gaulle's government for having authorized immigration in the first place and wanting to create housing for "people of 'Algerian' nationality while the French" were inadequately housed.[99]

Publicly, Médecin claimed that the problem was the cost of real estate. Under the proposed SONACOTRAL contracts, the city needed to provide the land. According to Médecin, the high price of bare ground in Nice made it impossible for the city to provide such a property. But there was more going on. Like many of his constituents, Médecin's resistance to public housing for North Africans resulted from a sense that they should ultimately disappear. In December 1960 Médecin argued that every time the municipality considered even temporary housing for North Africans, "we run into a veto from the local population." Médecin claimed in 1963 that "the bidonvilles are inhabited by a large number of unemployed Algerians, who need to be sent back to where they came from. For those who do work, they need to be housed by the company that uses them. Movable barracks on construction sites would suffice."[100] Médecin was here reflecting widely held views but not reality. Although Algerians' work was often precarious, meaning they were frequently forced to change jobs, the prefecture's repeated investigations of bidonvilles from the 1950s to the 1970s showed that the men were employed. Moreover, employers could not be legally bound to provide housing, however much the mayor may have hoped they would do so.

Nice's approach also resulted from Médecin's intense anti-Gaullism, including a desire to continue the war in Algeria. As he put it, "I can only regret that the Évian Accords have permitted Algerians to move to France, but since the consequences result from a governmental decision, it is the government that must assume the responsibility for its decisions." Clearly,

Médecin blamed the national government for the bidonvilles: "If, from the beginning, the bidonvilles had not been tolerated, North Africans who earn the same salaries as their French comrades would have taken care of their lodging by normal means."[101] Of course, this argument rests on the idea that North Africans had comparable salaries, which was not true as they occupied unskilled and semiskilled positions, even if employers were willing to hire them legally. Médecin's argument also rests on the presumption that landlords were willing to rent to North Africans, which was not true, as other officials admitted.[102]

In addition, Nice, like the Riviera generally, skewed markedly to the right electorally. Jean Médecin was to the right of de Gaulle, at the opposite end of the public spectrum from communist mayors just outside Paris who had accepted SONACOTRA structures. Even the prefecture admitted, in an internal memo in 1963, "No municipality [in Alpes-Maritimes] would have the courage to build *foyers* for Algerians, while thousands of their voters, and notably thousands of repatriated from Algeria, were still without housing."[103] The Médecins knew their political base. As the police RG reported in April 1970, Jacques Médecin told a delegation from the CGT, "I don't give a damn about Algerian workers and construction workers who don't vote for me anyway."[104]

To the Médecins and many of their supporters, North Africans were temporary workers. If the city accommodated them, they and eventually their families would settle permanently. There was also a fear that decent lodging would lead more North Africans to migrate to Nice. The prefect was caught between demands from Paris and local opposition to construction of housing for North African workers. In 1963 the prime minister's deputy charged with Algerian affairs urged the prefect to steamroll local opposition, arguing that Lyon had built housing and there had been no deluge of additional North Africans in the city. He even laid out the process of requisition and expropriation used in the department of the Seine to procure property for building.[105] The prefect blamed Médecin and other local mayors for their opposition. The slow progress of HLMs generally in Alpes-Maritimes meant that new housing for North Africans—even though the funding stream differed—would face resentment from locals with inadequate housing. Moreover, the "presence in Nice of a large colony of European *rapatriés* from North Africa, who themselves have great difficulties finding lodging, would make very delicate the application of procedures of requisition and expropriation on behalf of Algerian workers."[106] The same was true in Toulon; in 1966 pieds noirs there had vehemently opposed the construction of a *foyer* for single North Africans.[107]

In 1970, as a portion of French public opinion became more sympathetic to North Africans stuck living in bidonvilles, Eugène Claudius-Petit, head of SONACOTRA and long-standing advocate for decent housing in postwar France, traveled to Nice in order to set Jacques Médecin and other opponents of SONACOTRA structures straight. Claudius-Petit took on a host of preconceived notions about North Africans, "especially the ideas developed in the course of one hundred years of colonization: (1) They are not dirty, they are clean; because if we lived in their bidonvilles, we would be dirty. But they manage to have clean laundry. (2) They do not refuse to pay their rent. They are good at paying. (3) They send what they can to their families, but they do not avoid decent conditions here. We don't offer them anything else." Claudius-Petit denied longtime assertions that North Africans preferred bidonvilles for their low cost. Moreover, in housing North Africans, "we have never had a problem with morals." He argued that SONACOTRA had had far more problems with Sicilians and Yugoslavians.[108] This claim repeated that of local police, who noted that few North Africans or Africans ran afoul of the law, in marked contrast to the Croatian refugees from Tito's Yugoslavia.[109]

Claudius-Petit and other officials also challenged Jacques Médecin's essentialist generalizations about North Africans while often deploying their own. Médecin, like many on the Riviera at the time, denied he was racist or "anti-Arab" but simultaneously contrasted North Africans with Italians, who had earlier done the jobs the French avoided. Erasing just how much discrimination Italians had faced early in the twentieth century, Médecin claimed that Italians "never gathered together in bidonvilles; that is a North African specificity. It is a well-established fact that the problem they are causing us results from a certain number of particularities of their race." For example, Médecin claimed that Algerians "have no sense of family." Bighetti de Flogny corrected the record, noting in his own essentialist way that "they have a very well developed one: they don't even spank their children." Médecin even attributed North Africans' rates of hospitalization to their "race." "Forty percent of hospital beds are occupied by North Africans. That is abnormal. I believe that the climate, with a cold to which they are not habituated, creates conditions causing them to have more frequent illnesses." Médecin clearly wanted to clear bidonvilles without providing alternative housing. That had certainly been the official practice, but by 1970 there were few isolated spaces remaining to which North Africans might go and, more importantly, the national government had changed tack. As Claudius-Petit put it, in a heated exchange with Médecin, a bidonville cannot "be liquidated because one wants to build there without taking into account those living there. You will not put men under bulldozers. Are these men workers or are they not workers? Are they useful or are they not useful?"[110]

The mayor of Antibes, Pierre Delmas, similarly resisted the SONACOTRA. In 1963, when the police estimated that there were seven hundred North African laborers living in Antibes, the mayor rejected the option of constructing housing through SONACOTRA because Antibes still had "1,200 requests for public housing from local French and 400 requests from *rapatriés* that had not been filled." His constituents, conditioned to see the world through the colonial racial hierarchy, would presumably not understand why North Africans should have new housing while Europeans remained on waiting lists. The mayor's deputy, Dr. Michel Hébert, went farther, arguing that North African workers were incapable of "adapting to the norms of living in public housing," which was tantamount to saying that they were not civilized enough to live like Europeans. The prefect pointed out to Delmas, as he had Médecin, that SONACOTRA constructions had separate, dedicated funding (the Fonds d'action sociale), so the dormitory-like SONACOTRA buildings, designated solely for housing North African workers, in no way interfered with other public housing priorities.[111]

Nice and Antibes were not alone, as other mayors and municipal councilors along the Riviera rejected SONACOTRA constructions. Before the launch of SONACOTRA, the only place dedicated to housing North African workers was a twenty-four-bed center (expanded to eighty beds by 1961) at l'Aubarède, at the edge of le Cannet—a town adjacent to Cannes and a good deal less bourgeois. For the most part, the Association pour les travailleurs Nord-Africains, a benevolent group, limited its efforts to giving North African workers food, clothing, and administrative help in dealing with authorities. At l'Aubarède, the association also oversaw the center, which received modest subsidies from the French state and the departmental assembly. Built on a half hectare of pines, it was consistently full.[112] When the idea for a similar center in Cannes arose in 1959, the municipal councilors were outraged at the very idea, one proclaiming, "If we establish a housing center here, we will collect all of the riffraff [*racaille*] of France." Another flatly stated, "We don't want to keep them here; it is in the interest of the city of Cannes to eliminate them. It is necessary that this labor be sufficiently hidden." Georges Gelineau, charged by the city with the issue, argued, "It is necessary to show them that Cannes is the least welcoming city of France."[113]

Given mayors' (and their constituents') resistance, in 1970 there were about thirty thousand migrant workers in the department but only two *foyers*, at l'Aubarède in le Cannet, and a second, new one at Saint-André to the northeast of Nice, the two with a total capacity of five hundred.

Meanwhile, there were six important bidonvilles, in addition to overpopulated slums in Vieux Nice and Grasse. As late as 1974, Nice had only the *foyer* at Saint-André, while there were 216 across France, housing sixty thousand men. The highest concentrations were on the outskirts of Paris, notably at Saint-Denis.[114] As the prefect of Alpes-Maritimes set about to eliminate the remaining bidonvilles in the department, there was much work to be done.

Saint-André

Public housing for North African workers came late to Nice. L'Aubarède had opened in le Cannet in the 1950s, but it was isolated. The Médecins' resistance delayed any such construction in Nice until SONACOTRA itself acquired the land and opened the first *foyer* for single workers in March 1968.[115] As the prefect had suggested in a memo to Paris, the *foyer* needed to be at the edge of Nice, far from the eyes of tourists. With a capacity of 298 individual rooms, the *foyer* of Saint-André was supposed to house workers as authorities destroyed bidonvilles. Rent was 110 francs per month and included sheets, blankets, hot and cold water, and access to common areas, including a kitchen. On paper the *foyer* was a solution to bidonvilles. In practice, North Africans avoided it. One month after its opening, the *foyer* was running a deficit, as it was nearly empty with only thirty-six inhabitants. Having invested so much, there was frustration in the prefecture when it remained largely empty. Officials lashed out at North African workers, blaming them for their reluctance. According to Bighetti de Flogny, North African workers were not signing up due to their "scorn for comfort" and their "desire to save as much as possible, preferring to remain in bidonvilles or move to another when one closed down."[116] North Africans and Portuguese laborers were regularly reputed to send at least half of their earnings home, as remittances to support their families, so they wanted to economize on housing; tellingly, the residence at l'Aubarède in le Cannet, which cost only thirty francs per month in 1968, was always full.[117] When the bidonville at Rimiez in Nice was destroyed, with eighty-three men evicted, only a half dozen moved into Saint-André. As the bidonvilles at Ariane and 105, route de Marseille were about to be cleared, Bighetti de Flogny suggested a "continued harassment" of the evicted to try to get them to move into Saint-André.[118] In the pages of *L'Espoir*, Roger Cans piled on, claiming with more than a tinge of racism that North Africans avoided Saint-André for several reasons. Presumably, they didn't like rules of hygiene, cohabiting with other nationalities, or not being able to make noise after 10:00 p.m. "In short they won't accept even a minimal collective discipline, preferring instead the organized anarchy of the bidonville, without administrative hassles, forms to fill out, bills to pay." Given that retired military officers who had served in Algeria generally ran SONACOTRA *foyers*, the discipline at Saint-André may not have been as minimal as Cans implied. Only fifty men lived at Saint-André by late August 1968.[119]

North Africans' reasons for avoiding Saint-André differed markedly from those asserted in the press and the halls of the prefecture. While Cans implied that the North Africans were irresponsible, their own objections to Saint-André reveal concerns about getting to and from work. The men claimed that it was too far away and had inadequate bus service. They told Bighetti de Flogny in 1970 that workers living there could not get to construction worksites by 7:00 a.m.[120] As bad, the last bus ran to Saint-André at 7:00 p.m.; workers in western Nice had considerable difficulty returning, sometimes forced to pool together for a long and expensive taxi ride. For Tunisians, often working illegally for employers insisting on that status, Saint-André was an impossibility because residents needed to have a residency card. In November 1968, the city wanted immediately to expel more than fifty North Africans living at 280, boulevard de la Madeleine in an old villa with twenty rooms but no water, gas or electricity.[121] The prefecture had informed them that they could move to the newly completed *foyer* at Saint-André. Fifty-one North Africans signed a letter to the prefect, reminding him that the *foyer* accepted only single men, whereas their group included "families, one of which has six children." They also threatened the "trouble their expulsion during the winter would cause for public order."[122] Clearly understanding that evictions were usually delayed until spring and authorities' fears of active resistance, signatories did not accept the city's efforts to evict them immediately. The laborers also knew that their presence at la Madeleine resulted from the fact that they had worked on the nearby construction of HLM apartments for European families, and that they were being evicted so that another HLM building could be built on the site of their squat. It too would be for European families, as well as students attending the University of Nice.[123] The language of the letter and its use of third person indicate that the letter was written on their behalf. In all but two cases, the signatures included only a last name with no first name; many were in Arabic script; and those in Latin script were entirely in capital letters. In any case, the men understood the situation and the stakes. The prefect delayed the expulsion until spring.[124]

In May 1970, despite police pressure, including buses at each bidonville destruction to take workers to Saint-André, there were still sixty-three openings at the *foyer*, as many of those initially moving there subsequently left.

Officials in the prefecture were desperate to prove its worth, in part to save face with the mayor. Saint-André got a boost when the construction of the bypass around Nice began, as it ran close to the *foyer*. In essence, work came to the *foyer*, and it became, for a time, a more convenient place for those working on the autoroute to live.[125]

The Bidonville at the Digue des Français

In light of local resistance, it is not surprising that Alpes-Maritimes lagged behind other French departments in eliminating bidonvilles and finding alternative housing for their inhabitants. Nice trailed other large cities; Paris, Lyon, and Marseille had already begun the effort in the late 1950s. In 1975 Alpes-Maritimes had up to ten thousand people living in bidonvilles and other slumlike conditions, more than any other department.[126] In fact, the Digue des Français in Nice was France's largest remaining bidonville in 1975.

The Digue des Français (French dike) was an embankment on the left bank of the Var River that protected the flood plain when the Var crested. It was public land, part of the national Domaine Public Fluvial. As early as 1964–65, men built shacks next to the embankment, not far from Roma encamped there. In 1966 the head of the local police asked if three hundred inhabitants evicted from a bidonville across from the airport could move to the Var riverbed. In principle, the answer was no, as the prefect never authorized settlement there. In practice, when evicted, many men found their way to the Digue, where police tolerated their presence. When hundreds left the Domaine d'Olivetto, future site of the Musée Chagall, many of the evicted workers ended up at the Digue. Although there were complaints in 1973 that the bidonville was visible from the new sports stadium, the bidonville at the Digue was essentially out of sight and out of mind, far from the racist attacks that were becoming commonplace. In 1969 there were at least nine hundred North African men living at the Digue. Inhabitants worked on construction sites as far away as Fréjus. As authorities eliminated other bidonvilles and squats, and as there remained few abandoned properties as alternatives, more workers settled into the bidonville. About two thousand men lived there in 1973.

The Digue des Français ranged from 50 to 150 meters wide and was 1.5 kilometers in length.[127] The only cinder block constructions were along the principal street running north to south; the rest consisted of salvaged wood, paper, and tar paper, while cracks were sealed with pieces of aluminum or a plastic casing held on with strings attached to old beer cans. Light came from candles or lanterns. Bottled propane served as fuel for cooking. There

FIG. 2.1. This aerial view of the bidonville at the Digue des Français in the early 1970s shows both the main street and the alleys branching off to other shanties. Note the bidonville's placement just to the east of the earthen dike protecting the flood plain from the Var. Archives départementales des Alpes-Maritimes 207 W 125.

FIG. 2.2. Inside the bidonville at the Digue des Français in the early 1970s. The tar paper shacks, mud, and puddles were typical of bidonvilles. Archives départementales des Alpes-Maritimes 30 Fi 2434 1972 (collection Michou Strauch), rights held by the Conseil départemental des Alpes-Maritimes.

FIG. 2.3. Moving containers and trailers at the edge of the bidonville at the Digue des Français, visible from the new stadium, generated complaints in 1973. Here the view is from the bidonville toward the stadium. The prefecture and departmental archives of Alpes-Maritimes are today across the street from the stadium. Archives départementales des Alpes-Maritimes 207 W 134.

was no heat, save a few oil stoves in cafés. The typical dwelling was six square meters, with a ceiling 1.9 meters high, a space normally shared by three men. Men paid rent to owners (one man actually rented out ten separate shacks), up to thirty francs a month, or bought the spaces from others claiming to own them; ownership was a fluid concept in a community built on public land without authorization. The main north-south street included no fewer than "130 small businesses: fifty-one cafés-bars, thirty-four small groceries, fourteen butchers, twenty assorted artisans, from a haircutter to a tailor to a bicycle-motorcycle repairman. A tooth-puller came more or less regularly." Of the approximately two thousand inhabitants in 1973, two hundred made their living from business in the bidonville itself. About 40 percent of the population was Algerian and 60 percent Tunisian, and about 40 percent of this latter group were in France without a residency card.[128] The men self-segregated; Algerians cohabited with each other, as did Tunisians (usually by village of origin), and even whole sections of the bidonville were Algerian or Tunisian. They were all men, many from rural areas, notably southern Tunisia and Algerian territories just to the west. Most sent home remittances; 52 percent of the men had seven to twelve people they were supporting. Three-quarters of the Tunisians and 92 percent of the Algerians were employed, overwhelmingly in BTP.[129] The population doubled on weekends, as workers from the Var and even the Bouches-du-Rhône traveled there. By 1974, after the elimination of bidonvilles in Marseille, some North Africans frequently traveled from Marseille to the Digue des Français to shop and spend time.[130]

Some police reports also gave prurient attention to prostitutes working at the Digue on weekends. It was, according to one report, a "real center for debauchery" with twenty-eight to thirty prostitutes working there in 1970. Another report noted that some young Tunisian men also worked as prostitutes.[131] While prostitution was illegal in France, both Bighetti de Flogny and Claudius-Petit defended the government's toleration, using arguments familiar when prostitution had been legal and regulated in France. Bighetti de Flogny admitted that it was "frequent that young prostitutes come to the bidonvilles. Public security has everything to gain." For his part, Claudius-Petit asked critics, "The foreign workers that come here, leaving their families back home, are you convinced that they should all become eunuchs? Yes, we tolerate certain things."[132] For these officials, as prone as anyone to stereotypes of the hypersexualized Arab man, prostitution helped keep the men from the kind of prowling they were supposedly prone to do.

Authorities took the elimination of the bidonville seriously, attempting fitfully to understand the challenges from the point of view of residents. Having experienced eviction after eviction, residents were reluctant to speak to the police, who swooped in periodically to gather information. Whatever its inadequacies, the bidonville was a somewhat safe place for men threatened with assault when outside it. When SONACOTRA put a social worker in an office in the HLM complex nearby at Saint-Augustin, North Africans who stopped by faced threats of physical violence from nearby residents; SONACOTRA had to relocate the office in the bidonville itself. Repeatedly, official reports confirmed that young French men harassed and even assaulted North Africans in the Saint-Augustin neighborhood. "They are very sensitive to the rejection they have faced by the French population, which has spurred them to gather together in the bidonville, despite the very bad living conditions they have found there."[133]

As a result, SONACOTRA hired Pierre Espagne, a sociologist and ethnologist from the Universities of Paris VII and VIII to assist in preparing residents for the move. For eighteen months, Espagne and his Arabic-speaking students worked to gain the confidence of residents, finding out what they needed in order to accept a move. In his report, Espagne claimed that the men "don't refuse from the outset to give us the information that we need, but they are waiting for precise, definitive information about their future before responding." In particular, the Tunisian men, who had come to France as tourists and stayed, wanted residency cards so that they could remain in France legally.[134] In a sense, this problem had been of the government's own making. In 1970, concerned about the "invasive migration," the prefecture had refused to issue a residency card to Tunisians unless they already had a work contract approved by the National Office of Immigration.[135] At Espagne's urging, both Tunisians and Algerians got authorities' help in ensuring that their papers were in order. Moreover, residents of the Digue knew that any new *foyers* would cost them more, so they demanded subsidies to help with the rent in their new digs. The prefecture ultimately granted their wishes in order to persuade the men to leave peacefully.[136]

The newfound flexibility resulted partly from the changes in public opinion in the early 1970s. On 1 July 1974 a fire at the Digue des Français wiped out 250 shanties housing some 400 Algerian and Tunisian laborers.[137] The cause was never clear, leading many to speculate that it might not have been accidental. Not only did SONACOTRA provide tents for those rendered homeless, but each man also received 400 francs in compensation. Aid also flowed from the Union sociale du bâtiment et des travaux publics (the sector in which most men worked) and a host of nonprofits, including the Secours catholique, the Secours populaire, the Association de soutien des travailleurs émigrés des Alpes-Maritimes, the Comité catholique contre la faim et pour le développement, the French Red Cross, and the Amicale des Algériens et des Tunisiens en Europe. It was an unprecedented response, indicating a significant shift since the 1960s, when men pushed out of their shelters or victims of fires, both accidental and arson, lost everything with no effort on the part of either officialdom or mainstream French associations to come to their aid. Even in the pages of *Nice Matin* there was a recognition of the men's contributions to the construction of postwar tourist infrastructure: "The vast majority of the workers are participating directly in the expansion of the Côte d'Azur, particularly in the field of construction and public works."[138]

Of course, public opinion is never uniform, and alongside officials' more understanding approach to bidonvilles was ongoing resistance among the local population to North Africans' very presence. In 1975, as SONACOTRA sought locations for new *foyers* to house the men from the Digue, they ran into serious opposition in several neighborhoods. In les Moulins, which housed about fifteen thousand people in several large HLM blocks, residents were strongly opposed. SONACOTRA officials noted that about 50 percent of inhabitants of les Moulins were *rapatriés*, thus presumably even more hostile to North Africans in their midst. Although there is no evidence that pieds noirs were more hostile than other residents of les Moulins, the notion that pieds noirs were more racist than other French was already widespread in the early 1970s. In any case, the effort was successful, and SONACOTRA gave up; instead, SONACOTRA built temporary housing two kilometers north of the bidonville, as well as new *foyers* in other neighborhoods. In March 1976 bulldozers flattened the Digue des Français, eliminating the last large bidonville in France.[139]

The acute housing shortage, municipal resistance to building both HLMs and SONACOTRA *foyers*, and the mass arrival of pieds noirs meant that the Riviera was particularly slow in providing HLM apartments for North Africans. In 1961 the HLM office in Nice, deluged with demands, had just ten HLM apartments for North African and mixed North African–European families. In 1968 new HLMs set aside 6.25 percent of all apartments for immigrant workers, but most of those went to those of European descent.[140] Other French cities, including Marseille, had quotas or thresholds of tolerance (*seuils de tolérance*), that is, maximum percentages for North Africans in HLMs lest Europeans react (thus legitimizing their racist response by recognizing it as a sociological fact).[141] In Nice the point was essentially moot, as North Africans could not dream of many HLM apartments before the late 1970s. They generally got access to HLMs when Europeans moved out. Predictably, the worst constructed, such as the HLM Pasteur, had high turnover, and Europeans left as soon as they could afford to do so. Today, HLMs on the Riviera have large numbers of people who came, or whose parents came, from North Africa.

Given that up to 90 percent of North Africans in Alpes-Maritimes worked in construction, it is remarkable that so many struggled to have adequate potable water, flush toilets, or even waste removal. It was only when SONACOTRA prepared the way for bidonville destruction that the situation improved somewhat. Until SONACOTRA intervened, there was no garbage service at the Digue. The mayor had claimed that the bidonville was on national property, the Domaine Public Fluvial, not city property; therefore, it was not the city's responsibility. Moreover, the paths within the bidonville were too narrow for normal trash trucks, and the city deemed the expense too high to use the smaller, narrow vehicles purchased for Vieux Nice. There was instead a huge permanent pile of refuse, infested with rats. In 1973 there was only one well for almost two thousand men;

almost everyone had dysentery. By 1976 there were five additional wells pulling water from the aquifer, as authorities improved conditions to prove goodwill in preparation for the forced evacuation. There was never a sewage system.[142] Along the Riviera, North Africans dug the trenches and laid the pipe for expansions of water and sewage systems—but until 1976 many lived in bidonvilles without such niceties.

CHAPTER 3

Providing Potable Water and WCs

In August 1944 Allied troops invaded south-eastern France. They faced little German resistance and advanced rapidly. Months later, between January 1945 and January 1946, as the Riviera became a huge leave center, each week ten thousand US troops arrived. By the end of 1945, around 350,000 GIs had spent a week there.[1] For years thereafter, two stories about those American troops circulated widely. Both involved water. The first recounted that American soldiers initially refused to drink the water, as it did not smell right. The water in Nice had no odor. As the head of the Compagnie générale des eaux (General Water Company), the private company that supplied Nice's water, later put it, "The GIs were afraid to drink the water in Nice, so their quartermaster added chlorine to it, in order to reassure them. Ozonated water is not at all like the strongly chlorinated water that is still consumed across the Atlantic." Many of the men were accustomed to a whiff of chlorine, as US cities regularly used chlorine in the early twentieth century in order to neutralize any contaminants in drinking water.[2] Ignoring the fact that some Niçois had chlorinated water or no running water whatsoever, local notables were horrified that the American men had refused Nice's superior water, as Nice had long prided itself on its potable water. Using water from glacier-fed springs in the Alps and applying a process of ozonation since the turn of the twentieth century, Nice had provided those who could afford to subscribe to the water service with some of the best-tasting and safest water anywhere in the world. Repeated retelling of the story emphasized that unlike the United States, usually held up as the symbol of modernization after World War II, it was Nice that was at the global cutting edge of quality water production.[3] Whatever the postwar problems in Nice, in this respect at least, the city could claim to maintain its prestigious reputation.

The second story was about water off the coast of the Riviera. In 1945 American enlisted men took leave in Nice, while officers went to Cannes. Staying in requisitioned grand hotels, what better rest and recreation than to swim in the Bay of Cannes? Yet in the summer of 1945, the US military strictly forbade its officers from even entering the Mediterranean at Cannes.[4] Fecal matter in the bay risked the health of the Allied forces. For years afterward, as local officials struggled to upgrade the region's sewers, both officials and the press cited the embarrassing incident, a serious blow to the Riviera's reputation as a prestigious paradise for well-off foreigners. Given how thoroughly the United States stood for modernity in twentieth-century France, a polluted bay turned the Riviera into a backwater.[5] Much worse yet, it could scare away future tourists.

This chapter examines the rebuilding of infrastructures for potable water and sewage after World War II. In the wake of the war, as cities and towns struggled to expand their potable water supplies and sewer systems, they kept their eye on global standards of hygiene. Foreign tourists not only expected beautiful and water-hungry landscapes but also personally consumed prodigious quantities of water during the summer months. In the 1950s, while many homes in Vieux Nice had no running water, ritzy hotel rooms and rented luxury apartments did. Tourists wanted to bathe or shower daily, not to mention take additional showers after playing or swimming in the salty water of the Mediterranean. They expected flush toilets in their hotel rooms, and they flushed after every use. At the same time, those visitors expected the Mediterranean to be clean. But all of that wastewater had to go somewhere, and improving the sewer infrastructure became critical.

Authorities were obsessed with efforts to improve hygiene in postwar France, and municipalities on the Riviera especially so, as tourism depended on ever more potable water as well as safe water in the sea. The Riviera had long had more bathtubs and more WCs, better drinking water, and more sewer lines than much of France, but the desire to be internationally competitive as a tourist destination meant that local communities remained preoccupied with clean water and effective waste removal. In France as a whole, there were two changes afoot. The first was the expectation on the part of French citizens that all French deserved running water and flush toilets. The second was the role of the postwar French state in delivering that comfort. Although France had been a centralized country since Louis XIV, the national government did little to fund water and sewage systems until the Fourth Republic.[6] The successive postwar French economic plans laid out precise objectives for modernization, and the state funded initiatives as never before. In essence, potable water plumbed into homes became a public rather than a private good. Water and waste removal became rights for French citizens, delivered to all, rather than the privileges they had been. Along the way, the French state and municipalities implicitly worked to erase a long-standing class divide. Indoor running water and flush toilets had signified a social hierarchy into the early twentieth century. After the war, as potable water and sewer lines became the norm, class difference on the Riviera was increasingly measured not by access to potable water or flush toilets but by how many bathrooms one had or whether one had a swimming pool. Meanwhile, in tourists' eyes, abundant clean water for drinking and washing as well as clean seawater for swimming became primary criteria for measuring the Riviera against other beach destinations.

Potable Water and Class Difference

Potable water became a commodity in the nineteenth century, sold and delivered to the rich. In theory, water, like air, is natural, available to all.[7] In practice, the availability of good potable water tracked social status in late nineteenth-century French cities. The wealthy could afford abundant potable water that increasingly ran into their homes. On the Riviera, they even got clear mountain water from the Alps, while the poor carried water of varying quality from nearby wells or public fountains. Although Nice was in the avant-garde of French cities in the quantity and quality of water, its experience embodied the challenges of water provisioning in the nineteenth century.[8]

Contrary to widespread assumptions among summer visitors, the Riviera is not arid. Part of the Mediterranean bioregion, it does have hot, dry summers, but winter months see more rain, some of which falls in torrential downpours. Especially during storms, the mountainous terrain causes much of the rainwater to flow quickly down small valleys (*vallons*) and rivers into the sea. In 1860, when France annexed Nice and Savoy from the Kingdom of Piedmont, the people of Nice got most of their water from numerous wells throughout the city as well as some natural springs near the port. The aquifer under the Paillon River was large and shallow, adequate for a city of fewer than fifty thousand. However, by the time of the census of 1911, Nice had just over 105,000 year-round residents—plus about 100,000 winter residents. These winter residents, or *hivernants*, were part of a global elite with expectations for high-quality, abundant water for their bodies and their gardens. As a result of nineteenth-century cholera outbreaks, wealthy travelers knew well the dangers of waterborne illnesses. The city worked to keep up with increasing demand for safe water, fearing the loss of *hivernants'* expenditures.[9]

Class difference determined who got the best water. After the annexation, Mayor François Malausséna oversaw the purchase of the spring at Sainte-Thècle in the valley of the Paillon and granted a concession to the private Compagnie générale des eaux to supply the city with potable water (it was quite usual for municipalities both in Europe and beyond to sign contracts with private companies for water delivery).[10] In 1866 the company opened an aqueduct from the spring at Sainte-Thècle, about ten kilometers long, which supplied the city with nine to ten thousand cubic meters of water per day.[11] However, little of that water ended up where most Niçois lived, in or near Vieux Nice. Their water came either from a second aqueduct just upstream, with water that had already passed through several villages, or from the old wells and springs in the city. The water from Sainte-Thècle ended up on the western side of the Paillon, where *hivernants* had rented or built villas. The aqueduct's origin was high enough in the Alps that gravity could also bring water to the new villas springing up in the hills north of the city. Water from Sainte-Thècle required a subscription costing a minimum of twenty francs a year, while the average worker earned only two francs per day and often faced bouts of unemployment; the subscriptions were too expensive for most inhabitants of the city.[12] For those who could afford the subscription, there was unlimited water unless the source ran low. With no meters, well-off inhabitants and *hivernants* not only bathed in the water but also used extraordinary amounts to water their large, elaborate gardens. British owners were even known to ship in sod from England then water it heavily to try to keep grass green. In general, much of the appeal of villas on the Riviera consisted of their surrounding gardens, where owners had their gardeners plant and water an impressive array of water-thirsty subtropical plants not native to the region, plants that would never survive dry summer months without a huge amount of water.[13] For those who could not afford to subscribe, let alone live in an apartment with indoor plumbing, procuring water consisted of going down to the well or spigot in the courtyard, or down the street to the local public fountain, and hauling it back in pails and bottles. Running water was a privilege for the few, not a right for the majority.

As numbers of both inhabitants and *hivernants* in Nice increased, demand for water grew quickly. Because more water could mean more subscribers, it was profitable for the Compagnie générale des eaux to increase the water supply. The company opened another aqueduct in 1883, providing an additional ninety thousand cubic meters per day. This time, water came from a tributary of the Var River, the Vésubie, just upstream from the village of Saint-Jean-la-Rivière. Flowing in an open canal for twenty-nine kilometers, the water arrived north of the city at Gairaut, where it underwent filtration. The cascade de Gairaut's villa-like structure with artificial falls became a tourist sight known for its aesthetics and its engineering.[14] Because the water was less pure than that arriving from Sainte-Thècle, even after filtration, the water from the Vésubie was originally destined for agriculture and gardens, but was also increasingly used for toilets. At the turn of the twentieth century, buildings were even plumbed with two systems, one for potable water, the other for unpotable. In an effort to improve the quality of water, the Compagnie générale des eaux opened the ozonation facility in 1907 so that water from the Vésubie could be purified. The northern city of Lille had already adopted the new technology, as had the town of Cosne. Ozonation

FIG. 3.1.   The cascade de Gairaut, where water from the Vésubie canal arrives in Nice. The half-timbered villa-like structure overlooking the waterfalls became, and remains, a tourist sight. Photo by Kheper—own work. Licensed under Creative Commons Attribution-Share Alike 3.0: https://creativecommons.org/licenses/by-sa/3.0/deed.en. Unported via Wikimedia Commons.

offered Nice a water supply both abundant and excellent, except when heavy rains overwhelmed the ozonation facility.[15]

Summer Demand

In the 1930s continued population growth and an increasing number of summer tourists led the Compagnie générale des eaux to pump water from the Var aquifer, providing an emergency backup for the Vésubie, when production often fell short in the summer months.[16] Tapping the Var water table proved a flexible strategy; electricity (rather than gravity, as in the case of the aqueducts) could be used as necessary to provide sufficient water on demand, but pumps could be turned off in order to avoid overcapacity. Barring inordinate storage capacity, an additional aqueduct would have yielded too much water particularly in the wintertime rainy season, much as hydro-electric dams sometimes produce more electricity than the grid can handle. The importance of the Var aquifer became clear in 1944, when Allied forces aiming for the road and rail bridges over the Var bombed water processing facilities along the river. As a result, in the summer of 1945 the Compagnie générale des eaux needed periodically to cut off the water supply to homes in western Nice.[17]

Across Nice, demand for water grew exponentially. In 1865 the daily consumption of water in Nice had been five liters per day per inhabitant, at a time when the year-round population consisted of fewer than fifty thousand. In 1965, when the winter population was 320,000 but the summer population was 500,000, the daily consumption of water was 500 liters per inhabitant (in 1982 the French national median was 210 liters per inhabitant).[18] Thus, while the summer population increased tenfold in Nice, water consumption per capita increased hundredfold. Clearly, population growth alone does not explain the phenomenal increase in consumption. The proportion of households with flush toilets grew. The city used more water for public gardens and for washing the streets. People bathed and showered much more frequently than in the past. Clothes washing also consumed considerable water. For many, public washhouses and the Paillon riverbank had been the primary loci for washing. By contrast, postwar washing machines "take a lot of water," as one reporter put it.[19] Swimming pools became important status symbols for wealthy villa owners; Jacques Deray's popular 1969 thriller set on the Riviera was titled simply *La piscine* (The Swimming Pool).

Nice's rapid postwar growth led to a patchwork of makeshift solutions for new neighborhoods. As Nice expanded into the hills overlooking the city and westward into what had been agricultural land, developers built houses and new apartment blocks without waiting for an adequate infrastructure for potable water. In the 1950s neighborhoods of las Planas and Fabron had water, but it got muddy and undrinkable in times of heavy rain, forcing inhabitants to trek downhill to a public fountain.[20] Caucade and Sainte-Marguerite, near the airport, had water, but there was not enough and the quality was not that of neighborhoods closer to the center of the city. In 1958 there were sixty-three days when there was too little water at Caucade and Sainte-Marguerite, and what was available was not potable. Periods of heavy rainfall stirred up so much muddy sediment that even chlorination could not work, as the application would have to be so heavy that the water would have been undrinkable. As reported in *Nice Matin*, "One inhabitant had filled a container with twelve liters of water, and once it settled the water included 1.2 kilograms of mud!" An association representing four thousand inhabitants petitioned authorities, requesting that they receive the same "privileges of urban distribution [of other inhabitants of Nice]: that is, consistent flow, abundance, and especially that the water be potable."[21] The problem for the Caucade and Sainte-Marguerite neighborhoods was that the system for distribution of water was the same in 1958 as it had been in 1878, when the canal from the Vésubie first opened. The canal had not been designed for drinking water, even though some of its waters had, since the first decade of the twentieth century, undergone ozonation and were used as potable by some Niçois. Caucade and Sainte-Marguerite areas had been agricultural, so the water had never undergone ozonation. Yet developers ran the water into faucets in new homes.[22] In short, as developers threw up housing after World War II, as *Nice Matin* reported in 1959, "It is relatively easy to give a suburb potable water using the existing pipes, coming from the Vésubie, but the establishment of a second network creates a problem costing several billion francs." In the late 1950s, one-fifth of subscribers in Nice still got the chlorinated water of the Vésubie.[23] Only in 1982 did Nice get a unitary water system with all sources undergoing ozonation. No longer did water from the Vésubie or the Var aquifer carry that whiff of chlorine. Niçois saw outside validation in the fact that the city of Moscow adopted the ozonation process used in Nice, granting a contract to the Compagnie générale des eaux for an enormous ozonation plant.[24]

Construction, Water, and Resistance

Such water consumption came at a price. In the postwar years an increasing proportion of the city's water came from the Var aquifer, an indispensable part of the city's water network after World War II. Here local farmers' needs for water directly conflicted with the city's rapid development. As early as 1958, the departmental association of farmers, the Fédération des exploitants agricoles des Alpes-Maritimes, warned that construction companies were removing too much stone from the bed of the Var. The removal caused a progressive decline of the level of the Var aquifer and a related decline in the volume of available water.[25] Farmers feared their wells would soon run dry.

Farmers' predictions soon proved true. In 1964 *Le Patriote* reported that the city had eight wells, up to four meters in diameter, drilled into the Var aquifer.[26] New wells had been necessary because the "three oldest, the closest to the water plant, were predicted originally to produce one hundred liters per second. Unfortunately, it has been found that the removal of materials from the bed of the Var, for the establishment of the airport and the seaside road, have had the result of lowering the water table and slowing the flow of water." In 1964 there was already a ban on taking stone downstream from the wells. Newer wells further upstream had, for the time being, adequate flow.[27]

The threat came from the considerable extractions of stone for the building projects in the region. In the mid-1960s about one million cubic meters of extractions took place each year, while the river deposited only 250,000 to 300,000 cubic meters each year. Crisis seemed imminent. Some of the farmers' wells dried up. There was a serious risk that seawater would seep into the reduced water table, causing the Compagnie générale des eaux to pump salt—rather than fresh—water for the inhabitants of Nice. The nature of the Var itself was at issue. Unlike the Loire or the Garonne, where water flows continuously, the Var is little more than a stream amid stones until there is a heavy rain and it becomes a fast-moving, torrential river.[28] The water table is not constantly replenished as is the case with most rivers.

Amid the controversy, in 1967 geologist Jean-Philippe Mangin of the newly founded University of Nice issued a report on the state of the Var. His findings were shocking. In May 1965 the Var water table upstream from the water processing plant was no more than 1.5 meters under the riverbed when the river's waters were at their lowest. In May 1967, just two years later, it had fallen to eight meters below the riverbed. All of the wells in a two-kilometer radius dried up, requiring redrilling—if farmers could afford it. The dramatic shift in the aquifer had some surprising effects. One farmer, on the left bank of the Var, claimed that when the water level was at 1.5 meters, the water kept the ground a bit warmer in the winter months, so that in 1958, when frost destroyed many plants farther from the river, his own survived. He was convinced that the same temperature in the winter of 1967–68 would cause a total loss. The stakes were high. In 1967 some five hundred farm families risked not having water to irrigate their fields; they provided at the time an estimated twenty-five thousand metric tons of vegetables, a quarter of the consumption of the entirety of Alpes-Maritimes.[29] These were the beautiful vegetables that filled local open-air markets.

Farmers took action, declaring in July 1967 that if authorities did not act within the week, they would block (no doubt with tractors as became the norm when farmers demonstrated in postwar France)[30] not only the entrance to the Spada construction company's quarry site but also the promenade des Anglais itself—this at the peak of the summer tourist season. One farmer noted that Spada was primarily responsible, having created through its extractions a valley within the riverbed some twenty meters wide and fifteen to twenty meters deep, a practice that eventually drained water from the surrounding water table. Local farmers were sure that other construction firms, including Nicoletti and Detragiache, as well as Spada, had removed stone and sand for the construction of luxury apartment buildings—not just for the public works projects, such as the construction of the airport and roads that authorities had approved. The airport itself was now in jeopardy; Mangin claimed there was a serious risk of flooding in the case of heavy rains. It had been easier for construction companies to dig vertically, close to their processing facilities, but that practice created veritable canyons. In case of heavy rains, water would speed up, resulting in a flood inundating the airport.[31]

The risks were considerable, and authorities sprang into action in August 1967. The solution was to fill in the deep trenches that construction firms had created. Mangin had suggested that the large rocks and public dump of rocks and soil at the eastern end of the airport runway instead be used to close off the canyons.[32] The three firms Spada, Nicoletti, and Detragiache, nervous that they could lose access to the stone of the Var, quickly created three separate earthen dams near their quarries. Farmers argued that there should be a moratorium on any extractions from the riverbed downstream from the dams for four to six months. Nicoletti and Detragiache decided to lay new roads to the riverbed over two kilometers upstream, between Saint-Isidore and Lingostière, where there were more stones.[33] In 1970 there were ten separate earthen dams, extractions were more tightly regulated, and a tax of 1,50 francs was levied on each ton of materials removed.[34]

Water in Cannes

As in Nice, elsewhere on the Riviera potable water supplies depended on local geography. To the east of Nice, there was generally adequate potable water. Like Nice, Villefranche received water from the spring at Sainte-Thècle. Farther to the east, from Menton at the Italian border to Beaulieu, coastal towns got their water, as Nice did, from the Vésubie. The situation was much worse to the west of Nice. From the city's western edge to le Trayas at the boundary with the department of the Var, towns got most of their water from the canal de la Siagne or the canal du Loup, as did Cannes.[35] There was simply not enough water to keep up with demand. Until 1964, Antibes restricted delivery of water during the summer, despite efforts to draw tourists who inevitably demanded adequate water. Other communities west of the Var River also faced regular, embarrassing shortages during the summer months.[36]

Cannes was particularly hard hit, and the water shortage undermined the city's attempts, including costly international advertising and the film festival, to maintain its reputation as a center for elite tourism. As one engineer wrote in 1947, "The importation of foreign currency that the 'pearl of the Côte d'Azur' provides our country cannot develop, or even be maintained" without significant improvements in the supply and distribution of potable water.[37] He knew of what he spoke. In 1945 Americans in Cannes were angry when there was no water for baths or showers, and the municipal council had long discussions for the next three decades about avoiding a recurrence.[38]

Cannes, like Nice, had once been a pioneer in providing potable water for the well-off by signing a concession with a private company to provide abundant, high-quality potable water. Cannes had signed with the Société lyonnaise des eaux (the Lyon Water Company, later named Société lyonnaise des eaux et de l'électricité, or SLEE) in 1864. The company built a canal to bring water from the Siagne River, just upstream from Saint-Cézaire-sur-Siagne (thirty kilometers to the northwest of Cannes), to Cannois who signed up for the service. As the city grew, the company also built a canal from the headwaters of the Loup River near Gréolières (thirty-five kilometers to the north of Cannes), completed in 1911.[39]

In part, the problem after World War II was simply that the growing population and mass tourism caused water usage to outstrip supply. In 1911 Cannes had 30,000 inhabitants. By 1954 the city had 50,192 inhabitants, and by 1959 between 60,000 and 65,000, as many former colonizers, other

French, and foreigners moved to Cannes for retirement. During the peak summer months, counting visitors, there were a hundred thousand people living in the city in 1959. As had been recognized since the 1920s, the problem was also an aging infrastructure, as old technology developed for well-off subscribers could not efficiently scale up for mass consumption of water and widespread use of indoor plumbing. Waste was another problem. In 1945, fifty thousand cubic meters of potable water arrived in Cannes. The city consumed a fair amount in watering gardens, supplying public fountains and the port, and cleaning streets. Yet much of the rest went straight down the drain. Customers subscribed for a set amount of water, choosing the quantity they thought they would need, and that amount was pumped into their reservoirs. When the reservoir was full, the excess water ran out, often directly into the storm sewer system. Most surprising, many users had only second homes in Cannes, and their water subscription kept dumping more water into their reservoirs year-round, only to run directly out. In the late 1940s and 1950s each Cannois consumed up to eight times the amount of water per capita of the average French person.[40]

There were significant water shortages. Rolling cutoffs of the water supply, from twelve to forty-eight hours long, became the summer norm in Cannes from the 1940s into the early 1960s.[41] The water situation promised to get worse. After the Allies bombed a hydroelectric facility at the Pont du Loup, it no longer functioned, so Cannes had been able to take additional water into the canal du Loup. However, immediately after the war, the newly formed national electric company, Électricité de France, repaired the factory and then needed the water Cannes had been diverting.[42] Cannes could, and did, continue taking water directly from the Loup downstream (where it was much dirtier than upstream, where the original canal du Loup had been placed), and the water was brown when there were heavy rains. The water required heavy chlorination.[43]

The Challenges of Conservation

The obvious solution was to replace the reservoirs with metered water. In the wake of dry years, in 1921, 1931, 1945, and 1955, there were calls in Cannes's municipal council for the installation of water meters in subscribers' homes and businesses. This meant a fundamental rebuilding of the entire system, including both larger, stronger pipes—some thirty-nine kilometers' worth—that could take the increased pressure that metered water required and larger city reservoirs that would supply the water and increase the pressure. In the 1950s Cannes was one of the last cities in France to make

widespread use of a system of customer reservoirs. The system had historically worked for the affluent, as those who could afford to subscribe to the
service got abundant water. But as indoor plumbing and changing norms
of hygiene became expectations across traditional divides of social class,
Cannes required extensive upgrades that practically amounted to a whole
new system of distribution.[44]

The cost seemed prohibitive. In 1959 the estimated price was 800 to 900 million francs for a job that would take, with that level of investment, up to
ten years, even with state subsidies.[45] Unlike Grasse, Cannes had passed on
using 300 million francs of Marshall Plan money, which would have covered
part of the cost after the war—before it became clear that both the permanent and summer populations would grow so quickly. Of course, costs are
always relative. As local communists pointed out repeatedly, potable water
in Cannes could have taken precedence over the rebuilding of the Croisette
beachfront after World War II. As for support from Paris, communists sting-
ingly argued that the entire project, assuming a cost of one billion francs, was
only one-third the cost of a single day of what France spent fighting the war
in Algeria.[46] Meanwhile, even the center-right *Nice Matin* noted the workings of water and social class in Cannes. It was clear that costs for existing
subscribers would rise, particularly for those who used a lot of water. By the
1950s the rich in greater Cannes were increasingly not only watering their
gardens but also filling and topping off their private swimming pools, which
lost considerable water to evaporation.[47]

Fill valves (*flotteurs*, literally "floaters"—at the time fill valves in France
as in North America often had floating balls as part of fill valve assemblies) seemed to be an intermediate solution, as they could work in reservoirs as they did in toilets, shutting off incoming water once the water
reached a certain level. The technology was simple and cheap in theory. In
practice, however, reservoir systems relied on a small, not terribly strong
and often lead pipe that carried the water from underground to the roof
or attic of a building (it is not cold enough on the Riviera that such pipes
could freeze). Fill valves themselves were not expensive, but normally
new pipe had to be run from the main valve to the reservoir, pipe that
could withstand eight to nine kilograms of pressure, since the fill valve
would stop the water and pressure would build up in the pipe.[48] The new
plumbing could be costly.

Given the likely fiasco for postwar tourism in Cannes, urgent measures
seemed necessary. After all, why would international tourists visit a place
where there was no water in summer? Exercising the kind of power French
prefects were famous for, in January 1946 the prefect of Alpes-Maritimes

gave Cannes the authority to force residents to install fill valves, at the latter's expense. By May 1947 some 1,700 of the more than 7,000 property owners who needed to install fill valves had complied.[49]

Rich Resistance

Other property owners were outraged at the imposition. The property owners' association protested to the mayor. In large apartment buildings and co-ops, there was an array of systems, some of which could make the installation of new pipes and fill valves especially expensive. About a thousand buildings had a simple reservoir, and a single pipe leading to it. When the reservoir was full, excess water went into the sewer. Installation of fill valves here was low-hanging fruit. In five hundred or so buildings, there were several reservoirs, all with separate incoming pipes, and here too any excess went directly into the sewer. Another 3,500 buildings had reservoirs on different floors, and the excess drained into secondary reservoirs for washing and watering. Where there was more than one reservoir and more than one pipe, the cost of the renovations seemed prohibitive. In the logic of the association, since saving water was for the good of the city as a whole, so all had access without interruption, all should pay for it, through their taxes.[50] These were, after all, folks accustomed to abundant water, and if their reservoirs were full, the impact of rolling cutoffs of the supply minimal. For many other users with water meters, including inhabitants of newer buildings, the cutoff meant no water at all. In essence, Cannes was attempting to engineer the conversion of a private system built for the wealthy into a public water system; from the perspective of the more affluent, the public as a whole should pay.

In order to placate well-off voters, in May 1947 the municipal council decided to install all of the fill valves on all reservoirs, borrowing 3 million francs, which would be amortized over ten years, as users across the city paid the city back. Before administrative decentralization of the French state in the early 1980s, a city needed the prefect's approval for almost all decisions, particularly one this significant involving debt. The prefect rejected the city's request. The city did get authorization to advance the money to the SLEE, which could then pay it back slowly by charging customers, but the prefect was clearly worried about the city taking on the liability of fixing what would turn out to be a very complex and costly reconstruction of the plumbing in some buildings.[51] It looked like a subsidy for the wealthy.

As late as 1982, fully one-third of the old reservoirs in Cannes had not yet been replaced with water meters. In the meantime, as the population increased and water usage increased, the city continued to use water from the Loup River, chlorinating heavily. Cannes also tapped into new sources, pumping water from the aquifer of the Siagne, twenty kilometers from Cannes.[52] Proposed in 1945, the project remained in the planning stage until the early 1960s. In the meantime, some neighborhoods in Cannes had serious water shortages. In l'Aubarède, a neighborhood in Rocheville–le Cannet in the northwestern quadrant of greater Cannes, 90 percent of residents lacked potable water between May 15 and September 15, 1961 (this was the same marginalized area where the first *foyer* for North African workers was built). The local homeowners' association got the mayor to have a public fountain installed. Placed where there was water, a full five hundred meters from some residents' homes and on a busy street, the fountain's location was blamed for an auto accident in which several people fetching water were injured. In 1962 Cannes had to pressure the SLEE to establish the pumps in the Siagne. Pumping from the water table of the Siagne took care of summer shortages in 1963.[53] As with Nice's pumping of water from the Var aquifer, Cannes could adjust the quantity of water arriving in the city, pumping more water during the summer months as needed. The downside was that chlorine was required to make water safe during summer months of increased demand, and that seemed to undermine the reputation of Cannes. It was an imperfect yet cheaper solution to increase the water supply, as compared to upgrading the entire system in order to mandate metered water.[54]

Cannes was not alone in slow adoption of water meters. Despite a local effort after 1952 and a national effort since the early 1960s, many homes in Nice still did not have water meters in 1982. Instead, older apartment buildings continued to use reservoirs on the roof or in the attic.[55] Nevertheless, lest it sound like the Cannois and the Niçois were particularly wasteful in still having reservoir systems in the 1980s, it is worth noting that despite water shortages in California, state law has only required water meters on new houses since 1992, and older structures are not required to have meters until 2025. There the issue has not been one of laying new pipe to handle increased water pressure, but of wealthy communities accustomed to wasting water on big green lawns and swimming pools.[56]

Sewage and the Sea in Cannes

In French, wastewater is known as *eaux usées*, literally "used water." Conceptually the term is helpful, because it reminds us of the direct link between increased consumption of water and increased water flowing into sewers.

With the exception of water used in watering and swimming pools, once-potable water had to be evacuated. The baths, showers, and flush toilets for tourists and residents left behind more dirty water than ever. The problem of wastewater was not new to the postwar era; in Cannes much of it already ran into sewers and then into the sea. In the late nineteenth century, as the development of flush toilets and sanitary sewer systems displaced cesspools with night soil (picked up and used as agricultural fertilizer), wastewater flowed untreated into nearby waterways; as elsewhere, water quality declined as a result of flush toilets.[57] In the interwar years, as Cannes gradually morphed into a summer tourist destination, sewage in the sea became a problem. As all along the coast, Cannes pumped its sewage into the sea through marine outfalls (*émissaires*), underwater pipes that carried waste away from the beach. Sewage had long ended up in the Mediterranean. What changed after World War II was the amount of waste and the fact that tourists and locals now wanted to spend significant time in the water and on the beach during summer months.

In the early twentieth century the French state did little to control or develop sewage systems, even after the creation in 1906 of the Conseil supérieur d'hygiène publique de France (CSHP), a national health board. For funding, Cannes and other municipalities were on their own; they needed the prefect's approval for the debt, but it was the city, not the state, which was on the hook for paying it back. Already well aware of human and household waste floating along the coastline, in October 1930 Cannes's municipal council contracted with architect and engineer Ernest Fournier to design an improved sewer system. Fournier was something of an expert in sewage, serving as a technical adviser to towns outside Alpes-Maritimes, including Cassis, le Levandou, Montargis, Orange, Tours, and Valence. Fournier drew up plans, and the municipal council approved the project unanimously in January 1931. The Fournier plan called for the *dilacération*, or grinding up of waste, before sending it out to sea. Two long submarine outfalls, one to the east of Cannes and one to the west, would combine and replace the outfalls of some seventeen separate short pipes that dumped waste along the coastline.[58] The timing was not good; the Depression that began in the United States in 1929 hit France in 1931.

Local architect François Arluc immediately began a virulent campaign of opposition. The projected cost of the Fournier project—45 million francs—was Arluc's rallying cry during elections for the *conseil général*, the department's deliberative body, in October 1931. Once elected, here Arluc had a forum for his criticism. In the wake of the attacks, municipal council members resigned their posts, and a newly elected council rejected Fournier's plan. Instead, the city pursued a cheaper solution in 1933–34, costing less than 1.3 million francs. It consisted of continuing to allow sewage to go into the sea along the famed Croisette. Here a couple of pumps pushed sewage slightly farther out to sea, assisting gravity. Not surprisingly, the new solution did little to reduce sewage in the bay. In the meantime, Arluc's media campaign was so over the top that Fournier sued for defamation, and the appeals court in Aix twice condemned Arluc, fining him.[59]

In the wake of trains of working-class vacationers sponsored by the Popular Front descending on the Riviera in 1936, city leaders worked to preserve Cannes's reputation as an elite destination. The founding of the film festival was an important step. Ensuring clean water in the bay was another. Yet as the prefect of Alpes-Maritimes put it to the minister of the interior, "as a result of a faulty system dumping sewage into the sea, the water quality leaves much to be desired; it is the cause of frequent complaints and this situation cannot continue without causing serious damage to [the reputation of Cannes]." Despite Arluc's continuing opposition, the municipal council again approved the Fournier project in 1938. Arluc persisted, and the prefect claimed that Arluc mobilized twelve separate associations in Cannes concerned about an increase in taxes; petitions came from an array of civic and professional associations.[60] Notably absent were any professional groupings of hotel and restaurant owners or workers. At stake, in essence, were competing visions for Cannes. Would it remain a provincial town with some winter visitors who rarely got in the sea? Or would it adapt to changing tourist expectations for summer sun and the sea? To succeed as a summer tourist destination, Cannes needed cleaner seawater.

In 1938 the CSHP approved the revised version of Fournier's plan for Cannes, just as it had his project for Antibes, implemented already in 1934. However, the CSHP recommended full-blown sewage treatment plants and not just the grinding up of waste before pumping it to sea, as laid out in the revised Fournier project. The CSHP's approval of dilacération of waste was provisional; the Fournier plan called for the eventual construction of treatment plants at each outfall, and the CSHP endorsed that longer-term solution.[61] Dilacération was a lower-cost but imperfect solution as regards bacteria. In a process pioneered on the Atlantic coast in an effort to save oyster beds, experiments with grinding up human waste sped the dissolution of fecal matter in the sea. In the late 1930s the approach seemed to be working in Antibes, as well as in Cassis and le Levandou.[62] Of course, dilacération did not eliminate the bacteria. Arluc's orchestrated campaign against the revised

Fournier project caused further delay, and all efforts to upgrade the system came to a halt with the outbreak of World War II. Despite the upheaval and controversy, Cannes continued to pump its sewage just off the coast in 1945 in much the same way it had in 1930.

After the Liberation, the tide turned. Dr. Raymond Picaud, who as assistant mayor had resigned along with other municipal council members in 1932, became mayor of Cannes in 1945.[63] After the disastrous and embarrassing summer of 1945, when American brass forbade soldiers from entering the Mediterranean, it was clear that immediate action was needed. In December 1945 the city and Fournier at last signed a new contract, which relieved Cannes of obligations to Fournier and gave the city the right to use as much of his plan as it wished.[64] Picaud understood the stakes: "We need to move fast. The situation is catastrophic for Cannes. We want tourists this summer, and we have to give them assurance that the right decisions have been made regarding the cleanliness of our beaches. It is unnecessary to remind everyone of the adverse and harmful American policy resulting from the filth of our beaches. It is thus essential that we clean up the sea."[65]

The Ministry of the Interior approved a newly revised sewer project, largely paid for by the French state as part of the Plan d'équipement national. The first priority was to extend the sewer system to the entire city, so that no sewage ended up in valleys between hills, getting washed into the sea during rainstorms. The second priority was the construction of much longer marine outfall. Antibes served as a model, as it already had a system of dilacération, followed by fermentation, as set up twelve years earlier. In Antibes there was no toxicity three hundred meters beyond the marine outfall. In the words of Mayor Picaud, the Antibes system worked "so well that the famous beach at la Garoupe, just over 1,000 meters from the point of emergence of the marine outfall, still has exceptionally clear water."[66] In 1946, as had been the case since 1931, the mayor of Mandelieu, just to the west of Cannes, protested the marine outfalls at the western edge of Cannes. Since the Ligurian current along the coast flows from east to west, it seemed logical that waste pumped out in Cannes would end up in the water off Mandelieu. Picaud claimed that a new marine outfall would go three hundred meters out to sea and would be a full 1,400 meters to the east of Mandelieu, so waste would go out to sea rather than toward Mandelieu.[67] Because dilacération and longer outfalls seemed to solve the problem, Cannes resisted building a sewer treatment plant that purified the water before its release.

Yet the city implemented only part of the project in the late 1940s. Engineers divided sewage into two large zones, one to the east and another to the west, with the boulevard Carno as the dividing line. Engineers built a submarine outfall to the east, designed to protect the beach along the Croisette by eliminating the various outfalls along the famous beachfront. The outfall to the east took waste 650 meters away from the coast and 17 meters deep. The resulting pollution was not detectable more than 300 meters from the outfall. The beach at Cannes seemed safe. However, nothing at all happened in the western zone. There two older pumping stations pumped waste just 160 and 420 meters from the coast. Waste found its way to the beaches to the west of Cannes, including at Mandelieu.[68] Strong currents swept bacteria to the north, to the beach, where in the late 1950s there were dangerous concentrations of *E. coli* even though the water appeared clear. The problem was obvious and immediate. Beachfront tourism was developing rapidly. "An enormous crowd" of tourists arriving by car swamped the beaches to the west of Cannes. One proposed solution, extending the length of outfalls, was not feasible because of the depth of the sea, one hundred meters deep just five hundred meters from the beach. At the time, such a deep outfall would have been technologically impossible to monitor, maintain, or repair.[69]

Polio and the Valleys

Automobiles made it possible for postwar tourists to change plans quickly when at all dissatisfied with beachfront conditions. A news report could lead to a quick change of plans before or after arriving, badly damaging local businesses catering to tourists. In 1957 and 1960 public health authorities worked to keep a lid on public knowledge of polio outbreaks for fear of scaring tourists. In April 1957 polio struck children in Antibes, Cannes, le Cannet–Rocheville, Mouans-Sartoux, and Vallauris. Parents panicked. Tourists did too, and changed their summer plans. Press reports about the scare received much of the blame for a bad tourist season in the summer of 1957.[70]

In June 1960 directors of local summer camps received a confidential letter dated 14 June, referring to the existence of "malady no. 14" in Cannes and some surrounding communities. In an effort to avoid panic, the word "polio" did not appear. In principle, children had to be vaccinated to go to summer camp, but in practice public health authorities were worried many had not been. The press did not report the story in 1960. *Le Patriote* reported the second polio outbreak only in 1961, nearly a full year later, admitting that the editors knew of the incidents at the time. *Le Patriote* justified its silence by pointing out that it had published the news in 1957 on the front page, using five full columns, and that this time around the newspaper did not want to be "accused of sowing panic in a population sensitized by the outbreak of April 1957" and ruining the tourist season. Even in May 1961, almost a full year later but before the high season that year, the editors predicted that critics would accuse them of damaging the Riviera's tourist season.[71]

Water was to blame. One cause seemed to be contamination of the canal de la Siagne. Long-standing complaints about the safety of water coming through the canal had led to a new water treatment plant in the town of Mougins, up the hill from Cannes. However, the treated water then flowed to Vallauris and le Cannet in an open canal, where it was used for public washing at Rocheville. Refuse and even dead animals also found their way into it. In addition, Cannes's three outfalls were suspect.[72] Yet the most likely culprits were the six different valleys in and around Cannes that continued to drain water from the hills down into the sea. In 1961 there were some fifty kilometers of such valleys, but only nine kilometers of the total length were covered. They served as natural drainage, a sort of open-air storm sewer as Cannes struggled to build an effective sewage system.[73] The valley of the Foux was the worst, symbolizing the problem of valleys along the Riviera as development in the hills had polluted streams. Running from way up in the hills of le Cannet down through Cannes to the sea, some 1,700 meters in length, the Foux served as a veritable sewer. In principle, it carried rainwater. In practice, clandestine sewer hookups had fed it since before World War II. Some residents without sewer lines placed their waste directly in it or ran household sewer lines into it. The Foux was slow-moving, drawing flies and mosquitoes.[74] As it reached the sea, the water went underground into a collector running under city streets. But much more water and waste found its way into the Foux than when the collector had opened in 1890. In periods of heavy rain, everything went directly into the sea, contaminating it. In the end, the precise cause of the polio outbreaks, besides the fact that not all of the children had gotten the vaccine, remained unclear. The incidents highlighted existing concerns about water and sewage.

Valleys remained a major cause of pollution in the 1970s. The solution was to build collector pipes large enough, then to pipe everything out to sea in longer outfalls. In 1972 Cannes and the surrounding communities of le Cannet, Mandelieu, Mougins, and la Roquette-sur-Siagne installed a new marine outfall west of Cannes at Béal, 1,200 meters long and 100 meters deep. This single outfall handled the waste of 300,000 residents during the summer months. The next step, achieved in the mid-1970s, was the collection of waters from the valleys and storm sewers, which then also went out through the outfall. The problem seemed to be solved. Then in the summer of 1975, Cannes witnessed an algae bloom lasting two weeks in the high tourist season. Since it had not occurred before, the concentration of nitrogen around the new outfall was suspect. Now there was fear that tourists would avoid Cannes because of the algae.[75]

Sewage in the Sea at Nice

Nice had long taken sewage seriously, even if the increased number of tourists and population growth consistently outpaced the extension of the sewer system. Nice founded a municipal hygiene office in 1887, fifteen years before the law of 15 February 1902 mandated one for each French municipality.[76]

FIG. 3.2. Nice's sewer trunk line runs under the promenade des Anglais in what is here an open space during reconstruction in 1947. Note also the complete absence of beach at the base of the wall protecting the promenade. Archives Nice Côte d'Azur—Ville de Nice, 1064 W 538 (collection of the photographic service of the city).

FIG. 3.3.   Sewer lines exposed in this hole at the intersection of the boulevards Tzaréwitch and Gambetta in Nice in 1941. The crisscrossed lines reveal the complexity of the separate systems for waste and rainwater. Archives Nice Côte d'Azur—Ville de Nice, 1064 W 537 (collection of the photographic service of the city).

Wealthy international visitors had high expectations, and for the most part city leaders catered to them. Nice already had something of a storm sewer system as early as 1832, when the population of the city was concentrated in Vieux Nice. As new villas appeared on the right bank of the Paillon, the city extended the system in that direction. Because of the dominant westbound Ligurian coastal current, the outfall was to the west of the city. By the early twentieth century, Nice had a unitary sewer system, combining rainwater and human waste in one network. A huge (2.5-meter-diameter) collector ran east to west under the promenade des Anglais, culminating in an outfall that took waste to sea off the coast at Carras. When the outfall opened in 1910, it was far from the center of Nice, four kilometers from Vieux Nice. The system worked except in the case of heavy rains, when it overflowed and raw sewage poured into the sea.[77]

In the 1930s Nice pioneered a "separate sewer system," meaning that in one part of the system rainwater drained through several outfalls into the sea, while sewage used a separate part of the system. As sewers went, it was the gold standard. Sewage continued to flow through pipes to the collector under the promenade, then to the outfall at Carras. There it underwent limited dilacération before going out to sea.[78] In principle, the current took the waste westward, where it met water coming down the Var, which pushed the waste farther out to sea. Nevertheless, the system had serious problems, some of which resulted simply from the unique geography of the Riviera. The narrow coastal plain on which much of Nice sits is not far above sea level. Despite the nearby mountains, there is very little grade on the plain. Sewer lines running toward the collector have a pitch of only five millimeters per meter. The general collector that runs under the promenade falls only three-tenths of one millimeter per meter. The sewer lines in some neighborhoods were actually below sea level and required pumps to move the waste.[79] Sewer lines were too narrow for a person to stand upright within them, and some were virtually impossible to enter even on all fours. In the early twentieth century, sanitation workers used sewer dogs (*chiens-égoutiers*) to clean narrow lines. With a cable attached to the dog's harness, the dog ran down the pipe to the next manhole. Sewer workers could then use the cable to knock waste off the inside of the pipe. In Nice criticism from foreign tourists led to its abandonment, and the practice was condemned at the World Federation of Societies for the Protection of Animals meeting in the Hague in 1952. (French cities less dominated by tourism, notably Rennes, continued to use sewer dogs, as late as the 1980s.)[80]

Runoff and Marine Outfalls

Runoff posed a bigger problem. After Marseille, Nice was France's largest Mediterranean city. In the late 1950s and 1960s, Nice added about five thousand homes a year as the number of inhabitants grew by ten to fifteen thousand per year. Unbridled development quickly covered bare ground with buildings, cement, and asphalt, significantly increasing runoff. Sections of the system for rainwater dated from 1880; the storm sewers were not designed for the increased volume. Both the Paillon River and the Magnan stream were covered before they reached the sea, limiting the volume of runoff they could carry. In addition, when the promenade was enlarged and extended toward the sea in the 1930s, it was also raised so that storm surges from the sea would not flood it. As a result, streets just inland from the promenade, such as the rue de France, which runs parallel to the promenade just to the north, is at a lower elevation than the promenade. When the storm sewers could not handle the flow, water flooded nearby streets. Those areas most recently developed, notably the westernmost areas of the city near the Var, had no storm sewers until the 1960s, so flooding was common. Worse yet, heavy rains overwhelmed both parts of the system, temporarily turning it into a veritable combined sewer system as rainwater and sewage mixed and flowed into the sea at several points along the coast.[81]

The system had been designed for a city of about 100,000, but in 1960 Nice had 500,000 summer residents. In 1970 Nice pumped 1.5 cubic meters of sewage into the Mediterranean per second.[82] During the high tourist season, the city avoided releasing waste from the Carras outfall, letting it build up in the grand collector under the promenade des Anglais, as there was always a risk of sewage ending up on the beach should the current change. The westbound Ligurian current is dominant; however, occasionally an exceptionally strong mistral, from which Nice is usually protected by the Alps, blew in from the northwest and caused waste from Carras to spread eastward along the beach at Nice. So the city played it safe by only releasing sewage in the off-season.[83]

The sewage outfall at Carras had repeated problems. A leak erupted just sixty meters from the coast, until it was repaired in 1949. Underwater detonations during the war had caused a second breech 170 meters from the coast; it went unrepaired for several years. On occasions when the Carras outfall failed entirely, its waste went to Magnan to the storm sewer outfall, where raw sewage mixed with rainwater and flowed into the sea just off the beach. In the early 1950s the Fabron neighborhood, west of Magnan, got a rainwater outfall also used when that of Carras failed. Since Fabron was 800 meters to the west of Magnan, waste from that outfall was less likely to end up on the beach near the center of the city, thus less likely to ruin the tourist season if an overflow occurred during the summer.[84]

Beginning in the early 1960s, there were plans to move the outfall at Carras westward to Ferber, just to the east of the airport. At the time, the outfall at Carras went 189 meters out to sea, and there was a strong contamination at least 500 meters from the marine outlet, but water was reasonably clean

800 meters from outlet. The idea was that relocation to the edge of the airport "would make it possible to 'liberate' 700 meters of beach." In principle, sewage would flow toward the mouth of the Var, where its waters would push waste farther out to sea. Communities to the west of Nice protested angrily that the sewage from Nice would end up on their beaches. Except in periods of heavy rain, the Var does not release much water into the sea, so it did little to push sewage away from the coast.[85] The communities failed in their quest; in 1972 Nice's sewage outfall moved to Ferber. It was ten meters deep and six hundred meters long, far enough out to sea that when seagulls gathered to snack on the waste they would not get caught in airplane engines.[86] The move made little difference in water quality, even in Nice. As reported in *Nice Matin* in 1974, waste found its way back to the beach at Nice in the form of minuscule debris that was "inaesthetic" and made the water "dirty and nauseating." In an ongoing effort to dodge the more expensive solution of a treatment plant that would purify the water, recommended by the CSHP since the end of World War II, Nice had moved and lengthened the outfall (further lengthened to one kilometer in the early 1980s).[87] In simply pushing sewage farther out to sea, Nice was not alone. Cannes of course followed a similar strategy, as did Antibes, Golfe-Juan Vallauris, Menton, Roquebrune-Cap-Martin, Saint-Jean-Cap-Ferrat, and Théoule. Nearby in Monaco, where Prince Rainier considered himself an environmentalist, the outfall was just 750 meters in length.[88]

As in Cannes, valleys in Nice presented a major challenge, as they caused the content of rainwater outfalls to resemble that of the sewage outfalls. While most of the city had sewer lines (only 92 hectares of the city's 3,192 total hectares had no lines in 1959), not all homes were hooked into the system. Some homes had underground connections not to the waste sewers but to the rainwater system. Other residents simply dumped waste into the valleys, many of which went into underground rainwater pipes as they approached more populated parts of the city. Dog excrement, trash, and dead rats made their way to the beach through the valleys and storm sewers.[89] In western Nice the rainwater outfall at Magnan was consistently problematic. In the words of a local resident, Dr. P. D., "My home is just above the mouth of the Magnan. It has become an open sewer where residents regularly throw waste. In addition, some of them do not hesitate to dump the waste of their workshops (soap makers, etc.) so that the stream looks like a cesspool upon its arrival at the sea. There is an outfall fifty meters off the coast, at this same spot, which allows one to see the surrounding beaches invaded by excrement."[90]

Swimming in Sewage

Sewage in the sea was a recurrent problem, one that threatened to destroy the very reason most tourists came to Nice after World War II. There was irony in the city's efforts to keep sewage away from visitors. Tourists created considerable additional sewage, but they expected protection from their own waste; in 1967, Nice produced an average of 180,000 m³ of sewage per day from May to October, but only 130,000 m³ per day the rest of the year.[91] Mass tourism depended on heavy use of natural resources, but the landscape, whatever its real state, needed to seem unaffected. For decades after 1945, tourists noted and judged local water quality. In the 1950s tourists repeatedly complained of tar, trash, and excrement in the water.[92] In 1957 a Briton living in Nice complained that it was a "scandal to be in the water among trash." *Nice Matin* claimed in 1961 that the newspaper received many complaints, by mail and in person, about pollution on the beaches at Cannes as well. There was fear that tourists would move on to another less-polluted place on the coast. Complaints from tourists and locals, especially those who made their living from tourism, continued into the 1970s. In 1972 the owner of a beach concession (*plagiste*) in Nice noted that when the mistral blew, "a sort of creamy residue comes back toward the beach."[93]

In 1976, of forty-five kilometers of beachfront in Alpes-Maritimes, on only three kilometers was swimming banned, consisting mostly of the beaches of western Nice, where outfalls continued to dump sewage into the sea.[94] But those three kilometers were in the city of Nice, where both tourists and locals expected to be able to swim and play in the water. In the summer of 1976 *Nice Matin* published a series of readers' letters. G. B. explained, "The baie des Anges has become a vast latrine. Swimming has become dangerous. I've heard many tourists very unhappy about what they call a real scandal. To promote tourism in the region of Nice without securing the healthfulness of the summer season is an enterprise destined for failure." A group of German tourists sarcastically informed a reporter, as they fled Nice, that they would "long remember sea-bathing in the baie des Anges!" Another reader of the newspaper remarked that in the baie des Anges the obstacle to swimming was not the *dents de mer* (literally "teeth of the sea," the French title of the film *Jaws* about shark attacks, which had just appeared in France), but the rather the *crottes de mer* (turds of the sea). Madame C. de S. claimed that the baie des Anges had become the "bay of turds," wondering whether authorities should post signs recommending against swimming given the number of tourists who unknowingly undressed their small children and let them play in and near the water, risking their health. J. R. M. wrote that the promenade des Anglais had become a vast sidewalk alongside an "immense sewer" and that the city's moniker "Nice-the-Beautiful had become Nice-the-Smelly."[95]

In 1977 the water was so bad that authorities forbade swimming in western Nice, at Ferber and Carras.[96] Mayor Jacques Médecin's efforts to defend the city rang hollow. Although he accurately pointed out that in 1979 Nice tested seawater at some twenty-four different places along the beach for viruses and that none was ever found, he remained silent about the existence of bacteria. He also declared, "50,000 people swim each summer in Nice. But there are no more infectious illnesses in summer than in winter."[97] Of course, such an assertion rested on medical statistics, generated by doctor and hospital visits, so if medical assistance was not sought, there was no paper trail. It was not a denial that there was raw sewage in the sea. Not surprisingly, a survey undertaken by the Ministry for the Quality of Life in 1975 found that summer tourists to Alpes-Maritimes clamored for treatment plants.[98]

Whatever its reputation for natural beauty, the coastline of Alpes-Maritimes was essentially a long, narrow urban agglomeration by the 1970s. Despite the obvious challenges, the Riviera was actually on the cutting edge of French coastal cleanliness at the end of the Thirty Glorious Years, a reminder that the area's reputation as paradise raised expectations and thus generated complaints. As of 1974, as reported in Le Monde, Cannes had the longest outfall, at 1,200 meters, and the deepest, at eighty-five meters, of any municipality on the French Mediterranean or Atlantic coasts. In Alpes-Maritimes generally, rigorous testing along the coast proved that there was less bacteria than allowed in French public pools. The department had six long marine outfalls and three more under consideration. Four treatment plants were under study. The biggest danger was still from valleys, which brought bacteria into the sea during heavy rains, but both Nice and Cannes were completing central collection systems to treat all water from every source, purifying it before putting it into the sea.[99]

Water, Sewage, and Race

From the vantage point of 1975, water provisioning and the extension of sewage systems over the previous thirty years were indeed glorious. Interwar inaction and a shortage of funds had led to the international embarrassment of the American ban on officers so much as entering the sea at Cannes in 1945, not to mention the summer shortages of potable water in Antibes and

Cannes. However, by the 1970s, because funding had flowed from Paris, water systems kept pace with tourists' and residents' ever more intense consumption of water. In the meantime, expectations for clean seawater grew during the period. In the 1980s, as treatment plants were complete, the water off the coast was safer for swimming than it had been for much of the twentieth century. For tourists and most residents, potable water and effective sewer systems became the norm.

There remained an important exception. Many North Africans did not enjoy those comforts. Ironically, North African labor was critical in constructing postwar water and sewage infrastructure, both on the Riviera and inland.[100] North Africans were also well represented on building sites, where workers installed plumbing for kitchens and bathrooms, the amenities they lacked themselves. Many had neither running water nor WCs where they lived. In fact, in neighbors' complaints about nearby squats and bidonvilles, the absence of potable water and WCs was a frequent refrain. Yet the lack of water and WCs in North African dwellings was not attributed to a failing of French society or government. Rather, it was inevitably assumed to be the fault of North Africans themselves, leading to assertions that they did not care about cleanliness, or did not fully understand French mores—in short, that they were not fully civilized. They faced incessant criticism for not using enough water, for drinking nonpotable water intended for gardening, for stealing water, and for using public fountains for water. There was even more scorn for the fact that squats and bidonvilles did not have proper WCs and that the men either reserved a floor for excrement, dug a latrine, or did their business at the edge of a villa's lawn (that is, far from where they slept, though closer to passers-by).

In the seemingly inclusive postwar French language about a right to comfort, North Africans faced exclusion. Access to clean water was a class privilege in the nineteenth century. In a sense, it became a racial privilege in the mid-twentieth century. North Africans' contributions to French economic growth and tourists' comfort did not entitle them to the same comfort, even potable water and WCs. To a large extent, French government policy after World War II delivered the goods for those of European descent, including pieds noirs, erasing some of the acute class differentiation of the nineteenth century. Although race is not an official category of differentiation in France, notions of racial difference nevertheless divided the people living in postwar France, including Algerians who were legally French citizens before 1962, before they became "immigrants" upon Algerian independence.[101]

The dynamic only began to change in the 1970s when, under increasing public pressure, authorities took a few halting steps to ensure potable water supplies at the bidonvilles across from the airport and at the Digue des Français in order to prove goodwill before persuading the men to leave.[102] Nevertheless, it is worth remembering that the destruction of bidonvilles was not primarily for the welfare or comfort of their inhabitants. Rather, their elimination was above all to improve the aesthetics of western Nice for tourists arriving to enjoy the promenade des Anglais and the beach.

CHAPTER 4

Fattening Up Beaches and Polluting the Mediterranean

As a destination for northern European visitors since the late eighteenth and early nineteenth centuries, the Riviera owed its existence to an early shift in Europeans' cultural understandings of the sea. In his now classic work *The Lure of the Sea*, Alain Corbin showed how Europeans gave up deep-seated fears of the sea, instead seeking it out as a romanticized source of inspiration. Maritime air also became a cure for a variety of ailments, and a host of seaside resorts emerged in the eighteenth and nineteenth centuries.[1]

The early nineteenth-century "lure of the sea" was above all an interest in the sight of the sea and the presumed healthfulness of sea air, not the beach. In France Hyères-les-Palmiers was the first important winter destination, where visitors came for the season in order to breathe sea air and enjoy warmer weather than in northern Europe.[2] Adored by Britons, the center of Hyères is a full five kilometers from the nearest beach. In Nice foreigners rented and built villas near the sea but not necessarily on the beachfront itself; in fact, the hill of Cimiez was a much sought after locale, the site of grand hotels and grand villas occupied by northern Europeans during the winter months. Visitors liked to walk or ride alongside the sea, but they did not spend much time in the water or on the beach.

Twentieth-century tourism brought two critical changes to the Riviera. First, summer tourism largely displaced long winter stays. Second, the number of visitors exploded after World War II, as salaried employees and managers, the lower middle class, and even some workers joined the rich in visiting the Riviera. Expectations for use of the sea and the beach shifted dramatically. After 1945 ever more visitors sought the sun, the sea itself, and beaches where they tanned, played, and swam much of the day. The water and the beach became the point in traveling to the Riviera in the first place.

This chapter examines the re-forming of the Mediterranean seaside after 1945. While beachgoers enjoyed "nature," immersing their bodies in the water, lying on the sand, and boating, those activities required an infrastructure and continual maintenance, not to mention considerable expense. Tourists' own presence significantly altered the environment, even as they were supposed to appreciate spending their vacations in a "natural" setting of sea air, sand, and the Mediterranean—distinguishing vacation from their usual, presumably "artificial" urban existence.[3]

Beachfronts were a draw after World War II, necessitating intervention if the Riviera were to meet changing expectations among tourists. In sync with postwar preoccupations with hygiene, visitors expected clean beaches. They wanted beaches to be wide. Most preferred them with sand rather than stones. In a cultural reversal since the early nineteenth century, when advancing coastal sand dunes in the Landes seemed such a threat that the French state undertook massive afforestation,[4] now sand became the objective for tourists and the communities hoping to lure them.

Beachgoers loved sand, creating a challenge for the Riviera. On sand, they could go barefoot to, from, and along the water. They liked to lie on the sand for hours, play games, and build sandcastles with their children. As one Parisian put it, "What pleasures for children and adults to experience the joys of sand! Sand pâtés, holes, castles."[5] The desire for large sandy beaches lay in the words themselves. *Plages*, or "beaches," became the destination. Yet the paucity of wide, sandy beaches in Alpes-Maritimes initially caused some commentators to avoid the word *plage* to describe the beaches of the Riviera, preferring the term *grève*, which means "shore" or "strand." In the pages of *L'Espoir*, reporter Marcel Rovère wrote that it was ridiculous to use the word "beach" to describe the "thin" and "scrawny" coastline of Nice.[6] He and many others over the years visualized the narrow coastline as a physical problem requiring remedy; it was a skinny body that needed to be fattened up. Not coincidentally, the French term for widening a beach by dumping additional stone or sand and spreading it around is *engraissement*, the "fattening up" of the beach. Since World War II most beaches on the Riviera have undergone regular, often annual engraissement; it occurs after the winter storms but before summer tourists arrive, thus is largely invisible to them. A notion of the right kind of coastline emerged after World War II, and communities on the Riviera scrambled to meet the new standard lest they lose the tourist trade.[7] Spain offered sandy beaches.[8] And in the early 1960s the French state invested heavily in developing Languedoc-Roussillon for tourism; there wide, sandy beaches and dunes seemed a direct threat to tourism on the Riviera. Ironically, beginning in the late 1960s the French state also undertook development of the sandy coastline of the Gironde and Landes, where advancing sands had been the perceived problem a century earlier.[9]

As is clear from the preoccupation with sewers and submarine outfalls after the war, clean seawater presented as much of a challenge as wide beaches. Yet even as sewage diminished off the coast, a host of new pollutants arrived. Detergents from household cleaning, oil spills, waste from yachts and small pleasure craft, and beachgoing tourists themselves presented obstacles for authorities attempting to make the Mediterranean as sterile as a chlorinated public swimming pool. To be sure, the preoccupation was with clean water for tourists' use. Until the early 1970s there was little concern with conservation of natural flora and fauna. When an environmental movement focused on conservation did emerge, it had relatively little impact on the coastline, beyond cleaning up beaches and the water for tourists' use.

The Promenade des Anglais

In 1945 the beachfront in Nice consisted of the promenade des Anglais and the stony shore alongside it. The promenade des Anglais began as a small walkway in the 1830s, when English visitors paid unemployed local workers to build a beachfront trail west of the mouth of the Paillon. As the director of the oceanographic center at Antibes later put it, "In the nineteenth century, almost no one, save a few eccentric foreigners, was on the stony beach."[10] Visitors preferred an even, level surface not too close to the water. Over the course of the nineteenth and early twentieth centuries, the promenade became a frequent destination for carriage rides and strolling. The sun, the air, the view, and people watching—not the beach—were the attractions. By the interwar years the promenade was a touristic icon, filled with people and cars. Elected mayor in 1928, Jean Médecin initiated a major widening, extending it some fifteen meters over what had been the beach, creating space for beachfront concessions with changing rooms and bathrooms under the promenade but reducing the width of the beach significantly.[11] There was irony in the timing, as the widening of the promenade came just as winter tourism was giving way to summer tourism, and interest in lying on the beach soon rivaled desire for a promenade.

In addition to fifteen meters of lost beach, the widened promenade became the cause of considerable erosion of the remaining beach. By the early 1950s the ecological effects of the widening were clear. The promenade altered the natural process by which the waves of the Mediterranean built up the beach. Strong waves had long deposited stones before receding. But the wall that made it possible to widen the promenade kept waves from advancing and depositing stones. Instead, during storms the waves crashed against the wall, then swept back, eroding what little beach was left and sometimes damaging the wall itself. The problem was compounded by the current, which swept stones from east to west, toward the western parts of the beach and away from those areas where most tourists stayed. The Paillon had always deposited stones along the coast, but many of these were now swept farther westward rather than back onto the beach. Along much of the promenade, the beach was disappearing. There was so little beach near the Hôtel Ruhl, today the site of the Hôtel Méridien, that holders of beach concessions (*plagistes*) had to set up a solarium on pylons. The beach had been

FIG. 4.1. The iconic view of the promenade des Anglais and the baie des Anges as seen from the hill of the château. Vieux Nice is in the foreground to the right; the flat terrain in the distance is the airport. Photo by Reinhold Möller—own work. Licensed under Creative Commons Attribution-Share Alike 4.0 International: https://creativecommons.org/licenses/by-sa/4.0/deed.en, via Wikimedia Commons.

more than twenty meters wide across from the Negresco hotel, at the western end of the tourist area when the promenade was widened in 1930–31, but it barely existed in the early 1950s. The beach entirely disappeared at several spots along the promenade, while waves repeatedly threatened the integrity of the wall itself in the winter months.[12]

Tourists noticed. As reporter Michel Vives put it in 1958, "The beach of Nice (thus will we name the narrow band of stones that lines the shoreline of the baie des Anges) is the object of permanent criticism on the part of tourists." If the situation continues, the "beachgoers will leave our beach for good." Locals were well aware of the problem. As *Le Patriote* wrote in 1963, "It is well known that Niçois, whenever they can, go swimming elsewhere. There isn't really a beach at Nice, just a narrow band of coastline along the promenade in most areas. There is no space for walking or playing on the beach."[13] With the beach disappearing, the promenade itself was in danger. The city had already placed huge rocks and chunks of concrete along the wall in order to save it and had dumped several thousands of tons of stones to save the beach, not to mention authorizing dumps (*décharges publiques*) along the promenade. In principle the fill was clean, free of garbage, metal, and wood. In the early 1950s dumps along the promenade provided about ten thousand metric tons of materials each year, or about half the tonnage of stones the Paillon brought down to the sea.[14]

Groynes and Engraissement

The 1950s saw repeated efforts to build groynes to block erosion along the promenade des Anglais in efforts to create a beach for tourists. Called *épis* in French, they consisted of walls of rocks, sometimes topped with cement, going out into the sea perpendicular to the coast. They look like small jetties. Groynes had already worked well in stabilizing beaches in Spain. On the Riviera, groynes established before World War II succeeded in creating the plage du Midi, forming an almost uninterrupted beach between Cannes and la Napoule. In Nice the Jetty Promenade, a pier extending out into the sea, had done much to protect the nearby beach before the war (think Brighton Palace Pier in the United Kingdom, albeit of smaller size). Its destruction at the hands of the Germans led in subsequent years to serious erosion of the beach just west of where the Jetty Promenade had stood. In addition, in 1937 engineer Charles Chauve had overseen the placement of several groynes near the airstrip to the west of Nice, and they had been somewhat effective in maintaining the beach. In 1942 a forty-meter groyne, a veritable jetty, was built just east of the mouth of the Paillon River, and it had stabilized the beach between the Paillon and Rauba-Capeù. The challenge was in the area west of the Paillon where most tourists congregated. In 1950 the city built groynes, some ten meters long, westward from the Paillon.[15] While Chauve continued to study the possibilities and the municipal council considered the price tag of various actions, catastrophic weather provided a test case. Many of the stones along the coastline of Nice came from the Paillon. In a normal year about twenty thousand metric tons of stone came down the Paillon to the beachfront. However, heavy rainfall and flooding in the fall of 1951 and the spring of 1952 brought approximately forty thousand metric tons of stone down the Paillon to the sea. The city built two more groynes

FIG. 4.2. The beach across from the Hôtel Ruhl in 1950. Note the tiny groyne, narrow beach, and the small solarium platform constructed up to, and even over, the sea. Archives Nice Côte d'Azur—Ville de Nice, 1064 W 192 (collection of the photographic service of the city).

in April 1952 in hopes of keeping the stone from being washed westward. The makeshift experiment seemed to work at first, giving some credibility to long-standing plans to use groynes to rebuild the beach along the promenade.[16] However, subsequent winter storms in the 1950s revealed that the groynes did little to preserve the beach.

By the 1960s, the city realized that the cost of having a beach was constant engraissement. The solution was ever more fill. During the intense reconstruction of postwar Nice, companies generated considerable building waste that went directly into the sea at several spots along the promenade. Also, in 1963 the city hired the Nicoletti construction company to remove the stones that had built up where the Paillon was covered. In heavy rains, stones had always come down the Paillon, just as they did the Var. However, once the Paillon was covered, a process that began in the late nineteenth century, stones built up within the arches that channeled water down to the sea. In the winter of 1963–64, a steady stream of ten dump trucks moved down the Paillon and along the beach, where bulldozers spread the stones out. Nicoletti took some sixty thousand cubic meters of stone from the covered areas of the Paillon and used them to build up the beach, widening it by seven to ten meters, making it twenty-five meters wide from the Palais de la Méditerranée to the boulevard Gambetta. Nicoletti took an additional twenty thousand cubic meters from Var once done with the Paillon arches. In yet another attempt, a groyne forty meters in length was constructed in the winter of 1964–65 as an experiment, to see if it would hold the engraissement of 1963–64 in place. It had very limited success.[17] The city instead accepted that each spring dump trucks hauled tons of fill and stone to the beach, where bulldozers spread them out in time for the summer tourist season. Winter storms swept some away, and the next year the spring engraissement began anew. Nature proved unruly, hard to control even with twentieth-century technology.[18]

Groynes did not turn out to be a long-term solution. Storm surges damaged the groynes and even the wall of the promenade des Anglais. In-depth hydraulic studies indicated the reason that groynes, effective on many French and Dutch beaches, simply would never work at Nice. The grade is so steep that just three kilometers off the coast the water is almost one kilometer deep. Moreover, groynes were not pretty. Nice was no ordinary seaside city. Larger groynes would have blocked the trademark expansive views along the promenade and were thus deemed insufficiently "aesthetic" for such an emblematic space as the promenade.[19]

Towns to the west of Nice faced comparable challenges. Beachfronts were damaged during the war, as Germans had built blockhouses, laid

FIG. 4.3. Storm surges, such as this one in 1948, hammered the wall protecting the promenade des Anglais and often left water on streets near the sea. Archives Nice Côte d'Azur—Ville de Nice, 1064 W 187 (collection of the photographic service of the city).

mines, and run barbed wire. In some areas, such as at Juan-les-Pins, Germans had removed sand and gravel in order to make the cement used for blockhouses and other fortifications.[20] After 1945 the postwar building boom had a direct impact on beaches to the west of Nice. The Var River was an important source of stones that came down the river in torrential downpours, entered the sea, and were spread by the current onto the beaches west of Nice. However, heavy extraction of stones from the river for public works and building projects removed stones that had naturally replenished beaches to the west. Finally, the wall protecting the new beachfront road constructed to the west of Nice, like the promenade des Anglais, interrupted the natural replenishment of beaches. When the beachfront road was constructed between Cros-de-Cagnes and the Var River between 1936 and 1938, it was thirty meters from the sea. In the early 1950s the sea was eroding the road itself. At Cros-de-Cagnes, to protect the wall along the road, the department had to dump fill, expanding the beach. Farther to the west, winter storms repeatedly damaged RN 559 running near the Château la Napoule, as the road interfered with the natural process of the beach's replenishment. Here too the solution was to dump fill and build up the beach in order to protect the road.[21]

Departmental engineers were well aware of the Riviera's comparatively small beaches and advised use of heavy machinery to widen them. In their view, without the large tidal waves that created wide beaches, as on the Atlantic coast, the beaches of Alpes-Maritimes were too narrow, leading to a serious density of beachgoers on local beaches. Small beaches constituted a "problem," and there were two potential solutions, particularly west of Nice. The first was to move the coastal road and the nineteenth-century rail line, both of which ran near the sea. In the twentieth century the railroad in particular seemed to use valuable beachfront as well as cutting smaller towns off from their beaches. But most of the coastline along the Riviera was already built up by the 1950s, making relocation of the railroad financially impossible. And the road quickly became a popular artery for tourism. The second, more practical solution for the Riviera in general was, as for Nice, to dump ever more construction waste, stone, and sand in order to increase the size of the beaches. The twentieth-century invention of the dump truck and the bulldozer made earthmoving possible on a scale hitherto unimaginable; newspapers across the political spectrum were fascinated with the bulldozers for a reason. As *Le Patriote* pointed out with amazement, the bulldozers could accomplish in minutes what had taken men with shovels days to do.[22]

La Croisette

Municipal authorities in Cannes also desired a beach that would appeal to tourists, in their case along the famed Croisette. The Croisette is to Cannes what the promenade des Anglais is to Nice, a place to see and be seen along the coastline. The boulevard de la Croisette began as a trail connecting the center of Cannes to Croisette Cape to the east. A small cross stood on the cape, hence the name Croisette. The cape was the closest landmass to the Lérins islands; in the Middle Ages the cape served as a departure point for religious faithful going to the well-known Abbey de Lérins located there. The nineteenth century saw the draining of swampland along what is today the boulevard de la Croisette and the construction of villas and ultimately hotels. The Croisette became a smaller version of the promenade des Anglais for a smaller city. Both the promenade des Anglais and the Croisette were visual focal points of critical importance, emblematic of Nice, Cannes, and the Riviera more generally. Both the promenade and the Croisette predated postcards, but both became iconic partly as a result of them, as those postcards became the models for photos that tourists assumed they needed to take. Nice and Cannes are imagined not in their fullness but in their promenades. From the late nineteenth century onward, after Paris, the Riviera was the primary French locale featured on postcards. Most of those cards showed the promenade des Anglais or the Croisette.[23]

Cannes, like all communities along the coast of the Riviera, was saturated with automobiles after World War II. As the city looked to widen the boulevard de la Croisette along the coastline, the widened promenade des Anglais was a model both of the value of a wide avenue and the problem of building a wall along the sea. Options were laid out by departmental engineers, part of the Corps des Ponts et Chaussées (literally "bridges and highways corps"), the prestigious state engineers, who had since the eighteenth century overseen French public works projects. One option was for Cannes to build a wall much like that of the promenade des Anglais or along the seaside road at Cros-de-Cagnes. But those walls hastened the erosion of the beaches.[24] Cannes, which wanted both to widen the Croisette and to maintain, even expand beaches, chose instead an unprecedented and preventive widening of the beach, both as a destination for tourists, and as a buffer that kept storm surges from destroying the wall between the beach and the boulevard.

In Cannes the historical precedent of dumping fill into the sea in order to expand the beach also indicated likely success. Before the widening of the beach began in earnest in 1960, it was already wider than in the cadastral survey of 1814 as a result of fill over the years, including dirt from the construction of the railway, fill from building construction, and the digging of foundations for the grand hotels, not to mention an effort by Alexandre Arluc to widen the beach by dumping sand to create an "artificial beach."[25] Moreover, at the turn of the twentieth century, as the port at Cannes grew, the Albert-Édouard jetty was constructed. By 1906 it had caused enough sand to collect to the east that some seventy meters had been claimed from the sea, making it possible for the site to be used for the construction of the municipal casino (today the site of the Palais des Festivals et des Congrès). Between 1906 and 1926 additional fill to the east was meant to protect the casino from the sea. During the construction of the Martinez and Miramar hotels in 1926–28, fill from those construction projects also ended up in the sea along the Croisette.[26]

Between 1928 and 1952, however, the beach eroded. The wall of protection of the Esplanade des Alliés (the plaza just to the east of the Palais des Festivals today) was too close to the sea, so the waves tended to cut into the beach. Moreover, during the war Germans removed sand from the beach in order make cement. In 1952 efforts to increase the size of the beach began again. In the mid-1950s there were several dumps along the Croisette, and the beach slowly expanded in size. Older postcards were evidence that the beach was larger in the mid-1950s than it had been a decade earlier, as projects emerged to get sand from elsewhere, as far away as the beach of Pampelonne, just south of Saint-Tropez and soon to be made famous by Brigitte Bardot's performance in *Et Dieu créa la femme*.[27]

"Artificial Beaches"

Several studies revealed that engineers could successfully build what they called an "artificial beach" along the Croisette. Cannes had a distinct advantage over Nice. Whereas the sea gets deep quickly at Nice, the coastline at Cannes has a more gentle slope, which not only reduces the impact of the waves but also made it practical to build hundred-meter groynes of reinforced concrete into the sea (only about forty centimeters of which were above water in order to preserve views), blocking the force of the current. The Iles des Lérins also protects the harbor at Cannes from some storm surges.[28] Finally, the Croisette point juts out into the sea at the extreme east of the harbor, further sheltering the beachfront in Cannes. Beginning in November 1960, as this sort of work was always done in the winter when few tourists were present, a grand experiment began. For the first time in France, enormous amounts of sand were dumped along the coast in order to create a larger beach. In November and December 1960 convoys of some seventeen dump trucks daily hauled 1,100 cubic meters of sand from Fréjus to Cannes, forty-two kilometers, and placed it in front of the Martinez and Carlton hotels, on a stretch about 300 meters long, with sand-filled nylon groynes established on either side in order to mitigate the waves. The sand at Fréjus was not only plentiful due to natural dunes south of town; it was also only slightly more ochre in color than that at Cannes, and the grains slightly larger, thus harder for waves to wash the new sand into the sea. The sand seemed to hold during subsequent winter storms.[29]

Dump trucks had hauled 135,000 cubic meters of sand from Fréjus to Cannes by 1962, more than the total volume of the Hôtel Carlton. The sand remained in place, so the beach was then widened along the full length of the Croisette. Whereas the beach at Cannes had had only about one hectare of surface, it had four hectares after the engraissement. In some areas, to the east, the beach had been nonexistent, so that after the work, the beach was a full kilometer in length instead of only 700 meters. Its width ranged up to forty meters. By 1963 an astonishing 200,000 cubic meters of sand had been hauled in to widen Cannes's beaches.[30]

Cannes managed the cost by essentially privatizing much of the beach. At la Croisette engineers designed a cantilevered platform, anchored by cement groynes, under which plagistes could run concessions. New national rules for beachfront concessions became law in 1963. While only 30 percent of an existing beach could be leased and each plagiste could occupy only twenty-five meters of frontage, in the case of new "artificial beaches" (plages artifici-elles) fully 75 percent of the beachfront could be leased.[31] Cannes privatized as much as it could, granting some twenty-six concessions, 832 meters of a little over 1,100 meters of beachfront. All concessions had WCs "endowed with modern facilities appropriate for [Cannes's] reputation."[32] In Cannes as elsewhere, because municipalities were charged by the prefecture with keeping beachfronts clean, there was always a strong additional incentive to lease out concessions, so that the plagiste would take care of cleaning the beach in front of the establishment. The lease gave the plagistes the right to occupy the space almost up to the water's edge. They rented out lounge chairs, paddleboats, canoes, and rafts, and served drinks and light meals. They offered not only WCs but also places to change into swimwear. For the less well-heeled, both visitors and locals, concessions' costs were prohibitive, pushing those beachgoers to unimproved sections of the beach.[33] In principle everyone may have been wearing a swimsuit, seemingly equal, but in practice class difference was still manifest on the postwar beach. As a reader of Le Patriote complained, "Workers are forced to be content with a few square meters, where they are crammed in like sardines."[34]

Cannes's success in creating what was known as an "artificial beach" with sand quickly led to comparable efforts elsewhere on the Riviera. The problem was that just as Alpes-Maritimes did not have many sandy beaches, it also lacked much sand at all. In 1958 municipal employees in Antibes had attempted, unsuccessfully, to create sand by grinding stones.[35] Using dump trucks to ship in sand, as in Cannes, seemed a solution, though it proved impractical to get that sand from Fréjus, as the cost of transport was high. Also, since Alpes-Maritimes forbade the movement of sand out of the department, it could not expect the Var to allow much more sand to continue to come to the department of Alpes-Maritimes. So for the development of the beach at Salis in Antibes in the early 1960s, sand came from a quarry in Biot, the only locale in Alpes-Maritimes with decent surplus sand. Antibes had 22,000 cubic meters of sand trucked in, creating a beach three hundred meters long and twenty meters wide. The sand largely stayed in place and the beach became quite popular, in part because it remained free of concessionary interests, thus entirely free to the public.[36] Salis had long had the nickname among locals as the "beach of the Niçois," as the latter flocked there for a bit of sand on a free beach with a less dramatic drop-off than at Nice. Salis soon began attracting tourists as well. By the summer of 1965, each day there were five thousand people squeezed onto the beach of Salis. The success of the beach at Salis became a model for other beaches in the community of Antibes-Juan-les-Pins, and regular additions of sand became the norm all along the coast of the municipality.[37] In the Var, Saint-Raphaël followed suit. By the early 1970s small sandy "artificial" beaches also existed in Beaulieu-sur-Mer, Menton, Saint-Jean-Cap-Ferrat, and Théoule-sur-Mer. The cost, due to transportation, ranged from 100 to 350 francs per square meter.[38]

Even Nice briefly attempted to create a sandy beach just west of the mouth of the Paillon in 1964–65, hauling in seven hundred cubic meters of sand to create a modest beach two hundred meters long and ten meters wide.[39] The sea washed it away. Moreover, plagistes interviewed in November 1964 about the experiment were opposed. Although they claimed their opposition resulted from the fact that sand "goes everywhere, on chairs, mattresses, plates, and glasses," it seems as likely that sand would erode their profits. Plagistes made a lot of their money renting lounge chairs and small mattresses that made the stone beach at Nice far more comfortable for anyone sitting or lying in the sun.[40]

Marinas for Pleasure Craft

After World War II the rapid expansion of marinas to accommodate yachts and other pleasure craft also transformed the beachfront and the sea. Before the war most ports on the Riviera had been for commerce or fishing. In the decades after the war, almost all were marinas for yachts, motorboats, and sailboats. In 1939 there were twelve thousand pleasure craft registered in France. However, in 1962 there were at least forty thousand registered on the Côte d'Azur alone. Here as in so many domains, marinas seemed critical if the Riviera were to compete with other locales in France and beyond.[41] In the development of marinas catering to yachts, Cannes led the way, setting a model followed by other municipalities.

The original port at Cannes dated from 1838, when Lord Brougham, the veritable founder of Cannes as a winter destination, intervened with King

Louis-Philippe to ensure its construction. Docking at Cannes had been dangerous, and Brougham and other wealthy foreigners wintering in Cannes wanted the port. By the twentieth century it was large, welcoming the transatlantic liners that regularly docked there. But the port was not large enough for the increase in yachts docking there. In 1957 the municipal council deliberated the need for a second port, dedicated exclusively to the yachts proliferating off the coast. The original port was already incredibly busy, and tourism to the city would suffer if it could not accommodate all of the yacht owners desirous of docking there. With an area of eleven hectares, it was the most visited on the entire Mediterranean in 1957. A total of 660 boats from large yachts to fishing boats sheltered there permanently. In the first ten months of 1957 there were 1,178 embarkations, an increase of 150 boats over the twelve months of 1956. In the summer of 1957 the port received eight hundred boats from twenty-nine different countries. The port was so often full that many yachts were regularly denied entry.[42]

In 1960 Pierre Canto laid out a detailed plan for a private marina, to be run by the International Sporting Club de la Mer, made up of four hundred French and foreign stockholders. He proposed a large marina with access to potable water, electricity, fuel, telephones, and garbage collection on the quais, protected by full-time guards.[43] The city of Cannes approved the project. Although Cannes set an important precedent in establishing a private port, even local communists approved of a proposal that promised construction jobs. *Le Patriote* proudly announced that Cannes already had the leading marina in the world and endorsed the views of one of its readers, who noted that the new marina was a way to preserve the renown and prosperity of the city in the face of local competition: "Monaco and Nice would love to see this project taking place in their cities. Remember when we had horse racing and polo at Mandelieu, the airport of Saint-Cassien, pigeon shooting at la Bocca [all three of these places being on the outskirts of Cannes], Carnival, etc.? All of that has disappeared, forfeited to these two cities."[44] Interestingly, the opposition that did emerge was aesthetic, not political or environmental. In 1961, in the weekly *Arts*, Yvon Christ called the project a "massacre of the Cannes harbor. Nineteenth-century French author Prosper Mérimée had already mocked the 'abracadabra' (orientalist) villas denaturing the Cannes port; imagine what he would say about this new port that would "amputate ten hectares of the harbor."[45]

In 1964 Canto launched the construction of the private marina, subsequently named for him, at the far eastern end of the Croisette. Largely suspended during the summer tourist season, construction was intense during the winter months. Supervising the project were the departmental engineers of the Corps des Ponts et Chaussées. One hundred dump trucks did the relay from the quarry at Sarrée, near Gourdon, nearly thirty kilometers away, hauling 600,000 metric tons of rock, four times the volume of the Carlton hotel. A cement factory appeared on the construction site to produce the prodigious amounts of necessary cement. Inaugurated in 1965, the new port occupied nine hectares, with a 550-meter-long primary jetty fully 3.5 meters above sea level. Quais were one kilometer long, with 450 places for boats, thus accommodating 175 large yachts of 20 to 50 meters in length, 175 medium ones measuring 8.25 to 20 meters, and 200 small yachts measuring less than 8.25 meters. There were electricity hookups with three different international voltages, each with a telephone jack and access to the two French television stations, as well as those from Italy and Monaco. There was an elevator for getting boats onto land for repairs. Despite nearby land that was originally swampy, developers managed nonetheless to build an underground service station that could fuel twelve boats at once, with diesel or gasoline as well as a 12,500 m^2 parking garage, topped by a three-hectare garden. There were changing rooms for five hundred people, toilets, and trash containers every thirty meters, a bank branch, a waiting and reading room, a bar, a restaurant, a library, a post office, and shops. The clubhouse had a heated swimming pool.[46]

A sizable investment of 20 million (new) francs, the new port served as a model for the rash of marinas built in France in its wake.[47] The French state, department, and municipality contributed nothing to its financing. The marina was legally a private concession, on which the city imposed requirements, such as a supplemental jetty to the north designed to protect gardens belonging to the city, and the extension of marine sewage outfalls up to eight hundred meters long into the Mediterranean. Finally, in a precedent important all along the Mediterranean coast, since the marina jutted out into the sea, thus forming a protective barrier, developers were also required to build a new beach, 350 meters in length, at the eastern end of the Croisette. In the next ten years, forty-one other private marinas appeared in France, following the concessionary model used in Cannes. Developers still struggled to meet strong demand. In 1968 there were already ninety hectares of ports along the coast of Alpes-Maritimes and the Var.[48] While there had been 75,000 registered pleasure craft in France in 1965, there were 350,000 in 1975. With both Atlantic and Mediterranean coastlines, France witnessed the largest expansion of marine tourism in Western Europe.[49] The largest share of marinas was in Alpes-Maritimes, where there were 7,600 boats in August 1966 and 11,500 in August 1973. The rate of visits to local marinas grew by 6.5 to 10.15 percent per annum in the late 1960s and early 1970s.[50]

Cannes's Port Canto was a pioneer in one more respect. Concerned about stagnant water that would annoy rich yacht owners, the port had a system for renewing the water. The Société grenobloise d'études et d'applications hydrauliques set up a cascade of water at the entry, pushing water from the port out into the sea. There was also a "curtain of bubbles" developed by Albert Tardieu and Francis Giordan of Nice; large pumps created a permanent current within the port, bringing water in from the sea and pushing water from within the port out to sea, thus renewing the water within the port every five days or so. It was the first such installation in the world. It was by no means the norm on the Riviera. Most marinas, veritable "'boat garages,' became zones of stagnant water, polluted by fuel, inert matter that floats on the surface or covers the bottom, bacteria, rotting algae, and sewage." Some yacht owners used their craft essentially as houseboats (themselves formally banned), releasing their sewage into marinas.[51]

Marinas soon became the linchpin in even bigger development schemes. Here Monaco was the pioneer, setting an example adapted by other communities along the coast. After opening the area's first casino in the 1860s, the principality had managed to attract a well-heeled global elite. In 1956 the marriage of Prince Rainier and Grace Kelly was a choreographed media event, a splashy advertisement for the elegant, gambling haven without income taxes. Ever ready to attract rich foreigners, Rainier oversaw unbridled urbanization in a principality that ran three kilometers along the coast but is on average only five hundred meters wide, giving it an area of only about 1.5 square kilometers. As increasing numbers of well-off tourists arrived after World War II, Rainier opted to build vertically and to put up buildings on platforms with cement pilings on what had been the sea, increasing the size of Monaco by approximately 30 percent by the late 1960s.[52] The process began intensely in the 1950s, with the construction of a tunnel for the rail line, a project that freed up space for construction above ground and kept the railway from cutting most of the principality off from the sea. The work on the tunnel generated considerable fill, which was dumped into the sea. Construction waste also found its way into the water, creating the platform at Portier measuring thirty-five thousand square meters, ready for the construction of buildings. Along with boulders and seven thousand cubic meters of concrete, more than a million metric tons of fill created a second platform at Larvotto, which occupied more than fifty thousand square meters. Rainier then built literally on top of what had been the Mediterranean Sea. Alongside a new marina, developers created an artificial beach of ground rock as an answer to the sandy beaches so popular after the war.[53] Soon, as reported by the national French news weekly *Le Point*, "From Menton to Marseille, mayors are ecstatic before the Monaco Manhattan; they are ready to sacrifice the coastline to compete with the principality," whatever the cost to the environment.[54]

Sure enough, other communities approved development schemes that combined a new marina; new buildings, including apartment buildings for second-home owners; and a small public beach in return for the privatization of a chunk of the coastline. In Menton there had been no natural port, just a jetty for unloading cargo itself badly damaged during World War II. In 1967 Menton inaugurated the private port modeled on that of Cannes with room for a thousand boats. As at Cannes, the scale was remarkable, requiring some 600,000 tons of rock from la Turbie.[55] The development only whetted Mayor Francis Palmero's appetite. In 1976 he announced another development project on the beachfront of Menton. The plan called for a pleasure craft marina of eight hectares, with spaces for five hundred boats, and a platform of ten hectares, on which there would be a tourist complex including both a pool and a casino. Additional beaches would cover the seaside from Menton to Roquebrune. Local fishermen opposed the destruction of the fish habitat near the coast.[56] Local conservationists were opposed, as were local communists, who accused Palmero, an ally of Mayor Jacques Médecin of Nice, of the kind of graft (affairisme) for which Médecin was well known. Le Patriote also referred to such privatization of the beachfront as "segregation," as development of beaches allowed private developers to lease out up to 75 percent of the improved beachfront at the expense of the public, be they tourists or locals.[57] The collective opposition was of little avail. Construction proceeded apace.

In the early 1970s the coastline of a Napoule-Mandelieu was also transformed beyond recognition. Just up the Siagne, a navigable river, a marina with an area of 10.8 hectares was dug out of the plain. Apartment blocks arose alongside it. At Saint-Laurent-du-Var, the Association nationale des amis de la mer, founded in 1969, fought yet another massive project, arguing to Prime Minister Jacques Chirac in 1975 that the work would eliminate public beachfront for the sake of private profiteering and that the marina itself would damage the underwater plain along some 1.2 kilometers of beachfront. There was further concern that large buildings near the sea would block views from the town and hills behind them. The association took the government, which had approved the plan, to court in the Administrative Tribunal in Nice; the court decided against the group. Even the scathing book-length indictment of development projects tied to marinas, The Côte d'Azur Assassinated, had little immediate impact. Although an elaborate scheme to build yet another marina off the pointe de la Croisette failed in the face of residents' opposition in 1974, an enormous expansion of the Port Vauban in Antibes proceeded unhindered in the 1980s.[58]

Environmental Pushback

Given the profound changes to the beach and the sea in the years after World War II, it is astounding in retrospect just how infrequently opposition arose. When there was resistance, it was usually aesthetic; the Riviera had a prestigious reputation for beauty to maintain, and anything that might harm tourists' experience was anathema. As in France generally, there had long been an appreciation of physical space as manipulated by and for humans, though not a desire to preserve nature for nature's sake. However, in the early 1970s concerns about ecological degradation emerged strongly on the Riviera as they did in France generally.[59] In 1970 thirty-two separate neighborhood associations, representing thirty-five thousand households in the Alpes-Maritimes and the Var, argued that the coastline risked becoming a "wall of concrete" with high-rises lining the coastline.[60] In the early 1970s scientists, activists, and the press increasingly pushed back against the plans of developers and officials. Their focus was especially on the beachfront and nearby waters. Despite valiant efforts, environmentalists on the Riviera had limited success. When an environmentalist agenda was effective, it was because it complemented longer-term concerns with maintaining either the aesthetic appeal of the space or its cleanliness for human use.

In late 1974 Mayor Jacques Médecin and the municipal council of Nice approved a project to develop the eastern end of the beachfront of Nice, in the cove of Ponchettes at the base of the hill of the chateau. By the summer of 1975 the proposal had morphed into a huge scheme to take sixteen thousand square meters from the beach and the Mediterranean (along about four hundred meters of coastline) in order to build a hotel, a casino, a shopping mall, restaurants, a health spa, nightclubs, and a swimming pool.[61] In the pages of Nice Matin, frequent ally of the mayor and local developers, Médecin defended the project by arguing that "often visitors ask us if there exists in Nice an establishment comparable to Monte Carlo Beach [in Monaco] or Palm Beach at Cannes."[62] Reaction was swift and effective. The Comité de défense de la baie des Anges (the Committee for the Defense of the Baie des Anges), while twice writing French president Valéry Giscard d'Estaing, in the meantime managed to interest France's leading center-right daily Le Figaro. The newspaper sent a reporter who proceeded to criticize the plan, interviewing Prof. Alexandre Meinesz, a biologist and specialist in algae. Meinesz pointed out that expansion of the airport of Nice (occupying two hundred hectares) and the planned marina at Saint-Laurent-du-Var already reduced by half the area zero to twenty meters in depth reached by sunlight and inhabited by thousands of species. In Meinesz's words, "Half of this ecological complex has already been destroyed; that's enough."[63]

It was an argument that Meinesz had used unsuccessfully against other proposed projects. In this case, however, the aesthetics of the coastline were also at issue. The *International Herald Tribune* was critical of the plan, quoting the Comité de défense de la baie des Anges: "The defacement of the shore and the sea will be inflicted on us in the name of profit for a few private firms." The mayor's office could not have been more dismissive, claiming that the organization "is made up of a bunch of emotional old ladies." When the Comité reserved a public auditorium for a large meeting, the mayor's office forbade usage of the public space. When Médecin was out of town, the Comité held the meeting anyway and began a petition that got more than fifteen thousand signatures.[64] Letters of protest arrived at the Ministry of Equipment (which oversaw development projects), the Ministry for the Quality of Life (charged with the environment), and the president's office.[65] X. de C., president of the Ligue urbaine et rurale, argued that public opinion was now opposed to such *urbanisation sauvage*. A former ambassador living in the upscale Cimiez neighborhood of Nice declared that the development project was a "real massacre of the baie des Anges" on the part of a municipal government with "megalomaniacal tendencies and a well-developed taste for business but no artistic sense whatsoever." A former architect who divided his time between Cimiez and the well-heeled Parisian sixteenth arrondissement wrote Giscard d'Estaing in order to point out that the project would, if realized, eliminate a public beach for the sake of private interests. It was the only public beach completely without any private concessions, and the beach closest to Vieux Nice, inhabited by a "modest population." But the icing on the cake was aesthetic: "The inevitably modernist architecture of such a project would damage the beauty of the site."[66] The mobilization worked. The city abandoned the project.

However, when the damage was completely underwater, having no impact on sightlines, criticism fell flat. For years fishermen had complained about dumps, indicating that they were not as clean as authorities maintained. In 1964 fishermen asserted that fill included pieces of wood and iron that got caught in nets. As reported in *L'Indépendant*, "It is a real disaster for us, because it is our livelihood that is in the process of being destroyed. Already for several weeks now we can't catch any fish. 'You understand, these tons of fifth have caused the fish to flee.'" The mayor's office did nothing.[67] Professional fishing was disappearing from the coastline. It became more lucrative to captain a rich family's yacht, do guard duty and maintenance on yachts, or sail tourists out into the sea on excursions. Fishermen could earn as much in three months assisting tourists during the high season as they earned all year from fishing.[68] Destruction of fish habitat further aggravated the situation.

Seaside dumping continued into the 1970s. In 1976 Madame D., president of the Comité de la défense de la baie des Anges, complained that the Spada construction company was dumping tons of material from its autoroute construction site into the cove at Ponchettes. In principle the materials were supposed to be of high quality. In fact they contained the fine particles that clouded the water. Both the prefecture and the mayor's office asserted that the materials were clean and necessary to keep the beach from disappearing during storms. The dump of ten thousand cubic meters proceeded unimpeded.[69] At Roquebrune-Cap-Martin and Menton, builders complained that they had no place to dump. The department worked with municipalities to locate sites on land or, if materials were considered "noble," meaning without metal, wood, or trash mixed in, at sites on the coastline. The Fédération départementale du bâtiment et des travaux publics estimated in 1975 that there were two to three million metric tons of excess material from earthmoving. The prefecture's solution was to find specific sites for dumping, which would be more hidden, and to charge fifteen francs per square meter of material dumped, a fee that would allow the landfills to be monitored and eventually covered over and for professional fishermen to be compensated for their losses when waste material was dumped into the sea.[70]

When scientists raised serious concerns about the state of flora and fauna just off the coast, they got little traction. In the 1970s Meinesz and his team at the University of Nice studied the area zero to twenty meters deep along the coast. That depth gets sufficient sunlight for photosynthesis, so algae and marine phanerogams grow, serving as shelter and food for fauna. Fish hunt and reproduce there. But given its proximity to the coastline, this was the area jeopardized by the construction of marinas, buildings on platforms gained from the sea, and beaches. Construction of groynes and platforms destroyed large surfaces of Neptune grass or *Posidonia oceanica*, which created oxygen and were indispensable for underwater wildlife. Pleasure craft dragged anchors. Moreover, sewage from boats, oil, gasoline, and even paint and paint thinners entered the water. Beaches nearly enclosed by groynes and jetties, as at Beaulieu, Monaco, and Menton, may have protected swimmers, but they left the water stagnant and bereft of ecological diversity. In 1975 already 328.74 hectares between le Trayas (just east of Saint-Raphaël, thus at the westernmost extreme of the department of Alpes-Maritimes) and Ponchettes, at the eastern end of the promenade des Anglais in Nice, measuring zero to twenty meters deep, had been developed. Overall, 263.15 hectares had been made into marinas, 23.25 into beaches, and 42.32 into platforms on which buildings were constructed. In Monaco the area zero to twenty meters deep consisted of 89.57 hectares, of which only 22.04 remained in 1975, thus a reduction of 75.39 percent. In 1975 a fair amount of the flora and fauna immediately off the coast of the Riviera was already dead.[71]

Rainier and RAMOGE

Prince Rainier of Monaco symbolized the ironies of growing environmental awareness along the coast. The same Rainier who appointed Jacques Cousteau director of the Oceanographic Museum of Monaco in 1957 also undertook an expansion of his principality that increased its territory by 30 percent, all at the expense of the sea. Having just reduced the coastal area zero to twenty meters deep to less than 25 percent of its original surface, Rainier fashioned himself a champion of international cooperation in tackling ecological threats to the Mediterranean.[72] In 1970, at the general assembly of the Commission internationale pour l'exploration scientifique de la Méditerranée (CIESM), Rainier called for the creation of a transnational body to fight pollution on the French and Italian Rivieras. When formed, the body took the name RAMOGE, for the areas to be covered: the French coast from Saint-Raphaël (RA) but soon extended to Hyères, past the coastline of Monaco (MO) to Genoa (GE). Because petroleum shipments fell under existing international agreements, that source of pollution was not subject to RAMOGE, so the intergovernmental group focused on industrial waste drifting in from Italy, sewage, beachfront waste, and detritus left by pleasure craft. The accord was signed in 1976.[73] RAMOGE expanded to include the coastline from Marseille to La Spezia in 1981. The value of RAMOGE was as intergovernmental cooperation to reduce pollution all along the coast. The French government committed resources from the Fonds interministériels pour l'aménagement du territoire (FIAT), the Ministry for the Quality of Life, and the Fonds interministériels pour la nature et l'environnement (FIANE), resulting in increased funding for treatment plants and longer outfalls.[74] Similar efforts increased in Italy. The need seemed obvious; before the implementation of RAMOGE, Italian authorities approved the release of toxins from the Montedison Company, near Grossetto, into the Tyrrhenian Sea.[75] The waste was from the manufacture of titanium dioxide and vanadium. The release of three to six thousand metric tons daily was to be an experiment for six months. Professor Vassière of the Centre scientifique de Monaco, a lab focused on combating pollution in the Mediterranean, argued that the sea simply could not absorb it. Sure enough, a reddish mud drifted from Italy and threatened the Riviera and Corsica. Pointing out the devastating effects of the Chisso company's mercury poisoning at Minamata Bay in Japan, Dr. Maurice Aubert, director of the Centre d'études et de recherches de biologie et d'océanographie médicale (CERBOM) in Nice, declared that titanium and vanadium were also deadly. Titanium killed phytoplankton and zooplankton. Moreover, its diffusion by sea current produced aerosols that harmed the lungs of people living near the coast. Vanadium, a rare element, is even worse, as it can interrupt the creation of blood cells. In 1974 the CEO and four other executives of Montedison of Scarlino were condemned to three months and twelve days' suspended sentence for the plant's release of titanium dioxide into Italian territorial waters. The resulting "red mud" (*boues rouges*) ruined tourism in nearby Fallonica.[76] RAMOGE would prove effective in limiting this sort of industrial pollution, which threatened tourism, but it did little to conserve the natural habitat along the coast. Worse yet, it did not grow to include cooperation around the entire Mediterranean basin.[77]

Oil

During the Thirty Glorious Years, particularly in the 1960s, oil consumption in France grew dramatically, complementing the country's historic reliance on coal. Oil fueled the airplanes, automobiles, boats, and diesel-powered trains that brought tourists to the Riviera before electrification of rail lines. Although no one talked of a carbon footprint in those days, tourists left an increasingly large one. More immediately, a fair amount of oil ended up in the water and on the shore, as oil washed up frequently on the beaches of the Riviera. Oil got on people, on swimwear, and on the equipment that plagistes rented out to beachgoers. In 1958 participants in a swim meet found themselves covered with it. A forty-year-old Niçois attested that same year that he "had never seen the water or the shore so dirty."[78] In 1966 "there was a nasty surprise . . . for the numerous people on the beaches of Nice" as a small oil slick made its way to shore. When they got out of the water, they had black splotches on their legs. "Some of those running private beach concessions even had to put pails of gasoline out for their clients, where they took unanticipated footbaths." Experienced in the matter after so many earlier incidents, plagistes knew that a petroleum product always works better to remove oil than a water-based one.[79] When oil washed ashore, tourists fled Nice, looking for a beach without an oil slick. But slicks appeared nearby as well. In 1958 tourists avoiding the beach at Nice quickly found that the oil was also at Saint-Jean-Cap-Ferrat and Èze to the east, and was heading to Cannes in the west.[80] The solution was to leave the Riviera altogether.

Ships were sometimes at fault. *Le Patriote* reported in 1965 that the US Navy was responsible for a spill, noting that "public condemnation had borne fruit and sailors from the [US] fleet had to clean the shore with detergent, which was effective."[81] Clearly, the US Navy did not need bad public relations, particularly given the rocky relationship between de Gaulle and NATO in the mid-1960s. In 1975 there was an oil slick spreading across three hundred meters of the beach between Cannes and Cannes la Bocca. The Greek cruise ship *Delphi* was suspected, as it had been in harbor and had just lifted anchor for Mallorca. Walking a fine line, the mayor of Cannes wanted to communicate the problem to the guilty party without undermining tourism. In describing his contact with the company, he noted that "it is not an issue of showing toward them any sort of hostility that risks eventually discouraging them from dropping anchor in Cannes, but to lead them, with a moderate but constant pressure, toward a better behavior and to get them to understand the disastrous effect of an oil slick landing on the beaches of a city like Cannes."[82]

However, most oil slicks came from tankers that hauled the oil tourists and other consumers burned. Oil en route to northern Europe passed through the Mediterranean. Oil imports coming from Haifa, Tripoli, and Mina-el-Ahmadi (from Kuwait, via the Suez Canal) went to refineries in France, notably to the huge refinery installation at Berre, near Marseille. The spills were in no way accidental. Rather, after tankers emptied at refineries, the tanks still had corrosive deposits that could generate explosive gases. So the maintenance of the tanker required a cleaning after each delivery. At port, the tankers were half filled with water in order to assure the stability of the ship, then once the tanker was away from the coast, crews dumped the oily residue into the sea and refilled the tanks with water.[83] This process, called *dégazage*, literally "degassing," allowed about one percent of a tanker's original oil cargo to be dumped into the sea. Under the best of circumstances, the petroleum spread out as a thick layer, suppressing photosynthesis and modifying biological cycles. Under the worst, oil came ashore. Given the heavy traffic of oil tankers in and out of the refineries at Berre, the amounts added up. As French oil consumption grew, the problem got worse; there were frequent oil slicks several dozen meters in width, all along the coast from Menton to Saint-Raphaël. Although in Nantes there was already a facility for cleaning the tankers in that port in 1958, in the 1970s oil tankers in the Mediterranean were still conducting *dégazage*.[84]

Municipalities were on the hook for cleanup. On stony beaches, the remedy was simple. The city contracted with a local construction company to turn over a layer of stones so that oily ones were buried and others put on the surface of the beach. In Nice construction firm Spada's technique was to create a deep trench in which the oily stones could be buried in one spot, facilitating later cleanups because the fouled stones were localized. On large sandy beaches, as at Cannes, bulldozers and backhoes could shift the sand around, burying the oil. However, on small beaches, as at Menton in the late 1950s, there was not room for heavy equipment to move the gravel around, delaying cleanup and driving up the cost.[85]

The experience of regular oil slicks made mayors particularly skittish about oil exploration off the coast. In 1972 the Compagnie française des pétroles, the Entreprise de recherches et d'activités pétrolières, and the Société nationale des pétroles d'Aquitaine all filed requests for five-year leases for oil exploration with the prefectures of Alpes-Maritimes, the Bouches-du-Rhône, the Var, and Corsica. About twenty kilometers from the coast, thus within French territorial waters (which extended to twenty-two kilometers from the coast), Jacques Cousteau had discovered salt domes in the area in 1957, thus indicating the possibility of oil.[86] Although the technology did not yet exist to drill the necessary 2,000 to 2,700 meters deep, the companies eventually hoped to compensate for France's paucity of oil reserves. After Algerian nationalization of oil and gas in 1971, it was clear that France was heavily dependent on external sources for petroleum; French sources seemed a godsend.

Ecologists and the mayors of coastal towns reacted swiftly to the news. Thirty-five researchers affiliated with the CERBOM sent an open letter to the prefect of Alpes-Maritimes. They noted the threat to the ecology of the flora and fauna, the threat to seafood (citing the dead zones created by oil spills in the étang de Berre and the golfe de Fos near Marseille), and the threat that spills posed to tourism along the coast. More significant was the mobilization of mayors. Gaullist mayor of Cannes Bernard Cornut-Gentille led the charge. He wrote other mayors in the department of Alpes-Maritimes, requesting that they lodge protests with the prefect, just as he did. Cornut-Gentille reminded authorities and the press of the huge oil spill, of some three million gallons, from an offshore drilling platform off the coast of Santa Barbara in 1969. He corresponded, in English, with Santa Barbara resident Lois Sidenberg, the president of GET OIL OUT, who advised him how best to mobilize public opinion.[87] When Yvonne Rebeyrol wrote in the pages of *Le Monde* that an oil spill amounted to less oil than already resulted from the cleaning of oil tankers and that the crash of a tanker could release more oil than an offshore platform, Cornut-Gentille corrected the record in *Le Monde*, reminding readers of the disaster at Santa Barbara.[88] The mayor succeeded, for the time being. Just two years later, Cornut-Gentille wrote the mayors of coastal towns in Alpes-Maritimes once more. When the mayor of Menton (and French senator) Francis Palmero asked the minister of industrial and scientific development for assurances, he could get no promise from the minister that the stay on exploration was anything more than temporary. Cornut-Gentille, in his capacity as deputy in the National Assembly, raised the same issue, reminding his colleagues that the oil leaking from the sea floor off the coast of Santa Barbara had still not stopped in 1974, five years after the initial disaster.[89]

The American Sixth Fleet

The American Sixth Fleet, stationed in the Mediterranean, was an imposing presence at the height of the Cold War. Often putting down anchor in the well-protected deepwater natural harbor in Villefranche, just east of Nice, and in the port at Cannes, the Americans and their ships were impossible to miss along the postwar Riviera. And when pollution appeared off the coast, how could such huge ships carrying so many men not be responsible? It was widely and persistently assumed that the American ships were major polluters, an idea often repeated by local communists. The claim worked well for them politically, as they could link communist geopolitical opposition to the American nuclear-armed fleet off the coast with the local pollution it caused. The popularity of communists in postwar France hinged on local, not international issues, but here was an ongoing opportunity to fuse the two.

In 1961 *Nice Matin* did an inquiry. Reporter Pierre Dany interviewed the men, Messieurs Detante and Garino, whose company had the contract to remove the waste from US Navy ships and take it out to sea. They were categorical: "It is the American ships that pollute the harbor the least." The two men described their routine. Aircraft carriers, for example, required three evacuations daily, at 800, 1300, and 1800 hours. One of the men's boats gathered solid trash while the other pumped out liquid waste. They then, depending on weather conditions, sailed six to ten nautical miles from the coast, where they dumped the waste while a navy helicopter observed. The men claimed that, given stringent penalties for throwing trash in the sea, sailors never did so. They claimed to have witnessed the lowering of a small boat from a battleship in order to pick up a single piece of paper that had fallen into the water. During the three years that the men had had the contract, they had only one accident. After Detante and Garino hauled waste from the "Cambrera" (no doubt the USS *Canberra*) out to sea, a strong current from the south washed waste onto the shoreline; the commander sent sailors to shore to clean the beach, then insisted that a new contract locate the dumpsite two additional nautical miles away from the coast.[90] The US Navy was attempting to maintain good public relations by hiring a local firm to dump its considerable waste miles away from shore. What all parties took for granted was that the trash would not make its way back to the beach. When engineer Guy Palausi compiled a report on the findings of a committee of a dozen specialists examining pollution for the city of Cannes in 1971, he too argued that contrary to ongoing, widespread assumptions, the Sixth Fleet was not a primary source of local water pollution. Palausi confirmed that locals were contracted to collect the entirety of the waste and haul it six nautical miles out to sea. However, Palausi noted, when the sea was rough, and when the *ponant* (a wind from the west) blew, a surface current carried everything floating in the water into the Gulf of Napoule and the Cannes harbor. Palausi isolated noise and air pollution of the Sixth Fleet as more important; the jets on aircraft carriers were exceedingly noisy, and the smoke from their engines definitely fouled the air.[91]

Cruise ships and yachts got more of the blame for water pollution. While usually difficult to pinpoint a source, there were exceptions. In 1954 a cruise ship left the harbor at Villefranche. A few hours later a layer of oil and orange and grapefruit rinds arrived on the beach at Nice. While a ship remaining in the harbor at Villefranche was required to have small boats evacuate the waste out to sea, waste remained on board during short trips. Even if regulations were respected, which required the ship to be three nautical miles offshore before the release of waste, some of it still ended up on local beaches.[92]

The rapid increase in the number of pleasure craft after the war drew particular attention. When Pierre Dany interviewed plagistes about pollution, they pointed out that yachts anchored both offshore and in marinas had no easy means of disposing of waste. "They eat and drink onboard. It is easy to throw cans and melon rinds off the deck. In the port of Cannes, there are yachts that have not left the quai for twenty years. Ask them where they drain their waste." Monsieur Garino, whose livelihood consisted of ensuring the emptying of waste of military and civilian ships, noted at six in the morning, there was a "river" of waste slowly floating out to sea from the old port of Cannes. "The floating city [of pleasure craft] of Cannes houses up to 5,000 people," and rare were those even bothering to use trash cans at the port. Just as bad were the dripping oil containers, which, whether new or old, left oil on the ground on the quais.[93]

Palausi's committee agreed that pleasure craft were a major source of pollution. He noted that water that had circulated in natural bodies of water, even natural harbors, got trapped within the jetties built to create marinas. Spilled fuel and oil had nowhere to go and usually ended up in the sea. Some boaters continued to dump trash into the sea, including in port. And when in port, few yachts connected to a sanitary system, even when one was present, so human waste went directly into the port's water. The "curtain of bubbles" of the new Port Canto apparently made little difference. Palausi instead argued that the ports of Cannes adopt the Liljendhal system of aspiration of waste to which boats could connect; Sweden used such a system for trailers in campgrounds, and a prototype was already in operation in Saint-Jean-Cap-Ferrat. Without mandating compliance, Palausi was pessimistic about outcomes. His report blamed pollution of the sea on the "indiscipline of the French in general and of tourists in particular," noting the problems of increased chemicals from synthetic materials to hydrocarbons. Among the worst problems were the oil changes of pleasure craft engines in port; used oil sometimes went directly into the sea.[94]

Beachgoers as Polluters

As the number of people on the beaches and in the water grew, beachgoers themselves became an important source of pollution. Despite the creation of artificial beaches and constant engraissement along the coast, Riviera beaches were nevertheless quite crowded. Between 1965 and 1973 the total area of beaches in Alpes-Maritimes increased by 40 percent. However, in 1973, when averaging out the entirety of beachgoers on the beaches of Alpes-Maritimes during the summer, there were only two square meters per person.[95] Worse yet, people were not spread evenly on the available beaches but were instead crowded onto the more accessible of them, so many were lucky to have room for a beach towel. Trash collection on land and sea, adequate WCs, and disinfection of beaches became summertime preoccupations for municipalities along the coast.

Trash was a particular problem. Plagistes cleaned their concessions and emptied trash cans, but on the rest of the beachfront, municipalities were responsible. In 1954 Nice had eight employees charged with keeping the beach clean. Much to employees' chagrin, beachgoers generated considerable waste, as many ate their meals then left paper and food waste on the beach. In the water refuse from visitors mixed with that from valleys and that brought in by the sea from pleasure craft, cruise ships, and other towns; its collection presented more of a challenge. Water off the beach could be clean in the morning, but when the wind increased, the current brought in trash. To collect waterborne trash, Nice pioneered a solution in 1954. Louis Icart, an assistant mayor, oversaw the creation of a small boat with an apparatus for skimming trash out of the water. Eventually nicknamed the "pelican," the boat patrolled all day. On its first day of operation, it collected fifty kilos of trash. By 1976 four separate boats patrolled the beaches of Alpes-Maritimes. In addition to picking up trash, the newer prototypes, called "sea sweepers," tested water quality and hosed down the beaches every morning. In the late 1970s they also had air support, on the lookout for floating piles of waste and oil slicks; pelicans could get radio orders to go after the trash before it got too near the beach.[96]

There was widespread speculation that the human waste occasionally found in the sea came from fellow beachgoers. Some beaches had no toilets, and others had few. The plagiste J. Burdin noted in 1972 that there were few WCs along the beach at Nice. "Along six kilometers, there are only three WCs that are open." It seemed obvious that with so many people and so few toilets, many people used the sea.[97] In 1971, on the plage du Midi between Mandelieu-la Napoule and Cannes, there were no WCs. About 60 percent of tourists on the beach were staying in campgrounds in the backcountry but spent all day long at the beach. It was obvious that the Mediterranean served as their toilet. In his report about pollution in Cannes, Guy Palausi delicately wrote, "In the absence of any sanitary facilities, this results in a very significant coastal pollution."[98] By the early 1970s it was clear that beachgoers themselves were an important source of pathogens. Even if most germs could only survive on the sand or stones for several hours, there was turnover during the day and new germs with each visitor. Athlete's foot, yeast infections, and various types of dermatitis were widespread, particularly in the humid sands barely touched by waves—that is, the very area where people most liked to walk and play with children.[99]

Tourists' and locals' dogs were another source of pollution. In 1972 there was a single sign along the promenade des Anglais forbidding dogs on the beach, and police did nothing to enforce the ban. The journalist Jean Magnet noted that dog excrement was "bad enough on sidewalks, where it is not nice to step onto something that slides, but it becomes utterly unpleasant when it comes to a hand." In the words of the plagiste J. B., "The whole beach at Nice is for dogs. Every morning, dog owners come and let their dogs loose on the beach. In the afternoon, children play on the soiled stones."[100] In 1976 a tourist wrote to *Nice Matin* informing the newspaper that she would never return to Nice given the dog feces on the beach.[101]

Municipalities proceeded to disinfect their beaches nightly (thus invisible to tourists), using solutions perfumed with lemon, lavender, or carnations in order to mask unpleasant odors. In the early 1970s municipal employees in Nice sprayed six hundred liters of disinfectant twice weekly on six kilometers of beachfront. It cost 650,000 francs. Even small communities, such as Èze-sur-Mer, Roquebrune-Cap-Martin, and Saint-Jean-Cap-Ferrat, spent 100,000 francs each, solely for cleaning the beaches. In Cannes in the summer months, forty to fifty city employees were deployed to clean eight kilometers of coastline. For years the solutions included insecticide. In 1986 *Nice Matin* reported that the city disinfected the beach with a combination of ammonium, chlorine, formaldehyde, and phenol.[102] In a sense, this sanitation of the beach resembled that of homes. Municipalities' disinfectants ended up in the sea, just as detergents and other toxic cleaning agents used to clean homes, hotels, and clothing did. Fishermen on the Riviera complained that cleaning solutions killed fish. The postwar sense of human hygiene had an impact on the sea largely ignored by tourists and those welcoming their visits.[103]

In 1974 Maurice Aubert of CERBOM claimed that the bacterial level just off the beach at Nice was no higher than that permitted for public swimming pools in France.[104] In essence, the notion that the Mediterranean had to be clean for swimming was an expectation that it was essentially a large swimming pool. Any chemicals were permissible to keep the beach and water usable for tourists, regardless of the impact of the flora and fauna in the sea.

In 1975 the Ministry for the Quality of Life conducted a survey in coastal departments of both the Atlantic and the Mediterranean. It found that the two most frequent complaints on the part of tourists were an "absence of sanitary equipment," meaning WCs (64 percent of respondents), and "trash left by summer tourists" (59 percent). The next five important concerns all ranked between 30 and 35 percent: "tar on the beach, absence of trash cans, floating waste, waste brought in by the sea, and questionable water." Tellingly, tourists believed that the primary cause of pollution was first fellow tourists (34 percent), followed by boats (22 percent) and only then municipalities' waste (19 percent). The department in France most heavily criticized and most visited was Alpes-Maritimes, followed by the Var.[105]

Class and Race on the Beach

As the postwar masses descended onto Mediterranean beaches, class status took different forms than in the past. Before World War II most visitors to the

Riviera were wealthy. After the war, they were increasingly middle class and even lower middle class. Most workers who went to the beach lived nearby, as few workers could afford an extended beachfront vacation, particularly in an area such as the Riviera. Among people who could afford the trip, in principle the beach was "natural" and could be the great equalizer; swimsuits can reveal a lot of skin but do not necessarily reveal social station.

Nevertheless, *where* people could afford to appear in a swimsuit certainly reflected social class. Those on pleasure craft showed their wealth or at least their connection to it. However, social position could also be clear on beaches near the new marinas. In Beaulieu-sur-Mer, for example, the shortest route from the center of town to the beach named Petite Afrique (a name evoking both its sheltered warmth and colonial nostalgia) is through the marina—the only place I have ever seen a drinking fountain with sparkling water. Even away from the yachts, as the hoi polloi in wet swimsuits and flip-flops traipse past people arriving in Bentleys, Jaguars, and Porsches, everyone knows the pecking order. Moreover, the creation of new beaches allowed for extensive private beach concessions with expensive fees. Most people crammed onto free public beaches bereft of amenities. A few feet away were the better off with chaises longues, walkways down to the water, bathrooms, changing rooms, and drinks with little umbrellas served by waiters.

The racial divide was yet deeper. Of course, North Africans spent a lot of time on and near the beach—working. North Africans worked for the construction companies that got the contracts to renovate the Croisette, to repair the promenade des Anglais, to dump fill all along the coastline, to do the annual engraissement of beaches, to build the new marinas, and to clean up oil spills. The men were clearly visible as they worked manually with tools, drove trucks, and operated backhoes, cranes, and bulldozers. Yet at the same time, the men were unseen, at least by tourists. Since much construction work took place in the off-season, it was easier for tourists to overlook the men's work and life on the Riviera. And one might argue that because some of the construction on the promenade and the Croisette was night work and a disproportionate share of second- and third-shift work was done by foreign workers, it was somewhat easier for others not to notice or care about them.[106] The men's work developing the coastline was overlooked in the way that custodians' work is often unseen as they labor on behalf of us all.

North African construction workers helped remake the Riviera during the Thirty Glorious Years, but there is no evidence that they enjoyed much fruit of that labor. Police surveillance and racist harassment followed them if they attempted to use the beaches. In the abundant documentation on squatting and bidonvilles, I have found no evidence that the men succeeded in sleeping on the beach. I have seen considerable evidence of obsession with young backpackers, dubbed "beatniks" during the late 1960s and early 1970s. These latter were blamed for leaving trash and human waste on the beach. The mayor's office in Nice complained to the prefect in 1969, "There are twice as many beatniks this year compared to last and they use our beaches as bedrooms and WCs."[107] Plagistes complained, "It is scandalous that these people, with no money, lie all night on the beach, throw out their trash, use the beach as a WC, shave, and wash themselves in the public showers."[108] Citing the municipal decree against vagabondage, the police conducted regular raids.[109] Given the police crackdown on young, mostly white backpackers, we can be sure that North Africans did not successfully set up camp on the beach. In fact, laws against vagabondage could keep North Africans from even entering ritzy towns on the Riviera. In 1954, as Ahsene Draa, thirty-three, and Abdellah Zebouchi, twenty-four, were entering Villefranche, they were stopped by the police. They had been employed at the dam project at Tigne, in Haute-Savoie, but were now looking for work. They were immediately jailed for vagabondage.[110] Clearly, the many North African workers without work or residency cards risked such charges if caught in public spaces where they were not wanted.

Even in isolated spaces, neighbors rejected the men's presence on prime real estate near the sea. In May 1958 two North African workers in Saint-Jean-Cap-Ferrat, employed by local construction firms, approached the mayor. Pushed from place to place, they, in his words, "declared rather aggressively that they were 'French citizens and have the same rights.'" The men wanted to know where they might place a small (two-by-three-meter) wooden shed to serve as their shelter. The mayor directed them to the plage des Fosses, one hundred meters from a public washhouse and WC; the men placed the shed on a cement base, painted it, and furnished it with a table and a couple of iron frame beds. According to the police, it was well maintained, and only two men lived there. Placed on the Domaine Public Maritime, thus territory officially belonging to the French state but normally overseen by municipalities, the shed was close to the gated entries to nearby villas Les Embruns and La Carrière. But these owners rarely used their gated access to the beach, as sewage ran into the water and algae had taken over.[111]

The mayor did not expect the virulent reaction, or political connections, of the villa owners. In June 1958 Commander H. W. A. A. of the British Royal Navy complained to the prefect. He claimed that the men "mixing with tourists" were probably of bad character "as one never knows the character of these people, and their presence diminishes property values."[112] When the prefect did not immediately force the mayor to make the men move on, the commander wrote to Antoine Pinay, former French prime minister and minister of finances and economic affairs. Pinay's deputy wrote the prefect on the commander's behalf, noting that Pinay "attached a definite personal importance" to the need for the mayor to reverse his decision. Pinay's deputy accepted the commander's word that several North Africans lived in the structure and that "a horrible crime" could take place because his villa had many valuable objects. Pinay repeated the commander's claim that "my little ones and their nurse can no longer go out in the garden in the evening, and our nights are filled with nightmares." Moreover, housing "such people without guarantee of character on a public beach" constituted "risks and perils for neighboring property owners." The men were a "danger" and a "menace." And since the US ambassador was supposed to spend several weeks at the villa in September, the commander was very upset about "running such a risk." At the mayor's direction, the North Africans removed the shed, borrowing a truck from their employer.[113]

In another instance, in Saint-Laurent-du-Var, there was a bidonville along the neglected beachfront in the quartier du Lac (near what is today the large shopping mall on the right bank of the Var as it flows into the Mediterranean, just across the river from the airport). There, in 1966, lived just over two hundred North Africans (and seven people of French nationality, including five French women, likely partners of North African men). The number had increased in 1966; when the bidonville at Olivetto was destroyed for the construction of the Musée Chagall, residents scattered, and some ended up in the bidonville of Saint-Laurent-du-Var. They lived in wooden shanties, moving containers, disabled buses and trailers, and five cement blockhouses, remnants of German wartime fortifications. Complaints from neighbors ensued, including a petition demanding that the prefecture eliminate "Arab bidonvilles, in order to preserve the unique site of Saint-Laurent-du-Var so that the tourists are not scared off."[114] The mayor of Saint-Laurent-du-Var refused to cooperate with SONACOTRA in constructing a workers' *foyer* for them, because of the 196 men living there, only nineteen worked in Saint-Laurent-du-Var, while 118 were employed in Nice, eight in Monaco, and the rest in other nearby communities. Saint-Laurent-du-Var aspired to attract more tourists and second home buyers, not to house North Africans. All of the North Africans were evicted in 1966, and many moved just across the Var to bidonvilles at the Digue des Français and the airport, where many of them worked for the construction companies contracted to expand the airport.[115]

CHAPTER 5

Erecting an Airport and Living with Jet Planes

Airplanes seized the collective imagination in the twentieth century. The appeal was not just functional. Of course, airplanes and especially jets were faster than trains. But airplanes also allowed human beings to fly, as if birds. They sparked human imaginings of what the future might bring. Just as the ultimate technological invention of the nineteenth century, the railroad, shortened distances and led to different ways of seeing and touring, airplanes and their airports became sites of modern dreaming.[1] Even those who had not yet flown, perhaps especially those who had not yet flown, found themselves attracted to airports. In the wake of 9/11, airport observation decks are gone, but they were once evidence of the fascination people had with flight. In the early 1950s, 90 percent of the visitors to New York airports were not flying.[2] Between 1956 and 1966 in the Paris area, only the Palace of Versailles got more annual visitors than the terraces that served as observation decks at the Orly airport south of the city. French families rode down to Orly, paid the fee to enter, and spent the day watching jets take off and land. With both restaurants and a sandbox for the kids, Orly was a destination for those not traveling; the Sunday ritual was so popular that Gilbert Bécaud immortalized the practice with a hit song in 1963, "Dimanche à Orly."[3]

A new commercial airport opened in Nice just after the war. Families did not go there to watch the planes. They did not need to. The airport of

Nice was *in* rather than near the city, placed on a patch of earth practically in the sea at the city's edge; Christiane and Jean-Marie Spill compared it to an aircraft carrier.[4] Part of the appeal of Orly was its proximity to Paris, just fifteen kilometers from the Cathedral of Notre-Dame. However, the airport in Nice is only seven kilometers from Vieux Nice, just at the other end of the promenade des Anglais. From the beach, high ground, or balconies in the city, Niçois and tourists could watch airplanes land and take off. In essence, the city itself was an observation deck. Airplanes flew directly over the beach, climbing quickly over the Colline du Château and Mont Boron. From those natural observation decks, an onlooker could appreciate the curve of the baie des Anges, the promenade, and the airplanes flying over them. For beachgoers, what could be more modern than to watch the airplanes take off while getting a tan?[5]

At the Nice airport as elsewhere, the aesthetics of the airport mattered. Like Orly, the airport terminal at Nice did not have a particularly innovative design. It was not the TWA terminal shaped like a bird at JFK airport in New York. Nor was it the modernist circular structure of the first terminal at Charles de Gaulle airport north of Paris. In the case of Nice, it was the airport's natural setting that constituted its allure. One of the engineers building the airport noted that they hoped "to have given France and the Côte d'Azur a new aerial entry, aesthetically worthy of its natural setting and ready to welcome modern commercial aviation for many years."[6] From hills surrounding Nice, from the beach, and from the promenade des Anglais, those on the ground watched the flights. As important, those coming by air could fly over and into the city at the same time, appreciating the sweep of the baie des Anges, the azure blues of the Mediterranean, and the Alps. By day, the symmetry of the palms on the promenade framed the image; by night, symmetrically spaced streetlamps did the same. The airport's aesthetic appeal could easily cause one to ignore the impact of the airport and airplanes on the sea and on the city—the subject of this chapter.

Trains and Planes before 1945

As a leading global tourist destination before World War II, the Riviera owed its importance to the train. Although a small number of visitors arrived by ocean liner in the port of Cannes, most foreign and French tourists came by rail. For a time in the late nineteenth century, Nice was the fastest growing city in Europe; that rapid growth resulted from the train. Until the establishment of the state-owned rail company, the Société nationale des chemins de fer français (SNCF), in 1938, private companies had the authorization to exploit different routes to the French provinces. After the French annexation of Nice in 1860, the Chemins de fer de Paris à Lyon et à la Méditerranée (PLM) company extended its rail line eastward, reaching Cannes in 1863 and Nice in 1864, en route to the Italian border. Northern Europeans departing Paris could henceforth sleep on the train and arrive the next day on the Riviera. Britons could take an exclusively first-class express train from Calais, known after 1923 as the "blue train" because the sleeping cars were blue and gold. Wealthy Americans joined them, after arriving in northern ports and usually staying for a time in Paris. In the interwar years, the blue train was the stuff of legend for Britons and Americans. Celebrities from Charlie Chaplin and F. Scott Fitzgerald to Winston Churchill and Somerset Maugham took the well-known train, which was even the setting for an Agatha Christie mystery aptly titled *The Mystery of the Blue Train*. Thanks to the Popular Front, when Parisian workers got the chance to take a vacation on the Riviera, they too came by train.[7] In fact, the primary reason that much of the coast of the department of the Var remained "undiscovered" until after World War II was that it was not served by a rail line, as the line goes inland from Toulon to Saint-Raphaël and then along the coast to the Italian border. On the Riviera, even the smallest of towns had a train station where visitors might disembark.

By contrast, air tourism barely existed despite efforts to promote it. Michelin produced guidebooks to airfields in the 1930s in the expectation that air tourism would eventually take off just as automobile tourism had.[8] Like automobiles in the 1890s, airplanes were playthings for the rich in the 1930s. They did not go far, and they cost a lot. However, wealthy amateur pilots were precisely the demographic that appealed; it was not a big stretch to imagine an expansion of private air travel. Already in the 1930s there were a number of plans to transform the aerodromes of Cannes and Nice into airports worthy of the name. Aerodrome (literally "air race course"), a term rarely used today, connotes hippodromes for horse racing and velodromes for bike racing, reminding us that aerodromes were conceived as airfields for stunts, shows, and competition. Despite several plans for improved airports in both Cannes and Nice, they came to naught before the war.

On the eve of World War II, the aerodrome at Nice had an unpaved landing strip, eight hundred meters long, once used by Ferdinand Ferber and other aviation pioneers. Set on just thirteen hectares, on the floodplain where the Var meets the Mediterranean, there were significant obstacles to any potential expansion. There was a hippodrome to the northwest far more popular among visitors than the aerodrome. There were private properties to the north and east, and French law before 1935 made expropriation extremely difficult. The bridge over the Var and its connection to the promenade des Anglais were also in the path of any longer runway. The Mediterranean lay to the south. Despite plans in the late 1930s to move the horse-racing track, and even the bank of the Var River, the landing strip remained as it had been since the glory days of Ferber at the turn of the century. Then, in 1943–44, German preparations for an allied invasion included blockhouses and other fortifications on the airfield. Both the aerodrome and the nearby hippodrome, like the aerodrome at Cannes, took heavy hits from Allied forces, ruining what limited runway there was.[9]

On August 15, 1944, Allied forces invaded Provence; they reached Nice at the end of the month. American military engineers worked quickly around German blockhouses and other detritus of the war in order to find room for a runway on what had been the old aerodrome and hippodrome. Initially, the airstrip was for reconnaissance aircraft. Soon engineers extended the runway to 1,350 meters in length, strengthened the foundation, and asphalted it for use by heavy aircraft delivering materiel. In 1945 the US Army used the airport for Douglas Dakota DC-3s and DC-4s, Constellations, and Super Constellations full of American soldiers on leave.[10]

The Aéroport de Nice–Le Var

For proponents of a commercial airport on the Riviera, the Liberation provided an unprecedented opportunity. Americans repaired the damage their bombardment had done to the aerodrome at Cannes, but it became clear that the topography was inadequate for any aircraft weighing more than twenty metric tons.[11] Instead, Cannes maintained a small airport for private planes. In Nice, however, the Americans had already built a paved runway that could accommodate heavy aircraft. The Americans had also destroyed the Var bridge; there was no longer a grand entry into Nice along the promenade, so the bridge and the street could be moved. American bombs had destroyed 80 percent of the horse-racing track and its stands. As important, the Germans had demanded the evacuation of properties near the sea, several of which also sustained heavy damages. Advocates for an airport, particularly the local chamber of commerce, realized that it was time to strike, before those displaced by the war rebuilt.[12]

As the war was ending, engineer Louis Lessieux of the Corps des Ponts et Chaussées developed a plan for an airport in Nice. He presented the project to the Special Delegation of Nice, headed by Virgile Barel, which ran the city when Resistance groups seized control of local government as the Germans withdrew. The delegation approved of the plan, and Barel buttonholed the minister of air, Charles Tillon, at a reception in the prefecture of Alpes-Maritimes and convinced him to listen to Lessieux's ideas. Tillon liked what he heard, returned to Paris, and immediately ensured state funding. Engineers soon dumped approximately 700,000 cubic meters of stones from the Var riverbed onto the area and construction of the Aéroport de Nice–Le Var began.[13]

The new airport had a distinct advantage over others: the climate. While the Riviera gets torrential rainfalls, especially in the late fall and winter, they are usually short. There is no fog, as clouds very rarely descend lower than fifty meters. The new airport lost only portions of three days per year due to foul weather, staying open 99 percent of the time. Nice could accept flights diverted from Marseille-Marignane due to snow, because the Alps protected Nice, giving it a superior microclimate.[14] Since Marseille-Marignane was the closest commercial airport, Nice seemed to have an important niche. In 1950 there were flights to Algiers, Amsterdam, Geneva, London, Paris, and Rome, and, with numerous stops as these were propeller planes, New York.

As engineers, local business leaders, and officials set about selling the new airport to the public, they relied heavily on a language of progress and modernity. The airport was to preserve the Riviera's place as an elite tourist destination, since those who could afford to fly just after the war were, by definition, wealthy. Local advocates for tourism saw the new airport as key for future economic growth. And no advocate was more vocal than the local chamber of commerce, the powerful Chambre de commerce et d'industrie de Nice, which received the concession to run the new, ever-expanding airport. The arrangement was not unique. Local chambers of commerce also ran regional airports of Bordeaux, Marseille, and Toulouse; Paris was the standout in having a distinct nonprofit entity, Aéroports de Paris (ADP), which managed the airports of Bourget, Orly, and eventually Charles de Gaulle. For Nice's chamber of commerce, the airport was a key to ensuring local economic growth by maintaining and even increasing the number of well-off tourists choosing the Riviera as their vacation destination.

Expropriations

Although western Nice was not nearly as built up in 1945 as it would be in the succeeding decades, the area did not consist of bare land. There were already homes, businesses, and small farms. Historically, payments for declarations of eminent domain (*déclaration d'utilité publique*) had been quite high in France, prohibitively so according to developers, because property owners had made up a majority of members on the juries that determined payments. But in 1935 French law changed, and henceforth a commission of only five members adjudicated any payments for declarations of eminent domain; of the five members, three were government officials, one an owner of property, and one a notary (*notaires* in France are more like property lawyers and have considerable status, not at all like American notary publics). As might be expected, the "reform" of 1935 led to low reimbursements for owners facing expropriation of their properties.[15]

Local property owners fought the airport project. The Committee for the Defense of Interests of the Neighborhoods Lavallière-St.-Augustin-Arénas represented about two hundred families and gathered hundreds of signatures opposed to the placement of the airport. Particularly given the organization's name, it is obvious that the committee's opposition involved, above all, petitioners' own expropriations and forced moves. But in petitioning authorities, notably the Ministry of Air, the committee argued more broadly for the interests of Nice and taxpayers generally. They claimed that the airport should instead be located on the plaine de la Brague, near Antibes. The committee cited small plane accidents in the past, due to airflows along the Mediterranean and the Var. It noted that the recently built road along the sea, having cost 50 to 60 million francs, was now being torn up, forsaking the grand western entry into Nice so long envisaged and realized just before the war. The committee argued that aircraft noise would effectively ruin the Victorine movie studio in western Nice, ending local aspirations to become a French Hollywood. The committee confidently proclaimed that the population of Nice was not convinced that one of the most beautiful parts of Nice should be destroyed, along with one of the most popular horse-racing tracks in France, long a fixture of the social scene. Finally, the committee bemoaned the elimination of two hundred hectares of farmland producing approximately four hundred metric tons of fruits and vegetables.[16]

Opponents also attempted to wield a new law on rents. France faced an acute housing shortage after World War II; rent controls in place since the First World War and the economic crisis of the 1930s had already been obstacles to new construction in the interwar years. Then the war wrought widespread destruction. To protect the eviction of people with nowhere to go, the law on rents of 1 September 1948 specifically addressed the issue of expropriation for eminent domain, requiring the authorities to "ensure alternate housing for renters or occupants, [subsequently read to include owners], expelled from buildings acquired or expropriated as a result of a declaration of eminent domain."[17] Since the housing shortage in Nice was acute, and there were few suitable alternative dwellings, proprietors and tenants tried to use the law as part of their broader strategy of resistance; two owner-occupants and six tenants cited the law in refusing to leave their dwellings, causing work on the airport to grind to a halt. The chamber of commerce fought back, mobilizing other French chambers of commerce and lobbying the prefect, local deputies, Prime Minister Georges Bidault, and all 169 national deputies who had voted against the measure originally. Arguing for the broader economic interest represented by the airport, the chamber of commerce wanted the measure overturned "due to the almost total impossibility of acquiring apartments for the tenants or occupants" of the buildings slated for demolition on the site of the new airport.[18] Clearly the chamber of commerce believed that the price of progress might include homelessness for some Niçois. The result of opponents' actions was not an end to the airport but merely delays in its completion. Although unsuccessful in their quest, property owners had been clairvoyant in opposing a project that turned out badly for them. Three hundred families lost their homes between 1945 and 1950, this after having already been forced to evacuate by the Germans in 1943–44. To add insult to injury, some owners were still awaiting payment five years after expropriation.[19]

The Aéroport de Nice–Côte d'Azur

In the twentieth century, chambers of commerce generally cared about airports, as a well-run airport with good connections facilitated business. The same was true in Nice, though on the Riviera the focus was particularly on tourist travel. The chamber of commerce's interest in tourism extended to the airport's name. As early as 1951, long before the completion of the main terminal, the chamber of commerce petitioned the Ministry of Public Works, Transport, and Tourism to have the name of the airport changed from Aéroport de Nice–Le Var to Aéroport de Nice–Côte d'Azur so that it might be better identified with coastal tourism for potential visitors. The ministry resisted. Officially airports had two-part names, the first indicating the city, the second indicating a prominent geographical feature that facilitated recognition for a navigator and appeared on the aeronautic map with the scale 500,000 to 1. The chamber of commerce persisted, and in 1955 the ministry relented, allowing the airport to carry the more evocative name, Aéroport de Nice–Côte d'Azur.[20]

Although most visitors continued to come by train in the 1950s and by automobile thereafter, well-heeled travelers to the Riviera increasingly abandoned the blue train for the airplane. Air travel quickly reduced travel times. Whereas the rich had once lingered, now they were preoccupied with speed. The blue train had been the quickest way to get from the gray north to the sunny Riviera in its day. After 1945 airplanes allowed a passenger to fly from Paris to Nice and back to Paris in the course of a single day; in 1957 jets would soon reduce the flying time from Paris to Nice to a couple of hours.[21]

Expansion was swift, from 34,230 passengers in 1946, to 562,672 in 1956, to 729,616 in 1959, to 940,144 in 1962, allowing the Nice–Côte d'Azur airport to surpass Marseille and become the busiest airport in France after Orly.[22] Almost every year broke the previous year's record, as the growth of air travel after World War II was rapid. Growth came in the number of planes, the size of planes, and the number of passengers. In the 1950s, an era still dominated by passenger propeller planes, the new airport became an important stopover for flights en route to North Africa and for those bound for locales to the east; 40 percent of arriving passengers in the late 1950s were those on layover.[23]

Because of the astonishing growth in demand, the airport was under constant construction. That made it typical of airports in Europe and

FIG. 5.1. Workers paving the runway of the Nice airport in 1954. Note that the men standing appear to be North Africans, who frequently laid asphalt. Archives départementales des Alpes-Maritimes 598 W 28 (image, Centre d'études techniques de l'équipement).

North America after World War II; they were quickly obsolete. In Nice as elsewhere, some of the work was organizational, a matter of moving people more quickly and efficiently from curb to plane.[24] But Nice was also unique. While at most airports a runway could be added or extended with comparatively little engineering by simply strengthening the base and increasing the length, in Nice the Var River and the Mediterranean Sea were at either end of the runway. Early construction and expansion to the edge of the Var extended the short runway paved by the Americans to 1,700 meters in 1947. However, as aircraft grew in size, the runway remained too small, and in 1953 work began on a runway measuring 2,200 meters long, which could handle the tonnage of larger aircraft. As would happen repeatedly in the postwar years, the engineers of Ponts et Chaussées oversaw a reengineering of the riverbed and coastline near the airport. In order to force the Var to flow more toward the west, construction firms built a dike of huge boulders, each weighing three to five metric tons, one kilometer long, forming an outer barrier into which they dumped 600,000 cubic meters of stone from the riverbed upstream.[25]

In 1957 Édouard Bonnefous, the minister of public works, transport, and tourism, came to Nice to inaugurate the new 2,200-meter cement runway and the completed terminal. He reminded the audience of the importance of the airport's beauty, even for those passengers en route to another destination. Adapting the language always used in France to describe the Champs-Elysées, "la plus belle avenue du monde," Bonnefous proclaimed the Nice airport "la plus belle escale du monde" (the most beautiful stopover in the world). Referring to those for whom Nice was their final destination, Bonnefous felt the need to warn listeners that the mass of tourists "will not resemble those who were our guests during the Victorian era. They will have neither the outdated grace nor the refined elegance." Many more Americans would soon be arriving as airlines restructured their aircraft to include a new economy class fare. "These new visitors will arrive with the same craving, the same enthusiasm, the same earnest impatience which, thousands of kilometers from here and everywhere in the world, seizes those who want to see, for once in their lives, this Côte d'Azur which, like Paris or Versailles, is one of the highlights of our country."[26]

Bonnefous was referring to the economy class on transatlantic flights on new Boeing 707 jets. Not surprisingly given the reference, planning for another expansion began before the inauguration. In 1957 French Caravelles and American Boeing 707s could now land. But they could not have a full load of fuel and still take off, thus negating the reason for longer-range aircraft in the first place. Work soon began to extend the runway to the east, at the expense of the Mediterranean and the coastline.[27] In 1961, after 270,000 m³ of fill (from a dump strategically placed along the sea) and an additional 270,000 m³ of stone from the Var were placed behind a dike of 12,000-metric-ton rocks, the runway grew to 2,700 meters so that it could accommodate the passenger jets in the air at the time.[28] Increases in aircraft size, passenger numbers, and runway length were dizzying. As the French regional director of the American carrier Pan Am put it in 1960, "Ten years ago, the big airplanes carried forty passengers. Now they have eighty. In another month, we will be putting into service four-engine DC-8s, which have a capacity of 130 passengers." The longer runway made it possible for Nice to receive nonstop Pan Am flights from New York.[29] In 1962 the chamber of commerce asked arriving passengers to fill out a survey during the period August 6–14, that is, the peak of the summer season for French tourists. More than 15 percent of all arrivals consisted of US Americans. Only the English and French outnumbered them.

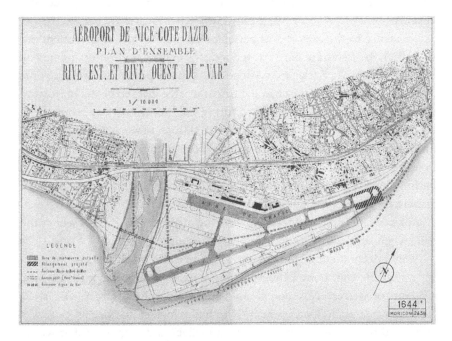

FIG. 5.2. The Aéroport de Nice-Côte d'Azur in 1959. Dotted lines show the original coastline (cutting through the airport), the earlier bridge over the Var, and the original path of the Var River to the sea. Hash marks show the proposed extension of the runway, labeled here "Piste I." Archives départementales des Alpes-Maritimes 142 W 14.

Jets for the Jet-Setters, Noise for the Neighbors

Culturally, the postwar years were the jet age. In novels, films, advertising and an array of cultural artifacts, jet travel was an important theme. Even the designs of automobiles, that quintessential symbol of twentieth-century mobility, sometimes resembled those of jets. People who could afford to fly might imagine themselves as part of the jet set, like the movie stars who flew to Cannes for the film festival. Jets whisked travelers across the globe in pressurized cabins, a far cry from the vibrations, frequent fuel stops, and oxygen masks of earlier propeller planes.

Alongside that imagined world of jet flight were those who lived near airports, who heard the roar of early jet engines and inhaled their fumes. As well-off tourists arrived by plane to experience the fabled Riviera, they made a lot of noise. Of course, trains with steam engines had made significant noise. So did diesel engines; electrification of the train line through Nice was complete only in 1969. Loading of rail freight was also noisy.[30] What made airplanes and particularly jets different is that they were new, they were even louder, and they often affected neighborhoods not already subject to deafening noise.

Resistance to the airport was never for the sake of the environment per se. Rather, the airport at Nice created a classic case of opposition defined by NIMBY (Not In My Back Yard). Those living in the proximity of the airport despised it. Meanwhile, the chamber of commerce, backed by the mayor and the French state, argued on behalf of future visitors. Tourists were omnipresent in the discourse promoting the airport, though never actually present in the meetings and correspondence among locals with much to gain, and lose, from the airport and its subsequent expansions. In the end, those mobilizing the imagined hordes of future tourists for the sake of local business interests, namely, the chamber of commerce, consistently won out—much to the chagrin of residents and hotel owners near the airport, who had no seat at the table when airport expansion was at stake.

Neighborhood complaints about airplane noise began almost immediately after the war. Long before passenger jet service began at the airport, residents of western Nice complained about the noise of propeller planes, particularly at night. One resident, who had relocated to Nice in 1948, was impressed by the "incredible nocturnal racket" and wondered if it would cause tourists to call Nice the "city where one cannot sleep" because "each night, and particularly about two o'clock in the morning, one is awakened by the passage of large aircraft flying over the city at low altitude. The vibrations, which make the tiles tremble and make everything in the apartment dance, are such that it seems difficult, for even the deepest sleepers, not to wake up." According to the resident, the interwar ban on flying at low altitude over cities seemed to have disappeared entirely.[31] In 1952 a group of residents and hotel owners on the promenade des Anglais petitioned Mayor Jean Médecin to do something about the noise, posing their complaint as a question. "Why do all airplanes leaving the airport of Nice persist, especially at night, to offer their passengers a view of the promenade at an altitude of about 150 meters, while the regulations prohibit their flying over the promenade at that altitude?" At the airport there were clear directions for pilots forbidding the practice; however, as petitioners suggested, it was not enforced.[32]

Things got worse before they got better. In 1957, as jets were replacing propeller planes, residents in the vicinity of the airport complained vociferously. Residents used a local association, the Syndicat de défense des intérêts généraux de Caucade-Sainte-Marguerite, to fight the noise. Some 150 members of the group gathered two hundred signatures on a formal complaint in the summer of 1960, demanding the suppression of night flights and the elimination of all jet traffic even during the day. The group had assistance from an association fighting noise in general, the Comité de lutte contre le bruit dans les Alpes-Maritimes, which had a Dr. Klinger as its president. Klinger laid out alarming details about what he considered the specifics of medical problems resulting from the noise, which he had treated. In one case a forty-eight-year-old man moving to the neighborhood could no longer sleep without sleeping pills. After a month, he was depressive, unable to eat properly. He developed "character problems" such as "beating his child (which he had never done before), [he] neglected his business, and (the reason he decided to consult a doctor) had a sexual anomaly: sudden impotence. Despite diverse treatments, the man did not get better." Then he moved to a different town, and ten days later he could sleep without medication, recovered his appetite, and gained weight. After twenty days, he was no longer impotent. In a second case, a two-and-a-half-month-old had not gained weight since birth; he awoke each time an airplane flew overhead, cried, and became agitated. He vomited frequently and his gastrointestinal problems did not respond to the usual treatments. Nor could his mother sleep, developing alarming signs of nervousness. The baby developed a laryngospasm with a cyanosis (a muscle spasm in the throat with bluish membranes due to low oxygen levels in red blood cells), and the parents left Nice, the father having found a job in Languedoc. Dr. Klinger later inquired about the baby, and as soon as he was not subject to the noise of airplanes, he quickly gained weight and no longer had any symptoms.[33]

In September 1961 now long-standing concerns about the noise generated by jets led to the creation of a "sound map" (*carte sonore*) of the area around the airport, based on assessments done by four mobile sound labs that tested various spots on nearby streets. *Nice Matin* used the occasion to interview several residents who complained about what they considered an untenable situation. One woman claimed that the situation "is dreadful. We do not have an instant of rest. We have to live with all of the windows closed, in the middle of summer," this in a brand-new (thus presumably somewhat soundproof) building on the avenue de la Californie. Nearby, in another new building, the Palais Vénus, a tenant noted, "the vibrations that shake the entire building broke two vases" on her buffet. Moreover, her "young child is awakened almost every night. Each time he hears a jet, he puts his hands over his ears and closes his eyes." On the promenade des Anglais, a former Resistance fighter mentioned her nervous condition dating from the war and the need for rest, and night flights robbed her of any sleep. The newspaper made clear that it was in no way cherry-picking the evidence, as it received many letters from inhabitants of the area who could not manage to sleep since the introduction of jet service, particularly that of "the four-engine jets that caused deafening vibrations." Jets made the walls shake. Noise at the airport was like "cancer."[34]

The location of the airport seemed partly responsible. It was a point of pride that the airport was only seven kilometers from Vieux Nice, since such proximity meant incredibly easy access to the airport from the city. For tourists staying in the many hotels and apartments on the promenade, the airport was even closer. But the airport also made deafening noise an inevitable fact of life in western Nice. According to Commander Allégret, who was in charge of the airport, the problem was that the location gave pilots little room to maneuver. As soon as their planes reached a safe altitude, pilots were supposed to veer to the south, head out over the sea, and climb as rapidly as possible. Allégret was confident that "sixty percent of the pilots of the [two-engine, French-built] Caravelle applied the instructions and turned to the south quickly." However, he claimed that it was "almost impossible for the pilots of four-engine [American-built Boeing 707 and Douglas DC-8] jets to undertake such a maneuver. From the time that the plane gets to the runway, pilots and the rest of their flight crew are absorbed with a series of complicated controls and movements." Moreover, the wind, tied to the prevailing current along the coast, presented a problem for all jets. "Whenever possible we have the planes take off toward the west since the population of Saint-Laurent-du-Var is less dense and especially since the trajectory off the runway is farther from the coast." Of course, this only worked when the wind was out of the west, assisting lift during take-off, but the wind at Nice is usually from the east, just as the Ligurian current comes from the east. In 1962, after two full years of consideration and innumerable complaints, the Ministry of Transport at last gave the green light for the airport of Nice to ban night flights between 11:00 p.m. and 6:00 a.m., following the lead of Orly in Île-de-France and Croydon airport near London.[35] It was a tacit admission of the noise residents suffered.

Suing Air France

Affected parties upped the ante by suing the French national airline, Air France, drawing the attention of authorities so ready to dismiss the protests of residents. In 1962 a construction company, the Société de construction Evré, filed suit against Air France, the airline with the largest presence at the airport. Evré had constructed a residential building, the Oiseau Bleu, near the airport in 1956. At the time of its completion, jet service began at the airport, so that each time someone visited an apartment, "an airplane passed and the [potential] buyer went home."[36] Only one apartment sold. Pieds noirs, arriving in droves in 1962 and unable to find other housing, initially rented apartments, but they moved out when their leases expired six months later. Evré claimed that the company lost 2 million (new) francs and that Air France bore the responsibility because the noise of jet aircraft scared away buyers.[37] Two individual owners joined the suit; M. Vomero was the only person to have bought one of Evré's apartments, and he claimed a personal loss of 100,000 francs. A second family, the Bondars, had built a nearby residence, a reconstruction of one bombed during the war, and claimed 180,000 francs (in order to get reconstruction funds, they had been required to rebuild on the same site).[38] In addition, the Syndicat du Caucade-Sainte-Marguerite, whose petition years earlier had been ignored, also joined the suit; as longtime residents, its two hundred members could not prove immediate financial loss, but they wanted a cessation of the noise, with Air France facing a 500-franc fine each time the airline surpassed acceptable noise levels. In the words of their attorney, their "paradise had become hell." The fine was to serve as a guarantee that nearby residents affected by the noise, estimated to be as high as 50,000 out of a total population in Nice of under 300,000, would get a reprieve. The noise was not nothing; jets regularly caused the din to reach the level of 115 decibels in apartments with the windows closed (not a small imposition in such a warm, sunny summer climate at a time without air-conditioning), while doctors agreed that any level above ninety decibels was unhealthful.[39]

Air France fought back by attempting to change the court venue. By arguing that the problem was the location of the airport, thus the responsibility of government, the airline wanted to move the suit to the administrative tribunal (*tribunal administratif*), where French citizens could challenge the government. Air France further argued that the petitioners' choice of a civil court was merely tactical; though Air France was legally a private company, thus subject to civil claims, the French state owned 98 percent of its shares at the time.[40] Air France also created a diversion by attempting to get thirteen other airlines added to the suit alongside Air France. In August 1963, the high tourist season, Air France had 132 incoming jet flights while all of the others combined had eighty-one.[41] The company's legal team knew full well that foreign firms, including Pan American Airways and Swissair, could not be held liable due to international agreements governing their presence in France; the strategy was to release Air France from responsibility. Finally, Air France claimed that some propeller planes, notably the DC-3, DC-4, and DC-6, could also surpass ninety-five decibels.[42]

In the meantime, support for Air France mobilized. For local officials, progress and the economic development of the Riviera seemed to be under siege, particularly when the head of Air France, Joseph Roos, threatened that if Air France lost the case, the company might simply terminate all service to Nice. Nice mayor Jean Médecin noted that any reduction in air traffic would have "disastrous economic consequences" for the region. Pierre Pasquini, Gaullist deputy and vice president of the National Assembly, commented that "even for an instant there can be no question of eliminating or moving the airport for the private interests of a few compared to the general interest" of the public. Joseph Raybaud (independent), senator, mayor of Levens, and president of the departmental *conseil général*, pointed out that if Air France were held liable, it was inevitable that the company and other airlines would pull out of the airport, and the result would be catastrophic for tourism on the Riviera. He too made clear that the public interest should prevail over that of individuals. Gaullist deputy Diomède Catroux noted that a loss in court would cause both domestic and international carriers to abandon Nice in favor of Marseille or even Genoa. Francis Palmero (right-wing, non-Gaullist), deputy and mayor of Menton and protégé of Jean Médecin, said that the airport in Nice, like those elsewhere, simply needed to be accepted as part of living in the modern world. Louis Magnan, president of the chamber of commerce, focused on the fact that night flights had ended and that flight paths already minimized what would have been even higher noise levels.[43]

In the end, the court largely sided with Air France, a decision upheld on appeal. Although Air France did pay indemnities to the individual property owners for their losses, the Syndicat du Caucade-Sainte-Marguerite lost its bid to require a 500-franc payment each time a plane took off, thus the company and other airlines could continue service to Nice without any liability for the noise generated. In Nice, as at Orly and elsewhere, the growth in airline traffic was now unbridled.[44] Noise from the airport, particularly as the number of flights increased each day, effectively shut down the Victorine movie studio, as it became nearly impossible to shoot. In his film about making a film, *La nuit américaine* (1973), François Truffaut repeatedly shows that already in the early 1970s jet takeoffs were a serious obstacle to production by featuring the planes' noise as they flew over the set at Victorine.

Noise remained a problem for other communities along the coast as well. Airplanes needed to be at a low altitude as they approached the airport, and the flight path was directly over Antibes. There inhabitants complained that evening flights regularly woke up their children.[45] In 1977 *Nice Matin* interviewed Commander Provot, then in charge of the airport, who explained, "It so happens that Antibes is an *obligatory crossing point*. It is situated on the approach path—about nine kilometers—from the airport" (emphasis in the original). The landing path went directly over Juan-les-Pins and then over the historic Fort Carré at the edge of Antibes. The noise only grew as the airplanes approached Nice.[46]

The Airport and the Sea

As air travel increased in the 1960s, the terminal expanded. Jets had longer range, and Nice became the destination, not the stopover. The airport remained the busiest airport in France outside Île-de-France. As air traffic grew, the chamber of commerce worked to accommodate the projected growth with more construction projects. In 1969 the runway extended once more to the east, as the airport absorbed five additional hectares of the Mediterranean. Yet even that was inadequate as projected growth in air travel indicated that the airport would need to welcome 7 to 8 million passengers per annum by 1981. The physical space of the airport was tiny given its traffic. In 1971 the airport occupied 200 hectares of land, while the less busy Marseille-Marignane airport occupied 500. Since the airport at Nice was already squeezed into the edge of the city, along the coast and the river, and had already created serious noise pollution in western Nice, there was no room for expansion. Engineers seemed to have reached the limit in 1973, when they took an additional twenty-four hectares from the Var so that the runway could grow to 3,000 meters, the minimum necessary for fully loaded Boeing 747s. There was simply no room for a second runway.[47]

As in Île-de-France, where the new (eventually named Charles de Gaulle) airport at Roissy was rising to the northeast of Paris, the initial solution was to build another airport somewhere else in Alpes-Maritimes. Given the mountainous terrain of the department anywhere but along the coastline and the natural limits of the small airport at Cannes, engineers were unsuccessful in locating a suitable alternative site. Instead, the chamber of commerce decided to expand the existing airport at the expense of the Mediterranean. By filling in seabed, engineers could build a platform of 200 hectares just south of the existing airport. Monaco had already successfully built a huge platform with several large buildings over what had been the sea, setting the model.[48]

Interestingly, the chamber of commerce sold the idea with a promise to reduce noise pollution in western Nice. The plan faced no significant resistance; in a sense, Niçois seemed to be trading the flora and fauna of the sea for less noise. The new longer runway, measuring 3,200 meters, would be farther from the old coastline. In essence, the principal runway was moving 500 meters into what had been the sea. Engineers studied the likely sound impact. What they found was promising. Before the construction, 114 hectares nearest the airport (zone A, of intense noise) were officially *non aedificandi*, meaning that no construction whatsoever was possible; that number could be reduced to one hectare after the expansion. A second section (zone B, of loud noise), a bit farther from the airport, measuring 139 hectares, had commercial buildings but no residences; the new runway would reduce that area to fifty-seven hectares. Finally, the third area measuring 264 hectares (zone C, of medium noise), even farther from the airport, permitted residences with considerable soundproofing; the new runway would reduce that area to ninety-six hectares. Thus might a large portion of western Nice be available for new development, impossible since the arrival of jets in the late 1950s.[49]

The scale of the project was enormous, doubling the size of the existing airport. The company formed to do the work, the Société niçoise pour l'extension de l'aéroport (SONEXA) brought together ten companies: five national, two Dutch, and three Niçois, including both Nicoletti and Spada. Over the centuries, stone coming down the Var had created an alluvial plateau in the Mediterranean near the airport, so it was only ten to fifteen meters deep, making the whole project possible along a coastline known for its otherwise steep drop-off.[50] Taking more fill from the Var riverbed was out of the question; there simply were not enough materials. One solution was to follow in the footsteps of the Dutch and pull materials from the sea, along the coastline. Engineers ruled out this option for fear it would ruin the beaches, already facing erosion each winter. Instead, engineers flattened the hill of Crémat. A projected thirty million metric tons could be trucked down then dumped into the sea.[51] Crémat had distinct advantages. Due to its rugged terrain, it would not otherwise have been suitable for development; it had no roads, only old mule trails crossing it. Moreover, it was just eleven kilometers upriver, on the left bank of the Var, so it would not be necessary for the huge dump trucks to cross the river. Crémat also had pudding stone, perfect for fill. Finally, there were only twenty-five property owners, facilitating expropriation. After the removal of the pudding stone, bulldozers could simply level off what was left of the hill "for aesthetic reasons" and it would be suitable for development.[52]

From the mid-1970s to the early 1980s, construction continued. Boulders from Spada's quarries at Roquefort-les-Pins (in Alpes-Maritimes, not the Roquefort of famed cheese in the Aveyron) and Saint-André formed a sort of dike, filled in with about thirty million metric tons of pudding stone from Crémat. Huge excavators loaded twenty-five metric tons per shovelful into dump trucks with trailers that hauled the fill to the airport. Thirty trucks, weighing 140 metric tons each, formed a nonstop convoy for months. Construction companies laid a roadbed in the Var River valley later used for

FIG. 5.3. After the completion of the second runway in 1983, the airport resembled an aircraft carrier off the coast of Nice. The original coastline ran near the buildings standing on the left of the image. Archives départementales des Alpes-Maritimes 1504 W 11.

the bypass around Nice, completely avoiding existing public roads. Trucks dumped the fill into the sea, where some of it stayed in place, and some seeped past the rocks and ended as silt in the sea. After the fill settled for months in different sections of the project, a massive compacting machine dropped a 160-ton mass onto the fill, turning former sea into stable land. The project employed 350 people, including North Africans, for many years.[53] The new runway opened in 1983.

Clearly, the environmental impact of the Nice–Côte d'Azur airport was significant. However, neither air pollution nor the effects of plants and marine life got as much attention as noise did. Successive expansions of the airport, not to mention its doubling in size in the late 1970s and early 1980s, wiped out the flora and fauna in its path. There were sporadic complaints about air quality near the airport; for example, in 1961 the same Syndicat de Caucade-Sainte-Marguerite that sued Air France also complained to journalists about the exhaust of jet engines. *Le Patriote* claimed in 1962 that twelve departures and arrivals each day produced as much exhaust as eighty thousand additional vehicles on the streets of Nice.[54] But concern about air quality did not get as much traction on the Riviera as it was garnering nationally; the relative absence of industry and coastal breezes made air pollution a less immediate problem than in many French regions.[55] Instead, in a frequent formulation in favor of more roads, advocates of a bigger airport argued that it could also help Nice "breathe." In announcing the pending arrival of Boeing 727s in 1969 and Boeing 747s in 1970, André Luchesi of *Nice Matin* called the airport a "lung" for the Riviera, apparently breathing new life, or at least more tourism, into it.[56]

The Jet Set and the Rest

From the beginning, commercial airplane travel denoted social difference. However, whereas staying on the Riviera for months had been the marker of status in the Belle Époque, by the 1950s the jet set often opted for rapid movement and short stays. Speed, not quiet leisure, became a norm for the rich. To attract them and other well-heeled visitors, the chamber of commerce sought to keep pace with rapidly changing expectations for airports and runways. In the meantime, the chamber of commerce, state engineers, and officials at all levels were unconcerned with the environmental impact of airport expansion into the Var and the Mediterranean, let alone the effects on nearby residents' peace and quiet.

The racial divide was pronounced, as the noise was a good deal worse for North Africans living nearby. They worked for the firms that got the contracts for the initial construction and repeated expansions of the airport. Since they had work but nowhere to live, they ended up squatting and erecting bidonvilles in the area designated *non aedificandi*, too noisy even for commercial building. Throughout the Thirty Glorious Years there would remain abandoned structures and bidonvilles in the vicinity of the airport. In fact, the first bidonville in Nice seems to have appeared in 1946, near the new airport, as initial airport construction began.[57] It was only the first of several bidonvilles that emerged near the airport between 1946 and the elimination of the last in 1976. Throughout the period, workers living across from the airport in mere shacks were subject to far more noise than the European residents who complained so vociferously.

In 1958 fifty-seven men lived in a bidonville on the route de Marseille across from the airport.[58] It was close to the hundreds of private construction sites as the western edge of Nice metamorphosed from farmland and villas to apartment blocks. Public works projects were also nearby. When the police inquired as to the workers' employers, they heard the names Borie, Cecchi, Fassi, Gandolfo, Martin, Nicoletti, and Tirverio, companies that regularly got the contracts for public and private construction projects.[59] The airport bidonville drew the attention of authorities, who described it as an eyesore. Officials and promoters of tourism to Nice saw the area near the airport as a sort of grand entry into the city. As tourists left the terminal, the first thing they saw was a bidonville. In addition, most travelers by car also entered Nice from the west, and they drove right past the bidonville.[60]

Evictions were a regular occurrence, causing the men to find another abandoned property and start all over again. In 1959 the police expelled fifty North Africans from a building at the block straddling 133, avenue de la Californie and 213, promenade des Anglais, to the east of the airport. It had no water and no sewer, and trash accumulated in all rooms. The prefecture oversaw their expulsion and the destruction of the building in order to prevent reoccupation, with full knowledge that "the interested parties have found lodging in nearby buildings also in ruins."[61] In 1961 North Africans were living in a bidonville at 179, route de Marseille. Although the men "reacted violently and absolutely did not want to leave" when the company charged with its destruction arrived to begin demolition, they were still evicted.[62] They moved down the street.

After the airport expansion in the mid-1960s, the existence of a bidonville across the street preoccupied the chamber of commerce. The argument for its removal was, above all, that its existence interfered with tourists' enjoyment of Nice, as it was impossible to miss. In the words of *L'Espoir*, the bidonville "constitutes a 'black spot' in the otherwise generally welcoming aspect of the neighborhood; for the tourist, arrival at Nice is by [its presence] rendered rather depressing. It always surprises tourists arriving on the coast."[63] Attempts at visual barriers had not worked; in 1967 a solid fence painted the blue of the Rotary Club emblem at the time of its international meeting in Nice was supposed to block the sight of the bidonville, but soon damage to it revealed the bidonville behind it.[64] By June 1967 there had been three fires, but North Africans rebuilt each time. The land was private property, but building on it had been prohibited so that later growth of the airport could take over the area; this had been the case since 1945.[65]

Not far away were two additional bidonvilles, along the avenue Lindbergh, directly across the street from the airport, just west of what is today the Musée des arts asiatiques. The two small bidonvilles (twelve men living in one and eight in another) were on abandoned properties. They had once been part of one large parcel, belonging to the Cicion family, since divided into three. The middle parcel had been sold to the Société Charles Martin, an asphalting company, and the men living in sheds on the other two parcels, just to the north and south of Martin's firm, worked for Martin. There was no sewage hookup, and water came from a spigot on Martin's property.[66] This was typical of many properties near the airport; they were abandoned, subject to expropriation in case of airport expansion, and of limited value given the noise from the airport.

In 1971 the chamber of commerce again pressured owners to evict the North Africans out of a "concern for the aesthetic" as tourists arrived at the airport only to see small bidonvilles directly across from it.[67] A. T., whose wife had inherited one of the properties in question, replied that there was nothing he could do. The North Africans had "invaded" the property, forcing open the door of the shed and moving in. When A. T. had gone in, removed the men's possessions, and then put a chain and lock on the shed, the police let him know that he risked a charge for theft. He had no right to remove the men's things, no doubt because the men had been living there for more than two weeks, giving them the right to the due process of proper eviction. The men moved back in. A. T. laid the problem at the feet of the chamber of commerce and the city, suggesting sarcastically they buy him out and put in a flower garden. He let them know that the entire property had once been enclosed, but when the state expropriated a portion for a "little bit of nothing," they took the locked entrance and left the rest of the property open. Because the property was so close to the airport, it had limited value because it was in the zone where residential development was banned due to aircraft noise.[68]

Frustrated, the chamber of commerce asked the prefect to intervene. He did so, asking departmental director of sanitary and social action Robini to compile a report, noting the "inaesthetic character" of such habitations "along a touristic approach" to the city, where the airport met the coastal road. Initiating inspections in order to clear the area, the director agreed that the bidonville "does not flatter the entry to Nice" with "rubbish and excrement spread about." He advised that the authorities could use the public health code in order to evict the men. The men were soon evicted.[69]

At the end of 1973 there were 450 North African workers living in another bidonville across from the airport.[70] At 203, route de Marseille the bidonville began as a simple rental, when the owner G. P. had rented the property to L. G., an Algerian. A scrap metal merchant, L. G. in turn rented out rooms in the two houses, a basement, the garage, and some twenty old buses, trucks, and trailers he moved onto the property, ultimately earning more than he paid G. P., 24,000 francs per month. However, when L. G. returned to Algeria for a visit, the French government blocked his return. The men on the property remained. Incrementally, the workers removed the vehicles, replacing them with small structures of cinderblock, with canvas roofs. On adjacent property next door, two to three hundred workers constructed additional structures. The bidonville grew even larger when a fire destroyed another near the airport, located at 104, route de Marseille, in March 1973.[71]

After investigating, police claimed that the men asked, in case of eviction, for lodging nearby so that they would still be near their work (indicating they were working for firms on the expansion of the airport or on apartment blocks in western Nice). Mayor Jacques Médecin was vehemently opposed to a SONACOTRA structure across from the airport: "It is certain that the airport of the capital of tourism of the Côte d'Azur has a vocation to receive hotels and not housing. Across from the airport, given the paucity of land in our city, it would be indecent to build anything else but tourist establishments." For their part, the men refused to leave the property because they were near their worksites; the only openings in a SONACOTRA structure were at Saint-André, too far away for the men to get to work on time. G. P. was in the process of selling the property to the chamber of commerce for airport expansion. He was so eager to get rid of the men that he said that once they were removed, "I will have guards with dogs do surveillance and stop any return" of North Africans. But authorities had no idea where the men might be rehoused, so they ignored the court order for eviction G. P. acquired.[72]

In the end, the building of a second runway and the construction of the autoroute bypass around Nice coincided with the elimination of bidonvilles both at the Digue des Français and across from the airport. The chamber of commerce not only wanted room for airport freight on G. P.'s property; it also needed the considerable fill from the hill of Crémat. Engineers laid a roadbed along the Var, used first for the airport fill and then as a foundation for the autoroute to circle around Nice. In March 1976, after eighteen months of preparation, authorities cleared both the Digue des Français and the airport bidonvilles, precluding any efforts of the men to move from one to the other. A parade of huge dump trucks began to haul the hill down to the sea. North Africans, including no doubt many of the men recently evicted, worked for the construction companies that got the contracts for both the airport expansion and the extension of the autoroute.

CHAPTER 6

Remaking Roads and Disciplining Drivers

In Alfred Hitchcock's *To Catch a Thief* (1955) the roads of the Riviera play an important role. Starring Grace Kelly (as Frances) and Cary Grant (as Robie), the film is a mystery about a cat burglary that includes an astonishing number of car scenes. From the initial car chase to Frances's fast drive in a convertible to the couple's picnic site overlooking the sea, *To Catch a Thief* is a veritable advertisement for the wonders of motoring on the Riviera. The panoramas are breathtaking, the curves fun, and there is, except for a bit of comedy as Frances enjoys scaring Robie on the way to the picnic, almost no one else on the road. Because Hitchcock interspersed views of the sea into car scenes, the film suggests that much of the driving takes place on the *moyenne corniche*, already an important tourist sight in the 1950s. *To Catch a Thief* reveals how many potential tourists imagined the Riviera immediately after World War II, an ideal place to be in an automobile. Significantly, Hitchcock actually shot the road scenes several kilometers from the coast, free of the constant traffic jams, noise, and air pollution that typified the Riviera after World War II.[1]

The Riviera by car was of course a twentieth-century development. Visitors, like the advertising designed to attract them, had long imagined the Riviera differently. Posters for the PLM train line featured modern trains against the beautiful backdrop of the Alps and the sea; would-be tourists could easily imagine the Riviera by train. Postcards frequently featured the promenade des Anglais in Nice and the Croisette in Cannes, inviting visitors to see themselves riding in a carriage or strolling along those famous promenades. Alternatively, postcards and hotel advertisements for grand hotels invited potential tourists to stay on the Riviera, from the grand Hôtel Carlton (another setting for *To Catch a Thief*) to Frank Jay Gould's art deco Palais de la Méditerranée. Villas required a private invitation, and they seemed to embody how the Riviera might be imagined as modernist, orientalist, and often garish, always with views of the sea.[2]

In the twentieth century the automobile found its place in the mythical Riviera, as it did in *To Catch a Thief*. From the turn of the twentieth century onward, wealthy tourists used automobiles to enjoy driving on winding, vertiginous roads with incredible views. Panoramas accessible by car rivaled those by train.[3] Cars quickly took the wealthy out to villas, away from the other visitors to the Riviera. The tourist infrastructure adapted accordingly. Already in the interwar years, officials in Alpes-Maritimes completed the *moyenne corniche* to ready it for tourism. After World War II, as automobile ownership and automobile tourism exploded in France, the roads of the Riviera became an important draw. No object better represented the economic growth and individualistic consumerism in the Thirty Glorious Years than the automobile.[4] It became a permanent feature of both the imagined Riviera and the real one, remade to accommodate it. Like the airport, roads were not finished public works so much as ongoing projects requiring constant maintenance, expansion, and transformation.

Corniches and Automobile Tourism in the Early Twentieth Century

Corniche, which means "ledge" or "cliff," also refers to a cliff road, literally perched on a ledge, with a mountain on one side and a drop-off on the other. In the early twentieth century, corniches and their spectacular views became the rage among automobile tourists. A train line must avoid steep grades, and the line along the coast of the Riviera stays close to the sea. When the mountains fall directly into the sea, the rail line goes inland or through a tunnel until rejoining the narrow plain next to the sea. By its nature, a train simply could not climb to roadside viewpoints accessible by car. The automobile opened up vistas.

Tourist aesthetics drove road development on the Riviera. The Touring club de France (TCF) launched automobilists' fascination with corniches. An association promoting tourism, the TCF raised money to finance road building in areas its members deemed worthy of touring.[5] In 1903 the organization inaugurated the *corniche d'or* (the golden cliff road), which ran along the coast from Saint-Raphaël to Cannes. For part of the forty-kilometer trajectory, on one side of the road is the sea, on the other the Estérel mountain range, famous for its reddish, rusty hue resulting from iron deposits in the rock. The *corniche d'or*, also known as the *corniche de l'Estérel*, quickly became a popular icon among wealthy tourists with cars, and an example of how the Riviera might draw and retain well-heeled visitors.[6]

In the interwar years, French officials followed suit in accentuating beauty in road development. The *corniche d'or* was a model for a new thirty-kilometer through road running east of Nice to Menton near the Italian border. Between Nice and Menton ran two roads in the early twentieth century. One, known today as the *grande corniche*, goes inland. Constructed by Napoleon, far enough inland to avoid naval bombardment in the early nineteenth century, it partly retraces the Roman Via Julia Augusta through la Turbie. It has some beautiful views but for long stretches is too far inland for drivers to see the Mediterranean at all. A second road ran along the coastline. It too was popular with car owners. In the fetishization of anything that might be called a corniche, it is today called the *corniche inférieure*, *basse corniche*, or *corniche du littoral*. However, the most spectacular vistas of the sea are from areas between these two roads. So the prefecture charged the Corps des Ponts et Chaussées with connecting the roads between the other two roads into a *moyenne corniche*, opened in 1928. The *moyenne corniche* is replete with incredible views. There were thus three options for a driver headed to Menton from Nice: one could choose the *grande corniche*, *moyenne corniche*, or *corniche inférieure*. In the interwar years, when long-distance freight went by rail, as did most business travel, these were roads for tourists. Gorgeous panoramas were the point, and the routes quickly found their way into tourist guidebooks. By the 1950s they were clogged, with particularly acute jams on the *moyenne corniche*. The supposedly open roads of *To Catch a Thief* did not exist on the corniches, especially in the summer months.

Postwar Automobilism

The reality of postwar driving was a far cry from the imagined landscape of the movies. As automobile ownership among the French and other Europeans exploded after World War II, they took to roads and streets not designed for cars. In cities, French drivers sat in traffic. When they went on vacation, they sat in traffic. On the Riviera, the most frequent destination for French tourists besides Paris, they arrived in an area that already had high rates of automobile ownership. Without counting second homeowners and tourists, or allowing for the fact that most cars were on the coast and not spread throughout the department evenly, Alpes-Maritimes in 1962 already had the second highest rate of automobile ownership of French departments. It tied the department of the Rhône (Lyon), at one car for seven inhabitants, immediately behind the Seine (Paris), at one car for five inhabitants. Once summer visitors arrived in the months of July and August, Nice had the densest concentration of automobiles in France (in essence surpassing Paris because many Parisians were in Nice). The number of cars coming into Nice from the west, measured at the bridge over the Var River, doubled between 1953 and 1956. In 1951, 60 percent of tourists to the Alpes-Maritimes and the Var came by train, falling to 46 percent by 1957; those coming in private cars (not including buses) climbed from 24 percent in 1951 to 41 percent in 1957. By the 1960s, the majority came by private automobile.[7]

Cars were an important cultural preoccupation in postwar France.[8] The Riviera, like urban France generally, was already a densely built area when the automobile came onto the scene. Theoretical objects of individual mobility, automobiles actually required huge investment to remake cities to accommodate them. The same would be true of the roads leading to cities, from the famous Route Nationale (RN) 7 to the local corniches. As in France generally, local officials worked to keep up with the growth of automobiles, but then that growth further outpaced the new infrastructure. In the early 1950s French central planners assumed that vehicular ownership would double every decade; in Alpes-Maritimes it doubled every five years. The stakes seemed high. Government economic plans in the 1950s saw tourism as critical in maintaining France's international balance of payments, to the tune of 140 billion francs in the mid-1950s. Since fully 56 percent of tourists in France hit the road each year, any growth in tourism seemed to depend on upgrading the infrastructure for automobiles. As France was losing its empire and many French worried about American hegemony, even the maintenance of French "civilization" could appear to be at issue. In 1957 Jean Filippi, president of the Association technique de la route, stated, "No observer in the world would contest that the road has not become an important element of national infrastructure in the countries with a high degree of civilization."[9]

The Promenade des Anglais and the Croisette

As tourists arrived in droves, both Nice and Cannes undertook extensions and major renovations of their historic seaside thoroughfares in order to provide aesthetically pleasing entries for automobile tourists. Postwar changes were not the first updates. In Nice the promenade des Anglais, initially called the camin dei Angles, began at the Paillon as a dirt walkway in 1824. In 1844 the original promenade grew from two to eight meters wide and lengthened westward to Magnan, two kilometers from the Paillon. After 1864 it was twelve meters wide and had gas lighting. In 1882 it stretched to Carras (four kilometers from the Paillon) and in 1903 to the horse-racing track alongside the Var, where the airport now sits (seven kilometers from the Paillon). In 1930, in the area close to the Paillon, the promenade became a divided street, the sidewalk widened and electric lighting installed. This last change both accommodated automobiles and enhanced the aesthetic appeal of the promenade for tourists arriving in Nice by car. During World War II, after attempting to rename the promenade to eliminate the reminder of the English, Germans prohibited people from being on it (walls were built at the end of streets perpendicular to the promenade and those living in adjacent buildings evacuated). Then the Germans installed barbed wire, artillery, blockhouses, and anti-tank spikes expecting that Allied troops might land there.[10]

Between 1949 and 1951, between the boulevard Gambetta and rue Rosa Bonheur, near the center of the city, the postwar Médecin administration installed a small central garden with Mediterranean plants and palm trees in the median. As viewed by *L'Espoir*, "this construction has brought a cachet of grand luxury," enough so that it would eventually be replicated along the length of the promenade. In 1951 work began on the widening of the promenade from the Hôpital Lanval westward to Ferber. Not only was this a step toward the construction of a uniform look for the promenade, since both ends could match, but the development created a "triumphant arrival on the baie des Anges" near the airport, where motorists entered the promenade from RN 7. Because much of the new paving immediately after the war required manual labor, with shovels and picks, *Le Patriote* pointed out that some worked very hard so that others could "taste the pleasures of vacation."[11]

The stretch between Rosa Bonheur and Lanval presented a serious challenge. The Magnan stream flowed into the sea in that area, and waves during storms tended to hit the section hard. The area required constant fill to protect even the narrow promenade in that sector.[12] In the winter months, a dump accepting supposedly clean fill helped keep the beach from washing away. On the eve of Carnival in January 1960, *Nice Matin* worried about what tourists would see if they stopped to take in the view: "For about one hundred meters, across the street from no. 287 of the promenade, there sit tires, containers, washtubs, barrels, scrap iron, carcasses of crates and of sheds, etc." It took until 1965 for the promenade to take on the appearance it maintains today, uniformly wide and beautiful from the airport to the center of the city.[13]

Widening of the promenade both before and after World War II was environmentally and financially costly. The promenade was not only built over what had been the beach; the wall protecting it also interrupted the natural cycle, so that even if fill were dumped to build up the beach, storm surges eroded the beach while damaging the wall. *Le Patriote* complained of the mounting costs of widening the promenade and maintaining both it and the adjacent beach when the city had a much more urgent need for housing.[14] In November 1951 storms brought in waves that breached and damaged the wall along the promenade. *Le Patriote* argued that "the widening of the promenade caused the death of the beach" and efforts to maintain both cause "incessant construction that is expensive, very expensive."[15]

The widening, which encouraged more automobile traffic, also reduced the extent to which the promenade was a pleasant promenade. Before stoplights (Nice had only two in the whole city in 1950), it was difficult for pedestrians to cross. So much money was spent on the roadway, as cars got priority, that the city could not afford to pave the entirety of the promenade for pedestrians along the sea, as late as 1958. In 1962 Pierre Mathis, the city's director of construction projects, noted that the promenade was no longer what it had been, instead becoming "an autoroute busier than those around Paris."[16] In 1968, as the number of automobiles increased (74,000 per day in the summer months), the promenade was surpassed in traffic only by roads connected to the Autoroute de l'Ouest and the Autoroute du Sud, which ran west and south out of Paris. With three eastbound lanes and two westbound in 1965, the promenade seemed to contemporaries more like an autoroute than a city street, as not even new timed stoplights managed to slow the traffic down.[17] In 1973 *Nice Matin* reported that drivers sometimes drove on the sidewalks in order to "avoid the traffic jams in the lanes." And the "'promenade' des Anglais is dangerously close to losing its original purpose which gives Nice, in large part, its worldwide reputation. It is time to realize this fact, as the tourist season begins, because if we are not on guard, a disastrous counter propaganda [against Nice] could feed off of this regrettable anarchy on the promenade."[18]

Whatever the challenges in Nice, the renovation of the promenade des Anglais nevertheless served as a model for that of the Croisette in Cannes. In Cannes the original road dated from 1856, when local property owners paid much of the cost to build a five-meter-wide road. The Croisette expanded in the late nineteenth and early twentieth centuries as grand hotels appeared on much of its length. As automobile traffic increased, the Croisette became one-way, yet there were still constant traffic jams after the war. In the early 1960s Mayor Bernard Cornut-Gentille oversaw the remaking of the Croisette.

Expanding it out toward the sea after building up the beach, Cannes created a promenade some ten meters wide alongside the road opened to two-way traffic, separated by a five-meter divider with palm trees and flowers. With the completion of the project in 1963, 215 palm trees framed the Croisette. It seemed an ideal setting for the international film festival held each year at the Palais des Festivals et des Congrès. Local communists noted that Cannes prioritized views for tourists over improved hygiene, as the city undertook renovation of the Croisette before improving much of the sewage system while local children fell victim to polio.[19]

Cannes grew after World War II, from approximately 45,500 inhabitants in 1946 to about 75,500 in 1975, and the fleet of automobiles expanded more quickly. Traffic in Cannes increased by 50 percent just between 1955 and 1960. After Monaco placed its rail station underground in order to relieve congestion, Cannes did the same. There was far too little parking; as part of the rebuilding of the Croisette, Cannes put up a 12,000 m^2 underground parking garage in 1965. It lay just north of the new Canto port at the eastern end of the Croisette and hid up to four thousand cars. It doubled as boat storage in winter. Built on pilings driven down into former marshland, the garage had a garden placed on top, to match the one at the Casino Municipal (now the site of the Palais des Festivals) on the western end. Symmetry mattered for the aesthetic appeal of the Croisette. Moreover, placing the parking lot underground preserved the Croisette's beauty. In the words of reporter Gilles Paillet, "To open a parking garage on the Croisette, a step away from the palace hotels, is to run the risk of offering tourists a view of cars lined up, surely practical, but inelegant."[20] However, more cars arrived in Cannes. By the late 1970s the streets near the Croisette were constantly jammed in summer, and despite many other parking lots, the city planned yet another subterranean one near the new Palais des Festivals.[21]

In Nice and Cannes it was important to have a triumphal entry of palm trees and streetlights. In Nice just before World War II, once cars crossed the bridge over the Var, they went straight onto the promenade. After the original bridge was destroyed by American bombers in the war, engineers situated a new bridge to order to accommodate the placement of the airport so that Nice would again have a grand entry. From there, cars passed under a gorgeous canopy for seven kilometers. By day, evenly spaced palm trees formed the canopy. Like so many of the subtropical plants and trees on the Riviera, the palms are not native. Count Vigier introduced the seeds of the *Phoenix tenuis* from the Canary Islands to his garden on the boulevard Frank-Pilatte in 1862. Their towering appearance lent a certain grandeur to the promenade, as they did the Croisette. By night, evenly spaced, uniform electric streetlights formed comparable triumphal canopies over both the promenade and the Croisette.[22]

Noise and Air Pollution

Automotive traffic brought noise and foul air. Of course, transport noises were not new. Trains were noisy until the electrification of rail lines.[23] Trams had made noise. In western Nice airplane noise competed with that from cars, motorcycles, trucks, and buses. However, in a region long known as a place of calm and respite, the transformation of neighborhoods once far from sources of noise seemed shocking. In Nice, whether uphill in Cimiez, where Queen Victoria had stayed with her retinue, or the posh villas near the coast, there was a certain tranquility that disappeared as motorized traffic became prevalent. Complaints from the (often literally) entitled ensued. In 1951 a "countess," precisely the kind of wealthy, elite visitor that once had been the norm, complained that she had three years prior purchased an apartment situated on the promenade des Anglais and was beginning to regret her acquisition "because the noise of traffic has become completely unbearable." When friends came to stay, they "repeatedly ask how we could put up with such a racket." Motorcycles made quite a din. "But the buses too make an infernal noise. As for the horns, I don't understand how they can be tolerated. I just returned from a stay in Stockholm, I go constantly to Brussels, and I can attest that in these large capitals, as well as in other Swedish and Belgian cities, such usage of horns is entirely forbidden." Jacques de Berny, a reporter for *L'Espoir*, agreed that drivers in Nice loved their horns, pointing out how much quieter Switzerland was because of the "discipline" of drivers who did not constantly honk their horns.[24]

In 1952 residents and hotel owners along the promenade addressed a petition to Mayor Jean Médecin. They claimed that it was impossible for anyone, from individual proprietor to hotel guest, to get any sleep at night along the promenade. Hotel owners said that their guests, "after spending one night, with the windows and *volets* closed, and sometimes with their heads buried under a pillow, pay the bill and go elsewhere, some also nicely adding, 'I have friends who need to come to the coast in order *to rest (!)*, but I will not recommend Nice, and certainly not the promenade.' *Certain (French and foreign newspapers) that have more or less the habit of speaking ill of Nice will have, justifiably in this case, cause to do so*" (emphasis in original).[25] Hotel owners demanded action, including the banning of motorcycles entirely from the promenade in the off hours. Their complaints drew attention to a problem throughout the city. The city of Nice took the issue seriously, issuing some

1,200 citations for noise violations in the first six months of 1952. But the problem persisted. In August 1952 a Belgian tourist complained, "I've been in Nice for two months. My apartment is on the boulevard Gambetta. I thought I was going to stay until September, but alas, I am returning to Belgium completely crazy with my nerves on end. It is impossible to rest. In the morning, starting at 5:00, the motorcycles start passing by." He blamed a "lack of discipline of the French."[26]

There seemed a serious risk of alienating tourists, retirees, and other residential tourists who could easily decide to pick up and go elsewhere. In the 1950s *Nice Matin* regularly published their letters in an effort to push authorities into action, saving the reputation of the city. In 1954 one reader wrote, "Having come and gotten settled in Nice barely three months ago, I am already thinking of abandoning this residence to set up 'my pleasant retirement' elsewhere, precisely due to the street noise, which makes any kind of rest illusory, day or night. You have to live in your own century and accept its inconveniences, certainly, but I have traveled a lot and visited large cities that, in terms of progress, are in no way put to shame by Nice. I have compared; nowhere have I been, as in Nice, as inconvenienced by such a racket."[27] Even Parisians agreed. Years later, in 1976, *Nice Matin* opened its pages to a tourist who complained that noise and air pollution were worse than back home in Paris: "After my 'vacation' I am certainly leaving tanned but also exhausted by the noise and gassed lungs. As paradoxical as it might appear, it is with pleasure that I return to calm in greater Paris. Incredible but true!"[28]

Both archival files and newspaper articles contain comparatively few complaints about air quality on the Riviera until the 1970s.[29] Trucks and buses got much of the blame, presumably due to inadequate regulation of diesel fuel injectors in France. As reported by Paul Thierry in the pages of *Nice Matin*, "It is regrettable to attest that foreign tourist buses, which are on the promenade des Anglais, do not emit these [diesel] clouds. Only French buses using diesel gratify us and with much abundance!"[30] Interestingly, though the term "asphyxiation" got wide use in the 1950s and 1960s, it referred less often to human beings suffocated by foul air than to the idea that economic prosperity was suffering from too few roads and too little parking. Journalist Claude Mercadié claimed in 1960 that while establishment of one-way streets had helped, Nice was already "asphyxiated" by too much traffic on too few streets.[31] Rapid population growth and increased automobile ownership in the early 1960s seemed to require new streets, wider existing streets, and more parking lots. In 1962 *Nice Matin* argued that the city was "asphyxiated" not by the automobile, its fumes, or its noise so much as the inability of city officials to adapt the city to the automobile quickly enough. In 1965, in the face of heavy traffic in Nice, *Le Provençal* asserted that Nice needed urban highways like those that were dissecting American cities at the time, lest Nice be "asphyxiated."[32] The head of the public transportation agency, the Compagnie des transports en commun à Nice, thought that slow traffic "asphyxiated" Nice. In 1974 he noted that once "tramways pulled by horses averaged 9 km/h. Buses now average about 11 km/h. Since the beginning of the [twentieth] century, we have gained only 2 km/h, while we need today, on average, a speed of 20–25 km/h." The only way to achieve that was to establish a "separate network," that is, special bus lanes, a process that began in 1974. *Nice Matin* endorsed the plan, arguing that earlier efforts to solve the "asphyxiation, with expedient measures," had been mere pyrrhic victories.[33]

Disciplining Drivers and Pedestrians

Nice, like cities across France, worked to accommodate drivers, and particularly tourists arriving by car. One-way streets appeared throughout the city. Parking lots proliferated. The city cut down plane trees in residential neighborhoods in order to make more room for parking on sidewalks. The very automobile tourists who were causing the necessary accommodation were impatient that the city did not do more, better, and faster. Visitors and those worried about losing the tourist trade fretted about jaywalking, inadequate parking, having to pay for parking, double-parking, lack of directional signs, speeding, and traffic jams. There was a widespread notion among both tourists and locals that the problem was "indiscipline," and Nice made repeated efforts during the Thirty Glorious Years to "discipline" both drivers and pedestrians.

Tourists especially complained about the "indiscipline" of drivers in Nice. In 1972 André Bergé, from Montélimar, noted that crazy driving began with one's arrival on the promenade des Anglais, where "speeding, lane changing, jack rabbit starting, and the cutting off of other cars sets the tone." Then, "within the city, invectives and nasty remarks gush out of the mouth of drivers, who otherwise look quite respectable, the second they have to wait for a tourist desperately seeking a parking space or who has the misfortune to stop while waiting for one opening up." Bergé suggested that drivers from Nice go watch their Italian counterparts in order to "observe the difference in behavior." *L'Espoir* similarly blamed the "imprudence, indiscipline, and insouciance" of French drivers for the accidents in Nice—and in France generally.[34]

There were complaints that speed caused accidents. While the accidents along RN 7 were legendary, accidents occurred throughout Alpes-Maritimes in disproportionate numbers. Alpes-Maritimes was consistently near the top of departments in terms of the number of automobile accidents; in 1961 it was behind only Seine and Seine-et-Oise in greater Paris and the department of the Nord. In Nice there were frequent complaints about speed and the subsequent accidents. Already in 1952 *Nice Matin* compared the promenade to a racetrack; the posted speed limit was 40 kilometers per hour, but no one followed it. Particularly given the volume of traffic, accidents were frequent on the promenade. In 1964 *Le Patriote* declared it a "veritable hecatomb" all the way from the boulevard Gambetta to the airport. One cause was the many drivers from elsewhere who were unfamiliar with city streets, and the city was not eager to annoy visitors. *L'Espoir* reported that police were directed "not to punish tourists [with traffic violations] with the same rigor as Niçois." Reminding its readers of the empire France was in the process of losing, *Le Patriote* criticized the policy, implying that well-off tourists were colonizers, as opposed to local *indigènes* (natives) who got moving violations.[35]

Indiscipline supposedly characterized pedestrians who jaywalked, particularly in the eyes of northern European visitors.[36] Only a sometime offense in twentieth-century France, jaywalking could not really exist before the automobile dominated streets to the exclusion of horse-drawn conveyances, tramways, and pedestrians. Nice, like other cities, worked to control pedestrians' movements. Pedestrian crossings (designated by raised metal caps in the road that resembled the tops of huge nails, hence the French term *passages cloutés*) increased in number after the war. In the 1950s Nice began to install signals for lights at pedestrian crossings. As the city did so, both drivers and pedestrians received specific instructions about how they functioned—instructions that remind us how technologies now taken for granted were once new and unfamiliar. "These signals, at the disposal of pedestrians, are activated by a button left at the disposal of users wanting passage. This type of light exists in Paris on the quais of the Seine, between the place de la Concorde and the pont d'Austerlitz. In pressing the button, the pedestrians make a red light appear, which stops traffic for a short period of time. Lest drivers be horrified, know that the pedestrians won't be able to stop traffic permanently. The button will remain without effect for three to five minutes after each usage."[37] Not surprisingly, given how long pedestrians were to wait, few did, and jaywalking was rampant. In May 1963, for the first time, Nice began issuing tickets for jaywalking.[38] *Le Provençal* believed that "the pedestrian is becoming more disciplined and the driver, in turn, pays more attention to the pedestrian, notably in stopping at pedestrian crossings." The battle soon seemed useless; as late as November (the rainy season, not the high tourist season) 1965, police cited almost one hundred people for jaywalking in a single day.[39]

Parking was a constant problem. As parked cars made it difficult to walk on many sidewalks, tourists noticed and complained. Belgian newspapers even asserted that it was the reason that increasing numbers of tourists were going to Italy instead of staying on the Riviera.[40] On the one hand, there were simply not enough spaces, despite new parking lots, including a huge one built on the platform covering the Paillon (today the site of a park, next to the tramway). On the other, drivers had not been accustomed to paying for parking. *Le Patriote* claimed that the "French don't like to pay for parking," which is why the big new parking lots in Toulouse were always three-quarters empty in 1963. In the meantime, small streets were nearly impassible even with cars on sidewalks. "Narrow streets have really become garages."[41]

FIG. 6.1. On the quai des États-Unis in Nice on 10 August 1965, parked cars limited traffic flow despite motorists' efforts to park on the sidewalk. Traffic jams were frequent in the summer months. Archives départementales des Alpes-Maritimes 22 Fi 65081015 (image, Centre d'études techniques de l'équipement).

FIG. 6.2. Beachgoers' makeshift parking along the coastal road at Golfe-Juan, 1956. Like the railway line alongside it, the road constitutes a barrier between the town and the sea. Archives départementales des Alpes-Maritimes 598 W 16 (image, Centre d'études techniques de l'équipement).

Tourists also complained that Nice lacked directional, one-way street, and parking signs. A Belgian tourist who arrived in Nice for the first time told *L'Espoir* in 1951, "I crossed all of France without a problem. Everywhere I found adequate signage. In Lyon, for example, where crossing the city is difficult and complicated, I did not have to ask anyone to find my way. In Nice, I got lost after asking my way three or four times." *L'Espoir* claimed that it was a frequent criticism on the part of visitors by car.[42] When most people traveled by train, signs had been unnecessary. Only in the early twentieth century had the Touring club de France and the Michelin tire company begun to set road signs, an effort taken over by the French state. However, mayors had the responsibility for road signs in their municipalities. At least some tourists thought the city a laggard.

Before extensive signage, drivers stopped to ask for directions, often bringing traffic to a halt by asking traffic cops. Traffic cops stood in intersections and directed traffic with whistles and hand motions. After 1956 they stood on small raised platforms called *fromages* (because they resembled large rounds of cheese). It is today hard to imagine the mayhem as traffic cops gave directions to tourists (many of whom did not speak French) and directed traffic, motorists honked, and pedestrians darted through traffic. The problem was aggravated by the huge influx of cars each summer. In the late 1950s the number of cars quadrupled between June and September, when many traffic cops, like other French, took their annual vacation. Meanwhile, the number of traffic cops fell in Nice from 850 before the war to 670 in 1958. In the 1960s a shortage of municipal police combined with the influx of tourists caused the national government to deploy one hundred French national police officers (CRS, or Compagnies républicaines de sécurité) in the summer and during the usually busy holiday weekends of Easter and Pentecost.[43] By all accounts, traffic and parking remained horrendous. In 1978 a Parisian tourist claimed that returning to Nice from the *moyenne corniche* was worse than driving on the avenue de la Grande Armée in the direction of the Arc de Triomphe in evening rush hour. A fellow Parisian claimed that "large city for large city, I prefer Paris; it is easier to park."[44]

Doing Away with Dumps

As tourists increasingly arrived by car, efforts to promote the Riviera as a beautiful space for vacation came to include attention to everything tourists saw from their cars. Whereas tourists by train had access only to those areas near a train station, by car they could see the countryside and the coastline throughout the area. With the predominance of automobile travel, itself a generator of waste, came a desire to hide waste. Junked cars inside and outside junkyards became a preoccupation, as did both authorized dumps and unauthorized roadside dumping.[45] Traditionally, much trash had always ended up in the dry riverbeds of the Paillon and the Var, but now it became particularly unsightly and worthy of removal. Now junkyards needed greenery, screening them from roads. Dumps, long accepted along the beachfront, became problematic. In the words of the prefect, "it is necessary to aid towns to put into place means of waste treatment that do not cause either aesthetic pollution or water pollution."[46]

Sensitivity to the sight of refuse, not presence of waste itself, was the new development. The seaside had once been liminal space. Coastal dwellers had long accepted wrecked ships, rotten organic material, and their own trash near the sea. Completion of the road along the seaside, and then the explosive growth of tourists taking it, exposed waste at the same time that postwar consumer society was generating more than ever. In the 1950s it became obvious just how much trash was ending up near and in the sea.[47]

To be sure, the new concern was less with the environment per se than with the aesthetics for tourists. As reporter Paul Thierry put it, "Situated near built-up areas, along roads in general, these mountains of nauseating and sometimes fuming waste swarming with rats disfigure a site that should be kept impeccably clean. It is always upsetting and unpleasantly surprising to discover piles of filth in the middle of sunny nature, sometimes in the most charming of places. We have already said it and we will repeat it endlessly: such stains are unworthy of the Côte d'Azur, which is supposed to be the paradise of tourism."[48]

There was limited space away from the coast for the detritus of consumerism. Historically, the ritzy communities just to the east of Nice, Villefranche-sur-Mer, Saint-Jean-Cap-Ferrat, and Beaulieu-sur-Mer, dumped their household waste into the sea. Since the current brought that trash to the beach at Nice, in the early 1950s Nice had come to an agreement with all three that their waste would go to Nice's incinerator at Ariane. Farther to the east, Monaco accepted waste from Èze-sur-Mer, Cap d'Ail, and Beausoleil as well as some of the trash from Menton, while Èze-Village, la Turbie, and Roquebrune-Cap-Martin piled it up. To the west of Nice, where the coastal road was under construction, only Cannes had a processing facility, fermenting garbage in silos. Cagnes-sur-Mer, Biot, Vallauris, Golfe-Juan, le Cannet, and Mandelieu, la Napoule piled it up, while Saint-Laurent-du-Var and Villeneuve-Loubet burned trash in the open air. One coastal town in Alpes-Maritimes, Théoule-sur-Mer, continued to dump all household garbage directly into the Mediterranean. Only Antibes and Juan-les-Pins had an actual landfill, where employees periodically covered the waste with dirt.[49]

In the mid-1950s, under pressure from the *conseil général* of the department, the departmental division of Ponts et Chaussées studied the options, and the prefecture chose landfills as the solution. Although *Nice Matin* dubbed the "provisional" solution "better than nothing," at least landfills would avoid direct dumps of waste into the sea and piles of waste near the sea. New rules stipulated that liquids from landfills could not leech into the groundwater, that the waste be covered with a layer of dirt every seventy-two hours, and that greenery hide the sites as necessary.[50] Tourists and locals continued to generate more waste, but that waste was now buried, hidden from tourists. Beachfronts themselves needed to look clean. As the prefect reminded mayors of all coastal communities in 1969, they were responsible for keeping their beaches clean, emptying garbage cans placed on the beach and cleaning the beach daily.[51]

Camping

The automobile did much to make camping possible, as visitors could haul their equipment and locate campsites far from train stations. Pitching tents along the beach, many campers did *camping sauvage* (primitive camping), a term that can connote "returning" to nature but was also weighted with notions of European empires and Western civilization. By 1951 campgrounds, both authorized and illegal, appeared near the beach from Menton to Saint-Raphaël. In 1951 there were already 4,300 campers in forty-seven campgrounds in Alpes-Maritimes.[52] In 1954, in la Napoule alone, there were twenty thousand campers, of whom 80 percent arrived by car. There campgrounds had water, electricity, WCs, and outdoor sinks for laundry and dishes. In 1956, in the whole of Alpes-Maritimes, there were 130 campgrounds (all but ten in communities along the coast) with an official capacity of thirteen thousand campers, a number that expanded to fifty thousand actual campers in July and August. There was even a Tourisme et Travail (Tourism and Work) campground at Golfe-Juan specifically for working-class tourists (Tourisme et Travail was an association close to the Communist Party that organized worker vacations).[53]

The rapid expansion of both authorized and illegal camping alarmed authorities and newspapers concerned about the damage it could do to the prestige of the Riviera. After all, just as cars brought campers, they also brought tourists who expected the beachfront to be aesthetically pleasing. In the words of reporter Claude Mercadié, "Camping, it must be said, does not correspond to the needs, the possibilities, or the aesthetics" of the Riviera.[54] In 1960 the prefecture of Alpes-Maritimes severely regulated camping in the entire department. The department was divided into zones. West of the Var River, between the railway line and the sea, and east of the Var River between the *corniche inférieure* and the sea, camping was strictly forbidden; that took care of much of the presumably unsightly *camping sauvage*. In a second zone, west of the Var River, between the autoroute and the rail line, and east of the Var between the *corniche inférieure* and the *grande corniche*, camping could only be authorized if "of quality, notably as concerns aesthetics and hygiene." In a third zone, that is, the interior of the rest of the department, camping could be widely authorized. The move forbade most camping near the sea in Alpes-Maritimes, closing down many campsites frequented by workers, notably the Tourisme et Travail site at Golfe-Juan. *Le Patriote* argued that unless part of a Tourisme et Travail establishment, camping may have seemed more affordable but was still middle and lower middle class, not working class; camping usually required a car and camping equipment, still beyond the means of many workers in the 1950s.[55]

By contrast, the department of the Var did not have a prestigious reputation to maintain, so rules were less strict there. As more working people
took vacations, tourists sought more affordable accommodations. In 1957
the prefect of the Var laid out the economics of camping, noting that three
weeks in a hotel would cost a family of four about 100,000 francs, far beyond
the reach of most French families. Camping cost a fraction of that, even in
well-appointed campgrounds with running water, WCs, and electricity. The
Var, which had not historically seen nearly the number of tourists that Alpes-
Maritimes did, encouraged the development of campgrounds. Growth was
marked. To give but one example, Hyères-les-Palmiers alone had 205,800
camping nights (each person spending one night camping constituted a
camping night) in 1955 but 455,800 in 1957. The Var quickly became the
French department with the most campsites.[56]

Whatever camping's successes in the Var, the notion of camping as ugly,
lower-class, and damaging to the reputation of the Riviera persisted. In the
words of René Bardy, the permanent representative of the French Commissariat général du tourisme in New York, *"we are partisans of a policy
of selectivity as regards the Côte d'Azur. It is absolutely essential to eliminate that
part of camping that dishonors the Côte d'Azur"* (emphasis in the original). He
added that the Riviera was not made for the workers of Sarcelles, a reference
to the community best known for HLM high-rises. Instead, Bardy argued
that the focus in Alpes-Maritimes and the Var should be on well-off foreigners who already had a notion of the prestige of the Riviera: "We need to turn
to those who want to see, once in their lives, the ex-paradise of millionaires."
The vast state-sponsored development of Languedoc-Roussillon, considered
decidedly low-brow by tourism officials, was under way. It seemed to Bardy
and others a more suitable place for camping.[57] Bardy was not alone in seeing camping as decidedly déclassé. As late as the 1980s, after large bidonvilles
had been cleared from Alpes-Maritimes as from France generally, Jacques
Bruyas compared campgrounds to them. "Camping . . . remains too often a
synonym for bidonville."[58]

Route Nationale 7 and the "Route de l'Intérieur"

In 1959 popular French singer Charles Trenet recorded "Route Nationale 7"
about the mythic *route des vacances* taken by so many seeking the sun. RN 7
ran southbound from Paris, through Burgundy, down the Rhône River valley, eastward to Fréjus, on the west side of the highest of the Estérel mountains, then near the coast from west of Cannes, through Cannes, and to Nice.
Although sections of the roadway had existed since the Romans, Napoleon
oversaw the building of the continuous Route Impériale between 1805 and

1812.[59] Republican France later renamed the road and all major "national roads." Originally designed for marching troops and moving materiel, in postwar France RN 7 carried both trucks and tourists to southern France. As it wended its way through small towns and cities, the road's traffic jams also became infamous, particularly during the summer months.[60] In 1955 RN 7 handled more traffic than any other road in France besides the first limited-access highway built in the interwar years to the west of Paris. It was also dangerous, particularly in the departments of Bouches-du-Rhône and Alpes-Maritimes.[61] In the postwar years, RN 7 had the nickname "the road of death."

RN 7 was *the* road artery connecting Cannes and Nice to northern France. When the *corniche d'or* opened, it provided an additional route from Fréjus and Saint-Raphaël to Cannes. Officially RN 98, the *corniche d'or* was even more sinuous than RN 7; in both cases, the terrain dictated speeds of 20 to 40 kilometers per hour in several spots.[62] Average speeds on both roads were even slower in town, particularly in the summer. RN 98 ended in Cannes, and that traffic also took RN 7 to Nice, adding to congestion in Cannes, Antibes, and other communities en route to Nice. The worst bottleneck was between Cannes and Nice. On that stretch of RN 7, there were already seven to nine thousand vehicles daily in 1950. The number then grew 14 percent per year between 1950 and 1954, double the growth of 7 percent per year, the median planned for France as a whole. The section between Cannes and Nice was a problem because through traffic, local traffic, and tourist traffic all took the same road, whereas to the east of Nice, traffic was split among the *grande corniche*, the *moyenne corniche*, and the *corniche inférieure*.[63]

Summertime congestion on RN 7 became the stuff of legend in the 1950s. On the western side of the Estérel, the road had steep grades. Heavy trucks in that era were not powerful enough to maintain speed; in some areas they traveled only 15 kilometers per hour for up to ten kilometers on the two-lane road. In 1960 it could easily take six hours to travel the seventy kilometers from Fréjus and Saint-Raphaël to Nice. Between Cannes and Nice, just twenty-five kilometers, the trip regularly took two hours.[64] In 1956 writer and filmmaker Jean Cocteau spent two and a half hours to go forty kilometers from Vallauris to Cap Ferrat. On 15 August 1960, on the feast of the Assumption, during the absolute peak of the tourist season, a traffic jam between Cannes and Juan-les-Pins was five kilometers long. It took hours for two hundred CRS officers to clear. There developed widespread concern that well-off tourists would avoid a tourist destination so difficult to get to, particularly in the 1950s when the average stay of tourists was only a couple of days.[65]

Already well aware of the problem, engineers of Ponts et Chaussées had begun planning an "interior road" in 1953, built farther inland than RN 7 with less steep grades. They did not initially envision an autoroute, of which France had only one (the Autoroute de l'Ouest) at the time, constructed to the west of Paris before World War II. Even the engineers' project name, route de l'intérieur, as opposed to its eventual name, autoroute, is a reminder that engineers did not initially see their project as part of a whole, dense network of toll roads in postwar France. Instead, the objective was to remove heavy trucks from RN 7, where they held up traffic. According to engineers, the new road would reduce accidents by 75 percent.[66] They assumed that tourists would remain concentrated on the existing roads, particularly RN 7 and the corniche d'or.[67]

An Autoroute to the Riviera

In 1955 the French National Assembly approved construction of what was now billed as the first postwar French autoroute, from Puget-sur-Argens, just inland from Fréjus and Saint-Raphaël, to the outskirts of Nice. The original completion date was 1960, just in time to mark the centenary of France's acquisition of Nice and Savoy. The new limited-access highway was to have two lanes in each direction, separated by a median, with enough room on either side to add an additional lane. As was the case in many postwar infrastructure projects, the contract for the actual building of the autoroute went to a société d'économie mixte. This newly formed public-private company went by the acronym ESCOTA, short for Société de l'autoroute Estérel-Côte d'Azur. ESCOTA received a concession to exploit the new road, that is, to charge tolls on it, for thirty-five years.[68]

By the time the autoroute opened in 1961, French planners considered it an early piece of a massive network of two thousand kilometers of autoroutes across France, a project designed to try to catch up with the Germans and the Italians, a preoccupation of advocates of tourism in postwar France. The German Federal Republic already had a well-developed and underused network of Autobahnen in 1945 while postwar Italian governments built on Mussolini's early autostrada—compared by Le Provençal with the art of "Michelangelo, Donatello, and Botticelli." In practical terms, the threat was that efficient German Autobahnen and beautiful Italian autostrada would deliver tourists to the sunny and cheaper Italian shoreline. Statistics were meant to alarm the French public, stoke nationalism, and build support for autoroutes; in 1961 West Germany had 2,700 kilometers of Autobahnen and Italy 1,100 kilometers of autostrada, while France had all of 170 kilometers of autoroutes—this after the opening of the new autoroute in the Var and Alpes-Maritimes.[69] France had long had the most developed, most dense network of roads in Europe, as well as more cars per capita than Germany and Italy; the problem was that long-distance travelers jammed key roads such as RN 7. Officials and promoters of tourism called for a network of autoroutes that would allow the Riviera to maintain "its essentially touristic renown."[70] Local and national officials worried that the increasing density of Autobahnen from northern Europe to autostrada through Italy would cause tourists to bypass southeastern France entirely. As Édouard Bonnefous, the minister of public works, put it, foreign tourist infrastructure could *deliver a deadly blow to French tourism. That's why we have to catch up as quickly as possible.* The autoroute Savona-Turin is being built. There is talk of a tunnel under Saint-Bernard. These projects will permit the linking of German and Italian autoroutes, which will redirect much of the traffic away from French territory, menacing our country with a 'scorched earth of tourism'" (emphasis in the original).[71] Contemporaries frequently pointed out that the new European Economic Community increased the likelihood of competition for European and international tourists among member states. It was an issue not only of northern European tourists seeking the sun but also of transatlantic ones visiting Europe. Their ships often arrived in "Anvers, Rotterdam, Amsterdam, [and] Hamburg, and the disparity of traffic conditions will turn away from French roads the ever increasing wave of tourists going from northern Europe to the Mediterranean."[72]

In order to foster passage by such tourists to, from, and through the Riviera, even before the completion of the autoroute from Puget-sur-Argens to Nice, planning began for an extension to the Italian border. Francis Palmero, longtime mayor of Menton and deputy to the National Assembly, began strong advocacy in the fall of 1960.[73] In the National Assembly, Palmero reminded deputies that tourism was an "industry," and "tourist traffic is essentially itinerant and optional. The most convenient route to sunshine and to the Mediterranean for the English and Northern Europeans passes through the valley of the Rhône and the Côte d'Azur." The Swiss and Italians were undertaking massive road construction that could connect to France through Basel or a tunnel under Mont Blanc, marginalizing southeastern France, notably that most visited of regions, the Riviera.[74]

Once more, the metaphor of suffocation served to justify a major building project, regardless of the effects of air quality for residents living near the new highway. *Nice Matin* argued that the Riviera was being "asphyxiated" by traffic jams. In *Constellation* Étienne Thil wrote, "From year to year the Mediterranean paradise of France is seriously threatened by asphyxia." When luminaries visited the "tourist sights" on the half-complete autoroute between Mandelieu and the Estérel at 140 kilometers per hour, Jean Médecin declared that the autoroute would allow the region to avoid "asphyxia." In the pages of *Ouest France*, reporter François Lemarié argued that without a system of autoroutes, France as a whole would suffer from a "slow asphyxia" while "international tourism will have a tendency to turn away from France."[75]

Given the acute traffic congestion on RN 7 and the limits of environmental conservationism in the late 1950s and early 1960s, it is perhaps no surprise that there was little opposition to the construction of a new autoroute—only to its path and its tolls. Affected residents and town leaders, alongside local communists (championing local causes, including those of property owners), protested vehemently against the trajectory during both the planning stages and the construction. As the engineers planned the autoroute, they decided to cut south of the towns Mougins and Biot, thus between the centers of the towns and the sea, a decision that would provide drivers with panoramas of the Mediterranean but cut these small towns in two. Locals wanted the autoroute to pass north of the towns on largely undeveloped wooded land. In the case of Mandelieu, the autoroute went right through the center of town. There residents had hoped for a tunnel. For many, the decision to make the drive more stunning for tourists would doom the development of tourism in their towns.[76] In Cannes a local association, the Groupement de défense des riverains de la route de l'intérieur, also protested the projected path of the autoroute on the hill overlooking Cannes. The group wanted the autoroute to pass behind the hill, where the French national electric company, the EDF, was running high-voltage electrical lines, in an area neither farmed nor developed.[77]

As the autoroute went to the very edge of Nice, eventually through the towns of Cagnes-sur-Mer and Saint-Laurent-du-Var, they were to be cut in two by the autoroute. Their departmental representative (*conseiller général*) Léon Bérenger protested that the autoroute—requiring at least a width of twenty-five meters, and running close to the road along the sea, the rail line, and RN 7—cut towns off from the sea, thus impeding their development as tourist resorts. At least twenty thousand inhabitants would feel the effects of such a "dam of asphalt and concrete."[78]

Despite a few slight changes in the planned trajectory of the autoroute, officials essentially stuck to the engineers' plans, ignoring local opposition. *Nice Midi* summarized what it called the "principal ravages."

In Mandelieu, the autoroute crosses through the locality over an embankment seven meters in height. In Cannes–la Bocca, the housing developments [earlier] authorized by the prefect and very beautiful properties are pillaged. In Mougins, the town is cut in two, with one part pushed toward the mountain and the other toward the sea. In le Cannet, there is a flattening and clearing of hills that overlook the locality and form the backdrop of Cannes. Moreover, the residential neighborhood of Bréguières is pillaged. For all of these localities, normal urban development has been halted by the creation of this modern railroad.[79]

Residents complained that now the autoroute was doing precisely what the railroad had: dividing towns in two and cutting the centers of towns off from the beach.[80] Of course, in the 1860s, when the PLM put down the track, few people went to the beach, and coastal towns were not developing toward it. The autoroute seemed different, as it was already clear to all that the economic futures of coastal communities depended on the appeal of their beachfronts.

Autoroute Aesthetics

In the twentieth century, like rockets, jets, and eventually high-speed trains, the automobile offered speed. On the new autoroute, unprecedented speed for long distances was certainly an appeal. In 1961 there was no speed limit between Fréjus and Mandelieu; contemporaries justified it by arguing that many drivers were already going up to 150 kilometers per hour on any open stretches of RN 7 east of Aix-en-Provence.[81] However, engineers did not always promote the autoroute with appeals to speed and functionalist efficiency. As in the case of airplanes and airports, cars and autoroutes were sold to the public as beautiful. It was not only in the United States, where creatively designed cars with tail fins mimicking jets hit the new interstates, that the link between airplanes and cars was explicit; in France a series of articles in *Ouest France* specifically situated the new autoroutes in the "aeronautic age."[82] For engineers, officials, and much of the press, there was no contradiction in their coupling of speed and aesthetic appreciation on the autoroute. From the overpasses to the bridges, the exits, and the panoramas, autoroutes offered both beautiful design and spectacular views engineered to please the aesthetic sensibilities of motorists.[83]

In France the language of travel on an autoroute is in itself evocative. On French autoroutes, as on the rail lines that preceded them, a viaduct, an overpass, a tunnel, and a bridge are all *ouvrages d'art* (works of art); both the most elaborate bridge and the humblest overpass are examples of how engineers produce a form of architecture worthy of being called art. When the autoroute opened in 1961, *Nice Matin* dutifully repeated the official press release in reporting that the new road had 130 *ouvrages d'art*, of which 87 were in Alpes-Maritimes.[84] Highway ramps, which seem straightforward in English, are in French *bretelles*, a term that also refers to straps on a woman's dress as well as suspenders for a man's pants. Traffic jams and the lack of them are, in France, suggestive of a good bottle of wine. If traffic flows, it is *fluide*, like wine flowing out of a bottle. If traffic is jammed, it is *embouteillée* (bottled up). A traffic jam is a *bouchon* (a cork) or an *embouteillage* (a bottling up).[85] On the Riviera, the autoroute bore the name A8, as the new network of roads needed numbers for clarity. However, letters and numbers hardly evoked the regions through which they passed, let alone their perceived beauty. In 1973 a national competition sought new names for the major French autoroutes. A8 got the sobriquet "La Provençale."[86]

From the planning stages onward, the beauty of the autoroute was to constitute much of its appeal. Jean Mathieu, engineer of Ponts et Chaussées, emphasized the aesthetics of the project. There was to be, in the median, low-lying brush, "as in America, but this would be the first such realization in Europe." However, the autoroute would have "no advertising," that is, no billboards as along US interstates, but instead "a lawn, trees, and flowers."[87] Even service stations at autoroute rest areas needed to symbolize a beautifully designed future. In 1961 the French subsidiary of Shell asked seventy students of the École des beaux arts and the École spéciale d'architecture in Paris to propose plans for the first gas station on the new autoroute. Three young Parisian architects won the competition for the elegantly designed "service station of the future."[88]

Once it opened, articles in the press celebrated the beauty of the autoroute itself. For *L'Indépendant*, the autoroute was a "work of art, a magnificent realization, a sensational realization."[89] In the pages of *L'Espoir*, reporter Robert Buson noted the importance of autoroutes for "prosperity" and "progress" but quickly connected that modern agenda to the aesthetics of the autoroute. "Autoroutes have been studied in detail with attention to the aesthetic lay of the landscape in a way that satisfies the eye. This result was obtained by caring for the appearance of the *ouvrages d'art* and the choice of the colors of trees and plants that line it." *Nice Matin* wrote, "At the end of each curve, one discovers a new landscape. It is a constant enchantment, and no matter the weather, the view of the mountains is magnificent, even if it takes on a different character. One could not even dream of creating a more beautiful arrival on the Côte d'Azur, from Puget to the last bridge at Mandelieu, to the harbor at Cannes."[90] Another article in the same newspaper linked the beauty of the autoroute to speed and futuristic design in a language reminiscent of contemporary descriptions of jets and airports: "Now thirty-seven minutes suffices to go from Villeneuve-Loubet to Puget-sur-Argens. The roadway is a marvelous work [with] majestic curves. The autoroute, stretched here and there across bridges with futuristic lines and much elegance, founded with much happiness in the ravishingly beautiful countryside of Antibes and Mougins, practically abolishes distance." After motorists appreciated the "ravishing" beauty of the natural setting, they could appreciate the beauty of carefully chosen young women meeting them at their destination. In the early days local *syndicats d'initiative* hired young hostesses to welcome tourists (modeled after Air France's *hôtesses de l'air* [stewardesses]).[91]

Ignoring destruction of natural landscape wrought by the new autoroute, officials focused instead on anything ramshackle once hidden from tourists but now in full view. This was an extension of the postwar concern about dumps and junkyards along the seaside, where tourists might be disgusted. Along the autoroute, "garbage, the carcasses of old cars, and various sorts of debris" lined the route between Cannes and Antibes. Well aware of the fact that the Riviera was supposed to be "one of the most beautiful places in the world," the prefect ordered mayors to clean up the "makeshift sheds and workshops as well as junkyards" that lined the autoroute.[92]

Interestingly, opposition to the path of the autoroute also made aesthetic appeals, though clearly with a different sensibility. One of the more pitched battles was over a proposed viewpoint at the top of the hill at Piccolaret in le Cannet, overlooking Cannes and the Mediterranean. In a sense, the proposed belvedere viewpoint symbolized the contradiction inherent in the autoroute project. While the initial road proposal in the early 1950s called for a road that would drain truck traffic and through traffic away from the coast, by the late 1950s engineers billed the autoroute as a primary way for tourists to make their way to the Riviera and to appreciate its natural beauty. On the Riviera, because the views from the hills toward the sea are stunning, engineers wanted to incorporate panoramas of the sea into the autoroute.

To make the panorama at le Cannet possible, the autoroute rounded a hill. In order to keep the grade from being too steep, the plans called for the removal of some 450,000 m^3 of earth on just 1,200 meters of the roadway, at an early estimated cost of 5 to 6 million francs.[93] Opposition was virulent. Critics argued that the autoroute could pass on the backside of the hill, in the valley of Valmasque with no view of the sea. Their argument, like the arguments about the trajectory in Mandelieu and Mougins, was also aesthetic.

For critics of the Piccolaret viewpoint, the project cut down too many trees; large pines, olive trees, green oaks, and cypress trees were dominant. Such clear-cutting would be "inaesthetic" and would slice through the neighborhood much as the railroad had Cannes proper, all at a time of increased interest in France in the foundation of departmental forests and parks. After local opposition "animated by [famous authors] Georges Duhamel, Jules Romains, [and] André Siegfried" responded with "emotional shock," engineers altered the plan slightly. Instead of essentially removing the top of the mountain, engineers skirted around the top of it. In 1966 an effort to stabilize the hillside and create a third lane for trucks on the grade resulted in the leveling of the hilltop anyway.[94] Today the aire de Piccolaret, a small rest area with a table of orientation and restrooms, allows motorists to stop and see the blues of the Mediterranean. Yet it seems neither fish nor fowl, as it is not quite high enough for one to take in the full view, and at the same time the autoroute creates considerable noise and exhaust on the once wooded and quiet hill. Another rest area, with the usual array of amenities on French autoroutes (gas station, boutique, café) is only 1.8 kilometers away at the aire de Bréguières.[95]

FIG. 6.3. The autoroute as seen from Gorbio. A spectacular *ouvrage d'art*, this enormous viaduct, on tall cement columns, soars over the buildings and trees in the valley below. Roquebrune-Cap-Martin and the Mediterranean are in the distance. Photo by MOSSOT—own work. Licensed under Creative Commons Attribution 3.0: https://creativecommons.org/licenses/by/3.0/deed. en. Unported via Wikimedia Commons.

Tolls

The planning and construction of the new autoroute came during what Herrick Chapman calls "France's long reconstruction."[96] The country faced an acute housing shortage, requiring investment of public funds, while also fighting two colonial wars, first in Indochina and then in Algeria. Highway construction does not come cheap, and it competed with a host of other priorities. Meanwhile, the highway was severely over budget. Projected to cost 15 billion old francs, it ended up costing over double that amount. Expropriations ran up the tab. In some areas, as around Mandelieu, clay proved very difficult and costly to stabilize; after the disastrous failure of the dam at Malpasset near Fréjus (killing 423 people in 1959), engineers took no chances in stabilizing the foundation of the autoroute.[97] Moreover, the prohibition of billboards enhanced the aesthetics of the highway but increased cost.

Since the Italians had successfully used concessionary companies for new autostrada, it made sense to consider a toll road. French officials claimed that without the concessionary company and tolls, it would have taken another twenty-five years to build the autoroute.[98] France's only interwar limited access highway, the Autoroute de l'Ouest had been free, as were other French roads. But the new autoroute, like the entire new French network, relied on concessionary companies that charged steep tolls. Users of the autoroute felt the pinch.

While individual motorists groused about the costs, local communists led the organized opposition. They did not criticize the autoroute per se; like communists generally, they embraced and celebrated new infrastructure. Rather, local communists opposed the tolls. On the one hand, it was good politics. Postwar French communists owed their popularity to communists' role in the Resistance and to their attention to domestic political issues after the war. On the other, the financing of the autoroute seemed an object lesson in the problems of capitalism, in the ways that the private interests could ruin the public good. Framing opposition historically, *Le Patriote* rightly noted that tolls had been widespread in the Middle Ages and the Old Regime, but they had been abolished during the French Revolution. It made for a good rhetorical question: how could a modern road could be paid for with "medieval" financing, as if the French Revolution had never taken place?[99]

Assurances that the United States, that symbol of modernity in the aftermath of the world wars, also had toll roads hardly endeared the financing scheme to communist deputies. The ESCOTA was a classic postwar French fusion of private and public monies, and the tolls would pay investors, or as the communists put it, capitalists. If anything went wrong, taxpayers would provide the bailout. To Jean Médecin's argument that users had a choice and could take RN 7 instead, Virgile Barel and other local communists pointed out that next the public school, swimming pool, and hospital would be neglected, with those unsatisfied with the public option having to pay for a private alternative, from which investors profited.[100]

The response of government planners was that France needed to build autoroutes quickly, lest France lose out to Italy and Germany. Tolls were, according to Minister of Public Works Bonnefous, the only way to build quickly. For their part, engineers at Ponts et Chaussées claimed that the new French autoroute, in collecting tolls, resembled those of the United States and West Germany; they were wrong on both counts. After passage of the Interstate Highway Act in 1955, new US interstates were free to users. German Autobahnen always had been.[101]

Through and around Nice

The autoroute from Puget-sur-Argens to the edge of Nice opened in April 1961, in time for summer tourist season. Surveys showed that up to a quarter of cars in the first couple of months were foreign. The volume of traffic increased by 25 percent annually. Most vehicles arriving to the west of Nice proceeded to take the bridge over the Var into the city. In 1962, 42,000 crossed the bridge each day. In 1963, in the month of August, an average of 67,850 vehicles crossed the bridge daily. Even Mayor Jean Médecin, who had been delighted with an autoroute that deposited tourists at Nice's doorstep, could see the problem created by the quantity of cars now entering the promenade des Anglais from the bridge. A fair amount seemed to be through traffic that might be diverted onto a bypass or a route that sliced through the city much as American expressways did.[102]

As early as the 1930s, there existed plans for a street that would take trucks through a tunnel under the Cimiez hill. In the early 1960s one plan was to extend the autoroute right through Nice, taking a tunnel under Cimiez, passing over the Paillon, then into another tunnel under Mont Boron.[103] Patterned after "les express-ways américaines," work began in 1962. Completed in 1977, it resulted in Nice's *voie rapide*, which runs from western Nice, mostly along the rail line. It is raised above city streets except when it descends under the Cimiez hill, then it ends at the Paillon. Eight and a half kilometers long, like many US expressways it cuts right through the city, though in a much more confined space, sometimes near buildings on either side. Pierre Mathis, who planned the road, was already sure in 1963 that it was only an interim solution, as it would be saturated with traffic as soon as it opened.[104] By that time, the second solution, a bypass around Nice, was also in the works.

Prefect Pierre-Jean Moatti had been working with Minister of Public Works Marc Jacquet since 1963 to build a bypass circling to the north of Nice.[105] By 1965 work on the autoroute to the east of Nice had begun, initially in the sector of Roquebrune-Cap-Martin and Menton, connecting ultimately to Italian autostrada. Construction of the bypass around Nice did not begin until 1973. The causes were delays in funding and significant opposition

FIG. 6.4. Nice's expressway (*voie rapide*) near the boulevard Grosso in 1963. Running alongside the railroad tracks on the left of the image, the road passes through both relatively empty stretches in the foreground as well as dense residential areas in the background. Archives Nice Côte d'Azur–Ville de Nice, 1064 W 323 (collection of the photographic service of the city).

to various paths for the highway. In the early 1970s the project called for deep trenches into hillsides and considerable fill across the valleys. Farmers dreaded the loss of what little arable land still existed in the area. Residents of the hills above Nice joined them, fearing a destruction of the countryside. The municipal council of Nice also expressed its opposition. Many property owners feared the "mutilation" and "devastation" of the hillsides. The cost of the proposed project escalated quickly in the course of the 1970s, as tunnels replaced trenches in order to allay opposition. Not completed until the early 1980s, one section of the bypass has 1.8 kilometers of tunnels in a stretch only 3 kilometers long.[106]

Impacts and Complaints

The autoroute quickly became the subject of complaints about both air and noise pollution. In Cagnes-sur-Mer and Villeneuve-Loubet, three local residents' associations banded together in order to improve a situation they found completely untenable. In November 1976, just four months after the opening of that sector of the autoroute, they wrote key ministries, ESCOTA, and local leaders in protest. They gathered 630 signatures supporting their complaints about air pollution, the lack of vegetation, and particularly the noise generated by traffic. They called for a series of measures: the planting of the thousands of trees that had been promised; a reduction of speed on that sector of the autoroute to 60 kilometers per hour; compensation for residents and business owners hurt by the autoroute; soundproofing and air-conditioning for those residences most affected; and a covering of the autoroute, essentially creating a tunnel through their towns.[107] Given various complaints about the new autoroute, their demands were pretty typical.

The head of ESCOTA, A. Ponton, laid out explicitly for the Ministry of Equipment in Paris how he handled such complaints, thus revealing how little the management of the autoroute cared about residents' concerns. In essence, Ponton defended the interests of the autoroute and denied the legitimacy of inhabitants' claims. Implausibly, he claimed that higher speeds on the autoroute produced less noise than lower speeds. Nevertheless, since the mayor of Cannes had called for reducing the speed for cars through his town from 110 kilometers per hour to 90, a partial reduction of the speed limit could be granted for its "psychological impact." Ponton called demands for compensation "demagogic." Ponton's comments about noise are revealing. He noted that the issue was not whether residents now had to put up with considerable noise but whether it was an "abnormal annoyance." He said that twenty different specific instances had come to his attention, but he was working in each case to clarify that the autoroute was, in fact, the sole source of the noise. But while there were constant promises of studies about noise, Ponton asked rhetorically, "Is it really opportune to do studies, to let their results be known, to undertake the work, to reimburse those requesting it? It seems far more preferable to let the courts decide [on a case-by-case basis, for those willing to file suit]. For my part, [if a study is undertaken], I consider it dangerous to publish the results. In effect, one resident will be upset about 68 dbA, while another won't be about 73 dbA." Similarly, he did not believe that the autoroute should undertake measures to reduce noise, as they would be expensive and there would still be complaints about the autoroute's effects on views, sunshine, and sea breezes that could never be resolved to residents' satisfaction. Meanwhile, compensation for the decline in value of their property would just lead to unrealistic requests. Instead, he argued that better plantings and a reduction in speed on that sector of the autoroute be granted, while individual residents could, if they desired, file suit with the *tribunal administratif*. By 1978 the speed limit had fallen to 90 kilometers per hour, but residents were still waiting for the promised plantings.[108]

The bypass around Nice was also a source of grief. R. C., who resided on the avenue de Pessicart, lived atop a tunnel of the autoroute after the expropriation of land beneath his house. He complained of the noise that emanated from trucks in the tunnel.[109] There is no evidence that R. C. got any redress; a residence with his address, like many in the hills of northern Nice, still stands atop the autoroute. On avenue Gravier, the Colonel G. and Monsieur and Madame C. received the sound waves from the interchange of northern Nice. Nighttime noise of trucks was especially bad. Colonel G. in particular argued that the autoroute should ban truck traffic between 10:00 p.m. and 6:00 a.m., since there "were precedents in other communities." Moreover, Colonel G. and Monsieur and Madame C. were concerned about the aesthetics of the autoroute. "In the place of the dozens of oaks and olive trees, there is now assorted vegetation that has already turned brown, where it stagnates. Why not replant with local vegetation that grows so densely near Nice (oaks, green oaks, arbutus, olive trees, carob trees, etc), getting inspiration from what was done in the last century on [the hill] of the Château and on Mont Boron." Both of those hillsides had been denuded in the early modern period, as it was easy to cut the wood and let it slide down to the ports at Nice and Villefranche-sur-Mer, before reforestation in the nineteenth century. Colonel G. and Monsieur and Madame C., like others, pointed out the irony of the situation at the same time that France's political leaders "spoke in favor of respect and protection of the environment." However, all were out of luck. On the subject of noise in particular, Ponton of ESCOTA claimed that the decibel level was mostly below 70 dBA and that there was no legal precedent for limiting nighttime traffic on any autoroute in France.[110]

Just down the street, Monsieur M. and Madame P. lived at 32, vieux chemin de Gairaut and 34, vieux chemin de Gairaut, respectively, right next to the autoroute in northern Nice. Having written the mayor's office and the Ministry of Equipment twenty-six times without redress between 1972 and 1978, the two Niçois continued to complain that they and their neighbors suffered from "assaults of untenable levels of noise," forcing them to leave their windows closed during hot weather and abandon use of their terraces. They were disappointed that the plantings meant to screen the autoroute were gangly and planted in stone, thus were barely alive. Like many complainants, they noted that discussions about the environment and preservation of nature were increasingly important in French political discourse in the 1970s; as political leaders made public commitments to conservation, the natural setting of the hills of Nice disappeared before the correspondents' eyes. Madame P. insisted on the fact that residents were putting up with a decibel level of 70 dBA at a time when the president of the republic himself, Valéry Giscard d'Estaing, "was saying specifically on the radio that measures would be taken to protect inhabitants of buildings near autoroutes."[111]

The new expressway within Nice also had a severe impact on nearby residents, who claimed compensation for its effects on their lives. Near the Saint-Philippe exit, residents complained of noise, dust, obstructed views, and obscured sunlight. As the attorney, Me. Luiguegha, stated on behalf of Mme. Caviorno, who lived in the Les Palombes building on the rue de Châteauneuf, "Before, my client could see le Mont Gros and the Saint-Philippe hill. She could see the sky. Now it has all disappeared, and she can't see anything but a bloc of concrete [towering] seven meters above her house." Another attorney, Me. Scherbatoff, representing several residents down the street claimed, "Several of these unfortunate folks have to keep their windows closed day and night due to the dust and noise. In this section of the expressway 35,204 vehicles pass each day, a number that includes numerous trucks that rattle the windows of residents." Another resident's windows were entirely blocked by a wall of concrete and metal girding. Most complaints saw no redress. However, a resident who lived very close to the new expressway did receive compensation because the structure of the new route was within 60 centimeters of his bedroom window![112] For residents of Nice in general, there was no solution to the increased levels of pollution caused by automobile traffic.

Automobiles and Bidonvilles

Symbol of modern individualism, the automobile required an important, state-financed remaking of the roads to the Riviera, between towns, and within city centers. New and rebuilt roads could be fast and aesthetically pleasing, but they also brought a host of problems, from accidents to noise and air pollution. They cost a lot to build and maintain. Roads also took enormous amounts of concrete and asphalt, arguably the long-term physical legacy of the twentieth century.[113]

A powerful myth of the visible Riviera—driving on the corniches and appreciating the views like Grace Kelly and Cary Grant—obscures the invisible reality, including North African workers' critical role in the expansion of automobile tourism after World War II. In France as a whole, it was estimated in 1975 that foreign workers (including North Africans) built one automobile of every two, and ninety kilometers of autoroute out of every one hundred. State-owned automaker Renault was in the vanguard in hiring Algerians.[114] We have no statistics for exactly how many North Africans worked on the autoroutes in France in general or Alpes-Maritimes in particular. In neither archival files nor local newspaper articles about the autoroute are North Africans featured. However, in the voluminous files on bidonvilles, there are interesting traces of the men's contributions.

North Africans worked for the construction companies building the new autoroute, often sleeping in makeshift housing near the worksites. For example, in Mandelieu, North African workers lived in horse stalls while employed on the autoroute. Brothers A. M. and L. M. bought a horse-training track and related buildings in 1956. Beginning in 1958, while contracted to work on the road, three construction firms—Labelette, Lowe, and Wandevalle—leased horse stalls from the brothers M. for North African workers. As work on the autoroute advanced, Labelette and Wandevalle moved some of their workers elsewhere, and the companies' leases with the brothers M. expired. Based in Mandelieu, Lowe had other construction projects as well, and continued to house some twenty-three laborers in the stalls until 1962. Another fifty-seven people, mostly North African men but also including two Yugoslavian families, also continued to live there until 1962. The brothers M. received rent from only some of the residents and were concerned about electricity and water consumption by so many people. So when the M. brothers realized that there was a major horse competition in Cannes in 1962, for which lodging for horses would be in demand, they began the process to evict the workers in favor of horses. The expulsion did not happen in time, as the prefecture feared the optics of such a move as French and Algerian negotiators finalized the Évian Accords ending the war. Once finalized, however, authorities quickly evicted the workers. Tellingly, as the brothers M. attempted to throw out the North Africans, they thought it would help to tell authorities that they would instead be willing to rent to pieds noirs.[115]

Beginning in the late 1950s, North Africans employed on the autoroute running through the town of le Cannet, just north of Cannes, began squatting in the neighborhood of Serra-Capeou, near what is today the aire du Piccolaret. Almost five hundred workers lived at the site in 1969. Angry neighbors argued that the bidonville was out of place near the famed villa Yakymour of Aga Khan, overlooking Cannes and the Mediterranean. Much to the frustration of the absentee owner of some of the property, J.-J. L., neither the town of le Cannet nor the prefecture followed through in evicting the men. The absentee owner himself noted why, in one of his letters of complaint; the men had jobs and regular paychecks, but no one would rent to them, so they threatened to stop their work, hurting the construction of the autoroute. Le Cannet had even asked the local water provider, the SLEE, to run a water line so that the men would have potable water. Not coincidentally, authorities did not evict the men, still numbering 150, until March 1970, when the widening of the autoroute in the vicinity and changes to the aire du Piccolaret were complete. Unconcerned about where the men would go but preoccupied with "public hygiene," the local press joined officials in noting that it was for reasons of "sanitation" that local firefighters burned down the bidonville.[116]

Many of the men who worked on the autoroute lived in the bidonville at the Digue des Français. Hidden near the Var, the bidonville seemed isolated, but it was in fact integral to the construction of western Nice.[117] In the end, even the elimination of this last, large bidonville in France was intricately tied to the autoroute. In March 1976 residents moved out of the bidonville and into temporary SONACOTRA housing upstream, far from the sight of tourists arriving by plane or car. Press accounts marveled at what quick work bulldozers made of destruction, much as they marveled at the modern backhoes, cranes, and supersized dump trucks used in the building of the autoroute and the airport. In the words of Nice Matin, "The bulldozers will come and clean up the place."[118] Nicoletti, which employed many North Africans who lived in the bidonville at the Digue, got the contract for the destruction of that same bidonville. It is entirely likely that some of Nicoletti's workers who bulldozed the bidonville had lived there. After laying a new roadbed over what had been the bidonville, construction workers leveled the hill of Crémat and hauled it down to the airport for its expansion out into the sea. The long-planned construction of the bypass around Nice then commenced. Fill from the tunneling for the bypass built up the area for the construction of the autoroute.[119] As at other sites, inhabitants lost any investment they had made in structures, whether they had bought them or built them, as well as any possessions too large to haul away. When Nicoletti bulldozed the bidonville, SONACOTRA contracted a company to gather the remaining scrap metal and sell it. Remaining cinder blocks, cement, and stone became fill in the construction of the new bypass, which ran right on top of what was once the bidonville, covering some 10 percent of its original surface.[120] Clearly, if we dig deep in the archives, we find a good deal more to motoring on the Riviera than *To Catch a Thief* would have us believe.

Epilogue

The More Things Change

Yves Boisset's film *Dupont Lajoie* appeared in cinemas in 1975. The film reflected a growing recognition that North African workers in France were subject to racism. As a last name, "Dupont" is the equivalent of "Jones" or "Smith," indicating that the main character, Georges Lajoie, could be any Frenchman; the English title of the film, "The Common Man," indicates just how normal Lajoie and his friends were supposed to be. In the film Lajoie, a café owner from Paris (thus, again, a quintessentially French man), goes on vacation with his wife and son. They tow a travel trailer behind their car to a campground near the Mediterranean. There Georges ogles Brigitte (Isabelle Huppert), the daughter of campground friends. He then finds her sunbathing in the dunes and rapes her. When she resists, he tries to silence her and kills her. To hide his crime, Lajoie drags her body to a construction site where Algerian workers live in a shack next to the vacation rentals they are building. Lajoie figures the Algerians will take the rap. Frustrated by the slow response of the police, campers, including Lajoie, form a vigilante group and attack the Algerians, murdering an innocent man, Saïd. In the aftermath, during the police investigation, viewers witness yet more evidence of European racism as well as a cover-up.

The message resonated; *Dupont Lajoie* was a box-office success, selling more than 1.5 million tickets. The film subsequently became an important cultural artifact, as critics use it to discuss issues of race and sexuality.[1] On a basic level, the film is evidence of an acknowledgment in the early 1970s that North Africans had been critical in the development of France's postwar tourist infrastructure while simultaneously being subject to widespread racism. Certainly, there was racism on the part of the common men and women who wrote letters to complain about North Africans squatting in their midst. However, policies, and not just attitudes, were also at issue. The very social and economic structure of postwar France marginalized North African workers, and officials in the police and the prefecture were important in enforcing the social divide. On the Riviera only Virgile Barel and fellow communists consistently explained, from the 1950s until the late 1970s, how the exploitation of North African workers facilitated the exploitation of the working class more generally.

Interestingly, the dunes featured in *Dupont Lajoie* are actually those at the beach of Saint-Aygulf, at the edge of Fréjus, where the sand to build up the beach at la Croisette originated. Today, the southern edge of Fréjus continues to embody many of the ironies of tourism and race in contemporary France. It has long had a popular nude beach frequented mostly by northern European tourists. But in late summer 2016, in the wake of the terror attack on the promenade des Anglais of July 14, Fréjus was one of the first municipalities in France—along with Cannes and Nice—to ban the burkini (a modest, nearly full-length swimsuit deriving its name from "burqa" and "bikini").[2] Thus, Fréjus allowed full nudity but banned the burkini. In Nice a monokini, meaning a bikini without the top, was legal on the beach, while the burkini was not. Right-wing former president and candidate Nicolas Sarkozy went so far as to claim that the burkini was a "provocation." Socialist prime minister Manuel Valls, himself eyeing a run for the presidency at the time, also spoke in favor of the bans. Officially, mayors instituting the bans claimed that they were preserving French *laïcité*, the strict separation of church and state; the argument seemed a stretch, even in a country that bans the hijab in schools and the burqa on the street. Overturned in court, the ban nevertheless revealed that the burkini touched a nerve. Politicians clearly hoped that their criticism of the burkini would assist their electoral chances with the common man. We may not have come all that far in the past sixty years or so. There remains a certain way that the Riviera is imagined as a paradise for tourists of European descent, and burkini-clad women in 2016 could seem for some as provocative as North African men on the beach and in other public places in the 1950s and 1960s.

Housing the Rich and the Rest

After the dramatic changes of the Thirty Glorious Years, the Riviera remained largely in a holding pattern as the growth in tourism and population slowed. The hotel stock has not changed markedly since the 1970s. In 1974 the Méridien opened on the site of the historic Hôtel Ruhl on the promenade des Anglais. Today usually seen as a modernist monstrosity, the luxurious four-star hotel with 444 rooms was part of a broad modernization of hotels to meet the expectations of postwar tourists.[3] In March 1977 Serge Benedetti reported that in the previous year and a half, 870 new hotel rooms appeared in Nice, doubling the number of luxury accommodations in the city, driving down the rate of occupancy from 61 to 57 percent, and introducing cut-throat competition among the hotels due to overcapacity. In addition to the Méridien, the Continental-Masséna, the Frantel, the Aston, and the Novotel appeared.[4] Cannes and Nice, intently focused on business travel, became important sites for conventions, in ongoing efforts to keep hotels occupied in the off-season. Residential tourism became yet more prevalent. In 1990, in several coastal communities, about half of residences were second homes, a number that climbed to 72.09 percent in Théoule-sur-Mer.[5] After more than a century of rapid growth, the permanent population of Nice peaked at just under 350,000 souls and stabilized there. Particularly along the coast, the population continued to skew older; in 1982, 22 percent of the population of Nice was over sixty-five, and much of the turnover in real estate consisted of new retirees moving in as older ones died.[6]

Demand for housing caught up with supply in the late 1970s, once huge housing blocks, including thousands of HLM apartments, sprang up. Families in HLMs could upgrade to private apartments rendered more affordable by their abundance as population growth tapered off.[7] They left behind quickly built, already dilapidated buildings now occupied by minorities and the poor, in some cases the progeny of the North African men who constructed them. As Algerian women and children arrived in Alpes-Maritimes in the late 1970s and after, Algerian families often ended up in the worst of the HLMs. The large bidonvilles are long gone, as is the temporary housing where many men from the Digue des Français moved in 1976. However, SONACOTRA dormitories for single immigrant workers, as at Canta-Galet, remain in operation. Meanwhile, the gentrification of old town centers completely displaced the working poor, including North Africans, who once lived there. In 1989 renovated apartments in Vieux Nice were as expensive as luxury apartments at Cimiez. The vast disparities of wealth, and thus access to upscale housing, remained intact. Since the end of the Cold War, as the number of middle-class American tourists fell, wealthy Russian oligarchs have arrived for months at a time, harkening back to Nice's Belle Époque heyday as a second home for Russian aristocrats.[8]

Politically, the Riviera continued to be a right-wing stronghold with disproportionately strong support for the National Front by the 1980s. Although pieds noirs often got the blame for the success of the Far Right given the local strength of pied noir associations, the explanation is simplistic.[9] The Médecins seem emblematic. Jean Médecin was as strong a critic of the Évian Accords as Jean-Marie Le Pen would be, undertaking the same kind of race-baiting that the French center-right has regularly done to pick off potential National Front voters. Jacques Médecin, after his indictment for corruption, even endorsed the National Front. It was a view that resonated among many of his former constituents. In the second round of voting in the legislative elections in 1994, 43.51 percent of Niçois voted National Front, and in the first round of the presidential election of 1995, 23.75 percent did so.[10] It is perhaps fitting that Jean Raspail's dystopian novel imagining a brown invasion of France, wildly popular in far right-wing, anti-immigrant circles, is set on the Riviera.[11]

Waste and Water

In the early 1970s there emerged in France a notion that the natural environment should be preserved for its own sake. Environmental awareness grew markedly in France in the 1970s, reflected in French laws of 15 July 1975 and 10 July 1976 banning pollutants damaging to flora and fauna. On the Riviera much of the damage had been done. In Alpes-Maritimes, in 1977, 15 percent of the underwater area one hundred meters out from the coastline had already been destroyed.[12] The angel sharks that gave the baie des Anges its name were so long gone that most tourists thought the name referred to Christian angels, as in the azure blue skies of some religious paintings. In 1990, 25 percent of the coastline of Alpes-Maritimes had been developed. Marinas (twenty-eight with a total of fifteen thousand boats), man-made beaches, and huge second home apartment blocks already covered the coastline.[13] In such a context, efforts at environmental preservation were sometimes laughable. Interest in a marine sanctuary in the 1970s resulted in an underwater reserve off the coast of Golfe-Juan. Some fifty hectares were set aside, amounting to a rectangle off the coast of the pointe Fourcade, with depths of twenty-five to forty-five meters. It was closed to professional and pleasure fishing so that fish could reproduce. However, since the area was devoid of rocks, the Cellule d'intervention contre la pollution dans les Alpes-Maritimes (CIPALM) oversaw the creation of an artificial reef in 1979 made up of some eleven thousand tires dumped into the reserve in five groups thirty to forty meters from each other. Studies showed that the *Posidonia oceanica* remained in regression anyway. It seemed a sign of the times; tires had often ended up in the sea in barely regulated dumps along the Riviera in the immediate postwar years. Now they could be dumped on behalf of the environment.[14]

Water quality improved, not for the sake of the flora and fauna, but because tourism depended on meeting higher expectations of tourists who might choose other venues. After World War II the national Conseil supérieur d'hygiène publique advised both Cannes and Nice to build treatment plants. Both repeatedly flinched at the cost, opting instead to push waste farther out to sea. Finally, in 1979 Cannes opened a treatment plant at its outfall at Béal, west of the city. In Nice the treatment plant awaited the massive expansion of the airport into what had been the sea, freeing up some six hectares just east of the airport. At last, in 1988 Nice opened a treatment plant at Ferber. Experts created a completely enclosed facility in order to control odors, which could "risk the tourist reputation" of the city. The plant is underground, hidden from tourists on the promenade.[15] In both Cannes and Nice, treatment plants handled both sewage and rainwater, eliminating the long-standing challenge of the valleys during heavy downpours. They also worked to remove the nitrates and phosphates that became important threats to water quality by the 1970s.[16] In the larger region of Provence–Côte d'Azur, in the early 1990s fully 75 percent of sewage went through treatment plants, a larger percentage than in Greece, Italy, Spain, or other countries bordering the Mediterranean.

Yachts and marinas became leading polluters. As reported by *Nice Matin*, "pleasure craft became campgrounds on the water. In summer, three to four people live on a boat, and for 1,000 boats there are 4,000 people whose waste escapes any collection" and treatment. The marinas represented a permanent transformation of the coastline. In the words of Charles Boudouresque, "The construction of marinas is the worst pollution, because it is irreversible. Cement is irreversible. I prefer a sewer to a marina, because one can fix it."[17] Boudouresque's words could apply to the postwar transformation of the Riviera generally. Reinforced concrete was the dominant construction material for apartment blocks, villas, hotels, the airport, roads, bridges, overpasses, and underpasses, as well as marinas. It left behind a legacy as enduring as the industrial pollution that lingers in the soil of the calanques near Marseille.[18]

Along the coast of Alpes-Maritimes, the "fattening up" of beaches has continued. Into the 1980s, construction waste was still dumped along the promenade des Anglais at Magnan in an effort to build up that area of the beach. In 1989 there were still eight quarries along the Var, some of whose stone was dedicated each year to replenishing the beach at Nice. In the early 1990s Nice dumped nearly forty thousand cubic meters of stones each year along the promenade des Anglais. Today, the city continues to dump stones, though not construction waste, to replace what is washed away each winter.[19]

Although the department of the Var displaced Alpes-Maritimes as the most visited French provincial department by the 1980s, the Riviera remained every bit as crowded in the summer. Stone beaches continued to create particular problems for municipal employees charged with cleaning them, as there was no machine capable of cleaning stones below the surface. Instead, employees sprayed fungicides laced with chlorine onto the stones, letting the liquid penetrate and, ideally, disinfect a couple of centimeters deep.[20] Beaches and nearby water did seem cleaner in the eyes of locals. In 1988, as the new treatment plant was opening in Nice, *Nice Matin* reported that 81 percent of Niçois surveyed believed the water just off the coast to be polluted. However, fully 51 percent of those surveyed went to the beach anyway. Among those surveyed, 85 percent did not believe that pollution kept tourists away. Most telling, the majority of retirees surveyed thought that over the decades the cleanliness of the beach had definitely improved.[21]

Planes, Trains, and Automobiles

In the 1960s automobiles displaced trains as the primary means of transport to the Riviera. But while the advent of the high-speed TGV (Train à grande vitesse) revolutionized travel in much of France, where high-speed trains easily compete with planes, the Riviera still has no TGV line (the terrain makes laying new track very expensive). The trains called TGVs take high-speed tracks from Paris and to Lyon down the Rhône valley, but once they turn eastward, they take standard tracks. As a result, it still takes nearly six hours by train to go from Paris to Nice. That fact has made air travel to the Riviera as attractive as ever, even for people traveling within France. With nearly fourteen million passengers each year, the airport Nice–Côte d'Azur remains the busiest in France outside greater Paris.

According to residents of Nice, though the placement of the new runway (opened in 1983) was supposed to lower the noise by twenty decibels, it did not. Turbofan engines probably made more of a difference, but residents remained unconvinced that noise had declined substantially in western Nice.

In 1984, as residents complained about the noise, *Nice Matin* argued that the noise had declined, implying that Niçois (and others living near other airports) had become more sensitive to noise levels, with higher expectations than before. Even if the noise of each jet decreased, residents noted that there were more takeoffs and landings than ever. Moreover, asserting that now jets made less noise, the airport also began to accept flights between 11:00 p.m. and 6:00 a.m., hours formerly forbidden to flights as a compromise in 1962.[22]

The situation in Antibes was less ambiguous. The flight path remained directly over the town. Efforts to have the runway placed differently and to change the path of approach failed. The Association for the Defense of the Environment in Antibes petitioned the head of civilian aviation in France to ensure the planes were not violating rules by dropping below an altitude of 900 meters when flying over Antibes. They also complained that jet engines lost some fuel in descent. In 1986 the municipal newsletter asked rhetorically, "Who does not suffer from having to interrupt a conversation [or] not to hear the sound of the television in the big tourism season when the rhythm of landings reaches one hundred planes a day?"[23]

The Riviera, and Nice in particular, continued to have a notorious reputation for automobile traffic, bested only by Paris. In 1991 the promenade des Anglais was ranked the second busiest roadway in France, right after the Champs-Élysées. Moreover, traffic was, according to residents, still noisy. In 1991 the average noise level along the promenade averaged 75 decibels. As a result, relatively few inhabitants of Nice lived there, ceding the place to Scandinavians, Middle Easterners, and French from Paris and other provincial cities more in the grip of the image—rather than the reality—of life on the promenade.[24] Traffic jams, noise, and air pollution all caused Nice eventually to build a tramway, now the vogue in any French city worth its salt. It was a back-to-the-future moment, as 1953 had seen the elimination of the last tramway track in favor of buses. In 2007 the first new tramline opened in Nice, followed by second and third lines by 2019. Now trams run from the center of the city not only to the airport but also to the prefecture and the departmental archives of Alpes-Maritimes.

For decades now, as the sheer volume of postwar records and the number of researchers overwhelm French archives, they move out of the center of cities to new facilities in outlying areas. In Nice the departmental archives moved alongside the prefecture to the western end of the city, just north of the airport and just east of the Var. The archives are now just a stone's throw away from the site of the former bidonville of the Digue des Français. Significantly, there is no historical marker near the site, no notice in the archives, no sign whatsoever that up to two thousand men lived there, nor any evidence that they worked to build the autoroute that now runs through the area, the airport less than four kilometers away, or the thousands of apartments in the vicinity. As in much of the historical record of the remaking of the Riviera, the men's contributions have left few traces. It has taken archival files and old newspaper articles to reveal their work and their living conditions.

I think I understand why, at least in part. We are accustomed, particularly as tourists, to seeing places in a certain way prescribed by guidebooks, tales of others' visits, views on postcards, and culture both high and low. There is a certain "tourist gaze."[25] I can wax as nostalgic as anyone: the natural setting of the Riviera is unquestionably beautiful, particularly when seen from on high. While I did research in the summer of 2015, my wife Lisa and I rented the ground floor of a tiny villa up on the hill overlooking the city in the foreground and the sea in the background. At dinner, we sat on the terrace, watching the planes arrive and depart until well after dark. I liked how easy it had been for us to arrive practically in the center of the city, before taking a short cab ride on the expressway to get to our apartment. I took for granted that we had running water; it is phenomenally good tap water, as good as any bottled water I have tasted. As the weather was very hot that summer, I often showered several times daily in order to cool off. Of course, the toilet flushed waste out of sight and out of mind. On Sundays we took walks along the promenade des Anglais and swam in the Mediterranean, usually entering the water on the "artificial" sand beaches at Villefranche and Beaulieu. When I rented cars to go to the departmental archives of the Var and to municipal archives in Antibes, Cannes, Hyères-les-Palmiers, and Saint-Tropez, I happily took the autoroute. To be honest, had I not been working on this book, I might not have thought twice about the profound transformations that the Riviera underwent in the twentieth century.

At the same time, the hidden Riviera was right there in front of me. Since air pollution in Nice is worse in the hills surrounding the city, we got a heavy dose during rush hour and every time we climbed or descended the hill. I have never in Europe breathed in so much automobile exhaust; like the rest of the world, we only learned later that VW and other automakers had been cheating for years on emissions tests, designing cars that illegally spewed nitrogen oxides into the air. Moreover, while the panoramic view to our left was of the sea, on the right were the high-rises of Saint-Roch, where inhabitants who cannot afford hillside villas are stacked like cordwood. Our landlady criticized "those people." I can only imagine her analysis on Bastille Day the next year, when Mohamed Lahouaiej Bouhlela, a Tunisian living in Saint-Roch, committed the horrific terrorist attack on the promenade des Anglais—let alone the subsequent attack at the Nice basilica in 2020.[26] A retiree from northern France (thus not one of the pieds noirs often blamed for racism in contemporary France), our landlady was sure that North Africans were ruining Nice and France generally. "I am no racist," she assured me. "I love my little Tunisian baker." She spoke approvingly of both Jean-Marie and Marine Le Pen. Her perspective seemed little different from those of wealthy villa owners in the 1950s writing the mayor, the prefect, and the police to complain about nearby bidonville residents.

After soldiering through an entire book, I hope you will agree that the touristic myth of the Riviera, or any other tourist sight, is not nearly enough for us to understand that place. In the end, it is all too easy to miss the changes wrought by our very presence. Those changes are more profound in areas that have welcomed large numbers of tourists and that have been transformed repeatedly over time to keep pace with changing expectations. The Riviera was an earlier tourist destination than most, grew bigger than most, and underwent more overhauls than most. The Riviera is not typical as much as archetypal. If we want to travel, I would argue in conclusion that we might consider the history of our destinations, and the impact we and our fellow travelers have had on them.

Notes

Foreword

1. Dean MacCannell, *The Tourist: A New Theory of the Leisure Class* (Berkeley: University of California Press, 1999), 91–107.
2. John Urry and Jonas Larsen, *The Tourist Gaze 3.0* (Los Angeles: Sage, 2011), 1–3.
3. Ning Wang, "Rethinking Authenticity in Tourism Experience," *Annals of Tourism Research* 26, no. 2 (April 1999): 349–70. For the classic discussion of "aura," see Walter Benjamin, *Illuminations: Essays and Reflections*, ed. Hannah Arendt (New York: Schocken Books, 1988).
4. The Minute Man National Historical Park in Massachusetts is a wonderful example, its landscape carefully tended to look as most would imagine it looked in 1775, not how it actually did. As David Lowenthal notes when describing the construction of the park: "the whole countryside ceased to bear any resemblance to the Revolutionary epoch's usage." See David Lowenthal, *The Past Is a Foreign Country* (Cambridge: Cambridge University Press, 1985), 360–61.
5. Rudy Koshar, "'What Ought to Be Seen': Tourists' Guidebooks and National Identities in Modern Germany and Europe," *Journal of Contemporary History* 33, no. 3 (July 1998): 326.
6. Jenny Chio, Tiffany Gill, Vernadette Vicuña Gonzalez, Stephen L. Harp, Kate McDonald, and Adam T. Rosenbaum, "Discussion: Tourism and Race," *Journal of Tourism History* 12, no. 2 (August 2020): 173–97.
7. Frank Schipper, Igor Tchoukarine, and Sune Bechmann Pedersen, *European Travel Commission: 1948–2018* (Brussels: European Travel Commission, 2018), 12–30; Richard Ivan Jobs, *Backpack Ambassadors: How Youth Travel Integrated Europe* (Chicago: University of Chicago Press, 2017). See also Eric G. E. Zuelow, *A History of Modern Tourism* (London: Palgrave, 2016), 149–55, 171–72.
8. Serge Benedetti, "Vieux-Nice: Spéculation interdite," *Nice Matin*, 23 December 1986.
9. R. L. Bianchini, "Six cents litres de parfum et de désinfectant," *Nice Matin*, 20 June 1973.

Introduction

1. "C'est pour dégager le terrain où sera édifié le Musée Chagall," *L'Espoir*, 12 August 1966; "Au bidonville de l'Oliveto [*sic*]," *Le Provençal*, 22 September 1965; in Archives départementales des Alpes-Maritimes (ADAM) 207 W 130, see record of phone call from Ahmed Ghemann of the Amicale des Algériens to the prefect, 25 June 1966; letters of complaint from the head of the Association des propriétaires

du Quartier de l'Olivetto of 10 March 1966, 27 July 1965, and 16 September 1965; complaint from a resident of the avenue Dr. Ménard, 29 July 1965; and a petition from residents, 26 October 1965.

2. "Les pompiers ont incendié un bidonville," *Nice Matin*, 13 August 1966; "C'est pour dégager le terrain où sera édifié le Musée Chagall," *L'Espoir*, 12 August 1966.

3. Jean Chatelain to the prefect, received 2 September 1966, in ADAM 207 W 130. Neither Chatelain nor others noted that the French state, known for its secularism, had just pushed hundreds of Muslim workers out of a space in order to build a national museum dedicated to Chagall's (Judeo-Christian) religious art.

4. In this sense the Riviera was an envirotechnical landscape with the technology and labor that made it possible largely invisible to tourists. On the concept of the envirotechnical, see Sara Pritchard, *Confluence: The Nature of Technology and the Remaking of the Rhône* (Cambridge, MA: Harvard University Press, 2011), 1–27.

5. Eric G. E. Zuelow, *A History of Modern Tourism* (New York: Palgrave Macmillan, 2015). A notable exception in focusing on locals affected by the advent of coastal tourism is Johan Vincent's *L'intrusion balnéaire: Les populations littorales bretonnes et vendéennes face au tourisme (1800–1945)* (Rennes: Presses universitaires de Rennes, 2007).

6. Jacques Gascuel, "L'importance du tourisme en France," *Nice Matin*, 2 July 1950. France was the world's most frequented international destination in the 1920s, a status it regained in 1948 and maintained until the COVID-19 pandemic. See World Atlas, "The World's Most Visited Countries," last updated 5 June 2020, https://www.worldatlas.com/articles/10-most-visited-countries-in-the-world.html.

7. Mary Blume, *Côte d'Azur: Inventing the French Riviera* (New York: Thames & Hudson, 1992); Michael Nelson, *Americans and the Making of the Riviera* (Jefferson, NC: McFarland, 2008); Kenneth E. Silver, *Making Paradise: Art, Modernity, and the Myth of the French Riviera* (Cambridge, MA: MIT Press, 2001).

8. Rosalind Williams, *Dream Worlds: Mass Consumption in Late Nineteenth-Century France* (Berkeley: University of California Press, 1982).

9. "Embouteillage Lapalisee Route Nationale 7 en 2018," 22 November 2018, https://www.youtube.com/watch?v=iR7tNdNWh3M.

10. On transatlantic American and French film culture, see Vanessa R. Schwartz, *It's So French: Hollywood, Paris, and the Making of Cosmopolitan Film Culture* (Chicago: University of Chicago Press, 2007).

11. Geneviève Massard-Guilbaud, "Aménager: pourquoi, au bénéfice de qui et à quel prix?" in Patrick Fournier and Geneviève Massard-Guilbaud, eds., *Aménagement et environnement: Perspectives historiques* (Rennes: Presses universitaires de Rennes, 2016), 231–45. Fournier's introduction to that volume surveys the historiography on development and the environment (7–21).

12. Thomas G. Andrews, *Killing for Coal: America's Deadliest Labor War* (Cambridge, MA: Harvard University Press, 2008); Andrews, "Work, Nature, and History: A Single Question, That Once Moved Like Light," in Andrew C. Isenberg, ed., *The Oxford Handbook of Environmental History* (New York: Oxford University Press, 2017), 423–66.

13. Jean Fourastié, *Les trente glorieuses, ou la révolution invisible de 1946 à 1975* (Paris: Fayard, 1979).

14. Céline Pessis, Sezin Topçu, and Christophe Bonneuil, eds., *Une autre histoire des "Trente Glorieuses": Modernisation, contestations et pollutions dans la France d'après guerre* (Paris: La Découverte, 2013).

15. Christian Pfister, "The '1950s Syndrome' and the Transition from Slow-Going to a Rapid Loss of Global Sustainability," in Frank Uekötter, ed., *The Turning Points of Environmental History* (Pittsburgh: University of Pittsburgh Press, 2010), 90–118.

16. Kristin Ross fuses postwar consumption with the often unseen production of North African laborers, such as in automobile manufacturing, in *Fast Cars, Clean Bodies: Decolonization and the Reordering of French Culture* (Cambridge, MA: MIT Press, 1996). On race in environmental history more generally, see Connie Y. Chiang, "Race and Ethnicity in Environmental History," in Isenberg, *Oxford Handbook of Environmental History*, 573–99.

17. Fourastié briefly refers to "immigrants," "foreigners," and *rapatriés*, essentially ignoring the importance of colonial and postcolonial labor in postwar France (*Les trente glorieuses*, 55). In doing so, Fourastié was typical of social scientists who participated fully in what Ann Stoler terms colonial aphasia in *Duress: Imperial Durabilities in Our Times* (Durham, NC: Duke University Press, 2016), chap. 4. Decolonization also has an astoundingly small place in classic surveys of twentieth-century European history, including Tony Judt, *Postwar: A History of Europe since 1945* (New York: Penguin, 2005), and Mark Mazower, *Dark Continent: Europe's Twentieth Century* (New York: Knopf, 1999). A notable exception, in the case of France, is Tyler Stovall's *Transnational France: The Modern History of a Universal Nation* (Boulder, CO: Westview, 2015). For a comparative history of European decolonization, see Elizabeth Buettner, *Europe after Empire: Decolonization, Society, and Culture* (Cambridge: Cambridge University Press, 2016).

18. On the postwar emergence of the occupational category of *cadres*, see Luc Boltanski, *Les cadres: La formation d'un groupe social* (Paris: Minuit, 1982).

19. This is the distinction made by the Encyclopedia Britannica. See "Riviera," last updated 29 January 2009, https://www.britannica.com/place/Riviera. There is some fluidity in the use of these terms. The Michelin guide *Côte d'Azur* (2013) even excludes Cannes from its section on "Nice and the Riviera." After World War II, tourist authorities in Alpes-Maritimes resisted efforts by their counterparts in the Var to have the latter joined for tourist propaganda under the rubric of Côte d'Azur, insisting that the coastline of the Var was merely the Côte varoise: "La Chambre de Commerce varoise demande que le Var soit rattaché touristiquement à Nice," *Nice Matin*, 26 June 1954; "Réunie en assemblée générale à Hyères," *Nice Matin*, 18 June 1961. Minister of Tourism Édouard Bonnefous made a distinction in 1957 between the Côte d'Azur and the Côte varoise: "Après la visite du ministre des 3 T," *Nice Matin*, 14 September 1957. Promoters of tourism in the Var readily acceded that only the Alpes-Maritimes was the Riviera. See "Tour d'horizon des problèmes touristiques," *Nice Matin*, Draguignan edition, 18 January 1961.

20. Stéphane Liégeard, *La Côte d'Azur* (Paris: Maison Quantin, 1887).

21. On the mistral, see Catherine T. Dunlop, "Looking at the Wind: Paintings of the Mistral in Fin-de-Siècle France," *Environmental History* 20 (2015): 505–18.

22. Ville de Nice, "Climat," accessed 27 March 2020, https://www.nice.fr/fr/le-climat; Robert Riem, "Pollution: Eau de mer; c'est (presque) tout bon entre Théoule et Menton," part 1, *Nice Matin*, 6 August 1978.

23. On the myth of Provence, see Helen Lefkowitz Horowitz, *A Taste for Provence* (Chicago: University of Chicago Press, 2016).

24. Riem, "Pollution."

25. Rosemary O'Neill, *Art and Visual Culture on the French Riviera, 1956–1971* (Farnham, UK: Ashgate, 2012), 9. On tourism and race in Miami, see Chanelle N. Rose, *The Struggle for Black Freedom in Miami: Civil Rights and America's Tourist Paradise, 1896–1968* (Baton Rouge: Louisiana State University Press, 2015).

26. *Bulletin d'information et recueil des actes administratifs* 20 (31 October 1970): 6–8, ADAM 207 W 125.

27. "Les possibilités touristiques de la Côte d'Azur," *Le Patriote*, 24 September 1961; Étienne Thil, "Des autoroutes-viaducs pour la Côte d'Azur," *Constellation*, July 1961, 36.

28. Dustin Harris notes that in 1976, the Gault et Millau restaurant guide warned tourists about North Africans in northern Marseille. Harris, "Maghrebis in Marseille: North African Immigration and French Social Welfare in the Late Colonial and Postcolonial Eras" (PhD diss., University of Toronto, 2018), 170. I have found no comparable references in the case of the Riviera, where authorities worked to keep North African workers out of public spaces and away from tourists.

29. Vincent Lemire, *La soif de Jérusalem: Essai d'hydrohistoire, 1840–1948* (Paris: Publications de la Sorbonne, 2011). See also Jamie Linton, *What Is Water? The History of a Modern Abstraction* (Vancouver: University of British Columbia Press, 2010); Peter Soppelsa, "Water and Power in Modern France," *French Politics, Culture and Society* 31 (2013): 117–32; Erik Swyngedouw, *Social Power and the Urbanization of Water: Flows of Power* (Oxford: Oxford University Press, 2004), 1–50.

30. In a book about successive waves of immigration in Nice, designed for a popular audience, Ralph Schor, Stéphane Mourlane, and Yvan Gastaut do include North African workers, though they mix Italian and North African workers with Russian, British, and American tourists, which together created a "cosmopolitan Nice" that they implicitly celebrate. See Schor et al., *Nice cosmopolite, 1860–2010* (Paris: Éditions Autrement, 2010). Jean-Paul Potron briefly mentions "a mass of displaced and illegal" North Africans who "worked illegally in construction," then claims that "fires, illnesses and corruption pushed authorities to make them move" out of shantytowns in *Les trente glorieuses: Nice, 1945–1975* (Nice: Gilletta, 2016), 43.

31. On environmental racism in the United States, see Carl A. Zimring, *Clean and White: A History of Environmental Racism in the United States* (New York: New York University Press, 2015); Andrew Hurley, *Class, Race, and Industrial Pollution in Gary, Indiana, 1945–1980* (Chapel Hill: University of North Carolina Press, 1995). William Cronon has argued that preoccupation with the wilderness (as opposed to the urban, built environment) among many environmentalists "excludes from the radical environmentalist agenda problems . . . of environmental justice." See Cronon, "The Trouble with Wilderness: Or, Getting Back to the Wrong Nature," in Ken Hiltner, ed., *Ecocriticism: The Essential Reader* (London: Routledge, 2015), 113.

1. Building Hotels and Housing for the Rich and the Rest

1. On Vigo, see Michel Estève, ed., *Jean Vigo* (Paris: Lettres Modernes, 1966); Pierre Lherminier, *Jean Vigo* (Paris: Éditions Seghers, 1967); Michael Temple, *Jean*

Vigo (Manchester: Manchester University Press, 1988); René Prédal, "À Propos de Nice: Le point de vue documenté de Jean Vigo," *Nice historique* 222 (1993): 62–69.

2. In 1946 the preamble to the Constitution of the Fourth Republic stated, "The nation shall provide the individual and the family with the conditions necessary to their development." In the words of the Assemblée départementale sur le logement social d'Alpes-Maritimes, "Housing is a natural right, recognized by the Constitution just like education, work, and health." Papers of Virgile Barel, 17 April 1966, ADAM 84 J 5. On the right to comfort, see Minayo A. Nasiali, *Native to the Republic: Empire, Social Citizenship, and Everyday Life in Marseille since 1945* (Ithaca, NY: Cornell University Press, 2016), chaps. 1–2; Nicole C. Rudolph, *At Home in Postwar France: Modern Mass Housing and the Right to Comfort* (New York: Berghahn, 2015), esp. 11–12, 17; Rebecca J. Pulju, *Women and Mass Consumer Society in Postwar France* (New York: Cambridge University Press, 2011), 3–4.

3. Christophe Granger, *Les corps d'été: Naissance d'une variation saisonnière, XXe siècle* (Paris: Éditions Autrement, 2009); Pascal Ory, *L'invention du bronzage: Essai d'une histoire culturelle* (Paris: Éditions Complexe, 2008). Tellingly, L'Oréal tested its first tanning lotion in 1935, on five people sent to the Côte d'Azur. See Geoffrey Jones, *Beauty Imagined: A History of the Global Beauty Industry* (Oxford: Oxford University Press, 2010), 118.

4. In the late 1950s only about one-quarter of French people went on vacation. "Selon l'Institut de la Statistique, pas de vacances pour trois Français sur quatre," *Le Patriote*, 29 May 1957.

5. Although both the tourist industry and SNCF, the national rail company (both of which wanted to spread the extra business over several months), pushed to alter the school holiday from the usual July and August, they were unsuccessful. The Conseil supérieur de l'éducation nationale refused to budge, keeping the school holiday in the late summer. "La question des grandes vacances scolaires," *Nice Matin*, 27 March 1952.

6. Georges Reymond, "L'évolution et les nouvelles formes de tourisme: Enquête," *L'Espoir*, 20 October 1956; Max Burlando, "Grande saison d'été sur la côte," *Le Patriote*, 19 September 1951; Marcel Rovère, "Premier bilan provisoire de la saison touristique estivale," *L'Espoir*, 20 September 1955; J.-C. Vérots, "Paradoxe du mois d'août à Nice," *Nice Matin*, 4 September 1957; Guy Riffet, "Malgré les efforts surhumains," *L'Espoir*, 14 August 1958. On the *syndicats d'initiative*, see Patrick Young, *Enacting Old Brittany: Tourism and Culture in Provincial France, 1871–1939* (Farnham, UK: Ashgate, 2012), 65–69.

7. "Tourisme et Côte d'Azur," part 4, "Un patrimoine hôtelier qu'on a laissé vieillir," *Le Patriote*, 26 November 1960; "Les ennemis du tourisme, le 'coup de fusil' et les parasites," *Nice Matin*, 18 November 1952; Roger Zuntini, "En Angleterre, on prépare les prochaines venues touristiques," *Le Patriote*, 6 May 1953; Antoine Giorgi, "À propos du caractère saisonnier du tourisme et de ses conséquences," *Le Patriote*, 7 June 1962; "L'avenir de la promenade des Anglais," *Nice Matin*, 6 December 1962; Peter Lyth, "Flying Visits: The Growth of British Air Package Tours, 1945–1975," in Luciano Segreto, Carles Manera, and Manfred Pohl, eds., *Europe at the Seaside: The Economic History of Mass Tourism in the Mediterranean* (New York: Berghahn, 2009), 11–30; Orvar Löfgren, *On Holiday: A History of Vacationing* (Berkeley: University of California Press, 1999), 172–82.

8. "Le Syndicat d'Initiative de Nice a discuté de la zone touristique Languedoc-Roussillon," *Le Patriote*, 19 June 1963.

9. "Pour conserver et accroître leurs profits," *Le Patriote*, 4 June 1952; "L'activité et l'évolution du tourisme à Nice," *Nice Matin*, 4 March 1958; Registre, Hôtel Beau Rivage, ADAM 18 J 253.

10. Georges Reymond, "L'évolution et les nouvelles formes du tourisme," part 9, "En hiver comme en été, Nice bénéficie d'une triple clientèle," *L'Espoir*, 1 November 1956; "Tourisme et Côte d'Azur," part 3, "Huit pays en huit jours," *Le Patriote*, 24 November 1960.

11. "Théories de l'enseignement moderne et problèmes de l'hôtellerie quotidienne," *Nice Matin*, 28 September 1961.

12. "Le Conseil municipal de Nice favorable au principe de la transformation de l'Hôtel Luxembourg," *Nice Matin*, 31 August 1962; "Tourisme et Côte d'Azur," part 4, "Un patrimoine hôtelier qu'on a laissé vieillir," *Le Patriote*, 26 November 1960; Georges Reymond, "Le client a le droit d'être exigeant," *L'Espoir*, 20 October 1956.

13. Diplomat, aviator, and author Romain Gary is the best known of those who fled the Soviet Union in the early years, to the extent that the historical library in Nice carries his name. See Romain Gary, *Promise at Dawn*, trans. John Markham Beach (New York: Harper, 1961).

14. Georges Reymond, "Le client a le droit d'être exigeant," *L'Espoir*, 20 October 1956; Antoine Giorgi, "À propos du caractère saisonnier du tourisme et de ses conséquences," *Le Patriote*, 7 June 1962; Georges Reymond, "L'évolution et les nouvelles formes du tourisme," part 4, "'Essayons de penser à l'avenir sans pessimisme,'" *L'Espoir*, 25 October 1956.

15. Marie-France Mortier, "Archives d'entreprise: L'Hôtel du Beau Rivage de Nice, 1882–1969," *Provence historique* 40 (1990): 217–32; "Pour conserver et accroître leurs profits," *Le Patriote*, 4 June 1952; *Trois siècles de tourisme dans les Alpes-Maritimes* (Milan: Silvana, 2013), 104.

16. "L'activité et l'évolution du tourisme à Nice," *Nice Matin*, 4 March 1958; Marcel Rovère, "Davantage de clients dans les hôtels," *L'Espoir*, 2 February 1951; "Les possibilités touristiques de la Côte d'Azur," *Le Patriote*, 24 September 1961.

17. Yves Dartois, "Le tourisme, industrie exportatrice no. 1," *Nice Matin*, 2 June 1949; "Théories de l'enseignement moderne et problèmes de l'hôtellerie quotidienne," *Nice Matin*, 28 September 1961.

18. Claude Mercadié, "Bilan du tourisme estival à Nice," part 4," *Nice Matin*, 11 October 1960; "Doléances," *L'Espoir*, 6 August 1963. On American expectations of bathrooms, see also Christopher Endy, *Cold War Holidays: American Tourism in France* (Chapel Hill: University of North Carolina Press, 2004), 87–88.

19. "Le problème de l'équipement hôtelier," *Le Patriote*, 13 May 1955; Serge Benedetti, "Ces palaces qui veulent vivre," *Nice Matin*, 27 March 1977.

20. "Immeubles en construction dans notre région," *Le Patriote*, 17 February 1952; "Les innombrables immeubles en construction," *Le Patriote*, 16 February 1952; Claude Mercadié, "La Côte d'Azur a besoin de 15,000 HLM!" part 1, *Nice Matin*, 15 October 1959; "Les problèmes du logement évoqués par M. Siadoux, Directeur Départemental de la Construction," *Nice Matin*, 25 December 1962; Roger Beccatini, "Rideaux entreouverts: Quand le bâtiment ne va plus," *Le Patriote*, 17 September

1958; "L'industrie du bâtiment connaît une période fébrile," *Le Monde*, 29 March 1955; Pierre Kerlouégan, "La patrie des retraités," *Le Figaro*, 25 October 1976.

21. In the 1960 revaluation of the franc, one hundred "old" francs became one "new" franc. However, many people continued to cite numbers in old francs, particularly as concerned large sums, such as in real estate transactions.

22. Claude Mercadić, "La Côte d'Azur a besoin de 15,000 HLM!" part 2, *Nice Matin*, 16 October 1959; J.-C. Vérots, "Le 'logement social,' bilan d'une faillite," part 2, *Nice Matin*, 21 November 1962; Médecin to Virgile Barel, 23 January 1963, in Barel's papers, ADAM 84 J 7; Gilles Roche, "Le feu trop souvent criminel, la spéculation immobilière éffrénée tuent le tourisme en Corse et sur la Côte d'Azur," *Carrefour*, 4 August 1965; "Les innombrables immeubles en construction," *Le Patriote*, 16 February 1952; Roger Beccatini, "Logement: De l'optimisme inaltérable de Médecin à la confession de M. Bosio," *Le Patriote*, 17 April 1958; William Caruchet, "Tout ce qu'il faut savoir sur la nouvelle législation des loyers," *Le Patriote*, 4 January 1959.

23. Beccatini, "Rideaux entreouverts"; Antoine Giorgi, "Quand le bâtiment ne va pas," *Le Patriote*, 28 March 1966; Jean-Paul Potron, *Les trente glorieuses: Nice, 1945–1975* (Nice: Gilletta, 2016), 69; Paul Thierry, "À la cité-jardin Saint-Roch," *Nice Matin*, 26 August 1955. Italian immigrants had founded both the Nicoletti and Spada firms, the largest on the Riviera. By the postwar years, Nicoletti had 400 employees and Spada 1,200. See Ralph Schor, Stéphane Mourlane, and Yvan Gastaut, *Nice cosmopolite, 1860–2010* (Paris: Éditions Autrement, 2010), 116–17. Max Gallo fictionalized Jean Spada in his well-known novels set in twentieth-century Nice: *La baie des Anges* (Paris: Robert Laffont, 1975); *Le Palais des Fêtes* (Paris: Robert Laffont, 1976); *La promenade des Anglais* (Paris: Robert Laffont, 1976).

24. "L'industrie du bâtiment connaît une période fébrile," *Le Monde*, 29 March 1955.

25. "L'industrie du bâtiment connaît une période fébrile"; Rachel Picard, "Un toit au soleil," part 8, *Le Patriote*, 31 August 1957; Beccatini, "Rideaux entreouverts"; Roger Beccatini, "Sur une décision de l'Office municipal des HLM de Nice," *Le Patriote*, 21 August 1962; Jean Claude, "Les acheteurs d'appartements sont pratiquement tous des étrangers aux Alpes-Maritimes," *Le Patriote*, 20 February 1952.

26. Maurice Huleu, "Les étrangers au paradis," *Nice Matin*, 19 September 1976; Potron, *Les trente glorieuses*, 31; Pierre Kerlouégan, "La patrie des retraités," *Le Figaro*, 25 October 1976. On second homes in France, see Françoise Dubost, ed., *L'autre maison: La 'résidence secondaire,' refuge des générations* (Paris: Éditions Autrement, 1998); Sarah Farmer, *Rural Inventions: The French Countryside after 1945* (New York: Oxford University Press, 2020), chap. 2.

27. William Caruchet, "Tout ce qu'il faut savoir sur la nouvelle législation des loyers," *Le Patriote*, 4 January 1959; Antoine Giorgi, "Quand le bâtiment ne va pas," part 2, *Le Patriote*, 29 March 1966; "L'industrie du bâtiment connaît une période fébrile," *Le Monde*, 29 March 1955.

28. Marcel Rudo, "L'hôtel le plus prospère de Nice s'appelle le 'Clandestin,'" *Le Patriote*, 7 August 1952; "Pratiquée à Nice sur une large échelle, la location clandestine 'en meublé,'" *L'Espoir*, 23 June 1955; Georges Reymond, "Le client a le droit d'être exigeant," *L'Espoir*, 20 October 1956; Georges Reymond, "L'évolution et les nouvelles formes du tourisme," part 5, "Le meublé rappelle l'ambiance du 'chez soi' à une clientèle avide d'indépendance," *L'Espoir*, 26 October 1956.

29. Marcel Rudo and Roger Beccatini, "Une première possibilité de résoudre la crise, les logements vides," *Le Patriote*, 10 April 1954.

30. Roger Beccatini, "Logement: Où en est-on réellement dans les Alpes-Maritimes?" *Le Patriote*, 16 April 1958; Danièle Voldman, *La Reconstruction des villes françaises de 1940 à 1954: Histoire d'une politique* (Paris: L'Harmattan, 1997), 25, 176; Rudolph, *At Home in Postwar France*, 34, 120.

31. Marcel Rovère, "Une enquête sur la 'crise du logement,'" *L'Espoir*, 16 November 1955; "Afin de réduire le nombre des taudis," *L'Espoir*, 11 September 1953; Antoine Giorgi, "Quand le bâtiment ne va pas," part 2, *Le Patriote*, 29 March 1966.

32. On rent controls and the percentage of income French families spent on rent, see Pulju, *Women and Mass Consumer Society*, 132–33; Rudolph, *At Home in Postwar France*, 41–42; Voldman, *La Reconstruction*, 330.

33. "Libération des loyers pour certains locaux," *Le Patriote*, 4 January 1959; Henri Faraut, "Le 'Martinez' sera-t-il bradé?" part 2, "L'expropriation, une solution de garantie," *Le Patriote*, Cannes edition, 29 June 1961.

34. "Ceux qui font les maisons n'en ont pas pour eux-mêmes," *Le Patriote*, 17 March 1954; "La guerre d'Indochine nous coûte un logement à la minute et plus," *Le Patriote*, 17 April 1954; "Une lettre terrible," *Le Patriote*, 15 April 1954.

35. "Osera-t-on mettre 11 familles à la rue?" *Le Patriote*, 21 January 1954; "Vâcherie Gorbella," *Le Patriote*, 18–19 April 1954.

36. Assemblée Départementale, "Motion," 17 April 1966, in Barel's papers, ADAM 84 J 5; "Conférence de presse, 5 April 1966, sur la question sociale, par Monsieur Pasquetti," in Barel's papers, ADAM 84 J 5.

37. Roger Beccatini, "Logement: Pas de faux-semblants, réquisition!" *Le Patriote*, 19 April 1958; "Ceux qui s'en vont chercher refuge dans les villages," *Le Patriote*, 14 April 1954; "Qu'en pensez-vous, M René Laniel?" *Le Patriote*, 18–19 April 1954; Marcel Rovère, "Visite au service municipal de logement: En cinq ans, 5,827 dossiers de réquisitions ont été constitués sur lesquels 1,272 ont obtenu satisfaction," *L'Espoir*, 16 August 1951; Marcel Rovère, "Visite au service municipal du logement: Grâce à des nouvelles constructions et des mesures efficaces la crise du logement pourrait être résorbée en peu de temps," *L'Espoir*, 17 August 1951; "On construit beaucoup, mais on loge moins," *Le Patriote*, 4 June 1958.

38. "Menacé par une maison (habitée) qui risque de s'écrouler, le lavoir de la rue des Serruriers vient d'être fermé," *Le Patriote*, 21 July 1955; Rachel Picard, "Un toit au soleil," part 1, *Le Patriote*, 21 August 1957. As it turned out, the fountain on the place Masséna was a particular waste of money. A larger-than-life Apollo is at its center, and the sculptor endowed Apollo with equally larger-than-life genitalia. Scandal ensued, and the sculptor reduced the size of Apollo's penis. Scandal continued, so the statue ended up at a local stadium, only returning to the place Masséna a few years ago. See Montmartre Secret, "Nice, Fontaine du Soleil, Apollon," 21 May 2013, http://www.montmartre-secret.com/article-nice-fontaine-du-soleil-apollon-alfred-janniot-117920805.html.

39. Jacques Herbey, "L'Assemblée du Comité National du Tourisme à Paris," *L'Espoir*, 14 May 1950; "Un taudis n'est jamais pittoresque," *Le Patriote*, 21 September 1951; "Le problème, c'est de loger décemment 25,000 hommes, femmes, enfants," *Le Patriote*, 22 September 1951; "Un jour, les rires des gosses sonneront plus clair dans les rues rajeunies," *Le Patriote*, 27 September 1951; "Toujours les

habitations à loyer modéré," *Le Patriote*, 31 March 1954; "Depuis le 26 mai 1944," *Le Patriote*, 16 April 1954.

40. "Le Vieux-Nice va être classé 'site pittoresque,'" *Nice Matin*, 21 August 1965.

41. Pepita Berardi, "Souvenirs, souvenirs, la Vieille Ville, avant 1936," *Le Niçois*, 24–30 January 1980.

42. C. James Haug, *Leisure and Urbanism in Nineteenth-Century Nice* (Lawrence: University Press of Kansas, 1982), 95–124; "Dans les rues du Vieux-Nice," *Le Patriote*, 29 November 1958; "Un taudis n'est jamais pittoresque," *Le Patriote*, 21 September 1951; "L'escalier merveilleux des Lascaris," *Le Patriote*, 7 April 1954; "La grosseur des rats effraie même les chats!" *Le Patriote*, 5 October 1951; "Le Vieux-Nice en chiffres," *Le Provençal*, 25 March 1966; "Le Vieux-Nice a trouvé un 'poumon,'" *Le Patriote*, 8 January 1950; "L'aménagement de l'îlot sinistré de la rue des Serruriers permettra de jouer au basket-ball dans le Vieux-Nice," *Nice Matin*, 8 June 1949.

43. "Le Vieux-Nice va être classé 'site pittoresque,'" *Nice Matin*, 21 August 1965; "L'escalier merveilleux des Lascaris."

44. "Des projets pour transformer le Vieux-Nice?" *Le Patriote*, 9 October 1952; "La transformation du Vieux-Nice," *Le Patriote*, 14 October 1952; "Un arc romain du XIIIe siècle mis à jour dans le Vieux-Nice," *Nice Matin*, 4 June 1963; "Promenades dans le Vieux-Nice," *L'Espoir*, 13 April 1955; "Un taudis n'est jamais pittoresque."

45. "Des projets pour transformer le Vieux-Nice?" *Le Patriote*, 9 October 1952; "La transformation du Vieux-Nice," *Le Patriote*, 14 October 1952; "Deuxième série de projets pour le Vieux-Nice," *Le Patriote*, 10 October 1952. On communists' embrace of consumerism, advocating that the working class have access, see Pulju, *Women and Mass Consumer Society*, esp. 161–72.

46. "Pour cause d'utilitié publique, dans le Vieux-Nice, un îlot insalubre où logent 89 familles, sera détruit," *Le Patriote*, 12 November 1954.

47. Paul Thierry, "La cité de relogement de Bon-Voyage est commencée," *Nice Matin*, 26 July 1953; "Pose de la couverture des immeubles de la 'Cité de Transit de Bon-Voyage,'" *L'Espoir*, 20 May 1955; "Un plan d'assainissement prévoit la destruction de certains îlots insalubres du Vieux-Nice," *Nice Matin*, 29 September 1955; "Le premier immeuble HLM," *Le Patriote*, 17 February 1954.

48. "Pour cause d'utilitié publique, dans le Vieux-Nice, un îlot insalubre où logent 89 familles, sera détruit," *Le Patriote*, 12 November 1954; "Les travaux d'assainissement du Vieux-Nice," *L'Espoir*, 31 October 1956; "À propos de la modernisation de Nice," *Le Patriote*, 16 May 1963; Roger Beccatini, "Logement: Pas de faux-semblants, réquisition!" *Le Patriote*, 19 April 1958; "Le Vieux-Nice va être classé 'site pittoresque,'" *Nice Matin*, 21 August 1965; J.-C. Vérots, "Vieux Nice: Il faudra plusieurs années avant qu'apparaissent les effets positifs de la création du 'secteur sauvegardé," *Nice Matin*, 2 October 1969. The historic preservation law of 1962, also known as the Malraux law after de Gaulle's well-known minister of culture, allowed the protection of whole neighborhoods as historic landmarks. On how the designation helped turn the Marais into a "virtual fantasyland," see Rosemary Wakeman, *The Heroic City, 1945–1958* (Chicago: University of Chicago Press, 2009), 327–40.

49. Prefectoral report generated just after a 9 June 1967 request from the prefect to the police to provide surveillance and protection for shantytowns in the department, ADAM 207 W 130; Procès-verbal of the police, 19 June 1967, ADAM 328 W 11. The police kept files on such establishments in order to track activity of the

Front de libération nationale (FLN). On their political function in Paris, see Neil MacMaster, "The Algerian Café-Hotel: Hub of the Nationalist Underground in Paris, 1926–1962," *French Politics, Culture, and Society* 34, no. 2 (2016): 57–77.

50. J.-C. Vérots, "Vieux Nice: Il faudra plusieurs années avant qu'apparaissent les effets positifs de la création du 'secteur sauvegardé,'" *Nice Matin*, 2 October 1969.

51. Serge Benedetti, "Vieux-Nice: Spéculation interdite," *Nice Matin*, 23 December 1986; "Le Vieux-Nice est en train de changer," *Nice Matin*, 17 February 1983.

52. "Public housing" is an inexact translation of *logement social*, which in the words of Amelia Lyons "refers to all housing projects, publicly and privately held single-family houses and multiunit apartments, for which rental or purchase prices are controlled in order to ensure residents do not pay exorbitant prices in relation to their income." Lyons, *The Civilizing Mission in the Metropole: Algerian Families and the French Welfare State during Decolonization* (Stanford, CA: Stanford University Press, 2013), 126. On LOGECO and the Courant Plan, see Rudolph, *At Home in Postwar France*, 121–22.

53. Marcel Rovère, "Une enquête sur la crise du logement," *L'Espoir*, 17 November 1955. On the *abbé* Pierre, urgent housing, and the so-called Opération Million Housing, see Rudolph, *At Home in Postwar France*, 122–26; Nasiali, *Native to the Republic*, 46–47.

54. "La situation de l'habitat à loyer modéré, à Nice," *Nice Matin*, 28 June 1955; Mercadié, "La Côte d'Azur a besoin de 15,000 HLM!" part 1.

55. "Monaco, un paradis, mais pour qui?" *Le Patriote*, 8 November 1960; Paul Thierry, "Les municipalités peuvent construire des immeubles d'habitation," *Nice Matin*, 2 July 1949; "Le premier immeuble HLM," *Le Patriote*, 17 February 1954; "Puisqu'on nous parle des HLM," *Le Patriote*, 30 March 1954.

56. Thierry, "À la cité-jardin Saint-Roch"; "Toujours les habitations à loyer modéré," *Le Patriote*, 31 March 1954; "Osera-t-on mettre 11 familles à la rue?" *Le Patriote*, 21 January 1954.

57. Roger Beccatini, "Logement: Le résultat d'un choix," *Le Patriote*, 18 April 1958; Mercadié, "La Côte d'Azur a besoin de 15,000 HLM!" part 1; "2,000 habitations à loyer modéré mises en chantier cette année dans les Alpes-Maritimes," *Nice Matin*, 9 January 1960; "Pierre-Jean Moatti et Jean Médecin visitent les chantiers de construction," *Nice Matin*, 15 November 1960; "Il faut que la France connaisse l'effort de Nice et du département," *Nice Matin*, 4 March 1961.

58. Marcel Rovère, "Une enquête sur la 'crise du logement,'" *L'Espoir*, 25 November 1955; J.-C. Vérots, "Le 'logement social,' bilan d'une faillite," part 1, *Nice Matin*, 20 November 1962; "Les 280 occupants des HLM du col de Villefranche," *Nice Matin*, 4 March 1975.

59. "Les grands ensembles HLM à Nice," part 2, *Nice Matin*, 10 April 1966; "Des cités nouvelles sont nées dans la ville," part 1, *Le Patriote*, 5 March 1961; "Des cités nouvelles sont nées dans la ville," part 2, *Le Patriote*, 7 March 1961; José Steve, "Des cités nouvelles sont nées dans la ville," part 4, *Le Patriote*, 21 April 1961; "Vivre dans les grands ensembles: Béton sur champ d'azur," part 3, *Nice Matin*, 10 January 1974.

60. José Steve, "Des cités nouvelles sont nées dans la ville," part 2, *Le Patriote*, 18 April 1961; José Steve, "Des cités nouvelles sont nées dans la ville," part 4, *Le Patriote*, 21 April 1961; José Steve, "Las Planas, cité du bout du monde," part 3, *Le Patriote*,

17 May 1962; "Vivre dans les grands ensembles: Béton sur champ d'azur," part 3, *Nice Matin*, 9 January 1974; "Vivre dans les grands ensembles: Béton sur champ d'azur," part 4, *Nice Matin*, 10 January 1974. On women's complaints about high-rise apartments in *grands ensembles*, including HLMs, in France generally, see Pulju, *Women and Mass Consumer Society*, 202–8; Rudolph, *At Home in Postwar France*, 175–78.

61. "Aux HLM Pasteur, à Nice, les gouttières mal installées," *Le Patriote*, 19 September 1960; José Steve, "Des cités nouvelles sont nées dans la ville," part 4, *Le Patriote*, 21 April 1961; José Steve, "Des cités nouvelles sont nées dans la ville," part 2, *Le Patriote*, 7 March 1961.

62. Paul Thierry, "153 nouveaux appartements ne vont pas tarder à être mis en chantier à la cité-jardin Saint-Roch," *Nice Matin*, 5 May 1954; José Steve, "Des cités nouvelles sont nées dans la ville," part 1, *Le Patriote*, 16 April 1961; José Steve, "Las Planas, cité du bout du monde," part 3, *Le Patriote*, 17 May 1962. On the danger of heat in apartments not built for it, as well as the social stratification revealed by them, see Richard C. Keller, *Fatal Isolation: The Devastating Paris Heat Wave of 2003* (Chicago: University of Chicago Press, 2015).

63. By December 1962 there were 18,000 households that had registered; assuming a household size of only three to four people, 60,000 may be on the conservative side. "18,000 familles rapatriées d'Algérie se sont installées dans les Alpes-Maritimes," *Nice Matin*, 2 December 1962. Schor et al. cite the number 40,000 (*Nice cosmopolite*, 143) while Dominique Olivesi claims there were 100,000 by the end of 1965, as pieds noirs who had initially arrived elsewhere in France settled Alpes-Maritimes. Dominique Olivesi, "L'utilisation des rapatriés dans les Alpes-Maritimes (1958–1965)," *Bulletin de l'Institut d'Histoire du Temps Présent* 79 (October 2002): 130.

64. Jean-Jacques Jordi, *De l'exode à l'exile: Rapatriés et pieds-noirs en France, l'exemple Marseillais, 1954–1992* (Paris: L'Harmattan, 1993); Sung-Eun Choi, *Decolonization and the French of Algeria: Bringing the Settler Colony Home* (Basingstoke, UK: Palgrave Macmillan, 2016), 1, 58; Yann Scioldo-Zürcher, *Devenir métropolitain: Politique d'intégration et parcours de rapatriés d'Algérie en métropole (1954–2005)* (Paris: Éditions de l'École des Hautes Études en Sciences Sociales, 2010), chap. 4; Todd Shepard, *The Invention of Decolonization: The Algerian War and the Remaking of France* (Ithaca, NY: Cornell University Press, 2006), chap. 8.

65. Beccatini, "Rideaux entreouverts"; "La guerre d'Indochine nous coûte un logement à la minute et plus," *Le Patriote*, 17 April 1954; Gruson, director general of the Institut national de la statistique et des études économiques, in an interview first printed in the *Journal du Bâtiment de Nice* and quoted in Antoine Giorgi, "Quand le bâtiment ne va pas," part 1, "5,000 appartements invendus à Nice," *Le Patriote*, 27 March 1966.

66. "Départ encourageant, à Nice, de 'l'Opération rapatriés,'" *Nice Matin*, 9 April 1963; "2,189 demandes d'emplois émanant des repliés d'Algérie dans les Alpes-Maritimes," *Le Patriote*, 9 April 1963; "Opération 'priorité' d'emploi aux rapatriés," *Nice Matin*, 16 April 1963; "La formation professionnelle des rapatriés sera intensifiée," *L'Espoir*, 6 April 1963; "'L'État doit assumer les conséquences financières de son changement de politique," *L'Espoir*, 26 June 1961; "Pour les rapatriés d'Algérie," *Nice Matin*, 11 December 1962.

67. Vérots, "Le 'logement social'"; "Les grands ensembles HLM à Nice," part 2, *Nice Matin*, 10 April 1966; "Le problème numéro un: Le logement social,"

L'Indépendant, 29 January 1965; "Conférence de presse, 5 April 1966, sur la question sociale, par Monsieur Pasquetti," in Barel's papers, ADAM 84 J 5; Roger Beccatini, "La cité de l'espoir pour 2,500 candidats prioritaires aux HLM," *Le Patriote*, 13 October 1965. Jean Médecin claimed in 1963 that there were only five thousand applicants for public housing in Nice, a much lower number than the prefecture used or the newspapers reported throughout the early 1960s. See Médecin to Virgile Barel, 23 January 1963, in Barel's papers, ADAM 84 J 7. On housing for pieds noirs elsewhere in France, see Nasiali, *Native to the Republic*, 89–93; Scioldo-Zürcher, *Devenir métropolitain*, chaps. 4–5; Choi, *Decolonization and the French of Algeria*.

68. "'L'état doit assumer les conséquences financières de son changement de politique," *L'Espoir*, 26 June 1961; "Les rapatriés des Alpes-Maritimes ont tenu leur congrès à Nice," *L'Espoir*, 1 July 1963; "M. Francis Jouhaud, adjoint au maire 'rapatrié' annonce: Trois mille logements pour les 'pieds-noirs' vont être construits en cinq ans à Nice," *Nice Matin*, 6 April 1965. On the Médecins' bond with pieds noirs, see Claire Eldridge, *From Empire to Exile: History and Memory within the Pied Noir and Harki Communities, 1962–2012* (Manchester: Manchester University Press, 2016), 183–84. On Gaston Defferre's doling out of housing and other benefits in Marseille, see Nasiali, *Native to the Republic*, chap. 1; Ed Naylor, "'A System That Resembles Both Colonialism and the Invasion of France': Gaston Defferre and the Politics of Immigration in 1973," in Emmanuel Godin and Natalya Vince, eds., *France and the Mediterranean: International Relations, Culture, and Politics* (Oxford: Peter Lang, 2012), 249–74; Ed Naylor, "'Un âne dans l'ascenseur': Late Colonial Welfare Services and Social Housing in Marseille after Decolonization," *French History* 27, no. 3 (2013): 422–47.

69. "Vivre dans les grands ensembles: Béton sur champ d'azur," part 1, *Nice Matin*, 7 January 1974; Roger-Louis Bianchini, "HLM: Ce qui ne va pas!" *Nice Matin*, 18 February 1976; "Les grands ensembles HLM à Nice," part 2, *Nice Matin*, 10 April 1966.

70. "List nominative des nord-africains occupant des baraquements situés sur la colline à proximité des HLM de Saint-Roch," 14 November 1959, ADAM 207 W 130; Report from Bighetti de Flogny to the prefect, 12 March 1963, ADAM 207 W 121; "L'histoire du bidonville de Saint-Roch ou les méandres d'une inertie préfectorale," *L'Action républicaine*, 29 September 1964.

71. "Motion présentée par l'Association des Locataires des HLM Saint-Roch," to the prefect, 20 February 1963, and the Association des locataires des HLM-Saint-Roch, Bloc E, 10 Étages, to the prefect, 30 December 1961 (this was signed by all fifty-eight adult inhabitants of that building; all of the names sound European), both in ADAM 207 W 130.

72. Président de l'office municipal d'habitations à loyer modéré to prefect, 5 November 1959, ADAM 207 W 130; "L'histoire du bidonville de Saint-Roch."

73. "Destruction d'un bidonville à Saint-Roch," *Nice Matin*, 10 September 1964; "Une partie du bidonville de Saint-Roch a été demolie ce matin," *L'Espoir*, 9 September 1964.

2. Reconstructing the Riviera, Sleeping in Squats and Shantytowns

1. Letter to the mayor of Cannes, 26 February 1955, Archives municipales de cannes (AMC) 22 W 400. On the myth that North Africans had endemic rates of

syphilis infection, see Ellen Amster, "The Syphilitic Arab? A Search for Civilization in Disease Etiology, Native Prostitution, and French Colonial Medicine," in Patricia M. E. Lorcin and Todd Shepard, eds., *French Mediterraneans: Transnational and Imperial Histories* (Lincoln: University of Nebraska Press, 2016), 320–46. In the case of tuberculosis, Ralph Schor notes that Algerians more often contracted it in metropolitan France than in Algeria. Schor, *Histoire de l'immigration en France de la fin du XIXe siècle à nos jours* (Paris: Armand Colin, 1996), 216–17.

2. Mlle. Guyot describing a letter in the meeting of the Commission chargée de l'étude des problèmes de la main d'oeuvre nord africaine, undated (likely 1959), and "Main d'oeuvre nord africaine: Note de M. Gelineau," 6 June 1959, both in AMC 22 W 400. On the supposed sexual threat of "Arab men," see Todd Shepard, *Sex, France and Arab Men, 1962–1979* (Chicago: University of Chicago Press, 2018); Yvan Gastaut, "Les travailleurs immigrés au prisme des sexualités en France (1962–1983)," in Gilles Boëtsch, Nicolas Bancel, Pascal Blanchard, Sylvie Chalaye, Fanny Robles, T. Denean Sharpley-Whiting, et al., eds., *Sexualités, identités et corps colonisés, XVe siècle–XXIe siècle* (Paris: CNRS, 2019), 173–81.

3. Commissaire principal of Antibes to the mayor, 12 April 1963, ADAM 207 W 121.

4. Jean Fourastié, *Les trente glorieuses, ou la révolution invisible de 1946 à 1975* (Paris: Fayard, 1979), chap. 3; Régis Boulat, *Jean Fourastié, un expert en productivité: La modernisation de la France (années trente-années cinquante)* (Besançon: Presses universitaires de Franche-Comté, 2008).

5. On the origin and use of the term *bidonville*, see Zeynep Çelik, *Urban Forms and Colonial Confrontations: Algiers under French Rule* (Berkeley: University of California Press, 1997); Jim House, "Shantytowns and Rehousing in Late Colonial Algiers and Casablanca," in Ed Naylor, ed., *France's Modernising Mission: Citizenship, Welfare and the Ends of Empire* (London: Palgrave Macmillan, 2018), 133–63; and the memo from the Ministry of the Interior to the prefect, 16 June 1966, ADAM 207 W 122. On colonial agriculture in Algeria, see Owen White, *The Blood of the Colony: Wine and the Rise and Fall of French Algeria* (Cambridge, MA: Harvard University Press, 2021).

6. François Chavaneau of SONACOTRA to subprefect, 16 October 1975, ADAM 207 W 135.

7. "Document établi par Madame Autunes, direction des études et programmes de la SONACOTRA," 29 October 1975, 27, in Virgile Barel's papers, ADAM 84 J 45. In 1958, 94 percent of Tunisian immigrants in Alpes-Maritimes worked in BTP. See Nadhem Yousfi, *Des Tunisiens dans les Alpes-Maritimes: Une histoire locale et nationale de la migration transméditerranéenne (1956–1984)* (Paris: L'Harmattan, 2013), 148.

8. Commissaire principal of Antibes to the mayor, 11 April 1967, ADAM 207 W 121.

9. A police report from 6 June 1961 (ADAM 207 W 130) notes that the shantytown near the airport was fifteen years old. See Ralph Schor, Stéphane Mourlane, and Yvan Gastaut, *Nice cosmopolite, 1860–2010* (Paris: Éditions Autrement, 2010), 134; Bighetti de Flogny to the prefect, 30 July 1957, ADAM 207 W 126; prefect to the Ministry of the Interior, 7 February 1958, ADAM 207 W 121; "Action en faveur des Français musulmans," 11 July 1959, ADAM 207 W 121; Bighetti de Flogny, report for the prefect, 24 June 1959, ADAM 207 W 121; "Les 'migrants': 20,000 travailleurs

dans les Alpes-Maritimes dont beaucoup peuplent encore bidonvilles," *Nice Matin*, 5 February 1970; "Résorption des bidonvilles," *Bulletin d'information et recueil des actes administratifs* 20 (31 October 1970): 6–8, ADAM 207 W 125; "Résumé du rapport de M. le Sous-Préfet," 28 July 1975, AMC 1 W 167.

10. "Action en faveur des Français musulmans," 11 July 1959, ADAM 207 W 121; Bighetti de Flogny, report for the prefect, 24 June 1959; "Travailleurs musulmans originaires d'Algérie: État des familles résidant dans les Alpes-Maritimes à la date du 1er mars 1962," ADAM 207 W 125; "Procès-verbal de la réunion du comité départ-mental du service de la main d'oeuvre étrangère, 4 May 1970," ADAM 207 W 121. On the migration of Algerian families elsewhere in France before 1962, see Amelia Lyons, *The Civilizing Mission in the Metropole: Algerian Families and the French Welfare State during Decolonization* (Stanford, CA: Stanford University Press, 2013).

11. Claudius-Petit, in the minutes of the meeting in the prefecture, 23 September 1970, ADAM 207 W 125. On the ways that North Africans were imagined to be single migrant workers even in regions where they were more likely to be skilled workers or accompanied by their families, see Muriel Cohen, "Les circulations entre France et Algérie: Un nouveau regard sur les migrants (post)coloniaux (1945–1985)," *French Politics, Culture, and Society* 34, no. 2 (2016): 78–100.

12. Tahar Ben Jellou, *French Hospitality: Racism and North African Immigrants*, trans. Barbara Bray (New York: Columbia University Press, 1999), 75; Ethan B. Katz, *The Burdens of Brotherhood: Jews and Muslims from North Africa to France* (Cambridge, MA: Harvard University Press, 2015), 282–83.

13. "Par décision préfectorale, le 'squatting' ne sera plus toléré," *Nice Matin*, 5 January 1956.

14. "Nouveaux squatters au bidonville de Cimiez, à Nice," *Le Patriote*, 5 January 1956. On the broader squatters' movement and the claims of squatters' rights to housing in France, see Minayo A. Nasiali, *Native to the Republic: Empire, Social Citizenship, and Everyday Life in Marseille since 1945* (Ithaca, NY: Cornell University Press, 2016), chap. 1.

15. R. L. to the prefect, 15 September 1958; police in Cagnes-sur-Mer to prefect, 1 December 1958; prefect to R. L. in Casablanca, 3 December 1958, all in ADAM 207 W 131; Jacques Biget, note for the prefect, 30 November 1961, ADAM 207 W 130.

16. Police in Antibes to the mayor, 12 April 1963, and "Rapport semestriel d'Antibes," 30 June 1967, both in ADAM 207 W 121.

17. Marc Bighetti de Flogny, "Pour Monsieur le Directeur," 27 June 1963, ADAM 207 W 121.

18. Police list dated 1 July 1963, ADAM 207 W 122; Secrétaire d'état auprès du premier ministre chargé des affaires algériennes to the prefect, 10 October 1963, ADAM 207 W 121. Amelia Lyons and Dustin Harris note that most Algerians in France did not live in bidonvilles. In Alpes-Maritimes, which was an outlier, most did in the early 1960s, though the proportion declined by the early 1970s. Lyons, *Civilizing Mission*, 279; Harris, "Maghrebis in Marseille: North African Immigration and French Social Welfare in the Late Colonial and Postcolonial Eras" (PhD diss., University of Toronto, 2018), 146.

19. Prefect to the president of the republic, 1 July 1963, ADAM 207 W 130; "10,000 habitants dans les bidonvilles de la Côte d'Azur," *Nice Matin*, 13 August 1974.

20. Internal report in the prefecture, 9 June 1967, ADAM 207 W 130; Bighetti de Flogny, "L'Action sociale en faveur des Français musulmans dans les Alpes-Maritimes," 20 October 1961, ADAM 207 W 125. Bighetti de Flogny was one of the *conseillers techniques aux affaires musulmanes* appointed to prefectures. Others made the same point. See Jean Le Camus, "Vivre dans un bidonville," *Nice Matin,* Cannes edition, 16 June 1967; commissaire de police of the 7e arrondissement of Nice to the commissaire divisionnaire, 28 January 1958, ADAM 207 W 130.

21. O. S. to the directeur des services de l'hygiène in Cannes, 15 July 1957, AMC 22 W 400. On the history of odor in modern France, notably the "stench of the poor," see Alain Corbin, *The Foul and the Fragrant: Odor and the French Social Imagination* (Cambridge, MA: Harvard University Press, 1986), esp. 142–60.

22. M. L. to the prefect, 21 July 1958; prefect to M. L., 4 August 1958; police to the prefect, 1 August 1958, all in ADAM 207 W 130.

23. "Dans le cadre du projet de résorption du bidonville de la digue des Français," *Nice Matin,* 6 February 1974; "Note pour M. le directeur du cabinet," 8 May 1963, ADAM 207 W 121; "Laissera-t-on proliférer des bidonvilles insalubres, inesthétiques, même au centre de Cagnes?" *Le Patriote,* Cannes edition, 17 June 1967; "Les bidonvilles, plaies purulentes au flanc de notre département," *Le Var: Information,* 3 June 1967; Prefect Thomas quoted in "Résorption des bidonvilles," 6–8, and his remarks in the minutes of the 23 September 1970 meeting with Claudius-Petit, both in ADAM 207 W 125; Bighetti de Flogny, "Pour M. le directeur, cabinet du préfet," 21 March 1966, ADAM 207 W 121; Georges Gelineau to mayor of Cannes, 5 October 1959, AMC 22 W 400.

24. "Saint-Augustin: Les bidonvilles, un problème national," *Nice Matin,* 30 October 1970; Thomas quoted in "Résorption des bidonvilles" and his remarks in the minutes of the 23 September 1970 meeting with Claudius-Petit; "Un problème à la fois humain, social, et esthétique: Le cancer des 'bidonvilles,'" *Nice Matin,* 22 May 1965. The comparison of bidonvilles to cancer or disease was of course not unique to the Riviera. See, for example, Harris, "Maghrebis in Marseille," chap. 3.

25. Bighetti de Flogny repeated the notion in "Pour Monsieur le directeur du cabinet," 27 June 1963, ADAM 207 W 121.

26. "L'Action sociale en faveur des français musulmans dans les Alpes-Maritimes." On the racialization of North African Muslims, see Naomi Davidson, *Only Muslim: Embodying Islam in Twentieth-Century France* (Ithaca, NY: Cornell University Press, 2012).

27. Kristin Ross, *Fast Cars, Clean Bodies: Decolonization and the Reordering of French Culture* (Cambridge, MA: MIT Press, 1996). On the newfound preoccupation with hygiene in the 1950s, see Steven Zdatny, "The French Hygiene Offensive of the 1950s: A Critical Moment in the History of Manners," *Journal of Modern History* 84 (December 2012): 897–932. For North Africans' views of bidonvilles, see the interviews in Monique Hervo and Marie-Ange Charras, *Bidonvilles: L'enlisement* (Paris: Maspero, 1971), and for the Alpes-Maritimes, see Riadh Ben Khalifa and Alain Bottaro, "Les archives orales et l'histoire de l'immigration," *Recherches régionales* 194 (July-December 2009): 71–80; Riadh Ben Khalifa, "Rapport sur une enquête orale concernant la population maghrébine et la digue des Français," *Recherches régionales* 196 (July-December 2010): 103–18. For information about medieval bathhouses, closed during the early modern period, I thank Ellen Wurzel for a copy of her paper "Pleasure, Passion and Purgation: Bathing Together in the Middle Ages."

28. On the "agency" of Algerians in France, see Cohen, "Les circulations," 79.

29. Michel de Certeau, *The Practice of Everyday Life*, trans. Steven F. Rendall (Berkeley: University of California Press, 1984). On the building of dwellings from the materials at hand, see also Tim Ingold, *The Perception of the Environment: Essays on Livelihood, Dwelling, and Skill* (London: Routledge, 2011), 172–88.

30. Bighetti de Flogny, for the prefect, to the Ministry of the Interior, 18 June 1958, ADAM 207 W 130.

31. Such as the Moroccan mason Mohammed Guezbiri whom Riadh Ben Khalifa interviewed for "Rapport sur une enquête orale."

32. Prefect (with Bighetti de Flogny's initials) to Raoul Bosio, of the mayor's office, 1 July 1958; Raoul Bosio of the Office Public Municipal HLM to the prefect, 4 June 1958; Bosio to the prefect, 23 January 1958, all in ADAM 207 W 130. Bosio also claimed that the Algerians threatened to kill the contractor and his workers, promising to use machine guns. Marginalia indicate that someone in the prefecture questioned the veracity of this claim.

33. Police report, 28 January 1958, ADAM 207 W 130.

34. Georges Gelineau reporting, in the meeting minutes of the Commission chargée de l'étude des problèmes de la main d'oeuvre nord africaine, undated (likely 1959); Georges Gelineau to mayor of Cannes, 5 October 1959, both in AMC 22 W 400.

35. "Note pour le secrétaire général pour les affaires économiques, la police et le personnel," initialed by Bighetti de Flogny, 24 August 1961, and police report to the Commissaire central in Menton, 1 September 1960, both in ADAM 207 W 131.

36. P. G. to the mayor of Roquebrune-Cap-Martin, 14 September 1961, and E. M. to the mayor of Roquebrune-Cap-Martin, 16 September 1961, both in ADAM 207 W 131.

37. Telephone message no. 76, from the police commissariat in Menton, January 1962, and police report, 1 September 1960, both in ADAM 207 W 131.

38. Police report, 14 September 1960, ADAM 207 W 131.

39. Petition addressed to the president, 15 June 1963, and report from RG to the Commissaire principal, 5 July 1963, both in ADAM 207 W 131.

40. General Consul of Algeria to the prefect, 22 June 1963; prefect to the general consul, 8 July 1963; note for the prefect, signed by the secrétaire général, 2 July 1963, all in ADAM 207 W 131.

41. "Fiches signalétiques des bidonvilles," September 1970, ADAM 207 W 125; R. Fouich, note for the prefect, 6 May 1974, ADAM 207 W 134.

42. D. de L. to prefect, 25 October 1960, ADAM 207 W 130.

43. Commissaire principal of 6e arrondissement to the prefect, 24 October 1960; prefect to D. de L. 16 November 1960; D. de L. to the prefect, 19 November 1960; Bighetti de Flogny to the prefect, 23 November 1960, all in ADAM 207 W 130.

44. "État d'esprit des travailleurs nord-africains," 7 July 1959, on RG stationery, ADAM 207 W 130. On FLN collections, see Lyons, *Civilizing Mission*, 144–45.

45. "Résorption des bidonvilles." On the broader context of migration to twentieth-century France, see Michael A. Kozakowski, "Making 'Mediterranean Migrants': Geopolitical Transitions, Migratory Policy, and French Conceptions of the Mediterranean in the 20th Century," *Cahiers de la Méditerranée* 89 (2014): 181–93; Gérard

Noiriel, *The French Melting Pot: Immigration, Citizenship, and National Identity*, trans. Geoffroy de Laforcade (Minneapolis: University of Minnesota Press, 1996); Schor, *Histoire de l'immigration*.

46. "Rapport semestriel d'Antibes," 30 June 1967, and Commissaire principal in Antibes to the mayor, 12 April 1963, both in ADAM 207 W 121.

47. Police reports, 20 September 1974 and 21 November 1974, ADAM 207 W 123.

48. Police reports, 20 November 1974 and 21 November 1974, ADAM 207 W 123.

49. Police report, 21 November 1974, ADAM 207 W 123.

50. Neil MacMaster has noted that Europeans of lower socioeconomic status were usually the least hostile to Algerian migrant workers. MacMaster, *Colonial Migrants and Racism: Algerians in France, 1900–62* (New York: St. Martin's, 1997), 190–91.

51. Bighetti de Flogny to the prefect on the views of Michel Massenet, Délégué de l'action sociale pour les Français musulmans, serving in Prime Minister Debré's cabinet, 24 November 1960, ADAM 207 W 121. On the Constantine Plan, see Herrick Chapman, *France's Long Reconstruction: In Search of the Modern Republic* (Cambridge, MA: Harvard University Press, 2018), 278–89; Muriam Haleh Davis, "Restaging Mise en Valeur: 'Postwar Imperialism' and the Plan de Constantine," *Review of Middle East Studies* 44, no. 2 (2010): 176–86; Muriam Haleh Davis, "'The Transformation of Man' in French Algeria: Economic Planning and the Postwar Social Sciences, 1958–62," *Journal of Contemporary History* 52 (2017): 73–94. On Massenet, see Vincent Viet, *La France immigrée: Construction d'une politique, 1914–1997* (Paris: Fayard, 1998), 190–205.

52. Police reports of 5 March 1963 and 12 April 1963, both in ADAM 207 W 121.

53. "L'Action sociale en faveur des Français Musulmans dans les Alpes-Maritimes"; "Document établi par Madame Autunes," 21–22; employer quoted in "La fin d'un bidonville," *Le Patriote*, 4–12 April 1970.

54. Chavaneau to subprefect, 16 October 1975, ADAM 207 W 135. To give but one example of North Africans' presumed responsibility for hospitalizations, Fernand Icart, deputy in the National Assembly and assistant mayor in Nice, pointed out North Africans' higher rates of hospitalization and thus higher health care costs. "Une question écrite de M Fernand Icart, député des Alpes-Maritimes, sur les problèmes posés par l'immigration algérienne," *Nice Matin*, 24 May 1970.

55. Joseph Bohling, *The Sober Revolution: Appellation Wine and the Transformation of France* (Ithaca, NY: Cornell University Press, 2018), 143, citing Raymond Girard, "Les Français malades de l'alcool," *Réalités*, September 1957, 71.

56. Marcel Rudo, "Pour éviter le chômage, l'Algérien devrait-il accepter toutes les illégalités?" *Le Patriote*, 3 January 1954. Accepting a job *non-déclaré* meant no *allocations familiales*, *sécurité sociale*, or worker protections, but small employers in construction could easily skirt the law and get recent arrivals to accept such a condition of employment. For those who arrived illegally, that is, Moroccans, Tunisians, and workers from sub-Saharan Africa, employers had even more leverage. See Yousfi, *Des Tunisiens*, chap. 2.

57. J. Tiberi, of the Union Syndicale de la Construction des Alpes-Maritimes, 21 November 1975, ADAM 207 W 134; Marcel Rudo, "Sur le toit de la maison le maçon ne chante pas," *Le Patriote*, 6 June 1952; Jean Claude, "Immeubles en construction sur la Côte d'Azur," *Le Patriote*, 22 February 1952.

58. Marcel Rudo, "De l'Oued [El] Kebir aux rives du Var," a series in *Le Patriote*, part 1, "Un homme cherche ses frères," 27 December 1953; part 2, "Comment Nice accueille Ali Draa," 29 December 1953; part 3, "Première ressource, l'asile de nuit," 30 December 1953; part 4, "Agressions nocturnes, coups de couteaux, légende colonialiste," 31 December 1953; part 5, "Pour éviter le chômage, l'Algérien devrait-il accepter toutes les illégalités?" 3 January 1954; part 6, "Où ils logent? Partout et nulle part," 5 January 1954. Amelia Lyons (*Civilizing Mission*, 96) estimates that in 1955, Algerian workers received 33 to 70 percent of the usual benefit, depending on the number of children.

59. Commissaire principal of Antibes to the mayor, 11 April 1967, ADAM 207 W 121; Aide aux travailleurs nord-africains, Nice, "Rapport Moral de l'Assistante Sociale Départementale," 29 April 1957, AMC 22 W 400.

60. Chapman, *France's Long Reconstruction*, 73–74; Marcel Berlinghoff, "'Faux Touristes'? Tourism in European Migration Regimes in the Long Sixties," *Comparativ* 24, no. 2 (2014): 88–99.

61. "Note pour M le Préfet (Cabinet)—Affaires musulmanes," 29 March 1963, and Commissaire principal, 6e arrondissement of Nice, report of 23 October 1962, both in ADAM 207 W 130.

62. Société des grands travaux de Marseille to Bighetti de Flogny, 15 December 1962; Société Clémente to the prefecture, 26 November 1962; Vultaggio maçonnerie to Bighetti de Flogny, 26 November 1962; Cecchi to Bighetti de Flogny, 27 November 1962; Nicoletti to Bighetti de Flogny, 28 November 1962, all in ADAM 207 W 130.

63. Procès-verbal/constat de l'huissier, 9 May 1963, and directeur du Bureau d'hygiène de Nice to the prefect, 30 May 1963, both in ADAM 207 W 121.

64. Prefect to the minister of the interior, 12 July 1966, ADAM 207 W 131.

65. General consulate of Tunisia in Marseille to the prefect, 9 June 1967; general consulate of Algeria in Marseille to the prefect, 17 August 1967; prefect to the Ministry of Foreign Affairs, copied to the Ministry of the Interior, 30 August 1967, all in ADAM 207 W 130. Setting fires had long been a political act in France and its empire. See C. Kieko Matteson, "Lucifer Sticks and Briquets Bics: Arson as Environmental Protest in France," paper presented at the annual meeting of the Western Society for French History, Bozeman, Montana, 3–5 October 2019; Christopher Church, *Paradise Destroyed: Catastrophe and Citizenship in the French Caribbean* (Lincoln: University of Nebraska Press, 2017).

66. "Un incendie a détruit le bidonville des Nord-Africains situé face à l'aéroport de Nice," *Nice Matin*, 11 May 1961; "Ce matin, au parc de l'Olivetto," *L'Espoir*, 21 September 1965; "Un incendie ravage la presque totalité d'un bidonville," *Nice Matin*, 22 September 1965; "Le bidonville est ravagé par un incendie," *Le Patriote*, 22 September 1965; "L'incendie du 'bidonville' de l'Olivetto," *L'Espoir*, 16 June 1966.

67. Commissaire principal 6e arrondissement of Nice to the commissaire divisionnaire, 7 June 1967, ADAM 207 W 130; "Un nouvel incendie ravage le bidonville de l'Arénas," *Le Patriote*, 8 June 1967.

68. Police in Cagnes-sur-Mer to the prefect, 9 June 1967, ADAM 207 W 122; note of telephone call from the police in Cagnes-sur-Mer to prefecture, 9 June 1967, ADAM 207 W 130; RG report of 9 June 1967, ADAM 207 W 122; police in Cagnes to prefect, 9 June 1967, ADAM 207 W 131 (quotation).

69. Police in Cannes to the subprefect in Grasse, 10 September 1966, ADAM 207 W 131; the tract and report about it in the 1967 internal prefectoral report about bidonvilles, 9 June 1967, ADAM 207 W 130.

70. Report from RG (2e Groupe, Section Afrique du Nord), 9 June 1967, ADAM 207 W 130; police report titled "Incendie du bidonville de l'Arénas," 14 June 1967, ADAM 207 W 122 (quotation).

71. "Rapport semestriel d'Antibes," 30 June 1967; prefect to the Ministry of the Interior and the Ministry of Foreign Affairs, 9 June 1967; Bigetti de Flogny to prefect, 5 May 1970, all in ADAM 207 W 130.

72. Laborie of SONACOTRA to prefect, 20 April 1970, ADAM 207 W 130; Mustapha Cherrak, Algerian consul, to the prefect, 27 November 1972, ADAM 207 W 123; M. A. Vidal, "Solidarité du PCF aux travailleurs immigrés au bidonville de la plaine du Var," *Le Patriote*, 22 June 1973.

73. Internal prefectoral report, ADAM 207 W 130, just after the 9 June 1967 instructions from prefect to police, requesting that they provide surveillance and protection for all shantytowns in the department of Alpes-Maritimes.

74. Commissaire divisionnaire to the prefect, 22 January 1971, ADAM 207 W 125.

75. Joanine Roy, "Le RACISME sous toutes ses formes entretient les bidonvilles," *Le Monde*, 17 April 1968.

76. Minister of the interior to the prefects of the region and of Alpes-Maritimes, 13 August 1970, ADAM 328 W 11. On the national policy and process of bidonville elimination, see Marie-Claude Blanc-Chaléard, *En finir avec les bidonvilles: Immigration et politique du logement dans la France des trente glorieuses* (Paris: Publications de la Sorbonne, 2016).

77. Despite their persistence, police did not find the extent of political activity on the part of North Africans that they expected. There were exceptions, such as F. K., a native of Algeria, who worked for the Grands Travaux de l'Est as a mason. When F. K., who belonged to the CGT, attempted to mobilize fellow workers, RG officers hauled him in and reminded him that, as a foreigner, if he did not respect political neutrality, he would be expelled from France. RG report, 15 December 1971, ADAM 328 W 11. For more on both the development of anti-racist sentiment in France after 1968 and the role of Algerians in developing it, see Daniel A. Gordon, *Immigrants and Intellectuals: May '68 and the Rise of Anti-Racism in France* (Pontypool, UK: Merlin Press, 2012).

78. "À propos du bidonville de la digue des Français," *Nice Matin*, 13 August 1974.

79. "Après les incendies des bidonvilles: Un communiqué de l'UD-CGT," *Le Patriote*, 11 June 1967. Virgile Barel was remarkably consistent; it was the same argument he had used in the 1930s, in defense of Italian immigrant workers. See Schor et al., *Nice cosmopolite*, 102. At the time of Barel's death in 1979, French communists were doing an about-face, attempting to use anti-immigrant sentiment among workers to increase political support (rather than educating European workers in order to avert racist responses as had been the norm after World War II). See Neil MacMaster, *Racism in Europe, 1870–2000* (New York: Palgrave Macmillan, 2001), 186–89.

80. Telegram from the Commissaire divisionnaire, 12 April 1970, ADAM 207 W 130.

81. RG report, 11 April 1970, and the attached CGT tract, ""Un scandale que les travailleurs ne veulent plus voir," ADAM 207 W 130.

82. Bighetti de Flogny, report for the prefect, 5 May 1970, ADAM 207 W 130; RG report, 14 April 1970, ADAM 328 W 11.

83. Report from gendarmerie in Nice to the prefect, 7 January 1970, with an attached political tract, ADAM 328 W 11; report from RG to prefect, 11 April 1970, ADAM 207 W 130.

84. RG report to the prefect, 11 April 1970, and the attached Gauche prolétarienne tract, "On voit qui sont nos amis et nos ennemis," ADAM 207 W 130 (quotation); RG report to the prefect with the tract attached, 23 October 1970, ADAM 328 W 11.

85. RG report to the prefect, 28 June 1971, and RG report with the tract attached, 14 June 1971, both ADAM 328 W 11.

86. Schor et al., *Nice cosmopolite*, 146–47. Priest Aloys Carton, one of the religious leaders involved, has an interview in the Archives nationales collection "Histoire et mémoire de l'immigration, mobilisation et lutte pour l'égalité, 1968–1988," Centre des archives contemporaines, Archives nationales (CAC) 20160153/14. On the Tunisian hunger strikes and other North African political activity across France, see Gordon, *Immigrants and Intellectuals*, 127–30; Katz, *Burdens of Brotherhood*, 282–93; Maud S. Mandel, *Muslims and Jews in France: History of a Conflict* (Princeton, NJ: Princeton University Press, 2014), chap. 5. In essence, the Tunisians had been caught by the Marcellin-Fontanet decrees, which required workers to have a job contract before they could get a residency card, thus changing the long-standing practice of normalizing workers' status after they entered as tourists or clandestinely.

87. Dr. Motte, "Rapport sur la lutte contre l'habitat insalubre dans les Alpes-Maritimes," 22 February 1973, ADAM 207 W 124; "La résorption de l'habitat insalubre," *Le Moniteur*, 11 September 1971.

88. Prime minister to other ministers and the prefects, 26 June 1973, ADAM 207 W 124 and AMC 60 W 63.

89. "Les bidonvilles de Nice," *L'Espoir*, 10 September 1971; "Après le dramatique incendie du bidonville de la route de Marseille: Le problème du logement des travailleurs migrants," *Nice Matin*, 14 September 1971; M. A. Vidal, "Solidarité du PCF aux travailleurs immigrés au bidonville de la plaine du Var," *Le Patriote*, 22 June 1973; on Pompidou's abstract condemnation of racism as well as the wave of violence in Marseille that caused a sense of crisis, see Ed Naylor, "'A System That Resembles Both Colonialism and the Invasion of France': Gaston Defferre and the Politics of Immigration in 1973," in Emmanuel Godin and Natalya Vince, eds., *France and the Mediterranean: International Relations, Culture, and Politics* (Oxford: Peter Lang, 2012), 257–58.

90. François Chavaneau, "À Nice, l'Oued, dernier grand bidonville de France, vient d'être résorbé," *Bulletin GIP: Groupe interministériel permanent pour la résorption de l'habitat insalubre* 20 (2e trimestre 1976): 4–9.

91. Brain-damaged, Bougrine killed a French bus driver in Marseille in August 1973, setting off right-wing violence to which Algerians responded with strikes. See Gordon, *Immigrants and Intellectuals*, 145.

92. M. A. Vidal, "Solidarité du PCF aux travailleurs immigrés au bidonville de la plaine du Var," *Le Patriote*, 22 June 1973; Chavaneau, "À Nice, l'Oued"; Schor et al., *Nice cosmopolite*, 146.

93. Bighetti de Flogny to the prefect on the views of Michel Massenet, 24 November 1960.

94. Minister of the interior to prefects, 6 December 1957, ADAM 207 W 121.

95. Claudius-Petit, in the minutes of the meeting in the prefecture, 23 September 1970, ADAM 207 W 125.

96. On the SONACOTRA generally, see Marc Bernardot, *Loger les immigrés: La Sonacotra, 1956–2006* (Paris: Éditions du Croquant, 2008); Nasiali, *Native to the Republic*, 78–82, 94–99; Lyons, *Civilizing Mission*, esp. chap. 4.

97. Bighetti de Flogny, report for the prefect, 16 January 1961, and prefect to the Ministry of the Interior, 7 February 1958, both in ADAM 207 W 121.

98. Prefect (written by Bighetti de Flogny) to Jean Médecin, 15 March 1964, ADAM 207 W 130.

99. "Algerian" is in quotation marks in the original as if to suggest that it did not exist as a category, a denial of the legitimacy of the Évian Accords. "L'histoire du bidonville de Saint-Roch où les méandres d'une inertie préfectorale," *L'Action républicaine*, 29 September 1964. On the influence of mayors in housing policy regarding North Africans, see Ed Naylor, "'Un âne dans l'ascenseur': Late Colonial Welfare Services and Social Housing in Marseille after Decolonization," *French History* 27, no. 3 (2013): 422–47; Nasiali, *Native to the Republic*.

100. Note for the prefect, 1 April 1966, in folder "Note détaillée sur tout ce que nous avons fait depuis 7 ans pour convaincre le maire," ADAM 207 W 121; mayor to the prefect, 21 March 1963, ADAM 207 W 130.

101. Mayor to the prefect, 22 July 1963, ADAM 207 W 121; mayor to the prefect, 21 March 1963.

102. Bighetti de Flogny's draft for the prefect's letter to the head of the Office Public d'HLMs, 18 November 1959, ADAM 207 W 130.

103. Bighetti de Flogny, "Pour Monsieur le Directeur," 27 June 1963, ADAM 207 W 121.

104. This was according to the CGT delegates, reported by RG to prefecture, 20 April 1970, ADAM 207 W 130.

105. Secrétaire d'état auprès du premier ministre chargé des affaires algériennes to prefect, 10 October 1963, ADAM 207 W 121. Médecin, for his part, claimed in 1960 that the *foyers* for North Africans in Lyon caused the city to be "invaded" by them, so that there were now twenty-five thousand in Lyon. Mayor to prefect, 9 December 1960, ADAM 207 W 121.

106. The prefect to the secrétaire d'état auprès du premier ministre chargé des affaires algériennes, 20 December 1963, ADAM 207 W 121. That sentiment was already well established in 1959, well before the independence of Algeria. At that time, Europeans from Indochina, Morocco, Tunisia, and Algeria were, despite assumptions in France to the contrary, not always well heeled, and their associations vocalized resentment about any priority given to the problems of Algerians in France. "Action en faveur des Français musulmans," 11 July 1959, ADAM 207 W 121.

107. "Des rapatriés s'opposent à la construction d'un foyer pour célibataires où habiteraient des Nords-Africains," *Le Monde*, 12 October 1966.

108. Claudius-Petit, in the minutes of the meeting in the prefecture, 23 September 1970, ADAM 207 W 125.

109. Commissaire divisionnaire to the prefect, 22 January 1971, ADAM 207 W 125.

110. Minutes of the meeting in the prefecture, 23 September 1970, ADAM 207 W 125.

111. Michel Hébert to the prefect, 21 May 1963, and prefect to the mayor of Antibes, 28 May 1963, both in ADAM 207 W 121.

112. "Une solution positive au problème du logement des migrants," Nice Matin, 13 December 1973.

113. "Procès-verbal de la réunion de la commission chargée au logement des travailleurs nord-africains," 24 August 1959, AMC 22 W 400.

114. RG report to the prefect, 6 April 1970, ADAM 207 W 130; "Dans le cadre du projet de résorption du bidonville de la digue des Français," Nice Matin, 6 February 1974.

115. Bighetti de Flogny to the prefect, 27 March 1968, ADAM 207 W 130.

116. Draft of memo to police by Bighetti de Flogny on behalf of prefect, undated but clearly from March 1968, ADAM 207 W 130.

117. Prefect to the minister of the interior, 27 May 1968, ADAM 207 W 127; "Les 'migrants': 20,000 travailleurs dans les Alpes-Maritimes dont beaucoup peuplent encore bidonvilles," Nice Matin, 5 February 1970; meeting minutes of the departmental commission des bidonvilles, 21 June 1968, ADAM 207 W 121.

118. Bighetti de Flogny to the prefect, 27 March 1968, ADAM 207 W 130.

119. Roger Cans, "Les bidonvilles de Nice," L'Espoir, 15 September 1971; Bernardot, Loger les immigrés, 60–61; prefect to the commissariat central, 29 August 1968, ADAM 207 W 130.

120. Bighetti de Flogny called the city bus service and confirmed that the first bus left at 6:00 a.m., but with one bus per hour, a worker arriving just after 6:00 would need to wait for the 7:00 bus. "Compte-rendu d'audience," for the prefect, 8 April 1970, ADAM 207 W 130. Just as significant, other files indicate that some workers began work as early as 3:00 a.m., long before the bus ran.

121. "Après le dramatique incendie"; "Les 'migrants'"; Commissaire principal to the commissaire divisionnaire, 27 November 1968, ADAM 207 W 130.

122. Letter to the prefect, 26 November 1968, ADAM 207 W 130.

123. Président de l'Office Public Municipal d'HLM G. Blanchard to the prefect, 19 November 1968, ADAM 207 W 130.

124. Letter to the prefect, 26 November 1968, and "Note pour Monsieur le Préfet 'Cabinet,'" 13 March 1969, both in ADAM 207 W 130.

125. Bighetti de Flogny, report for the prefect, 5 May 1970, ADAM 207 W 130; "Les 'migrants.'"

126. Lyons, Civilizing Mission, 179; Jean-Pierre Perrin, "La résorption des bidonvilles entre 1970 et 1975: Présentation statistique," Bulletin GIP: Groupe interministériel permanent pour la résorption de l'habitat insalubre 20 (2e trimester 1976): 2–3; "10,000 habitants dans les bidonvilles de la Côte d'Azur," Nice Matin, 13 August 1974. The number ten thousand includes both the large, well-established bidonvilles and the smaller locaux insalubres embedded in neighborhoods such as Vieux Nice. R. Fouich, note for the prefect, 6 May 1974, ADAM 207 W 134; subprefect of Grasse, "Recensement des bidonvilles dans le département des Alpes-Maritimes, 13 March 1975," ADAM 207 W 121.

127. "Les bidonvilles de Nice," L'Espoir, 10 September 1971.

128. "Opération de résorption des bidonvilles de Nice," 10 September 1973, ADAM 207 W 134.

129. "Les travailleurs immigrés dans les Alpes-Maritimes," SONACOTRA, 29 October 1975, in Barel's papers, ADAM 89 J 45; Nadhem Yousfi, "Les Tunisiens dans le bidonville de 'la digue des Français,'" *Recherches régionales* 194 (July-December 2009): 57–69.

130. Chavaneau, "À Nice, l'Oued"; R. Fouich, note for the prefect, 6 May 1974.

131. Lieutenant-Colonel Bagarie of the gendarmerie to the prefect of AM, 16 July 1970, ADAM 328 W 11; Commissaire divisionnaire to the prefect, 22 January 1971, ADAM 207 W 125; RG report to the prefect of the region, copied to the prefect, 20 February 1970, ADAM 328 W 11.

132. Bighetti de Flogny, note for the prefect, 12 January 1968, ADAM 207 W 130; Claudius-Petit, in the minutes of the meeting in the prefecture, 23 September 1970, ADAM 207 W 125.

133. Chavaneau to the prefect, 1 August 1975; R. Fouich, note for the prefect, 6 May 1974; and "Objet: Opération de résorption des bidonvilles de Nice," 10 September 1973, all in ADAM 207 W 134; quotation from "Les travailleurs immigrés dans les Alpes-Maritimes," SONACOTRA, 29 October 1975, in Barel's papers, ADAM 89 J 45.

134. Pierre Espagne, "Note concernant les travailleurs maghrébins du bidonville de la digue des Français," July 1975; Bernard Boucault, "À l'attention de Monsieur Fouich," 22 October 1973; J. Hubert, "Note pour le secrétaire général," 29 April 1974; prefect to the mayor of Nice, 14 September 1971, all in ADAM 207 W 134.

135. RG report to the prefect of the region, copied to the prefect of Alpes-Maritimes, 20 February 1970, ADAM 328 W 11. In 1972 the Marcellin-Fontanet decrees made the same requirement for France as a whole. On the Office national d'immigration, see Chapman, *France's Long Reconstruction*, 63–74.

136. Pierre Espagne to Subprefect Pascal, chargé de mission, 28 November 1975, and "Note d'information: La résorption des bidonvilles de Nice," 11 March 1976, both in ADAM 207 W 134.

137. "Le quartier du bidonville de la digue des Français ravagé par un violent incendie," *Nice Matin*, 2 July 1974.

138. "Le problème du logement des travailleurs immigrés," *Nice Matin*, 13 August 1974.

139. SONACOTRA, report titled "Nice: Mission d'information de la population à l'occasion de la résorption du bidonville de la digue des Français," 16 July 1975, ADAM 207 W 134; Chavaneau, "À Nice, l'Oued." On the notion that pieds noirs were inevitably racist, see Todd Shepard, "Pieds-Noirs, Bêtes Noires: Anti-'European of Algeria' Racism and the Close of the French Empire," in Patricia M. E. Lorcin, ed., *Algeria and France, 1800–2000: Identity, Memory, Nostalgia* (Syracuse, NY: Syracuse University Press, 2006), 150–63.

140. Bighetti de Flogny's report, "L'Action sociale en faveur des Français musulmans dans les Alpes-Maritimes," 20 October 1961; Bighetti de Flogny, "Note pour M. le directeur, cabinet du préfet," 29 September 1970; Balarello in the minutes of the meeting in the prefecture, 23 September 1970, all in ADAM 207 W 125.

141. Claudius-Petit, in the minutes of the meeting in the prefecture, 23 September 1970, ADAM 207 W 125; Pierre Costa, note for the prefect, 2 August 1973, ADAM

207 W 134. See also Nasiali, *Native to the Republic*, 100–108; Naylor, "'System,'" 249–74; Shepard, *Sex, France and Arab Men*, 232–34.

142. M. A. Vidal, "Solidarité du PCF aux travailleurs immigrés au bidonville de la plaine du Var," *Le Patriote*, 22 June 1973; Chavaneau, "À Nice, l'Oued"; Direction de l'équipement et du logement to the prefect, 8 February 1973, ADAM 175 W 176; J. Hubert, "Note pour le secrétaire général, 29 April 1974; "Compte rendu de la réunion à l'aéroport," 31 August 1973; Directeur départemental de l'action sanitaire et sociale Raymond Anquetin to the prefect, 29 November 1970, both in ADAM 207 W 134.

3. Providing Potable Water and WCs

1. Alain Ruggiero, *Nouvelle histoire de Nice* (Toulouse: Privat, 2006), 249; Jean-Louis Panicacci, *Les Alpes-Maritimes 1939–1945: Un département dans la tourmente* (Nice: Serre, 1989), 283. The men followed in the footsteps of the doughboys; 150,000 American soldiers had taken leave on the Riviera at the end of World War I. See Robert Rudney, "From Luxury to Popular Tourism: The Transformation of the Resort City of Nice" (PhD diss., University of Michigan, 1979), 110; Harvey Levenstein, *Seductive Journey: American Tourists in France from Jefferson to the Jazz Age* (Chicago: University of Chicago Press, 1998), 223.

2. Hélène Vuischard, "L'usine d'ozonisation de Moscou," *Nice Matin*, 26 July 1970. During World War I the US Army in France chlorinated drinking water as did the French army in the Verdun sector, hence the French term *verdunisation* to refer to the process. After initial use in Paris in 1911, other French municipalities began chlorinating water supplies in the 1920s. See Stéphane Frioux, *Les batailles de l'hygiène: De Pasteur aux trente glorieuses* (Paris: Presses universitaires de France, 2013), 299–313.

3. Virgile Barel, *Cinquante années de luttes* (Paris: Éditions Sociales, 1967), 310. In the pages of *Nice Matin*, reporter Serge Benedetti insisted as late as 1982 that "in the United States, the hygiene maniacs prefer the tenacious odor of bleach." Benedetti, "Adieu le chlore; voici l'ozone," *Nice Matin*, 5 November 1982.

4. Ingénieur en chef des Ponts et Chaussées Méchin to the Ministry of the Interior, 27 July 1946, ADAM 60 W 6; Paul Thierry, "La baie des Anges pourra être bientôt assainie," *Nice Matin*, 17 July 1949.

5. On the United States as a symbol of modernity in twentieth-century France, see Christopher Endy, *Cold War Holidays: American Tourism in France* (Chapel Hill: University of North Carolina Press, 2004); Victoria de Grazia, *Irresistible Empire: America's Advance through Twentieth-Century Europe* (Cambridge, MA: Harvard University Press, 2006); Richard F. Kuisel, *The French Way: How France Embraced and Rejected American Values and Power* (Princeton, NJ: Princeton University Press, 2012); Richard F. Kuisel, *Seducing the French: The Dilemma of Americanization* (Berkeley: University of California Press, 1997).

6. Frioux, *Les batailles de l'hygiène*; William B. Cohen, *Urban Government and the Rise of the French City* (New York: St. Martin's, 1998), chap. 7. For the global historical context of water provisioning and sewage removal, see Ian Douglas, *Cities: An Environmental History* (London: I. B. Taurus, 2013), chaps. 5–6.

7. Alison Frank's description of air applies to water: "Even if no human labor went into making air, a great deal of human ingenuity, of mental and physical work, went into creating the demand for certain types of air, in gaining access to those types of air, in storing, marketing, and packaging it for sale, and in distributing access to it." Just as alpine air underwent commodification as tourist infrastructure made it both accessible to some people while inaccessible to most, water also become a commodity. Alison F. Frank, "The Air Cure Town: Commodifying Mountain Air in Alpine Central Europe," *Central European History* 45 (June 2012): 186.

8. C. James Haug, *Leisure and Urbanism in Nineteenth-Century Nice* (Lawrence: University Press of Kansas, 1982), 95–108. For a comparative perspective, see David Soll, *Empire of Water: An Environmental and Political History of the New York City Water Supply* (Ithaca, NY: Cornell University Press, 2013).

9. Haug, *Leisure and Urbanism*, 107; Steven Johnson, *The Ghost Map: The Story of London's Most Terrifying Epidemic and How It Changed Science, Cities, and the Modern World* (New York: Riverhead, 2006).

10. "1864–1964," *Nice Matin*, 16 January 1964; Michel Savini, "Il y a 101 ans, la ville de Nice achetait les sources de Sainte-Thècle pour 90 francs," *Nice Matin*, 7 September 1965. One main went to Nice while a second went directly to Villefranche. Although the granting of private concessions for the development of municipal water supplies began only in the Second Empire, it became the norm in France. As late as 1964 the Compagnie générale des eaux alone still supplied one out of every five French people with potable water. Compagnie générale des eaux, "Cent années à Nice et dans les Alpes-Maritimes, 1864–1964," in Virgile Barel's papers, ADAM 89 J 63. On the use of private companies to supply water to wealthy subscribers in the late nineteenth century, see Erik Swyngedouw, *Social Power and the Urbanization of Water: Flows of Power* (Oxford: Oxford University Press, 2004), 38–39.

11. "L'alimentation en eau de la ville de Nice et du département sera-t-elle suffisante cet été?" *Le Patriote*, 28 May 1953; "L'usine de traitement de Super-Rimiez," *Nice Matin*, 28 October 1972; Jean Bernard Lacroix and Jérôme Bracq, eds., *L'eau douce et la mer: Du Mercantour à la Méditerranée* (Vence: Trulli, 2007), 79.

12. Haug, *Leisure and Urbanism*, 99.

13. *Du mélèze au palmier: Nature, cultures et paysages des Alpes-Maritimes* (Nice: Imprimix, 2006), 127–45.

14. "L'alimentation en eau de la ville de Nice"; Jean Bomy, "Visite aux laboratoires du Bureau d'Hygiène de Nice," *Nice Matin*, 22 November 1960.

15. "L'usine de traitement de Super-Rimiez," *Nice Matin*, 28 October 1972; Benedetti, "Adieu le chlore"; Haug, *Leisure and Urbanism*, 107–8. On the specific process itself, invented by the Niçois Marius-Paul Otto, and the competing technology, see Frioux, *Les batailles de l'hygiène*, xx–xxiii.

16. "La distribution de l'eau à Nice," *Nice Matin*, 6 October 1961; Lacroix and Bracq, *L'eau douce*, 95.

17. René Rousseau, "Le risque du manque d'eau s'éloigne de Nice de jour en jour," *Nice Matin*, 1 June 1951; "L'alimentation en eau de la ville de Nice"; "Pour célébrer le centenaire de sa présence à Nice, La Compagnie Générale des Eaux a inauguré, hier, la station de pompage de Saint-Sylvestre," *Nice Matin*, 7 July 1964; Lacroix and Bracq, *L'eau douce*, 97.

18. José Steve, "Côte d'Azur, pays de la soif?" *Le Patriote*, 17 August 1965; Benedetti, "Adieu le chlore."

19. Jean Magnet, "La ville de Nice manquera-t-elle d'eau?" *L'Espoir*, 3 July 1964.

20. "Temps modernes à Nice: Dans certains quartiers l'eau coule du robinet, mais elle est vaseuse," *Le Patriote*, 1 July 1955.

21. "Le problème de la distribution d'eau potable dans les quartiers ouest de Nice," *Nice Matin*, 27 December 1959.

22. "Alors que Nice était ville pilote pour l'ozonation, à cause de l'emploi du chlore, allons-nous boire une eau qui aura un goût moins bon?" *Le Patriote*, 26 February 1961; "Le problème de la distribution d'eau potable dans les quartiers ouest de Nice"; Bomy, "Visite aux laboratoires."

23. "Le problème de la distribution d'eau potable dans les quartiers ouest de Nice"; "L'eau potable à Nice: 8.000 abonnés sur 40.000 sont encore desservis en 'Eau-Vésubie' javelisée," *Le Patriote*, 7 August 1957.

24. Benedetti, "Adieu le chlore."

25. Fédération départementale des syndicats d'exploitants agricoles to Virgile Barel, thanking him for his work on their behalf, 5 August 1967, in Barel's papers, ADAM 84 J 63; R.-L. Bianchini, "Par suite d'extractions de graviers et sables, le lit du Var a baissé causant trois graves dangers," *Nice Matin*, 9 August 1967.

26. "Hier a été inaugurée la station de pompage de St-Sylvestre," *Le Patriote*, 7 July 1964.

27. Magnet, "Nice manquera-t-elle d'eau?"

28. Bianchini, "Par suite d'extractions de graviers et sables"; "La nappe phréatique du Var," *Nice Matin*, 14 September 1967.

29. Report by Jean-Philippe Mangin, dated February 1968, in Barel's papers, ADAM 84 J 63; Bianchini, "Par suite d'extractions de graviers et sables"; "Nice, va-t-elle boire de l'eau salée? Les agriculteurs qui manquent d'eau parlent de barrer les routes," *Le Patriote*, 31 July 1967.

30. Venus Bivar, *Organic Resistance: The Struggle over Industrial Farming in Postwar France* (Chapel Hill: University of North Carolina Press, 2018), 38.

31. Mangin report, February 1968; Bianchini, "Par suite d'extractions de graviers et sables"; "Nice, va-t-elle boire de l'eau salée?"

32. Bianchini, "Par suite d'extractions de graviers et sables."

33. P.-F. Leonetti, "Trois barrages aménagés dans le lit du Var pour relever le niveau de la nappe phréatique," *Nice Matin*, 10 August 1967; "Transfert des lieux d'extraction du sable dans le lit du Var," *Nice Matin*, 18 August 1967; "Construction immédiate d'un quatrième barrage pour remonter le niveau de la nappe phréatique du Var," *Nice Matin*, 30 August 1967.

34. "Des 'seuils' sont construits en travers du lit du Var pour sauvegarder la nappe phréatique et relever son niveau," *Nice Matin*, 13 August 1970; "Réglementation plus stricte pour l'extraction des matériaux du lit du Var," *Nice Matin*, 5 May 1968.

35. Vuischard, "L'usine d'ozonisation."

36. "Après l'inauguration du tronçon Villeneuve-Loubet-Antibes de la conduit d'adduction des eaux de la nappe souterraine du Var," *L'Indépendant*, 24 January 1964; "Problème d'un autre âge et pourtant Cannes et le Cannet–Rocheville manquent d'eau," *Le Patriote*, 14 February 1961; Steve, "Côte d'Azur, pays de la soif?"

37. Report of the chief engineer of Génie Rural to the prefect, 10 March 1947, ADAM 60 W 5.

38. Mayor of Cannes to prefect, 30 July 1945; deliberations of the municipal council of Cannes, 27 November 1945; report of the chief engineer of Génie Rural, 12 January 1946; deliberations of the municipal council of Cannes, 23 January 1947, all in ADAM 60 W 5.

39. Henri Faraut, "Un problème important pour Cannes, l'alimentation en eau potable: Bref historique de la question," Le Patriote, 22 November 1959; Lacroix and Bracq, L'eau douce, 79.

40. Henri Faraut, "Un problème important pour Cannes, l'alimentation en eau potable: La jauge, une gangrène," Le Patriote, 24 November 1959; Gilles Paillet, "Avant de substituer le compteur à la jauge," Nice Matin, Cannes edition, 18 November 1959; deliberations of the municipal council of Cannes, 27 November 1945, ADAM 60 W 5.

41. Paillet, "Avant de substituer"; deliberations of the municipal council of Cannes, 27 November 1945, ADAM 60 W 5.

42. Report of the chief engineer of the Génie Rural to the prefect, 27 May 1947, ADAM 60 W 5.

43. "Le problème de la javelisation de l'eau potable à Cannes," Nice Matin, 10 February 1957; "Un problème crucial pour la ville de Cannes: L'eau domestique ou de consommation," Le Patriote, Cannes edition, 31 January 1957; Hubert Germain, "'La guerre contre la pollution' intensifiée: Bientôt de l'eau limpide et pure," Le Provençal, 4 March 1966.

44. Report of the chief engineer of the Génie Rural to the prefect, 10 March 1947, ADAM 60 W 5; Paillet, "Avant de substituer."

45. Paillet, "Avant de substituer."

46. Henri Faraut, "Un problème important pour Cannes, l'alimentation en eau potable: Les compteurs," Le Patriote, 27 November 1959.

47. Paillet, "Avant de substituer."

48. Report of the chief engineer of the Génie Rural to the prefect, 27 May 1947, ADAM 60 W 5.

49. Report of the chief engineer of the Génie Rural to the prefect, 27 May 1947; report of the chief engineer of the Génie Rural to the prefect, 12 January 1946, ADAM 60 W 5.

50. Chambre syndicale des propriétés immobilières du Canton de Cannes to the mayor of Cannes, 15 February 1946, in prefecture files, ADAM 60 W 5; report of the chief engineer of the Génie Rural to the prefect, 27 May 1947.

51. Prefect to the mayor of Cannes, 23 September 1947, ADAM 60 W 5; report of the chief engineer of the Génie Rural to the prefect, 27 May 1947.

52. Paul Raphaël, "L'eau de robinet: Potable à 100%," Nice Matin, Cannes-Grasse edition, 11 March 1982; deliberations of the municipal council of Cannes, 27 November 1945, ADAM 60 W 5; Henri Faraut, "Un problème important pour Cannes, l'alimentation en eau potable: La jauge, une gangrène"; Gilles Paillet, "Les flotteurs étant insuffisants, pour assurer l'alimentation de Cannes en eau potable il faut envisager la refection du réseau de distribution et la pose de compteurs individuels," Nice Matin, 4 February 1954.

53. "Cannes: À l'Aubarède, les propriétaires en ont assez," Le Patriote, 11 August 1962; "Conseil Municipal: Le délicat problème de l'eau trouvera-t-il une solution?"

L'Indépendant, 28 September 1962; "Cannes, une solution heureuse," *l'Indépendant*, 10 January 1964.

54. Conseil départemental d'hygiène, Extrait du registre des délibérations, 4 March 1963, as reported by Directeur du laboratoire municipal de contrôle des eaux de Nice Lebout, ADAM 201 W 60.

55. "Eau potable: La fin du forfait?" *Nice Matin*, 3 December 1981; Benedetti, "Adieu le chlore"; "Une mesure d'hygiène: Le remplacement du 'réservoir sur le toit' par le compteur d'eau individuel," *Nice Matin*, 24 October 1964.

56. "California Homes Lack Meters during Drought," *Los Angeles Daily News*, 6 September 2014.

57. Frioux, *Les batailles de l'hygiène*, chap. 1; Johnson, *Ghost Map*, 1–22.

58. Ernest Fournier to the prefect, 1 December 1941, ADAM 60 W 5; Ingénieur en chef des Ponts et Chaussées Méchin to the Ministry of the Interior, 27 July 1946, ADAM 60 W 6; "Sur l'assainissement des plages," *Le Patriote*, Cannes edition, 14 May 1960.

59. Fournier to the prefect, 1 December 1941, ADAM 60 W 5; Ingénieur en chef des Ponts et Chaussées Méchin to the Ministry of the Interior, 27 July 1946; "Projet d'assainissement des plages, Commune de Cannes," by Vignerot of the CSHP, 11 April 1938, ADAM 201 W 58. Arluc's personal papers at the ADAM (series 82 J) include tens of thousands of pages of correspondence, press clippings, and trial records.

60. These included the Comité de défense des quartiers du vieux Cannes, the Syndicat des patrons bouchers, Association des descendants des vieilles familles cannois, the Chambre syndicale des propriétés immobilières, the Association syndicale des architectes de Cannes, the Syndicat professionnel des entrepreneurs de maçonnerie de Cannes, the Syndicat de l'epicérie, the Chambre syndicale des coiffeurs-parfumiers, the Syndicat des détaillants de la chaussure, the Union des commerçants de Cannes, the Cercle d'études économiques et sociales, and the Cercle de défense des quartiers du vieux Cannes. Prefect to the Ministry of the Interior, 2 February 1939, ADAM 201 W 60.

61. Prefect to the Ministry of the Interior, 2 February 1939; Ministry of Public Health to the prefect, 20 April 1938, ADAM 201 W 58.

62. "Projet d'assainissement des plages, Commune de Cannes," 11 April 1938, ADAM 201 W 58.

63. Ingénieur en chef des Ponts et Chaussées Méchin to the Ministry of the Interior, 27 July 1946, ADAM 60 W 6.

64. Prefect to the Ministry of Reconstruction and Urbanism, 23 February 1948, ADAM 60 W 5.

65. Deliberations of the municipal council of Cannes, 6 December 1945, ADAM 60 W 6.

66. Mayor of Cannes to the prefect, 16 December 1946, ADAM 60 W 5.

67. Mayor of Cannes to the prefect, 3 December 1946, ADAM 60 W 6.

68. CSHP de France, Section des eaux et de l'assainissement, meeting on 22 December 1958, Ville de Cannes, and deliberations of the municipal council of Cannes, 20 February 1958, both in ADAM 201 W 58.

69. "Demande en modification d'éléments du projet général d'assainissement des plages de Cannes approuvé par le CSHP de France, 11 April 1938," ADAM 201 W 58.

70. E. Bouchéry, "Menaces sur la ville, la maladie no. 14: 'Vous n'êtes pas sans savoir," *Le Patriote*, Cannes edition, 2 May 1961.

71. Bouchéry, "Menaces sur la ville, la maladie no. 14: 'Vous n'êtes pas sans savoir."

72. E. Bouchéry, "Menaces sur la ville, la maladie no. 14: Par le canal, d'un canal," *Le Patriote*, Cannes edition, 4 May 1961; an observation of famed scuba diver Dimitri Rebikoff cited in E. Bouchéry, "Menaces sur la ville, la maladie no. 14: À base d'eau d'égouts," *Le Patriote*, Cannes edition, 3 May 1961.

73. "Une question d'intendance, l'assainissement de Cannes," *Le Patriote*, 2 April 1961; deliberations of the municipal council of Cannes, 29 April 1960, ADAM 201 W 61.

74. E. Bouchéry, "Menaces sur la ville, la maladie no. 14: Par le canal, d'un canal"; "Une intervention fortement accrue de l'état," *Le Patriote*, Cannes edition, 13 May 1961.

75. Directeur des services techniques of Cannes to mayor, 5 June 1974, AMC 43 W 357; "Mise en place à Cannes–la Bocca de l'émissaire en mer destiné à rejeter à 1,200 du rivage et à 100 mètres de profondeur les eaux usées," *Nice Matin*, 24 September 1972; "Nouvelle étape vers l'assainissement de la rade," 21 June 1973; Compte rendu de la réunion tenue à la mairie de Cannes, 21 August 1975, au sujet du rapport de Mme. Stevenino, 21 August 1975, AMC 43 W 357.

76. Bomy, "Visite aux laboratoires."

77. Haug, *Leisure and Urbanism*, 122–24; Thierry, "La baie des Anges pourra"; Henri Bartoli, "Des égouts et des hommes," *Le Patriote*, 12 November 1960; Lacroix and Bracq, *L'eau douce*, 141.

78. Thierry, "La baie des Anges pourra"; Paul Thierry, "La baie des Anges sera plus claire," *Nice Matin*, 19 September 1951; Michel Vivès, "Nice souterraine: L'extension de la ville et l'accroissement de la population ont mis l'accent sur la gravité du problème des égouts," *Nice Matin*, 9 October 1959; Lacroix and Bracq, *L'eau douce*, 147.

79. Bartoli, "Des égouts."

80. "Comment on écrit l'histoire ou la fable des chiens-égoutiers de Nice telle qu'on la raconte à l'étranger," *L'Espoir* 6 May 1952; Henri Bartoli, "Les égoutiers," *Le Patriote*, 6 November 1960. Sewer workers claimed, by contrast, that they treated the dogs well. Sewer workers in Rennes claimed the same in 1982. See "Les égoutiers de l'impossible," 2 January 1982, at the Institut national de l'audiovisuel, https://www.ina.fr/video/CPA8205229901.

81. "Le système collecteur des eaux pluviales, à Nice, est périmé," *L'Espoir*, 5 November 1959; "Nice, ville noble, a les égouts les plus modernes d'Europe," *Nice Matin*, 9 September 1965; Vivès, "Nice souterraine"; Henri Bartoli, "Des égouts"; "En face de l'Hôtel Ruhl on construit un 'emissaire' pour les eaux de pluies," *Le Patriote*, 8 February 1952.

82. Robert Gelly, "Cri d'alarme aux journées d'études du CERBOM à Nice sur les dangers encourus par la Méditerranée," *Nice Matin*, 1 October 1970.

83. "Le problème de l'assainissement de la baie des Anges," *Nice Matin*, 3 February 1960; Vivès, "Nice souterraine."

84. Thierry, "La baie des Anges sera plus claire"; Michel Vivès, "Nice souterraine"; Paul Thierry, "Un nouvel émissaire sera construit," *Nice Matin*, 17 February 1952; Paul Thierry, "Les grands travaux à Nice," *Nice Matin*, 24 August 1952.

85. "La délibération municipale contre le rejet en mer des eaux-vannes de Nice," *Nice Matin*, 9 November 1961; "Le problème de l'assainissement de la baie des Anges," *Nice Matin*, 4 November 1961; "Les mouettes vont-elles retarder la réalisation du projet d'assainissement de la baie des Anges," *Nice Matin*, 5 December 1962; "Les problèmes de la promenade," *Le Patriote*, 2 December 1962.

86. "L'usine de pré-traitement des eaux usées de Ferber," *Nice Matin*, 18 May 1972; "Station d'épuration," *Nice Matin*, 24 September 1980; Jean Magnet, "Usine d'épuration de Ferber," *Nice Matin*, 6 November 1987.

87. R. L. Bianchini, "La pollution des plages," *Nice Matin*, 26 May 1974; "Projet d'assainissement," *Nice Matin*, 17 September 1978.

88. "Note sommaire sur la politique de lutte contre la pollution dans le département des Alpes-Maritimes," undated but clearly from 1974 or 1975, ADAM 173 W 701; "Construction d'un émissaire de 750 meters et création d'un laboratoire flottant en Principauté," *Nice Matin*, 10 December 1974.

89. "Nice, ville noble, a les égouts les plus modernes d'Europe"; Vivès, "Nice souterraine"; "Plan de sauvegarde contre la pollution des eaux," *L'Indépendant*, 31 January 1964; "Journal d'un parisien en vacances: Peaux noires et peaux rouges sur la plage de Nice," *Le Patriote*, 3 September 1953.

90. Jean Magnet, "L'assainissement de la plage de Nice: Il y a encore beaucoup à faire, estiment nos lecteurs," *Nice Matin*, 18 July 1972.

91. Jacques Gantié, "L'assainissement de la baie des Anges," *Nice Matin*, 17 November 1977.

92. "Le problème de l'assainissement de la baie des Anges," *Nice Matin*, 3 February 1960; "Le problème de l'assainissement de la baie des Anges," *Nice Matin*, 4 November 1961; "Les problèmes de la promenade: De l'assainissement de la baie des Anges (à coups de digues) à l'engraissement de la plage," *Le Patriote*, 2 December 1962; "Que fait-on à Nice pour protéger la salubrité de nos plages?" *Réalités niçoises*, September 1962.

93. "Au sujet de la propreté de la plage de Nice," *Nice Matin*, 11 July 1957; Pierre Dany, "D'où vient le salissement de nos plages et par quelles mesures y porter remède?" *Nice Matin*, Cannes edition, 1 November 1961; "Le projet d'assainissement de la baie des Anges est en bonne voie de réalisation," *Le Patriote*, 26 June 1962; Magnet, "L'assainissement de la plage."

94. "Sur les 45 km de plages des Alpes-Maritimes, 30 sont exempts de toute pollution," *Nice Matin*, 29 August 1976.

95. "Une tribune pour nos lecteurs," *Nice Matin*, 13 April 1976.

96. "Les plages, bonne pour la baignade estime Dr. Moreno: Plusieurs secteurs sont toutefois interdits," *Nice Matin*, 17 June 1977.

97. "Pollution atmosphérique: Un laboratoire de pointe à Nice," *Nice Matin*, 29 September 1979.

98. "Les résultats d'une enquête effectuée par le Ministère de la Qualité de Vie: Les vacanciers face à la plage," *Nice Matin*, 20 June 1975.

99. Guy Porte, "Côte d'Azur, chers émissaires," *Le Monde*, 22 June 1974; Robert Riem, "Pollution: Eau de mer; c'est (presque) tout bon entre Théoule et Menton," part 1, *Nice Matin*, 6 August 1978.

100. Aide aux travailleurs nord-africains en Nice, "Rapport Moral de l'Assistante Sociale Départementale," 29 April 1957, AMC 22 W 400.

101. For a sophisticated analysis of how Algerians were supposed to earn a right to comfort by "evolving" sufficiently, see Amelia Lyons, *The Civilizing Mission in the Metropole: Algerian Families and the French Welfare State during Decolonization* (Stanford, CA: Stanford University Press, 2013).

102. At the long-occupied bidonville across from the airport, at 201, route de Marseille, the Compagnie générale des eaux removed water meters and cut off the water supply to more than one hundred North Africans living there in 1972. Only after the intervention of both the local Association de soutien aux travailleurs immigrés des Alpes-Maritimes and the Ligue française pour la défense des droits de l'homme et du citoyen did the men get permission to install a hand pump on a well, drawing water from the local water table. At the bidonville de la Digue des Français, authorities drilled wells into the Var aquifer as a temporary solution and in order to gain the trust of men there, as preparations for the elimination of the bidonville proceeded. Ligue française pour la défense des droits de l'homme et du citoyen, Section de Nice, to the prefect, 7 April 1972, and the Directeur du bureau d'hygiène of Nice to the Directeur départemental de l'action sanitaire et sociale of Alpes-Maritimes, 9 May 1972, both in ADAM 207 W 134; François Chavaneau, "À Nice, l'Oued, dernier grand bidonville de France, vient d'être résorbé," *Bulletin GIP: Groupe interministériel permanent pour la résorption de l'habitat insalubre* 20 (2e trimestre 1976): 4–9.

4. Fattening Up Beaches and Polluting the Mediterranean

1. Alain Corbin, *The Lure of the Sea: The Discovery of the Seaside, 1750–1840*, trans. Jocelyn Phelps (New York: Penguin, 1994). On the broader context, see also John R. Gillis, *The Human Shore: Seacoasts in History* (Chicago: University of Chicago Press, 2012), esp. chap. 5; Vincent Andreu-Boussut, *La nature et le balnéaire: Le littoral de l'Aude* (Paris: L'Harmattan, 2008); Gabriel Désert, *La vie quotidienne sur les plages normandes du Second Empire aux années folles* (Paris: Hachette, 1983); Alice Garner, *A Shifting Shore: Locals, Outsiders, and the Transformation of a French Fishing Town, 1823–2000* (Ithaca, NY: Cornell University Press, 2005).

2. Marc Boyer, *L'invention de la Côte d'Azur: L'hiver dans le Midi* (La Tour d'Aigues: Éditions de l'Aube, 2002).

3. Jean-Didier Urbain, *At the Beach*, trans. Catherine Porter (Minneapolis: University of Minnesota Press, 2003).

4. Samuel Temple, "The Natures of Nation: Negotiating Modernity in the Landes de Gascogne," *French Historical Studies* 32, no. 3 (Summer 2009): 419–46; John Croumbie Brown, *Pine Plantations on the Sand-Wastes of France* (Edinburgh: Oliver & Boyd, 1883); Caroline Ford, "Shifting Grounds: From Profit to Patrimony in the Landes of Gascony, 1780–1980," paper presented at the annual meeting of the Western Society for French History, Bozeman, Montana, 3–5 October 2019; Diana K. Davis, *The Arid Lands: History, Power, Knowledge* (Cambridge, MA: MIT Press, 2016), 76–78.

5. "Journal d'un parisien en vacances: Peaux noires et peaux rouges sur la plage de Nice," *Le Patriote*, 4 September 1953.

6. Marcel Rovère, "Depuis 14 mois les baigneurs attendent la construction," *L'Espoir*, 26 July 1952.

7. Francis Brugna, "Après l'expérience (heureuse) de la plage artificielle de la Salis, Antibes veut agrandir son domaine balnéaire," *L'Espoir*, 11 January 1964; "Dans le Languedoc-Roussillon les moustiques compromettront-ils le succès du futur complexe balnéaire," *L'Espoir*, 4 July 1962; "Au comité régional de sauvegarde des eaux," *Le Patriote*, 25 August 1963; Marc d'Amato, "'Baie des Anges' ou 'baie des Fanges'?" *Le Patriote*, 10 April 1964; Roger-Louis Bianchini, "L'aménagement du rivage dans les Alpes-Maritimes," *Nice Matin*, 22 August 1974; Maurice Huleu, "Plages, pénurie d'espace," part 3, "Pour un meilleur confort des baigneurs, augmenter les superficies disponibles et faciliter l'accès à la mer," *Nice Matin*, 9 July 1975.

8. On Spain as a destination for northern Europeans, see Sasha D. Pack, *Tourism and Dictatorship: Europe's Peaceful Invasion of Franco's Spain* (New York: Palgrave Macmillan, 2006).

9. Mikael Noailles, *La construction d'une économie touristique sur la Côte Aquitaine des années 1820 aux années 1980: Pratiques sociales, politiques d'aménagement et développement local* (Toulouse: Méridiennes-Alphil, 2012).

10. André Company, "Il y a cent ans, la promenade des Anglais en 1860," *Nice Matin*, 27 August 1960; A. Johan Foucaud, "Belle Côte d'Azur," *L'Espoir*, 3 April 1953.

11. "À Nice, le problème d'une plage," *Le Patriote*, 30 August 1963.

12. Michel Vives, "Le problème de la reconstitution et la protection de la plage de Nice," *Nice Matin*, 30 July 1958; "Ceux qui se disent 'administrateurs,'" *Le Patriote*, 1 April 1953; Foucaud, "Belle Côte d'Azur"; Rachel Picard, "'Les techniciens: 'Voici 40,000 tonnes de rochers,'" *Le Patriote*, 30 July 1958; "Les travaux d'engraissement de la plage s'achèvent," *L'Espoir*, 11 May 1957; "Travaux d'enrochement sur la plage de Nice," *L'Espoir*, 7 April 1955.

13. Vives, "Le problème de la reconstitution"; "À Nice, le problème d'une plage," *Le Patriote*, 30 August 1963.

14. Vives, "Le problème de la reconstitution"; "Les galets pris, à Risso, dans le lit du Paillon," *L'Espoir*, 3 April 1953; Paul Thierry, "Est-il possible de défendre la plage de Nice contre les effets des tempêtes?" *Nice Matin*, 13 February 1953.

15. Gilles Paillet, "En attendant la réalisation du plan d'urbanisme et l'encorbellement de la Croisette," *L'Espoir*, 7 October 1954; "Les travaux d'engraissement de la plage s'achèvent"; Thierry, "Est-il possible?"; deliberations of the municipal council of Nice, 4 April 1951, ADAM 59 W 92; "Promenade des Anglais, Notice technique, Mairie de Nice," 17 March 1951, ADAM 59 W 92; Rovère, "Depuis 14 mois"; "Les travaux 'engraissement' de la plage," *Le Patriote*, 29 February 1952.

16. Thierry, "Est-il possible"; Marcel Rovère, "Mesure provisoire en attendant l'application d'un important projet d'engraissement de la plage," *L'Espoir*, 21 October 1954; "Y aura-t-il une vraie plage de Nice?" *Le Patriote*, 24 June 1956.

17. "70,000 mètres cubes de galets pour 'engraisser' la plage de Nice," *Nice Matin*, 12 January 1964; "Puisés sous une seule arche du Paillon," *Nice Matin*, 7 February 1964; "Pour stabiliser la plage de Nice," *Nice Matin*, 8 October 1964; "Un 'épi' de 40 mètres va être construit sur la plage," part 1, *Le Patriote*, 17 November 1964; "Un 'épi' de 40 mètres va être construit sur la plage," part 2, *Le Patriote*, 18 November 1964; "L'engraissement de la plage de Nice," *Nice Matin*, 15 April 1964.

18. On the notion of "agency" of nature, not easily controlled by human beings, see Linda Nash, "The Agency of Nature or the Nature of Agency?" *Environmental History* 10 (2005): 67–69; Anna Lowenhaupt Tsing, *The Mushroom at the End of the*

World: On the Possibility of Life in Capitalist Ruins (Princeton, NJ: Princeton University Press, 2015).

19. Foucaud, "Belle Côte d'Azur"; "Ceux qui se disent 'administrateurs,'" *Le Patriote*, 1 April 1953; Rachel Picard, "'Les techniciens: 'Voici 40,000 tonnes de rochers,'" *Le Patriote*, 30 July 1958; "Travaux d'enrochement sur la plage de Nice," *L'Espoir*, 7 April 1955; Inspecteur général des Ponts et Chaussées A. de Rouville, Note récapitulative des essais concernant la défense de la plage de Nice, 13 March 1954, ADAM 824 W 26; Vives, "Le problème de la reconstitution."

20. Rapport de l'ingénieur des TPE subdivisionnaire, 22 September 1950, ADAM 60 W 2.

21. L'ingénieur en chef des Ponts et Chaussées to the conseil général, 24 November 1964, ADAM 173 W 707; Foucaud, "Belle Côte d'Azur"; Report of l'ingénieur de l'arrondissement Lerebour, Ponts et Chaussées, 25 November 1961, ADAM 201 W 61; L'ingénieur en chef des Ponts et Chaussées to the prefect, 16 April 1964, ADAM 718 W 81.

22. Ingénieur de l'arrondissement Lerebour, Ponts et Chaussées, 25 November 1961, ADAM 201 W 61; "Une nappe de mazout a incommodé les baigneurs," *Nice Matin*, 23 July 1966; "Assez de mazout sur les plages de Nice!" *Le Patriote*, 24 July 1966; "À coups de bulldozer, la plage de la promenade termine sa toilette," *L'Espoir*, 19 June 1958; "Mazout et goudron à l'assaut de nos rivages," *Le Patriote*, 7 June 1958 (quotation).

23. "Cartes postales en noir et en couleurs," *Le Patriote*, 21 September 1963; Patricia Namvrine, "La naissance du boulevard de la Croisette," *Recherches régionales* 136 (1996): 139–58.

24. Ingénieur de l'arrondissement Lerebour, Ponts et Chaussées, 25 November 1961, ADAM 201 W 61.

25. Directeur général des services techniques, ville de Cannes, "Élargissement de la promenade de la Croisette: Notice justificative," 22 April 1960, ADAM 201 W 61. Engineer Alexandre Arluc oversaw an effort to create a beach at Cannes, most of which washed away in subsequent storms. See Jean Bresson, "La Croisette," part 2, "Des palaces avec vue sur la mer," *Nice Matin*, Cannes-Grasse edition, 11 April 1980; Ernest Hildesheimer, "La plage artificielle de Cannes: Le projet d'Alexandre Arluc," *Annales de la Société Scientifique et Littéraire de Cannes et de l'Arrondissement de Grasse* 31 (1985): 17–34. Alexandre Arluc was the father of François Arluc of sewer fame in Cannes, and the papers of the latter (ADAM 82 J 2) include files about his father's efforts to widen the beach at Cannes.

26. "Rien de nouveau sous le soleil de Cannes," *L'Indépendant*, 3 November 1961.

27. "Rien de nouveau sous le soleil de Cannes"; Gilles Paillet, "Grâce aux apports de terre effectués chaque hiver, la plage de la Croisette s'élargit de façon constante," *L'Espoir*, Cannes edition, 15 February 1957.

28. Gilles Paillet, "Les travaux de la Croisette," *Nice Matin*, 16 February 1963; "Impératifs des grands travaux de la Croisette," *Le Patriote*, Cannes edition, 17 September 1961; Directeur général des services techniques, ville de Cannes, "Élargissement de la promenade de la Croisette."

29. Gilles Paillet, "Une expérience unique en France," *Nice Midi Cannes*, 26 November 1960; Gilles Paillet, "Les chances d'élargir la plage de la Croisette se

précisent," *Nice Matin*, 22 December 1960; Gilles Paillet, "L'engraissement de la plage de la Croisette, expérience concluante," *Nice Midi Cannes*, 23 February 1961.

30. Bresson, "La Croisette: Des palaces"; Gilles Paillet, "Les embellissements de Cannes," *Nice Matin*, 23 July 1963; Gilles Paillet, "Les 2,870 mètres de la Croisette, à Cannes, sont désormais à double chaussée," *L'Espoir*, 9 April 1964; Gilles Paillet, "Les travaux de la Croisette," *Nice Matin*, 16 February 1963; Jean Bresson, "La Croisette: La construction du port Canto," *Nice Matin*, Cannes-Grasse edition, 12 April 1980; "À Cannes, un problème," *Le Patriote*, 18 August 1963.

31. "Impératifs des grands travaux de la Croisette," *Le Patriote*, Cannes edition, 17 September 1961; Roger-Louis Bianchini, "L'aménagement du rivage dans les Alpes-Maritimes," *Nice Matin*, 22 August 1974.

32. Paillet, "Les travaux de la Croisette."

33. "Rapport de l'ingénieur des travaux publics de l'état," 13 August 1969, ADAM 173 W 706; "À Nice, le problème d'une plage," *Le Patriote*, 30 August 1963.

34. "Journal d'un parisien en vacances."

35. A. Johan Foucaud, "Côte d'Azur," *L'Espoir*, 21 February 1958.

36. Deliberations of the municipal council of Antibes, 16 February 1963, and "Rapport de l'ingénieur des TPE subdivisionnaire," both in ADAM 28 W 265; A. Johan Foucaud, "La plage de la Salis sera aménagée avant la saison d'été prochaine," *L'Espoir*, 20 April 1962; "Antibes-Juan-les-Pins," *Le Patriote*, 21 August 1963.

37. A. Johan Foucaud, "'La plage des Niçois' à la Salis d'Antibes," *L'Espoir*, 17 February 1965; T. Rosselli, "À Antibes, cinq mille personnes se sont dorées chaque jour sur la plage de la Salis," *L'Espoir*, 9 September 1965; Brugna, "Après l'expérience."

38. "La politique des plages 'améliorées,'" *L'Espoir*, 7 June 1963; "Le domaine maritime sera aménagé à Antibes," *Nice Matin*, 19 January 1972.

39. "'L'engraissement' de la plage de Nice," *L'Espoir*, 30 April 1964; "Un cargo a 'arrosé' de sable 400 mètres carrés de la plage de Nice," *Nice Matin*, 5 May 1964; "La première plage de sable niçoise est ouverte aujourd'hui aux baigneurs," *Nice Matin*, 6 May 1964.

40. "Un 'épi' de 40 mètres va être construit sur la plage" part 2, *Le Patriote*, 18 November 1964.

41. Roger Beccatini, "La 4e marine à vague ouverte," part 1, "Une invasion," *Le Patriote*, 31 July 1962; J.-C. Vérots, "À Menton, un nouveau port de plaisance pourra accueillir 750 bateaux dès juin 1967," *Nice Matin*, 30 April 1967.

42. "Il y a cent vingt-six ans les cloches carillonnaient en l'honneur de la pose de la première pierre de ce que est aujourd'hui le port de Cannes," *L'Espoir*, 24 July 1964; "Un deuxième port pourrait être créé à la Croisette," *Nice Matin*, Cannes edition, 27 February 1957; André Clément, "Tous les records ont été battus cet été," *Nice Matin*, 17 November 1957.

43. "Le second port de Cannes," *Cannes Nice Midi*, 18 August 1960.

44. "Un deuxième port de plaisance," *Cannes Nice Midi*, 28 July 1960; "Un lecteur pose un problème (vital)," *Le Patriote*, 17 February 1961.

45. "Quand 'Arts' dénonce le scandale: La rade de Cannes massacrée?" *Le Patriote*, 26 January 1961.

46. Bresson, "La Croisette: La construction du port Canto"; "Intense activité au port de Cannes," *Nice Matin*, 14 July 1965; "La construction du nouveau port de Cannes," *L'Espoir*, 4 January 1964; J.-C. Vérots, "Cannes: Avec le nouveau port

privé qui sera inauguré après-demain redevient la capitale du yachting," *Nice Matin*, 17 July 1965.

47. Vérots, "Cannes: Avec le nouveau port privé." Enamored with the concessionary model, in 1964 Cannes mayor Bernard Cornut-Gentille invited the CCIN to take over management of the old port at Cannes. It did so, with a concession from the Ministry of Public Works and Transport. In return for taking it over, the CCIN was allowed to triple taxes for its use, in order to provide electricity, telephone, potable water, renovated quais, and WCs. "Les problèmes du port et de l'aérodrome de Cannes," *L'Espoir*, 23 January 1964; "Un cadeau (désagréable) de nouvel an pour les plaisanciers," *Le Provençal*, Cannes edition, 15 December 1965.

48. "Deux millions de francs de travaux d'intérêt public," *Nice Matin*, 17 July 1965; Claude Berneaud, "Les ports de plaisance devant le congrès des hygiénistes et techniciens municipaux à Menton," *L'Espoir*, 27 September 1968.

49. According to Marc Jacquet, who had been minister of transport in 1965, and Secrétaire d'état du tourisme Gérard Ducray, in 1975, cited in "Le Xe anniversaire du Port Canto," *Nice Matin*, 20 July 1975.

50. Roger-Louis Bianchini, "L'aménagement du rivage dans les Alpes-Maritimes," part 2, "8,000 nouvelles places d'ici 1985," *Nice Matin*, 24 August 1974.

51. O. de Pignol, "Le nouveau port assurera l'avenir de notre ville," *Cannes Nice Midi*, 6 October 1960; "L'eau du bassin renouvelée tous les cinq jours," *Nice Matin*, 17 July 1965; Robert Gelly, "Cri d'alarme aux journées d'études du CERBOM à Nice sur les dangers encourus par la Méditerranée," *Nice Matin*, 1 October 1970 (quotation); "Les maisons flottantes devront disparaître des ports de la Côte d'Azur," *Nice Matin*, 23 August 1973; "L'interdiction des 'maisons flottantes,'" *Nice Matin*, 25 August 1973.

52. "La principauté de Monaco: Un état moderne confirmant par d'importants travaux sa vocation de grand standing," *L'Espoir*, 29 March 1966. See also Jean-Baptiste Robert, "État et structures urbaines à Monaco de 1949 à 1974," *Villes du littoral: Annales de la Faculté des Lettres et Sciences Humaines de Nice* 25 (1975): 169–92. On the history of Monaco, see Mark Braude, *Making Monte Carlo: A History of Speculation and Spectacle* (New York: Simon & Schuster, 2016).

53. "Monaco, la centenaire prend le virage de sa vie,'" *Le Provençal*, 11 October 1965; Jacques Nimeskern, "Monaco demain," *Le Provençal*, 14 October 1965; "L'équipement touristique monégasque en pleine expansion," *Le Provençal*, 20 September 1965. In some places, the cement jetties of the marinas blocked current and assisted in the development and maintenance of new beaches; the same occurred at Santa Monica, California. Elsa Devienne, "Agrandir la plage: Une histoire de la construction des plages de Los Angeles (années 1930–1960)," in Patrick Fournier and Geneviève Massard-Guilbaud, eds., *Aménagement et environnement: Perspectives historiques* (Rennes: Presses Universitaires de Rennes, 2016), 231–45.

54. Denis Jeambar, "Monaco fascine la Côte d'Azur," in the section "Ville-Environnement," *Le Point*, 22 December 1975.

55. Paul Deverdun, "Le port, jadis, aujourd'hui, demain," *Nice Matin*, 28 January 1958; J.-C. Vérots, "Le port privé de Menton-Garavan," *Nice Matin*, 20 July 1967.

56. Mayor Francis Palmero to prefect, 14 March 1975; Directeur de l'équipement et du logement to prefect, 29 January 1975, Administrateur en Chef des Affaires Maritimes Pennec to the directeur de l'équipement et du logement, 18 December 1974; and mayor of Menton to prefect, 7 October 1974, all in ADAM 173 W 701.

57. M. A. Vidal, "La côte à l'encan, à Menton aussi," *Le Patriote*, 20–26 August 1976; "Plages 'privées,'" *Le Patriote*, 13–19 August 1976.

58. R. Chausserie-Laprée to Prime Minister Jacques Chirac, 30 October 1975; Judgment of the Tribunal administratif de Nice, 13 November 1979; Directeur de l'équipement et du logement Tanzi to the prefect, 24 June 1976, all in ADAM 447 W 15; René Richard and Camille Bartoli, *La Côte d'Azur assassinée* (Paris: Roudil, 1971); *Trois siècles de tourisme dans les Alpes-Maritimes* (Milan: Silvana, 2013), 181–82; Richard Zanelli, "La restructuration du port Vauban d'Antibes," *Recherches régionales* 94 (1986): 2–25.

59. Michael Bess, *The Light-Green Society: Ecology and Technological Modernity in France, 1960–2000* (Chicago: University of Chicago Press, 2003). Caroline Ford distinguishes between a long-standing French awareness of the natural world, with human beings in it, and the more Anglo-American idea that the natural environment should somehow be unspoiled, preserved from human actions; this latter notion became more important in France in the 1970s. Ford, *Natural Interests: The Contest over Environment in Modern France* (Cambridge, MA: Harvard University Press, 2016). On conservation before use of the term *environnement*, see also Charles-François Mathis and Jean-François Mouhot, eds., *Une protection de l'environnement à la française, XIXe–XXe siècles* (Seyssel: Champ Vallon, 2013); Anne Cadoret, ed., *Protection de la nature* (Paris: L'Harmattan, 1985).

60. Catherine Dreyfus and Jean-Paul Pigeat, *Les maladies de l'environnement: La France en saccage* (Paris: Denoël, 1971), 13.

61. Jeffrey Robinson, "Will Nice Become the Las Vegas of France?" *International Herald Tribune*, 13 August 1975.

62. "Un avant-project à l'étude pour l'aménagement du quai des États-Unis," *Nice Matin*, 27 July 1975.

63. Laurent Greilsamer, "Menaces sur la baie des Anges," *Le Figaro*, 8 July 1975.

64. Robinson, "Will Nice Become the Las Vegas of France?"

65. On the limits of environmental enforcement as well as the succession of ministries charged with environmental issues, see Bess, *Light-Green Society*.

66. X. de C. au ministère de la qualité de vie, 25 September 1975; Édouard-Félix Guyon to Robert Galley, ministre de l'équipement, 11 July 1975; J. Zimmermann to President Giscard d'Estaing, 18 July 1975, all in ADAM 447 W 15.

67. Marc d'Amato, "'Baie des Anges' ou 'baie des Fanges'?" *Le Patriote*, 10 April 1964.

68. "Le tourisme maritime et la mort du pêcheur," *L'Indépendant*, 2 February 1962.

69. Délégué adjoint du maire de Nice to Madame D., 20 December 1976; Directeur d'équipement et du logement J. Tanzi au directeur général des services techniques de la ville de Nice (with copy to mayor), 2 March 1976; Madame D. to prefect, 16 April 1976, all in ADAM 447 W 15. Interestingly, when Madame D. got in touch with a contact in the Service des Ponts et Chaussées, she learned that that ten thousand cubic meters of construction waste were to be dumped (someone in the prefecture was not happy with this sharing of information, as the margin of the document includes a note questioning who had talked with her).

70. "Réflexions sur le problème posé par les excédents de produits de terrassements," issued by C. Pradon, 10 December 1975; Prefect Lambertin to the mayor of

Roquebrune-Cap-Martin, 17 October 1975; Prefect Lambertin to the president of the Fédération départementale du bâtiment et des travaux publics, 17 October 1975, all in ADAM 173 W 701.

71. "Ce ravage, ces établissements, ces immeubles, ce sont les plages de la Principauté de Monaco," *Le Patriote*, 31 July 1954; Hélène Vuischard, "Vers la création de réserves marines le long de la côte?" *Nice Matin*, 19 January 1975; M. A. Vidal, "La Côte à l'encan," *Le Patriote*, 20–26 August 1976.

72. On Cousteau's own ambiguous environmental legacy, see Bess, *Light-Green Society*, 72–74, and the contents of *Le monde du silence* (1956), the film he directed with Louis Malle.

73. "Lutte contre la pollution de la Méditerranée: Projet Ramoge, Rapport général sur les plans administratifs et scientifiques et propositions concernant le département des Alpes-Maritimes, la province d'Imperia et la principauté de Monaco," 1972, ADAM 173 W 705; Jean Bomy, "La France, l'Italie et Monaco signent aujourd'hui un accord de protection des eaux du littoral," *Nice Matin*, 10 May 1976.

74. "Le plan RAMOGE, sauver la mer," *Nice Matin*, 10 June 1976.

75. "Méditerranée: Un nouveau cri d'alarme du prince Rainier," *Nice Matin*, 8 June 1976; "Sauver la Méditerranée," *Le Patriote*, 14 and 20 July 1978.

76. "'Boues rouges,'" *Nice Matin*, 24 May 1972; "Le déversement des 'boues rouges' dans la Méditerranée," *Nice Matin*, 25 May 1972; François Guarnieri, "Dans un an, plus d'immersion des boues rouges dans la mer Tyrrhénienne," *Nice Matin*, 6 December 1974; "Pour sauver la Méditerranée," *Nice Matin*, 5 June 1973.

77. David Abulafia points to a "fragmented Mediterranean" in the twentieth century, noting the collective inability to regulate overfishing of tuna, but his characterization applies every bit as well to the absence of pollution control. Abulafia, *The Great Sea: A Human History of the Mediterranean* (New York: Penguin, 2011), 613–27, 640.

78. "À coups de bulldozer, la plage de la promenade termine sa toilette," *L'Espoir*, 19 June 1958; "La pollution des plages de la côte par du mazout et du goudron," *Nice Matin*, 5 June 1958; "Le problème du goudron sur les plages revient à la surface," *L'Espoir*, 4 June 1958; "Du cambouis à 'gogo' le long de la côte," *Le Patriote*, 5 June 1958; "Mazout et goudron à l'assaut de nos rivages," *Le Patriote*, 7 June 1958 (quotation).

79. "Une nappe de mazout a incommodé les baigneurs," *Nice Matin*, 23 July 1966; "Assez de mazout sur les plages de Nice!" *Le Patriote*, 24 July 1966; "La pollution des plages de la côte par du mazout et du goudron," *Nice Matin*, 5 June 1958.

80. "Mazout et goudron à l'assaut de nos rivages."

81. "Assez de mazout sur les plages de Nice!"

82. Mayor Georges-Charles Ladevèze of Cannes to CIPALM, 14 November 1975, AMC 43 W 357.

83. Jean des Chaumes, "Du mazout sur la plage," *Nice Matin*, 14 August 1963; Henri de Monléon, "Tant que les pétroliers feront leur toilette en pleine mer il y aura du goudron sur les plages de la Côte," *L'Espoir*, 19 August 1958. On oil refineries at the étang de Berre, see Xavier Daumalin and Olivier Raveux, "L'industrialisation du littoral de Fos/étang de Berre: Modalités, résistances, arbitrages (1809–1957)," in Mauve Carbonell, Xavier Daumalin, Ivan Kharaba, Olivier Lambert, and Olivier Raveux, eds., *Industrie entre Méditerranée et Europe, XIXe–XXIe siècle* (Aix-en-Provence: Presses Universitaires de Provence, 2019), 256–59; Clara Osadtchy, "Conflits

environnementaux en territoire industriel: Réappropriation territoriale et émergence d'une justice environnementale; L'étang de Berre et de Fos-sur-Mer" (thèse de doctorat, University of Nantes, Angers, Le Mans, 2015).

84. Guy Palausi, "Rapport préliminaire adressé à Monsieur le Maire de Cannes par le Comité paramunicipal pour la lutte contre les nuisances et pollutions," 1 December 1971, 10, ADAM 89 J 383 and AMC 1 W 146; "Plus de vidange en Méditerranée?" *Le Patriote*, Menton edition, 24 June 1962; Marcel Rovère, "La pollution de la mer et du rivage risque de nuire à notre saison estivale," *Nice Matin*, Menton edition, 7 June 1958; Henri de Monléon, "Tant que les pétroliers feront leur toilette en pleine mer il y aura du goudron sur les plages de la côte," *L'Espoir*, 19 August 1958.

85. "À coups de bulldozer, la plage de la promenade termine sa toilette," *L'Espoir*, 19 June 1958; Rovère, "La pollution de la mer."

86. J.-C. Vérots, "Des forages en Méditerranée?" *Nice Matin*, 9 August 1972; "En Méditerranée, le pétrole pourrait se trouver à 20 km des côtes," *Nice Matin*, 23 July 1972; "Pétrole: Les compagnies françaises veulent entreprendre des recherches dans les eaux de la Côte d'Azur et de la Corse," *Nice Matin*, 6 July 1972.

87. Yves Hilaire, "Recherche pétrolière sur la façade méditerranéenne," *Le Figaro*, 25 July 1972; "À propos des recherches de pétrole dans les eaux de la Côte d'Azur," *Nice Matin*, 11 July 1972; Lois Sidenberg to Cornut-Gentille, 14 August 1972, and Cornut-Gentille to Sidenberg, 21 August 1972, both in AMC 1 W 146.

88. Yvonne Rebeyrol, "Recherche pétrolière et pollution?" *Le Monde*, 22 November 1972; Bernard Cornut-Gentille, "Point de vue: Le pétrole en Méditerranée," *Le Monde*, 9 December 1972.

89. Bernard Cornut-Gentille, "Projet de lettre-circulaire, à adresser à tous les maires des communes limitrophes des Alpes-Maritimes" and the printed debate of 4 January 1974, which appeared in the *Journal officiel* of 2 March 1974, both in AMC 1 W 146.

90. Pierre Dany, "D'où vient le salissement de nos plages et par quelles mesures y porter remède?" *Nice Matin*, Cannes edition, 1 November 1961.

91. Palausi, "Rapport."

92. Paul Thierry, "Au sujet de la propreté de la plage de Nice," *Nice Matin*, 16 June 1954.

93. Dany, "D'où vient le salissement."

94. Palausi, "Rapport"; Palausi to the mayor of Cannes, 26 July 1971, AMC 43 W 709.

95. Porte, "Côte d'Azur"; Jean Magnet, "Les plages des Alpes-Maritimes ont augmenté leur surface," *Nice Matin*, 6 September 1973.

96. "Au sujet de la propreté de la plage de Nice," *Nice Matin*, 18 July 1954; "Ce 'rateau de mer' va nettoyer la baie des Anges," *L'Espoir*, 14 July 1955; "Trois bateaux seront employés cet été à la propreté des plages," *Nice Matin*, 22 June 1973; André Luchesi, "Une lance d'incendie et un tapis roulant," *Nice Matin*, 13 September 1978; "Conférence de presse de M. le Préfet des Alpes-Maritimes sur le thème de la lutte contre la pollution," 31 July 1975, ADAM 173 W 701.

97. Jean Magnet, "L'assainissement de la plage de Nice: Il y a encore beaucoup à faire, estiment nos lecteurs," *Nice Matin*, 18 July 1972.

98. Palausi, "Rapport."

99. Robert Riem, "Pollution: Eau de mer, c'est (presque) tout bon entre Théoule et Menton," *Nice Matin*, 6 August 1978.

100. Magnet, "L'assainissement de la plage." On the controversies over dog droppings in twentieth-century Paris, see Chris Pearson, "Combating Canine 'Visiting Cards': Public Hygiene and the Management of Dog Mess in Paris since the 1920s," *Social History of Medicine* 32 (2017): 143–65.

101. "Une tribune pour nos lecteurs," *Nice Matin*, 13 April 1976.

102. Porte, "Côte d'Azur"; Maurice Huleu, "Plages: La propreté coûte cher," part 2, "Un avion, des bateaux, des laboratoires pour surveillance," *Nice Matin*, 8 July 1975; R. L. Bianchini, "Six cents litres de parfum et de désinfectant," *Nice Matin*, 20 June 1973; "Trois bateaux seront employés"; Jean-Paul Fronzes, "Plages, faut-il désinfecter sable et galets," *Nice Matin*, 10 July 1986.

103. "Un projet qui contenterait plus d'un Niçois," *Le Patriote*, 12 November 1959.

104. R. L. Bianchini, "La pollution des plages," *Nice Matin*, 26 May 1974.

105. "Les résultats d'une enquête effectuée," *Nice Matin*, 20 June 1975.

106. "Document établi par Madame Autunes, direction des études et programmes de la SONACOTRA," 29 October 1975, 27, in Barel's papers, ADAM 84 J 45. Catherine Dreyfus and Jean-Paul Pigeat estimated that 80 percent of the coastline of the Côte d'Azur was privately controlled. *Les maladies de l'environnement*, 13, 234.

107. Assistant Mayor H. Bailet of Nice to the prefect, 14 August 1969, ADAM 173 W 706.

108. Magnet, "L'assainissement de la plage." On youth backpackers, see Richard Ivan Jobs, *Backpack Ambassadors: How Youth Travel Integrated Europe* (Chicago: University of Chicago Press, 2017).

109. Michel Barelli, "Ratissage nocturne contre les squatters," *Nice Matin*, 9 August 1979.

110. Marcel Rudo, "De l'Oued [El] Kebir aux rives du Var," part 6, "Où ils logent? Partout et nulle part," *Le Patriote*, 5 January 1954.

111. Procès-verbal by Émile Pommier to the prefect, 16 July 1958, ADAM 207 W 131.

112. Commander H. W. A. A. to the prefect, 24 June 1958, ADAM 207 W 131.

113. E. Faller to the prefect, 23 October 1958, with annexes; Mayor Albert Allari of Saint-Jean-Cap-Ferrat to the prefect, 9 February 1959; prefect to E. Faller of the Ministry of Finance, 11 February 1959, all in ADAM 207 W 131.

114. Gendarmerie to the prefect, 5 August 1966; "Note pour M. le directeur, cabinet du préfet," 22 August 1966; "Pétition en date du 8 novembre 1965 des habitants du quartier des Palluds et du boulevard de la plage à Saint-Laurent-du-Var, contre l'existence d'un bidonville," to the prefect, all in ADAM 207 W 131.

115. Prefect to the minister of the interior, 12 July 1966, ADAM 207 W 131.

5. Erecting an Airport and Living with Jet Planes

1. On the impact of trains in the nineteenth-century imagination, see Wolfgang Schivelbusch, *The Railway Journey: The Industrialization of Time and Space in the Nineteenth Century* (Berkeley: University of California Press, 1986).

2. Nathalie Roseau, "Le paradigme de la frontière: L'aéroport, miroir de la condition urbaine," in Nathalie Roseau and Marie Thébaud-Sorger, eds., *L'emprise du vol: De l'invention à la massification, histoire d'une culture moderne* (Paris: Metispresses, 2013), 185.

3. Robert Wohl, *The Spectacle of Flight: Aviation and the Western Imagination, 1920–1950* (New Haven, CT: Yale University Press, 2005); Vanessa R. Schwartz, *Jet Age Aesthetic: The Glamour of Media in Motion* (New Haven, CT: Yale University Press, 2020), esp. chap. 1. Already in the 1930s and 1940s, up to a hundred thousand people per month visited the Pan Am Dinner Key Terminal in Miami in order to watch the Clipper flying boats take off and land. Jenifer Van Vleck, *Empire of the Air: Aviation and American Ascendancy* (Cambridge, MA: Harvard University Press, 2013), 2.

4. Christiane Spill and Jean-Michel Spill, "L'insertion de l'aéroport en milieu urbanisé: L'exemple Marseille-Marignane et Nice-Côte d'Azur," *Méditerranée* 4 (1973): 49–72.

5. On the modernity of swimsuits on beaches, see Orvar Löfgren, *On Holiday: A History of Vacationing* (Berkeley: University of California Press, 1999), 240–41.

6. Paul Mari, "Nice, 3e aéroport de France, part 3," *Le Patriote*, 6 December 1957.

7. Though the arrival of working-class visitors was both well known and even contentious, only about fifteen hundred arrived on the Riviera in 1936, and two thousand in 1937. See Françoise Cribier, *La grande migration d'été des citadins en France* (Paris: CNRS, 1969), 46–49.

8. Stephen L. Harp, *Marketing Michelin: Advertising and Cultural Identity in Twentieth-Century France* (Baltimore: Johns Hopkins University Press, 2001), 184–85.

9. "Un million de voyageurs utiliseront en 1960 l'aéroport de Nice," *Le Patriote*, 22 November 1956; J. Lassalle, "Note descriptive," 8 September 1957, ADAM 717 W 1352.

10. Inspecteur d'arrondissement, division des bases aériennes, "Notice sur les pistes d'envol et de circulation," 11 April 1946, ADAM 717 W 1353; "Il était une fois l'aéroport de Nice," *Nice Matin*, 30 December 1982.

11. Pierre Montaigne, "Le problème de la circulation dans la région cannoise," part 5, *Nice Matin*, 7 October 1954.

12. "Aéroport: Rendons à César ce qui est à Virgile Barel!" *Le Patriote*, 3 February 1968; Jean-Bernard Lacroix and Hélène Cavalié, eds., *Cent ans d'aviation dans les Alpes-Maritimes* (Milan: Silvana, 2011), 128.

13. "Aéroport: Rendons à César ce qui est à Virgile Barel!"; Exposé de la question de l'aérodrome de Nice-Californie devant la Chambre de commerce et de l'industrie de Nice Côte d'Azur (CCIN), Commission spéciale d'aviation, Séance du 9 octobre 1945, ADAM 213 J 100.

14. "Les liaisons aériennes, maritimes, et routières conditionnent la prospérité de la Côte d'Azur," *Le Figaro*, 7–8 February 1959; "Aéroport Nice–Côte d'Azur," of the Commission de la CCIN, undated but from context 1973 or 1974, in Barel's papers, ADAM 84 J 10; "L'aérodrome de Nice remplace celui de Marignane," *Nice Matin*, 29 January 1947.

15. "Indemnité d'expropriation pour cause d'utilité publique," Chambre de commerce de Paris, 26 January 1950, in CCIN files, ADAM 213 J 100.

16. Petition stamped 26 February 1945 and two undated petitions from the same group from approximately the same period, ADAM 213 J 100.

17. "Relogement préalable en cas d'expropriation pour cause d'utilité publique," from the February 1950 assembly of presidents of chambers of commerce, ADAM 213 J 100.

18. "H. Woefflé to the ingénieur en chef des Ponts et Chaussées," 19 December 1949, and H. Woefflé to Georges Bideaut, 19 December 1949, both in ADAM 213 J 100.

19. E. R. of the Syndicat de défense des expropriés du nouvel aéroport de Nice to Virgile Barel, 15 February 1950, in Barel's papers, ADAM 84 J 10; "Les expropriés de la Californie sont outrés de l'attitude prise à leur égard par l'administration," *Nice Matin*, 17 December 1949.

20. CCIN, meeting of 5 May 1955, and the Ministère des travaux publics, transport, et tourisme to the CCIN, both in ADAM 213 J 105.

21. "L'avenir de la promenade des Anglais," *Nice Matin*, 6 December 1962.

22. Jean Malausséna, "En dix ans de 1946 à 1956, l'aéroport de Nice–Côte d'Azur a multiplié par 16 son mouvement de passagers," *L'Espoir*, 5 September 1957; "En 1959, l'aéroport de Nice–Côte d'Azur," *Nice Matin*, 21 January 1960; "Deuxième de France par l'importance de son traffic, l'aéroport de Nice-Côte d'Azur," *Le Patriote*, 25 July 1963.

23. Paul Mari, "Nice, 3e aéroport de France," *Le Patriote*, 4 December 1957.

24. Schwartz, *Jet Age Aesthetic*, 23.

25. J. Lassalle, "Note sur le nouvel aéroport de Nice–Côte d'Azur," 12 September 1957, ADAM 717 W 1352; Paul Mari, "Nice, 3e aéroport de France, part 3," *Le Patriote*, 6 December 1957. On the constant rebuilding of airports, see Hugh Pearman, *Airports: A Century of Architecture* (New York: Harry N. Abrams, 2004); Vanessa Schwartz, "Le Jet Age: Optimisme technologique et la pensée de l'obsolescence," in Roseau and Thébaud-Sorger, *L'emprise du vol*, 165–83.

26. Bonnefous cited in "L'aéroport de Nice offre depuis hier la plus belle escale du monde," *L'Espoir*, 2 December 1957. On the introduction of economy class fares, see Christopher Endy, *Cold War Holidays: American Tourism in France* (Chapel Hill: University of North Carolina Press, 2004), 128–29.

27. "Les liaisons aériennes, maritimes, et routières conditionnent la prospérité de la Côte d'Azur," *Le Figaro*, 7–8 February 1959; Mari, "Nice, 3e Aéroport de France, part 3."

28. Riou Rouvet, "Aéroport de Nice, été 60," *Le Patriote*, 6 September 1960.

29. "En 1959, l'aéroport de Nice–Côte d'Azur."

30. Daniel Provence, "La Compagnie Air France réfute les accusations portées contre ses réacteurs et rejette sa responsabilité civile," *Nice Matin*, 16 October 1964.

31. Escarletti, "Nice, revendique-t-il le titre de Ville la plus bruyante?" *Nice Matin*, 8 August 1951.

32. "Doit-on dénommer 'motodrome' la promenade des Anglais?" *Nice Matin*, 31 July 1952 (quotation); Paul Thierry, "La circulation des motos sera-t-elle interdite sur la promenade des Anglais," *Nice Matin*, 9 August 1952.

33. "Santé de dizaines de milliers de personnes habitant à proximité de l'aéroport de Nice menacées par le bruit des avions," *Le Patriote*, 4 June 1963.

34. "Une source de bruits souvent intolérable: Le décollage des avions à reaction!" *Nice Matin*, 6 September 1961; André Sallat, "Avantages et inconvénients de l'Aéroport de Nice," *Journal du Bâtiment*, February 1962; F. R. Valvy, "De l'aéroport au centre de la ville," *Le Patriote*, 24 July 1962.

35. "Une source de bruits souvent intolérable"; "Des mesures vont être prises à l'aéroport," *Nice Matin*, 19 July 1962. On the global context of airports' noise pollution, see Ian Douglas, *Cities: An Environmental History* (London: I. B. Taurus, 2013), chap. 7.

36. "Le bruit des avions à réaction est-il un 'danger social'?" *L'Espoir*, 14 October 1964.

37. "Le procès intenté contre Air France," *Nice Matin*, 30 January 1963; "Une société privée affronte Air France devant la 1ère Chambre du Tribunal de Grande Instance à Nice," *L'Espoir*, 22 May 1963.

38. Provence, "La Compagnie Air France réfute les accusations."

39. "Flots d'éloquence au Tribunal de Nice à propos du bruit des avions à réaction," *L'Espoir*, 15 October 1964 (quotation); "L'affaire des préjudices causés par le bruit des avions à réaction sur l'aérodrome," *Le Patriote*, 23 May 1963; Daniel Provence, "Rebondissement du conflit opposant les riverains de l'aéroport de Nice à Air France," *Nice Matin*, 3 June 1964; "Le bruit des avions à réaction est-il un 'danger social'?" *L'Espoir*, 14 October 1964.

40. "Flots d'éloquence au Tribunal de Nice à propos du bruit des avions à réaction."

41. Provence, "Rebondissement du conflit."

42. Provence, "La Compagnie Air France réfute les accusations."

43. "L'avenir de l'aéroport de Nice-CdA menacé?" *Nice Matin*, 13 December 1964.

44. J.-C. Vérots, "Le 'procès du bruit' de Nice devant la Cour d'Appel d'Aix," *Nice Matin*, 8 February 1966; "Le procès du bruit," *Nice Matin*, 19 February 1966; J.-C. Vérots, "La cour d'appel d'Aix a rejeté le recours du syndicat des quartiers Caucade, Sainte-Marguerite, Corniche-Fleurie," *Nice Matin*, 20 February 1966; "Faire face aux exigences de la navigation aérienne sans sacrifier les intérêts légitimes des particuliers," *Nice Matin*, 22 February 1966; "Dix communes riveraines d'Orly 'partent en guerre' contre le bruit des avions," *Nice Matin*, 23 June 1967.

45. A. Johan Foucaud, "Le Ministre des Transports se préoccupe des plaintes contre le bruit des avions passant sur Antibes," *L'Espoir*, 16 August 1965.

46. "Le survol des zones côtières à basse altitude par les avions," *Nice Matin*, 14 May 1977 (quotation); "Les décibels et la santé de l'homme," *Nice Matin*, 14 May 1977.

47. Jacques de Barrin, "Deux cent vingt hectares gagnés sur la mer," *Le Monde*, 13 December 1972; "Pour agrandir l'aéroport de Nice–Côte d'Azur de 300 ha," *Nice Matin*, 4 February 1970.

48. de Barrin, "Deux cent vingt hectares."

49. "Aéroport Nice–Côte d'Azur," Commission de la CCIN; for maps of the noise and a chart illustrating the difference the new runway would make, see Spill and Spill, "L'insertion de l'aéroport."

50. "Aéroport Nice–Côte d'Azur," Commission de la CCIN.

51. "Pour agrandir l'aéroport de Nice–Côte d'Azur"; "Les travaux d'extension sud de l'aéroport de Nice," *Nice Matin*, 13 December 1975.

52. "La SONEXA et l'extension de l'aéroport," *La Tribune: Hebdomadaire économique des Alpes-Maritimes*, 22 May 1976.

53. Brochure, "Aéroport Nice–Côte d'Azur, Aérodrome de Cannes-Mandelieu, Rapports d'Activités," 1975, in Barel's papers, ADAM 84 J 10; "La SONEXA et l'extension de l'aéroport."

54. "À propos du bruit du trafic aérien à Nice," *Le Patriote*, 18 November 1961; José Steve, "Alerte à la pollution atmosphérique," part 7, "Nice est-elle favorisée?" *Le Patriote*, 24 February 1962.

55. On air pollution in France, see Stéphane Frioux, "La pollution de l'air, un mal nécessaire? La gestion du problème durant les 'trente pollueuses,'" in Céline Pessis, Sezin Topçu, and Christophe Bonneuil, eds., *Une autre histoire des "Trente Glorieuses": modernisation, contestations et pollutions dans la France d'après guerre* (Paris: La Découverte, 2013), 99–115.

56. André Luchesi, "L'aéroport de Nice: 'Poumon' de la Côte d'Azur," part 1, *Nice Matin*, 12 March 1968.

57. A police report from 1961 notes that the shantytown near the airport was fifteen years old. Commissaire principal of 6e arrondissement to the Commissaire divisionnaire, 6 June 1961, ADAM 207 W 130.

58. Marc Bighetti de Flogny, for the prefect in a missive to the Ministry of the Interior, 18 June 1958, and Blanchard of the Ministry of the Interior to the prefect, 22 May 1958, both in ADAM 207 W 130.

59. Commissaire principal, "État des nord-africains logeant au bidonville, route de Marseille," 11 June 1958, ADAM 207 W 130.

60. E. Bonnaud to prefect, 9 May 1961, ADAM 207 W 130.

61. Secrétaire général, note for the prefect, 25 July 1959, ADAM 207 W 130.

62. E. Bonnaud to prefect, 1 June 1961, ADAM 207 W 130.

63. "Spectacle désolant à l'entrée ouest de Nice," *L'Espoir*, 22 June 1967.

64. "Un nouvel incendie ravage le bidonville de l'Arénas," *Le Patriote*, 8 June 1967. On the importance of Rotary Clubs in the modernization and "Americanization" of twentieth-century Europe, see Victoria de Grazia, *Irresistible Empire: America's Advance through Twentieth-Century Europe* (Cambridge, MA: Harvard University Press, 2006).

65. "Spectacle désolant."

66. M. Robini, Rapport du conseil départemental de l'hygiène, 27 March 1972, ADAM 207 W 123.

67. Letter from the CCIN to A. Talladoire, undated but clearly just before Talladoire's response on 17 February 1971, ADAM 207 W 123.

68. A. T. to J. Bona, president of the CCIN, 17 February 1971, ADAM 207 W 123.

69. Prefect to the directeur départemental de l'action sanitaire et sociale, 27 January 1971, and M. Robini, Rapport du conseil départemental de l'hygiène, 27 March 1972, both in ADAM 207 W 123.

70. "Les travailleurs immigrés dans les Alpes-Maritimes," SONACOTRA, 29 October 1975, in Barel's papers, ADAM 89 J 45.

71. Directeur du bureau d'hygiène of Nice to the conseil départemental d'hygiène, 18 October 1971; Commissaire principal to the prefect, 25 June 1972; Commissaire principal to the prefect, 23 March 1973; Commissaire principal to the prefect, 23 March 1973, all in ADAM 207 W 134.

72. Jacques Médecin in the minutes of the meeting on 23 September 1970, ADAM 207 W 125; François Chavaneau, "À Nice, l'Oued, dernier grand bidonville de France, vient d'être résorbé," *Bulletin GIP: Groupe interministériel permanent pour la résorption de l'habitat insalubre* 20 (2nd trimester 1976): 4–9; Commissaire principal to the prefect, 8 August 1973; Pierre Costa's note for the prefect, 2 August 1973; directeur du bureau d'hygiène of Nice to the Conseil départemental d'hygiène, 18 October 1971; police report, 3 May 1973 (quotation from G. P.); directeur départemental du travail et de l'emploi to the prefect, 13 June 1974, all in ADAM 207 W 134.

6. Remaking Roads and Disciplining Drivers

1. Alain Kerzoncuf and Nándor Bokor, "'To Catch a Thief,'" Alfred Hitchcock Wiki, accessed 13 December 2020, https://the.hitchcock.zone/cgi-bin/maps/googlemap.pl?txt=To%20Catch%20a%20Thief%20(1955). On the film as an advertisement for travel to the Riviera, see Christopher Endy, *Cold War Holidays: American Tourism in France* (Chapel Hill: University of North Carolina Press, 2004), 130.

2. On architecture along the Riviera, see Maureen Emerson, *Riviera Dreaming: Love and War on the Côte d'Azur* (London: I. B. Taurus, 2018); Charles Bilas, Lucien Rosso, and Thomas Bilanges, *French Riviera: The 20s and 30s* (Paris: Telleri, 1999).

3. For the novelty of the speedy, panoramic view by train in the nineteenth century, see Wolfgang Schivelbusch, *The Railway Journey: The Industrialization of Time and Space in the Nineteenth Century* (Berkeley: University of California Press, 1986).

4. Mathieu Flonneau, *L'automobile au temps des trente glorieuses: Un rêve d'automobilisme* (Carbonne: Loubatières, 2016); Jean-Louis Loubet, *Histoire de l'automobile française* (Paris: Seuil, 2001).

5. On the TCF, see Catherine Bertho Lavenir, *La roue et le stylo: Comment nous sommes devenus touristes* (Paris: Éditions Odile Jacob, 1999); Patrick Young, *Enacting Old Brittany: Tourism and Culture in Provincial France, 1871–1939* (Farnham, UK: Ashgate, 2012).

6. *Trois siècles de tourisme dans les Alpes-Maritimes* (Milan: Silvana, 2013), 111–12; Georges Reverdy, *Les routes de France du XXe siècle, 1900–1951* (Paris: Presses de l'École nationale des Ponts et Chaussées, 2007), 10–16.

7. "Un véhicule pour sept habitants dans les Alpes-Maritimes," *Nice Matin*, 2 February 1962; Jean Magnet, "Nice, la signalisation lumineuse devient 'pensante,'" *Nice Matin*, 10 July 1967; Maurice Huleu, "La 'grande saison' est commencée," *L'Espoir*, 16 July 1958; "En 1957, dix millions de Français ont pris des vacances," *Le Patriote*, 30 April 1958.

8. Kristin Ross, *Fast Cars, Clean Bodies: Decolonization and the Reordering of French Culture* (Cambridge, MA: MIT Press, 1996).

9. Marie Brun, "Les journées techniques de la route à St.-Raphaël,'" *Nice Matin*, 13 November 1957.

10. Ralph Schor, "La promenade des Anglais et les événements: Un haut lieu de la vie niçoise," in *Promenade(s) des Anglais, Nice 2015* (Paris: Lienart, 2015), 186–94; André Company, "Il y a cent ans, la promenade des Anglais en 1860," *Nice Matin*, 27 August 1960; Joseph Suppo, "Les transformations de la promenade des Anglais depuis sa création à nos jours," *Éclaireur de Nice et du Sud-Est*, 29 January 1931; René

Rousseau, "En juillet prochain, les derniers embellissements de la promenade des Anglais," *Nice Matin*, 24 April 1953; Graziella Le Breton and Alain Nissim, "Nice 1930, de la promenade au palais," *Nice historique* 222 (1993): 14–29.

11. Paul Thierry, "L'élargissement de la promenade des Anglais," *Nice Matin*, 8 March 1951; "Les travaux de l'élargissement de la promenade des Anglais," *L'Espoir*, 28 March 1952; "L'élargissement de la promenade," *Nice Matin*, 30 August 1951; Paul Thierry, "Les travaux d'élargissement de la promenade des Anglais," *Nice Matin*, 14 May 1952; "Sous le soleil ardent, par le travail pénible des ouvriers, l'élargissement de la promenade des Anglais s'édifie peu à peu," *Le Patriote*, 9 July 1952.

12. "La promenade des Anglais sera plus belle," *Nice Matin*, 21 April 1954.

13. "Bureau de réclamations," *Nice Matin*, 20 January 1960; "Chaussée sud de la promenade des Anglais," *Le Patriote*, 21 March 1965.

14. "L'entretien et les travaux de la promenade des Anglais," *Le Patriote*, 29 March 1951.

15. "Comme nous l'avons prévu, des blocs doivent être déposés sur la plage pour protéger la promenade des Anglais," *Le Patriote*, 16 November 1951.

16. "Travaux sur la promenade des Anglais prolongée," *Le Patriote*, 3 December 1958; Mathis quoted in "L'avenir de la promenade des Anglais," *Nice Matin*, 6 December 1962.

17. Jean Magnet, "Circulation à Nice," *L'Espoir*, 4 April 1968; "Circulation 'programmée' à partir de juillet sur la promenade des Anglais," *Nice Matin*, 12 April 1973; "La promenade des Anglais ne doit pas perdre sa destination première!" *Nice Matin*, 28 June 1973; Jean-Paul Potron, *Les trente glorieuses: Nice, 1945–1975* (Nice: Gilletta, 2016), 38; Jean-Bernard Lacroix and Jérôme Bracq, eds., *Une formidable invention à hauts risques: L'automobile dans les Alpes-Maritimes* (Vence: Trulli, 2008), 154.

18. "La promenade des Anglais ne doit pas perdre sa destination première!"

19. Jean Bresson, "La Croisette," part 1, "Sur le chemin modestement vicinal, l'impératrice de toutes les Russies," *Nice Matin*, Cannes-Grasse edition, 10 April 1980; "Impératifs des grands travaux de la Croisette," *Le Patriote*, Cannes edition, 17 September 1961; Gilles Paillet, "Les embellissements de Cannes," *Nice Matin*, 23 July 1963; E. Bouchéry, "Menaces sur la ville, la maladie no. 14: Par le canal, d'un canal," *Le Patriote*, Cannes edition, 4 May 1961; "Un problème peu spectaculaire, l'assainissement," *Le Patriote*, 1 April 1961.

20. Directeur général des services techniques, ville de Cannes, "Élargissement de la promenade de la Croisette," 22 April 1960, ADAM 201 W 61; Pierre Montaigne, "Le problème de la circulation dans la région cannoise," *Nice Matin*, 29 September 1954; Gilles Paillet, "Dès le printemps prochain à Cannes, le nouveau parking souterrain de la Croisette," *L'Espoir*, 20 November 1965.

21. Jean Bresson, "La Croisette: La construction du port Canto," *Nice Matin*, Cannes-Grasse edition, 12 April 1980.

22. Huleu, "La 'grande saison'"; Martine Pons, "La petite histoire des arbres de notre région," *Nice Matin*, 29 August 1973; Jean Bernard Lacroix and Jérôme Bracq, eds., *L'eau douce et la mer: Du Mercantour à la Méditerranée* (Vence: Trulli, 2007), 122; "L'embellissement de l'entrée de Nice," *L'Espoir*, 22 October 1954; "La promenade des Anglais et le jardin Albert 1er sont dotés de leur nouvel éclairage," *Nice Matin*, 12 July 1955; Gilles Paillet, "La ville de Cannes consomme annuellement pour l'éclairage public plus de trois millions de kilowatts," *Nice Matin*, 27 February 1959.

23. "Les bruits de la gare de Nice," *Nice Matin*, 21 September 1955. In his history of silence, Alain Corbin points out that urban life was not noisier in the twentieth century than in the nineteenth, so much as different. Corbin, *A History of Silence: From the Renaissance to the Present Day*, trans. Jean Birell (Cambridge: Polity, 2018), 2–3.

24. Escarletti, "Nice, revendique-t-il le titre de Ville la plus bruyante?" *Nice Matin*, 8 August 1951; Jacques de Berny, "Retour de vacances et réflexions après quelques jours passés en Suisse," *L'Espoir*, 8 October 1954.

25. "Doit-on dénommer 'motodrome' la promenade des Anglais?" *Nice Matin*, 31 July 1952.

26. Paul Thierry, "La circulation des motos sera-t-elle interdite sur la promenade des Anglais," *Nice Matin*, 9 August 1952; Paul Thierry, "Premier bilan de 'l'opération antibruit' à Nice," *Nice Matin*, 1 July 1952; Paul Thierry, "La lutte contre les bruits," *Nice Matin*, 1 August 1952 (quotations).

27. Paul Thierry, "Une sévère action antibruit est entreprise par la police niçoise," *Nice Matin*, 6 May 1954.

28. "Une tribune pour nos lecteurs," *Nice Matin*, 13 April 1976.

29. Stéphane Frioux notes that air pollution from automobiles received little attention anywhere in France in the 1960s. Frioux, *Les batailles de l'hygiène: De Pasteur aux trente glorieuses* (Paris: Presses universitaires de France, 2013, 65.

30. Thierry, "Une sévère action."

31. Claude Mercadié, "Quand l'asphyxie gagne la ville," *Nice Matin*, 7 January 1960.

32. "Nice asphyxiée par les embouteillages: Une situation abérrante, conséquence de très rapide développement de la circulation automobile que la municipalité n'a pas su prévoir," *Nice Matin*, 3 October 1962; "Nice asphyxiée par les embouteillages: Des projets de parking dont on parle depuis des années mais dont la réalisation se fait attendre," *Nice Matin*, 5 October 1962; "Pour éviter une asphyxie totale de la cité, une autoroute traversera Nice," *Le Provençal*, 17 July 1965.

33. René Cenni, "Circulation urbaine: La nostalgie du tramway," *Nice Matin*, 8 November 1978.

34. Bergé quoted in "L'indiscipline niçoise dans la moyenne française," *Nice Matin*, 4 September 1972; "À Nice comme dans le reste de la France, le nombre d'accidents de la circulation ne cesse de croître par suite de l'imprudence, l'indiscipline ou l'insouciance des usagers," *L'Espoir*, 10 May 1955.

35. "Comment résoudre le casse-tête de la circulation," *Le Patriote*, 16 August 1963; "On 'roule' trop vite à Nice," *Nice Matin*, 26 August 1976; "Doit-on dénommer 'motodrome' la promenade des Anglais?" *Nice Matin*, 31 July 1952; "Durant le mois d'août à Nice, 326 accidents de la circulation ont fait 3 morts et 119 blessés," *Le Patriote*, 2 October 1964; "Il reste un mois, avant le 'rush' d'été," *L'Espoir*, 16 April 1958; "Les torturés par l'avion, le camion, le wagon," *Le Patriote*, 23 November 1960.

36. Jean Malausséna, "L'indiscipline des piétons et la 'mauvaise conduite' des automobilistes," *L'Espoir*, 30 August 1957.

37. "L'opération 'réglementation de la circulation' déclenchée à la veille de la grande saison," *L'Espoir*, 19 May 1956.

38. "Premier bilan de la nouvelle réglementation," *Nice Matin*, 17 May 1963.

39. "98 PV distribués hier: Le piéton niçois, indiscipliné mais compréhensif," *Le Provençal*, 26 November 1965.

40. "À Nice, faudra-t-il supprimer le pauvre piéton?" *Cannes, Nice, Midi*, 20 November 1958.

41. "Comment résoudre le casse-tête de la circulation," *Le Patriote*, 16 August 1963.

42. "Nice, ville de grand tourisme se doit de posséder un jalonnement routier complet et précis," *L'Espoir*, 2 November 1951.

43. Potron, *Les trente glorieuses*, 56; "L'opération 'réglementation de la circulation' déclenchée à la veille de la grande saison," *L'Espoir*, 19 May 1956; "La circulation à Nice," *Le Patriote*, 1 September 1954; Huleu, "La 'grande saison'"; "L'opération 'primevère' sera permanente cet été dans les Alpes-Maritimes," *Nice Matin*, 1 July 1966.

44. "La circulation estivale sur la Côte d'Azur," *Nice Matin*, 27 July 1978.

45. Hubert Germain, "Nos bords de route des décharges publiques!" *Le Provençal*, 15 February 1966.

46. Document titled "Conférence de presse de M le Préfet des Alpes-Maritimes sur le thème de la lutte contre la pollution," 31 July 1975, ADAM 173 W 701.

47. "Le Conseil Général se penche sur la question de destruction des ordures ménagères dans les agglomérations de la Côte," *Nice Matin*, 4 October 1953.

48. Paul Thierry, "Le problème de la destruction des ordures ménagères dans les agglomérations de la Côte d'Azur," *Nice Matin*, 28 October 1953.

49. Michel Vives, "Construite pour une ville de 150,000 habitants, l'usine d'incinération des ordures ménagères de l'Ariane est devenue insuffisante," *Nice Matin*, 15 August 1959; Thierry, "Le problème de la destruction"; "Revivifiée par sa municipalisation, l'usine d'incineration de l'Ariane ne doit pas retourner à la SITAU," *Le Patriote*, 25 February 1950; Paul Thierry, "Au sujet de la propreté de la plage de Nice," *Nice Matin*, 16 June 1954.

50. "Le problème de la destruction des ordures ménagères sur la Côte d'Azur," *Nice Matin*, 8 October 1954.

51. Prefect to the mayors in Alpes-Maritimes, 6 August 1969, ADAM 173 W 706.

52. Max Burlando, "Grande saison d'été sur la côte," *Le Patriote*, 19 September 1951; "Ouvrons les écluses du tourisme populaire," *Le Patriote*, 13 June 1953.

53. Gilles Paillet, "Village de toile sous les pins," *Nice Matin*, 17 July 1954; Georges Reymond, "L'évolution et les nouvelles formes du tourisme," part 2, "Le campeur doit être considéré aussi comme un client," *L'Espoir*, 23 October 1956; *Trois siècles*, 120–23. On Tourisme et Travail, see Ellen Furlough, "Making Mass Vacations: Tourism and Consumer Culture in France, 1930s to 1970s," *Comparative Studies in Society and History* 40, no. 2 (April 1998): 267–70; Sylvain Pattieu, *Tourisme et Travail: De l'éducation populaire au secteur marchand (1945–1985)* (Paris: Presses de Sciences Po, 2009).

54. Claude Mercadié, "Bilan du tourisme estival à Nice," part 5, *Nice Matin*, 13 October 1960.

55. "Tourisme et la Côte d'Azur," part 7, "Tourisme et Travail," *Le Patriote*, 3 December 1960 (quotation); "Le tourisme social est menacé," *Le Patriote*, 13 March 1967; "Bon milléisme pour l'hôtellerie de la Côte d'Azur," part 3, "Ne pas confondre 'camping' et tourisme populaire," *Le Patriote*, 22 October 1955.

56. "Le tourisme dans le Var," *Nice Matin*, 1 January 1957; Nicole Mofflin, "Le Var, premier département touristique du sud-est: Un bilan au début des années 80," *Recherches régionales* 80 (1982): 2–40.

57. "La Côte d'Azur interdite aux congés payés?" *Le Patriote*, 21 April 1966.

58. Jacques Bruyas, "Les épines sous la plage," *L'Action Nice Côte d'Azur*, nos. 141–42 (1981): 29–31.

59. Ponts et Chaussées report, 1961, ADAM 660 W 128.

60. On summer travelers, RN 7, and twenty-first-century nostalgic recreations of summer traffic jams, see Mathieu Flonneau, *Les cultures du volant: Essai sur les mondes de l'automobilisme, XXe–XXIe siècles* (Paris: Éditions Autrement, 2008).

61. "Partant de Nice, une 'autoroute de l'intérieur,'" *Libération*, 15 January 1955; Riou Rouvet, "La route des sept douleurs," *Le Patriote*, 7 September 1958.

62. Ponts et Chaussées report, 1961.

63. "La route de l'intérieur, pièce maîtresse du programme des aménagements routiers," *Le Patriote*, 8 September 1954.

64. Roger Coulbois, "Où en est la construction des autoroutes françaises?" *L'Auto-Journal* 15, May 1959; Étienne Thil, "Des autoroutes-viaducs pour la Côte d'Azur," *Constellation*, July 1961, 35–39; "Tout doit être mis en oeuvre pour la réalisation rapide de l'autoroute Estérel-Côte d'Azur," *Nice Matin*, 8 September 1957.

65. Potron, *Les trente glorieuses*, 51; Thil, "Des autoroutes-viaducs," 36; "M. Marc Jacquet, Ministre des TP a examiné les problèmes routiers," *Nice Matin*, 12 March 1963.

66. "L'autoroute de l'Estérel qui accueillera 2500 à 5000 véhicules par jour sera mise en service vers 1960," *Le Patriote*, 14 November 1957.

67. "Des projets prévoient la création d'une voie 'poids lourds' qui éviterait la côte de l'Estérel," *Le Patriote*, 8 October 1953.

68. "La creation d'une société d'économie mixte pour la construction et l'exploitation de l'autoroute Var-Côte d'Azur," *Nice Matin*, 18 October 1955; Yves Florenne, "Histoire d'une route devenue folle," *Cannes Nice Midi*, 2 April 1959.

69. Louis Deville, "De l'Estérel aux Appenins par les routes de l'avenir," *Le Provençal*, 10 May 1961; "Une autostrade à l'échelle européenne," *Nice Matin*, 26 April 1961; François Lemarié, "À l'âge astronautique, l'autoroute," part 1, "De la voie appienne à l'autoroute ultra-moderne italienne," *Ouest France*, 9 May 1961. On the expansion of the French autoroute network, see Nicolas Neiertz, *La coordination des transports en France de 1918 à nos jours* (Paris: Comité pour l'histoire économique et financière de la France, 1999), esp. 305, 377, 455.

70. "Un programme de 2,000 km d'autoroutes a été arrêté," *L'Espoir*, 21 January 1956. When Autobahnen were first proposed in the Weimar Republic and then developed during the Third Reich, the aesthetics of the roadway landscape had been critical; however, in engineers' postwar efforts to distance themselves and the West German government from the Third Reich, efficiency replaced aesthetics in the placement and design of Autobahnen. See Thomas Zeller, *Driving Germany: The Landscape of the German Autobahn, 1930–1970*, trans. Thomas Dunlap (New York: Berghahn, 2006). After World War II, in both Italy and West Germany, where systems had served propaganda purposes, there were more limited-access highways than demand. France was more like the United States before the Interstate Highway Act, saturated with cars awaiting governmental intervention for highway construction.

71. "Le tracé de l'autoroute Estérel-Côte d'Azur est définitif," *L'Espoir*, 12 September 1957; J.-F. Simon, "Première voie française à péage," *Le Monde*, 6 July 1961.

72. "Un impératif: Les routes de péage," *L'Indépendant*, 3 April 1959.

73. "Quelques réflexions sur nos routes: L'accès est de l'autoroute se dessine sur le terrain," *Le Patriote*, 21 August 1960; J.-F. Simon, "Première voie française à péage," *Le Monde*, 6 July 1961; Marcel Rovère, "Une autoroute reliant la France à l'Italie va-t-elle être construite prochainement?" *Nice Matin*, Menton edition, 18 November 1960.

74. "À l'Assemblée Nationale, une intervention de M. Francis Palmero sur l'éventualité d'une autoroute France-Italie," *L'Espoir*, Menton edition, 23 November 1960.

75. "La route de l'intérieur est indispensable," *Nice Matin*, 22 January 1956; Thil, "Des autoroutes-viaducs," 36; Paul Raphaël, "À 140 kilomètres à l'heure, un cortège conduit par le préfet des Alpes-Maritimes a parcouru, hier après-midi, l'autoroute Estérel-Côte d'Azur," *Nice Matin*, 30 July 1960, quoting Médecin; François Lemarié, "À l'âge astronautique, l'autoroute," part 2, "Estérel-Côte d'Azur, timides essais français," *Ouest France*, 10 and 11 May 1961.

76. Roger Beccatini, "Sur les traces du premier autostrade à péage," *Le Patriote*, 20 November 1955; Roger Beccatini, "Sur les traces du premier autostrade à péage," *Le Patriote*, 25 November 1955.

77. "Autoroute Estérel-Côte d'Azur," *Cannes Nice Midi*, 5 March 1959; Yves Florenne, "Histoire d'une route devenue folle," *Cannes Nice Midi*, 2 April 1959.

78. "La traversée de Cagnes et de St-Laurent-du-Var par l'autoroute," *Le Patriote*, Cagnes edition, 21 December 1960; "Cagnes et St-Laurent seront-elles sacrifiées par le tracé définitif de l'autoroute," *Provençal*, 18 July 1965.

79. "Autoroute 'Estérel Côte d'Azur,'" *Nice Midi*, 1 May 1958.

80. Yves Florenne, "Histoire d'une route devenue folle," *Cannes Nice Midi*, 2 April 1959.

81. "Trente-sept minutes suffiront pour aller de Villeneuve-Loubet à Puget-sur-Argens," *Nice Matin*, 30 June 1961; "De Fréjus à Mandelieu: En 3 mois l'autoroute a absorbé 400,000 véhicules," *Nice Matin*, 14 June 1961.

82. François Lemarié, "À l'âge astronautique, l'autoroute," part 1, "De la voie appienne à l'autoroute ultra-moderne italienne," *Ouest France*, 9 May 1961; François Lemarié, "À l'âge astronautique, l'autoroute," part 2, "Estérel-Côte d'Azur." On the aesthetics of flight, see Robert Wohl, *The Spectacle of Flight: Aviation and the Western Imagination, 1920–1950* (New Haven, CT: Yale University Press, 2005), 1–2; Vanessa R. Schwartz, *Jet Age Aesthetic: The Glamour of Media in Motion* (New Haven, CT: Yale University Press, 2020).

83. Like airports, the nuclear reactor at Chinon welcomed visitors, who came to admire its modernist beauty. See Gabrielle Hecht, *The Radiance of France: Nuclear Power and National Identity after World War II* (Cambridge, MA: MIT Press, 1998), 13, 41–42, 224. Similarly, engineers compared the Donzère-Mondragon hydroelectric complex on the Rhône to a "modern-day Notre Dame or Chartres." See Sara Pritchard, "Reconstructing the Rhône: The Cultural Politics of Nature and the Nation in Contemporary France, 1945–1997," *French Historical Studies* 27 (2004): 781.

84. "De Fréjus à Mandelieu: En 3 mois l'autoroute a absorbé 400,000 véhicules," *Nice Matin*, 14 June 1961.

85. The metaphor is particularly ironic given postwar campaigns to end drinking and driving. See Joseph Bohling, *The Sober Revolution: Appellation Wine and the Transformation of France* (Ithaca, NY: Cornell University Press, 2018), chap. 4.

86. "Les autoroutes de France ont été baptisées hier," *Nice Matin*, 20 December 1973.

87. "La route de l'intérieur est indispensable," *Nice Matin*, 22 January 1956.

88. "La station-service 'futuriste' de l'autoroute Estérel-Côte d'Azur," *Nice Matin*, 11 June 1964.

89. "Une réalisation magnifique: L'autoroute Estérel-Côte d'Azur," *L'Indépendant*, 7 July 1961; "Autoroute Estérel-Côte d'Azur, oeuvre d'art," *L'Indépendant*, 8 March 1963.

90. Robert Buson, "L'autoroute, facteur de prospérité, est aussi la voie du progrès," *L'Espoir*, 30 July 1963; "L'autoroute permet de partir à la découverte," *Nice Matin*, Cannes edition, 27 June 1963.

91. "Trente-sept minutes suffiront pour aller de Villeneuve-Loubet à Puget-sur-Argens," *Nice Matin*, 30 June 1961; "Une nouvelle réalisation du Syndicat d'Initiative," *L'Espoir*, 10 August 1963.

92. "L'Autoroute A8: Pour l'automobiliste qui la parcourt, elle doit être le reflet de la Côte d'Azur," *Nice Matin*, 11 September 1974.

93. Marie Brun, "Le tronçon varois de l'autoroute sera ouvert à la circulation en 1960," *Nice Matin*, 14 November 1957; "Autoroute 'Estérel Côte d'Azur," *Nice Midi*, 1 May 1958.

94. Yves Florenne, "Histoire d'une route devenue folle," *Cannes Nice Midi*, 2 April 1959; "Vingt millions de véhicules ont emprunté, depuis juillet 1961, l'autoroute Estérel-Côte d'Azur," *Nice Matin*, 13 January 1966.

95. "La montagne est en grossesse: Une (belle) fille naîtra bientôt, l'Autoroute Estérel-Côte d'Azur," *L'Indépendant*, 16 December 1960.

96. Herrick Chapman, *France's Long Reconstruction: In Search of the Modern Republic* (Cambridge, MA: Harvard University Press, 2018).

97. "Le chantier de l'autoroute est ouvert aux Bréguières," *Le Patriote*, 23 March 1957; J.-F. Simon, "Première voie française à péage," *Le Monde*, 6 July 1961.

98. Thil, "Des autoroutes-viaducs," 37. Pierre Massé, head of the Commissariat général du plan and thus of French economic planning, later claimed that he had crafted the compromise of toll roads owned by concessionary companies in order to secure support from the ministry of finances. See Neiertz, *La coordination*, 375–76.

99. "Le droit de péage renaîtra-t-il?" *Le Patriote*, 28 December 1954.

100. "Le droit de péage renaîtra-t-il?"; "Sur les traces du premier autostrade à péage," *Le Patriote*, 27 November 1955; Max Burlando, "À propos de la route de l'intérieur," *Le Patriote*, 5 May 1955.

101. "L'autoroute de l'Estérel qui accueillera 2500 à 5000 véhicules par jour sera mise en service vers 1960," *Le Patriote*, 14 November 1957.

102. "Les torturés par l'avion, le camion, le wagon," *Le Patriote*, 23 November 1960; "De Fréjus à Mandelieu: En 3 mois l'autoroute a absorbé 400,000 véhicules," *Nice Matin*, 14 June 1961; "M. Marc Jacquet, Ministre des TP, a examiné les problèmes routiers," *Nice Matin*, 12 March 1963; "Nécessité vitale pour le Sud-Est: L'autoroute Menton-Aix-en-Provence doit être entreprise de toute urgence," *Nice Matin*, 21 September 1963.

103. "Depuis plus de 25 ans que sa construction a été envisagé, le boulevard de l'ouest est toujours à l'état de projet," *Nice Matin*, 27 December 1956; "Quelques

réflexions sur nos routes: L'accès est de l'autoroute se dessine sur le terrain," *Le Patriote*, 21 August 1960.

104. Jean Magnet, "Cinquante-huit kilomètres d'autoroutes sont nécessaires à Nice," *L'Espoir*, 9 May 1968; Potron, *Les trente glorieuses*, 55; "Comment résoudre le casse-tête de la circulation," *Le Patriote*, 14 August 1963.

105. "Deux cent millions prévus au Ve Plan pour l'équipement routier de l'agglomération niçoise," *Nice Matin*, 17 June 1967.

106. Thil, "Des autoroutes-viaducs," 38; "À propos de l'autoroute nord de Nice," *Nice Matin*, 16 January 1972; "Le conseil municipal renouvelle son opposition à la construction en tranchée de l'autoroute urbaine nord," *Nice Matin*, 16 May 1972; "L'autoroute de contournement de Nice," *Nice Matin*, 20 May 1972; "Les habitants de St-Pierre-de-Féric hostiles au nouveau tracé (en tranchées) de l'autoroute nord," *Nice Matin*, 23 May 1972; Jean Magnet, "Le contournement de Nice devient autoroute," *Nice Matin*, 15 January 1982.

107. The Association pour la protection de l'environnement du littoral de Cagnes, the Association de défense des Bréguières (in Cros-de-Cagnes) and the Association pour la sauvegarde de Saint-Laurent-du-Var to the Ministry of Equipment, the Ministry for the Quality of Life, the mayor of Cagnes-sur-Mer, the mayor of Saint-Laurent-du-Var, the prefect, the president of the *conseil général*, and ESCOTA, 4 November 1976, ADAM 660 W 115.

108. A. Ponton of ESCOTA to the Ministry of Equipment, 31 May 1977, ADAM 660 W 115; "Le piège magistral de l'autoroute A8," *Nice Matin*, 27 September 1978.

109. R. C., 438 avenue de Pessicart, to ESCOTA, 31 January 1978, ADAM 660 W 115.

110. Letters to the prefect, 19 February 1978; Colonel G. to the mayor of Nice, 29 December 1976; Directeur Général Ponton to the directeur départemental de l'équipement, 25 March 1977, all in ADAM 660 W 115.

111. Letters to the Ministry of Equipment, 28 November 1978; Mme. P. to the directeur de l'équipement, 18 July 1977, both in ADAM 660 W 115.

112. "Les nuisances de la voie rapide évoquées au tribunal administratif," *Nice Matin*, 7 May 1981 (quotation); J.-C. Vérots, "L'enfer de la 'voie rapide' évoqué devant le Tribunal Administratif de Nice," *Nice Matin*, 13 May 1978.

113. On the history of concrete, see Gabriel Lee, "Concrete Dreams: The Second Nature of American Progressivism" (PhD diss., Stanford University, 2019).

114. François Chavaneau to the subprefect, 16 October 1975, ADAM 207 W 135; Chapman, *France's Long Reconstruction*, 261–62, 278–90; Laure Pitti, "Ouvriers algériens à Renault-Billancourt de la guerre d'Algérie aux grèves d'OS des années 1970: Contribution à l'histoire sociale et politique des ouvriers étrangers en France" (thèse de doctorat, University of Paris VIII, 2002).

115. A. M. and L. M. to the prefect, 21 June 1962; prefect to minister of the interior, 14 April 1964; subprefect of Grasse to the prefect, 30 June 1962, all in ADAM 207 W 131.

116. J.-J. L. to the mayor of le Cannet, 1 August 1969; petition from residents near the bidonville to the mayor of le Cannet, 24 May 1963; subprefect of Grasse to the prefect, 9 October 1969; police report, Cannes, 26 March 1970, all in ADAM 207 W 131; "Hier, au Cannet, un bidonville détruit par le feu," *Nice Matin*, 27 March 1970; "Un bidonville de Nord-Africains détruit ce matin au Cannet," *L'Espoir*, 26 March 1970.

117. "Le problème du logement des travailleurs immigrés," *Nice Matin*, 13 August 1974; police report, Nice, 7 June 1971, ADAM 207 W 125.

118. Jacques Gantié, "Opération 'bidonville' réussie à Nice," *Nice Matin*, 17 March 1976, with pictures of bulldozers and the caption "Les bulldozers éventrent les baraques aussitôt après le départ des derniers occupants"; "Le bidonville de la Digue des Français," *Nice Matin*, 3 February 1976 (quotation).

119. Directeur Départemental de l'Équipement et du Logement A. Gautier au SONACOTRA, 9 November 1972, ADAM 207 W 134.

120. Prefect to the subprefect, chargé de mission, 5 April 1976, and R. Jamois of the Société centrale d'études et de réalisations routières to SONACOTRA, 12 March 1976, both in ADAM 207 W 134.

Epilogue

1. Thanks to Brett Bowles for first telling me about the film and Éric Zemmour's diatribe in reaction to it. See Todd Shepard, *Sex, France and Arab Men, 1962–1979* (Chicago: University of Chicago Press, 2018), 238–40.

2. Robert Gildea argues that "local authorities on the Côte d'Azur took their revenge" by banning the burkini. Gildea, *Empires of the Mind: The Colonial Past and the Politics of the Present* (Cambridge: Cambridge University Press, 2019), 229.

3. "Ouverture en 1974, promenade des Anglais, du Méridien-Nice," *Nice Matin*, 6 April 1973.

4. Serge Benedetti, "Ces palaces qui veulent vivre," *Nice Matin*, 27 March 1977.

5. *Trois siècles de tourisme dans les Alpes-Maritimes* (Milan: Silvana, 2013), 142.

6. Alain Ruggiero, *Nouvelle histoire de Nice* (Toulouse: Privat, 2006), 257.

7. "Le prix des loyers à Nice," *Nice Matin*, 25 June 1974.

8. "Le dernier bidonville de Nice a été détruit," *Nice Matin*, 3 November 1979; "Le bidonville de la Digue des Français," *Nice Matin*, 3 February 1976; Serge Benedetti, "Vieux Nice: L'or des vieilles pierres," *Nice Matin*, 27 February 1989; Ralph Schor, Stéphane Mourlane, and Yvan Gastaut, *Nice cosmopolite, 1860–2010* (Paris: Éditions Autrement, 2010), 131–32.

9. On the strength of pied noir associations in Nice, leading to the city hosting a twenty-fifth-year reunion in 1987 of pieds noirs that drew at least forty thousand (with associations claiming up to 300,000 attendees), see Claire Eldridge, *From Empire to Exile: History and Memory within the Pied Noir and Harki Communities, 1962–2012* (Manchester: Manchester University Press, 2016), 122–24.

10. Schor et al., *Nice cosmopolite*, 162; Ruggiero, *Nouvelle histoire*, 305. On the corruption and mafia connections of the Médecin régime, see Graham Greene, *J'accuse: The Dark Side of Nice* (London: Bodley Head, 1982).

11. Jean Raspail, *Le camp des saints* (Paris: Robert Laffont, 1973).

12. Jean Bernard Lacroix and Jérôme Bracq, eds., *L'eau douce et la mer: Du Mercantour à la Méditerranée* (Vence: Trulli, 2007), 52; Claude Vadrot, *Mort de la Méditerranée* (Paris: Seuil, 1977), 94, summarizing the work of Alexandre Meinesz.

13. Andrée Dagorne, "La Côte d'Azur, un mur de béton? Alpes-Maritimes et Monaco," *Recherches régionales* 131 (July-September 1995): 163–213.

14. CIPALM, "Réserve Sous-Marine de Golfe-Juan," September 1980, ADAM 447 W 15.

15. "Égouts: Les 'parfums' ne passeront pas," *Nice Matin*, 23 September 1986; Benedetti, "La baie des Anges"; Lacroix and Bracq, *L'eau douce*, 148.

16. Tristan Roux, "Colloque international à Nice pour la protection du littoral méditerranéen," *Nice Matin*, 13 April 1979.

17. "L'herbier de posidonies: Témoin du mieux-être du milieu marin," *Nice Matin*, 15 November 1993.

18. Xavier Daumalin and Isabelle Laffont-Schwob, eds., *Les calanques industrielles et leurs pollutions: Une histoire au présent* (Aix-en-Provence: REF.2C Éditions, 2016).

19. "La plage s'en va: Pour la retenir des tonnes de sable et de gravier ont été déversées," *Nice Matin*, 13 January 1986; Lacroix and Bracq, *L'eau douce*, 45; Valérie Tripoldi, "Opération plages propres," *Nice Matin*, 1 June 1993; Chef du Service Maritime, Hydraulique et Assainissment G. Leccia to mayor of Nice, 12 November 1998, ADAM 824 W 26; "Des tonnes de galets déversés sur les plages de Nice jusqu'à la fin du mois de janvier," *France 3, Régions: Provence, Alpes, Côte d'Azur*, 10 January 2020. The Riviera has not been unique in "fattening up" its beaches. Several Spanish resorts ship in sand from the Canary Islands to augment their beaches and to have light-colored, rather than black/volcanic, sand. See Stephen Mosley, "Coastal Cities and Environmental Change," *Environment and History* 20 (2014): 528.

20. Tripoldi, "Opération plages propres."

21. Benedetti, "La baie des Anges."

22. "Aéroport de Nice: Le bruit des avions fantômes," *Nice Matin*, 26 June 1984.

23. Jean-Bernard Lacroix and Hélène Cavalié, eds., *Cent ans d'aviation dans les Alpes-Maritimes* (Milan: Silvana, 2011), citing the *Revue municipale d'Antibes*.

24. Pierre Hillion, "'Vivre sur la Prom': Le meilleur et le pire," *Nice Matin*, 20 April 1991; "'Le bruit': Ça ne s'arrête jamais" and "Les Niçois n'y habitent pas," both in *Nice Matin*, 20 April 1991.

25. John Urry, *The Tourist Gaze: Leisure and Travel in Contemporary Societies* (London: Sage, 1990).

26. On the varieties of immediate remembrance of the 2016 attack, see Annette Becker, "Faire parler les objets," *Mémoires en jeu* 4 (2017): 60–64.

BIBLIOGRAPHIC ESSAY

The primary sources for this book are largely local, as I relied on the abundant holdings and excellent organization of the archives of the department of Alpes-Maritimes. Created during the Revolution, French departments have stood at the nexus between the national government and municipalities. Since Napoleon, each department has had a prefect, appointed by Paris, through whose prefecture administrative information flowed. Until the move to decentralization in the 1980s, municipal decisions required approval by the prefecture before implementation. As a result, departmental archives in France, housing the records of each prefecture, have the paper trail of communications between Paris and French towns. Most local issues were not important enough to make their way to Paris, but they almost always found their way to the prefecture. While sources consulted in the Centre des archives contemporaines at Fontainebleau (now mostly available at the new facility in Pierrefitte-sur-Seine) offer an aerial view of events on the ground, they proved less useful as I attempted to dig deeper into both construction projects and the lives of North African laborers. At the other end of the spectrum are municipal archives. In Alpes-Maritimes as in other French departments, municipal archives are highly uneven in both holdings and organization. There I found good if scattered evidence, particularly for Cannes after 1945 (and for Nice before 1945 and after 1980). However, the actions of communities all along the Riviera are well documented at the departmental level. At the Archives départementales des Alpes-Maritimes I used the voluminous files of the prefecture, the personal papers of François Arluc and Virgile Barel, and the records of the local chamber of commerce and of the Hôtel Beau Rivage. Because this book cuts across several topics often considered separately, it goes (almost) without saying that the documentation in Alpes-Maritimes would support further work on any one of them. For scholars and students interested in doing research on the history of tourism farther west along the Côte d'Azur, the departmental archives of the Var and the municipal archives of Hyères-les-Palmiers and Saint-Tropez have important holdings.

I also made considerable use of the press for the years 1945–75. Articles about the Riviera appeared regularly in international and French national newspapers. In addition, there were many local newspapers, the most important of which were *Nice Matin* on the political right and *Le Patriote* on the left. *Nice Matin* often backed the policies of longtime mayor of Nice Jean Médecin, even though he had a separate newspaper, *L'Action républicaine*, which leaned farther right. *Le Patriote*, by contrast, was the paper of Virgile Barel and local communists. *Le Patriote* was communist in the way that many French communists were after World War II; while critical of the United States and the rich, the paper's interests were overwhelmingly local and domestic, featuring the issues of work and housing critical for workers. *L'Espoir* filled the center/center left of the political spectrum, alongside less important and often short-lived publications. For the immediate postwar years, newspapers remained the primary organs for local news. Increasingly displaced by television news in the 1960s and 1970s, local newspapers underwent ruthless consolidation—even before the advent of the internet, which usually receives the blame for the crisis in local news. *Nice Matin* absorbed *L'Espoir* in 1966. In 1967 *Le Patriote* became a weekly. *Nice Matin* was dominant, maintaining a circulation of three hundred thousand copies in the 1970s. It still exists today. Long articles in these local newspapers provide granular detail that would be unavailable for anyone studying the 1980s and after.

Because of the legal requirement that French publishers submit a copy of publications to the Bibliothèque nationale de France (the *dépôt légal*), both national and local newspapers are available there (as are French radio and television programs in the BNF Inathèque; I found those much less useful). In addition, the Archives départementales des Alpes-Maritimes have many of the local publications in their library; the archives also maintain files of press clippings, organized by theme.

Although my secondary sources rarely cut across the various chapters of this book, they collectively reveal the richness of contemporary historiography on modern France. When it first appeared, most historians read Jean Fourastié's *Les trente glorieuses, ou la révolution invisible de 1946 à 1975* (Paris: Fayard, 1979) as a secondary source. Now, it seems a primary source, providing evidence of a contemporary view of postwar modernization that historians increasingly consider simplistic, if not downright misleading. The most direct corrective is Céline Pessis, Sezin Topçu, and Christophe Bonneuil, eds., *Une autre histoire des "Trente Glorieuses": Modernisation, contestations et pollutions dans la France d'après guerre* (Paris: La Découverte, 2013). Other historians provide explicit and implicit qualifications on the use of the term *trente glorieuses* and Fourastié's periodization: Dominique Lejeune, *La France des trente glorieuses, 1945–1974* (Paris: Armand Colin, 2015); Philip Nord, *France's New Deal: From the Thirties to the Postwar Era* (Princeton, NJ:

Princeton University Press, 2010); Jean-François Sirinelli, *Les vingt décisives: Le passé proche de notre avenir, 1965–1985* (Paris: Fayard, 2007); and Jean-Claude Daumas, *La révolution matérielle: Une histoire de la consommation, France XIXe–XXIe siècle* (Paris: Flammarion, 2018). Régis Boulat considers Fourastié himself as the historical subject in *Jean Fourastié, un expert en productivité: La modernisation de la France (années trente-années cinquante)* (Besançon: Presses universitaires de Franche-Comté, 2008).

In the past twenty years, scholars have significantly deepened our understanding of the environmental history of modern France, including the Thirty Glorious Years. Michael Bess's *The Light-Green Society: Ecology and Technological Modernity in France, 1960–2000* (Chicago: University of Chicago Press, 2003) highlights the ambivalent nature of environmental mobilization in postwar France. More recently, Caroline Ford, Charles-François Mathis, Jean-François Mouhot, and others have persuasively argued that there was a certain environmentalism in France long before the word *environnement* emerged, and that conservationism did not assume a wilderness bereft of human intervention as was the case in the United States: Caroline Ford, *Natural Interests: The Contest over Environment in Modern France* (Cambridge, MA: Harvard University Press, 2016); Charles-François Mathis and Jean-François Mouhot, eds., *Une protection de l'environnement à la française, XIXe–XXe siècles* (Seyssel: Champ Vallon, 2013). Patrick Fournier and Geneviève Massard-Guilbaud have combined the study of development, or *aménagement*, and its environmental impact in their edited volume *Aménagement et environnement: Perspectives historiques* (Rennes: Presses universitaires de Rennes, 2016). Xavier Daumalin and Isabelle Laffont-Schwob have led an interdisciplinary, multiauthored, and well-funded effort to study industrial development, labor, pollution, and environmental restoration in the calanques south of Marseille: *Les calanques industrielles et leurs pollutions: Une histoire au présent* (Aix-en-Provence: REF.2C Éditions, 2016).

Postwar reconstruction, the context for the significant increase in French housing stock, is the subject of Danièle Voldman, *La reconstruction des villes françaises de 1940 à 1954: Histoire d'une politique* (Paris: L'Harmattan, 1997) and Herrick Chapman, *France's Long Reconstruction: In Search of the Modern Republic* (Cambridge, MA: Harvard University Press, 2018). Nicole C. Rudolph (*At Home in Postwar France: Modern Mass Housing and the Right to Comfort* [New York: Berghahn, 2015]) and W. Brian Newsome (*French Urban Planning, 1940–1968: The Construction and Deconstruction of an Authoritarian System* [New York: Peter Lang, 2009]) describe the creation of the huge public housing estates at the edge of French cities. While such *grands ensembles* have been bemoaned by residents and most observers since their construction, Kenny Cupers has made clear just how aspirational the initial Le Corbusier–inspired visions of such high-rise apartments were: *The Social Project: Housing in Postwar France* (Minneapolis: University of Minnesota Press, 2014). Using housing requests addressed to longtime socialist mayor Gaston Defferre, Minayo A. Nasiali reveals the dynamics of who could get public housing in Marseille and how they did so, in *Native to the Republic: Empire, Social Citizenship, and Everyday Life in Marseille since 1945* (Ithaca, NY: Cornell University Press, 2016). Like Nasiali, Amelia Lyons describes the role of race in French housing policy: *The Civilizing Mission in the Metropole: Algerian Families and the French Welfare State during Decolonization* (Stanford, CA: Stanford University Press, 2013).

Given historians' former neglect of immigration to France as a subject of scholarship, it is noteworthy that works on immigrants in general, and North Africans in particular, gave chapter 2 an especially rich secondary source base. On immigration in general, see the classic works by Gérard Noiriel, *The French Melting Pot: Immigration, Citizenship, and National Identity*, trans. Geoffroy de Laforcade (Minneapolis: University of Minnesota Press, 1996); Ralph Schor, *L'opinion française et les étrangers en France, 1919–1939* (Paris: Publications de la Sorbonne, 1985); Schor, *Histoire de l'immigration en France de la fin du XIXe siècle à nos jours* (Paris: Armand Colin, 1996); and Vincent Viet, *La France immigrée: Construction d'une politique, 1914–1997* (Paris: Fayard, 1998); as well as the more recent work by Benjamin Stora and Émile Temime, eds., *Immigrances: L'immigration en France au XXe siècle* (Paris: Hachette, 2007). On immigration to Nice and the Alpes-Maritimes, see Ralph Schor, Stéphane Mourlane, and Yvan Gastaut, *Nice cosmopolite, 1860–2010* (Paris: Éditions Autrement, 2010), and Nadhem Yousfi, *Des Tunisiens dans les Alpes-Maritimes: Une histoire locale et nationale de la migration transméditerranéenne (1956–1984)* (Paris: L'Harmattan, 2013). In his now classic *The Invention of Decolonization: The Algerian War and the Remaking of France* (Ithaca, NY: Cornell University Press, 2006), Todd Shepard tracks just how quickly Algerians lost their French citizenship and became immigrants in the eyes of the French state and the public more generally.

On the origin and use of the term *bidonville*, see Zeynep Çelik, *Urban Forms and Colonial Confrontations: Algiers under French Rule* (Berkeley: University of California Press, 1997) and Jim House, "Shantytowns and Rehousing in Late Colonial Algiers and Casablanca," in *France's Modernising Mission: Citizenship, Welfare and the Ends of Empire*, ed. Ed Naylor (London: Palgrave Macmillan, 2018), 133–63. Monique Hervo and Marie-Ange Charras's books about bidonvilles remain as fascinating as when first published: Monique Hervo and Marie-Ange Charras, *Bidonvilles: L'enlisement* (Paris: Maspero, 1971); and Monique Hervo, *Chroniques des bidonvilles: Nanterre en guerre d'Algérie*

1959–1962 (Paris: Seuil, 2001). Marie-Claude Blanc-Chaléard provides a comprehensive look at their elimination in *En finir avec les bidonvilles: Immigration et politique du logement dans la France des trente glorieuses* (Paris: Publications de la Sorbonne, 2016). Marc Bernardot's history of the SONACOTRA lays out the politics of rehousing North African migrants as the bidonvilles disappeared: *Loger les immigrés: La Sonacotra, 1956–2006* (Paris: Éditions du Croquant, 2008).

Several scholars have examined the racism faced by North Africans in France: Tahar Ben Jellou, *French Hospitality: Racism and North African Immigrants*, trans. Barbara Bray (New York: Columbia University Press, 1999); Neil MacMaster, *Colonial Migrants and Racism: Algerians in France, 1900–62* (New York: St. Martin's, 1997); and Naomi Davidson, *Only Muslim: Embodying Islam in Twentieth-Century France* (Ithaca, NY: Cornell University Press, 2012). In *Sex, France and Arab Men, 1962–1979* (Chicago: University of Chicago Press, 2018), Todd Shepard offers an intriguing study of the presumed sexual threat of Arab men after the Algerian War. Daniel A. Gordon considers the emergence of anti-racism after 1968 in *Immigrants and Intellectuals: May '68 and the Rise of Anti-Racism in France* (Pontypool, UK: Merlin Press, 2012). To a large degree, the reaction of French society to Algerians has dominated the narrative of North Africans' experience, at times obscuring the agency of the migrants themselves. Muriel Cohen shatters many of the usual generalizations about North Africans' lives in "Les circulations entre France et Algérie: Un nouveau regard sur les migrants (post)coloniaux (1945–1985)," *French Politics, Culture, and Society* 34, no. 2 (2016): 78–100. In that same special issue, Neil MacMaster's article focuses on Algerian political activity centered in cafés that also lodged migrants: "The Algerian Café-Hotel: Hub of the Nationalist Underground in Paris, 1926–1962," *French Politics, Culture, and Society* 34, no. 2 (2016): 57–77. Both Ethan Katz and Maud Mandel historicize and correct the long-standing assumption that there was some inevitable tension and conflict between Muslims and Jews in France: Ethan B. Katz, *The Burdens of Brotherhood: Jews and Muslims from North Africa to France* (Cambridge, MA: Harvard University Press, 2015); Maud S. Mandel, *Muslims and Jews in France: History of a Conflict* (Princeton, NJ: Princeton University Press, 2014).

The other migrants from North Africa, the pieds noirs, are the subject of several books: Jean-Jacques Jordi, *De l'exode à l'exile: Rapatriés et pieds-noirs en France, l'exemple Marseillais, 1954–1992* (Paris: Harmattan, 1993); Yann Scioldo-Zürcher, *Devenir métropolitain: Politique d'intégration et parcours de rapatriés d'Algérie en metropole (1954–2005)* (Paris: Éditions de l'École des Hautes Études en Sciences Sociales, 2010); Sung-Eun Choi, *Decolonization and the French of Algeria: Bringing the Settler Colony Home* (Basingstoke, UK: Palgrave Macmillan, 2016); and Claire Eldridge, *From Empire to Exile: History and Memory within the Pied Noir and Harki Communities, 1962–2012* (Manchester: Manchester University Press, 2016).

Kristin Ross's *Fast Cars, Clean Bodies: Decolonization and the Reordering of French Culture* (Cambridge, MA: MIT Press, 1996) considers a few of the themes embedded in several chapters of this book. For Ross, the French learned to forget the empire as they embraced postwar modernity in the form of consumer products and scrupulous hygiene (dependent on running water in French homes). Stéphane Frioux's work is pioneering not only in considering the infrastructure of public hygiene in municipalities across France but also in spotlighting the unprecedented intervention of the French state after World War II: *Les batailles de l'hygiène: De Pasteur aux trente glorieuses* (Paris: Presses universitaires de France, 2013). Steven Zdatny focuses on the rapid transformation of hygiene in postwar France in "The French Hygiene Offensive of the 1950s: A Critical Moment in the History of Manners," *Journal of Modern History* 84 (December 2012): 897–932. Although C. James Haug considers the nineteenth century, his *Leisure and Urbanism in Nineteenth-Century Nice* (Lawrence: University Press of Kansas, 1982) provides invaluable information about water and sewage infrastructures for *hivernants* in late nineteenth-century Nice, laying out the historical context for twentieth-century changes.

In the eighteenth and nineteenth centuries, Europeans learned to appreciate the seaside: Alain Corbin, *The Lure of the Sea: The Discovery of the Seaside, 1750–1840*, trans. Jocelyn Phelps (New York: Penguin, 1994); Johan Vincent, *L'intrusion balnéaire: Les populations littorales bretonnes et vendéennes face au tourisme (1800–1945)* (Rennes: Presses universitaires de Rennes, 2007); Dominique Barjot, Eric Anceau, and Nicolas Stoskopf, eds., *Morny et l'invention de Deauville* (Paris: Armand Colin, 2010); and John R. Gillis, *The Human Shore: Seacoasts in History* (Chicago: University of Chicago Press, 2012). In the twentieth century, tourists sought the beach, the sand, and the summer sun: Jean-Didier Urbain, *At the Beach*, trans. Catherine Porter (Minneapolis: University of Minnesota Press, 2003); Gabriel Désert, *La vie quotidienne sur les plages normandes du Second Empire aux années folles* (Paris: Hachette, 1983); Christophe Granger, *Les corps d'été: Naissance d'une variation saisonnière, XXe siècle* (Paris: Éditions Autrement, 2009); Pascal Ory, *L'invention du bronzage: Essai d'une histoire culturelle* (Paris: Éditions Complexe, 2008); and Stephen L. Harp, *Au Naturel: Naturism, Nudism and Tourism in Twentieth-Century France* (Baton Rouge: Louisiana State University Press, 2014).

In an effort to lure tourists headed to Spain's wide, sandy beaches on the Costa Brava, the French state engineered an environmental makeover of the coasts of Languedoc-Roussillon in the 1960s and 1970s, and Aquitaine in the 1970s and 1980s: on Languedoc-Roussillon, see Pierre Racine, *Mission impossible? L'aménagement touristique du littoral Languedoc-Roussillon* (Montpellier: Midi Libre, 1980); Ellen Furlough and Rosemary Wakeman, "Composing a Landscape: Coastal Mass Tourism and Regional Development in Languedoc," *International Journal of Maritime History* 9, no. 1 (1997): 187–211; Furlough and Wakeman, "La Grande Motte: Regional Development, Tourism, and the State," in Shelley Baranowski and Ellen Furlough, eds., *Being Elsewhere: Tourism, Consumer Culture, and Identity in Modern Europe and North America* (Ann Arbor: University of Michigan Press, 2001), 348–72; Giacomo Parrinello and Renaud Bécot, "Regional Planning and the Environmental Impact of Coastal Tourism: The Mission Racine for the Redevelopment of Languedoc-Roussillon's Littoral," *Humanities* 8 (2019): 1–13; and Vincent Andreu-Boussut, *La nature et le balnéaire: Le littoral de l'Aude* (Paris: L'Harmattan, 2008). On coastal Aquitaine, see Alice Garner, *A Shifting Shore: Locals, Outsiders, and the Transformation of a French Fishing Town, 1823–2000* (Ithaca, NY: Cornell University Press, 2005) and Mikael Noailles, *La construction d'une économie touristique sur la Côte Aquitaine des années 1820 aux années 1980: Pratiques sociales, politiques d'aménagement et développement local* (Toulouse: Méridiennes-Alphil, 2012).

Histories of transportation, including by air and auto, have taken a cultural turn. In recreating its novelty for contemporaries, Robert Wohl, Vanessa R. Schwartz, Nathalie Roseau, Marie Thébaud-Sorger, and others have done for the airplane what Wolfgang Schivelbusch did for the train: Robert Wohl, *The Spectacle of Flight: Aviation and the Western Imagination, 1920–1950* (New Haven, CT: Yale University Press, 2005); Vanessa R. Schwartz, *Jet Age Aesthetic: The Glamour of Media in Motion* (New Haven, CT: Yale University Press, 2020); Nathalie Roseau and Marie Thébaud-Sorger, eds., *L'emprise du vol: De l'invention à la massification, histoire d'une culture moderne* (Paris: Metispresses, 2013); and Wolfgang Schivelbusch, *The Railway Journey: The Industrialization of Time and Space in the Nineteenth Century* (Berkeley: University of California Press, 1986).

Studies of what we might call French car culture include Catherine Bertho Lavenir, *La roue et le stylo: Comment nous sommes devenus touristes* (Paris: Éditions Odile Jacob, 1999); Mathieu Flonneau, *Les cultures du volant: Essai sur les mondes de l'automobilisme, XXe–XXIe siècles* (Paris: Éditions Autrement, 2008); Flonneau, *L'automobile au temps des trente glorieuses: Un rêve d'automobilisme* (Carbonne: Loubatières, 2016); and Stephen L. Harp, *Marketing Michelin:*

Advertising and Cultural Identity in Twentieth-Century France (Baltimore: Johns Hopkins University Press, 2001). Georges Reverdy considers the history of French roadbuilding in *Les routes de France du XXe siècle, 1900–1951* (Paris: Presses de l'École nationale des Ponts et Chaussées, 2007), while Nicolas Neiertz's *La coordination des transports en France de 1918 à nos jours* (Paris: Comité pour l'histoire économique et financière de la France, 1999) situates the construction of autoroutes in French planning of roads, airports, and train lines. On the German and Italian models for the French autoroute system, see Thomas Zeller, *Driving Germany: The Landscape of the German Autobahn, 1930–1970*, trans. Thomas Dunlap (New York: Berghahn, 2006); James Shand, "The *Reichsautobahnen*: Symbol for the Third Reich," *Journal of Contemporary History* 19, no. 2 (1984): 189–200; and Massimo Moraglio, *Driving Modernity: Technology, Experts, Politics, and Fascist Motorways, 1922–1943*, trans. Erin O'Loughlin (New York: Berghahn, 2017).

Popular histories that keep the imagined Riviera alive in the Anglophone world include John Baxter, *French Riviera and Its Artists: Art, Literature, Love and Life on the Côte d'Azur* (New York: Museyon, 2015); Mary Blume, *Côte d'Azur: Inventing the French Riviera* (New York: Thames & Hudson, 1992); Philippe Collas and Eric Villedary, *Edith Wharton's French Riviera* (Paris: Flammarion, 2002); Anne de Courcy, *Chanel's Riviera: Glamour, Decadence, and Survival in Peace and War, 1930–1944* (New York: St. Martin's, 2020); Julian Hale, *The French Riviera: A Cultural History* (Oxford: Oxford University Press, 2009); Patrick Howarth, *When the Riviera Was Ours* (London: Routledge & Kegan Paul, 1977); Robert Kanigel, *High Season: How One French Riviera Town Has Seduced Travelers for Two Thousand Years* (New York: Viking, 2002); Mary S. Lovell, *The Riviera Set: Glitz, Glamour, and the Hidden World of High Society* (New York: Pegasus Books, 2017); Michael Nelson, *Americans and the Making of the Riviera* (Jefferson, NC: McFarland, 2008); Nelson, *The French Riviera: A History* (Kibworth Beauchamp, UK: Matador, 2017); Nelson, *Queen Victoria and the Discovery of the Riviera* (London: I. B. Taurus, 2001); Kenneth E. Silver, *Making Paradise: Art, Modernity, and the Myth of the French Riviera* (Cambridge, MA: MIT Press, 2001); and Amanda Vaill, *Everybody Was So Young, George and Sara Murphy: A Lost Generation Love Story* (Boston: Houghton Mifflin, 1998). In *Riviera: The Rise and Rise of the Côte d'Azur* (London: John Murray, 2004), Jim Ring interestingly bookends his history of foreigners' "invention" of the Riviera with short critiques of pollution, public housing, and stone beaches.

On the notion of urban metabolism, see Nektarios Chrysoulakis, Eduardo Anselmo de Castro, and Eddy J. Moors, eds., *Understanding Urban Metabolism: A Tool for Urban Planning* (London: Routledge, 2015); Ian Douglas, *Cities: An*

Environmental History (London: I. B. Taurus, 2013); Paulo Ferrão and John E. Fernández, *Sustainable Urban Metabolism* (Cambridge, MA: MIT Press, 2013); Nik Heynen, Maria Kaika, and Erik Swyngedouw, eds., *In the Nature of Cities: Urban Political Ecology and the Politics of Urban Metabolism* (London: Routledge, 2006); Joel A. Tarr, "The Metabolism of the Industrial City: The Case of Pittsburgh," *Journal of Urban History* 28 (2002): 511–45; Sabine Barles, "Urban Metabolism and River Systems: An Historical Perspective. Paris and the Seine, 1790–1970," *Hydrology and Earth System Science* 11 (2007): 1757–69; Sabine Barles and Laurence Lestel, "The Nitrogen Question: Urbanisation, Industrialisation and River Quality in Paris (France), 1830–1939," *Journal of Urban History* 33 (2007): 794–812; Erik Swyngedouw, "Circulations and Metabolisms: (Hybrid) Natures and (Cyborg) Cities," *Science as Culture* 15 (2006): 105–21; and Matthew Gandy, "Rethinking Urban Metabolism: Water, Space and the Modern City," *City* 8 (2004): 363–79.

For examples of the connections between the environment and labor, see Thomas G. Andrews, *Killing for Coal: America's Deadliest Labor War* (Cambridge, MA: Harvard University Press, 2008); Andrews, "Work, Nature, and History: A Single Question, That Once Moved Like Light," in Andrew C. Isenberg, ed., *The Oxford Handbook of Environmental History* (New York: Oxford University Press, 2017), 423–66; Stéphane Kronenberger, "Les ouvriers des calanques," in Xavier Daumalin and Isabelle Laffont-Schwob, eds., *Les calanques industrielles et leurs pollutions: Une histoire au présent* (Aix-en-Provence: REF.2C Éditions, 2016), 93–129; Annie Gilbert Coleman, "The Rise of the House of Leisure: Outdoor Guides, Practical Knowledge, and Industrialization," *Western Historical Quarterly* 42 (2011): 436–57; Raymond Williams, *The Country and the City* (New York: Oxford University Press, 1973); Richard White, "Are You an Environmentalist or Do You Work for a Living? Work and Nature," in William Cronon, ed., *Uncommon Ground: Rethinking the Human Place in Nature* (New York: Norton, 1995), 171–85; and Geneviève Massard-Guilbaud and Stephen Mosley, eds., *Common Ground: Integrating the Social and Environmental in History* (Newcastle upon Tyne: Cambridge Scholars, 2011).

Finally, moving well beyond the borders of France, several intriguing recent studies of the social and environmental impacts of tourism flesh out parts of the global context for the profound changes on the Riviera: Scott Moranda, *The People's Own Landscape: Nature, Tourism, and Dictatorship in East Germany* (Ann Arbor: University of Michigan Press, 2014); Jenny Chio, *A Landscape of Travel: The Work of Tourism in Rural Ethnic China* (Seattle: University of Washington Press, 2014); Connie Chiang, *Shaping the Shoreline: Fisheries and Tourism on the Monterey Coast* (Seattle: University of Washington

Press, 2011); Chanelle N. Rose, *The Struggle for Black Freedom in Miami: Civil Rights and America's Tourist Paradise, 1896–1968* (Baton Rouge: Louisiana State University Press, 2015); Andrew W. Kahrl, *The Land Was Ours: How Black Beaches Became White Wealth in the Coastal South* (Cambridge, MA: Harvard University Press, 2012); and William Philpott, *Vacationland: Tourism and the Environment in the Colorado High Country* (Seattle: University of Washington Press, 2014).

Index

Page numbers in *italics* refer to figures.

A SHEARWATER BOOK

All the WILD *and* LONELY PLACES

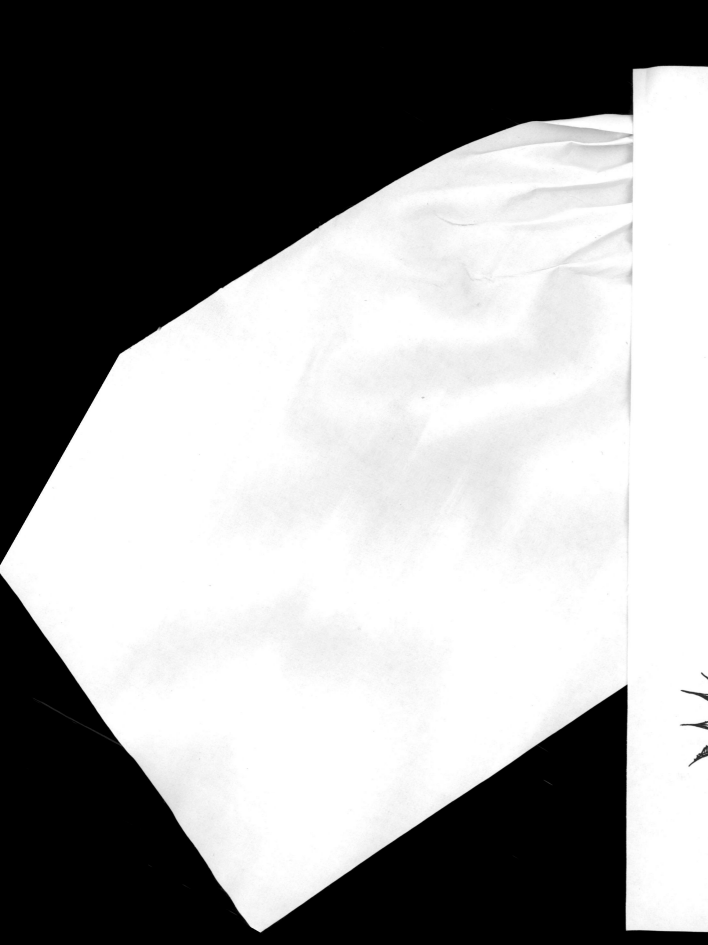

All the WILD
and LONELY
PLACES
JOURNEYS
in a DESERT
LANDSCAPE

LAWRENCE HOGUE

Island Press / SHEARWATER BOOKS

Washington, D.C. • *Covelo, California*

A Shearwater Book
published by Island Press

Copyright © 2000 Lawrence Hogue

Shearwater Books is a trademark of The

"Domelands: Reading the Desert" ap'
fall 1998.
"Epilogue: Eyes in the Dark" app
January 1997, as "Ghosts in th

Library of Congress Catalo
Hogue, Lawrence, 196
All the wild and lone'
by Lawrence Hog'
p. cm.
Includes bibliog.
ISBN 1-55963-651-3
1. Anza-Borrego Desert
Desert State Park (Calif.)—De
(Calif.)—Environmental conditions.
History. 5. Landscape—California—Ai.
6. Natural history—California—Anza-Borre
I. Title.
F868.S15 H68 2000
917.94'98—dc21   00-008181

Printed on recycled, acid-free paper
Manufactured in the United States of America

10 9 8 7 6 5 4 3 2 1

Contents

The love of wilderness is more than a hunger for
what is always beyond reach; it is also an expression
of loyalty to the earth, the earth which bore us and
sustains us, the only home we shall ever know, the only
paradise we ever need. . . . A civilization which destroys
what little remains of the wild, the spare, the original,
is cutting itself off from its origins and betraying the
principle of civilization itself.

      EDWARD ABBEY, *Desert Solitaire*

All the wild and lonely places, the mountain springs
are called now. They were not lonely or wild places in
the past days—no. They were the homes of my people,
who lived contented and happy. Sometimes an Indian
goes back into the mountains to a spring of water.
There
he visits, alone, the home of his ancestors.

      CHIEF FRANCISCO PATENCIO,
      Stories and Legends of the Palm Springs Indians

PART I

INTRODUCTORY

Chapter 1

THE VIEW
FROM GARNET PEAK

IMAGINE the shape of the land here in California's southwestern corner. As you move inland from the coast, it rises gently in successive mesas and canyons for twenty miles until you reach the first foothills. The grade becomes steeper then as you travel through hills and valleys to the summits of the Laguna Mountains, part of the Peninsular Ranges, the long backbone running north to Mt. San Jacinto, towering above Palm Springs, and south to the tip of Baja California. To the east from that crest, the land falls away in one dramatic plunge to the Anza-Borrego Desert, five thousand feet below. The mountains create the aridity of the country to the east, blocking moisture from Pacific storms. Beyond them, there's nothing but desert—desert plains, desert sinks, desert peaks. On a clear day, peaks in Arizona float on the horizon, their bases obscured by the curve of the earth.

In a good year, three inches of rain fall beyond the mountains. Temperatures in summer often reach 115 degrees Fahrenheit; in winter, they sometimes dip below freezing. The wind howls much of the time. Everything out here, plant and animal, has had to adapt to these harsh circumstances. It's a land of dreams and nightmares, where the waking world meets the fantastic shapes and bent forms of imagination: spiny, many-armed chollas; agaves growing like clustered daggers; the tall, whiplike wands of ocotillos. It is a landscape laid bare, showing the effects of water everywhere, though water itself is seldom seen.

If you stand facing east on Garnet Peak in the Laguna Mountains, you

can see it all, the entire sixty- by thirty-mile expanse of Anza-Borrego Desert State Park and the country beyond. This is the western edge of the Southwest. Behind you, it's all California; to the east, the land has more to do, ecologically and culturally, with Arizona and the Colorado River country. Basin and range country begins here, too—isolated summits jutting from the Peninsular Ranges alternate with badland basins and dry sinks. Those peaks literally slid off the Peninsular crest. Crowned with juniper and pinyon pine, they look like ships sailing out into the desert sea. Here and there, springs well up to create lush oases. Deep canyons cut the mountain flanks, tracing courses across alluvial fans covered with agave and barrel cactus, through flats covered with creosote bush, and over contorted badlands—a landscape of mud hills that look like giant, multi-colored layer cakes in cross section. The desert washes run eventually into the largest basin of them all, the Salton Trough.

None of the water that occasionally fills these washes finds its way to the ocean. All the land visible eastward from Garnet Peak—a great half-circle that extends down the entire eastern flank of the Peninsular Ranges, from the San Jacinto and Santa Rosa Mountains in the north through the San Ysidro, Volcan, and Laguna Mountains above the heart of Anza-Borrego to the In-Ko-Pah and Jacumba Mountains in the south, then across the vague, flat expanse toward the Gulf of California and back north on the other side of the basin through the Chocolate and Orocopia Mountains—all that land tilts into this long trough, a trench 225 feet below sea

View from Garnet Peak

level containing the Imperial and Coachella Valleys and the pale blue waters of the Salton Sea. The effect is that of looking into a vast, oblong bowl with a blue center, scalloped around its edges with beaches of white sand.

The entire region between the Peninsular Ranges and the Colorado River is known as the Colorado Desert, itself a subsection of the Sonoran Desert, which extends into Arizona and northern Mexico. The Anza-Borrego Desert is, then, a land of edges: the western edge of the Colorado Desert, on the western edge of the Sonoran Desert; edged by the burgeoning population of coastal southern California to the west and the reclaimed desert and towns of the Imperial Valley to the east. Most important, it's a desert at the verge of the mountains. In that meeting of alpine and desert habitats, an astonishing diversity of plants and animals emerges. This is the country encompassed by Anza-Borrego Desert State Park, a 600,000-acre expanse of some of the most varied terrain and habitat in the United States.

The place has a hold on me that is hard to describe. Its vastness draws me with a force I don't quite understand. The expanse of rock, sand, and sky seems timeless; the bizarre shapes of desert plants seem prehistoric, even prehuman. Compared with the rest of southern California, a region where landscapes are transformed with the rapidity of a sea breeze shifting to become a hot, dry Santa Ana, Anza-Borrego seems immune to change. It's a country so sere and rugged that it's easy to imagine no one has ever set foot there—a wilderness waiting to be explored.

On my first visit there, in 1987, Anza-Borrego's wilderness promised an escape from human problems—all those ills associated with the crowded city, even a comfortable one such as San Diego. In the desert, I hoped to find pure nature, in its canyons the keys to mysteries, on its peaks perhaps even transcendence. So I unconsciously cropped my view, just as photographers do to avoid the annoying telephone wire or building they don't want to intrude on the scene they are constructing for their viewers.

In a sense, though, the place was already framed for me by the boundaries of the state park. Inside was the sanctioned playground. Outside, the boundaries suggested, I was more likely to run into someone I didn't want to meet: an off-roader, a target shooter, a psycho with a car full of guns, or

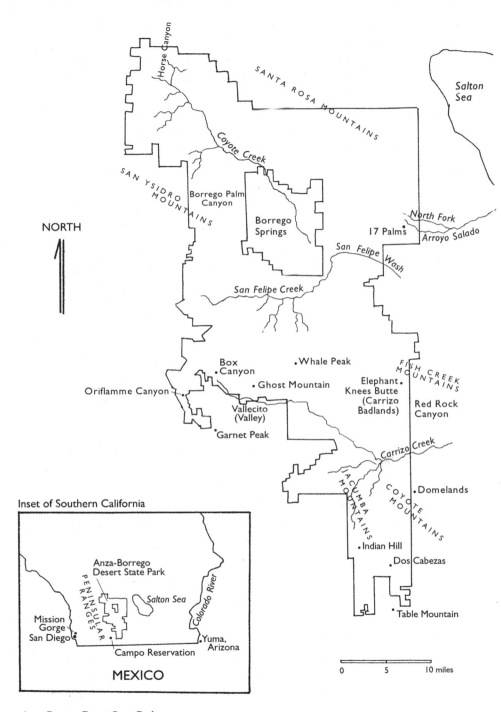

NORTH

Horse Canyon

SANTA ROSA MOUNTAINS

Salton Sea

Coyote Creek

SAN YSIDRO MOUNTAINS

Borrego Palm Canyon

Borrego Springs

North Fork

17 Palms

Arroyo Salado

San Felipe Wash

San Felipe Creek

•Whale Peak

Box Canyon

•Ghost Mountain

FISH CREEK MOUNTAINS

Oriflamme Canyon

Elephant Knees Butte (Carrizo Badlands)

Red Rock Canyon

Vallecito (Valley)

•Garnet Peak

Carrizo Creek

JACUMBA MOUNTAINS

COYOTE MOUNTAINS

•Domelands

•Indian Hill

•Dos Cabezas

•Table Mountain

Inset of Southern California

Anza-Borrego Desert State Park

PENINSULAR RANGES

Salton Sea

Colorado River

Mission Gorge San Diego•

•Yuma, Arizona

Campo Reservation

MEXICO

0   5   10 miles

Anza-Borrego Desert State Park

maybe just the desert rats who I thought were crazy to live out on the flats where the wind never stops. Inside the park boundaries, tucked up against the protecting wall of the mountains, it all seemed safe—just a few rattlesnakes and tarantulas, mountain lions and coyotes to avoid.

Within the park, I had to keep cropping the view to see the place as pure nature. Even its hyphenated name suggested a confluence of the human and the natural: *Anza* refers to an early Spanish explorer, *borrego* to the bighorn sheep that are the park's most widely known denizens. Even though the evidence of human occupation was obvious, I kept it stored carefully in one corner of my mind. Indians had dwelt here for thousands of years before Europeans came. Footpaths, rock art, pieces of pottery, even remnants of ancient dwellings dot the landscape; the changes these first inhabitants made to the landscape itself were at first less apparent. To the Indians, this was home; today, we call much of it a wilderness.

Following the first peoples to dwell on the land, the Spanish, after a few tentative explorations, colonized the region two centuries ago. They were followed in the nineteenth century by American mountain men, pioneers, and forty-niners. Many of these successive waves of immigrants passed through the badlands and the valley directly below Garnet Peak, where old wheel ruts can still be seen. More recently, ranchers ran cattle in the desert, fattening them on the spring wildflower bloom. Early in the twentieth century, a twisting, impossible rail line was built through Carrizo Gorge, down near the border. Although the state park was created in the 1930s, preservation was put on hold for World War II, when the navy used the desert as a bombing range. Now, half a million visitors each year come to see the sunrise paint the rocks red, to smell the flowers in April, and to try to find a moment of silence.

Anza-Borrego is a romantic landscape, a place for photographers to snap pictures of sunsets, a place to get lost in silent slot canyons. This is the side of the desert that drew me back every fall for ten years. But the desert is also a place where people intrude. Initially, I viewed the pottery shards and rock art, the line shacks and broken water troughs as part of that romance of the past, but it was harder to ignore the dirt roads snaking across the park and the cars and trucks that used them.

I use those roads, too, driving to favorite hiking spots. I plan elaborate expeditions to get as far from the roads as possible. But even this isn't

enough to escape the marks left by humans. Hiking ten miles into the backcountry, I see a Peninsular bighorn sheep. Chances are that animal has been radio-collared, weighed, and tested, all in an attempt to keep this subspecies from going extinct. (There is no chance I'll see a desert prong-horn, which disappeared locally back in the 1940s.) Or I hike up what seemed to be a pristine desert canyon and find a pretty green shrub with reddish bark and a spray of pink flowers. It is a tamarisk, which doesn't belong there; the tamarisk is an invading species, another threat to local diversity that our species seems to bring everywhere it goes. If I don't find a tamarisk, it could be that a restoration crew has removed it—grooming the wilderness.

But the image that I keep coming back to is that of the Salton Sea, the most telling scene in the panorama visible from Garnet Peak. From there, it looks like a natural lake filling the Salton Trough. But that view is decep-tive: the lake is actually the result of a poorly engineered 1904 irrigation project intended to bring the water of the Colorado River to the Imperial Valley. The Salton Sea is thus in part a human-made lake, but it simulates a natural body of water, the ancient Lake Cahuilla, which filled the basin as recently as 500 years ago. Today, it is an important stop on the Pacific flyway for hundreds of thousands of migratory geese, pelicans, and other shorebirds. Nearly every year, thousands, sometimes hundreds of thou-sands, of those birds die from mysterious causes associated with the lake's rising salinity and toxicity.

The Salton Sea owes its continued existence to runoff from Imperial and Coachella Valley fields; its fate, and that of the fish and birds that depend on it, is in our hands. Some people want to "save" the Salton Sea, and others want to "let nature take its course." But the lake is such a blend of the human and the natural that "nature's course" is far from clear.

This book tells the story of the Anza-Borrego Desert region, the peo-ple who have lived there, the different ways these people have treated the desert, and the plans for its future. It also tells the story of how my view of Anza-Borrego has changed, from that of a wilderness to something more like home. Along the way, I've had to question all my thoughts and beliefs about nature and wilderness. Humans have always played a role in nature. We're too deeply involved to simply leave it alone. Yet like many others who are distressed by the overmanipulation and outright destruc-

tion going on everywhere around us, I find something deeply attractive in the nonhuman, the prehuman. How, then, to chart a course between these two extremes—absolute human domination and absolute human absence—to find an honorable role for humans in nature?

Chapter 2

DOS CABEZAS:
INITIATION

O N MY first visit to the Anza-Borrego Desert, no one had to tell me that it was a wilderness. That much seemed obvious at first sight—a glimpse of dry, tan hills in the distance as our car swooped around the curves of Interstate 8 on its plunge down the eastern scarp of the Jacumba Mountains. Beyond those distant hills was nothing but clear, luminous space, lit by the sun as it pecked through gaps in a receding band of clouds. Much was promised in that single glimpse, cut off by a bend of boulder-strewn canyon wall.

It was 1987, and my wife, Diane, and I were on our way to the first outing of the Sierra Club's Basic Mountaineering Course. Diane had backpacked for years with the Girl Scouts, but except for a few nights of carcamping, I was a novice. This first trip would introduce us to the basics of low-impact camping and to the desert environment.

As we emerged onto the desert floor near the little town of Ocotillo, the hills we had seen from above grew into mountains, rising from the plains in striated reds, tans, browns, and whites. We turned north and then west onto a jeep trail and moved back toward the high mountains, regaining a thousand feet of the elevation we had just lost. The road crossed a *bajada*, a broad gravel-and-sand skirt created by the combined flood debris of many alluvial fans flowing together. Tall sprays of ocotillos and the twisted shapes of chollas lined the route as if greeting us.

It's hard to recapture how new the desert seemed to us. We didn't even know the name of the valley we were driving through or the names of the

mountains on either side. To the north, more peaks rose up, thirty, forty miles distant, all nameless, all waiting to be explored. I remember thinking that the cacti and succulents we passed seemed aquatic, grotesque. I could imagine their many-armed branches waving to the rhythm of sea currents instead of a light breeze making its way down from the mountains.

After setting up camp, we went for a hike with our group. Our instructor began introducing us to the more obvious and dangerous plants. First, the Big Three. The chollas, branching cacti covered in barbed, needle-sharp spines, were the most plentiful. We were to watch out for the cholla balls, segments of the cactus that drop off and attach themselves to pant-legs, boots, and skin. Growing among the chollas were clusters of agaves, sometimes called century plants, with sharp, daggerlike fronds radiating from the ground. After ten or twelve years of growth during which the agave puts out more and more fronds, the plant concentrates all its energy into sending up a single, twelve-foot stalk topped by white flowers. Dead agave stalks can stand for years; the desert around us was dotted with them, standing like scattered sentinels. Ocotillos, or coachwhips, were less plentiful here but still dangerous. Their barbed, polelike branches end in slender tips, making them look like bundles of whips.

There was yet another plant to watch for, though at first it looked harmless: the catclaw acacia. Its soft green leaves hide sharp, curved thorns that hook clothing and skin. Once hooked, a hiker usually has to back up and go around, earning this small tree the Sierra Club nickname of the "wait-a-minute bush."

Spines and daggers, thorns and claws: the list makes the desert sound forbidding. But on that winter day, with the temperature in the low seventies and the sun shining, a slight breeze waving the ocotillos, the desert seemed benign, even welcoming. The sun sparkled gold and silver off the chollas, and there were countless more innocuous plants whose names we hadn't learned. It would take me years to begin to discover their names: cheesebush and brittlebush, white sage and white bur sage, Mormon tea and desert lavender. The creosote bush—slender, rangy branches cloaked in drab olive green leaves—was perhaps the most common, giving the desert its characteristic tangy smell. Biologists now think that creosote bushes, growing in colonies that reproduce clonally, are one of the oldest

living single organisms on earth. The plants we were walking among could have been more ancient than the sequoias.

We hiked over a pass between two hills and entered a landscape out of an old Western: blind draws and labyrinthine canyons and high, rocky passes. A group of peaks on our right, known as the Volcanic Hills, were capped with the telltale purple and red rock of lava flows. On the left, granitic outcrops thrust toward the sky, tan and gold quartz diorite and tonalite, sometimes burnished dark brown with desert varnish. The boulders in these outcrops were piled in improbable formations—balance rocks, leaning rocks, arch rocks. Who knew how they had come to rest this way? The formations seemed almost arranged, as if some giant invisible hand had been at work here.

The ground we covered was composed of the same granitic rock crushed down to a coarse sand. It made for a quick-draining soil on which the desert plants thrived. "Because it's clean" was Lawrence of Arabia's famous response when asked why he loved the desert, and I recognized how he felt: there was no dirt, no dust, very little organic matter to rot or cling or smear. You could roll in this sand and come up clean. I began to feel I was experiencing a kind of spiritual cleansing, mysterious and subtle, but growing as the day progressed.

We paused at an old cowboy's or shepherd's shack, probably built in the 1890s. Tucked away in a little draw, it was barely visible from the wash below. Its wooden beams had fallen in, and its tin roof had torn and rusted. The dirt floor was covered with cholla balls, a pack rat's hoard. A set of rusted bedsprings rested against the back wall, lonely and forgotten, the only evidence of a human life lived here. The desert had slowly begun to absorb the building, making it increasingly a part of the landscape.

Farther on, we came to a railway camp that had been built to service the construction of the San Diego and Arizona Eastern Railroad in the early 1900s. The camp was perched on a sandy slope, with bits of machinery and rusted five-gallon tin cans lying about. A shack had been made from these cans cut lengthwise. A couple of posts stood out away from the shack, an iron bar suspended between them. Even out in the open, and as out of place as this machinery was, the camp seemed to fit in the desert. The rusted metal scraps looked as if they could have erupted from the earth along with the nearby Volcanic Hills.

At Indian Hill, we saw evidence of a much older culture, one that had left fewer traces on the land. By now, whatever marks the Kumeyaay Indians and earlier indigenous peoples made here have mostly been absorbed by the desert or stolen by amateur archaeologists. We found a low overhang blackened by centuries of fire, a flat rock covered with *morteros* (grinding holes for mesquite beans and other plant foods), and a couple of pieces of broken pottery on the ground nearby. But the most obvious remnants were the thousand-year-old pictographs our group leader had told us about: bizarre, one-eyed anthropomorphs, sunbursts in red and yellow, and schematics of lizards and bighorn sheep, none of which held much meaning for me. Scattered among these were geometric figures that held no meaning at all.

My companions had a similar response. After taking a quick look at the pictographs, their gaze turned out to the desert, as if they were hoping to find an object these designs represented. We had expected some message from the past, a picture that would show us the lives of these artists and perhaps illuminate our own. We expected representation and got abstract art. The figures seemed to come from that Dreamtime we call prehistory—the time before white people got here to write it all down. And what would there have been to record? Indian occupation of the rock shelter near there dated back almost six thousand years. Yet other than those paintings and a scattering of potsherds, the Indians seemed to have left few traces, or so it seemed to me at the time. History, I thought, must be the story of change, and change, it seemed clear, began only with the coming of Europeans to this desert, the people who had built the shack and the railroad camp and the rail line that ran nearby.

I hadn't really come for a cultural tour, so I was glad when we left behind this evidence of human occupation and dropped into a steep canyon containing a grove of California fan palms. We were told these were natives, not the ersatz imported palms lining our streets back in San Diego. I had read about them before. "They survive in the wild now by having the audacity to stand in any available water source and shade out or shrug off everything else," one writer had said. "If you take the time to stalk them into the broken hills you can see them wild." We looked for the water that supported the trees but found none, just a musky, damp feeling in the air around the grove. There were perhaps a dozen palms, some of them dis-

playing full skirts of dried fronds that made them look like tall grass shacks. These were trees that had never been touched by vandals' fires.

Even the more obvious human marks we had seen on our journey so far couldn't dim my conviction that this place was essentially a wilderness. People had lived and worked here in various ways, but compared with, say, San Diego, the area was untouched, pristine—virgin desert. Or perhaps I just saw what I wanted to see—an untracked wilderness.

From the lectures we were given on low-impact camping to the mottoes of backpacking stores where we bought our gear ("Leave only footprints, take only memories") to the signs posted at some nature preserves ("Wildlife Habitat—Keep Out"), the message was that humans are invaders in the wilderness. Left alone, nature is a delicately balanced machine, like a Swiss watch, and humans are like sand in its gears, grinding it to a halt. This view is enshrined in the Wilderness Act of 1964, which defines wilderness as a place where "man is a visitor who does not remain"—a definition just short of saying that wilderness is a place where humans don't belong. Others are more explicit. In *The End of Nature*, Bill McKibben comments, "If we can't have places where no man has ever been, we can at least have spots where no man is at the moment."

Even as visitors to these natural places, our proper relationship to the land seemed to be one of looking, never of touching, tasting, or interacting. The wilderness might become part of us, but we could never become part of it. We were like visitors to a museum, looking at displays in a glass case.

THAT night, we camped right up against the base of the Jacumba Mountains at Dos Cabezas, a place named for the two house-size boulders that perch above it, watching over the desert like strange guardians. Nearby, catclaws and desert willows grew around a piped spring feeding an old water trough. Looking back across the valley, I could see the Coyote Mountains, the setting sun sculpting their contorted outlines. The canyons cutting into their flanks were shadowed, dark, mysterious. I wondered where those canyons led, how it was in the heart of those mountains. The Jacumba Mountains rising behind me looked barren from a distance, yet here we were camped at their feet near a spring surrounded by green trees filled with the chatter of birds. Did the mountains across

the valley hold equal surprises? Beyond them, there seemed to be nothing but infinite space. Something in me hungered for an escape into those canyons and into that void beyond. I wanted to leave behind all that was human, to find emptiness, a space in which to lose myself.

IT TOOK me another six years to make that trip to the Coyote Mountains. In between, I explored other areas of Anza-Borrego. I went on trips with the Sierra Club, with friends, and with Diane. I hiked and drove the jeep roads, car-camped, and backpacked. I learned to use a map and compass so I could navigate convoluted terrain where there was no trail—or only faint, ancient Indian paths. I became obsessed with having the best back-packing gear. I learned climbing techniques in case I needed to scale an unexpected dry waterfall blocking a canyon route or climb a difficult boulder on a mountaintop.

As goals for many of these trips, I chose particular summits, granite-topped knobs jutting from the main crest of the Peninsular Ranges: the Vallecito Mountains in the middle of the park and the higher, wilder Santa Rosa Mountains in the north. I was drawn by the impression of depth and space these peaks afforded—a sense of the three-dimensionality of the world, something I missed, living near the ocean.

I spent time on canyon floors, too, in the deep slots carving the sides of the mountains, their walls often fifty or a hundred feet high and so close together I had to squeeze through. There was a pattern common to the canyon excursions that made each journey familiar, like a trip home. First, there was a rugged approach across a rocky, cactus-dotted alluvial fan where the canyon opened onto the flats below it. Beyond the canyon mouth, patches of sandy streambed alternated with boulder jams and the hard bedrock of dry falls, like a set of stairs climbing the canyon. The walls of the canyon crowded in closer and closer and the rock steps became higher and higher, sometimes impassable. Beyond these slots, the canyon often opened into a broad bowl encircled by steep mountain flanks.

Despite this regular pattern, each canyon had its own character: a group of strange, twisted elephant trees in Torote Canyon, outcrops of rose quartz flecked with black rock in Bighorn Canyon, a hodgepodge of rock colors and shapes in Canyon Sin Nombre, rock tanks in Smoke Tree Canyon. Desert writers from Mary Austin to Edward Abbey have noted

the mysterious quality of the desert, that it seems to hold out a promise. This is what these canyons seemed to hold for me: a promise of treasure, of secrets to be revealed to those who enter. The desert always seemed about to speak, if only I could listen closely enough.

As the years progressed, I found myself going alone to the desert more often. At first, this was because of my schedule, which left me free to hike on weekdays, when neither Diane nor my friends could join me. Later, after the birth of our son, solo trips were the only option if I wanted to go very far or for very long. But mostly I believed that by myself I would have better access to the true nature of the desert. So I went to the Coyote Mountains alone, to pierce the heart of the desert, to learn what secrets it would reveal.

Chapter 3

DOMELANDS:
READING THE DESERT

I<small>T'S AN</small> unusual desert day when I begin my journey: cool, overcast, drizzling off and on since early morning. To the west, thick clouds pour over the crest of the Laguna Mountains like waves rolling ashore, turning to foam as they hit the dry air of the desert. Above me, only a thin cloud cover remains, turning the sun to a light smear in the gray dome of sky. In contrast to the storm over the mountains, everything out here is still—only puffs of wind now and then, an occasional bird swooping by.

None of this fits the story I've brought with me, a story of sun-baked rocks, clear skies, lonely expanses stretching to the horizon. These badlands should be ablaze, illuminated by that absolute clarity of light found only in the desert. Instead, the mud hills seem muted, dormant. Even the new leaves of the ocotillos look dull. The desert in my mind struggles against this actual, rainy-day desert.

I'm walking toward the Coyote Mountains on a dirt road just east of the boundary of Anza-Borrego Desert State Park. Behind me, the mile-high mountains of the Peninsular Ranges stretch from northwest to southeast into Mexico. Ahead of me, to the east, the Coyote Mountains look small in comparison. I know more about them now, from talking with friends and reading guidebooks, than I did when I first gazed across the valley, six years ago. I expect to find 5-million-year-old seashell fossils, wind caves carved in the twisted sandstone that was once seafloor, grand views out over the badlands, and, if I'm lucky, solitude—all rarities that make this place precious.

Nearing the mountains, I come upon two signs beside the road. One, placed by the Bureau of Land Management, declares the Coyote Mountains an "Area of Critical Environmental Concern" because of their easily vandalized fossil resources and because they are habitat for the endangered Peninsular bighorn sheep (one of several subspecies commonly referred to as desert bighorn). An older sign put up by a mining company warns, "No Shooting." Both signs are riddled with bullet holes, statements as powerful as the words they partially obliterate. These signs, I've begun to realize, have become palimpsests, like the desert itself: a manuscript of overlaid marks and erasures. Jeep roads run over old wagon trails; dirt-bike tracks mar thousand-year-old intaglios; moviemakers embellish ancient pictographs; aqueducts and highways cut straight lines where none existed before. The markings have increased dramatically in recent years as more and more people have discovered the desert. To some, it's just a motorized playground or a target range; to others, it's a storehouse of natural resources or a place of beauty.

Today, I want to dig down past all these stories to see the desert as it

Ocotillo

really is. I want to look past all the marks and erasures on this palimpsest and find the original manuscript. Somewhere, I think, under all the marks we've made and all the assumptions we have, I can find the true thing, the desert on its own terms.

For the rest of the hike, I resolve to put aside the impressions in my head and concentrate on the things in front of me: Yellow mud hills in the distance, as barren as any place I've seen in the desert. Creosote bushes closer at hand, their masses of olive-green leaves looking newly washed and covered in yellow flowers. The smell of wet creosote—clean, acrid; sweet, too. The ocotillos have greened up nicely, adding a coat of fresh leaves. In a week or so, bright red flowers will appear at the tip of each branch.

I cross a dry, sandy wash filled with smoke trees. They are only ten or twelve feet tall, and their masses of gray-green twigs make them look like puffs of smoke from a distance. One catches my attention, the only one in bloom among hundreds in the wash. And here's a further singularity: only one of its branches carries the lurid purple flowers. Why just this one branch? Why now, in October? The field guide I am carrying describes the leaves and flowers accurately enough but tells me only that smoke trees usually bloom in June. Let down by the field guide, I make up my own story about the smoke tree. Except for its flowers, the tree doesn't seem quite as healthy as the others near it. One branch is split partway off near the trunk; the others are covered with dried tan stems. Perhaps this is a species survival technique, one last stab at reproduction before the tree dies of some disease or injury.

I pass a quarry with blasted rock and heaved earth. The jeep road turns left and rises steeply into the mountains, becoming fainter the farther I follow it. It was probably built a half century ago, but it's already eroding badly, a trace on the land erased further with every rain. Because it's here, I'll follow it, a strand in a story of mining and resource extraction that I use for my own purposes. Other marks, like the scars of the quarry, will take longer to disappear.

As I enter an enclosed valley, I lose the road entirely and have to find my own way. I can see the Domelands across the valley, maybe half a mile away. They're two or three hundred feet above the valley floor and are capped with outcrops of white rock. I can even make out wind caves pock-

ing the face of the cliffs. But something looks awry. I pull out a U.S. Geological Survey topographic map—another kind of story about the landscape.

At home, I had spent hours staring at the map, translating its symbols and contour lines—representations of changes in elevation—into an image of what the terrain would look like. I pictured myself moving through that image, across the sloping valley the map shows and up into the hills on the opposite side. Now, as I try to relate that image to the actual world, nothing seems to fit. Instead of the gently sloping valley I expected, I see a confusion of twenty-foot mud hills cut by a labyrinth of washes. My imaginings of an easy approach to the summit where I'll camp unravel into a series of detours over and around these hummocks. One wash narrows so much that I can't squeeze through with my backpack. I retreat and scramble up another rise to get my bearings. Finally, I spot a series of hills that thread together into a route toward the peak I'm aiming for.

Near the summit, I discover a little swale between three peaks—a good spot to camp for the night. From a low ridge nearby, I gain a wider view of Anza-Borrego. Carrizo Creek cuts across the badlands in the foreground, out through the gap between the Coyote and Fish Creek Mountains, and on across miles of sandy flats to the Salton Sea in the northeast. This wash drains a vast area beginning southwest of here in the Jacumba Mountains, where the creek passes through Carrizo Gorge. Entering the badlands, it collects runoff from the flanks of the Laguna Mountains in the west and from the Vallecito Mountains in the north. The water mostly stays underground, but it wells up at this confluence of washes to create a green oasis at Carrizo Marsh.

Colors I can see from here: the yellow, cocoa brown, burnt umber, pink, and white of the mud hills; the green swaths of mesquite and tamarisk at the marsh; and the blue of the Salton Sea. In the background, behind the Vallecito Mountains and higher than anything else, the Santa Rosa Mountains rise up from the desert in a long ascending arc. The dark summits of Villager and Rabbit Peaks, forty miles away, are lost in clouds.

More names. Every little broken ridge of the Peninsular Ranges has one. The In-Ko-Pah Mountains, the Sawtooth Mountains, the Tierra Blanca Mountains, on and on until the names become a litany. Some of

these names attempt description, mostly those given two hundred years ago by Spaniards heading north to the missions or chasing deserters through the badlands. There are hundreds of washes with names like Arroyo Hueso (Bone Wash, or perhaps Wash of Drudgery) and Arroyo Seco del Diablo (Devil's Dry Wash). These names tell us less about the actual places than about the people who named them. Still, they have a lilting, musical quality, in contrast to the newer American place-names. Whereas the Spanish attempted description, American settlers named places after themselves: Clark Dry Lake, Harper Flat, McCain Valley— memorials to ownership, to men who ran cattle here, dug wells, and tried to claim the land for themselves.

Even when the American names are descriptive, they are more fanciful than useful, though they sometimes reveal the uses to which Americans put the land. Hellhole Canyon, for instance, isn't particularly hellish; it has a pleasant waterfall enjoyed by modern-day hikers. But for a cattle rancher, it *was* a hell of a hole from which to retrieve stray cattle. In other cases, the names are pure whimsy. Twenty miles northwest of me, the Vallecito Mountains are crowned by a summit with the odd name of Whale Peak. The mountain does look something like the hump of a breaching whale, but only from certain angles. From others, it looks like a large, dark welt on a forehead, a black spider with steep avalanche chutes for legs, or a circus tent propped over a dirt lot. From here, it's just a bump on a long, high ridge.

I SPEND the afternoon exploring the Domelands, picking through the litter of fossilized sand dollars and poking into the wind caves. I hike down a canyon that cuts into the convoluted hills south of my campsite. For most of the way, I follow a single set of footprints in the sandy wash. I recognize the outline of a large man's boot, but I can't tell how old these prints are. Who left these tracks? Just another hiker in search of solitude, like me? Probably. There are other possibilities: a lost border crosser, a drug smuggler out to hide his stash? Both possible but not likely. Now I don't know whether I'm alone out here or not. I'm glad when I lose the tracks as I circle back by way of the steep ridge above the canyon.

It's late afternoon by the time I return to my pack. There's something forlorn in the way it sits on the ground, as if abandoned. I remember now

that my truck was the only vehicle parked at the trailhead. That solitary hiker must have been here some other day. With evening approaching, I have the place to myself. I realize, as if it weren't obvious, that I'll have to spend the long hours of darkness alone.

This is silly. I've come here to be alone, and now, only a few hours since leaving town, I feel not only alone but also lonely. Part of this is residual bogeyman fear from childhood. But there's more, a nameless dread I can't put my finger on.

The drizzle has let up, and the sun makes a last appearance before sinking behind the mountains. The storm has washed all the dust and haze out of the air; the atmosphere is scrubbed clean. There is energy in a storm, and this one seems to leave some of it behind as it moves east. Even the birds seem invigorated, frolicking in the gusting, groaning winds. Swallows swoop in the breeze above the peak. I hear a long birdsong, a quick upward scale and a longer descending arc. Another bird makes a single loud chirp. Shafts of golden light march across the badlands, playing across the mud hills, teasing, bathing some of them in yellow light and leaving others in shadow. In the movies, this is how it looks when God is about to speak.

The scene should make me feel better, but it doesn't. No voice accompanies these shafts of light. As beautiful as these badlands are with their range of light and color, there's also something daunting about them. I watch the birds, the light, and the storm, trying to see how they all fit together. They don't. They seem as isolated from one another as people on a busy city street. I don't fit here either. I've left behind everything that tells me who I am—my wife and son, my extended family, my friends, the people and things that keep me placed. Now I don't know why I'm here. I've been fighting this feeling all day, keeping myself busy, hiking and exploring. As I come to rest, with nothing to do, the feeling crowds in on me.

I had dreamed of losing myself in the vastness of the desert. But now, in that vastness, no vision comes. What I'm left with is simple fear—fear that I have no significance here; worse, that nothing around me has significance. When I strip the human stories from the desert, I'm left with nothing but rock so ancient it means nothing to me. All the geologic

knowledge in the world won't illuminate the rock I'm standing on. It seems like any other rock, belonging only to the quotidian present.

All day, I've tried to leave behind my stories and let the desert speak to me on its own terms. Now that I've succeeded, I find that the desert doesn't speak at all. This is the mirror that the desert holds up for me—a nothingness reflecting back nothing. It's as if, having rubbed out all the marks and erasures on this page, I've torn a hole in the manuscript. The cacti, the ocotillos, the birds flitting about: they don't mean anything; they just *are*, and who knows why? There is no story here if I don't supply one. I've brought myself to the edge of an abyss deeper and blacker than any vastness the desert has to offer. Psychologists call this state narrative dysfunction. To lose the story of who you are and where you are is to lose your mind.

MORNING. Clouds pour over the Laguna Mountains, but it's clear out here. A dark shape lands on the ridge opposite me: a raven. It gives out several *aaak*s and then flies up behind the dome near my campsite, its wings whooshing through the still air. I eat my breakfast of instant oatmeal and coffee and watch the light hit the Carrizo Badlands, playing across the angles of ridges. Last night's terror is gone, perhaps only because I know I'll be going home today.

Above Whale Peak, a cloud catches the sun's first rays, reflecting them onto the granite-covered mountain and bathing it in an orange glow. Even though it's not the most prominent landmark I can see, Whale Peak draws my attention. I can't look at its rocky bulk without remembering the times I've been up there. The inadequacy of its name again strikes me. I want a new name for the mountain, one that captures what it means to me: "Boulder-juniper-pinyon-covered maze; Barton proposed to Viraj there New Year's Day 1988; I nearly got lost on the north side last spring; I gathered pinyon nuts there, planted them in pots on our front porch." A true name, true for me at least, and one that's never finished. Whenever a friend mentions Whale Peak, this is the name I really hear.

Last night, I realized that I can't escape from stories to see some true essence of the desert. If the desert is a palimpsest, then I can't dig down to an original manuscript. There are only layers and more layers; all the

marks and erasures are part of what this place is. Geology shows me one strand of that story, Indian creation tales another. Sheep trails, Indian footpaths, mining roads, jeep tracks, hikers' paths: each can bring me closer to the heart of this desert. By returning again and again, I can gain new strands of the story, weaving in stories of my own, making this place part of my internal landscape, making it part of my home.

PART II

DEEP TIME

Chapter 4

CARRIZO BADLANDS:
WALKING ON THE
BOTTOM OF THE SEA

I'M SITTING on Elephant Knees Butte, just south of Split Mountain and Fish Creek Wash, a popular jeep route in the center of Anza-Borrego Desert State Park. The butte is a 600-foot block of sculpted mud whose lower portion has eroded into truncated ridges that look from a distance like the knees of a kneeling elephant. From up here, though, they look like a series of ski jumps. I imagine gliding down the initial steep ramp and then shooting into space from the upturned end of the ridge. But the maze of low mud hills below would make for a hard landing.

From this vantage, the mud hills radiate out in all directions. To the west, the badland topography is interrupted by the flat plain of East Mesa and then continues nearly to the mile-high wall of the Laguna Mountains. To the south and east, the hills stretch even farther, a convoluted jumble of water-sculpted forms, pale yellow and tan mostly, with subtle shadings of light pink and chocolate brown. Some are layered like a tiered cake; others are a uniform yellow. In one spot to the east, there is a swath of unearthly, blood-red rock, a shade that is deep but bright at the same time. And these are just the colors I see now, at noon. Toward sunset, the colors will deepen to bright oranges and reds.

This is the most desertlike of any place I've been in the park. The mud hills are completely barren, too alkaline to support even the hardiest desert plant. Walking through them, I feel as if I could be Lawrence of Arabia, or

Clint Eastwood in the beginning of *The Good, the Bad, and the Ugly*. Instead of shifting dunes of sand, however, these hills are made of loose clay and silt. My boots sink several inches with each step. Viewed from the top of the butte, the mud hills stand like frozen waves surrounding a tiny island. Two or three other buttes dot the horizon, an archipelago of islands separated by the rolling hills. The ocean metaphor is fitting: 5 million years ago, these badlands at the eastern edge of Anza-Borrego were underneath the waters of the Gulf of California, and I would have needed diving gear to get to this spot.

Remnants of that ocean are everywhere. The top of this butte is made of coquina shell beds, a hard, reddish brown matrix of sandstone and oyster and scallop shells. This hard cap has protected the mud underneath from erosion, allowing the butte to remain standing while the exposed hills around it were melting away. Each small chunk of the coquina contains hundreds of shell fragments, shiny oyster shells, and delicately fluted shells of pectens, or scallops. The fossils are fragile—many have broken out of the loose sandstone where they've lain embedded for eons, and they now lie strewn in fragments across the slope. I pick up the loose ones, taking care not to break them as I inspect the delicate fluting of the shells' imprints.

Think in deep time. That's the lesson of standing on an ancient seabed at 1,000 feet elevation. Keep in mind the malleability—the unpredictability—of this landscape. What I see here now might be radically different from what was here even a thousand years ago, let alone a million. Thinking in geologic time is the only way to begin to understand this place.

The Indians who lived in Anza-Borrego knew this. The Cahuilla Indians even had a word that embodied the constantly changing nature of their environment: ˀivaˀa was the motivating power for the entire universe, a power that was "quixotic" and therefore unpredictable. This concept, according to Lowell John Bean, an expert on the Cahuilla, conveyed the "all-pervasive and intense feeling of apprehension of the Cahuilla toward the present and future." "When the time comes," they would say, meaning that catastrophe could strike at any moment.

Cahuilla stories tell of streams changing course or becoming intermittent, of springs going dry. Four hundred years after Lake Cahuilla evaporated, the Cahuilla were still telling of the time when their grandfathers

were fishermen. Everything had changed, and they had been forced to find another way to live. Such stories encouraged the Cahuilla to stay mobile and adaptable—though they had permanent villages, they could easily rebuild in a new place when an earthquake or a flood wiped out their homes. They didn't accumulate many things that could be lost: when a person died, the family burned the deceased's hut and possessions to the ground.

Today, we've developed a different adaptation to the desert. Out in the Imperial Valley, we've made it adapt to us. Irrigated with Colorado River water, the valley's green fields give the lie to their desert heritage. New subdivisions deny what the valley could one day become: the northern tip of the Gulf of California. Our stories tell us that most of the time, we can control nature. But the land has its own stories to tell.

It wasn't so long ago that this region was home to saber-toothed cats, mastodons, camels, and the tropical Sabal palm. Then everything changed. The geologic story of how the desert came to be is a dramatic one, filled with seas rising and receding, tectonic plates colliding, rock twisting into fantastic shapes, and mountain blocks falling like dominoes. It explains why the peoples who have lived there—at least until recently—have had to rely on sophisticated adaptations to an arid, hot environment. And it explains why all our stories that would make us masters of nature are, ultimately, just idle fantasies.

IF THE desert is a palimpsest, then its geology comes the closest to an original manuscript, itself constantly shifting, erasing, and starting the story over. More, through the constant process of mountain building and erosion, the pages of the manuscript have been thrown into disarray. It's as if someone had hurled the pages out the window of a speeding car. Now the task of geologists is to piece together that scattered story, which has some pages missing, many out of order, and some smudged beyond recognition. The narrative has been deconstructed in the most physical sense. Although geologists have reconstructed the story to a remarkable extent, it still makes for confusing reading. For the Anza-Borrego region, park ranger/geologist Paul Remeika and guidebook author Lowell Lindsay have gone a long way toward putting the story in order with their book *Geology of Anza-Borrego: Edge of Creation.*

Two caveats. First, to think of the events of this story happening where San Diego County sits today is a little misleading. The earth's crust is made up of giant plates that move independently over the viscous outer mantle, sometimes moving apart, sometimes colliding with or grinding against one another. Five million years ago, what is now the Anza-Borrego Desert was 200 miles farther south, much closer to the mouth of the Colorado River; 50 million years ago, it was so far south (and the earth was so much warmer) that it had a climate similar to that of modern-day Central America. To say that these rocks or fossils or oceans were "here" is like driving from Los Angeles to San Francisco and saying you're still in the same place—in the driver's seat.

Second, as San Diego State University geologist Patrick Abbott points out, any linear version of events in the region is complicated by the interaction of three independent systems: plate tectonics, the action of the Colorado River, and climate change. These three factors, working sometimes in concert with one another and sometimes in opposition, made the creation of the desert a halting, circuitous process.

But one chapter in the creation of Anza-Borrego is clear: the building of the Peninsular Ranges. An understanding of this process tells us much about the nature of the region today. The dramatic plunge of the mountains down to the desert is the most obvious feature that greets visitors, and that simple, awe-inspiring element of topography is the most obvious factor creating the desert beyond.

The first stage in the building of the Peninsular Ranges began about 150 million years ago as one large chunk of the earth's crust, the west-moving North American Plate, collided with the east-moving Farallon Plate. The North American won the battle, riding over the Farallon and driving it deep below the surface of the earth. The resulting pressure heated the sedimentary rock on top of the Farallon Plate until it melted and welled up underneath the rock of the North American Plate. Instead of bursting through the surface to become a lava flow, the magma cooled slowly deep underground, crystallizing into balloons of hard, granitic rock called plutons. Together, these plutons formed a massive batholith, or "deep rock," stretching nearly a thousand miles. That batholith would become the building blocks of today's Peninsular Ranges and of several earlier mountain ranges that rose up and then eroded away.

Another stage in the creation of today's mountains and desert came some 45 million years ago. Geologists believe that the region that is now Anza-Borrego was then a level plain hundreds of miles south of its present location, with rivers running all the way from the mountains of Sonora, Mexico, to the coast. Think of that vast plain as a seesaw. For millions of years, it had remained poised at equilibrium. Then, with North America having completely overrun the Farallon Plate, the continent came into contact with the Pacific Plate, which began grinding northwest along North America's western edge. As a result of these forces, about 24 million years ago, the western end of the seesaw began to rise. The granitic bedrock of the Peninsular Ranges batholith was thrust upward to elevations more than a mile above sea level. As the bedrock rose, the steep eastern slope became a launching ramp, with great chunks of the batholith breaking away and sliding east like newly christened boats into the sea. The blocks created a series of steps from the crest, visible today in the descent from Yaqui Ridge to the Vallecito Mountains and finally the Fish Creek Mountains. The block that slid the farthest east formed the Superstition Hills, low outcrops barely poking above the sand that will one day drown them. Yet although this mountain-building phase had placed the mountain blocks in roughly their present position by about 12 million years ago, the creation of the desert was still far in the future.

Now the story moves ahead to about 5 million years ago. As the tectonic plates continued grinding against each other, the Baja California peninsula split off from mainland Mexico and began riding north on the Pacific Plate. As it did so, Baja's southern end rotated west, away from the mainland, and a great trench began to open in between, creating the Gulf of California. When the spreading and sinking of that trench reached the Anza-Borrego region, the eastern end of our seesaw tipped downward, plunging into the depression that would become the Salton Trough, geologically a northern extension of the Gulf of California. The basement rocks in that trough are as much as 14,000 feet below sea level, creating a total descent from the top of the Peninsular Ranges of more than 20,000 feet. For a time, Gulf waters filled the entire basin, including what is now the eastern Anza-Borrego Desert; the marine fossils visible today at Elephant Knees Butte and in the Coyote Mountains were laid down during this period.

So why isn't the entire Salton Trough, from El Centro up to Palm Springs, covered by the Gulf of California today? And why isn't that body of water still 14,000 feet deep? The answer can be found in that second factor operating in the region, the Colorado River, and in forty feet of unconsolidated sand south of the Mexican border—all that separates the farms and towns of the Imperial Valley from the waters of the Gulf.

For millennia, the Colorado River has been carving down into the rising Colorado Plateau. Think of the vast trench of the Grand Canyon; now picture where all that excavated sediment went—enough rock and gravel and sand to build mountains, a whole upside-down mountain range, carried by the Colorado River to its delta on the Gulf of California. As the Gulf spread and sank, the Colorado dumped enough sediment to nearly keep up with the sinking, burying the deep bedrock of the Salton Trough under 14,000 feet of sand. Sometime between 2 and 4 million years ago, at a point just south of today's boundary between Mexico and the United States, the river did keep up with the sinking, building a bar of sand and silt across the neck of the newly formed trench. Thirty miles wide and just forty feet above sea level, the sandbar blocked the Gulf's waters from reaching the Salton Trough.

After creating this dam across the nascent Gulf, the fickle Colorado sometimes ran south of the dam and into the Gulf; at other times it turned north and ran into the dry Salton Trough, forming a vast freshwater lake, Lake Cahuilla, in the basin. When the lake appeared, it would crest at an elevation of 40 feet and then spill over the delta dam and back into the Gulf. Each appearance of the lake could last for hundreds of years; then the Colorado would shift its course once again, leaving the Salton Trough to revert to a dry basin 274 feet below sea level.

The role of the third factor, climate change, can also be seen in this period, from 1 to 5 million years ago, when Anza-Borrego was anything but a desert. A cooler, wetter climate, perhaps combined with the near disappearance of the Peninsular Ranges, created what geologists describe as a "lush, well-watered plain with grasslands and scattered forests, much like modern East Africa." The abundant rainfall supported an array of larger flora such as avocado, bay laurel, ash, buckeye, walnut, and *Sabal* palm. Mastodons, mammoths, horses, camels, giant zebras, and dozens of species of smaller animals roamed these plains, preyed on by saber-

toothed cats, cheetahs, bobcats, a condor with a wingspan of seventeen feet, and two canines with the ominous-sounding names of dire wolf and bone-crushing dog. This was a wilderness if ever there was one.

Finally, what geologists call the current uplift of the Peninsular Ranges began only about 1 or 2 million years ago, initiating the transition to the modern desert. At elevations of 6,000 feet on Anza-Borrego's western edge and of more than 10,000 feet on Mt. San Jacinto, farther north, the mountains are tall enough to block many of the winter storms that move in from the Pacific Ocean. As the clouds rise to pass over the mountains, they release much of their moisture on the western slope; then they hit the dry air of the desert and evaporate. But even after the current uplift, ice ages provided a series of wetter, cooler periods that punctuated the overall trend toward desert.

In addition to explaining the desert climate, the presence of the Peninsular Ranges also explains eastern Anza-Borrego's badland topography and the peculiar effect of being on the bottom of the ocean. As the mountains rose, rain and snowmelt drained more quickly across the flat marine and alluvial deposits of the basins, which were themselves rising slightly. The result was like a knife slicing down into a vast layer cake, creating the convoluted mud hills and sinuous washes of the Carrizo and Borrego badlands. The cutting action of water also revealed what Paul Remeika describes as "four million seasons" of sediments and fossil records, the remnants of that diverse flora and fauna that inhabited the region more

Mud hills in the Carrizo Badlands

than a million years ago. Now eastern Anza-Borrego is a playground for amateur and professional paleontologists searching for the bones of camels, mastodons, and saber-toothed cats.

Today, with the Colorado River tamed by dams, only plate tectonics and climate change are left to shape the landscape. The Peninsular Ranges continue to rise, and the Salton Trough continues to sink. Earthquake "swarms" plague the Imperial Valley, posing a greater threat to humans than the swarms of killer bees that arrived in the mid-1990s. Baja California and southwestern California keep moving north; one day, San Diegans and San Franciscans will be neighbors. And one day, the floor of the Gulf of California will spread and sink enough to breach the delta dam. It's even conceivable that global warming could further this process by raising the level of the Gulf. No engineering fix can stop such forces. Inevitably, the Gulf will invade its northern extension in the Salton Trough.

In geologic time, that day isn't too far off. A study by a graduate student at San Diego State University suggests that it will take more than a single cataclysmic event to breach the dam. Still, the people of the Imperial Valley can only hope that the inevitable breach, so close in geologic time, remains far off on the human time scale. They might do well to imitate the Cahuilla: when the time comes, they'll need to be ready to head for higher ground.

BY THE end of the last ice age, roughly twelve thousand years ago, the landscape of Anza-Borrego and the Colorado Desert looked much like the landscape we see today: the Peninsular Ranges rising in the west, desert plains sloping toward the Salton Trough in the east, rugged badlands and isolated peaks momentarily interrupting that eastern drainage. With the retreat of the glaciers that had pushed into the middle of the continent, climatic conditions also began to resemble those of today: a cool, arid climate on the coast, a hot Mediterranean climate in the inland valleys and western foothills, a temperate climate at the highest elevations, and a hot, arid climate in the desert. The mountains can get thirty inches of rain in a year, and the elevations above 8,000 feet often hold snow into June and sometimes July. The desert just east of the mountains, in the Coachella, Borrego, and Imperial Valleys, gets as little as three

inches of rain per year. Out on the creosote flats below sea level lies some of the hottest, driest land anywhere in North America.

Yet the mountains also act as storehouses of moisture. Right at the edge of the desert, in places such as Borrego Palm Canyon and Coyote Canyon, a kind of natural paradise appears where year-round streams bring water out of the mountains or where faults allow water to spring from underground. Formally known as the Desert Riparian and Palm Oasis subzones of the Desert Scrub biotic zone, these are the oases where the California fan palm grows, as well as cottonwood, willow, alder, mesquite, cattails, reeds, and yerba mansa. Farther out on the desert plain, year-round wetlands rise at junctures of streams in Carrizo and San Felipe Creeks. These oases seem out of place, green ribbons laid across the burning sand. Birds come to feast on the berries and seeds and to roost and nest in the branches, and bighorn sheep browse on the grass and leaves. Before the last of them were killed, in the 1940s, desert pronghorn roamed these canyons and plains.

The streams and oases are not the only pockets of abundance on this desert margin. The breathtaking rise of the Peninsular Ranges from the desert floor creates a variety of ecological life zones, from low desert (Lower Sonoran life zone) to alpine (Canadian-Hudsonian life zone). One can, in terms of plant communities, travel from the subtropics nearly to the Arctic Circle in a matter of miles. Each of these life zones contains a number of different habitats and plant associations, depending on type of soil, angle of slope in relation to the sun, and supply of water. Today, this variety in flora and topography attracts hundreds of thousands of visitors to Anza-Borrego each year. Hundreds of years ago, it made life possible for the Indians of the desert and foothills.

The Lower Sonoran life zone is what most people think of when they think *desert:* a land of sand and dry washes, coyotes and roadrunners, and a flora that could have come from the mind of Salvador Dalí. Where it is flat—and generally at elevations below 1,000 feet—this life zone is dominated by the drab brown to olive-green creosote bush and a small sage, the white bur sage. This is the monotonous landscape one sees when driving the interstate highways through much of western Arizona and southeastern California. Temperatures here stay above 100 degrees Fahrenheit

throughout the summer, and the thought of moisture is like a faded memory.

Closer to the mountains, where the alluvial fans begin sloping upward, other plant forms take over, taking advantage of the coarser soils and increased moisture—the cacti: cholla, barrel, and beavertail; the succulents: agave and many varieties of yucca; the subtrees: palo verde, mesquite, catclaw, and desert apricot; other shrubs: Mormon tea and brittlebush, which turns desert slopes yellow with flowers in spring.

Farther up in the mountains, juniper appears. The pinyon pine begins a little higher, usually around 5,000 feet. This pinyon-juniper association is characteristic of what is known as the Upper Sonoran life zone. Manzanita and scrub oak also grows here, as do other shrubby chaparral plants such as chamise and ceanothus (California lilac). Boulders seem to grow here, too, some as large as houses. They've fractured away from the granitic bedrock that forms these mountains, and they're just beginning their journey down into the desert flats. By the time they get that far, they will have eroded into fine sand. Up here, they provide welcome shade on a hot day, creating a microtopography to match the macrotopography of the mountains.

Life here is tenacious. From the barrel cacti clinging to vertical canyon walls to the groves of pinyon pine cloaking the mountaintops above 5,000 feet, life seems perched on the edge, isolated, provisional. In October, before the first winter rains, the plants of the desert are hunkered down, the ocotillo gathered in upon itself, gray and leafless, the cheesebush and brittlebush nothing but bare branches poking out of the sand. But within days of a rain shower, the desert bursts out in green profusion; the ocotillos' branches open like umbrellas and put out new, velvety green leaves. In a week or so, the ocotillos will sport crowns of red flowers.

Farther west and higher still is the crest of the Peninsular Ranges, a place of transition between desert and alpine habitats. Because these summits are the first to receive moisture from Pacific storms, they support different plant associations from those found on summits of equal height farther east. An elevation of 4,500 feet in the Cuyamaca Mountains can support lush meadows and oak forests. A little higher, especially on north-facing slopes, forests of incense cedar and ponderosa pine, Coulter pine, and sugar pine appear. Even during the hottest Santa Ana winds, these

mountains remain cool—the air rising rapidly from the desert floor is cooled to a comfortable seventy degrees.

As one moves north along the spine of the Peninsular Ranges, elevations increase. The San Jacinto Mountains at the northern end of the range push up into the Canadian-Hudsonian life zone, above 8,000 feet. As the name suggests, this life zone has more in common with the boreal forests of the far north. Oaks have disappeared, leaving the high elevations to evergreens such as lodgepole pine. There are a few meadows here around 8,000 feet, but at the summits it's mostly rocks and trees and sky. The soil is coarse granitic sand; where the trees grow densely, the sand is sometimes covered with a layer of forest duff. Where water is abundant, ferns and a kind of heather grow. Summer temperatures rarely push above the mid-seventies, and winter can bring heavy snow.

Here is the variety that makes southern California too popular for its own good. Vacationers can stand in winter sun in Palm Springs and gaze up at the cloud-covered peaks as the San Jacinto Mountains receive a dusting of snow. After finishing a round of golf, they can drive for a couple of hours on the palms-to-pines highway and then throw snowballs at one another. Or they can ride the Palm Springs Aerial Tramway and stand in that snow in a matter of minutes. If permanent immigrants from the east begin to miss the seasons, they can just take a day trip into the mountains to see leaves turning color in fall. If they grow tired of the chaparral-covered hillsides and artificial environments along the coast, they can travel to those same mountains to stand in green forests.

A thousand years ago, this same diversity of landforms, climate, and plant communities made southern California a popular spot among Indians. Then, as now, this was one of the most densely populated areas of the continent north of Mexico. And places such as the Anza-Borrego Desert, which we now see as wilderness, were home to more people than live there today.

EDGE OF THE WORLD: CREATION

THE PEOPLE who lived in and around the Anza-Bor-rego Desert before Europeans arrived had their own stories of how this landscape came to be. One part of the Cahuilla creation tale, adapted here from the version related in the 1940s by Chief Francisco Patencio of the Palm Springs Cahuilla, explains the origin of red-rock outcrops in the desert:

"Coyote called out to the people, 'My sisters and brothers, our father has died!' Then every one of them, they cried, and this was the first time that the people knew how to cry." The people had killed Mo-Cot, their creator, because he was a troublemaker who brought disease, gave the rattlesnake poison, and taught the people to kill one another.

Now the people sent Coyote after the eastern fire, which Mo-Cot had drawn from his heart to light the first tobacco. While he was away, they made a fire from the palm tree and burned the body of Mo-Cot.

Coyote looked back and saw the smoke and ran back to the people. They tried to keep him away from Mo-Cot's body. Coyote said, "My brothers and my sisters, look at my face, the tears running out of my eyes. Let me get through and see my father." All of Mo-Cot's body was burned except the heart. Coyote jumped over the people and took up Mo-Cot's heart in his mouth and ran out with it.

Coyote ran east toward the end of the earth with Mo-Cot's heart. He passed over a great brushy mountain and through a great dry desert,

covered with many tracks. When he became tired, he would lay the heart down, leaving red stains on the ground.

When Coyote reached the end of the world, he ate his father's heart, spilling more blood on the ground.

Today, the marks of Coyote's journey remain in the form of red rock, Patencio claimed: "This ground is called good ground." The earth where Coyote ate Mo-Cot's heart "became clear, red paint. The Indians paint their faces red in memory of the blood that was spilled from the heart of their father. And for this reason red is the Indians' sacred color."

Red rock exists in a few spots in and around Anza-Borrego, most clearly at Red Rock Canyon, a vermilion streak visible from Elephant Knees Butte. How did the Cahuilla feel when they saw this red earth or when they painted their faces red? It seems impossible to know. Were they sad at the death of their creator? Humbled and awed by their own powers of destruction?

Some writers have compared the Cahuilla tale to the Judeo-Christian creation story. Both feature a capricious and often malevolent father figure as creator. In both stories, the people kill the god who created them. And even though it was an oral tale, the Cahuilla narrative is as sophisticated and complex as Judeo-Christian cosmology. The printed accounts we have today are the Cliffs Notes version of the original story, which took days to tell or sing. The tale was retold yearly at an annual rite for the dead held on the winter solstice.

The world, according to this tale, began as a void with an egg-shaped object floating in it. Out of this egg came the twin brothers Mo-Cot and Mo-Cot-tem-ma-ya-wit (sometimes just Tamayawet or Tamaioit). Like brothers everywhere, they argued: about who was the oldest, who should create the earth so they would have a place to stand, how they should create the people, whose people were better shaped, whether or not the people should die. Mo-Cot-tem-ma-ya-wit said there should be neither sickness nor aging among the people; "if they got old they could go into the water and come out young again." But Mo-Cot argued that the earth would soon overflow with people and there would not be enough for them to eat if they didn't die to make room for more.

The brothers continued to quarrel, and Mo-Cot-tem-ma-ya-wit took

his people underground. He tried to destroy the earth while Mo-Cot tried to hold it together. "Then there came an awful time," Patencio says in his version. "The sky blackened, and fire flew, and lightning. The earth rocked and rumbled. Earthquakes split the earth every way: Mo-Cot-tem-ma-ya-wit trying to destroy it, and Mo-Cot holding, holding down hard as he could, trying to save and protect it and his creations. Then came something worse than all: the smooth land was no more, the earth broke all in pieces, when up rose the mountains, which are here today." Finally, Mo-Cot-tem-ma-ya-wit gave up, and the earth became still again.

Victorious, Mo-Cot gave poison to the previously harmless rattlesnake, and the first people died. Then he taught them how to kill one another with bows and arrows. The people finally became tired of his trouble-making and poisoned him. After he died, the story continues, the people burned his body. Until recent times, the Indians followed this funeral rite in disposing of their own dead.

Like any good genesis story, the Cahuilla creation tale explains not only the creation of the world but also the people's place in it. Mo-Cot's insistence on the necessity of disease and death provided a clear lesson in how the people should relate to the earth. Their mandate was not to "go forth and multiply" but to maintain their population within ecological limits. In these tales, humans also were given a clear relationship to animals, a relationship stemming from the creation time, when humans, animals, and birds were all "people" who could understand one another. Patencio wrote that over time, this power of understanding became less and less until only a few "medicine men," or *puvalam*, possessed it. Still, animals were like brothers and sisters to humans; a reciprocal relationship was required, one involving ritual thanks to the animals for "giving themselves" to the hunters. The creation stories also prescribed relations within the human community. The cultural hero *Evon ga net* showed the people where to live, dividing the country among the different lineages. From stories such as these, the Cahuilla derived a functional worldview that showed them how to live together and how to inhabit the land.

Every spot in the Cahuilla landscape was named. *Evon ga net* and another cultural hero, *Esel i hut*, left their marks on places, named them, or gave them particular power. Others placed "friendship" rocks for the people, and some individuals became rocks that are still visible today.

These stories not only explain the creation of the landscape but also provide a kind of mapping system for the territory the Cahuilla inhabited. An observation that poet Gary Snyder made about the "songlines" of Australia's indigenous people seems to be at work here: the landscape itself became a kind of mnemonic device, with particular features triggering a particular story and the stories themselves becoming a way of navigating through the territory.

We moderns have our own explanation for the creation of the desert landscape, one that has mostly supplanted the Judeo-Christian cosmology out of which it grew. Instead of believing that Coyote spread drops of Mo-Cot's blood to create the red rock, we have an explanation based in our scientific worldview. Geology tells us that this red rock is sedimentary, "baked to a brick red by the heat of molten rock," in the words of geologist Paul Remeika. The sources of these sediments were the "ancestral Fish Creek and Vallecito Mountain ranges."

Yet explanations such as this don't seem quite sufficient; the Cahuilla story—or myth, as we call it—has its advantages. It offered values that guided the people in their relations to the place where they lived. Our story, couched in neutral, value-free terms, provides no such guidance, merely explanation. We may have gained much in our ability to explain nature, and therefore to control it, but we've also lost much if we believe that this explanation can fully replace creation stories like the Cahuilla's (or our own). Our modern, scientific worldview may have gained ascendancy, but it hasn't completely erased the older versions of the story. I try to hold both versions in my head at once, like interpretations of the same story printed side by side.

OUR OWN story of how people came to be in the Americas says that the first humans migrated from Siberia over the Bering land bridge shortly before the glaciers receded at the end of the last ice age. Some scholars, basing their dates on linguistic, dental, and genetic evidence, believe that people may have arrived even earlier, as much as 20,000 or even 40,000 years ago. But radiocarbon dating fails to support these theorics; archaeological findings once thought to be more than 20,000 years old, such as a skeleton discovered in 1971 in the Yuha Desert south of Anza-Borrego, have been redated to much more recent times. For the past three decades,

the consensus among most scholars has been that humans arrived in the Americas about 10,000 or 11,000 years ago, but recently these dates have been pushed back to about 13,000 to 14,000 years ago.

Whether the first humans arrived 14,000 years ago, 20,000 years ago, or at some other time, two distinct groups occupied the Anza-Borrego region at the time of the first contact with Europeans: the Cahuilla and the Kumeyaay. At least two cultures had preceded them: the hunters of the San Dieguito tradition and the hunter-gatherers of the Pinto Basin tradition. The "modern" Indians were distinguished from their predecessors by their increased reliance on plant foods and their development of projectile-tipped arrows and pottery containers for food storage. Archaeological evidence suggests that the immediate ancestors of the Cahuilla (Uto-Aztecans) and the Kumeyaay (Yumans) had brought these innovations to the area by at least 1,000 years ago, with the Yumans probably arriving first.

The Cahuilla lived in the northern portion of what is now Anza-Borrego Desert State Park, from the Borrego Valley up through Coyote Canyon and Rockhouse Valley. From there, their territory extended north to include the Santa Rosa and San Jacinto Mountains and San Gorgonio Pass, west to the San Jacinto Plain, and east to the Coachella Valley. South of them lived the Kumeyaay, separated from them by mountains, desert, the temporary appearance of Lake Cahuilla, and a completely different language. The Kumeyaay, previously known as Diegueño, lived in loosely affiliated bands extending east from the coast at San Diego (thus their Spanish name) nearly to the Colorado River, and from a northern limit roughly marked by modern Highway 78 and the Vallecito Mountains down into Baja California. The Cupeño were a third distinct people, closely related to the Cahuilla and living in two villages near modern-day Warner Springs in the mountains west of Anza-Borrego.

Sometime around A.D. 900 or 1000, the Colorado River once again shifted its course to the north, creating Lake Cahuilla and providing the desert-dwelling Cahuilla and Kumeyaay with ample food for the next 500 years. The lake teemed with fish, and it was a stop on the Pacific flyway for geese, ducks, cormorants, and grebes. Around its edges grew reeds, willows, cottonwoods, and palms—good habitat for game. The Indians probably had permanent villages around the shore of the lake: the Cahuilla

around the northern end, the Kumeyaay at the southern. Anthropologist Lowell John Bean estimated that the Cahuilla alone numbered approximately 10,000 during this period, giving them a population density of about 4 persons per square mile. They caught fish in stone traps or weirs built in the shallow margins of the lake. With the Santa Rosa Mountains nearby, they probably ventured into the canyons and up the slopes to supplement their diet with agave and other plant foods. The living must have been relatively easy. It's nice to imagine this half millennium as a kind of paradise.

The Colorado River continued to supply Lake Cahuilla with fresh water until sometime around A.D. 1500. Then the river shifted its course south to the Gulf of California. Within sixty years, the lake had vanished. No wonder the Cahuilla viewed the universe as unpredictable. Long before the lake's demise, the wetlands and the shore life around the lake's original margin would have died. The people would have continued fishing for a few more years, but at some point increasing salinity would have wiped out the aquatic animals. Cahuilla legend has it that the people fled the coyotes and predators that came down to feast on dead and dying fish. Eventually, the Cahuilla moved up into the mountains, making their homes around springs and streams. Deprived of the lake's bounty, the Cahuilla faced a harsher life, and their population shrank to an estimated 6,000. The Kumeyaay, who had lived on the lake's southern shore, retreated to New River, to the Colorado River, and west to the Laguna Mountains.

Later, around 1700, as mesquite colonized the dry lake bed, the Cahuilla moved back to reinhabit the Coachella Valley. In Cahuilla stories, Coyote is revered because he brought the mesquite seed down from the mountains. This is probably a literal version of events because coyotes are known to feed on mesquite beans and do not digest the seeds. In any case, the lake bed was soon filled with a sea of mesquite, providing the people with a high-energy food in the form of seedpods. After that, the Cahuilla held coyotes sacred and never killed them.

By the time Europeans arrived—in what anthropologists call the "pre-contact period"—mesquite was just one of the staples of the Cahuilla, who used an astonishing number of the plant species in their environment. Shortly after the mesquite harvest in July and August, the nuts of the pin-

yon pine ripened, followed by acorns in October or November. These harvests were so important that most of a village's members would make the trip to the mountains to gather and process pinyon nuts and acorns. These staples had to last for many months, stored in earthen pots and basket granaries. In winter, there was little to harvest except agave, which provided a concentrated food source. Groups of men and boys would travel the short distance to the agave stands, cut the cores from plants that were nearly ready to bloom, and roast them in pits lined with stones. In the spring, grass and other plants growing near the villages provided seeds from which the Cahuilla made a kind of mush. The people supplemented these staples with meat, mostly from rabbits and other small game but also from deer, bighorn sheep, and desert pronghorn. They also ate a variety of leafy greens, cactus fruits, and fruits from desert apricot, mountain cherry, and palm trees.

Although they were in large part hunter-gatherers, the Cahuilla were not at all nomadic. They followed what anthropologists call a sedentary lifeway, which means they had permanent villages where they lived year-round. Lowell John Bean pointed out that the villages were located not only near water but also near most major food sources. He estimated that 80 percent of the plant foods the Cahuilla used were within a two- to five-mile walk of their villages. They could thus pursue most of their gathering activities on day trips from home. The exceptions were the large harvesting trips for acorns and pinyon nuts, during which the gatherers would be away from home for two or three weeks at a time.

The Cahuilla's neighbors to the south, the Kumeyaay, relied on many of the same food sources but had a less settled lifeway. Early white observers called them nomadic, but they actually practiced what anthropologists call transhumance, or seasonal migration between village sites and temporary camps. In the conventional definition, this could mean living in a mountain village during summer and migrating down to a desert site for the winter. But such generalizations are difficult to make for the Kumeyaay, one of the most diverse indigenous peoples in North America. Even the mountain Kumeyaay would have needed to travel to the desert in summer to gather or trade for mesquite beans, so the simple model of biannual migration doesn't fit neatly. And the Kumeyaay territory covered such a diversity of landscapes that different groups followed differ-

ent lifeways in different places. Coastal Kumeyaay fished from ocean-going canoes and gathered shellfish, trading these to inland Kumeyaay, who hunted and gathered in much the same way as the Cahuilla. Desert-dwelling Kumeyaay living along New River raised corn and melons, a practice they apparently learned from the Yuma Indians of the Colorado River.

The broad outlines of Kumeyaay cosmology were similar to those of the Cahuilla, with important differences in detail. But both groups shared a core belief common among early peoples around the world: that the entire earth is alive. Not just humans and animals, but everything in it, plants and rocks and the earth itself, is sentient. Every object and phenomenon possesses mind, or intention. The world speaks in countless ways: the wind whistling through a canyon or waving the branches of an ocotillo, the sudden appearance or flight of a coyote, the call of a red-tailed hawk, even the mute presence of boulders along a trail. These communications were part of the everyday experience of the people.

As Lowell John Bean and Katherine Siva Saubel wrote in *Temalpakh*, plants, for example, "were not viewed [by the Cahuilla] simply as objects which might or might not be useful to man, but as living beings with whom one could communicate and interact. Plants were one of a number of life forms such as rocks, elemental forces, animals, birds, and spirits that could communicate with those who knew how to 'listen.'" Humans were part of a community in which each member had responsibility to the others. Both hunters and gatherers needed to approach animals and plants with respect, giving thanks to these beings for allowing themselves to be used. In Bean and Saubel's words, "A person gathering a plant would thank the plant for its use, apologizing in one sense for the harm inflicted on the plant, but also recognizing that it was natural that the plant submit to its predetermined use."

Thanks were expressed in the form of rituals dedicated to both the plants or animals themselves and the supernatural beings who watched over them. These rituals took the form of preparations for the hunt or first-fruit ceremonies for each major plant species. Key to all these rituals was a sense of reciprocity, of the need to give something back to a particular species or to repair damage done. Many rituals also served a practical ecological function, adjusting the timing of hunting and gathering activi-

ties, spreading them out geographically, or limiting the amount or number of a particular species that could be collected.

The people who oversaw these rituals were the *net*, or chief, who acted as an "economic executive, determining where and when people gathered foods or hunted game, [and] administering first-fruit rites," and the *puul*, or shaman, who acted as a mediator between the people and the animal and plant communities. The shamans, along with the *tingavish* (doctors), possessed most of the tribe's complex botanical knowledge. According to Bean and Saubel, the Cahuilla's knowledge and classification of plant types was as sophisticated as modern botanical taxonomies, in some cases matching our system species for species and family for family. But beyond this sophisticated knowledge, the *puvalam* (plural for *puul*) also had the power to communicate with other species and the spirits that guarded them. Much of the rock art still visible in the desert may have been tied to this ritual communication. The shamans were responsible, through properly performed rituals, for keeping the human community on good terms with the animal and plant communities. Some, it is said, were even capable of transforming themselves into particular animals.

At one time it seemed easy, from our modern, "rational" perspective, to view such beliefs as the superstitions of a childish people, an irrational darkness that we westerners have dispelled with the lamp of reason. Even for those not versed in the sciences, tribal beliefs such as these committed the obvious literary errors of anthropomorphism and the pathetic fallacy. But lately, as the drawbacks of modern scientific, technocratic control of nature have become more apparent, as destruction has mounted both outside our own doorsteps and around the globe, many people are realizing the limitations of this purely rational worldview. Beyond global warming and poisoned streams and acid rain, a kind of spiritual death has taken place, one that stems from seeing the earth as dead matter and animals as soulless machines. Presiding over this storehouse of "natural resources," we have become alienated and lonely, isolated by virtue of our special creation in God's image (in the Judeo-Christian version) or by having evolved a vast intellect, upright posture, opposable thumbs, and a self-consciousness that separates us from the rest of evolution (in the scientific version).

Instead of this dead world in which we are the only self-conscious

beings, imagine inhabiting a world that is wondrously alive, a place where you are surrounded by presences of animals and plants and rocks, where you are never alone, accompanied always by members of your extended family (with some of whom you are on better terms than others). This is the kind of world for which many in our modern industrial, high-tech culture have come to hunger. This hunger has taken some silly New Age forms, which often offend tribal peoples by appropriating their rituals and their sacred places. But it is an honest need, one that may hold the key to healing our relations with the earth.

So FAR, nothing in this account of the Kumeyaay and the Cahuilla peoples' practices as hunter-gatherers conflicts with the idea that the Indians lived "lightly on the land," changing it so little that the land the Europeans "discovered" was still a wilderness. If the desert is a palimpsest, then the manuscript at the time of European contact, in this view, was still in its original condition. God or nature had written the original story, and humans had yet to mark or erase it. Yet this account doesn't explain how hunter-gatherers had become sedentary (in the case of the Cahuilla) or near sedentary (in the case of the Kumeyaay). It doesn't explain how native peoples across California maintained a population density greater than any other in North America north of Mexico. And it doesn't explain the fact that their social structure was more complex than that of most hunter-gatherer societies.

The conventional explanation for these facts is that the natural bounty of California supported their large populations. But this theory overlooks the regularly occurring drought cycles in southern California, along with other natural catastrophes such as flash floods and earthquakes that could wipe out villages, food supplies, and water sources in a single event. Rather than seeing nature as a bountiful mother, the Indians saw it as capricious, an ever-changing set of circumstances to which they had to continually and aggressively adapt. Since the 1980s, cultural ecologists, a type of anthropologist, have been examining those adaptations in detail. What they have discovered profoundly changes our conception of the native peoples and the land they inhabited.

By the eighteenth century, the Cahuilla and the Kumeyaay were facing an environmental challenge more severe than any they had encountered.

As Lake Cahuilla evaporated and the Indians adapted to a new way of life, the Spanish explorations of California began. In 1540, Hernando de Alarcón sailed up the Gulf of California and explored the Colorado River as far as the Gila River. In 1542, the first sailing ships appeared in San Diego Bay, under the command of Juan Rodríguez Cabrillo, followed by the ships of Sebastián Vizcaíno in 1602. In 1769, more sails appeared, and this time the Spanish stayed. In the same year, Fathers Junípero Serra and Juan Crespi arrived overland from Baja California and founded the first mission in San Diego.

In 1774, when Juan Bautista de Anza came through the Colorado Desert with a party of soldiers, he found groups of desert Indians who were adapting successfully to a new set of environmental circumstances and evolving as a culture. But the Indians would find it harder to adapt to the Old World baggage the Spanish carried with them: plants, animals, disease, land management practices, and—perhaps most important for the way we see this landscape today—beliefs about the environment.

Chapter 6

MISSION GORGE:
FIRE AND WATER

O N A blustery, El Niño–soaked morning, anthropol-
ogist Florence Shipek and I venture out to Mission Trails Regional Park,
at the eastern edge of urban San Diego. The hills are cloaked in dense
stands of chaparral shrubs, along with patches of non-native grass. The
region has received double the normal rainfall this year, so the hills are
unusually green. We had hoped to stroll along one of the park's easier
trails, but the inclement weather drives us indoors, where we take up a
position in the visitor center's library. With its large picture windows overlooking the San Diego River and Mission Gorge, the room is an ideal spot
to view a landscape advertised as a window on San Diego's past, a rare remnant of the habitat that was here before the Spanish explorers arrived. I
wanted to be able to view this landscape as we discuss one of Shipek's
more radical notions: that the stands of chaparral we're looking at today
are neither purely natural nor indicative of what dominated the landscape
when the Spanish arrived more than 200 years ago. What we view as natural and even mostly pristine is actually, she believes, a modern invention.

Shipek wears a Barona Casino sweater and a Campo Environmental
Protection Agency baseball cap, tokens from two nearby Kumeyaay Indian reservations. Behind wide-rimmed glasses, her eyes sparkle as she
gestures toward the shrub-cloaked hills and tells me how they may have
looked 250 years ago. "The slopes and the mesas were all pastureland,
with shrubs dotted here and there," she tells me. "Between Ensenada and
San Juan Capistrano, there was one place that had some small shrubs. So

you see one little spot in the whole stretch of a couple of hundred miles. The rest was open grassland." It was the same in the desert, she says, where the first Spanish travelers again and again reported finding "good pasture."

The sources of these statements are the journals and other records of the Spanish soldiers and missionaries who entered southern California in 1769. As bigoted as their views of the area's original inhabitants were, their records are one of the few ways anthropologists have to reconstruct indigenous cultures and the environments in which the people lived at the time of first European contact. Shipek has devoted half of her seventy-something years to sifting the truth from the array of assumptions and prejudices set down in the journals and letters of the colonizers. She has also studied the Spanish records of harvests, baptisms, births, and deaths among converted Indians, an approach lacking in earlier studies, including those of Alfred Kroeber, the pioneering anthropologist in studies of the California Indians. Most important, Shipek has worked closely with the Kumeyaay since 1954, helping them defend their land rights. This earned her remarkable cooperation from tribal elders, who still remembered remnants of their traditional ways of life at the time Shipek interviewed them. Although some archaeologists criticize her work for a lack of hard, physical evidence, her ideas have become central to the emerging picture of the life of southern California Indians and the world they occupied.

The environment Shipek describes is far different from the one we see today. Now there are few areas of grassland left (almost none of it native grass), and chaparral has become one of the most common plant communities in southern California. Chaparral—an association of hardy shrubs such as chamise, ceanothus, toyon, laurel sumac, and lemonade berry and small trees such as scrub oak and manzanita—is almost synonymous with natural open space along the coast and in the foothills of southern California. In the Anza-Borrego Desert, the transition between desert and mountains is marked by dense stands of chaparral. One type of chaparral, the coastal sage scrub, has become the focus of conflict between developers and environmentalists. One of the rarest types of habitat in southern California, it is also home to the endangered California gnatcatcher as well as several endangered plants.

Some ecologists believe that natural fires kept the chaparral in check until modern methods of fire suppression allowed it to spread throughout the region, but Shipek has a more radical answer: the Indians themselves burned the chaparral, keeping the landscape open for their own purposes. And this was just one of the major changes they made in their environment, from the coast to the desert. Far from living in a natural paradise, the Kumeyaay and other Indians influenced almost every aspect of their surroundings. This means that places such as Mission Trails are not windows on San Diego's distant past, providing a comforting sense of continuity in nature amid a sea of change, but relatively recent results of a change in land management practices. This leads to an equally radical notion: if the landscape that was here 200 years ago was not a "natural" ecosystem but one shaped by humans, and if that landscape is nothing like what we see today, then what exactly are we protecting in habitat preserves such as Mission Trails—or in parks such as Anza-Borrego Desert State Park?

SAILING past San Diego Bay on November 9, 1602, Sebastián Vizcaíno wrote that he saw "so many columns of smoke on the mainland that at night it looked like a procession and in the daytime the sky was overcast." Fires set by Indians were so extensive that the Spanish soon gave the harbor the nickname "Bay of Smokes." After the missions were established, however, the soldiers and priests didn't find the fires quite so picturesque. On May 31, 1793, Governor Arrillaga called attention to "widespread damage which results to the public from the burning of the fields, customary up to now among both Christian and Gentile Indians in this country, whose childishness has been unduly tolerated."

Yet just a year earlier, naturalist José Longinos Martinez had found the burning reasonable. He wrote in his natural history journal that "the gentiles have the custom of burning the brush, for two purposes: one, for hunting rabbits and hares . . . ; second, so that with the first light rain or dew the shoots will come up which they call *pelillo* (little hair) and upon which they feed like cattle. . . ." Aside from the bigotry apparent in the cattle comparison, Longinos' description of the effects of burning sounds a lot like the findings of present-day fire ecologists, who study the effect of fire on plants. These researchers believe that the Indians burned the

chaparral not only to flush rabbits, as Longinos suggested, but also to increase the abundance of game by encouraging the sprouting of annuals and other plants for browsing and, possibly, to make travel easier. The Spanish did report great numbers of rabbits and deer, as did settlers on the Southern Emigrant Trail in 1848.

Shipek believes that the Indians burned the valleys, including some in the desert, every year, maintaining them as open grassland. On slopes and mesas, they followed a five- to ten-year burning sequence, creating a much more open landscape than the one we see today. "The first year," she tells me, "all your annuals will come up, and your chamise and chaparral plants will be spaced apart. The second year, you'll still have your annuals, but the chaparral plants will be getting bigger." As she describes indigenous practices, Shipek uses the second person more and more—not, it seems, because she thinks of herself as an Indian but because it is a way of emphasizing that these are things anyone would do in a similar situation. In all her work, she insists on the essential humanity of the Indians. They were neither noble nor degraded but simply people.

"By five years," she continues, "you've got just a little bit of the annuals left, and the roots of the chaparral plants are taking over everything, and the ground is bare in between. The rain can erode it, can't it? So by five years, you want to burn again. But you've had five years of annual gathering before you burn." The result was an increased diversity of plant and animal life. Instead of the dense brush on today's chaparral-covered slopes, including those on the western edge of Anza-Borrego, there would have been a mosaic of blackened patches, grassy openings covered with flowers, and stands of small, widely spaced shrubs. That kind of mosaic offers a greater number of ecotones, highly productive edges between different ecological communities, where diversity is often the greatest.

To keep their fires under control, the Indians burned each patch as it dried out after harvesting or after a foggy morning on the coast. In the chaparral, they burned just before a rainstorm. Natural fires also burned the chaparral, of course, but a human-caused increase in the frequency of fire would result in a vegetational structure different from that which would develop under a natural fire regime. Fire ecologists estimate that in other areas of the country, such as the Great Plains, Indians doubled the frequency of fires, an estimate that Shipek says is conservative for southern California. And whereas most natural fires would ignite during sum-

mer thunderstorms, the Indians changed the timing of fires by burning in spring and late fall. The more open structure of the chaparral meant that summer lightning fires wouldn't develop into the earth-scorching infernos that have plagued southern California for the past several decades. In many ways, the Indians were better fire managers than we are.

On the desert floor, fire had an even more extreme effect on the "natural" vegetation. Here, the Kumeyaay harvested and burned patches of grassland where canyons emptied onto the flats, near springs, and along intermittent streams such as the New River, far out in the desert. In 1785, for instance, as he looked down at the desert from the Sierra de Juarez, Spanish soldier José Velásquez saw a column of smoke. An Indian guide told him that this was an Indian village where "wheat" was planted. Instead of being allowed to germinate or resprout after fire as the chaparral did, many desert plants were simply pushed out of these frequently burned areas. Because grass provided better ground cover, it maintained soil moisture more effectively than did cacti and shrubs, creating a wetter microenvironment. Simply by using fire to promote grass instead of cactus, the Indians were changing the landscape from desert to something else.

To my surprise, I found that work done at Dos Cabezas provides some of the best evidence in support of Shipek's ideas. Instead of the cholla, ocotillo, and agave that I encountered there on my first experience in the desert—and which I assumed had "always" been there—botanist C. R. Orcutt found a far different plant association in 1889. What he described was a grassland savanna dominated by the native galleta grass, though by the late 1880s the non-native filaree (which he called Spanish clover) had begun to move in. The grass was so extensive that he described it as a "pasture." It may have served as pasture for the desert pronghorn that used to roam the area.

Ignoring what was once here can have grave consequences for conservation and restoration efforts. In a 1996 article, Manfred Knaak, a former archaeologist for Anza-Borrego Desert State Park, described the transition in Dos Cabezas' flora as desertification, a term that implies degradation. In one sense, that's true—the array of shrubs and cacti at Dos Cabezas probably wouldn't go very far to support pronghorn or other grazers. Instead of preserving a pristine landscape, we've preserved a degraded one here, mistaking it for untouched wilderness.

Leaving the desert shrubland alone at Dos Cabezas has not maintained

it in a stable, self-regulating state. Grassland specialist Craig Dremann warns that without its historic bunchgrass cover, the Colorado Desert is in decline. "If you don't factor in changes over the last 125 years," he told me, "you won't be able to predict trends for the future." And if you don't know what the trends are, you may not be able to save what's there now. This spot in Anza-Borrego is not a window on the past of this desert but something brand-new, another chapter in a story of continual change.

FIRE was just one of the ways the Indians managed their resources. They also planted and transplanted many kinds of "wild" plants, engaging in a kind of agriculture (or proto-agriculture). The annuals and grasses that came up after a burn were just some of the species the Indians planted, both on the coast and in the desert. "After they had burned," Shipek says, "they would broadcast [seeds of] the grass and some of the annuals they used for food." Early Spanish travelers even reported the Indians gathering the grass into sheaves like wheat, a technique associated with agriculture, not with hunting and gathering. Shipek has descriptions of the grass seeds as "half the size of wheat." Over centuries, by selecting the largest seeds for planting, the Indians had domesticated the grass into what we would think of as a grain. Today, we lament its extinction as part of California's "natural" heritage.

The Kumeyaay also changed the landscape by transporting plant seeds or cuttings from one plant community to another. The reason for this tactic has to do with California's varied and unpredictable climate. Although in some years the flora in southern California is remarkably productive, in other years drought can limit nature's bounty. During the time of the Kumeyaay, drought cycles occurred regularly, sometimes lasting more than twenty years. At other times, flash flooding or simply too much rain could limit harvests. In response to this unpredictability, the Kumeyaay experimented with growing food plants in areas where they wouldn't normally be found. They moved mountain flora down to the lowlands, desert plants to the coast, coastal shrubs to the desert. If drought limited the harvest of a water-dependent crop—acorns, for instance—drought-tolerant plants would help fill the gap.

Shipek tells a story of visiting a friend on the Campo Indian Reservation. She and her friend had previously surveyed the plants around the

house, and they thought they had identified all of them. "This year was a drought year," she tells me. "There were no acorns, there was no manzanita, there were no wild plums. We'd just had a rainfall, mid-September. You know, we don't often have rain in mid-September. And we got out there and the old lady said, 'Oh, Florence, we forgot all about this plant.' The whole hillside above the house was covered with this plant that I'd never seen before. It had responded to that one rainfall. She said that this plant is good to eat, and it was." Shipek believes that for the Indians, planting crops that would respond to this unusual rain pattern alongside plants that thrive in a normal season ensured that *something* would be available for harvest. It was a managed system for hedging their bets.

The person who managed this system was the shaman—the *kuseyaay*—for each village. He experimented with the different plants, decided which areas should be harvested when, and through a system of religious rewards, encouraged village members to develop knowledge of alternative food sources. As do modern grape growers in the Temecula Valley, these shamans recognized that southern California is a land of microclimates. They weren't interested in developing domesticated crops with larger seeds than their wild counterparts, though that did occur with the grass. Instead, by planting seeds and cuttings in as many of these niches as possible, they made more plant foods available at different times of year. Through fire and "plant husbandry," the Indians were managing for biological diversity long before Western science hit upon the concept.

IF THE Indians were so busy managing their landscape, why didn't the Spanish see and record these manipulations? Shipek points to the enormous cultural misunderstandings between the Indians and the Spanish. With their large four-footed animals, sticks that killed at a distance, and disrespect for the Indians' property, these newcomers fit easily into one of the Kumeyaay's cultural categories: the *kuseyaay* gone bad, using his power for evil purposes.

The Spanish view of the Kumeyaay and other southern California Indians was equally derogatory. The Spanish contrasted the Kumeyaay not only with their own Christian, European culture but also with the Central American cultures they had already conquered, with their elaborate and obvious technical and artistic advances. And just as the Kumeyaay

assumed that the Spanish were, in Shipek's phrase, "evil witches," the Spanish assumed that the Kumeyaay and other California Indians were simple hunter-gatherers, living off the fat of the land. They assumed that the abundance of game and the verdant pastures of southern California were "natural productions" from which the Indians derived an easy living. From this belief grew the stereotype of the "Digger Indian," who subsisted mainly on roots and nuts and never developed a more elaborate technology or culture.

This assumption obscured what the Kumeyaay and other Indian groups were actually doing on the land. The Spanish noticed some of the Indians' land management techniques, but most of the changes the Indians made blended into the landscape so well that the Spanish either didn't know what they were seeing or didn't take the time to understand. Sometimes, the "natural productions" of the landscape on which the Spanish did comment—lush grass, an abundance of small game—were products of those Indian manipulations.

In 1769, for example, Father Juan Crespi saw "wild" grapevines near the port of San Diego that looked "as if they had been planted." Farther north, he described the valley of San Luis Rey (present-day Oceanside) as "a large and beautiful valley so green that it seemed to us that it had been planted." If Shipek is right, it *had* been planted by means of broadcast sowing, in which the seed is simply spread over the surface of the field. This wilder form of agriculture blended in with its surroundings so well that it was nearly invisible to the newcomers. The grass was intercropped with other annuals, so it didn't look like the fields back in Spain. The Spanish wondered why, when they put their horses to pasture in these grainfields, the Indians protested.

If it was hard for the Spanish to recognize this cultivated grass, it was even harder for them to recognize that "wild" plants had been sown or cultivated in other ways. The Kumeyaay may have planted oak trees, with each family claiming ownership of the trees it planted. They planted chaparral species such as manzanita and ceanothus along the coast, as well as the desert mesquite. Near their homes, they maintained "kitchen gardens" in which they planted greens, sage, and cactus. There is some evidence that they raised corn, beans, and squash even farther west than the New River before the Spanish arrived, though there is debate on this topic.

The Spanish and other early settlers described numerous plants grow-ing in rows: wild plums in the high desert near the present-day town of Jacumba; oak trees in Escondido; pinyon pines from Warner Springs south to the Sierra de Juárez. Shipek has even found the remnants of these rows. "I remember seeing a steep slope in a canyon on Otay Mountain with row upon row of wild onions going two or three hundred feet up the slope. Those rows were eight inches apart." Besides including row plant-ing, the Kumeyaay's proto-agriculture paralleled modern agriculture in another way. With its unique soils, Otay Mountain was one of the best places to grow onions; the people around Otay traded these superior onions for other items they needed.

This, then, was a much more complex culture than our idea of simple hunter-gatherers would allow. "They were growing the things that did well in their area," Shipek says, "and trading them for the things they couldn't get where they lived. People who grew corn would trade it to the people on the coast, where corn doesn't do well. That's commercial agri-culture. I would call it a complex economy."

Desert-dwelling Kumeyaay also cultivated wild plants. They planted mesquite to increase its numbers, and they burned it once a year to remove yield-reducing parasites such as desert mistletoe. They may also have planted agave. In the desert, Shipek has found stands of the succu-lent planted in rows, which are visible from above. Did the Spanish ever climb to the peak of a hill and wonder at those lines of "wild" plants? More likely, they simply assumed these were more "natural productions" of the desert.

The Spanish weren't the only blind newcomers to this place. On arriv-ing at the New River in 1849, an American named Cave J. Couts wrote in his journal, "This particular place of the river, favored with such luxurious grass, can only be the work of an Invisible Hand, to aid the thousands of distressed emigrants." Mentally removing humanity from the landscape and looking instead for the hand of God (or nature) is a refrain that per-sists to this day.

IN *An Island Called California*, a classic in natural history, Elna S. Bakker takes two pages to describe the unlikely plant associations found in the deserts and mountains of southern California. Nothing stays where it's

supposed to. The region's flora has been moving around, intermingling like guests at a multicultural cocktail party for plants. She wrote:

> On both sides of the mountains that abut the deserts, many of the natural communities have been modified and their species rearranged to a bewildering degree. . . . California juniper, chamise, coast live oak, and cholla cactus, all distinctive members of four different natural communities, are closely associated in Big Tujunga Wash, a finger of semidesert that slips over a low ridge into the Los Angeles Basin. Another anomalous extension has found its way to the Coast Ranges, southwest of Bakersfield. Sagebrush, Mormon tea, pinyon pine, juniper, and rabbit-brush—all typical plants of the Great Basin—come within shouting distance of the sea. . . . Valley oaks, of all things, have crept through the Tehachapi Pass to the desert edge where they grow with Joshua trees and cactus. . . . Low passes, ranges of moderate elevation, and a climate of fairly uniform aridity permit such strange floristic goings-on.

Bakker assumes there must be a natural explanation for these seemingly unnatural plant associations. It's all part of the wonderful diversity of California. Plants haven't migrated across mountain boundaries; they've "leaked" as if by accident. She never considers the possibility that the plants might have been moved by humans. Despite California having the densest Indian population of any region north of Mexico, Bakker and other botanists often ignore the effects these hundreds of thousands of Indians must have had on the flora and fauna of the state. The same blind spot still affects the management of our parks and "nature" preserves.

If the managers of Mission Trails Regional Park really want to reproduce the conditions of San Diego before the arrival of the Spanish, Shipek says, they need to go back to what the Indians were doing: carrying out controlled burning of the landscape, transplanting native species from other areas, and allowing collection of certain plant materials. I ask her what purpose a preserve such as this serves, given that the landscape hasn't been in a "natural" state for thousands of years. "Do you think we could ever learn to manage it to where it looked like it did before the Spanish days?" she asks.

"Over here, there was a big old mesquite tree that the missionaries saw. I know [the park ranger] hasn't put one in, but I think he ought to." Yet

that suggestion runs up against the native plant doctrine. The mesquite tree is native to the desert, not the coast, so it doesn't "belong" out here. Moving these plants around would interfere with the presumed natural order of things.

But preserving a remnant of the past is not as important as conserving the species and habitats that are present today. Shipek is more concerned about the absence of fire in southern California. "Just look out at that slope," she says, gesturing toward the sage scrub-covered hillside visible from the library window; "that shrubbery is green right now, but unless they do a controlled burn, [it] will be subject to a wildfire in a year and a half. The Indians would have burned it. Fire is the best way to manage it, but you have to control the fire." The problem is that after years of fire suppression, a return to controlled burning takes more personnel than most parks can afford. So much fuel will have built up that it will need to be removed manually, especially in pine groves such as the ones at Torrey Pines State Reserve on the coast or on the peaks of the Laguna Mountains above Anza-Borrego.

In some of California's parks, managers are allowing some of these indigenous practices to be used. Yet they are hesitant to allow controlled burning, partly because of the danger to nearby homes. Others worry about air pollution caused by intentional burning. And in San Diego, some residents near controlled burn areas have complained about the fine ash that falls on their cars. A more important concern, especially in an area where mudslides are frequent, is the erosion that can follow a fire. Yet Shipek says that here, as with everything else, the Kumeyaay had an answer: they were as effective at managing water as they were fire.

Living in a land where the year's rainfall could come in a one-hour deluge, the desert Indians had to exploit every water resource available. And because gully-washers could wipe out large portions of their food supply, Indians had to control water as it moved across the land. Today, we think of water management in California as having got its start in the twentieth century, with William Mulholland pirating water for Los Angeles from the Owens Valley, or, to go back further, in the 1770s, when Spanish padres are credited with building the first dam on the San Diego River. But in contrast to these large-scale water projects, the Indians had devel-

oped a much more subtle way of conserving and controlling water to meet their needs.

One of the desert Cahuilla's methods of getting water wasn't too different from our own: they dug wells. These large excavations were probably the most elaborate and labor-intensive water projects the Indians undertook. Some of the wells were holes with steps leading down. Others were trenches dug back into alluvial fans, reaching depths of twenty-five feet and lengths of seventy feet. Francisco Patencio wrote that the first wells were dug at springs that were slowly drying. "The Indian people began digging to reach the water. As the water lowered, they dug deeper, until what had been a good spring came to be named 'Indian Well' by the first White People who came much time later. One side had steps going down to the water. Then often that one side was dug out slant-ways for the animals to go down to drink." The last of the wells were filled sometime after 1936, by landowners who didn't understand their significance. Now their memory is enshrined in such town names as Indian Wells.

The Indians also dug irrigation ditches and used them to water not only melons and other domesticated crops but also wild plants. Patencio described one of these ditches in Chino Canyon: "For much, much time the people had an open water ditch to irrigate with. . . . This ditch is there today. It follows the left side of the canyon going up. It is about two miles long." Another ditch near Tahquitz Canyon "was used so much that today it looks like a small dry creek bed."

The Cahuilla weren't the only ones using ditch irrigation. At the opposite end of the Salton Trough, near the Colorado River, the Yuma Indians used floodplain agriculture, but they appear to have dug ditches, too. After crossing the Colorado in 1848, Cave Couts noticed an area "which bears every sign of once having been *extensively* cultivated. The irrigating ditches are very numerous and as plain as if now in use. The whole is now but one mesquite thicket." Couts assumed that the irrigation was for cultivated crops; he never considered that the ditches might have been intended for the mesquite. He just couldn't believe his own eyes.

Wells and irrigating ditches were just two of the ways the Indians managed water, Florence Shipek believes. The picture she paints is of a much wetter southern California than the one we know today. Although the climate may have been wetter 200 years ago, Shipek says that changes in

water management have also contributed to the present conditions: "Everybody talks about [coastal San Diego] always being a desert—[but] *we've turned it into one.* You had the same system all over southern California. All the valleys were wetter then. You had marshes in valley after valley after valley."

On the San Diego River, for instance, Spanish missionaries placed their dam over a smaller boulder dam the Kumeyaay had already built. The resulting reservoir replaced what had been a marsh or a wet meadow. Shipek has found traces of the soil characteristic of these wet meadows in other locations, including one near her home in San Diego's Pt. Loma neighborhood. Although the indigenous techniques didn't create large bodies of water, they had other benefits, such as raising the surrounding water table and recharging nearby springs. This wet environment supported plants important both to the people and to the animals they hunted. The Indians practiced the same technique in the desert, creating wetlands where canyons emptied onto the desert floor. "You have a whole different behavior pattern," Shipek says, "keeping the water on the land, not letting it run away."

Shipek points to other elements of this behavior pattern, such as clearing shrubs back from springs to conserve water while allowing one tree to grow over the spring to provide shade and reduce evaporation. "This is what I learned from the old men," Shipek says. "If the old men knew this, [they were] managing their water supply."

The Kumeyaay also practiced erosion control, planting willows along streams to hold the banks and to ensure a supply of valuable basket materials. They used rock alignments to protect steep slopes from washing out. This practice was especially important after a controlled burn had exposed a patch of ground. The low rock walls slowed and spread the water as it traveled downhill. This technique prevented gullies from forming and protected areas where the people gathered grass seed, annuals, sage, and other plants. All this work was undertaken by families on their individual portions of a valley or by the village as a whole on communal land set aside for ceremonial purposes and for guests.

In the desert, rock alignments were placed across the slopes of alluvial fans—areas rich in agave and cactus. Few of these rock alignments exist today. "Once they're not maintained, storms start moving them around,"

Shipek says. "But we have found remnants of them, and I have Spanish descriptions of them. This is also part of what the old men told me they did."

All of the Indians' water management techniques—digging wells and ditches, building dams, constructing rock alignments, planting stream banks, and clearing springs—were the result of hundreds of years of experience with an unpredictable climate. "If you're in a land that has twenty-five-year droughts every couple of hundred years," Shipek says, "you'd better know what to do." These techniques, along with controlled burning and plant husbandry, add up to a kind of interior technology. They allowed the Kumeyaay to control three of southern California's most severe environmental variables: fire, flood, and drought.

In the story of this desert, the Kumeyaay and the Cahuilla acted as judicious editors, erasing here and adding there, illuminating the existing manuscript with skill and subtlety. Far from living at one with the land, these people sought to control it, just as all human societies have. Rather than attempting to suppress the forces of nature as we moderns do, however, they aimed many of their changes at intensifying or moderating natural processes. Most of those changes have vanished, erased by more than a century of our own more clumsy land management practices. Now we make the mistake of looking at the preserved landscape of today as the original story: the timeless, unchanging desert. Florence Shipek helped open my eyes to the changes people have made here.

Yet even after this visit with her, I still didn't want to believe, as she does, that there is "not a thing natural" in the landscape of southern California. There must be something that the Indians left untouched, something still wild in this semidomesticated landscape. And I thought I knew where to look for it.

FIRST GROVE:
GARDENS IN
THE WILDERNESS

I T'S THE first day of June, and I'm hiking up Borrego Palm Canyon toward a grove of California fan palms. The thermometer dangling from my backpack reads 100 degrees Fahrenheit. Up on the canyon's west-facing slopes, boulders the size of boxcars bake in the sun, radiating heat. My brain feels as if it's baking, too. I can't wait to get into the shade of the palms and take a dip in the natural pool at the heart of the grove.

As hot as it is, it feels good to be outside. It's four o'clock, and I've spent much of the day indoors, reading archaeological reports and old journals in the library of Anza-Borrego Desert State Park. After a swim, I plan to wait for the sun to disappear behind the mountains to the west. Then I'll hike farther up-canyon to bed down for the night—cheaper lodgings than either a hotel in town or the public campground at the mouth of the canyon.

I reach the first palm trees and experience immediate relief as I step into their shade. It feels twenty degrees cooler here. The younger trees sport tan skirts of dry fronds, making them look like high-rise grass huts. The older ones have bare trunks, blackened by fire. A slight breeze rustles the fronds. The trees grow thick near the little creek, covering both banks for maybe a hundred yards. There are 142 of these native palm groves in southern California and Baja California. This is one of the smaller ones, but the shade is just as sweet.

Rounding a boulder, I find the pool I've been daydreaming about for half an hour—it's about the size of a stand-alone backyard swimming pool and filled with teenagers. They splash in the water, shouting and laughing as they dunk one another under a waterfall. Someone's mom sits at the pond's edge, smoking a cigarette, ignoring them.

I drop my pack and sit down on a rock. After hiking just a mile, I'm feeling light-headed from the heat. I'll just sit here and wait my turn. Still, it's hard not to resent this crowd. When I come to the desert, I want to get away from people and every sign of their presence. I usually avoid busy places like this, only a mile from the visitor center and the most popular spot in the park. I have to remind myself that I'm here for a cheap place to sleep, not a wilderness experience.

Signs all around tell me this is a natural area, reminding me that this is a place where I should "Leave only footprints, take only memories." At the edge of the creek is a barricade made from downed palm trunks and a sign warning visitors not to cross it—people tramping around among the palms compact the ground and make life difficult for the trees. Beyond the barricade, dry palm fronds cover the ground. Another sign explains the blackened trunks on some trees: "This Fire Was Set by Careless Individuals."

That's one story about how the fires got started. *Gathering the Desert* tells a different tale, however. In it, Gary Paul Nabhan argues that the Cahuilla Indians burned these groves every four or five years. Although some careless individual may have set a fire here in the past century, there's a good chance that the older trees were burned by the Cahuilla.

Francisco Patencio reported that his ancestors burned the palms, stressing the practical purpose of the fires and denying reports that they were meant simply to drive away evil spirits. The palms were burned to increase their date yield, he claimed. Burning cleared out the old, dry fronds, leaving the fire-resistant trunks unscathed. It's basic fire ecology— fire returns nutrients to the soil, prompting new growth. And because the accumulated litter of palm fronds made good cover for rats, removing it was just good housekeeping. Burning also killed red spider mites and date scale, both of which reduced the date harvest. After years of research, the U.S. Department of Agriculture rediscovered this technique in the 1930s and recommended it to date farmers.

Besides burning the palms, the Cahuilla may also have planted them. Although coyotes can also disperse palm seeds after eating the dates, some palm groves are so remote from their nearest neighbors that humans must have planted them. Cahuilla legend also holds that the people distributed palm seeds from one original tree. In doing so, they may have extended the range of the fan palm beyond its "natural" boundaries. Genetic research is under way to determine whether these palms are truly native to California or whether, as some authorities suggest, they originally came from Mexico.

The Cahuilla were still carrying the seeds around in historical times. One account tells of a grove planted in the 1890s high on Mt. San Jacinto. Near some groves, the Cahuilla built villages, using the palm fronds to thatch their houses and ceremonial buildings. They channeled stream water to their garden patches or impounded it to create bathing ponds.

All these activities seemed to be good for both the palms and the Cahuilla. But when Americans took over these lands, just before the turn of the twentieth century, the numbers of palm trees began to decline. No one planted palm seeds or burned the groves. Our idea of preserving a place was to put a boundary around it and not touch it. James Cornett of the Palm Springs Desert Museum believes that this decline continued until 1945, when, ironically, a fire regime returned to the desert, triggered by an increase in visitors to the region—the "careless individuals" referred to on the sign here in Borrego Palm Canyon.

Now the descendants of the Anza-Borrego Cahuilla live in cities or on the reservations in the mountains west of here, and we view these partly fabricated oases as natural recreation areas. I'm not sure whether or not the Cahuilla planted this particular grove, but bedrock *morteros* in the canyon indicate that they were active here. The idea that the Cahuilla manipulated this grove for their own ends is just one more blow to my view of this place as a pure wilderness. Since my first trip to this desert, I've viewed these trees as the true wild palms of California. Unlike the glitzy imports lining the streets of Beverly Hills, these natives seemed to exist for their own sake, persisting in spite of changes to their environment. I have hiked for hours to find a remote, untouched grove and thought I was having a wilderness experience. Yet the scene I have before me right now—kids splashing in the water, enjoying the relief from the

surrounding heat—probably has a lot more in common with what this place was like 500 years ago than does my view of the desert as a vast emptiness.

MY FANTASY that the palm trees of the Anza-Borrego Desert represent the persistence of wild nature falls neatly into what William Denevan has called the pristine myth. According to this myth, life in North America before the arrival of Europeans was one big low-impact camping trip. The continent was a second Eden in which the Indians lived with the innocence of Adam and Eve, changing the land so little that it could still be considered basically untouched. But as soon as Europeans arrived, everything went downhill. They were the snakes in this New World Garden, which was lost in a swift second fall from grace. This myth tells us very little about actual Indian cultures, but it says a lot about what we Euro-Americans want them to be: the first ecologists, or environmental saints. We use this image of the ecologically noble savage to flagellate ourselves for what "we" have done to "them" and to the continent.

The pristine myth also tells us a lot about what we want nature to be. For a large segment of the environmental movement, the only nature worth saving is of the capital-*N* variety, Nature "untouched by the hand of man," as the saying goes. This is the kind of nature people had in mind in preserving wilderness areas, and it's a vision that applies not only to legally defined wilderness but also to the way we have managed national and state parks, monuments, and nature preserves. This is the nature that Kirkpatrick Sale, in *Conquest of Paradise*, says existed in America before 1492. It's also the nature whose demise Bill McKibben laments in *The End of Nature*. We've changed the climate of the planet so thoroughly, he says, that there is nowhere on earth that the "hand of man" hasn't touched. For McKibben, this is lamentable not only because of the negative effects of climate change but also because nature as Europeans have thought of it— "the world that existed outside human history"—no longer exists. This is not the death of a specific place, the end of a species or an ecosystem, but the death of an idea.

The reality is that the kind of untouched nature McKibben mourns hasn't existed in the Americas since the first peoples began to populate the hemisphere more than 10,000 years ago. Human history in the Americas

began in that dim past, not 500 years ago. Like any people, the newly arrived hunters had effects on the landscape—they made mistakes, over-extended themselves and their resources, faced environmental catastrophes. If geoscientist Paul Martin is right, they were largely responsible for the extinctions of the large mammals in North America between 10,000 and 12,000 years ago—the first erasures humans seem to have made in nature's original manuscript. As the sophisticated hunters from Siberia spread across the continent, they found easy prey in mammoths, giant bison, and other large animals unaccustomed to human hunting pressure. The end for this Pleistocene megafauna came quickly, in what Martin termed a blitzkrieg. Other scholars point out that climate change may have been a greater cause of these extinctions, but they still allow a role for humans in pushing many of these species over the edge.

Even more recently, certain Indian peoples may have brought environmental collapse upon themselves. Some researchers believe the Anasazi, the ancient people of the American Southwest who abandoned their elaborate cliff dwellings in the twelfth century, may have overrun the capacity of the area to sustain them. Anthropologist Shepard Krech III points out that they used more than 200,000 trees at one village alone. This kind of deforestation could have led to widespread erosion and flooding, wiping out the agricultural system on which their civilization depended. Pueblo ceremonies of more recent times seem to be warnings about what *not* to do in order to avoid a similar environmental catastrophe.

For a cynic, untouched by current romantic views of native peoples, this history might not come as much of a surprise. What might be more surprising is the news that—in some places, at some times—the Indians actually increased the biological diversity and health of the environments in which they lived. They weren't simple children of nature; instead, they developed sophisticated ecological knowledge through millennia of trial and error. The skill and subtlety with which Indians managed the landscape is perhaps best exemplified in California. Anthropologists Kat Anderson and Thomas Blackburn suggest that human population densities there may have been the highest of any society in the world without intensive agriculture. These peoples' success in maintaining a large population owed as much to their skilled management of the landscape as to the land's natural fecundity. Taken together, these management tech-

niques (including the use of fire, the sowing or broadcasting of seeds, transplantation of various species, irrigation, pruning, coppicing, weeding, and tilling) changed not only the appearance of the region's landscape but also its basic ecology. Anderson and Blackburn say that this effect went beyond control of specific resources to the essential domestication of certain habitats. Places such as Anza-Borrego's palm groves provide a good example of that domestication.

Other habitats that may *seem* natural to us, such as the dense stands of chaparral cloaking the mountain slopes above Anza-Borrego or the desert scrub at Dos Cabezas, may not be as natural as we think. The Indians' intentional burning changed these habitats in ways that go far beyond the cosmetic. It influenced everything else in the environment: the kinds of plants that could grow, the kinds and numbers of animals that depended on those plants, the amount of water available to plants, animals, and humans. The increased frequency of burning may even have changed the basic nature of the plants themselves. All the chaparral species have adapted to fire. Many of the shrubs resprout from the root crown after a fire, and the seeds of some annuals actually *require* a fire in order to sprout.

In 1959, geographer Homer Aschmann suggested that for as long as chaparral has grown in southern California, people have burned it. During the Wisconsin Glacial Stage, which ended about 10,000 years ago, the climate of southern California was much wetter and cooler, supporting forests of pine and fir trees. When the glaciers receded, creating more arid conditions, the drought-tolerant chaparral community began to dominate slopes below 5,000 feet. As the chaparral developed, the first humans moved into the area. If these hunter-gatherers used fire in the same way as did the Kumeyaay of the past one or two thousand years, there has never been a "primeval" chaparral, untouched by human hands. The chaparral has not just adapted to fire; it has adapted to the specific frequency of fire the Indians applied. It may be "natural" for chaparral to grow in dense stands, but such a natural state never existed in southern California. Likewise, the stands of cacti and desert shrubs at Dos Cabezas may not be a reversion to a long-ago natural state; they may be the first such plants ever to grow there.

The native peoples' transplantation of species from one region to another also changed the structure of the landscape in ways that challenge

our ideas of what makes up a natural community. Florence Shipek believes that by moving plants from one community to another, the Indians encouraged them to hybridize. Today, there are oak tree hybrids in southern California that are found nowhere else, crosses between varieties that don't naturally grow in the same area. The same is true with certain chaparral species. Botanists are still trying to classify the many hybridized species of cholla cactus in the desert.

The palm groves, the mesquite stands, and the oak groves are present in southern California partly because the Kumeyaay and the Cahuilla put them there. Other plants and habitats—such as the grassland at Dos Cabezas—have disappeared because the Indians are no longer around to tend them. The chaparral that we see today exists in such thick stands only because we have replaced the Indians' program of intentional burning with one of fire suppression. The wetlands the Indians created are gone, converted either to dry valleys traversed by eroding gullies or, in a few places, to deep lakes. We could bring those wetlands back if we wanted to. But the type of grass the Kumeyaay planted—the one with seeds half the size of wheat—is gone forever, the victim of overgrazing by European livestock and a disruption of the Indians' plant husbandry techniques. Now the loss of California's "native" grasses is one of the things we lament about the changes that have overtaken the state since the arrival of the Spanish. Across California, it turns out that many endangered species are disappearing because, in the words of one researcher, "the people no longer use them."

I take from all this a deep suspicion about what is natural or wild in southern California, or anywhere. This history—of palm groves that I presumed were wild, of desert habitat that I thought went back thousands of years—has shaken my long-cherished beliefs about wilderness and the environment. And histories like this one, replicated across the continent, have shaken some of the environmental movement's most basic assumptions. How do you call for protection of a natural area if you can't resort to terms such as *ancient, timeless, trackless,* and *pristine*? How do you argue for a universal need for wild, unpeopled places when that need seems so particular to our own culture, and to a minority in our culture at that? What argument can I make for greater protection of deserts beyond saying that I (and some others) like it that way?

Those who call attention to the implications of this environmental history, especially for wilderness preservation, are being labeled traitors to the cause. Yet learning to question these familiar terms should be more comforting than alarming. I could persist in seeing the desert as an emptiness, a place hostile to humans, an untouched wilderness, but it's better to see it as a place where ancient peoples tried to make their homes and succeeded. They didn't live according to some idealized notion of living lightly on the land, making no changes to their environment. They manipulated the natural world partly through technology and partly through elaborate knowledge and skill. Even though they were certainly less exploitative than their successors, our modern Western view sees any human changes to nature as destructive. But it was exactly this New World garden, cared for and shaped by its first human inhabitants, that helped form our most basic ideas about what is wild and natural. We can learn from what the Indians did here and use that knowledge to reinvigorate our concept of wildness. Humans are part of nature; it's still nature even when we change it.

AT LAST, the teenagers leave and I have the palm grove to myself. I wade into the cool water and then plunge in. When I climb out onto a smooth

California fan palm

boulder, I feel the chill of water evaporating from my skin. Suddenly, the place does feel empty, lonely. Now I have the solitude I've been looking for.

I try to imagine how this place might have looked a century and a half ago: the women using *manos*, or grinding stones, to crush hard date pits in stone *morteros*, the men getting ready for a hunt or an agave roast. But this kind of imagining only makes the place feel more desolate. The signs warning me not to touch make me feel like an outsider. On the other side of the fence, where I'm not supposed to walk, the creek bank is covered with the trash of fallen palm fronds. And the date scale and spider mites are back, ruining the date crop.

The Cahuilla never thought of this desert as a wilderness of solitude and hardship. In 1943, Chief Patencio put it this way: "All the wild and lonely places, the mountain springs are called now. They were not lonely or wild places in the past days—no. . . . Sometimes an Indian goes back into the mountains to a spring of water. There he visits, alone, the home of his ancestors." In our modern, crowded world, we long for that solitude. For Patencio, though, the word *alone* must have been a lament. Escaping from society—lighting out for territory, one of our culture's most cherished dreams—wouldn't have been a possibility or even a desire for him. Every place in this landscape was part of his people's history, from the time of creation to the present. Even the sacred places, where only the *puvalam* could go, were laden with stories.

This desert hasn't been a wilderness in the conventional sense for thousands of years. Two hundred years ago, it was the Indians' garden. Now it's a garden gone to seed.

COWBOYS *and* INDIANS

ORIFLAMME CANYON: BUSHWHACKING WITH PEDRO FAGES

I'M STRUGGLING through a stand of chaparral in the Laguna Mountains, trying to follow the trail of Pedro Fages, an eighteenth-century Spanish officer who traveled through this area in search of his men. The chaparral is head-high here. Sharp, stiff branches of chamise and manzanita clutch at my arms and legs. In some places, branches from two bushes have grown together and I have to unknit them by bashing through. One branch snaps back and whips me across the neck. Where the shrubs grow too thick, I back up and look for an easier route.

I hate bushwhacking. But at least it's not April, when blooming ceanothus fills the air with a nauseating aroma like very powerful Kool-Aid.

I'm twenty-five yards off the Pacific Crest Trail, and I have twenty-five more to go before I reach the top of this small rise. This is the northern end of the Laguna Mountains, though it's officially part of Anza-Borrego, a narrow finger of the park that extends up into the high country. Because the indigenous practice of frequent burning has been replaced by a policy of fire suppression, this dense chaparral is now typical of this transition zone between desert and mountain habitats. To the east of here and 2,000 feet lower lies the true desert of cactus and agave; west of here are golden meadows, stands of oak, and dense forests of Coulter pine and cedar. Here, in this in-between zone, chaparral cloaks the hillsides in a drab olive-green carpet.

I'm not having much luck in tracing Fages' route. He passed through here with a small band of soldiers in 1772, chasing deserters from San Diego. He would later become governor of California, but during this period he was a captain of the Catalonian Volunteers and *comandante* of the "New Establishments" in California. It was only three years after the first Alta California mission was established in San Diego, and Fages had just had a row with Father Junípero Serra over the number of soldiers the new missions would need. His problems in guarding the missions were compounded by desertions among his men, and this was at least the third in a string of them. According to one historian, Fages worked his men hard, a practice to which Spanish soldiers of the time were unaccustomed. Now he was in hot water with his superiors, and finding these men was important enough that he pursued them for 400 miles.

His trek took him on a grand tour of southern California: over the Cuyamaca and Laguna Mountains, down through what would become known as the Carrizo Corridor in the Anza-Borrego Desert, then north through Coyote Canyon to the San Bernardino plain. To avoid a conflict with another padre he'd antagonized, Fages bypassed Mission San Gabriel Arcángel and climbed north over Cajon Pass (where Interstate 15 now rises out of the Los Angeles Basin on its way to Las Vegas), skirted the western edge of the Mojave Desert until he reached what is now Palmdale, and then descended into the San Joaquin Valley, finishing his journey by turning west toward San Luis Obispo. He never caught up with the men he was chasing. They may have gone to live with the Indians, preferring their company to Fages' despotic rule.

This trek put Fages in contention for the title of First White Guy to cross Anza-Borrego. First White Guys get all the attention in popular history. Daniel Boone and Kit Carson, to name just two, became cultural heroes for their forays into "uncharted" territory. Local historians have made much of Fages' journey because it put him in the desert two years ahead of the more famous Juan Bautista de Anza. Whereas the Spanish used Anza's route through Coyote Canyon only a few times, Fages' route along the Carrizo Corridor later became an important link from desert to mountains for forty-niners on the Southern Emigrant Trail. But it was Anza's name that stuck to this desert while poor Pedro's name was lost in dusty history books.

Was Fages the first Spaniard to pass through Coyote Canyon? Today, I don't really care. This First White Guy myth is just that—a myth. We like to think of Daniel Boone carving a route through dense forest over the Cumberland Gap. But in reality, he just followed an Indian trail through a forest so open that he called it a park. I'm beginning to suspect it was the same with Fages. If the chaparral was as thick then as it is today, he would have had one bloody ride. Traces of Indian encampments have been found on this hill, so the vegetation must have been much more open at one time. This could account for a passage so easy it merits little notice in Fages' brief descriptions of the route.

I work my way around the southern side of the hill, hoping the chaparral will be less dense there. Near the top of the rise, I break out of the bushes into an open, rocky area, a tiny remnant of the way the whole hillside may once have looked. Perhaps coarser soil or heat radiating from the rocks has maintained this microenvironment. Yuccas and prickly pears have migrated up from the desert, and there's another heat-loving flower, the reddish orange Indian paintbrush.

After climbing a little farther, I crest the hill and get my first view of the desert. As many times as I've stood in these mountains and looked down into that brown expanse, the exhilaration has never worn off. The earth drops away beneath my feet, and I suck in my breath—it's almost like being punched in the stomach. The tan, muscular bulk of Whale Peak rises up directly opposite me, a dozen miles away across a valley 3,000 feet deep. Canyons and mountains overlap one another like cresting waves. The last of them, out near the horizon, fade ghostlike into the haze— smog spreading southeast from the Los Angeles Basin.

I imagine this view the way Fages might have seen it, the air crystal clear, his horse pulled up short at the sudden drop into the desert vastness. Approaching this rise after climbing the gentle western slopes of the mountains, he must have felt as if he were nearing the edge of something, maybe the edge of the world. I picture him pausing here, the horses shifting uneasily on their rocky footing. He dismounts and climbs the rocky hill for a better look. The men pass around a flask of water and curse under their breath at their *capitán*, who seems to be leading them on a fool's journey. Fages ignores them as he mentally traces a route down into the desert. Is he exhilarated, the way I am? A little afraid, confronted with this barren

country and the steep descent into it? Or just irritated by the thousands of square miles in which the deserters have lost themselves? On such matters, his writings tell us nothing.

Yet even then, the air may not have been as clear as I like to imagine it. Fages was here in late October, one of the times of year when the Indians intentionally set fires. The atmosphere could have been more smoke filled than the smoggy air over the Imperial Valley I see today. Perhaps he was already so used to the consequences of burning that he didn't mention it.

This hillside drops down to a sloping, mile-wide plateau, which in turn drops down into Oriflamme Canyon. On the far side of the bench, I can make out a bare strip of ground, perhaps a remnant of the trail Fages used. I can imagine it falling away into the canyon where chaparral grades into agave, cholla, and barrel cactus and the going gets easier. But between here and that bare ground, the brush makes a solid carpet, even denser than on the western side, where I came up.

Down in the desert, the route Fages took seems more obvious. Directly to the east, the way appears blocked by the mass of Whale Peak. But in the distance, twenty miles southeast of that peak, there is a clear gap in the mountains. This is the Carrizo Corridor, the route Carrizo Creek takes as it passes through the gap between the Coyote Mountains and the Fish Creek Mountains before turning north toward San Felipe Creek and the Salton Sea. Fages wound up on the shores of the ancient lake, which was dry during those years, and then headed back northwest through Coyote Canyon. The only tricky part of the route was right here, getting down into the desert.

The route must have been even more obvious to Fages. Not only was it probably more open from burning, but it was also part of a long-distance Indian path, possibly the major trade route known as the Yuma Trail. The Kumeyaay moved seasonally along this trail between the Cuyamaca Mountains and their wintering grounds in Mason Valley. Desert-dwelling Kumeyaay may have come the same way to gather acorns in the fall. And if it were a trade route, travelers from the Yuma Trail on the Colorado River and points east, as well as Kumeyaay from the coast, must have used it.

Did Fages think of himself as an explorer discovering this country or as just a man lucky to have found an Indian thoroughfare? Did he follow this trail on his own, or did he have guidance from the Indians? He didn't keep

a diary during this pursuit, but a passage from his *Historical, Political, and Natural Description of California* shows that he did look to the Indians for advice at other times. Regarding methods of communicating with Indians farther north, he wrote: "They in like manner indicated to us the road, the watering places, and other matters concerning which we required information for our guidance on the march." The image of a rugged pioneer entering an empty land is central to what we think of as wilderness travel, yet Fages hardly sounds like an intrepid explorer—more like a tourist asking directions.

MANY OF my hiking friends have the habit of knocking down "ducks"—the little rock cairns erected by Boy Scouts and other hikers to mark a cross-country route. On occasion, I've helped, gleefully kicking over the piles and listening to the stones clatter together as they fall. Although ducks are meant to serve as way-markers, many are poorly placed and almost useless to those making their own way through the landscape. That's one reason we dislike them. But we also relish the sense that we are exploring the country for ourselves. The ducks ruin the feeling that we're the first ones here. Others share our distaste for the cairns—planners of a Canada–Mexico desert route would ban not only the construction of trails but also the use of ducks in desert wilderness areas. And Steve Roper, author of *The Climber's Guide to the High Sierra*, has devoted whole guidebooks to wiping out ducks, even coming up with a half-baked ecological excuse: moving rocks disturbs the microenvironments underneath them. If we are concerned about that level of disturbance, we should stop hiking altogether.

Maintaining this illusion of discovery is half the argument for no-trace camping: in addition to the legitimate concerns about damage to the environment, we want those who come after us to feel just as we did: that they're the first ones in this spot. That this feeling is usually based on fantasy doesn't seem to bother anyone, even those who know better. It's almost a conscious act of the imagination. In *Wind in the Rock*, Ann Zwinger devotes a great deal of space to discussing the Anasazi culture of Utah's canyonlands and, a few pages later, berates a hiking group for building large bonfires. With this practice, she says, "the feeling that 'I am the first person here and I am alone,' is destroyed."

Another writer, Jack Turner, has an even stronger aversion to running

across people and their marks in the wilderness. Our purported wilderness areas have become so managed that no true wilderness is left, he says, just "a semblance of wild nature." In his essay "The Abstract Wild," he says: "We see signs and hike horse trails and cross sturdy bridges and find maps on large boards at trail junctions. We meet patrolling rangers, Boy Scout and Girl Scout troops working on character. . . . We meet trail crews, pack trains, and hikers galore." For Turner, any contact with other humans turns the wilderness into something else. How would he feel, I wonder, if he came across a party of Indians getting ready to burn a patch of grassland or chaparral?

Wanting to get away from humanity—in the words of one writer, to "wake to the sound of absolutely nothing human"—is certainly understandable, given our crowded, technological society. But insisting on seeing oneself as the first person in a place goes further. Doing so means living out a vision of pre-European North America as empty, "virgin" wilderness, as if the peoples who lived here for thousands of years never existed. Bill McKibben calls this the desire "to see surroundings unpolluted even by the knowledge that someone had been there before." One of the last to see these places in their purity, he says, was Bob Marshall.

Marshall, cofounder of The Wilderness Society, made finding uninhabited and uncharted territory the central point of wilderness recreation and preservation. He wrote of the sadness of visiting a place and wishing "that I might have had the joy of being the first person to discover it. . . . I yearned for adventures comparable to those of Lewis and Clark." Meriwether Lewis and William Clark, of course, weren't the first people to discover the Missouri River—Sacajawea and other Indians showed it to them. Likewise, Cabeza de Vaca wasn't the first person to discover the Southwest. He walked from village to village from Texas to Mexico. And Pedro Fages wasn't the first person to travel across Anza-Borrego.

But Marshall himself was inspired by this misconception to find places that (apparently) had never been seen, even by the continent's indigenous people. "There were no musty signs of human occupation," he wrote of exploring the upper reaches of Alaska's Koyukuk River in the 1930s. "This, beyond a doubt, was an unbeaten path." A few other explorers may have been the first to set foot in specific spots—John Charles Frémont on Fremont Peak or John Wesley Powell in the inner gorges of the Grand

Canyon. But for the most part, North America was already well known to the people who lived here. Even in the depths of the Grand Canyon, Powell and his men found an Indian garden of corn and squash, to which they helped themselves.

The problem comes when we use a vision of wilderness derived from rocky peaks, granite gorges, and truly barren deserts to drive people out of their homes in more hospitable territory. When Montana's Glacier National Park was created in 1910, for instance, the Blackfoot Indians were forced to stop hunting and carrying out other subsistence activities. The Tohono O'odham (formerly the Papago) were forced to move from Organ Pipe Cactus National Monument after its creation in 1937. When the monument's managers replaced the Tohono O'odham's techniques of burning, flood irrigation, transplanting, and seed sowing with a more "natural" regime, the biological diversity of Quitobaquito Springs began to decline. And the last of the Ahwahneechee, a subgroup of the Southern Miwok, were evicted from Yosemite National Park only in the middle of the twentieth century, as late as the 1960s. All this happened because we believe that people don't belong in wilderness and that hunting and gathering, intentional burning, and irrigating destroy the balance of nature.

The Indians of the Anza-Borrego area were dispossessed thirty to forty years before Anza-Borrego Desert State Park was created in the 1930s — long enough ago to assuage any guilt we might feel about their being removed for our own recreational needs. Still, we continue to cast ourselves in the role of the first European explorers, of Daniel Boone or Pedro Fages or Juan Bautista de Anza. We may abhor their treatment of Indians, yet that archetype of the self-reliant hero exploring unknown, unpopulated territory is still very much with us, and it still has consequences for the continent's indigenous peoples. Can we strip wilderness of these associations, learn to see it and experience it as something else, and still call it wilderness?

I sit down on a rock in the chaparral opening to make some notes. I try to picture the whole mountain slope looking as open as this spot, with a clear trail running down to the brink of Oriflamme Canyon. I can almost see the horses' tails disappearing over that edge, Fages' helmet glinting in the sun. Then I realize that Fages probably didn't wear a helmet. Most of

the Spanish army seems to have taken up some other headgear by this point. Pictures of the more famous Anza expedition show the soldiers wearing flat-brimmed and three-cornered hats.

Not that it much matters what he wore. I can't make up my mind what I think about Fages. Was he a daring explorer facing a harsh, unknown land? Part of me wants to see his journey as a trip into the unknown. This probably says a lot about the age I live in, when we know so much about almost every place on earth. The idea of encountering something unexpected holds an almost magical appeal.

As I stand here today looking down into that hazy, brown desert, his route certainly looks forbidding. It's seventy-five degrees Fahrenheit up here at 5,000 feet and probably twenty degrees hotter down in the desert. At those temperatures, even when just riding a horse, the human body needs at least a gallon of water a day to keep going. And there isn't much water between here and the Salton Sea. The "creeks" Fages' route follows are mostly dry, sandy washes, with two exceptions: Carrizo Marsh, where Vallecito and Carrizo Creeks join, and San Sebastian Marsh, near the Salton Sea. There are springs here and there, if you know where to find them, but only two or three sure sources of water in forty miles of hard slogging through sand. When I imagine that trip, I imagine a solitary march of four or five days, seeing no one the whole time.

But then I remind myself that Fages had four soldiers with him and that the journey would have been faster on horseback. I also know that there were native villages at points along the way where he could have received water. He may even have used a Kumeyaay guide. Maybe he was filled with wonder at this new place, or with dread at the expanse of terrain before him, but he wasn't discovering anything. The Indians who pointed out the way for him probably thought they were showing him around their neighborhood.

My reverie is interrupted by a deep roar coming from behind Granite Mountain, the dark, pyramidal peak just to the north. An F-14 jet fighter shoots up from behind the mountain and then banks left and levels out, heading east. Another jet follows a few seconds later. The sound of their engines remains long after they vanish in the distance.

I hate this intrusion. The jets are thousands of feet in the air now, but I wonder how low they were before I saw them. The navy, the Bureau of

Land Management, and the state park service have worked out regulations to keep the flyboys from going too low, but I see them breaking the rule all the time. Two decades ago, there were 1,200 bighorn sheep in the Peninsular Ranges. Now there are about 300. They have such a precarious hold on existence that any additional stress—such as the noise of those jets—could increase their susceptibility to disease and put them over the edge into extinction.

Still, I know that if I had a toy like that, I'd probably do the same thing.

I have a more selfish concern. Those jets may have started out from the air station at Miramar on the coast, thirty-five miles away, and probably took less than ten minutes to get here. They are just one more reminder of how small the world has become. They fly across the desert in a matter of minutes—this desert that had earned the Spanish description *la jornada del muerte,* "the journey of death"—and make a mockery of any notion of vastness this place conjures in me.

Now I realize at least part of what I'm doing out here: I'm imagining that this land is still as big as it was when Pedro Fages rode through it. This is one thing we can salvage from the age of explorers. Fages lived at a time when three miles per hour was the standard speed at which people moved through the world—ten, maybe, on horseback. Today, I can fly from San Diego to New York in less time than it would take to hike down into the desert from the spot where I'm sitting. That kind of compression of time and space makes the land in between seem unimportant. The world becomes a series of airport lounges and cab rides and Holiday Inn hotels, a world bounded by metal, concrete, and plastic. It's easy to forget that there's any world other than the one we've created. Some people have visions of a future in which the whole world has become a plastic bubble; some even think we could live that way.

Following an old trail like this is a way of keeping alive the idea that there is something bigger in the world than our own human pursuits. I don't have to pretend that I'm the first one here; I just need the possibility of finding something new and surprising (to me), a landscape that puts our human endeavors into perspective. I cling to that possibility as if it were a life preserver.

Chapter 9

BOX CANYON:
SOLDIERS AND
FORTY-NINERS

I'M SITTING in the shade of a mesquite tree in Box Canyon, enjoying a break from the heat. It's ninety-five degrees Fahrenheit with a light breeze, not bad for the desert in September. The dry air cools my sweat quickly, but the breeze isn't strong enough to keep down the flies and gnats that pester me whenever I stop. In the distance, I can hear the *scree-eee* of a hawk. The flies' buzzing and the swoosh of an occasional car passing on the road above the canyon are the only other sounds. A fat black lizard suns itself on the rocks across the wash.

The canyon here is formed by tilted layers of metamorphosed sandstone, baked to rust and slate and orange by lava welling up underneath it eons ago. The rushing of flash floods has carved a winding route down through this rock, exposing the layers and strewing boulders down the streambed. It's an interesting place for a geologist, but it wasn't so interesting 150 years ago for a party of soldiers trying to pull their wagons through.

On January 19, 1847, the Mormon Battalion forced a passage through this canyon on its way to join in the Mexican War. Their axes rang against stone as they tried to widen a spot in the canyon too narrow by a foot. The battalion of 350 men—Americans, provisionally at least, given that they had been run out of Illinois and Missouri for their religious beliefs—aimed to open a wagon road through the desert to the coast of California.

By these efforts, they hoped to earn the right to practice their religion and live unmolested by other Christians and the U.S. government. Utah, the territory in which many of them would find a home, fell almost incidentally into the lands the United States would acquire as it took Texas and California from Mexico.

The battalion had marched from Council Bluffs, Iowa, crossing New Mexico and traveling down the Gila River to its junction with the Colorado River. The men had just spent a week in the terrible *jornada del muerte* across the desert from the Colorado River to the Anza-Borrego area. They were following in the footsteps of Stephen Watts Kearny's Army of the West, which had passed through Box Canyon less than two months earlier. Riding and sometimes marching on foot to rest their worn-out horses and mules, broken down by the summer heat of the desert followed by a winter storm in the mountains, Kearny's men had arrived in poor condition at Warner's Ranch in Valle de San Jose, twenty-five miles northwest of Box Canyon. Three days later, their powder wet from a night of rain, Kearny's troops fell to the better-mounted, better-equipped lancers of General Andrés Pico in the Battle of San Pasqual.

The Mormon Battalion had just heard the news of Kearny's defeat, and now they found themselves enclosed in Box Canyon, between Granite Mountain and the Vallecito Mountains, in the heart of what is now Anza-Borrego Desert State Park. Like many of the gorges in this meeting of mountains and desert, this one narrows quickly from its wide-open mouth to a slot too narrow for a wagon to pass through. Its upper end was blocked by one of the dry waterfalls common to these canyons, a twenty-foot rock ledge that the waters of innumerable flash floods had been unable to erode. Here, in this confluence of mountain building and the intricacies of erosion, the battalion confronted the obstacle that would keep San Diego a sleepy backwater for another hundred years. The mountains that had risen up to create this desert would protect it for decades from the railroads and superhighways that lay in the American future. Here in Box Canyon, it was as if the water-polished and desert-varnished rock were speaking: "Turn back."

To one of the battalion's guides, a man named Weaver, this message seemed plain. "I believe we are penned up," he told the expedition leader, Colonel Philip St. George Cooke. For the colonel, though, with his Amer-

ican army background, the terrain of these desert passages was just another engineering problem. Cooke wrote in *The Conquest of New Mexico and California*, "I ordered him to find a crossing, or I should send a company who would soon do it."

This was at Campbell Grade, a two-hundred-foot rock-strewn hill separating Vallecito and Mason Valley. At Box Canyon, four miles farther on, the situation was even worse. Cooke wrote: "I came to the cañon and found it much worse than I had been led to expect; there were many rocks to surmount, but the worst was the narrow pass. Setting the example myself, there was much work done on it before the wagons came; the rock was hewn with axes to increase the opening." The battalion had lost most of its road-building tools in crossing the Colorado, so the men were reduced to widening the canyon with axes, a crowbar, and one or two spades. Fortunately for them, the dry fall at the head of the canyon was flanked by a low hill over which the wagons could be pulled. Had they been in many of Anza-Borrego's deeper canyons, with two-hundred-foot vertical walls, the fall would have been impassable.

Cooke returned to the first narrowing of the canyon, where the men were testing the lead wagon. The walls were still "too narrow by a foot of solid rock. More work was done, and several trials made. The sun was now only an hour high, and it was about seven miles to the first water. I had a wagon taken to pieces, and carried through." They were still seven miles from the next water source, with the sun sinking and at least one more rocky pass to get the wagons over.

Near sundown, they got another wagon through by removing its running gear. After still more hacking, they had mules pull the last two wagons through with their loads intact. The battalion made a dry camp in Blair Valley that night, where the livestock had "unusually good grass." The next day, they reached San Felipe Valley, where they found water and pasture, and the next day, the Valle de San Jose and Warner's Ranch, where they left the desert behind and entered the mountains proper. By the time they reached the coast, the war was over, but they had accomplished their mission: even though they arrived with only five wagons, they had opened the way for the thousands of emigrants that would follow.

Today, there is no obvious spot where the canyon becomes too narrow for a wagon. If the marks of axes are still visible, I can't find them. Perhaps

flooding has widened the canyon, erasing the marks. The dry fall is still there, a twenty-foot vertical chute of water-polished slate-and-white rock. The trail where the battalion pulled out of the canyon to bypass the dry fall is clear, and it's paralleled by a later wagon road used by the Butterfield Overland Mail Company. Well above the stream, modern construction crews have bulldozed a road over which cars glide effortlessly on pavement.

Although the immediate effects of this single act of trail blazing were relatively slight, the long-term consequences for the Anza-Borrego region would be large. Beyond their few tools and five wagons, Cooke and his men carried with them a new mind-set, one that would radically alter the region surrounding Anza-Borrego in the coming century. Cooke's exchange with the guide named Weaver best represents this sea change: an instinct to read the lay of the land and follow its contours gave way to a drive to subdue the landscape and bend it to human purposes. Cooke later wrote of the battalion's exploit, "With crowbar and pick and ax in hand we have worked our way over mountains which seemed to defy aught save the wild goat, and hewed a passage through a chasm of living rock more narrow than our wagons."

The Indians had changed the landscape, to be sure, yet most of their changes were intensifications of natural processes: they set fires, redirected water, and influenced the distribution of some plant species. Unlike the new road through Box Canyon, their paths followed natural contours, staying mostly to the ridges in mountainous country. The changes the Americans would make in the next century were orders of magnitude greater and aimed at defying natural processes rather than intensifying them. If a mountain stood in the newcomers' way, they would move it; if a river flooded, they would dam it; if fire threatened homes and timber, they would extinguish it. Americans believed in their Manifest Destiny to occupy the continent, to subdue not only the peoples of the West but also the landscape.

The most extreme intentional changes the newcomers would make were a half century in the future, but they wreaked a more immediate, unwitting havoc by means of the livestock they brought with them. The Mormon Battalion had eighty-eight sheep, at least forty-two mules, and ten cattle, all of them munching on the grass and mesquite beans and

desert shrubs along the way. They weren't the first herds to cross this desert, and by themselves, they probably had little effect. But these animals were just the first trickle in what would become a flood. In the next two decades, hundreds of thousands of cattle, sheep, horses, and mules would pour across the desert, generally following the path carved by the Mormons. Combined with the strange seeds they carried clinging to their hides, this rush of animals amounted to an invasion as devastating to indigenous species as the American invasion was to the Indians and the Mexicans. The livestock and plants the Americans brought west had their own destiny, manifest in the peculiar workings of a sheep's teeth on grass and in the digestive system of a cow.

THE COASTAL areas of San Diego had already experienced a similar environmental and social onslaught at the hands of the Spanish. The havoc the soldiers and missionaries wreaked on both the Kumeyaay Indians and the environment are incalculable. One of the most devastating of those effects undoubtedly reached farther inland than the Spanish themselves and may even have preceded them: the host of Old World diseases that the soldiers and missionaries brought with them. Like all indigenous people in the Americas, southern California's Indians fell quickly to these new diseases, to which they had no natural immunity. For example, the population of Cupeño Indians in Valle de San Jose (what would become Warner's Ranch) fell from 5,000 before 1769 to 2,000 in 1795. The culprits were at least one smallpox epidemic combined with several droughts. The Kumeyaay fared even worse, with their population plummeting from an estimated 12,000–14,000 in 1769 to about 4,000 in 1828. Droughts also played a part in that reduction, their effects intensified on people weakened by the new diseases. Anthropologist Florence Shipek estimates that disease doubled the death rate during this period. The situation was similar for the Cahuilla; Lowell John Bean wrote that "by 1875, European-introduced diseases had reduced the Cahuilla population to a fraction of its former numbers."

Other effects on the Indians were more intentional and confined more closely to the coast. The Spanish soldiers raped Indian women and girls, earning the early hostility of the Indians, and the priests and military commanders seemed unable to stop the sexual violence. The Spanish also

imposed forced labor on the converted Indians at Mission San Luis Rey and Mission San Diego de Alcalá. The converts, or "neophytes," were pulled away from their own subsistence activities to provide agricultural labor for the missions. This was the first step in breaking the people's intricately developed lifeway. (Neophytes of the more northern missions fared much worse because whole villages were brought into those missions year-round, thus preempting their traditional lifeways from the beginning.)

The livestock the Spanish brought with them had an immediate effect on the landscape the Kumeyaay inhabited. Some of the earliest accounts by the padres report soldiers turning their horses loose in Indian grainfields. To the Spanish, this was good pasture; to the Indians, it was their own food crop. Like the indigenous people, who had not developed immunities to European disease, the grass had not evolved with grazing by horses or cattle as the European grasses had, thus gaining "immunity" to livestock by developing seeds that passed through domestic animals' digestive systems. Lacking this ability, California's native grasses began to disappear, giving way to European grasses and weeds.

One outstanding example is the wild mustard, a beautiful but deadly invader made famous in Helen Hunt Jackson's novel *Ramona*. Early in the book, Father Salvierderra walks through a patch of the stuff. "As he proceeded he found the mustard thicker and thicker. . . . The plant is a tyrant and a nuisance,—the terror of the farmer; it takes riotous possession of a whole field in a season; once in, never out; for one plant this year, a million the next; but it is impossible to wish that the land were freed from it. Its gold is as distinct a value to the eye as the nugget gold is in the pocket."

That picturesque description didn't apply to another of the invaders, cheeseweed, or mallow. This weed, propagated accidentally from a batch of seeds sent from Spain, became such a nuisance that in the words of naturalist José Longinos Martinez, "it is cleared out every year only with great difficulty; indeed it grows so vigorously that in the vicinity of the missions and in the grain fields one cannot force a way through it." Other introduced species that began to crowd out native plants included redstem filaree, foxtail barley, knotweed, curly dock, prickly sow thistle, wild oat, slender oat, bur clover, Italian ryegrass, bluegrass, lamb's-quarter, Napa thistle (*Centaurea melitensis*, also commonly known as "tocalote"),

nettle-leaf goosefoot, rough pigweed, horehound, castor bean, tree tobacco, and anise.

Other than the new diseases, which probably spread rapidly inland, the changes wrought by the Spanish were confined to the coast. The Cahuilla and Kumeyaay peoples of the mountains and desert escaped Spanish influence almost entirely. Mission San Luis Rey's satellite, or *asistencia*, in Santa Ysabel, a mountain valley south of Valle de San Jose, was the farthest inland the padres reached. Large bands of Kumeyaay and Cahuilla remained independent and followed their original lifeways, especially in the deserts. Even in areas where the priests were most influential, the converted Indians adopted elements of Spanish agriculture, such as livestock raising and cultivation of fruit trees, but managed to maintain many of their traditional practices. The Cahuilla of the Los Coyotes area above Valle de San Jose, for instance, may have begun raising livestock as early as the 1830s. They probably moved the cattle down to the desert in winter, following the side canyons from the high grasslands down to Coyote Canyon. This would have been the first continual grazing of European livestock on the desert.

But most of the desert lands remained untouched by these changes throughout the early 1800s. The Spanish and Mexicans had little use for the desert. After Pedro Fages' last trip through the Carrizo Corridor in 1785, the desert saw little European traffic. The Spanish seem to have forgotten about Fages' route after the late 1780s, when the quarrelsome Yuma Indians made crossing the Colorado River problematic. Juan Bautista de Anza had been the first to drive livestock through the desert, but no one had used his route through Coyote Canyon since the 1780s.

In the 1820s, a newly independent Mexico realized that it had only a tenuous hold on Alta California and set about opening better communication to this northern region. In 1823 or 1824, Lieutenant Santiago Argüello discovered the link from the Valle de San Jose through San Felipe and Box Canyon to join Fages' route through the Carrizo Corridor. This route was known for the next twenty years as the Sonora Road to Los Angeles and San Diego. Still, it was used mostly by soldiers traveling on horseback, and their effect on the landscape and on the Indians was slight.

Even after Mexican independence, when the missions were taken over by the secular government and their lands doled out in grants to individ-

uals, ranching never took hold in or near the desert. Rancho San Felipe, the nearest land grant to the desert itself, wasn't used for grazing by its original owner, Luis Arenas, and was just beginning to be developed in the 1840s. The Kumeyaay of the inland areas were too numerous and hostile for the Mexicans to control. Repeated raids by the Indians kept the Mexicans near the coast. Florence Shipek believes that the Indians of southern California were so well organized that they would have eventually thrown the Mexicans out if Americans hadn't taken control of the territory in 1846.

The desert that Kearny's and Cooke's parties crossed in 1846 and 1847 on their way to San Diego was much the same as it had been for hundreds of years. The native grasses still grew at watering spots along the way. The cluster of palms between Carrizo Creek and Vallecito still called travelers to the water at their base. Lieutenant W. H. Emory, an officer with Kearny's Army of the West, who kept the best records of plants along the route, recorded no non-native species in the desert. And the Indians the party met at Vallecito and San Felipe were still following many of their traditional gathering methods. Although the Indians seemed glad to get the meat of animals that died along the way, they offered traditional foods such as pinole to the newcomers, a fact that led many Americans to call them impoverished.

But change came rapidly the following year with the single event that would transform the entire state: the discovery of gold on Sutter's Creek in January 1848.

THE FIRST gold rushers were not the forty-niners but Mexicans who either were still living in California or could make the relatively short journey from the state of Sonora. In 1848, they flooded the Sonora Road when they heard the news. Major Lawrence Pike Graham's troops were crossing to California at the same time, a fact that put them in an excellent position to observe the traffic on the trail. The men of the regiment were also catching gold fever. Cave J. Couts, a lieutenant with the regiment, wrote in his diary for December 17, 1848: "The mania that pervades the whole country, our camp included, is beyond all description or credibility. The whole state of Sonora is on the move, are passing us in gangs daily, and say they have not yet started."

By 1849, news of wild successes in the mines of California had sparked gold fever back in the United States. The Southern Emigrant Trail would become important as a winter route to California, enabling travelers to avoid the hardships of crossing the Sierra Nevada. Thousands of forty-niners couldn't wait for cooler weather and attempted crossing by the southern route in summer. By September, *la jornada del muerte* had lived up to its name.

In that month, Couts returned to the desert as head of a military escort for the boundary survey party of Amiel Weeks Whipple. Retracing his steps of only nine months earlier, he found that much had changed along the Carrizo Corridor. On September 22, with the temperature reaching 110 degrees, Couts wrote: "Arriving at Carrizo Creek, were much astonished at not finding a particle of cane for the poor animals, and more still at their not drinking the water. The little stream was running rather brisk, but not a horse or mule would put their nose to it. The water is the same as when we passed it on 2nd December last, but I judge that the number of dead animals around and in the water, was the reason they would not use it."

In Whipple's *Report*, the scene appears even more desolate: "Of food for them there was none; the emigrants had consumed every blade of grass and every stick of cane, so that our sorrowful animals are tied in groups to the wagons to ponder their fate upon the desert."

The number of people crossing the desert is perhaps best illustrated by Couts' journal entry for September 25: "If any are left in Arkansas, it is more numerously populated than I had anticipated." And with each party of travelers came a herd of livestock—cattle, oxen, horses, mules, or sheep. In the withering heat of the desert between the Colorado River and the mountains of the Peninsular Ranges, thousands of these animals died. The trail was littered with their rotting carcasses, and many of the watering places, as Couts found at Carrizo Creek, had been fouled.

William H. Chamberlin, who crossed the desert in August 1849, about a month before the Whipple party, found little but destitution and decay on the march through what is now Anza-Borrego. He called one of the wells along the way "a perfect Golgotha—the bones of thousands of animals lie strewed about in every direction; and a great number of carcasses of horses and mules that have died lately, pollute the atmosphere. Deserted wagons, harness, saddles, etc., add to this destructive and sickening scene."

Conditions were little better at Carrizo Creek, which his party reached on August 15. "The water, though clear as chrystal, has a peculiar and unpleasant taste. We ate a piece, but we could find nothing for our animals to feed upon." What had been the first almost-pleasant stop for Kearny's dragoons and Cooke's battalion, then, was already polluted and overgrazed. Chamberlin mentions a party of Sonorans camped at Carrizo Creek with a herd of several hundred horses. They were heading *east* on the trail toward home, either returning to bring their families back to California or driven out of the gold fields by Americans, a fate that would await many more of the Mexican miners.

Many animals had died here, too: "The stench arising from the number of dead animals strewed about is almost sickening." Later that day, Chamberlin's party moved on to the palm oasis, which they found also polluted by dead horses and mules, though they did find a "few bunches of bear grass." Three years earlier, Emory had called this a "small patch" of grass. Up the trail at Vallecito, where Emory had written that "the grass, which is coarse, extends a mile or two along the valley," Chamberlin found only a "fine green spot of grass containing a few acres."

Yet nature is resilient (or perhaps the Indians had been out replanting), for Benjamin Hayes, reaching Carrizo Creek on January 8, 1850, found short green grass. Farther on, he found "scattered tufts and patches of young grass under the bushes along most of the road." The grass had probably sprouted with one of the winter storms that push over the mountains and into the desert in mid- to late November. I find something heartening in that image of grass struggling back to life after the first onslaught of mass immigration.

Even in the summer of 1849, the desert wasn't entirely barren. Fortunately for the immigrants, the Colorado River overflowed its banks that year, sending water down its distributaries to the Salton Trough, right across the immigrants' path. Where Couts and all the previous American parties had found a dry, barren arroyo, the immigrants now found a flowing river, with grass growing along its banks and as far as two miles out on either side. "I was much astonished to find myself here with three wagons, and the horses, and on the prettiest grazing I ever saw," Couts wrote on his return in September. "Gamma, or Gramma, or buffalo grass, so called by emigrants. All this with the river, have sprung up since we passed last fall, though the river is probably as old as the desert."

If Couts was surprised at this sudden appearance of water, the Kumeyaay nearby were used to these changes. "The Indians about speak of it as an old thing, and are much astonished at our wonder." If he had pressed them further, they might have told him that they themselves had spread the seed for this grass the last time water had flowed this way; now they were returning to gather their harvest. This is the grass that Couts called the work of an "Invisible Hand"; the hands were right there in front of him.

As BAD as the destruction was in 1849, it was the result of only the first rush in a decades-long migration. During that year, the migration was mainly of people, bringing just enough stock for their own needs on the trail and at the mines. In years to come, however, ranchers would drive huge herds of livestock across the desert to feed the hungry miners or to begin ranching operations in California. They knew they would lose many animals in the desert, but the prices of beef and mutton in the early 1850s made the risk worthwhile.

It's hard to conceive of the numbers of animals crossing the desert in the 1850s, but it's not hard to imagine their effect on the land. Local historian Phil Brigandi combed the historical archives and came up with some astounding figures. From 1848 to 1870, more than 70,000 head of cattle made the trip. In just eight years, from 1850 to 1858, herders drove more than half a million sheep across the desert. Head for head, the sheep caused the worst damage because they crop the grass right down to the roots.

Half a million is an abstract number, hard to wrap the mind around, but the reality sinks in when one considers how many individual drives were involved. Historian Richard Pourade reported that 3,000 sheep arrived in San Diego in June 1851 after an arduous drive from Durango and Chihuahua, Mexico. In July, another 6,000 sheep arrived at the crossing of the Colorado River, and 4,000 more were farther back on the trail.

Brigandi lists dozens of cattle and sheep drives in his study of grazing in Anza-Borrego. One foresighted individual, T. J. Trimmier, drove 500 head of cattle from Texas to California as early as 1848. In March 1849, 3,000 to 4,000 horses and mules, along with herds of cattle, were "ready to start on the trail to California." Of course, starting from Texas and

reaching the coast are two different things; many of the drives lost half their herds, and some were reduced to one-tenth of the number that started out. One year, at least 50,000 cattle started from Texas, though as few as 5,000 completed the journey. Some were lost to Apache Indians in New Mexico and Arizona, and many died after crossing the Colorado River.

Still, in November 1850, 4,000 sheep passed by Vallecito. In July of the following year, 2,000 sheep died at Carrizo Creek (perhaps a portion of the 6,000 reported by Pourade). In 1852, 40,000 sheep were driven from New Mexico, most likely going through Anza-Borrego after crossing the Colorado. In September 1853, the *San Diego Herald* reported that 103,000 sheep were close to the crossing of the Colorado, and in the next month 1,200 Texas cattle crossed the Anza-Borrego region. A year later, 6,000 cattle crossed at Yuma in the space of two months. Two years later, in December 1856, Louis Iaeger ferried 19,000 to 28,000 sheep across the Colorado. He had ferried 8,322 sheep just a month earlier.

In the 1860s, the number of cattle crossing the desert increased. Drought years had decimated the California cattle herds, and ranchers from Arizona and Texas began driving cattle across the desert to replace them. In April 1869, about 1,400 cattle from Texas were successfully driven across the desert. Two months later, separate herds of 1,800 and 1,200 were on their way from New Mexico and Arizona, and "other parties, whose names we did not get, [had] large herds on the road."

These livestock drives killed grasses, fouled water sources, compacted soil, increased erosion, and introduced exotic species to the desert. But most of these effects were confined to the relatively narrow swath of the trail. In 1858, for instance, there was no native grass at Carrizo Creek. Henry Wilson, who was in charge of the Carrizo Creek station of the Butterfield Overland Mail, needed grass for horses. He reported, quite merrily, that the local Indian women would harvest the galleta grass farther afield from the creek and then the men would trade it to him for whiskey. This practice was probably more damaging to the Indians than to the grass itself: cutting it wouldn't harm the individual plant and might shake loose the seeds of mature grasses. It's not clear whether the Indians were still burning the grass at this point, but they seem to have been raising it as a trade crop. Indians were also paid to cut galleta grass at Algodones,

west of Yuma, in the early 1860s. Some of the Indians' traditional practices were becoming enmeshed with the American economy.

The survival of both the native grasses and the Indians' traditional way of life would become more difficult after the 1860s. During the Civil War, large numbers of Texans fled to California, and many of them settled in the mountains of San Diego, living closer to the desert than any Europeans had before. As they developed their herds of cattle and sheep, a different kind of grazing came to the mountains and desert. Now, instead of simply passing through on a narrow path, the livestock spread out across the countryside. And the animals stayed year-round, summering in the mountains and wintering in the desert. Some ranchers even pastured their cattle around the New River in late summer, when the Colorado overflowed its banks. The numbers were never as great as in the largest of the livestock drives, but the continual nature of the grazing must have had an even greater, more widespread effect on the indigenous plant species. Moreover, as Americans settled the mountains and desert east of San Diego, the Kumeyaay's way of life, even their very existence, came under attack.

FROM the Coyote Mountains to the south or the Vallecito Mountains to the north, Carrizo Creek is a narrow swath of green between lifeless mud hills. It seems a slim hope on which to risk crossing the desert. Had no water flowed to the surface here, had the peculiarities of stream confluences and depth of bedrock not produced this oasis, the crossing of the Colorado Desert by livestock and people on horseback might have been impossible. But it was just enough to get most of the people and many of the animals through to the gentler country at Warner's Ranch and beyond.

I imagine being one of those pioneers, a homesteader pulling my whole household in a covered wagon, risking everything I own in this crossing of the desert. Our wagon train has just crossed a hundred miles of sandy desert, dipping down into Mexico to avoid the sand dunes of what will one day be called the Imperial Valley. At our camps, there has been brackish water and little feed for our animals. Only a few of our cattle have made it this far. We've spent the last day and a half covering the thirty-two miles from Indian Wells with no sleep, pushing the oxen to this water and forage.

After weeks of crossing flat desert, our perspective flattened by that vastness stretching to the horizon, the world suddenly changes. We enter the sandy wash of Carrizo Creek and the world again becomes three-dimensional again. A jagged range of mountains rises up in the north, a more rounded set of hills in the south. As we pass between them, they almost reach out to embrace us. After miles of seeing nothing but creosote bush and bur sage, we enter the green oasis of Carrizo, and the next day, Palm Spring. The palms are long gone, having been cut down for firewood.

The coyotes—wolves, we call them—have followed in our tracks for a week now, waiting for another animal to drop. We're tired, worn down from the journey, too busy thinking about where we're going—the war, the gold fields, a homestead in gentler country—to look closely at this place, to think about it as something other than one more obstacle on our path. It is so different from the land back home: not a trace of green except here at the oasis, the cacti and agaves like strange figures from our nightmares, the smell of the creosote bushes reminding us of sulfur, a fitting complement to this landscape out of hell.

To the north, the mountains rise into a long, mile-high ridge paralleling our route. One of our fellow travelers will write that the mountains

Coyote

"had preyed on [the settlers'] minds for over a week, and as they approached nearer, grew more fearsome every day. It was that immense blue wall of mountain, like a cloud, rising three thousand to five thousand feet . . . before them. No pass through that was apparent. They had sorely learned how difficult it could be to travel over level country as it had nearly taken their lives. How much worse would that impassable wall be?"

Then I imagine I'm sitting on top of Whale Peak 150 years ago, watching from the shade of a pinyon pine as the pioneers follow Carrizo Creek and then Vallecito Creek. They struggle along, minute figures on the land, like pilgrims in a Japanese landscape. Their presence pales in comparison with the weight of the mountains surrounding them or the raven twisting and rolling in the wind blowing over the peak where I sit. Even the dust cloud they raise is a small thing drifting out toward the east. There is little to hint at the huge effect that they, and thousands more like them, will have on this land in years to come.

TABLE MOUNTAIN: COWBOYS AND THEIR COWS

O N A pleasant day one March, I return to the Table Mountain area, the site of my first backpacking trip and the place where I learned the intricacies of reading a map and using a compass. It's a well-used spot at the park's southern tip; most of the area isn't even part of the park, but rather Bureau of Land Management (BLM) territory. Home over the years to Indians, cattle ranchers, and prospectors and now open to target shooters and off-roaders, it's one of the most abused places in the Anza-Borrego region. Still, there's something magical about the place that draws me back.

The area I'm hiking through occupies a flat bench at the base of the Jacumba Mountains, which form a wall running along the northeast, and bounded by Table Mountain on the southeast, Gray Mountain directly south, and the steep drop into Carrizo Gorge on the west. The area encompasses only about six square miles, but it seems larger because of the many blind draws, parallel ridges, and isolated granite knobs that make it such a good place in which to get lost. Relatively flat on its eastern end, the land breaks apart as it drops toward the thousand-foot-deep Carrizo Gorge. The granitic bedrock eroded unevenly here, leaving a series of outcrops, piled turrets, sugarloaves, and balance rocks reminiscent of those at Joshua Tree National Park. The contour lines on the topographic map make patterns similar to those in a Rorschach test—sitting ducks,

toads, raven heads, ghost faces. As they trace a passage through this laby-rinth, the washes double back on themselves in sinuous S-curves. It's easy to feel as if you're in your own private sanctum here—though a jeep might come rumbling around the corner at any moment.

This spot was also a sanctum for the Kumeyaay, who had at least two villages in the area. At an average elevation of 3,000 feet, the village sites are located in that life zone known as the Upper Sonoran, where cactus and agave meet juniper, scrub oak, and manzanita and where most of the Indians' food sources were within a day's walk. From here, they could go west to the Laguna Mountains for acorns, south for pinyon nuts, and north and east into the low desert for mesquite beans. Dos Cabezas lies just on the other side of the Jacumba Mountains and a thousand feet lower—a formidable expedition for a modern day-hiker but all in a day's work for the Indian women who did the work of harvesting and planting grass. Closer at hand, deer, rabbits, and bighorn sheep were plentiful, and sta-ples such as agave grew nearby, along with such treats as desert apricot and juniper berry.

Remnants left by the Kumeyaay cover the whole bench in a thin scat-ter, though they're more concentrated at the village sites—one never need look far to find a potsherd or a worked stone. But these are not the only human leavings in the area. I stop to make a cairn of just the litter within sight, piling rusted nails, broken glass, and spent shells on a rock near the jeep road. It takes only a minute to find a piece of pottery to add to my found-object sculpture, a record of the various cultures that have occupied the place since the time of the Kumeyaay. Farther on, I find fence posts, an old outdoor fireplace and chimney, a dump of rusted tin cans, flakes of rubber tires. This is one reason for going cross-country, to leave these bits of modern Americana behind.

Everywhere, near the jeep roads and away from them, even up to the highest ridges and right through the Indian village, I find cow pies. Most of them are months old, but some are fresh. Coyotes have deposited their own scat on many of them: perhaps they perceive the cattle as some sort of threat. Or maybe these cairns of dung are signs of the coyotes' con-tempt for the hulking, dumb brutes that carve broad paths across the landscape.

At the end of my hike, as I am heading back up a jeep road, I come

across the culprits, two old black cows at the side of the road. Startled by my approach, they jump onto the track and lumber away. I have to drive them for half a mile before they pull off into a broad, flat spot where they can feel safe while I pass. Does their owner let them range down here on state park and BLM land, or are they lost and living here permanently? They could even be second- or third-generation feral cattle, a product of the days when the park leased grazing rights to local ranchers.

A few years ago, rangers tried to clear all the wild cattle out of the park. They had to use helicopters because not even the best cowboys from across the Southwest could find them all and drive them from this rugged country. Some of them still remain, a wild remnant of the desert's romantic ranching past but also one more threat to the park's native animal and plant life.

THE AREA'S cattle were hardly more tame a century ago, when Pete Larkin ran cattle here. This was in the days before fences, when ranchers let their cattle roam where they pleased. Once a year, the cowboys would round up the cattle and sort them by brand, and a judge, known as the "judge of the plains," would settle any disputes. Conscientious ranchers kept track of their cattle and herded them strictly to reduce the number of strays. But Larkin was different. Ella McCain, in her book *Memories of the Early Settlements*, says of Larkin's cattle: "Whenever one broke out of the herd, Mr. Larkin would say let it go. This mis-management made the cattle very hard to handle. It took someone that knew the country well, that was an expert rider and used to riding in rough country, and well trained horses to manage them." Mrs. McCain called Larkin's cattle "wild as deer."

Larkin had operated a stage station in the 1860s at Mountain Springs, just down the hill toward the desert, and maybe that life was more to his liking—less work and trouble. He seems to have tired of ranching and sold out in the 1880s to men who were better managers. Mrs. McCain wrote: "Mr. Chilwell and his cowboys had a tough job on their hands when they gathered those cattle and went to corral them. . . . The cowboys' lariats were in daily use for awhile and the cattle soon learned to respect the lariat, and were easily corralled." Still, perhaps some of Larkin's cattle escaped the notice of Chilwell's men. The cows I see today could be descendants of that herd.

Ella McCain had married into the second generation of George McCain's large ranching family. Like Chilwell, the McCains were strong believers in hard work, and eventually they bought or controlled large tracts of land on the eastern slope of the mountains and down into the desert. The McCain name is written all across the country: McCain Valley, a broad tableland between the lower Jacumba Valley on the east and the higher Laguna Mountains on the west; Jacumba Jim Canyon, a route over which Jim McCain took cattle from McCain Valley down to the desert; Dave McCain Spring in the Vallecito Mountains. Darrell McCain built the shack that now sits in ruins near Dos Cabezas and another cabin that gives Rockhouse Canyon its name. The McCains put in many of the water troughs and pipe works (now abandoned) that mark the canyon mouths around Dos Cabezas. They also pioneered many of the cattle trails from mountains to desert, and they built other roads, such as the one through Plum Canyon that let ranchers drive cattle from Julian and the San Felipe Valley down to the Borrego Valley.

The patriarch of this industrious family was George McCain, who had eighteen children from two marriages. McCain moved back and forth between Arkansas and California during the 1850s, settling in Mendocino County, California, with his second wife in 1857. Discouraged by the drought in the 1860s, the couple headed back to Arkansas in 1868 via the Southern Emigrant Trail. They had gone only as far as the Gila River when they learned of Indian massacres on the trail ahead and the impoverished condition of postwar Arkansas. They decided to turn back, crossed the Colorado Desert, and then turned southwest and headed into the mountains along the Mexican border.

The ascent into the mountains here passes through a set of terraces: first the stage station at Mountain Springs, where the McCains met Peter Larkin; then up a level higher to Jacumba; and finally, just below the Tecate Divide, to the Walker place at Boulevard. Walker himself greeted them: "Mr. McCain, you look like you had a kind of a hard time." "Yes," McCain replied, "we's kinda run down at the heel." Walker told them of a nearby valley still unsettled by Americans, free for the homesteading. "There's a nice valley over here," he told them. "It's a good place to rest; lots of feed, lots of water."

The valley occupies a 4,000-foot bench just below the higher peaks of

the Laguna Mountains and the Tecate Divide. "Grandpa went over and took a look at it," Darrell McCain recalled, "and he said it looked like a pretty good place." Darrell's daughter Mary remembered hearing that "the grass was real high, like it was up to the horse's belly, it was up to their necks. The grass was so high, he thought he'd really found something." Although these descriptions lack the drama of other pioneer accounts—of the Mormons arriving in Utah, for instance—the McCains sensed that this was a place where they could create a good life for themselves.

For many years, it was a good place. The McCains set to work immediately. They built their first house from tules and willow poles, the same materials used by the local Indians. Later, they would build an adobe house with fences and a garden. They also began developing the valley for cattle and sheep ranching. They piped springs to water troughs, built corrals for the stock, and forged trails down into the desert. Through a pattern of land purchase and leasing, George's son Robert came to control a corridor of land from the McCain Valley down through Bow Willow and Rockhouse Canyons to Carrizo Creek and out into the New River area. This added up to an area of 40,000 acres, where they ran 2,000 cattle and 1,200 sheep.

In addition to the family's holdings in the southern Laguna Mountains, in the early 1890s John McCain began running cattle in the Borrego Valley. Around the same time, the Clark brothers, Frank and Fred, began running cattle in Coyote Canyon and in what became known as Clark Valley, northeast of Borrego. The Sentenac brothers, and later George Sawday, ran cattle in the southern end of the San Felipe Valley around Sentenac Ciénega. The chain of valleys along the Southern Emigrant Trail—San Felipe, Earthquake, Mason, Vallecito, and Carrizo—all had cattle operations by the 1890s.

Like the Indians, many of the ranchers split their time between summers in the mountains and winters on the desert. After fattening the stock on spring grasses and wildflowers, they would head back into the mountains and their home place. Darrell McCain, who virtually grew up in the saddle, recalled fondly: "You worked and drove cattle every month of the year. I was in the saddle a month at a time, every day. Started out at four o'clock in the morning and stopped after it got too dark to see."

Lester Reed also found much to appreciate in the cowboy life. His *Old*

Time Cattlemen and Other Pioneers of the Anza-Borrego Area gives one of the clearest pictures of life for the earliest ranchers who ran cattle on the desert and of his own experiences as a desert cowboy in the early 1900s. "The old-time cowboys on such cattle drives had to endure many long, sleepless and thirsty hours, and there could not always be any great degree of regularity in getting their meals. . . . However, I don't believe there ever have been men working as a group, who apparently enjoyed their work—despite hardships—as did the old-time cowboys."

Reed's grandparents had come to California in 1867, traveling in covered wagons along the Southern Emigrant Trail, and homesteaded what became known as Reed Valley near Hemet, northwest of Borrego. Born in 1890, Reed had his own ranch and later worked as a cowboy for other ranchers and as a bounty hunter for the Department of Fish and Game. He got a taste of the old-time cowboy's life on cattle drives in the early 1900s and heard stories of the pioneers' experiences from his father, his uncle, and other ranchers. The book he fashioned out of these stories and reminiscences reflects not only an admiration for the struggles of the pioneers and the cowboys' way of life but also sympathy for the Indians they supplanted, whom he calls the first pioneers of the desert.

The back cover of Reed's book features a 1909 photograph of eight cowboys astride their horses, a clump of agaves in the foreground and distant desert hills in the back. The location was probably Borrego Valley, though it could have been anywhere between Borrego and Fish Creek. The striking thing about this photograph is the animation of the cowboys—young men in their twenties, hats in the air, an almost audible whoop rising from their throats as they await the click of the shutter. These are young men on a lark, an adventure for a week or two. Add a few women to the picture and they could be a group of recreational riders; take away the horses and give them day packs and they could be a hiking group from the Sierra Club. The message is clear: theirs seemed a good life on the land, with pleasures not too different from those I seek on my weekend hikes.

IT'S NOT so clear when that good life began to change. Ranching itself changed dramatically with the development of trucking and modern highways. The long cattle drives across the desert became things of the

past, fodder for old-timers' tales. Many of these accounts carry a sense of nostalgia for the cowboy life, a sentiment shared by Reed: "[Sal] Biles and I are nearing the end of the time that we can be 'wild' cowboys, but we have both enjoyed many experiences . . . [that] will not be a part of the lives of the young cowboys of today."

The old-timers missed not only the ranch life but also the land as it once was. By the 1950s, less than a hundred years after the first settlers arrived in the mountains and desert, the places that once held such promise had been depleted. In account after account, old-timers recall a land once rich with possibility now degraded, with dusty ravines and tough sagebrush where lush grass once grew. They watched it vanish, not quite understanding why the land was changing.

One can pick any spot in the backcountry, from mountains to desert, and find evidence of these changes. Warner's Ranch, that gateway between mountains and desert, was once lush with grass. Fray Juan Mariner was the first European to describe the valley, in 1795. He arrived in August, normally one of the driest times of year. "Here," he wrote in his diary, "we found a large gully of water which comes out of the sierra. . . . Also there are three springs which come out below the rancheria *Tauhi*, each with a good flow of water and below is much good land." His party also found, "very high up, a large swamp at the upper side of which there are three very large springs of water." Mariner noted that in a nearby valley, the gully was dry but the land was "good, with sufficient moisture." This seems to confirm Florence Shipek's contention that the Indians had traditionally maintained the water on the land rather than letting it run quickly into the streams and away.

In the 1850s, the valley was still verdant with grass, serving as a popular resting spot for travelers on the way to the gold mines. In January 1850, Judge Benjamin Hayes noted that "the bunch grass is fine, in thick bunches now about 6 inches high, green and tender. . . . Above our camp, within a hundred yards, is an excellent spring; in the valley below runs a small stream for the stock, over a bottom or flat half a mile broad; beyond, and on each side, rise up low hills, overlooked in the rear by the elevations of Agua Caliente, to any of which we may resort with a certainty of finding this bunch grass." Two miles beyond Warner's Ranch, Hayes found "good grass everywhere around, for miles."

Today, Hayes would hardly recognize the place. Viewed from Highway 79 or County Road S-2, the valley is still open pasture, but the grass is short and mixed with thistles. A green strip runs along the bottom of the valley, but the hillsides are brown even after a good rain. What little grass that does spring up is quickly eaten down by the cattle that still graze there. In 1957, a little more than a century after Hayes passed through, Emily Sawday was pessimistic about the potential for grazing at Warner's Ranch. The widow of George Sawday, one of the largest cattle ranchers in the mountains of San Diego County, she had been involved with cattle ranching since 1904. She described the prospects for grazing at Warner's this way: "We haven't any range of Palomar [the mountains west of Warner's Ranch] now and Warner's has been ruined with all the water pumped out. . . . I don't think Warner's will ever come back for range."

The southern end of the county's mountains had seen similar changes. Ella McCain, writing in 1955, remembered a valley near Campo: "During the time Mr. Ussery lived there it was a beautiful valley covered with grass, tules, and a stream of water running through it. . . . As a result of erosion and drought it is difficult to realize it was once a beautiful green valley."

The McCains' home place, McCain Valley, had gone the same way. Ella's son, "Tule" Jim McCain, was born in 1895 and watched the changes take place on the land he worked all his life. "I remember this country before the towns and villages were built," he told longtime backcountry writer Carl Woellwerts. "There was bunch grass all over the slopes and in the valleys. The streams ran good water and you could stand in one place and see the whole world and parts of Mexico." Wildlife was more abundant then, too, especially quail and ducks, which McCain remembered being present "by the thousands." Woellwerts went on to describe the same landscape in the 1970s: "Most of it is covered by chaparral, with occasional pockets of live oak trees. The chaparral has covered large tracts of land that in the early days supported the bunch grass on which the McCain herds fed. The streams are now empty dry washes and the only ponds are where man has built dams and impounded rain water draining from the heights." The land where Tule Jim's grandfather thought he'd "really found something" had almost completely dried out.

The desert was drying out, too, the galleta grass replaced by sage, cre-

osote, cactus, and exotic weeds. This happened not just at Dos Cabezas, as documented by C. R. Orcutt, but all over the desert. By 1934, even the old-time cattlemen were having a hard time imagining this desert as a grazing ground. Ed Mason returned to the valley named after his father after a thirty-year absence and was shocked by the changes, which he described to a reporter from the *San Diego Union*. "Decidedly, Mason says, the old-timers were not crazy; it's just that the water has gone away from that country. Warner's Ranch, the San Felipe grant, Paul Sentenac, Blair and Mason Valleys, and Vallecito all were passably green and fertile lands when the old-timers came. . . . The valleys, that were open grazing country, are overgrown with mesquite and sparse sage." Mason visited the valley during one of the driest years on record, which may account for some of the lack of grass. In recent wet years, spring flower enthusiasts have complained that grasses—mostly non-native—have drowned out the wildflower bloom. But despite these annual variations, the general trend has been a transition from grassland to desert scrub.

WHAT had changed to convert mountain grasslands to chaparral and desert grasslands to desert scrub? Several explanations make the rounds among historians and ecologists. Local historian Phil Brigandi attributes the change to generally drier weather. "The real impact on the vegetation of the Anza-Borrego Desert has not been due to grazing," he wrote; "it is due to water." Groundwater pumping for golf courses and citrus groves has been blamed for lowering the water table and drying up many of the springs around Borrego Valley. Brigandi pointed out that this pumping wouldn't have had much effect in places such as Mason Valley and Dos Cabezas and attributes the drying out of the country to a change in climate. Like Mason, he noted that this environmental change was evident by the 1930s, before pumping had much of an effect.

Many ecologists agree that a shift in climate occurred across the Southwest at the beginning of the twentieth century, when the Little Ice Age ended. This was a cooler period that began around 1500, creating ideal conditions for desert grasslands across the Southwest. When the Spanish arrived in the 1790s, as when the McCains arrived in the late 1860s, the prevailing weather patterns could have supported grassland in the mountains and savanna in the desert. But beginning about 1900, the

Southwest entered a hotter period with changed rainfall patterns that lasted into the 1940s, a period that favored the spread of chaparral and desert shrubs. By analyzing 12,000 years of faunal samples at a site in New Mexico, ecologists have concluded that similar fluctuations from grassland to desert scrub took place across the Southwest in two earlier periods, 2,500 and 990 years ago.

But weather patterns in San Diego County don't match the general trend across the Southwest. Tree-ring evidence from southern California mountains and weather data from San Diego County do show wet periods in the last half of the nineteenth century, especially in the late 1860s, when the McCains arrived to find lush grass. But the 1890s was one of the driest decades on record, and that dry year of 1933–1934, when Ed Mason returned to his homestead, came in the midst of a decade of above-average rainfall. If anything, the first half of the twentieth century in San Diego County was wetter than the last half of the nineteenth. Although many factors are involved and early rainfall and temperature records for the desert itself are lacking, it seems unlikely that climate alone explains the extreme changes in the desert landscape over the past 100 years, especially the erosion and the inability of the grass to renew itself during wetter periods.

To explain the severity of these changes, ecologists look to the new elements in the landscape, the presence of cattle and sheep. The hundreds of thousands of sheep and cattle that traveled across the desert, and the thousands that grazed there for months at a time, did have a real effect on the landscape, exacerbating the effect of any drying trends. Ecologists such as Ronald P. Neilson, who analyzed recent climate changes in the Southwest, argue that grazing acted in concert with climate change to increase the spread of desert scrub. Without the disturbances caused by grazing, he says, the grasslands might have been able to maintain themselves through the drier periods.

Grazing changes grasslands in two ways. Obviously, it removes the grass itself. If this happens before the grass produces seed, fewer new plants will sprout in following years. In addition, the native grass seed couldn't survive the trip through a cow's digestive tract, so even mature grass could fail to reproduce if it was grazed at the wrong time. Still, had this been the only adverse effect of grazing, the grassland might have sur-

vived. The bigger problem comes when a hard rain arrives after an area has been overgrazed. With no grass cover to hold it, the water runs off more rapidly, cutting new gullies in even ground. Unfortunately, the soil of the Anza-Borrego Desert is made up of decomposed granite, which is particularly susceptible to erosion. These gullies in turn carry water away more rapidly, making less water available to the remaining grass even in a wet year.

This is what ecologists call a feedback loop: grazing reduces the grass cover, which leads to more erosion; more erosion leads to more rapid runoff, which leads to less grass development, which in turn leads to more erosion. Once this kind of feedback loop is established, it is very hard to reverse. Unlike the situation during the earlier periods of desertification, the new areas of desert scrub might not shift back to grassland during a cooling period. There have been wet periods since grazing ended in Anza-Borrego, yet Dos Cabezas, for example, is still dominated by creosote bush, cholla, and bur sage. Where there is grass, it is mostly non-native varieties.

These non-native species, introduced mainly through grazing, are another element in the complex feedback loop that wiped out the native grass. C. R. Orcutt noticed a change in the desert beginning in the 1880s. In 1889, he wrote: "Eight years ago not a plant of alfilaria [which he called Spanish clover, and which is now known as filaree] was to be seen growing on this desert where now it is so abundant. It made its first appearance on the desert slope at about that time around the old stage station at Mountain Springs, where it is now luxuriant." Sheep grazing began at Mountain Springs in the early 1880s, and filaree seed may have arrived in the wool of the sheep or mixed with their feed. By 1889, after Marion Haydon had grazed cattle and horses in the area for several years, filaree had spread down to Dos Cabezas, where Orcutt described it as having "gained a good foothold." Like many weeds, filaree may have thrived in a disturbed environment, making it harder for the native grasses to survive.

This kind of feedback loop helps explain how the water "went away" from the desert country, as Mason put it. Yet at places such as Dos Cabezas, at least, the picture is made even more complicated by a third element, the presence of the Kumeyaay. If Florence Shipek is right, they not only maintained but also *created* the grasslands at places such as Dos Cabezas

and McCain Valley by planting, burning, and managing the flow of water. Indeed, 1880, not long before C. R. Orcutt recorded the occurrence of filaree at Dos Cabezas, was the last year in which the Indians lived there. Their presence in the landscape was as important as the climate in determining what the place looked like. Removing them was probably as big a disturbance to the local ecology as introducing livestock had been. These three elements—climate change, introduction of grazing, and the end of native management practices—seem to work together to explain the changes the desert underwent around the turn of the century. Deciding which one is the "real" adverse impact is probably impossible, but one thing seems certain: had the Kumeyaay been able to continue their traditional management practices in the desert, unmolested by Europeans or their livestock, then the droughts the area has experienced would have had much less effect. The Indians were already well adapted to these dry periods, and their management practices were intended to help reduce a drought's disturbance to the landscape. Without interference with their land management practices, the desert might look today much as it did in 1850.

LIKE the Spanish, the McCains and other pioneers thought they were entering a naturally verdant and thriving land; what they had really found was a carefully cultivated garden. Without the elaborate environmental knowledge of the Indians, the newcomers had no way of knowing how to maintain the lush grasslands onto which they turned their livestock; they had no way of knowing that their cattle and sheep were the very things that could change the landscape forever. Reading their reminiscences of the mountains and desert as these once were, one gets a sense of frustration and despair at this diminished landscape. Much of this anger was turned toward outside forces. "Now the cattle business is just about finished around this part of California," Jim McCain told Woellwerts. "The taxes are so high you can't hardly have a herd. The land values are going up, and this makes the land too expensive to use for cattle. They're weeding out the old timers like me."

For the cattle ranchers, the loss of grassland was certainly a negative effect, sometimes a devastating one. But what do this and other changes in the desert mean for the rest of us and for the ecology of the desert itself? Many of the plants that took over the desert grassland at Dos

Cabezas are native desert species. How can their spread be characterized as an invasion, as some ecologists have done? And how can any new change to this habitat be characterized as either good or bad? Again, I'm forced to wonder what we're protecting here if this stand of desert scrub is neither pristine nor ancient. If it's really a degraded landscape, how can I argue for its preservation?

If the answers to these questions are complicated by the fact that the Kumeyaay and Cahuilla used and changed this land for thousands of years, they are made even more complicated by the ideas of modern ecology. For much of its history, the dominant school of ecology used nature untouched by humans as a benchmark by which to judge the ecological character of a landscape. Left alone, ecosystems were self-regulating and stable, existing in what ecologists called a "climax state." Once disturbed—by fire, for instance—the ecosystem progressed through a series of successional stages until it returned to that stable climax state. A burned forest would regenerate through stages of open meadow followed by understory shrubs followed by a first stage of fast-growing trees followed by slower-growing hardwoods—the climax stand, or old-growth forest.

This was the view put forward by an ecologist named Frederic Clements in the 1920s, and it came to dominate the study of ecology as well as the environmental movement. This is the "balance of nature" to which environmentalists so often refer. The idea goes even deeper than that—it's simply *what we all know*. On a more sophisticated level, climax theory has shaped the philosophy of natural regulation espoused on the pages of *Audubon* magazine and adopted by the National Park Service. We think we can "preserve" the environment in its natural state and *nothing will change*. Like a good Swiss watch, nature will run indefinitely as long as we don't tamper with the mechanism.

Although Clements' ideas have persisted within the environmental movement and among resource managers, many ecologists have come to reject the idea that nature is balanced or stable. Instead, they see unremitting change and disturbance. Leave aside the fact that most of the habitats in North America were highly influenced by Indians—maintained at a successional stage somewhere below the climax stage. Even if we could imagine a landscape without those influences, the resulting habitats would be not stable climax stands but what ecologists call shifting mosaics.

Habitats do go through successional stages, but they rarely maintain

the climax stage for long. Natural disturbances—fire, storms, earthquakes, blowdowns, and changes in climate—are too frequent. Just as important, rather than being members of a closely knit community that evolved together (in the conventional ecological view), species evolved and function as individuals in "loosely knit, dynamic assemblages." In this view, put forth by taxonomist Henry A. Gleason and desert ecologist Forrest Shreve, individual species respond differently to the constant change in climate and other disturbances, and thus ecosystems rarely reach equilibrium. Change the conditions under which species must live and they come together in dramatically new assemblages. This happened on the dammed Colorado River, where newly clear water led to a new food chain that helped support bald eagles, and where the endangered southwestern willow flycatcher has found a home in the non-native tamarisk tree. This version of nature, far from being like a Swiss watch, is chaotic and unpredictable.

Both biologist Daniel Botkin, in his landmark work *Discordant Harmonies: A New Ecology for the Twenty-first Century*, and environmental historian Donald Worster, in *The Wealth of Nature*, have pointed out that this new theory pulls the rug out from under our usual way of thinking about the environment and why we should preserve it. Botkin observes that this new thinking seems to "open up a Pandora's box of terrible consequences. . . . If one admits that some changes are acceptable, how can one reject any changes?" He goes on: "As long as we could believe that nature undisturbed was constant, we were provided with a simple standard against which to judge our actions . . . providing us with a sense of continuity and permanence that was comforting. Abandoning these beliefs leaves us in an extreme existential position: we are like small boats without anchors in a sea of time; how we long for safe harbor on a shore."

Worster is even more suspicious of this new movement in ecology and its influence on the environmental movement. "Nature, many have begun to believe, is *fundamentally* erratic, discontinuous, and unpredictable. It is full of seemingly random events that elude our models of how things are supposed to work." This disorder, he says, undermines our attempts at preservation, making them into acts of quixotic nostalgia. "What is there to love or preserve in a universe of chaos? How are people supposed to behave in such a universe? If that is the kind of place we inhabit, why not

go ahead with all our private ambitions, free of any fear that we may be doing special damage?"

How do we judge the actions of the cattle ranchers who changed the face of the mountains and desert so drastically? After all, they weren't changing pristine nature but simply exchanging an aboriginal "ecosystem management practice" for a modern one. How can we call those aboriginal practices good and the modern ones bad? And this fluctuation could also have been caused, in large part, not by the ranchers but by a change in the weather.

I actually prefer desert flora to grassland, so the changes at Dos Cabezas suit me just fine. But if this is just my personal preference, then how can I argue with those people (who seem to be in the majority) who prefer lawns and golf courses? The desert flora is no more pristine than those lawns, no more permanent or stable, not even much more ancient. What sort of objective argument can I make to keep the off-roaders away from this patch of desert? What new sort of yardstick do we have to judge our actions in nature?

Botkin and others respond with just two words: biological diversity. Two words that embody a new relationship to nature, that can guide us past the seemingly insoluble question, What is natural?

INDIAN HILL:
HOMELESS

I'M SITTING atop Indian Hill, the hundred-foot boulder outcrop that I visited on that first trip to the Anza-Borrego Desert more than ten years ago. A vast expanse of desert spreads out before me, stretching across the Salton Sea to the Chocolate Mountains, a dark line undulating across the horizon. I come to places like this to touch base with something that seems more real and lasting than our human-manufactured world. Here, I can contemplate, as Edward Abbey put it, "a far larger world, one which extends into a past and into a future without any limits known to the human kind." Such reaches of time and space seem to dwarf my puny human concerns, a feeling that is at once terrifying and comforting.

As Abbey knew, and spent a whole book celebrating, such contemplation requires solitude. Today, I am absolutely alone. It's a weekday, and I have yet to see another visitor. Access to the park is restricted to highway-legal vehicles, so no off-roaders disturb the silence. Mining and quarrying are prohibited, so no heavy trucks rumble along nearby jeep roads. Thanks to a hurricane that washed out several bridges in 1976, the tracks of the San Diego and Arizona Eastern Railroad are silent, too, their black, horizontal line hardly disturbing the wild feeling of this place. Grazing was banned in the early 1970s, so no cowboys whoop at their cattle while driving them from the mountains.

But something else had to happen to create this solitude. Today, no bands of Kumeyaay Indians harvest native grass. No smoke from their

controlled burns pollutes the air. No parties of men set out to gather and roast agave. No grating of *mano* against *mortero* disturbs the silence. No shamans paint designs on rock canvases. No children laugh as they chase one another among the rocks. It's a perfect day in the wilderness.

This is how my precious solitude was purchased: On February 27, 1880, a group of ranchers, mostly teenagers, confronted a group of Indians at Table Mountain near Jacumba. The Indians, a band of the Kumeyaay, had been butchering the ranchers' cattle and perhaps stealing horses. Trouble had been brewing for some time as ranchers moved onto some of the Indians' best lands and fenced off the springs. In George McCain's eyes, the fault was all with the Indians and with the U.S. Cavalry, which failed to keep the Indians "in their place." "The Indians . . . are not kept on their reservation as they should be, but are allowed to run at large and are stealing stock when they get hard pressed," he told the *San Diego Union* a year after this battle.

Pete Larkin—the same man who was so careless about looking after his stray cattle—organized a posse of young cowboys that included two McCains. Depending on who tells the story, they intended to go out and negotiate with the Indians, to "look up" the missing cattle, or, in Ella McCain's version, to run the Indians out. One version has an Indian drawing a revolver and killing seventeen-year-old William McCain in cold blood and Will's young friends returning a day or two later to get their revenge. Another has the cowboys "suddenly confronted by a band of Indians in the rocks," after which "a hot fight ensued." Ella McCain said that the posse went ready for a fight, the older men coaching the teenagers in "Indian fighting," telling them to stay behind rocks and to move to a new position after taking a shot.

What became known as the Jacumba Massacre lasted nearly two hours. The Indians fought with rocks, javelins, and "a few shaky firearms." For their part, the cowboys seemed to take the battle as casually as a slingshot fight. Ella McCain wrote, "Jack McCain, the blacksmith at Campo, shot [an Indian] across the top of the head and yelled out, 'Whoops see the hair fly.'" Young Will McCain was a little too casual. Of the boy who would have been her brother-in-law, Ella McCain wrote: "As he raised his head above the rock, a bullet struck him in the head. They carried him out on a blanket, and he was buried in the little cemetery in Campo Valley. . . .

One can still read: William McCain, killed by Indians, February 27, 1880. Age, seventeen years, seven months, seven days."

The Kumeyaay fared worse, with estimates ranging from four dead and "more wounded" to nineteen men, women, and children killed ruthlessly by the young cowboys as revenge for Will McCain's death. Whatever the death toll, this was the last of this band of Kumeyaay in the Jacumba area. No one knows for sure what happened to the survivors because their side of the story has never been told. Ella McCain said simply that "the Indians moved away after this fight and in a measure stopped the killing of so many cattle." In a more fanciful version, the survivors retreated to Dos Cabezas, where "death would come slowly, from starvation, from thirst, from exposure. They knew that those who were left would gradually fall until the last survivor would curse the desert, curse his gods, and curse the guns of the white man before he died." Very poetic, and it could also be true; Florence Shipek reports that many Kumeyaay in the southern backcountry died of starvation during this time. But it's also possible that the survivors retreated into Mexico, leaving the green valleys of the mountains and the oases of the desert to the newcomers.

The Jacumba Massacre was just one in a series of conflicts in which the Indians were pushed off the best lands. Events such as this show the other side of that pioneer character Ella McCain and Lester Reed celebrate. Along with their hardiness and pioneer spirit—which would later become known as the "cowboy code"—the newcomers harbored a self-righteous certainty that they were meant to occupy the land, and typically they were ruthless in defending it. The worst of the American newcomers believed the cliché that "the only good Indian is a dead Indian" and killed as many as possible or petitioned for their removal to Oklahoma. Others, such as John Warner, saw the Indians as cheap labor. Even the best of the settlers, those who accepted the Indians as their neighbors and felt a measure of sympathy for their plight, spoke of "renegade" Indians who refused to obey the law. The pioneers believed that justice was on their side, and this was literally true—as historian Richard Carrico pointed out, "Justice was a concept usually extended by whites to other whites."

Some writers speak of the Jacumba Massacre as a tragedy for both sides. One mentions the lasting scars the massacre left on the cowboys themselves, the "terrible images" of death that would stay with them for

the rest of their lives. Others point to the violence on both sides, espe-cially the Indian attacks that many of the pioneers faced as they traveled across Arizona. Members of Ella McCain's family, for instance, encoun-tered the remains of the Oatman party, all of whom had been massacred by Apaches except for a boy who escaped and two young girls who were sold into slavery. Such episodes, whether rumored or real, made southern California pioneers distrustful and trigger-happy toward the much less hostile Kumeyaay and Cahuilla Indians.

All of this may be true—both sides perpetrated barbarous acts. But one side wound up with the land and the other with a shattered way of life. As anthropologist Bernard Fontana said, "Nobody has ever figured out a nice way, a proper way, to take somebody's land away from him." We are living on stolen land, and that simple fact makes our lives uneasy.

EVENTS such as the Jacumba Massacre were just the most obvious and lit-eral way in which the Indians were pushed off their land. By 1850, their population had already been more than halved by European diseases, coupled with droughts and the destruction of some of their food resources. This made it harder for them to hang on to their remaining lands and to support themselves in their traditional way. After 1850, the Indians con-tinued the pattern, begun under Spanish and Mexican rule, of integrating their own land management and food-gathering techniques with the farm-ing of European crops and the raising of some livestock.

If life for the Indians had been difficult under Spanish and then Mexi-can occupation, it was exponentially worse after the American conquest. Under American rule, more Kumeyaay land was taken over, beginning along the coast. Some Indian subagents, including our friend Cave Couts, abused their positions to acquire land that had belonged to Indians under Mexican law and should have been protected under the treaty the United States signed with Mexico. Couts seems to have interpreted loosely his instruction to prevent the Indians from "leading an idle and thriftless life"—he came to control a large number of Indian laborers who worked for little or no wages on land that had once been their own.

Conditions for many southern California Indians remained tolerable during the first fifteen years of American rule, in Florence Shipek's view. California's Act for the Government and Protection of Indians, passed in

1850, was enforced for a time by local sheriffs. This protection was based not on legal title, which the Indians effectively lost when the U.S. Senate failed to ratify treaties with them in 1852, but on the amount of land each sheriff felt to be "sufficient" for the Indians. Under this system, Shipek wrote, "most Indians remained in their villages, farming their lands and keeping some stock."

Richard Carrico paints a bleaker picture of these years, noting that the act for the protection of the Indians often worked against them. Section 10 of the act, for instance, prohibited the burning of grasslands. Carrico blames the federal government's policy of neglect at the time for the worsening conditions of San Diego's native peoples, who were "fair game for land hungry, self-centered whites who illegally expropriated hundreds of acres of Indian lands that were never returned to the Indian people."

After 1865, conditions worsened even further. First, immigration from southern states increased after the Civil War. Most of the land occupied by the Indians was legally open for homesteading by whites, and the new-comers simply moved onto Indian lands, telling the indigenous residents to go elsewhere. Of course, the best farming and grazing lands were the first taken. Some of the "pioneers" even moved into the adobe homes built by the Indians. Where were the sheriffs while all this was happening? Under the pressure of so much American immigration, the 1850 law pro-tecting the Indians simply was not enforced. Around the same time, news-papers and census takers began denying that Indians still lived on the land, especially in the valleys of San Pasqual and Pala. The fiction of whites entering an uninhabited wilderness had already begun.

It's tempting to believe, as some authors have, that this theft of Indian homes and land happened when the Indians were away on gathering trips, the whites apparently thinking the homes had been abandoned. But scenes like those in Helen Hunt Jackson's *Ramona*, set in the early 1880s, are probably closer to the truth. In one, the Indian Allesandro describes his father's removal from his home: "He would not come out of his house, and the men lifted him up and carried him out by force, and threw him on the ground; and then they threw out all the furniture we had; and when he saw them doing that, he put his hands up to his head, and called out. . . . Señorita, they said it was a voice to make the dead hear."

Later, when Allesandro and Ramona thought they had found a safe

home in San Pasqual, a white man approached and told them: "Look here! Be off, will you? This is my land. I'm going to build a house here." This scene is strikingly similar to what Julio Ortega, who was born in Santa Ysabel in 1882, remembers about his youth: "We lived here, there, just moving about. We'd live in one place and somebody would come along, 'Well this is my land, move out.' So we'd move."

By 1875, the Kumeyaay had become refugees in their own territory, southern California's first homeless people. A halfhearted attempt to create small reservations in rocky lands, meant to house *all* of southern California's Indians, was abandoned in 1871. Nine small reservations were created in 1875, but Americans continued to move onto these lands as well. Some Indians successfully filed for homesteads under the Indian Homestead Act of 1883, but many Indian homesteaders were pushed off their claims, and others resisted homesteading because it meant breaking affiliation with their tribe.

With their best lands gone, the Indians found it impossible to pursue the European farming practices they had adopted. But returning to their traditional lifeway was equally difficult. One reason was that once-cohesive bands of Indians had now dispersed into individual family groups living in isolated spots in the backcountry. Collective gathering efforts, such as the annual trips to oak or pinyon groves, became more difficult. Burning of the grasslands had already been banned. Another difficulty was that successive waves of European disease had decimated not only the population but also the knowledge base maintained by the *kuseyaay*, or plant specialists, who often died without training successors. The knowledge of when to burn and when to plant and harvest native foods began to disappear.

Perhaps most important, access to the entire range of habitats in southern California, on which the traditional gathering and management practices of the Indians depended, was no longer possible. The desert was still available to the Indians in 1880, as were acorn-gathering areas in the higher mountains. But mid-elevation areas such as Jacumba and the McCain Valley, places that provided quick access to a wide variety of plant sources, had been taken over by American ranchers. With these areas closed off, the Indians' whole subsistence pattern fell apart like a house of cards. It's no wonder that some Indians resorted to butchering American

cattle, animals they saw grazing on land that had once been theirs. During the 1880s and 1890s, some Indians simply starved.

Not all of southern California's Indians starved or eked out a marginal existence in the backcountry, however. Some began participating in the cash economy, hiring on at local ranches as shepherds and vaqueros. Others found work in the cities of San Diego and Los Angeles. Among their occupations, Shipek lists road and railroad work, stevedoring, painting, carpentry, bricklaying, blacksmithing, and butchering. "Some helped build Hotel del Coronado and paved the streets of the island town," she notes. Others shipped onto the whaling boats that visited San Diego.

Despite what might be seen as advances into the American capitalist economy, the Indians faced the same prejudice as did the newly arrived Chinese laborers. They were abused both by police and by vigilantes and drunken mobs whose idea of a good time was stoning an Indian to death. Murder, rape, and "accidental" hanging while in jail were common. Merchants tempted the Indian men with cheap liquor, which Richard Carrico argues was the source of much Indian degradation and violence, and young girls were lured into prostitution or short-lived marriages to whites. Once arrested, Indians were sentenced to indentured servitude in lieu of jail time, usually short-term service on government labor gangs or local ranches.

There was only one organized response to these abuses, and it came early in the American occupation, when local authorities decided to tax the Indians. In 1851, Antonio Garra, leader of the Cupeño Indians, began an unsuccessful rebellion that was to include Cupeño, Cahuilla, Luiseño, Kumeyaay, and Yuma Indians. But Garra failed to achieve widespread support among all Indian groups, and after two small raids he was captured by Chief Juan Antonio of the Cahuilla. Juan Antonio turned him over to the military in San Diego, where he was tried and executed. Another leader of the rebellion, Chief Chapuli of the Coyote Canyon Cahuilla, was killed in an attack on U.S. Army forces. The army burned the Cahuilla village in the canyon and captured four other leaders of the rebellion. They tried the Indians and executed them on Christmas Day at Middle Willows.

Desert historian Diana Lindsay wrote, "Village sites in Coyote Canyon were abandoned after the massacre, and for the next forty years the

Indians used the area as a gathering ground but not as a home." Eighty years after seeing the first whites enter their canyon, the Cahuilla had been driven from their homes by another group of white men. Today, Middle Willows is a popular spot for hikers drawn by Anza-Borrego's only year-round stream, most of them completely unaware of the area's dark history.

THE BRUTAL facts of 130 years of white contact and occupation can be seen in Florence Shipek's reconstruction of Kumeyaay population statistics. Drawing on statements made by the first Spanish occupiers and on early censuses, she estimated that in 1769 the Kumeyaay numbered 12,000 to 14,000 north of the present Mexican border and another 5,000 south of it. The diseases brought by the Europeans hit hardest in the following fifty years, combining with forced labor and disruption along the coast to reduce the Kumeyaay population north of the border to something more than 4,000. As Americans displaced the Indians after 1850, outright starvation played a greater role in their decline, along with a diminished birthrate, reducing the population to perhaps 1,500 by 1880. Despite efforts by crusaders such as Helen Hunt Jackson and the Sequoya League, abuses against Indians continued, reducing their numbers to a nadir of only 1,000 people by 1900, or less than one-tenth of their original population. As we know, similar rapid decimations destroyed indigenous peoples all across the Americas; these were the last of the American Indians to face such devastation.

By 1891, the federal government had been forced to create legitimate reservations, but even the Act for the Relief of the Mission Indians, fought for by honest advocates for Indian welfare, resulted in its own trail of tears. The act led to the creation of more than a dozen reservations in San Diego County for the Kumeyaay, Cupeño, Cahuilla, and Luiseño Indians as well as several reservations for the Cahuilla in Riverside and Imperial Counties. The commission appointed to choose the reservations, headed by Albert K. Smiley, attempted to provide the Indians with good land, but it was hampered by limited funds, mistakes in surveying the land, and resistance from the whites who owned land encompassing Indian villages.

At the large ranches along the old Southern Emigrant Trail leading down into the desert—Warner's, Mataguay, and San Felipe—the owners

demanded high prices for their entire grants and refused to sell just the land occupied by the dozen or so Cupeño, Cahuilla, and Kumeyaay villages located there. Some whites even argued that these were new villages and that the Indians had never lived there. Traditional stories that told of a creator giving the land to Indian people were cast aside as myths, replaced by the whites' own myth of the land as uninhabited wilderness, theirs for the taking. The United States Supreme Court sided with the Americans by affirming their ownership of the Indian villages. The government wouldn't pay the high prices the landowners demanded and apparently never considered acquiring it by eminent domain. Instead, another government commission was created in the late 1890s to find other lands for the Luiseño, Cupeño, and Kumeyaay of Warner's Ranch. This commission was chaired by Charles F. Lummis, founder of the Sequoya League, who also did his best to find good land for the Indians.

The difficulty was that the Indians didn't want to leave their homes, even if the new lands were "better" than their original home. Lummis knew this but saw no way around the problem. He publicized the plight of the Indians in his magazine, *Out West*, even as he pushed forward with a plan that would remove them from their homes and relocate them to Pala, thirty miles to the west. One article included the following speech by Chief Cecilio Blacktooth of the Cupeño, who spoke after the decision was made to expel his people:

> You ask us to think what place we like next best to this place where we always live. You see that graveyard out there? There are our fathers and our grandfathers. You see that Eagle-nest mountain and that Rabbit-hole mountain? When God made them, He gave us this place. We have always been here. We do not care for any other place. It may be good, but it is not ours. . . . If we cannot live here we want to go into those mountains and die.

Chief Blacktooth knew that moving spelled the erosion of his people's culture. When the people left their home place, they would lose the mnemonic triggers of the landscape—"that Eagle-nest mountain and that Rabbit-hole mountain"—and thereby much of the stories and beliefs that told them who they were as a people. Told at a distance from those physical features, the stories would become just so many empty words.

Blacktooth predicted correctly that some of his people would choose actual death over this cultural death. Florence Shipek reported that "a few elderly people hid in the hills to die there." But prospects weren't much better for the people who moved to the Pala Indian Reservation, which offered uninsulated housing and no sanitation. Many of the elders and children became sick or died under these conditions, which were little better than what they would have experienced hiding in the hills.

Lummis summed up the eviction of the people from Cupa and the surrounding villages in his own way: "The Warner's Ranch episode is closed. It was a tragedy; but that could not be helped. . . . The one comfort about it is that for the first time in our history, the Indians got more land and better land than that from which they were ousted."

With reservations established and no real alternative, the Indians gradually vacated the desert region around Anza-Borrego. The Cahuilla seem to have held out the longest, using Coyote Canyon as a gathering ground into the early 1890s and living in Rockhouse Valley even later than that. Lester Reed commented that Rockhouse was rightfully respected "as a place where the white man was not very welcome." As late as 1906, two prospectors were chased out of the valley and two others reported meeting an "old Indian" who carried a .30-30 rifle and told them to look for gold elsewhere. He may have been the last Indian to regularly occupy the area that would later become Anza-Borrego Desert State Park.

AFTER the Indian bands were expelled from the desert, the cowboys lasted nearly another century. Even after the creation of the park in the 1930s, grazing was permitted until 1972. Then permits were quickly allowed to expire. The politically correct notion is that the ranchers deserved it. They were the children and grandchildren of the people who had shut out the Indians. But the picture is not quite so simple. Some of the ranchers who could no longer graze their cattle in the park happened to be Indians, such as Alvino Siva, who ran his cattle in Coyote Canyon. And as Lester Reed pointed out, there was much to admire in the cowboy code. Even though their way of life was hard on the land, the ranchers were among the last people in the region to have the opportunity—it seems like a luxury now—to make their living outdoors, directly from the land.

Originally, park managers prohibited grazing not for environmental

reasons but because it conflicted with recreation. After all, I couldn't sit here at Indian Hill and experience solitude and the eternal nature of the desert while a herd of cows stomp past. The Indians are gone from this place, and so are the people who pushed them out. Now I can sit here with little to prompt remembrance of that history. Even the markings on these rocks seem to emerge from a time so distant that it has little effect on the present, on what this place is. In our minds, the Indians lived lightly as ghosts on the land in a dim long-ago. The further back in time we imagine that they left this place, the more comfortable we are with our idea of it as a wilderness. Even descriptions of Sierra Club hikes to this desert say that it is a "land of long-vanished Native Americans," as if a hundred years were as distant in time as the creation of Stonehenge.

In our conventional idea of wilderness, we have created an imagined past of emptiness and timelessness, the "back of beyond" where nature is the only player, where humans have changed nothing. Yet as at Stonehenge, the presence over centuries of the desert's former inhabitants continues to make itself felt, though not always in obvious ways.

Even now, as I climb down from my rocky perch, I spot one of the Indians' leavings, a diamond-shaped potsherd. I don't know what causes me to look down at this moment, but there it is, right at my feet as I'm about to step over it. At first, the piece seems no different from the hundreds of other pottery fragments I've found over the years. It's about two inches square and the usual tan color that blends so well with granitic sand. But something else catches my eye—a hole in one corner. Some sort of jewelry, a pendant maybe, worn on a thong necklace? But the piece is slightly curved, typical of fragments from large pots, or ollas. The pad of my index finger slides neatly into an indentation on the concave side. Suddenly, the piece takes on a more human dimension as I imagine the hands that worked this pot, and then, once it broke, bored a hole to make an ornament. The makers of this pottery and the paintings on the rocks nearby seem, for a moment, almost present here with me.

I have long felt that the desert has an aura of mystery, a sense of waiting to reveal something to me. When I stopped and listened, it seemed as if the desert itself was about to speak, to disclose something of its true nature. I spent years searching for that phantom *something* and always found the same silent slot canyons, the same mute badlands and *bajadas*

and desert peaks. But now I realize that the silence is what the desert has been speaking all along—a silence unheard here for 10,000 years or more. The erasures on this desert palimpsest speak more clearly than its legible markings. Now the desert is like an abandoned city—doors left open, kettles whistling on stoves, traffic signals flashing at empty vehicles with motors still idling. The spirits of the vanished citizens are all around, unseen but felt. I'm not walking through a wilderness here; I'm walking through a ghost town.

PART IV

A CENTURY
of WILDERNESS

SALTON SEA:
TAMING THE DESERT

Oɴ ᴀ warm late-winter day, I visit the Salton Sea National Wildlife Refuge, a narrow sliver of land wedged between the vast lake to the west and agricultural fields to the east. At 225 feet below sea level, the air is muggy, with a faint river-bottom smell to it, not like the desert at all. Viewed from the observation tower a quarter mile from the shoreline, the sea is a vast blue plate thirty-five miles long by seventeen wide—large enough to reveal a slight downward curve toward either end. With neither wind nor boats to disturb its surface, the water is smooth and placid.

To the east, the nearby Chocolate Mountains aren't merely brown but look like the frosting creation of a pastry chef on acid—a hodgepodge of rust reds, oranges, purples, grays, and whites. To the west, the mountains of the Anza-Borrego Desert seem far away. Except for the Santa Rosa Mountains hard by the northwestern corner of the Salton Sea, they look like low hills from this angle. In a trick of light and distance, the sea seems to stretch all the way to the base of those mountains; it almost seems as if I could hop in a boat and sail to Borrego Springs. It's ironic—from almost any vantage in Anza-Borrego, the Imperial Valley's outpost of hardscrabble civilization disappears in the haze. Now, surrounded as I am by those ragtag fields and dilapidated towns, it's Anza-Borrego that seems insignificant.

Closer at hand, birds are the most obvious presence. The abundant water flowing through the fields and the open water of the sea itself make

this the most important stopover and wintering ground on the Pacific flyway. From the tower, I look out over a green field filled with thousands of snow geese and Ross' geese. Occasionally they rise, honking, into the air and then glide as a flock to settle in another spot. A few white egrets ignore their jittery neighbors. A pond nearby holds terns, avocets, and green-winged teals, and on the sea itself, ducks, coots, and cormorants float and dive. A squadron of white pelicans, formal in winter plumage of white with black stripes, sails toward the southern shore, past the towers and steam plumes of a CalEnergy geothermal plant.

I decide to drive all the way around the sea today, to see where the waters flowing off the Peninsular Crest end up after crossing the desert. I leave the refuge and head north on Highway 111. Life here has a hard-bitten look. Most of the roads need repair, and the main streets of Calipatria and Niland are lined with shuttered cafés and bait shops, abandoned houses and trailers, and other houses that should be abandoned but aren't. Vacant lots are filled with irrigation piping, tractor parts, broken-down trucks, and more mundane household trash. In Niland, someone has turned a narrow strip between two rows of trees into a dump. Tons of winter vegetables and livestock feed flow out of the Imperial Valley, and with the produce must go most of the wealth. Everything seems temporary; the town looks more like a mining boom town than an agricultural community that has been here nearly a hundred years. *Valley Grower* magazine displays lavish farmhouses sitting in the middle of their fields, but none of those are apparent on my trip today. At the same time, the magazine's editorials warn about "threats" such as minimum wage hikes and eight-hour days for farmworkers, the people who live in many of those dilapidated houses.

Past Niland, the highway crosses a barren stretch of dried mud. This is the ancient playa of Lake Cahuilla, apparently unaltered by irrigation or plowing, the first undeveloped area I've seen since hitting sea level at El Centro. I get out of the car and walk across the barren mudflat toward the sea. I try to imagine how writer and art critic John C. Van Dyke saw it in 1898, before the Salton Sea was created, when the entire basin looked something like this. Standing at the bottom of the dry lake, Van Dyke had a vision of what the place would become. The combination of heat and the smooth white surface created "the one place in all the world where the

water-mirage appears to perfection." It was best to put your eye close to the ground to get the full effect, he wrote. "Now the water seems to creep up to you. You could throw a stone into it. The shore where the waves lap is just before you."

I try the experiment. As my eye approaches ground level, water does seem to rise out of the white expanse sloping toward the sea. And today, the illusory water of the mirage merges perfectly with the waters of the Salton Sea, both reflecting the same blue sky. I can't tell where the mirage ends and the real sea begins.

Finally, I walk all the way to the edge of the sea at Mecca Beach, a few miles farther north. There are shade trees here, and grass, and wooden tables out on the sand-and-shell beach—a nice place for a picnic. It's a weekday, though, and the park is nearly empty. It's now midday, and the sea has taken on a richer blue hue. But as I approach the shoreline, I can see below the blue surface a deeper darkness of mud-brown algae.

A salty stench assails my nostrils, the briny smell of water that is 25 percent saltier than the ocean mingled with the odor of dead fish. Now I notice carcasses floating belly-up in the water or resting on the shore, probably of tilapia, though I'm not sure. Birds have pecked the dead fishes' eyes out, and the hollow sockets gape up at the desert sun. A little farther up the beach, a line of seagulls squawks over hundreds of dead fish. At my feet, I see a few gray feathers and a limp webbed foot protruding from a lump of sand.

Salton Sea

This is the other face of the Salton Sea. A thriving spawning ground for transplanted fish and a haven for millions of migrating birds, it is, for many of them, a death trap. The numbers of fish and birds that live here are astounding—as are the numbers that die here. In 1992, 150,000 eared grebes breathed their last here, and the cause is still a mystery. Another 20,000 birds died in 1994 of undetermined causes, followed by 14,000 in 1996, a number that included 1,400 endangered brown pelicans. That time, the culprit was avian botulism. In 1998, 6,000 cormorants died, possibly of an illness known as Newcastle disease, and 17,600 birds of all species had died by the end of July that year. The causes of these diseases are uncertain, though the avian botulism was traced to the dead or dying tilapia that many of the birds eat. The most stunning figure came in August 1999, when more than 7 million fish died in one day. Conditions will only get worse as the sea's water becomes more saline through evaporation, as more water is redirected to urban uses on the coast, and as pollution pours in from both sides of the border.

Opinions abound about what, if anything, should be done about these problems. The Salton Sea Authority was created in 1993 to study the situation and develop a recovery plan. Congressman Sonny Bono championed a Salton Sea cleanup bill, and since his death in a skiing accident, the sea has been an environmental cause célèbre among Republicans. Meanwhile, environmental groups that had virtually ignored the sea—because they perceived it as neither natural nor very scenic—finally jumped on the bandwagon as flocks of birds began dying. In January 2000, the Department of the Interior published a draft Environmental Impact Report that presented a handful of immediate, medium-term, and long-term actions to restore the sea, mainly by reducing salinity.

Somewhere in this simulacrum of nature, in this story of boosterism gone wrong, lie clues to the way to see this whole desert. It's an example of how inextricably we're bound to and with the natural world, but it also shows how confused is our thinking about nature. Denver's abandoned Rocky Mountain Arsenal has been called "the nation's most ironic nature park" because years of being closed to the public made the twenty-seven-square-mile chemical weapons facility a great home for wildlife. But it's the Salton Sea, part natural and part human-made, part wildlife refuge and part death trap, that should really claim that title.

MOST of the forty-niners and other immigrants who passed through the desert west of the Colorado River in the nineteenth century thought of it as a desolate waste. They failed to recognize that much of it was home for the Indians there, and they didn't see it as a potential home for themselves. It was simply a wilderness to be crossed as quickly as possible on their journey to better lands. A few, however, recognized other possibilities. Toward the end of the century, some saw a wilderness that could be tamed and irrigated, while others, such as Van Dyke, saw a wilderness that needed to be preserved.

The first newcomer to promote the possibility of "reclaiming" the desert was Dr. Oliver Wozencraft, a forty-niner who got lost in the Colorado Desert's sand dunes. With two of his companions dying of thirst, he rode ahead, found water, and brought it back. Strangely, the experience convinced him that this was just the place for a farm: "It was then and there that I first conceived the idea of the reclamation of the desert," he said later. The valley did have fertile alluvial soil—if only water could be brought to it. A dry channel known as the Alamo River, Wozencraft argued, could be just the conduit to bring water from the Colorado.

The former forty-niner spent his life's savings in a futile attempt to convince Congress to back his plan. Too many doubted the fertility of the desert sands, and railroad surveyor William P. Blake in 1853 noted another problem: the elevation difference of 407 feet between the Colorado River and the floor of the Salton Basin made any water diversion project risky. Water seeks its lowest level, and any attempt to bring just a little of the Colorado's water to the desert would thus risk encouraging the entire river to shift its course, as it had many times in the past.

This, however, was the Age of Progress. Such little things as laws of nature couldn't be allowed to stand in the way. William E. Smythe's *Conquest of Arid America*, published in 1899, expressed the common view that this was an unmitigated wilderness but one that could be tamed: "It is popularly regarded as an empire of hopeless sterility, the silence of which will never be broken by the voices of men. . . . And yet it only awaits the touch of water and of labor to awaken it into opulent life . . . it will finally be reclaimed and sustain *tens of thousands* of prosperous people."

By the end of the century, two men had taken up Wozencraft's vision.

Charles Rockwood and George Chaffey established an umbrella corporation known as the California Development Company. They began by giving the place an expansive new name: the Imperial Valley. In their promotional literature, they denied that the valley was a desert at all, painting it as a fertile green plain. They dug a canal from the Colorado River south to the Alamo River, just as Wozencraft had suggested, which would then carry the water into the valley.

From the beginning of its operation in 1901, the canal required continual dredging because of the massive amounts of silt deposited in it. Still, the company delivered enough water to the valley to encourage rapid growth in agriculture. By 1904, more than 8,000 people had settled in the valley, farming 75,000 acres in wheat, corn, barley, and hay. This growth in turn placed more demands on the water system. Shortages had already hit the valley, and farmers were fighting over access to water.

Summer flooding in 1904 dumped so much silt into the canals that Rockwood realized he wouldn't be able to dredge them in time for the winter grain crop. Under pressure, he opened another intake in the banks of the Colorado, this one without a headgate to regulate channel flow. A scientist named Daniel MacDougal, who saw the cut shortly after it was made, later wrote, "Locks, control or headworks there were none . . . what pressure of necessity or overbold haste could lead to such unguarded opening of the cage of a sleeping tiger[?]" To be fair, MacDougal was writing with hindsight in 1908. Rockwood defended himself by pointing out that the cut was meant to be closed before the annual summer floods, a technique that had been used successfully in previous years. The chances of a winter flood were small, Rockwood believed, because in all of recorded history the river had flooded in winter only three times and never twice during the same winter. However, there was one small problem in his thinking: the recorded history of the Colorado River went back only twenty-seven years.

In the winter of 1904–1905, the Colorado River flooded five times. Despite the efforts of Rockwood and the California Development Company, much of the overflow passed through the new intake, increasing its dimensions to a width of 600 feet and a depth of 20 to 24 feet. Eventually, the entire flow of the river poured through the break. As Blake had predicted, the Colorado had returned to one of its historical courses. It

flooded the newly planted agricultural lands of the Imperial Valley, the tracks of the Southern Pacific Railroad, and the nearby towns of Mexicali and Calexico. It began recreating Lake Cahuilla, filling the basin at a rate of two inches per day, expanding it to an area ten miles wide and forty miles long. The town of Mecca in the Coachella Valley was flooded, as were lands of the Torres Martinez Indian Reservation (for which the tribe has only recently been repaid).

Although it had a large vision, the California Development Company was a small-time outfit. It didn't have the capital or the engineering know-how to deal with the force of the entire Colorado River. Five separate attempts to close the breach failed. The company brought in big money and engineering skill in the form of E. H. Harriman and his Southern Pacific Railroad; in return, Harriman gained control of the company. Even then, two more attempts were required to repair the breach and force the Colorado River back toward the Gulf of California. At one point, 4,200 railroad carloads of fill were dumped into the break over a twenty-one-day period. Finally, in February 1907, the hole was closed and the water stopped flowing uncontrolled into the basin.

Experts thought the newly formed Salton Sea would dry up, possibly as early as 1920, but inflows from agricultural runoff kept the sea partially filled. It retreated from a surface-level high of 195 feet below sea level (or about 80 feet in depth) to a low point of −250 feet in 1925 and then filled back to −234 feet in 1960. Today, it is up to −227 feet, or about 50 feet at its deepest. The sea is certainly here to stay as long as farmers practice flood irrigation, creating an inflow of more than a million acre-feet annually. It sits in the middle of the desert looking strangely out of place, a shimmering blue mirror reflecting whatever visions of nature we cast in its direction.

WATER in the desert, even agricultural runoff, is magic. The new sea soon became a recreation mecca thanks to the combined efforts of the California Department of Fish and Game (DFG) and local boosters. The DFG tried stocking the sea with different types of fish from the Gulf of California as early as the 1930s, but it wasn't until the 1950s that the department hit on corvina, a relative of the white sea bass that reproduced successfully in the sea's increasingly saline waters. A sportfishing industry developed around

the corvina, taking 500,000 fish per year in the mid-1960s. Along with the fishing came recreational boating, boat racing, water skiing, and bird hunting. More than a million people visited the lake each year. Resorts, yacht clubs, golf courses, restaurants, and nightclubs opened in an attempt to rival the popularity of Palm Springs. Celebrities such as Frank Sinatra and Dean Martin came down for the boat races, and later, the Beach Boys and the Pointer Sisters performed there. Sonny Bono's fondness for the sea stemmed from his learning to water ski on it.

The boom years from the 1950s to the 1970s were so heady that Mildred De Stanley, part Salton Sea historian and part promoter, seemed only to smile at concerns about the sea's rising salinity. In 1966, she predicted that the Salton Sea's fish production could be increased twentyfold, despite a study in the same year that warned, "The salt may begin to harm the fish as soon as 1970, and probably will destroy the fishery entirely by 1985." "Residents were not too upset" by the study, De Stanley reported, viewing salinity as just "another challenge by nature" that they would overcome, as they had others in the past.

In hindsight, such complacency seems absurd. Even though the report was off in its dates, many of its predictions were proving accurate by the 1990s. Continued inflows of naturally salty Colorado River water had caused the sea to become ever more saline. As the director of the Salton Sea Authority put it, agricultural runoff deposits enough salt in the sea each day to fill a mile-long freight train. That salt is left behind when the water evaporates, leaving the lake saltier while maintaining a relatively stable elevation.

But salt is not the sea's only problem. Fertilizers entering the sea from surrounding farms caused massive algal blooms and correspondingly massive fish kills. Although fish die-offs had been happening for years, these fish also carried botulism and other diseases, triggering the massive bird die-offs of the 1990s. High salinity, high nutrient levels, and high temperatures seem to have combined to multiply the sea's problems, and scientists are still trying to sort them all out.

Such are the Salton Sea's most significant biological problems, but none of them is responsible, by itself, for halting the boom in tourism and recreation. The first blow to these industries came in the late 1970s when two years of heavy rainfall raised the sea's level, flooding many shorefront

homes and resorts and closing the North Shore Beach and Yacht Club. Then, in the late 1980s, selenium was discovered in the fish, prompting warnings to limit consumption. Anglers began avoiding the sea, and once-busy bait shops closed their doors. When the birds began dying, this added to what has been dubbed the Salton Sea's "image problem." Newspapers and politicians called it a dead sea, and many believed them. Annual visitors to the Salton Sea State Recreation Area fell from 1 million in the early 1980s to approximately 100,000 in 1996.

In the late 1990s, however, the sea's prospects seemed to be improving. Anglers returned to the sea in increasing numbers (250,000 in 1998), either limiting their consumption of the fish or ignoring the health warnings entirely. One news article depicted a group fishing happily, waist-deep in the lake and surrounded by dead tilapia. Later studies have shown little selenium in the sea's water and fish. A 1999 study brought further good news, finding no pesticides, herbicides, or metals in the water. Then came the one-day die-off of more than 7 million fish. The lake may not be dead, but as a scientist studying the lake told a reporter, it's "an ecosystem in rapidly failing health."

The sea has been serving too many purposes. Promoters thought of it as a resort area. Sportsmen thought of it as a recreation area and hunting ground. Birders thought of it as a wildlife refuge. But farmers, the ones responsible for the sea's continued presence, had always thought of it as an agricultural sump. In 1966, the Imperial Irrigation District's M. J. Dowd pointed to the crucial role the Salton Sea played as a collecting basin for salts flushed out of Imperial Valley fields. At that time, the district and farmers were installing drain tiles and pipes to aid in maintaining a "favorable salt balance" in the fields—but obviously not in the Salton Sea. In 1993, a local farmer, John Benson, told a reporter: "The purpose of the sea is to receive agricultural drainage. That's what it's there for." Under so many conflicting demands, the Salton Sea is nearing ecological collapse; it seems likely that at least one of these demands will have to give way.

Opinions about the Salton Sea are as varied as the birds that visit it. Ken Sturm, biologist for the Salton Sea National Wildlife Refuge, refuses to eat fish from the sea, whereas longtime resident Norm Niver eats as much as he wants, claiming that a stalk of celery contains as much selenium as

the typical Salton Sea corvina. To one Imperial Valley biology teacher and Sierra Club member, the sea is completely unnatural because it has no outlet; he supported the option of building a canal from the sea to the Gulf of California. An op-ed writer for the *San Diego Union-Tribune* called the sea "a Frankenstein created by the blundering of man." A letter writer to the same paper argued that we should exercise benign neglect and let the sea follow its "natural course"—becoming increasingly saline until it turns into a virtual dead sea. And a geology professor called it "an environmental abscess on the southeastern California landscape," holding that the best solution is to let the sea dry up and revert to desert.

Taking the opposite view, Stuart H. Hurlbert of the Center for Inland Waters called this a solution "that only creosote bushes could view with equanimity." In his view, the sea is "the site of a tremendously positive symbiosis between agriculture, wildlife, human recreation, and, in the early days, commercial fisheries." Steve Horvitz, superintendent of the Salton Sea State Recreation Area, told a symposium audience: "I've found an Eden—here at the Salton Sea. Eden exists at California's largest lake in the vistas as one stands upon its shores and gazes at snow capped mountains. In the brilliant sunsets that reflect gold in the feathers of majestic pelicans, in the guttural cry of the snowy egret as the sun lowers into the horizon. Eden exists in the spirit of those people that use, enjoy and depend upon the Salton Sea for their state of mind; their state of soul."

Strangely enough, each of these opinions—portraying the sea as either natural or unnatural, an environmental abscess or a bit of Eden—has some truth. The sea is neither natural nor unnatural but a mix of both, a funhouse mirror that reflects and distorts all our ideas about nature. At this point, just about anything we do with the sea would be "natural." We could divert the flow of the Colorado River directly into the basin and bring back the Lake Cahuilla of A.D. 900–1400 at forty-two feet above sea level, flooding the towns and farms of the Imperial and Coachella Valleys in the process. This would also give the sea a "natural" outlet into the Gulf of California, maintaining its salinity at something less than that of ocean water. We could let things go the way they are until the sea becomes so salty that nothing will live in it but shrimp and brine flies, as must have happened when Lake Cahuilla was drying up around 1400. Or we could stop irrigating the Imperial Valley, let all that water run down the Col-

orado to renew the wetlands at its delta, and let the Salton Sea become the barren playa that existed there from 1400 to 1900.

All these conditions existed "naturally," so it's just a question of which period we want to preserve. Calling one period natural and the others unnatural makes no sense. Yet none of these alternatives would be wholly natural because we are inextricably involved with controlling where the water flows. Short of tearing down the dams on the Colorado and letting the river run where it will, asking what is natural for the Salton Sea cannot help us decide how to treat it.

Such conundrums are present all across the desert and all across the continent. The palm groves in the Anza-Borrego Desert and the mesquite groves near the Salton Sea depended to an extent on human care for their survival. Are they any less natural for that? Farther north, around Monterey Bay, ecologists have noticed that the threatened monarch butterfly seems to prefer the non-native eucalyptus tree over the native Monterey pine. Should they try to eradicate the eucalyptus and replant the pines, as the California Native Plant Society would have them do, or should they leave the eucalyptus for the butterflies? And forests in a variety of landscapes, from the Cathedral Pines in Connecticut to the North Woods of Minnesota to the Douglas fir forests of the Rocky Mountains, have changed significantly over the past 300 years, mostly because of the absence of fire, sometimes combined with logging. Which is the "natural" course: preserving those forests in their present condition or returning them to their historical state?

In all these situations, asking what is natural doesn't get us very far because this question is, at its heart, insoluble. Instead, we should think about what attracts us to "natural" areas in the first place. More often than not, the answer will have to do with the life that flourishes there. Here at the Salton Sea, it has to do with the astonishing numbers of birds that visit from fall to spring, with thousands upon thousands of wings lifting off the water at once, rising into the air to soar for a while, and then settling back on the water in a thousand V-wakes. In Anza-Borrego, it has to do with the variety of cacti, succulents, shrubs, trees, and grasses and the wildlife that feeds on them, all adding up to the "feeling of the desert." The fact that humans have had a hand in supporting this life makes it no less attractive.

Scientists use the word *biodiversity* to refer to this variety of life, in

terms of both the numbers of a given species, such as the millions upon millions of bison that once roamed North America, and the variety of species in any given area, from the smallest desert pond to the entire planet. Biodiversity is what Europeans marveled at in their first encounter with the Americas—the incredible abundance of open plains, temperate and tropical forests, even deserts. At one time, both Indians and European newcomers thought this abundance was inexhaustible. But we quickly reached the limits of that abundance, in 400 years wiping out dozens of species and pushing many more to the brink of extinction. Today, as we are increasingly becoming aware, despite numerous efforts at preservation, we are entering a sixth "great extinction," a period during which the diversity of life on earth will be drastically reduced. This extinction, unlike the previous five, has one root cause: the proliferation of humans on the planet.

Against this backdrop, we need to stop asking what is natural and start asking what will support diversity in a particular habitat, ecosystem, or region. The Salton Sea is still a haven of biodiversity, despite the fact that it is not purely natural and despite the impression many of us have that it is not a particularly pleasant place to visit. The birds don't care about our theories of nature or our sense of aesthetics. They care about such things as undisturbed nesting sites. The shorebirds care about getting their fill of fish, which the Salton Sea still provides in plenty. If this diversity of bird life is to continue, we must act to halt the decline of conditions in the sea, especially regarding the health of the fish. Exactly how to do that will always be a matter of contention. Scientists will argue about which is more urgent, stabilizing the sea's salinity or controlling the inflow of fertilizers.

Ultimately, however, the answer will depend on what we value. The decision of how best to maintain biodiversity is never made in a vacuum; human needs will always be considered and will often come first. (The recovery plan proposed in January 2000, for instance, was strangely silent on the issue of the heavy nutrient loads flowing into the sea.) But even here, the choice is not between birds and the economy. "Saving the Salton Sea" will also mean revitalizing the sportfishing industry and safeguarding the health of the thousands of anglers (some of them descendants of the original fisherfolk of Lake Cahuilla) who have returned to the sea in recent years. One economic study put a value of $360 million per year on

a restored Salton Sea. But if scientists are correct in thinking that fertiliz-ers are the most critical cause of bird and fish die-offs, then the choice may be between a thriving fishery and an agricultural economy providing plentiful produce. With decisions such as these facing us, being able to simply "let nature take its course" would be comforting. But we haven't been able to do that for a long time, if ever.

IN THE late nineteenth and early twentieth centuries, humans seemed to be getting the best of the "contest between man and nature," as it was often called. But in the Colorado Desert, nature dealt some blows of its own. The Colorado River defied those who underestimated its power. And in the Anza-Borrego region, the mountains of the Peninsular Crest presented a formidable barrier to transportation. While Los Angeles and San Francisco boomed, San Diego remained a sleepy coastal village rather than the center of national and international trade it aspired to be. By 1919, when the San Diego and Arizona Railroad finally linked San Diego directly to the East, it was too late for the city to catch up. Even then, the mountains seemed to begrudge the slender black thread of the railroad clinging to their flanks. The descent through Carrizo Gorge earned the line the nickname "the Impossible Railroad." The title would prove apt. On September 10, 1976, after the railroad had endured sixty years of slides, washouts, and tunnel fires, Hurricane Kathleen delivered the big-gest blow, destroying three trestles and washing out tracks in more than fifty places. A feeble attempt was made to reopen the route, but it was finally abandoned in 1983, after another tunnel fire and cave-in. The mountains had won. San Diego's boosters still dream of reopening the line one day, even expanding it to accommodate double-deck freight cars, but that day seems as far off as ever. For now, the trestles and tunnels in Carrizo Gorge are objects of curiosity to desert hikers.

But not everyone saw these forces of nature as something to be tamed or defeated. Writer and art critic John Van Dyke visited the desert and found a treasure more valuable than gold or agricultural wealth. Others would follow in his footsteps.

SEVENTEEN PALMS:
OUR LIMITS
TRANSGRESSED

I'M STANDING at the edge of the badlands around Arroyo Salado, a desiccated network of washes in the eastern part of Anza-Borrego Desert State Park. Behind me lies a gravel plain skirting the base of the Santa Rosa Mountains. Before me, to the south, the plain breaks apart in a jumble of chocolate-brown mud hills and twisting washes. Two forks of Arroyo Salado pass east through that convoluted terrain; I want to cross the north fork and then follow the main fork west to a spot known as Seventeen Palms Oasis. One dark palm standing alone in the west marks my goal, but first I head southeast. Somewhere out there, I hope to follow the path of J. Smeaton Chase, a writer who spent a night at the palms around 1918. He had already written two popular books, *California Coast Trails* and *Yosemite Trails*, and was at work on his third, *California Desert Trails*.

Chase knew many Cahuilla Indians (he bought his pony from Francisco Patencio), and he recognized their role in shaping the region's palm oases and other natural features. Although he celebrated the canyons near Palm Springs, forty miles to the north, he was drawn more to desolate wastes such as these badlands, which he called "the desert entire and austere, the realm of geology alone." He saw this as a wilderness, a place not to be hurried through or tamed by irrigation but to be enjoyed just as it was. Along with John C. Van Dyke and other writers, Chase is responsi-

ble for changing our view of deserts, and I want to see this place the way he saw it.

Walking across the plain to this point, I've dodged around widely spaced creosote bushes, bunches of galleta grass, and dormant ocotillos. Now, dropping into the badland maze, I leave even that sparse flora behind: few plants can grow in the gypsum of these mud hills. My feet sink into the clay earth as I descend from one sinuous ridge to another. I try to stay up high to keep my bearings, but soon I have to plunge down a steep slope to keep heading south.

Now I'm surrounded by the barren mud domes and have to use my compass to keep heading southeast. Watercourses barely a foot wide snake in and out among the hills. I wander up and down in this landscape for half an hour, with only an occasional glimpse of a peak in the Santa Rosas to hint of the world beyond. I could be walking on a lifeless planet. Flora and fauna, much less humans, have done little here to soften the harshness of bare rock and naked earth. There's not even a scrap of shade in which to rest. I feel like an outsider here, as if this is a place where I do not belong. It's the closest thing Anza-Borrego has to a wilderness, a landscape so barren and so little used that it can truly be called pristine.

The Indians didn't make their homes here; they only traveled through on their way to more hospitable spots. And maybe not even that, if one can believe Chase's quote of an Indian describing these badlands: "Cheechlicsh'-noo-ah, devil's house, we call that. Very bad place. Man get in there no can get out never." Wandering through this maze, I see how that could happen. I'm feeling disoriented myself.

Although the Indians may have avoided the area, plenty of people come here today—just not on foot. As I cross out of the park and into Bureau of Land Management (BLM) territory, I begin to see tracks of dirt bikes. The park allows only street-legal vehicles, and these have to stay on the jeep roads. BLM land is wide open; the few rules and the few rangers are widely ignored. Here, the tracks snake up and down the mud hills, leaving deep impressions. In the distance, I can hear the throaty *rat-tat-tat* of a dirt bike.

I cross the comparatively green strip of Arroyo Salado's north fork and then plunge into the mud hills once again. Here, they're larger, 80 or 100 feet high, and gravel topped, and they come in a wider variety of colors—

white, tan, and gray as well as the more common chocolate brown. In some places, the sediments have eroded into wide bowls that seem to have no outlet. At one point, I cross a five-acre playa that's absolutely barren.

When I'm halfway across, three riders crest the hill behind me. I've talked to enough BLM rangers and read enough statements from extremists in the Sahara Club—who boast that they'll shoot Sierra Club members on sight—to be wary of strangers on dirt bikes. I nod nonchalantly at them, but they seem to ignore me. One of them seems to be having trouble with his bike. I continue on and wonder what they make of me, a lone hiker out where no one ever hikes.

I climb to the southern rim of the bowl and wait for the bikers to pass through. From here, I can look down into the main fork of Arroyo Salado. Tracing its line to the west, I make out the single palm I saw earlier, now about three miles away. Off to the east, a dark, sloping plain descends to the Salton Sea, a faint, pale blue shimmer in the Imperial Valley haze. That seems to be the way Chase came, though judging from his description he was one wash farther south. The day is getting hot, and the palm is like a beacon. I decide to make straight for it and to strike Chase's route farther on.

After dropping into the arroyo, I pause to rest in the shade of a smoke tree. The weather report called for a temperature of eighty degrees Fahrenheit today, but it feels hotter. A light breeze cools me intermittently. When it dies, a faint briny smell rises from the wash. The creosote bushes here are covered in yellow flowers, and another bright green bush is putting out white blossoms. The dirt bikes are gone now; the only sounds are the drone of a distant airplane and the occasional buzz of a fly. I relax for half an hour, picking out shapes in the mud hills and rereading Chase's description of his journey in *California Desert Trails*.

CHASE's trip to Seventeen Palms was just one leg of a journey that lasted an entire summer. He didn't stay long in the cultivated canyon palm groves or the lush *ciénegas*, (wetlands) preferring instead the badlands in what would become Anza-Borrego Desert State Park and the shell-strewn sands near the Salton Sea. He had traveled here from Palm Springs, riding south along the shores of the Salton Sea and then around the southern arm of the Santa Rosa Mountains. From the palms, he continued west

to Borrego Springs, up Coyote and Cougar Canyons to Warner Springs, and then southeast to the valley of Vallecito. He took up with a prospector, and the two made a difficult crossing of the Carrizo Badlands, exiting at Split Mountain. After a break at San Sebastian Marsh and a side trip to Superstition Mountain, they traveled south, taking a "shortcut" around the eastern flanks of the Coyote Mountains, where they nearly died of thirst. Chase finished the trip with a long loop out to Yuma, north to Blythe, and then back west to Palm Springs. It would have been an ambitious journey if he had done it in winter; during the cauldron of summer it was audacious, even slightly crazy.

Chase was a transplanted Englishman, and maybe the comparison to mad dogs applies here. I try to imagine how he felt as he rode and walked through these badlands with temperatures thirty degrees hotter than what I'm feeling today. Chase had meant to start his journey earlier in the year, but he'd had trouble finding the right horse. That's one excuse, but the mad dogs and Englishmen adage probably has more to do with it. Later in the summer, while traveling through a slot canyon on Superstition Mountain—"It was midday and the place was like a furnace, the temperature not less, I think, than 150° in the sun"—he decided that a "billy" of hot tea would be just the thing.

Although Chase may have been crazy enough to travel in the heat of summer, he wasn't crazy enough to describe it as fun: "It was impossible to maintain any interest in the view, but that was no loss, since nothing changed, hour after hour. . . . It seemed a week that I had been creeping over this unending plain. Somehow I felt unreal, as if I were a picture of a man in my position, and wondered vaguely whether the man ever got anywhere." He found "no animal life either of beast, reptile, or bird, hardly of insect." Even the few shrubs and ocotillos offered little relief: "all looked at the point of death." It only got worse when he came to the clay hills, "the last extreme of the barren, dreary, and dangerous." He could have been any nineteenth-century immigrant who hurried across this desert seeing nothing but a barren waste, not an outdoorsman who was here partly for enjoyment and partly so he could write about it.

But these clay hills weren't the last extreme. Chase kept thinking he had found the absolute in desolation, only to find something worse, as when he approached Superstition Mountain across a level plain of silt

dotted with shells and an occasional mesquite clump: "I tried to imagine some addition or subtraction by which the landscape might be rendered more depressing, but had to admit that the maximum was reached: it was wholly, conscientiously bad." Ten pages later, describing the flanks of the Coyote Mountains, he wrote of finding an even more desolate spot: "I do not see how Sahara, Gobi, or Arabia could improve on this for rigid nakedness and sterility. One here sees Mother Earth scalped, flayed, and stripped to the skeleton."

What kept him tramping across these grim wastes? Chase struggled to explain the attraction. "Yet there is a strange beauty in it all" was about the best he could manage. "The magic of the desert is a riddle. . . . I have never found the person who felt that he could even shape it vaguely to himself in thought." At another point, he called the attraction "the fascination of repulsion or something near that, a morbid and dangerous thing in general, but which somehow I find invigorating." Even a respite in the mountains couldn't dull his appetite for the desert: "Already I felt the magic, the magnetism, of the old, wonderful desert, drawing me back: back to its dreariness, silence, and secrecy, its cruelty of heat and thirst, its infinite expanse, its ageless mystery and calm, its threat of death, its passionless repose." Like me, Chase seemed to be doing this for fun, but exactly where the fun lay remained something of a mystery.

It takes only an hour to hike the two or three miles to the palm, but that's long enough to make me feel somewhat as I imagine Chase did as he crossed his "unending plain." It seems an eternity that I've been walking up this same wash, with the same mud hills on either side, the same white sand and gravel passing beneath my feet. The southern Santa Rosa Mountains hardly seem to draw nearer as I walk. And that lone palm, the best gauge of my progress, has disappeared from view. I could be on a treadmill with a movie of passing desert scenery surrounding me. The only change seems to be the increasing temperature. I'm hiking along with the breeze, effectively negating its cooling effect. At times like these, the attraction of the desert seems a riddle even to me.

At last, the palm comes into closer view, and I leave the wash to cross directly toward it. The breeze has died, and all I can think of is that lone palm's shade. Half a mile below the grove, I pass a downed palm trunk,

and my brain is just active enough to wonder when there was ever enough water in this wash to carry it down here. I don't pause to examine the animal tracks I see, and even a bright glimmering on a nearby hill doesn't distract me from my course. It could be gold, but I don't care.

Nearing the lone palm, I realize that this must be Five Palms. It's up on a slope, whereas Seventeen Palms is in a hollow surrounded by mud hills, a quarter mile north. These palm groves were often named for the numbers of trees present at the time of their naming. Over time, of course, those numbers have changed. Climbing the slope, I realize there *are* five palms here, the tall one I've been approaching all day and four saplings. The large one is burned bare to within three feet of the green fronds at the top, making it look historically authentic. In my heat-addled state, I wonder whether the park service planted the four new ones in an attempt to make the place match its name.

As hot as I am and as much as I had looked forward to the shade of this palm, I don't pause but continue straight up the hillside to the top. The view out over the badlands is just too good. It's not beautiful in any conventional sense, though with some effort I can make out more varieties of color in the badlands: pale mauves and yellows and an eerie grayish green. But there's something voluptuous, almost erotic, about the undulating shapes of the mud hills that makes them attractive. That and the green of the palms, the wind rustling in their leaves, are the closest this landscape comes to conventional beauty.

Then what is the attraction? The sheer vastness of the place. I've hiked in a loop for most of the day, and none of the ground I've covered seems very far away. I can easily cast my eye over enough terrain for a hundred such hikes, and that's just down here on the flat. Mountains rise five or six thousand feet above me, encircling me in a horseshoe from south through west to north, mocking my puny eight- or ten-mile foray into the desert. I try to imagine the pinyon pines on Whale Peak to the south, the shady oak groves and cedar forests of the Laguna Mountains and the Cuyamaca Mountains, but I can't. From this angle, the mountains appear as Chase described them, having "a smoky, furnace-like hue as if the range were built of slag." In this landscape, I'm a tiny speck, no more important than the rocks or the shrubs or the fly buzzing near my face.

This is what Henry David Thoreau was talking about when he wrote:

"We must be refreshed by the sight of inexhaustible vigor, vast and Titanic features. . . . We need to witness our own limits transgressed, and some life pasturing freely where we never wander." And this is just what Chase, and others before him, found in the desert, what kept him going through months of journeying and led him to celebrate the desert over mountains or ocean. "Here Time and all things of Time seem to have ended or not to have begun," he wrote. "The sun rises, flames through the sky, and sets; the moon and stars look coldly down; the traveler seems to himself the last life on the planet. Awe that is close on terror grasps him: he feels himself alone in the universe—he, and God." There is something pagan in the kind of god Chase found in the desert: "Perhaps the dormant savage in the breast, some strain of the paleozoic, wakes up in the presence of these chaotic, barbaric shapes." Whereas others wanted to subdue that barbaric landscape, Chase found it whispering: "Your primal home. Come back."

IN 1918, the idea of finding God in the American desert was relatively new, at least for those of European descent. Only 50 years before, they had been more likely to describe the desert as a version of hell. And 150 years earlier, Father Pedro Font had described the mountains around Coyote Canyon as "the sweepings of the world." The only people who had seen other possibilities in the desert were the prospectors, with their dreams of lost gold mines, and irrigators such as Charles Rockwood and George Chaffey, with their dreams of an agricultural paradise.

Around the turn of the twentieth century, though, something changed. With the desert mostly emptied of its former inhabitants, it came to seem like a place that matched Thoreau's ideal of seeing "life pasturing freely where we never wander." With railways, improved wagon roads, and new wells making access easier, people began noticing an allure in even the dreariest and most austere of landscapes. And with desert lands in the Imperial and Coachella Valleys being converted to agriculture, a scarcity theory of value began to apply to the remaining desert areas.

Chase was not the first writer to both express and contribute to this shift in the way the nation looked at deserts. Three others had helped shape his own view. Instead of agricultural empires or rich gold mines, these writers found a different kind of treasure. They laid the ground-

work for protecting desert landscapes in parks, monuments, and wilderness areas. It's not too much to say that they made it possible for us to appreciate deserts as places of beauty as well as of aridity and desolation.

Their task was large. They had to retrain a largely eastern audience accustomed to bucolic scenes of forests and meadows, dramatic views of mountains and waterfalls, and most of all the color green as the symbol of vibrant nature. What could be beautiful in these brown wastes? If the desert wasn't beautiful in the traditional sense, it did have power, vastness, and mystery, qualities that both repelled and attracted, creating a feeling known as the sublime.

Although today the word *sublime* is often used to mean "extremely beautiful," in its original sense it described just this sensation of awe spiced with fear provoked by powerful forces of nature—storms, waterfalls, volcanoes, even sheer cliffs. For a long line of European thinkers starting with Edmund Burke, this was not just an aesthetic quality but a religious one as well. Experiencing the sublime was the closest thing to experiencing God.

The best place to experience the sublime, Chase and his predecessors claimed, was in the desert. John Van Dyke was the first to make that claim; *The Desert*, which he published in 1901, is widely credited as the book that turned the popular conception of deserts on its head, influencing later generations of desert writers right down to iconoclast and monkey-wrencher Edward Abbey. Van Dyke, an art critic first and desert traveler second, wrote, "In sublimity—the superlative degree of beauty—what land can equal the desert with its wide plains, its grim mountains, and its expanding canopy of sky!"

For Van Dyke, life's highest calling was the appreciation of beauty, and beauty found its highest expression in nature, especially the desert; therefore, the desert should be left in its natural state. Van Dyke's chapter titled "The Bottom of the Bowl" provides the best picture we have of the floor of the Salton Trough before it was inundated. His descriptions of the way the desert light played on the sand dunes or created the water mirage are wonders of detail and clarity. Alarmed at the effect irrigation would have on these qualities of light, Van Dyke made one of the first calls for desert preservation, warning that "the deserts should never be reclaimed."

There were almost no people in Van Dyke's desert—no Indians, no

railwaymen, no cowboys, no farmers—and he liked it that way. But George Wharton James, the second of Chase's predecessors, put people squarely in the foreground of *The Wonders of the Colorado Desert*. When James published his 536-page tome in 1906, some of what Van Dyke had foreseen had already come to pass: the newly named Imperial Valley had been irrigated and converted to farmland, and the Salton Trough was slowly filling with the floodwaters of the Colorado River. But surprisingly—considering that he celebrated the same qualities Van Dyke found in the desert—James was remarkably sanguine regarding these changes. If Van Dyke was an impressionist, then James was a social realist, showing farmers and engineers confidently taming the desert, with just a glimpse of pristine landscape visible in the background. In his attempts to blend preservation with boosterism, James came off as a mixture of John Muir and Floyd Dominy, that inveterate dam builder and foe of the Sierra Club. James concluded his book with the weak lament that "it would be a tremendous pity to reclaim all the desert. We need it for other and better things than growing melons and corn."

The viewpoint of Mary Austin, the third of these seminal desert writers, lies somewhere between these two extremes. Her desert is more like an Asian landscape, with tiny human figures occupying the middle ground. Published in 1903, *The Land of Little Rain* was not immediately popular in the United States, and it has never received as much credit as *The Desert* for changing our views of arid landscapes. But Austin's work was based on a longer and deeper experience with the region and its people. She had lived near the Mojave Desert since 1891 and was able to draw on a decade's worth of observing desert plants, animals, weather, and geography and of visiting with prospectors, ranchers, and Paiute Indians. She included those people throughout *Land of Little Rain*, asking how they affected the desert and, most of all, how the desert affected them. Austin was a bioregionalist before her time, and her work has something thoroughly modern about it. She seems to have had as great an influence as Van Dyke on later writers such as Edward Abbey, from expectations of what deserts have to offer right down to certain phrases. In his own book, Chase expressed doubt about whether any writer could ever capture the essence of the desert, but to my way of thinking, among this first generation of desert writers, Mary Austin came the closest.

Austin focused on the Mojave Desert and the nearby Sierra Nevada and Tehachapi Mountains. This leaves to Chase the distinction of being the best writer to focus on the Anza-Borrego region, blending an accurate eye for detail, an engaging sense of humor, and just enough purple-prosed celebration to let the reader feel his fascination. Although historians have cast doubt on whether Van Dyke really made his famously rugged journeys across the Southwest, Chase's description of his own trip is too accurate to have been fabricated. Whereas Van Dyke insisted on finding beauty and James insisted on finding "wonders," Chase was not afraid to admit that there is ugliness, dreariness, and even boredom in the desert.

Together, Van Dyke, James, and Austin had helped to change people's ideas about deserts. When Chase came along, he wrote that "a few people are just beginning to catch the idea" that the desert is a place of beauty, and he hoped that more would do so. By 1920, when he called for the creation of a desert park, the idea did not seem ludicrous, as it might have just twenty years earlier.

Today, I find good reason to be thankful for Van Dyke's and Chase's calls for preservation and the state park that eventually resulted. After a brief visit to Seventeen Palms—where Chase noted that the water gave his tea "a dirty gray curdle and a flavor like bilge"—I head home. On the way, I stop at an isolated mesa on the park's western edge. It is covered with desert pavement, a mosaic of rocks and pebbles created by wind and water eroding the sand in between. Soon I strike a trail, a slightly smoother, foot-wide track in the already even surface. Nearby, another trail runs parallel to this one, but it makes several S-shaped curves and doesn't seem to lead anywhere. A few feet away, a similar shape parallels the first.

I've seen aerial photographs of ancient ground figures, types of rock art known as intaglios or geoglyphs, and I wonder whether this might be one. Someone has left a single metal stake in the ground nearby as if to mark this as a significant spot. If this is a geoglyph, it was most likely left by the San Dieguito people, who inhabited the region long before either the Kumeyaay or the Cahuilla.

Farther on, I come to patterns of larger rocks in the trail. At first, I think they must be modern, but they are deeply imbedded, so they can't have been placed recently. One is an arrow pointing in the direction I'm

heading. The other is a vaguely circular shape. Together, the figures look something like the Shoshone "water marks" Mary Austin described in *Land of Little Rain*.

An ancient trail, a possible intaglio, and a possible water sign—I've hiked for a decade in this desert just to come across something like this, something I didn't expect, something not on the map or in the guidebook. I'm filled with wonder and respect for the people who left these traces and for the depths of time they represent. As a kind of offering, I add a rock to one of the ducks that marks the trail.

I'm glad these figures are in the state park and not on BLM land. In the BLM-controlled Yuha Desert, south of Anza-Borrego, dirt bikers deliberately carved "doughnuts" over two other intaglios, virtually destroying them. With the BLM's loose rules and loose enforcement, it would be just a matter of time before off-roaders headed this way. Even if they had no malicious intent—and most of them probably don't—they might not notice these faint tracings before the damage was done.

Chase made one of the first and strongest calls for preserving the desert, advocating the establishment of a national park centered on the lush palm canyons near Palm Springs. In *California Desert Trails*, he wrote, "Scenically the place is more than remarkable; it is strictly unique for this country, as well as strangely beautiful: while for its botanical rarity alone it should be preserved in the public interest." It's strange that he wanted to preserve these oases rather than the more austere regions that so captured his imagination; perhaps he was just guessing about what would draw tourists and support for a park. Palm Springs was the wrong place, though, partly because land prices there were already too high but mainly because the major canyons were owned by the Cahuilla.

Chase had the right idea, though, even if he chose the wrong spot. In 1927, when the newly formed State Park Commission began surveying lands for a state park system, members of the San Diego Society of Natural History lobbied for a desert park that would include the palm canyons near the Borrego Valley. The first proposal called for a park in the range of 150,000 to 300,000 acres, but the vision was soon expanded to a million-acre park connecting Borrego Valley and the Cuyamaca and San Jacinto Mountains and possibly extending all the way to the Salton Sea. Proponents pointed to many of the same desert qualities Van Dyke and Chase had extolled. The director of the park commission, Frederick Law

Olmsted Jr., a prominent landscape architect and the son of the designer of New York's Central Park, wrote in his report, "Certain desert areas have a distinctive and subtle charm, in part dependent on spaciousness, solitude, and escape from the evidence of human control and manipulation of the earth." He could have been quoting Van Dyke or Chase.

The first lands for what would become Anza-Borrego Desert State Park were turned over to the state in 1932, but it would take another fifteen years for the park to reach roughly its present shape. During that time, the dream of a million-acre park would vanish as the desert became a battleground between those who wanted to develop every available inch of land and those who wanted to preserve it for its scenic or botanical value. In *Our Historic Desert*, published in 1973, Diana Lindsay explored the machinations of county supervisors who saw the desert as a "tax base" and of boomers who bought land in or near the prospective park territory, hoping to either sell it for a high price or develop resorts near the park. She showed that the resulting compromises and delays in the state's land acquisitions forced major changes in the size and shape of the park.

The result is a crazy-quilt patchwork of boundaries defining the park and the many private inholdings still within it. The biggest of those inholdings is Borrego Springs, a thirty-five-square-mile chunk right in the middle of the park's northern section. Borrego Springs encompasses orange and grapefruit groves, luxury golf and tennis resorts, and a town of 3,000 people (double that in winter). All of that development relies on local groundwater, and as the town of Borrego Springs and the surrounding farms grew, the spring for which the town was named went dry. Today, farmers are moving into the area because, unlike the Colorado River water used to irrigate the Coachella and Imperial Valleys, the water here is free for the price of drilling and pumping. That pumping threatens even downstream oases such as San Sebastian Marsh.

In other places, private land or holdings of the federal government create strange gaps in the contour of the park's boundary. The Table Mountain area, for instance, is a block of BLM land surrounded on three sides by Anza-Borrego; it was withheld when other federal lands were transferred to the park because of potential mineral sources such as the Mica Gem Mine. And until 1998, the biologically rich Sentenac Ciénega, an obvious gateway to the park, was privately owned and heavily grazed.

Ideally, the park would have been based on some natural boundary,

such as a watershed or even a natural vista; instead, it was based on the whims of land speculators and those opposed to removing land from the tax base. The park expresses the contradictions in society's views of nature and the way it should be treated. It expressly protects "cultural features" such as these geoglyphs, but it fails to protect other cultural features, such as Indian land management practices, many of which would conflict with preservation of the park in its "natural state."

Yet every time I tread on BLM land, I am thankful for the park and the efforts of Van Dyke, Chase, Olmsted, and the San Diego Society of Natural History. The park effectively made a reality of Van Dyke's vision of the desert as a place devoid of people, but that was probably the only vision that would have protected it. In the Colorado Desert as a whole, on the other hand, it is George Wharton James' vision, not Van Dyke's or Austin's or Chase's, that has come to pass. Some desert areas are given over totally to human endeavors, while others are reserved for what we call pure nature. Areas managed as wilderness, where it is illegal to remove even a rock, sit next to off-road vehicle areas where it seems the purpose is to destroy every living thing. And these border on the fields of the Imperial Valley, where the desert has ceased to exist at all, having been replaced by another type of habitat. James wasn't successful in reconciling these competing demands, and neither are we today.

GHOST MOUNTAIN:
BAD DAYS
AT YAQUITEPEC

I T'S HALF past seven on a January morning. I'm work-
ing my way up the Ghost Mountain trail from Blair Valley, hiking fast to
keep warm. In the mountain's shadow, the temperature must be in the
thirties. A storm blew through yesterday, leaving the higher mountains to
the west dusted in snow and promising grand vistas today.

I am rewarded for my efforts. As I crest the ridge, the prospect opens
across the Imperial Valley and deep into Mexico, the kind of boundless
view that I look for on many of my hikes. To the southeast is a flat expanse
of desert stretching to the Gulf of California. The Sierra de las Cocopas
and Sierra de Juárez are directly south, misty, jagged outlines that make
me want to explore them. At the base of the Sierra de las Cocopas, the
Laguna Salada is an undulating brushstroke of burnished silver. Closer
in are the familiar ranges: the Coyote Mountains, the In-Ko-Pah Mountains, the Jacumba Mountains, and the main crest of the Laguna Mountains. The rays of sunlight warm my body, and the expansive feeling of
space warms my soul.

Others, too, have found this view alluring. A little farther up the ridge,
the trail ends at a two-acre flat. At its edge stand the remains of an adobe
and wood-frame cabin and several concrete cisterns. Inside the skeletal
cabin frame, the usual rusted bedsprings lie in one corner, though these
are from a double bed. At fifty feet by sixteen, the cabin itself was too big

to have been an ordinary cattleman's shack, and an arched doorway shows an attention to aesthetics unknown to typically primitive cowboy quarters.

This was the home of Marshal and Tanya South, two writers who hit on hard times during the Great Depression and moved out here to live off the land. Marshal was in his forties, a native of England and a writer of dime Westerns. Tanya, a Jewish woman from New York ten years his junior, was a poet. They hiked up here one February morning in 1932, fell in love with the view, and decided to stay. In Marshal's words, "We had found our Eden."

It *is* an attractive spot—if you overlook the lack of water. The terrain is covered with granitic boulders in all shapes and sizes, natural sculptural studies of varied line and form. Even for the high desert, the vegetation grows lush here—agave and juniper most prominently, but also yucca, cactus (cholla, barrel, fishhook, beavertail, and hedgehog), ocotillo, bunchgrass, jojoba, Mormon tea, chia, and several small shrubs I can't identify. The remains of the cabin hardly seem out of place—fragments of earthen walls, crumbling posts that look like old juniper branches, and concrete cisterns that blend with the local granite. Photographs of the cabin show that it was hardly more obtrusive when it was whole.

But with no water, living here was a foolish, romantic idea and bound to fail, as their friends told them. Why not settle lower down, near water? Much later, Marshal would write, as if justifying this choice: "One must have something of the poet or the artist or the dreamer to build his home upon a hilltop. Most men build theirs in holes and hollows. It is easier." A dreamer himself, he wasn't going to let realism interfere with his grand plan. He and Tanya would build the cabin, hauling water, supplies, and building materials 400 feet up the boulder-strewn hillside, clearing the agave and cholla with a stick and a small axe. They would endure freezing winter nights, blistering summer days, and howling winds—though the winds hardly ever blew for more than two weeks straight. They would wrestle ever larger water barrels up the hill, creating an elaborate water system that never met their needs. And all this for a view.

"Silence and peace!" exclaimed Marshal about the panorama at his feet. "Out over the rim, far below, in a shimmering pattern of barren ridge and thirsty wash, the desert rolled away into a blurring haze of gray-blue

that had for its bordering the jagged, pastel mountains of Mexico, the ghost-faint buttes of Arizona across the Rio Colorado. Distance and long leagues and mystery! But here were rest and silence and the roof of the world. . . . We knew suddenly that we had come home."

This was exactly the sort of sublime view that John C. Van Dyke and J. Smeaton Chase had celebrated. The Souths, however, didn't want just to look at it or travel through it; they wanted to live in it full-time. They were testing the ideals that Van Dyke had never lived up to—the idea that beauty is worth untold hardship. Marshal admitted that no reasonable person would choose such a place: "Sanity said that the thing was an impossible dream. But we were not, at that moment, sane." They named the place Yaquitepec, and they lasted there for fifteen years.

They were hippies thirty years before their time. They railed against the degradation of city life and maintained their pacifism even during World War II. When they weren't struggling to get water and fuel, they wrote and painted and practiced their crafts. They home-schooled their three children, Rider, Rudyard, and Victoria, raising them with "a new outlook on life and a new set of values," letting them grow their hair long and run barefoot over the rocks. Marshal dreamed of creating an arts and publishing community. They tried to live as they thought the Indians had, eating roasted agave, cactus fruit, and chia seeds and going naked much of the time. They made everything they needed by hand, especially at first, when they had little money: clothing, blankets, pottery, tools. In the early days, they harvested the agave with Indian digging sticks they had found. Later, when they had more cash, "romance yielded to utility" and they bought a hoe.

Cash came from occasional royalty payments for Marshal's books and, beginning in 1939, from articles he wrote about their way of life for the *Saturday Evening Post* and *Desert* magazine. Tanya began publishing her poems in *Desert* in 1941. Marshal didn't deny the difficulty of setting up their first camp and building the cabin. "There is nothing soft about Ghost Mountain," he wrote. "The wind and the sun fought us. The searing heat of summer and the bitter winter snows. . . . It was a fight every foot of the way." A photograph accompanying this *Saturday Evening Post* article indicates how difficult it was. The two of them, Marshal in his loincloth and Tanya in a short wrap, are lugging a ten-gallon container of

water up a forty-five-degree slope, stepping from boulder to boulder between cacti and agaves. I've hiked the same kind of slope with a backpack,
and this image makes me cringe.

The labor was good for the soul, at least the way Marshal described it,
with "the toughened muscles and the clear eyes and the peace of mind and
the health that [the desert] has given us." One gets the sense that by the
time he began publishing these articles, the worst of the physical hardship
was behind them. They really had found their Eden. But this one also had
its serpents.

MERGING with nature has its problems, not least that nature can as easily
hurt as nurture the human body and soul. As Herman Melville warned in
Moby Dick, drifting off into sublime reveries is a good way to get oneself
killed. Lulled by that vastness, the lookout in the crow's nest can easily be
thrown into the sea—the ultimate in merging with nature. The lure of the
abyss is always tempting, dangerous. What Melville called the "all" feeling is fine in small doses, but it is no way to go permanently through the
world. I call it the mountaintop feeling—that sensation of consciousness
expanding. I often feel it when I'm on any high point, though my mood,
my companions, and even the weather can affect the experience in different ways.

This expansive feeling is the main lure of climbing a peak to get a view.
In literary terms, it's a cliché, but it is, to use Mary Austin's words, "the
true movement of experience." It's a paradoxical sensation, one of sublime
awe mixed with comforting oneness. I feel tiny, even insignificant, in contrast to the far larger world at my feet, but at the same time my consciousness seems to expand outward to include the entire landscape. The
earth is my body; I am one small part of the earth's body.

The desert has a way of calling you back from that quasi-mystical state,
however. There is vastness, mystery, and power in desert expanses, but
there is also the cactus right at your feet. Pay attention only to the broad
vistas and you're repaid with a cholla ball in the thigh, an agave spine in
the ankle, or an ocotillo thorn in the eye. Distant objects are often farther
off than they appear, a trick of desert light that lured many early travelers
to their death. The desert tempts you with romantic vistas and then
bludgeons you with grim reality.

In *Desert Solitaire*, Edward Abbey tried to overcome "that gallant infirmity of the soul called romance—that illness, that disease, the insidious malignancy which must be chopped out of the heart once and for all, ground up, cooked, burnt to ashes." But he never overcame romanticism for long; it was a large part of his own attraction to the desert. "One whiff of juniper smoke" sent him back into the canyons, searching for the desert's heart, even though he was sure such a place didn't exist.

Others succumbed wholeheartedly to the lure of the desert. One response to that lure is to journey, preferably alone, as far into that sublime landscape as possible, as Van Dyke said he had done. In 1934, a youngster named Everett Ruess went into the canyon country of Utah to write about and paint the landscape that had captivated him. He never came back, thus entering the realm of desert legend. He became a semiannual subject in *Desert* magazine and a source of fascination for Edward Abbey, who, in his romantic mode, could understand "why Everett Ruess kept going deeper and deeper into the canyon country, until one day he lost the thread of the labyrinth." Although we live in a world that denies romanticism, we are captivated by romantic heroes who escape the bonds of civilization, whether as solitary wanderers like Ruess or, like the Souths, as settlers in the wilderness.

THERE is a telling moment in Marshal's writings about life at Yaquitepec. He was looking for the source of a whining birdcall, which turned out to be a roadrunner. As he followed the elusive bird, he "forgot caution—and trod squarely on a mescal spine." The wound smarted for weeks, reminding him of his foolhardiness. It seems that he heeded these warnings only in terms of the smaller things, in which he would sometimes allow "romance to give way to utility," but never in the one large fact of his choice of a homesite.

It's not clear when the reality of the desert began to puncture the Souths' dream, when the serpents slithered into the garden. Perhaps they had been there from the beginning. Although Marshal constantly used the word *we* in his writings, it is clear that he didn't always speak for the whole family. Later, he would admit that Tanya had never fully shared his dream, that he had, to some extent, dragged her to the desert. There were early hints of a split. On a winter visit, Grace Crawford noticed that Mar-

shal "stood there shiverin' and shiverin' and shiverin'" in order to live up to his clothes-free ideals. Tanya, on the other hand, was dressed to stay warm. One person's romantic heroism is another's megalomania, and by the mid-1940s Tanya had had enough.

Water was at the root of their problems. Building a sufficient catchment and storage system and getting additional water up the hill was not the heroic, soul-improving labor Marshal's writings implied. It was a Sisyphean task that colored everything in their lives. They were not living like Thoreau at Walden Pond but like the tenant of Baker Farm, who Thoreau chided because "he was discontented and wasted his life into the bargain." They were discovering that, as Mary Austin had warned, not the law (or even aesthetics) but the land sets the limit.

In an article in the *San Diego Reader*, Jeannette De Wyze dug into the actualities of the Souths' life on Ghost Mountain, and her observations contrast sharply with Marshal's romantic version. The family was, for example, more closely tied to civilization than Marshal's writings let on. Buzz Mushet, the son of ranchers in the area, told De Wyze that the Souths got much of their water from his family's ranch, even after the cisterns were fully developed. And Virginia Smith, who had visited Yaquitepec as a child, remembered, "They had the hugest can dump you ever did see." In Marshal's articles, it's all chia and cactus fruit, agave hearts and handmade tortillas, but they lived on a lot of store-bought food that Marshal neglected to mention. They were only dabbling in living on native plant foods, it seems. Water and canned food cost money, and for that the Souths wrote for a magazine supported by large advertisements from Imperial Valley tractor dealers. While those machines were converting the desert to agriculture, Marshal looked to the east and found only "distance and long leagues and mystery!"

Even if they had succeeded in disconnecting completely from society, the Souths weren't "living like the Indians," at least not like the local ones. The Kumeyaay never would have chosen for a home the top of a mountain with no water source. The Souths should have learned from the Kumeyaay village they visited at the base of Ghost Mountain, but "the call from the grim granite summit was stronger." The Kumeyaay didn't live in isolated families, either, but in communities of dozens or hundreds of people. So many of their hunting, gathering, and land management

efforts were community based that the kind of individualism the Souths pursued would have been inconceivable. And as anthropologists constantly remind us, the Indians were not "simple" people, nor was their lifestyle simple. Presuming to take up their way of life in isolation and with just a few years of practice is remarkably arrogant—especially when that way of life has been lost to those who originally followed it.

While Marshal's hubris was undermining the Souths' Eden, there was also a more classic temptation. In one of his first articles on their desert life, Marshal had proclaimed, "Lonely! How is it possible to be lonely in the desert? There are no two days the same." Yet by the 1940s, his need for companionship seems to have increased. He started an emotional, if not physical, affair with Myrtle Botts of the town of Julian, writing poetry to her and spending increasing amounts of time away from home, neglecting the work necessary to maintain his family on Ghost Mountain. The relationship doesn't seem to have bothered Mrs. Botts' husband, but one can imagine how it affected Tanya, after years of living Marshal's dream.

In 1947, Tanya filed for divorce, citing the affair, the bleak existence at Yaquitepec and its effect on the children, Marshal's refusal to help gather firewood, his absolute control of the family car, and a scheme of his to start a polygamous community in South America. She also charged him with physical abuse. Like many an idealist, Marshal turned out to have something of the despot about him. As his friend and *Desert* editor Randall Henderson later explained, "He despised the rules and taboos of the society he had left behind, and immediately set up a new and even more restrictive code."

The divorce shocked readers of *Desert* magazine, as it did Henderson, one of Marshal's closer friends. After the divorce, Marshal moved to Julian and took a menial job at the town library, where Myrtle Botts was the librarian. Tanya stayed for a short time at Yaquitepec and then moved with the children to San Diego. Later, she described life at Yaquitepec as a "stark, miserable existence" that Marshal had glorified in his articles.

Although his "Desert Refuge" column came to an end with the divorce, Marshal contributed several more articles about the Anza-Borrego area to *Desert*. He returned to the desert, camping at Burro Spring near Agua Caliente Hot Springs, and tried to put his life back together. His writing in this period shows him still focused on lofty ideals, though a note of sad-

ness has crept in. His article on a local cattleman's ruined and abandoned cabin could have been a eulogy for Yaquitepec: "The desert has a way of sapping dreams. And more often than not heroic plans wilt bit by bit— even during the sweaty labor of them—until the final result is another monument to futility."

Three months later, Marshal was dead, literally of a broken heart. He had been aware of his heart condition for some time. In print, he seemed to face death calmly, viewing it as "part of a mighty pattern that is free from fear. It is the pattern of Eternity." Finding such comfort in the cyclical nature of life is a common conceit in nature writing; it's a way of dealing with nature's dark side. Yet here, too, Marshal was playing the Pollyanna, brushing aside his increasing heart problems. Myrtle Botts' daughter Jeri still has letters Marshal wrote to her mother during this time that show him depressed and scared of death. "It's *mindboggling* to read his writings [in *Desert*] and then to read his letters," Jeri told De Wyze. In his published writing, "everything was so uplifting. And when these letters came there was such depression. No will to live." Another romantic illusion had proved to be a sham. That is the problem with romanticism: something always needs to be repressed to maintain the ideal. For John Van Dyke, it was the Pullman cars and his brother's porch from which he viewed the desert; for Edward Abbey, it was the wife he left out of *Desert Solitaire;* for Marshal South, it was the grip of civilization that he couldn't leave behind, a fear of death that wouldn't yield to ideas of eternity, and a lust that destroyed his ideal of family life in the wilderness.

I WORK my way farther up the ridge and find one of the Souths' agave-roasting pits, near the drop-off into Blair Valley. A large, flat rock rests on the brink of that precipice. Suddenly a picture flashes through my mind, a composite of Marshal's photographs from *Desert* magazine. Eight-year-old Rider South sits on the edge of that rock, one leg dangling into space, the other discreetly raised to shield his privates from the camera. His father is smoothing dirt over the baking agave hearts, his muscles taut on his small frame, his long, silver hair pulled back with a bandanna. They look, if not happy, at least content—a sublime view and dinner in the oven.

I look back at the cabin remnants. Something about it seems infinitely

forlorn, especially in contrast to the pictures of Tanya and the children, apparently happy in their wilderness home. Those pictures won't leave me alone. As an adult, Rider told a park ranger that life here "wasn't much fun at all." But they stayed in this place for fifteen years; there must have been happy moments in all that time.

Why does this affect me so strongly? The romantic in me dies hard. Something in me can't let go of Marshal South. I've had those dreams, too—of going to live in an isolated desert cabin, of disappearing into the desert vastness. It's a sick, romantic urge, as Abbey called it, but powerful nonetheless. The mountaintop feeling can be as addictive as a drug.

Abbey was right when he wrote, "The romantic view, while not the whole of truth, is a necessary part of the whole truth." Marshal South's problem was one of degree, not of kind. He took romanticism to the extreme. The sublime is not valuable in itself; it is not a state in which one can exist twenty-four hours a day. It is valuable as a reminder of our place in nature, but only if one can bring that feeling—what we now sometimes call a sense of the sacred—back to everyday life. That mountaintop feeling should enlighten action in the everyday world. In a sense, that is what South did. Through his writing, he reminded *Desert* readers of the sacred nature of life. We need extremists like South, despite their contradictions and impracticalities, to show that there is another way of being in the world.

But perhaps I'm wrong to find sadness in the ruin of Yaquitepec. What is sad about the desert reclaiming, through its own processes of erosion, a

Ruins of Yaquitepec

house that grew up partly from the desert itself? Perhaps I am clinging to illusions of permanence, as a Buddhist would put it. As Marshal himself wrote: "Human life is a fleeting thing. And after all it is not the physical that counts; nor the success or failure of earthly affairs." And elsewhere: "The feet come. The feet go. But the desert remains."

If only that were true everywhere in this land. But even as the Souths were living out their ideal, other forces were reshaping the Anza-Borrego Desert in a more permanent fashion.

RED ROCK CANYON: THE WAR ON THE DESERT

SOARING over a landscape as barren as the moon, two ravens dive-bomb a hawk. The hawk rolls and swoops, the ravens hot on its tail, and then pulls up for a moment as if catching its breath before the next attack. The battle swirls across the pale blue sky, the combatants unconcerned with our group of fifty or so people standing in a dry wash 500 feet below. Ranger Paul Remeika, his foot resting on the turret of a destroyed Sherman tank, interrupts his talk to watch the aerial combat. Someone clanks metal on metal, and suddenly the birds separate, like prizefighters at the end of a round.

Remeika has been telling us about a different kind of bombardment that took place in this desert half a century ago. From 1943 to 1959, the navy carried out a bombing campaign in the 30,000-acre expanse of badlands that had just been added to Anza-Borrego Desert State Park's eastern edge. In the name of defense, it bombed, shelled, strafed, and mortared land set aside for preservation and public enjoyment. It brought in fourteen tanker trucks, five Sherman tanks, and countless artillery pieces. Navy pilots flew thousands of missions over the area, aiming their bombs, rockets, and machine guns at the tanks and trucks or at the land itself. Even the McCains' home near the site of the Carrizo Stage Station wasn't safe. One ranger reported, "On many occasions, according to Mrs. McCain, planes have dropped bombs and made strafing runs perilously close to their home, so close, in fact, that bullets actually hit their chim-

ney." Earlier, the military had temporarily moved the Souths out of their home at Yaquitepec.

When the navy finished, it spent three years cleaning up after itself and then declared the area 90 percent decontaminated. Today, rangers still find unexploded bombs; my group will see two of them before the day is over. The U.S. Army Corps of Engineers has called this the most contaminated impact zone in the country. The old bombs tend to explode unexpectedly, as one scrap hunter found out back in 1959, prompting the park to close the place for good.

Evidence of the bombardment is everywhere, from the bullet holes in the tank and the soft sandstone nearby to the twisted, rusting remains of rockets and bombs we've been seeing all morning. Remeika, nervous about bringing so many people in here, has warned us to stay together and stay away from areas he knows contain "unexploded ordnance." We have to watch where we step to avoid cutting ourselves on the jagged edges of torn bomb casings and rocket fins. From a distance, the shards of shrapnel resemble the reddish brown Fish Creek Mountains northeast of here. Closer up, they look like machinery from some abandoned factory. The scraps don't look lethal, though their contorted shapes attest to the forces that ripped them apart. The unexploded bombs look even more benign, like old, rusted plumbing sticking out of the sand.

Today's trip is the first public viewing of this section of the park in thirty-five years. Organized as a benefit for the Anza-Borrego Foundation, the outing has attracted a mixed group of people who seem to know the park well: retired couples and several men and women in their twenties and thirties. Most of us already know much of the history the ranger has been relating; what we aren't prepared for is the rare beauty of this place. Remeika says that this is what he likes about the impact area: "You've got the good and you've got the bad, all in one place. Maybe after today's trip, you'll think a little differently about the Carrizo Impact Area."

We've seen places with names such as Lavender Canyon, with walls of brilliant purple volcanic rock, and Pink Valley, with a floor of sculpted pink sandstone and hillsides of tan-green and oxide red sediments, capped with a chocolate-brown layer of 4-million-year-old shell reef. Each time we've stopped, it has been for only a few minutes, just long enough to whet our appetites and help us form a mental image of what is off-limits to us here.

Remeika told us of a place we won't see today, a place we could have visited if we'd had more time: a valley with more fossil shell deposits like the ones we've been seeing everywhere. But these fossils are unlike anything else in the park—shark teeth, pancake-sized sea snails, and giant sand dollars. Now he tells us of yet another place in the impact area we won't see, one so precious that he'll never reveal its location: a petrified forest of hundred-foot trees. They grew here when the Anza-Borrego Desert lay near the Gulf of California, now 200 miles to the south. Remeika has a proprietary attitude toward this place, and with good reason: the beds of fossilized wood in accessible areas of the park have all been looted.

Our next stop is Red Rock Canyon. It's a spectacular spot, but we're given only fifteen or twenty minutes to take it all in, this place we've never seen before and aren't likely to see again. Approaching the canyon, we see a rock inscribed with block capitals dating from 1900: RED CANYON. Farther on, the canyon walls deepen to an unimaginable red. The red rock doesn't cover a large area, maybe one or two acres on both sides of the canyon. At first, I think of the cliffs in Zion National Park, but this hue seems deeper, richer, a blend of earth-tone reds and the Kodachrome colors of exotic birds. I realize I've never seen exactly this shade before; maybe it exists nowhere but here.

We pile out of the Jeeps and Explorers, gape at the rocks, snap a few pictures, and then follow Remeika up a low ridge on the western side of the canyon. My shoe knocks two pieces of shrapnel together—the metallic clatter sounds completely out of place in the desert. There's more of the navy's debris here than in the other places we've seen. Remeika explains that the bombers keyed on the red rock in this canyon when they couldn't find anything else to hit. He points out bomb craters that have filled with sand, now resembling what are sometimes called Indian sleeping circles—areas about ten feet wide cleared of large stones. "Now, I'm not saying this," he says, "but for two or three years during World War II the military bombed all over Anza-Borrego, and the archaeologists are finding a lot of sleeping circles."

At the top of the low ridge, we get a view to the west and to areas of the park with which many of us are familiar: the Carrizo Badlands, Whale Peak, the Tierra Blanca Mountains and the Sawtooth Mountains. Much of the low-lying mesa in between is part of the impact area. Somewhere

down there may be the petrified forest Remeika told us about or other treasures no one has seen for decades. Looking back at the red canyon we've just left, I realize there's no way to take it all in, no way at all to really know this place. It hurts to think of the time we could spend here exploring side canyons, climbing to the tops of the rock walls, or just watching the colors change throughout the day. But we don't have time. Soon, we'll have to get back into the vehicles and head home. I feel the way Edward Abbey did on his trip down Glen Canyon just before it was flooded to create Lake Powell, except that nothing here is going to be covered over. It's just closed to the public, and it will most likely remain closed forever.

It hurts, too, to think of what was done to this place. The shards of metal and the live bombs aren't the only remnants of the aerial campaign. Remeika points out the way the fragments of red rock lie on the hillside. To his geologist's eye, it doesn't look like natural erosion. "Ninety percent of the erosion we see here is from the bombing," he says. It's his rangerly, scientific way of saying what really can't be said: that the military carried out a war on one of the most precious places in this desert.

I pick up one of the rock fragments, this one such a deep red it could be a lump of congealed blood. I remember the story of Coyote dripping blood from Mukat's heart and realize that the Cahuilla creation story is still going on. It is as if God has been driven out of this place, hounded out by howitzers and bombs and missiles. Instead of the living world the Cahuilla inhabited, the earth for us has become simply a dead chunk of raw materials. Here and in ten thousand other such places, it is as if we are reenacting the killing of Mukat. Suddenly, I find myself choking back tears.

As BAD as Red Rock Canyon looks, it's worse near the village of Ocotillo Wells, ten miles north of the Carrizo Impact Area. On a windy spring day, I drive into the 42,000-acre Ocotillo Wells State Vehicular Recreation Area (SVRA) and park on a hill overlooking San Felipe Wash. On a map, the place doesn't look too different from any other spot in Anza-Borrego, though the concentration of jeep routes seems slightly greater. On the ground, though, the picture is far different. As I stand next to my car, parked in a wide spot next to the jeep route, a group of riders comes up the road toward me. Those in front apparently are going too slow because

two of the riders split off from the pack and come up the hill where there is no road. The riders pass by me on both sides.

The place has simply been overrun by an army of dirt bikes, all-terrain cycles, and dune buggies, which have created a spiderweb of overlapping trails and large bare patches. Whereas in the impact area, plants still grow relatively undisturbed, here the damage is not only geologic but also biological. Ocotillo Wells looks as if an army had carried out a scorched earth campaign there. I would guess that some 25 to 50 percent of the plant cover has been destroyed. The off-roaders seem to think that the desert is a barren place, and they've done their best to make that true. Here, it's open season on every living thing.

Off-roading got its start in the 1950s when desert rats began using army surplus jeeps to tour the desert on old mining roads. But in the 1960s, with newly popular dirt bikes making it possible to go almost anywhere, riding roughshod over the desert became an end in itself. Short on rangers and with no ban on off-road vehicles, the park became a popular spot for dirt-bike races and the bizarrely repetitive activity of "hill climbing"—riding up and down the steepest hill possible, usually a sand dune. Desert historian Diana Lindsay calls it "indiscriminate use" and says it "left a toll of destruction of natural vegetation and mud hills." I call it abuse. One ranger reported in the late 1960s: "At 1510 hours I am in Font's Wash and it looks like Cox's Army went through here. Dune buggy and bike tracks all over the place." Scars from those days are visible today, and park resources are still being used to restore the worst areas, at a cost of as much as $10,000 per acre.

Finally, in 1987, the California State Park and Recreation Commission approved a ban on non-street-legal or off-highway vehicles (OHVs) in the park. Park ecologist Mark Jorgensen and superintendent Dave Van Cleve risked their jobs fighting for the ban against the well-funded California Off Road Vehicle Association and the director of the state park system. The ban was a realistic, if not very fair, method of reducing damage to the park. Dirt bikers howled that they were being singled out unfairly because sport utility vehicles and highway-legal motorcycles, still allowed on park jeep trails, can do as much damage as off-highway vehicles. The ban was simply a good way to reduce the number of the most indiscriminately used vehicles.

Places such as Ocotillo Wells SVRA are sacrifice zones, areas that get trashed so that others can remain unscathed. They are a bone to throw to the off-roaders: "You've got 42,000 acres over here, so why can't you stay out of the park?" But the off-roaders see it differently; one told me that 42,000 acres is actually a small space when you're blasting around on a dirt bike. Because the SVRA abuts Anza-Borrego Desert State Park on the east, the off-roaders often do stray into the park, either intentionally or accidentally. Keeping them penned up in the SVRA and chasing strays are major tasks for park rangers. But the off-roaders are nothing like docile cattle. They're more like a modern version of the Wild West outlaw, flouting what they see as oppressive regulations wherever they can. On major holiday weekends, according to BLM estimates, hundreds of thousands of off-highway vehicle users descend on southern California's deserts. Having to contend with this number of off-roaders, many of whom are either armed, inebriated, or both, the combined forces of the BLM and local sheriff's departments are often unable to prevent illegal entries into park or wilderness areas.

This is where Edward Abbey's version of wilderness, or one part of it, falls flat on its face. Although he wrote in *Desert Solitaire* that wilderness is "an expression of loyalty to the earth," he also saw it as a place of almost anarchic freedom where he could leave rules and government signboards behind. Beginning his famous journey through Glen Canyon before it was dammed, he wrote, "Cutting the bloody cord, that's what we feel, the delirious exhilaration of independence, a rebirth backward in time and into primeval liberty, into freedom in the most simple, literal, primitive meaning of the word." In a typically Abbeyesque bit of hyperbole, that independence even included the freedom to murder his companion, Newcomb, with nothing but his conscience and his love for Newcomb to keep him from doing so.

This, I think, is just what the off-roaders want to feel when they ride off into the desert on their dirt bikes: that they have escaped from civilization with all its rules and codes of behavior. Like Abbey, they don't want to see government signboards encouraging good behavior or "cops in government uniforms" telling them not to ride over the creosote bushes. Unlike Abbey, though, too many of them have neither conscience nor love for the desert to keep them from destroying it. Far from feeling

"loyalty to the earth," they seem to be at war with it, as thoroughly as the navy once waged war on the desert just south of here. Seeing the desert as a wilderness is exactly what allows them to mistreat it.

If we want to preserve the desert, it cannot be a place of absolute personal freedom; it must be a place of restraint. For the Cahuilla and the Kumeyaay, that restraint grew out of seeing the earth as alive. Even the paths they traveled were alive; next to their trails, they built stone shrines, in which they placed offerings of juniper sprigs or food. Some Indian peoples added to the trail shrines whenever they accidentally stepped off the path, as reparation for any damage they might have caused. As places such as Ocotillo Wells SVRA show, we moderns are a long way from having that kind of self-restraint. Preserving habitat, and not merely places of absolute freedom, requires rules and regulations and cops in government uniforms. The wilderness needs to be a civilized place. It needs to be more like what it was when the Indians lived there—a part of our home.

BUT I, too, am no lover of government restrictions. I want to go back to Red Rock Canyon. That one glimpse just wasn't enough. Now I know how the off-roaders feel about Anza-Borrego, a piece of public land they believe has been locked up by the government. Of course, they are more than welcome in the park if they leave their machines behind, whereas everyone is banned from the impact area. Irrational as the off-roaders' argument is, their feeling is much the same as my own. It's our land, and we should be able to go there.

Some have called for the Carrizo Impact Area, or at least part of it, to be more thoroughly cleaned up and then reopened to the public. Yet as Paul Remeika told us, the bombs are so deeply buried that there's no way to remove them all. Over time, erosion will reveal even the deeply buried shells, so there's no way to ensure visitors' safety. Perhaps the actual danger is no greater than that of being bitten by a rattlesnake. "Don't bother the unexploded ordnance and it won't bother you" could be our motto. But this is a risk that the government is unwilling to take.

Even if it were to take that risk, there is another danger. Although I would like to see the area opened to foot travel only, park officials would probably open the area's existing jeep routes to highway-legal vehicles. Then the petrified trees and the shark-tooth fossils would be discovered

and would soon disappear. It's the old contradiction at the heart of the park's mission—how to protect the area's natural and cultural features while providing access to them. Perhaps keeping the area closed isn't so bad an approach after all. There's even something fitting in seeing a spot such as Red Rock Canyon only from a distance—it becomes almost a mythic place.

Some people, however, simply trespass in the impact area, as I am tempted to do. One Borrego Springs resident told me he hikes there all the time. Why shouldn't I do the same? Unlike the ban on oHVs, which protects the park's features, this closure is intended, ostensibly at least, to protect the public. Breaking a law intended for my own protection seems like a small transgression. But we can all make such rationalizations. Off-roaders trespassing in Anza-Borrego might tell themselves that their dirt bikes do no more harm to existing jeep routes than do highway-legal vehicles.

After two decades of state park authorities futilely relying on off-road-ers to exercise self-restraint, the ban on off-road vehicles was necessary. Further bans, similar to the closure of the middle section of Coyote Canyon to all vehicle traffic, may be necessary. But with each new regulation, more and more people grumble at limits on their "freedom"—just as I grumble at the ban on entering the impact area. And this is just in the state park; a ban on off-roading across the entire desert is unlikely to happen anytime soon, given its popularity and the strength of the oHV lobby.

What Edward Abbey called loyalty to the earth can't be legislated. Such changes ultimately have to come from within, from the kind of personal restraint of which humans have thus far shown too little. The off-roaders themselves must have a change of heart; they must learn to see the desert as a living place that can be harmed by their actions. But what will bring about that change of heart?

After Mukat died and went to the east, one man followed him. Mukat taught the man which plants were good to eat and how to grow them from seeds. We are still waiting to learn such a lesson, perhaps how to heal our relationship with the earth. But so far, our god has been silent. Having convinced ourselves so thoroughly that the earth is a dead place, where would we go to find our god now?

PART V

DESERT *at the* MILLENNIUM

HORSE CANYON: WEEDING THE WILDERNESS

"WOULD you look at this son of a bitch!" Mark Jorgensen exclaims, kicking at a tall shrub with his heavy-toed boot. The object of his wrath is a tamarisk, commonly called salt cedar. At first glance, the shrub doesn't look much different from the thousands of other tamarisks growing here in Horse Canyon at Anza-Borrego Desert State Park, or from the countless tamarisks that have invaded more than a million acres of streamside terrain throughout the Southwest. Just taller than Jorgensen's burly six-foot frame, the small tree has red bark, tiny green leaves, and sprays of pink flowers. It's a pretty shrub, which explains why nurserymen wanted to bring its ancestors from the Middle East to the United States in the early 1800s. But one thing sets this particular salt cedar apart from the others: it has grown up around a barrel cactus, embracing it the way a terrorist would hold a hostage as a human shield.

Now Jorgensen must decide whether to leave this tamarisk alone or spray it with weed killer and risk killing the cactus as well. His solution is simple. "Shoot 'em all and let God sort 'em out," he says. He sprays the exposed base of the tamarisk, making sure to coat several inches of bark with the bright blue liquid he carries in an awkward backpack sprayer. Inevitably, some of the concoction—the herbicide Garlon 4 blended with diesel fuel—splashes onto the cactus.

That barrel cactus is one of the native species that Jorgensen is sup-

posed to protect in his role as resource ecologist for Anza-Borrego and five other desert parks in southern California. But in canyons such as these, protecting native species—not only the barrel cactus but also such trees as willow and cottonwood and the birds and endangered bighorn sheep that depend on them—means eradicating the tamarisk, a prolific, fast-growing, water-guzzling, salt-producing import that is crowding out these natives. For Jorgensen, removing the tamarisk isn't just part of his job; it's a war—dirty, exhausting, expensive, and if you're a barrel cactus in the wrong place, risky. As with any war, collateral damage is unavoidable.

Today's foray into Horse Canyon is just a minor skirmish in Jorgensen's campaign. The major action is downstream in Coyote Canyon, where the tamarisk has a better foothold. There, Jorgensen hires a contractor—the Orkin of the wilderness. These crews use the cut-and-spray method of tamarisk control, cutting the trees at ground level with chain saws or loppers and then spraying the exposed stump with pure Garlon 4.

But removing the tamarisk from Coyote Canyon won't do any good as long as a seed bank of the trees thrives upstream. So today, Jorgensen and park aide Heidi Person are out to get the "mother of all trees" toward the head of Horse Canyon. This huge tamarisk may be responsible for a lot of the young seedlings down in the canyon's lower reaches. More than that, it provides Jorgensen and Person with a tangible goal in an otherwise Sisyphean effort. In this remote area, it's impractical to bring in equipment like chain saws. They'll spray as many of the smaller trees as they can, saving just enough for the main target up ahead. If they get 90 percent of the trees on this foray, they'll declare the mission a success.

The rangers make a good, if oddly matched, team. Jorgensen is forty-something, big, bearish, bearded, and balding. He wears a "park service green" baseball cap, sings country songs by Hank Williams Jr., and puffs on a cigar as he walks. Although he has survived in the state park system for more than twenty-five years, he has a carefully maintained reputation as a renegade and monkey-wrencher. Driving to the site this morning in the park's big Dodge Ram Charger,* Jorgensen had pointed out a new cit-

---

*A year after this trip, the Department of Parks and Recreation prohibited vehicle traffic in a one-and-one-half-mile stretch of the canyon to protect the stream environment at Middle Willows. Since then, the rangers have followed the no-vehicle rule as does everyone else, making jobs like this one even harder.

rus grove just outside the park boundary. "This used to be one of the finest stands of ocotillo anywhere around here," he said. "When they were clearing this field, it was all I could do to keep from coming down here and bustin' some 'dozers."

Now he calls to Person, "Get that one, Mama." Then he scrambles up a slope to get a particularly hard-to-reach plant. If Person minds Jorgensen calling her "Mama," she doesn't let on. She is a wiry five and a half feet tall but doesn't seem fazed by the thirty-five-pound pack on her back. She has short-cropped blond hair and wears wraparound shades. She has been Jorgensen's assistant for the past six years. The two are also golf partners. They won the last park service tournament, mainly because Person is good enough to have played on the professional tour in Europe.

Jorgensen has let me tag along to learn more about the spraying. I follow behind, helping where I can but mostly watching. The rangers dart back and forth across the dry streambed, squirting every salt cedar they can find. Sometimes they have to climb a steep canyon wall to get a salt cedar audacious enough to grow away from the stream. They avoid spraying around the few spots of running or standing water because Garlon 4 is toxic to aquatic animals. For these areas, they'll have to come back later with Rodeo, a less toxic and also less effective herbicide.

By ten o'clock, we've hiked a mile or so. It's the last day of May, and already the temperature is eighty-five or ninety degrees Fahrenheit. I call that hot; the rangers say it's just good hiking weather. I keep downing water to keep from dehydrating. Still, at 3,500 feet, we're in high desert; it's probably ten degrees cooler here than in the lowlands around Borrego Springs. Except for the smell of diesel fuel emanating from the rangers' backpacks, this could be just another pleasant nature walk. Lupines are still blooming here, though the wildflower show in the low desert finished a month ago. On the slopes leading away from stream banks, barrel and cholla cacti thrive, and on the ridges hundreds of feet above us, I spot the first junipers and pinyon pines. Near the streambed, there is room for other small trees such as desert apricot and catclaw acacia. Hawks soar in the sky, and an occasional raven flaps its wings. Even while Jorgensen is working, his senses are attuned to these signs of wildlife. Earlier, he spotted the print of a mountain lion in a muddy spot in the creek bed. The impression was as big as my fist.

Jorgensen has hiked, worked, and lived in and around Anza-Borrego for much of his life. Even as a boy, he would have his older brother drive him over from their home in San Diego so he could explore the park's canyons and peaks. He loves the place with the passion of a man who knows it better than almost anyone.

Before our trip up the canyon, he told me, "We're supposed to be out here hugging bunnies and feeling ferns, but instead we're spraying tamarisk with weed killer."

Person laughed at that. "I don't think I've hugged one bunny since I've been working for Mark."

In his head, Jorgensen carries two pictures. One is a view of the way he'd like to see this canyon someday: filled with the scent of blooming willows and the sound of wind rustling through cottonwood leaves, a home for the desert bighorn and least Bell's vireo, both endangered species. The other picture is bleaker, the future of these canyons if nothing is done to stop the tamarisk. Back in his office, he has an actual photograph of that future, an image that explains his willingness to spray Garlon 4 and diesel fuel in the wilderness. The photograph shows a stretch of the Colorado River 100 miles east of here. The riverbanks are covered with nothing but tamarisk. One surviving cottonwood pokes its head above the sea of salt cedar like a drowning victim going down for the last time. Considering that possibility, Jorgensen is willing to take his chances.

TAMARISK was first imported into the United States from Europe as an ornamental plant in the early nineteenth century. Some varieties can grow as tall as a good-sized eucalyptus, but the largest we'll see today is about twenty feet tall. Early in the twentieth century, ranchers in the Southwest planted tamarisk for shade, windbreaks, and stream bank consolidation. It began to spread rapidly across the region in the 1940s. Jorgensen said he guesses that tamarisk entered Coyote Canyon along with cattle feed, or maybe with the cattle themselves, because the shrub was never intentionally planted here. But he doesn't seem concerned with fixing blame for the tamarisk invasion. All those actions are far in the past, and now the only enemy is the tamarisk itself.

Since the 1940s, the shrublike tree has spread over more than a million acres, converting native riparian (streamside) areas to virtual monocultures. It has spread as far north as Oregon and Idaho and as far east as

Nebraska. It lives below sea level and, in the southern Rocky Mountains, at elevations as high as 7,000 feet. After cutting or burning, it grows right back, and it can survive as long as seventy days of total submergence.

Even in its home range, tamarisk is aggressive. The genus originated in India and the Middle East. From those two areas, it spread east to China and Japan and west to Africa and Europe. It's uniquely suited for colonizing riparian areas, especially those that have been disturbed. It grows as much as ten feet in a year, or two inches in a day.

Tamarisk is very efficient at taking water in but not very efficient at using it. Researchers can't agree on exactly how much water a mature tree uses, but 200 gallons per day is one estimate. Stands of tamarisk can dry up desert springs and seeps on which cottonwoods and wildlife depend, turn a perennial stream into a dry gulch, and even change the direction in which underground water flows. Perversely, even though tamarisk uses a lot of water, it can survive long periods of drought. Its native competitors are much better at water conservation, but they need a constant water supply.

Another weapon in tamarisk's arsenal is its ability to tolerate salinity. The tree passes the salt out to its leaves. When these drop to the ground, they create a salt crust around the tree's base, discouraging the growth of non-salt-tolerant natives.

But tamarisk's biggest weapon is its prodigious seed production—a single plant will produce as many as half a million tiny, almost weightless seeds per year. And it starts producing these seeds almost from its first moment of life. It just pokes its head up through the salty, sandy soil and puts out a few branches. Soon, one of those branches is covered with small pink flowers. On our trip to Horse Canyon today, we see several of these foot-high plants, probably just a month or two old, with four-inch sprays of tiny blossoms. Cottonwood and willow, on the other hand, take years to reach seed-bearing age. They're dioecious, meaning that male flowers are borne on separate plants from female flowers, so only about half the trees produce seeds, whereas every plant of the monoecious tamarisk produces seeds of its own. Tamarisk can also reproduce vegetatively: a stem broken off in a flood, for example, roots quickly if it comes to rest on moist sand. Cottonwood and willow can do the same thing but not as readily as tamarisk.

With all these advantages, tamarisk seems ideally equipped to create

monocultures. On a trip to the Dead Sea basin, that's exactly what Jorgensen found. "I had expected there would be a diversity of natives, like we find in a riparian area here," he says. Instead, the Dead Sea resembled the lower Colorado River: nothing but tamarisk.

The tamarisk invasion might not be so significant if it provided good habitat for native wildlife. Because it's an exotic, though, native animals don't make much use of it. Deer and bighorn sheep find little nourishment in tamarisk's tiny, scalelike leaves. Until recently, ecologists thought it made a poor home for birds. One study carried out on the lower Colorado River found that 100 acres of native vegetation supported 154 bird species, whereas 100 acres of tamarisk supported only 4. Dense tamarisk stands contain little in the way of food for birds: no fruit, no edible seeds, and few insects (though the latter point has since been challenged). Riparian bird habitat in the Southwest is especially important because more than 40 percent of native bird species depend on it. As good native habitat is replaced by poor tamarisk habitat, these species are pushed to the edge of extinction.

We're used to thinking about balance in nature—for every critter or shrub that's likely to overrun the planet, there's another shrub or critter that preys on it or competes with it, keeping it in check. For every elk herd, there's a pack of wolves; for every run of salmon, a family of grizzlies. And we're used to thinking that humans are the ones who upset this delicate balance—we wipe out the wolves and the elk population goes through the roof, or we wipe out both the grizzlies and the salmon. But a tree like tamarisk seems to defy these easy classifications. What was nature thinking when it created such a formidable plant?

Nature, of course, wasn't thinking anything. Random permutations happen; some succeed and others fail. At one time, ecologists thought that the process of evolution, if left alone, led to balance and diversity. It was supposed to work like one of those noncompetitive games the people in Outward Bound play, the ones in which no side wins. But increasingly, ecologists are discovering that nature often works more like a Monopoly game, in which one player ends up with all the real estate. Evolution can lead just as easily to species that wipe out everything else, creating monocultures instead of diversity.

This is the "devil theory" of tamarisk, the idea that it is an almost invin-

cible invader with malicious intent. Some researchers reject this idea, though, pointing out that tamarisk could never have spread so widely without human help. This is probably true on rivers that have been dammed. The new flood regime—the timing of high and low water— favors tamarisk over natives adapted to spring flooding. Ecologist Bertin Anderson questions earlier tamarisk research, holding that it overstated the shrub's water consumption and underestimated the number and amount of insects it harbored. He opposes the removal of tamarisk from dammed rivers because these habitats may no longer be able to support native species. Even a stand of tamarisk provides some ecological value compared with bare ground, which, he believes, may be the alternative.

Anza-Borrego's canyons have never been dammed, and tamarisk has done well there. Jorgensen believes that any disturbance, natural or human caused, will give tamarisk an advantage. "I call 'em catastrophes, whether they're fires or floods or droughts," he says. "They all favor tamarisk." In the case of Coyote Canyon, Jorgensen believes that natural flooding was the principal disturbance that let tamarisk get a foothold. In discrete, undammed canyons such as Coyote Canyon and Horse Canyon, removing the tamarisk can revive native species. Jorgensen's earliest success came in Borrego Palm Canyon, which now supports healthy stands of willow, alder, and cottonwood as well as of palm. Another success story is the Coachella Valley Preserve, near Palm Springs, where restoration-ist Cameron Barrows noticed such immediate benefits from tamarisk removal as the replenishment of once-dry pools, revival of near-dead cottonwoods, an additional kilometer of year-round creek flow, and an abundance of new species: six kinds of lizard, two of sparrow, and three of rodent, as well as the yellow-breasted chat.

Such evidence leads Jorgensen to believe that tamarisk removal, though an expensive, ongoing task, is vital for the health of these desert canyons. It's not that he is without qualms about the implications of invasive management in areas designated as wilderness. He worries about the effects of herbicides on the stream environments where they are applied. "It's a two-edged sword," he says. "Twenty years from now, we may find that Garlon has damaged these riparian areas. But the alternative is to wait for the tamarisk to wipe out all the native growth in the canyon."

The potential for damage from friendly fire in this war against the

tamarisk is real, though hard to measure. Accidental spraying of a native species is a concern, but a greater danger is the chance that Garlon 4 will linger in the environment longer than expected. The herbicide is supposed to break down quickly in soil, but some research suggests that minute amounts could persist for as long as two years. If a heavy thunderstorm hits Horse Canyon this summer, the remnants of today's spraying could wash down into the pools where tadpoles live. Unless the water is tested at just the right time, there is no way to know exactly how much Garlon 4 is actually entering these streams. Beyond that, there is debate over how much risk these tiny amounts—parts per million and even parts per billion—pose. (Diesel fuel, which helps transport the herbicide directly through the trees' bark, is also toxic. Jorgensen is exploring alternative surfactants, and his crews have begun using a tool called a weed wrench, which pulls entire plants out of the ground, avoiding the use of chemicals entirely.)

Another risky approach to tamarisk removal is biological control. Biologists have studied two insects that feed on tamarisk in its home territory in Asia and the Middle East and are prepared to release them in the United States. Although the insects would have no toxic effects, what would happen if they start feeding on native species here? Researchers have investigated this question and found little threat to native species, but Murphy's law would seem to have a wide application here. The release was held up temporarily, for another reason: the endangered southwestern willow flycatcher has begun nesting in tamarisk, giving this exotic species some ecological value in its new environment. The U.S. Fish and Wildlife Service withheld approval of the biological control for several years out of concern that it might be too successful against the tamarisk and natives might not take its place.

Proponents of biological control point out that the insects wouldn't wipe out all the tamarisk but would reduce its competitive advantage over native species. With "natural" competitors keeping it in check, tamarisk would take another step toward becoming "naturalized" in North America. How long does a species need to live in a new place before it is considered part of the native community? Bighorn sheep, after all, are thought to have come across the Bering land bridge only a little more than 10,000 years ago. The use of biological controls would let tamarisk become just

another member of a diverse community instead of the biological jugger-
naut it is now. And that's really the goal of all preservation efforts—to preserve not a single species but a diverse community of species.

As with most environmental issues, eliminating these kinds of risks
entirely is no longer a possibility; we're in too deep for that. Instead, Jorgensen had to weigh two kinds of risk in deciding whether to spray the
tamarisk, just as the U.S. Fish and Wildlife Service had to do in approv-
ing release of the exotic insects. The problem is that we don't know how
to measure such risks against one another. If the park stopped spraying
Garlon 4, the stream life would be safe from toxic effects, but the bighorn
sheep and the least Bell's vireo wouldn't be safe as long as tamarisk continues to dominate these canyons. How much are we willing to risk to
return Coyote Canyon to a more diverse, healthy condition? Despite the
input of science, it's really just a crapshoot.

SPRAYING of weed killer in the wilderness isn't the only intensive management regime Jorgensen has pursued in Anza-Borrego. After we picked
up Person early in the morning, the rangers paused to check traps that
had been set for cowbirds, exotic nest robbers that displace native birds.
The traps were empty. In the 1980s, Jorgensen oversaw the removal of
cattle from the park in an innovative helicopter netting operation. Next,
he wants to remove Coyote Canyon's horses—he calls them feral, but
local horse people call them wild. And at one time he wanted to reintro-
duce the locally extinct desert pronghorn, but range experts found that
there was too little grassland left in Anza-Borrego to support a herd. Jorgensen says the goal of these efforts is not to return the park to some
imagined perfect past but to restore the desert's natural processes.

The most intensively managed native species in the park is the Peninsular bighorn, whose numbers have been declining for decades. Tamarisk
control is part of the effort to maintain the sheep's habitat, but Jorgensen
has taken more direct measures to monitor and protect the bighorn. Park
staff members, along with researchers from the University of California,
Davis, began a radio-collaring program in the early 1990s to track bighorn
numbers. They netted the sheep from helicopters, tested them for disease, experimented with inoculations, placed radio collars around their
necks, and built watering devices known as "sheep guzzlers."

Spraying herbicide in the wilderness; capturing, studying, and even treating wild animals; reintroducing locally extinct species—these are the hallmarks and contradictions of ecological restoration. What kind of wilderness is left when we become so deeply involved in managing it? Are we just playing the role of God—and not even an omniscient god but a god who rolls dice to decide which species live and which ones die? Some argue that this kind of management is just another way of destroying wilderness. We've done enough to disrupt nature, this line of thinking goes; now we should just leave it alone.

In *The Abstract Wild*, Jack Turner argues that leaving the wilderness alone is exactly what we should do, though he puts a new spin on this familiar argument. Drawing on poststructuralist and chaos theories, he argues that the biological sciences are mired in a mechanistic worldview, obsessed with quantification and abstraction and, ultimately, with exertion of control over nature. Biologists, he says, are like emergency room physicians, using invasive medicine to treat the symptoms of disease instead of solving the root problems—in this case, overpopulation, overconsumption, and capitalism. Scientific management, in this view, runs the risk of killing the patient in order to save it, removing what little wildness is left in wild places—another "end of nature." Worse, the world is too chaotic and complex for these attempts at control to be successful. Turner concludes: "The 'preservation as management' tradition that began with [Aldo] Leopold is finished because there is little reason to trust the experts to make intelligent long-range decisions about nature." His solution is to "let whatever habitat we can preserve go back to its own self-order as much as possible. Let wilderness again become a blank on our maps."

Turner is certainly one of the smartest and most passionate thinkers about these issues, and much of what he says is spot on. But I think he makes a wrong turn, and it's in that phrase about wilderness as a "blank on our maps." *Whose* maps? This is the view of Christopher Columbus, of Daniel Boone, of Lewis and Clark, of the conquistadores. To its indigenous peoples, North America was not a blank but a known place. Turner admits as much, and he seems to contradict himself when he says that wilderness should not be defined by human absence or even the absence of human influence. Instead, he distinguishes between human influence and human control and points out that many native peoples influenced

the land in ways that let it follow its own principles of organization, that let it remain "self-willed land."

This is the crux move of Turner's argument, and a much more sophisticated definition of wilderness than the old one of a place where "man is a visitor who does not remain." But he doesn't follow it up. Where should we draw the line between influence and control? The Cahuilla and the Kumeyaay, like all people, also sought control over what they saw as a chaotic and unpredictable environment. They pursued control through both ritual and concrete actions such as controlled burning. The difference is that like many native peoples, they had the humility to know that absolute control is impossible—the kind of humility Turner wants contemporary biologists to feel.

Turner's attack on the biological sciences seems overly harsh. These disciplines have, after all, shown us the importance of biodiversity and the dangers associated with its loss. But now, awed and frightened and sickened by our own too-successful control of nature, should we shy away from playing any role in nature at all? Does the source of our knowledge in mechanistic or classical science mean that any given action we might take is bad? Or can we choose actions that "fit" self-willed land, that intensify natural processes, as the Cahuilla and the Kumeyaay sought to do?

Cutting and spraying the tamarisk is not too different from what the Cahuilla and the Kumeyaay did for millennia. Granted, the Indians never used herbicides, but their actions favored some species over others. Through burning, they chose game animals over chaparral and palms over cottonwoods. Today, we choose cottonwoods and willows and bighorn sheep over tamarisk.

We don't need sophisticated computer modeling or other kinds of technological information to tell us that something is wrong with a monoculture of tamarisk. Turner celebrates chaos, complexity, and dynamism as a kind of wildness, but there is little complexity or dynamism in these stands of a single species. Land overrun by a monoculture is no longer self-willed land—we have performed a kind of accidental control by loosing tamarisk on native species. By cutting and spraying the tamarisk, the rangers are liberating the land and its indigenous inhabitants. Instead of controlling the land, they are functioning as agents of chaos, of wildness.

Where Turner sees wildness disappearing, others see an opportunity

for humans to play a productive role in nature, a rarity in a time when much of what we do is destructive. John Rodman, environmental studies professor at Pitzer College in Claremont, California, and a volunteer in the tamarisk control efforts at the Coachella Valley Preserve, argues that those involved with ecological restoration become more than "mere esthetes entranced by pretty pink flowers . . . mere bird watchers or backpackers who pass like angelic, incorporeal tourists leaving no trace upon the land." Experiences of restoration can teach "what it feels like to participate once again as actors in a natural system." We long to be contributing members of a natural community, not estranged neighbors gazing in over a fence marking a wilderness boundary.

If some of these restoration actions are risky, then the concept of biodiversity gives us the best yardstick by which to judge them. Those plants and animals that fill niches in a diverse habitat are "good." A species such as tamarisk isn't bad because it doesn't "belong" or because it's not "wild"; it's bad because it wipes out diversity, the indigenous, the rare, and the unique. As eminent biologist Edward O. Wilson has pointed out, humans have a strong attraction to the variety of life on our planet, a built-in love for wildlife that he calls biophilia. We live in a time of rapid homogenization of life on earth, and as one species after another goes extinct, we lose something of the world's wonder, something of what sustains us spiritually, something of ourselves.

Will humans be able to survive—physically continue as a species—in a world depleted of diversity? It may be that we can. David Quammen, author of the popular, long-running "Natural Acts" column for *Outside* magazine and of the best-selling *Song of the Dodo*, believes that humans will survive the current (and coming) waves of extinction along with the planet's other "weedy" (rapidly reproducing and hard-to-kill) species. We may suffer spiritual death, a death of wonder, but we'll survive physically just fine, along with the tamarisk, cockroaches, and rats. But other observers aren't so sure. In pioneering work conducted at Cedar Creek Natural History Area in Minnesota, ecologist David Tilman has shown that biologically diverse grassland plots are more productive and recover from drought faster than do less diverse ones. This was one of the first studies to show that diversity has the benefits that many people have long suspected.

Mark Jorgensen makes the same argument for the desert. A community of diverse species, he believes, is more resistant to the inevitable catastrophes—disease, fire, floods, wind—than is a monoculture, such as one of tamarisk. And diversity doesn't necessarily mean stasis, stability, or even balance; it may require a dynamic landscape of "shifting mosaics," created by those very same events Jorgensen calls catastrophes. It is unclear how these theories based on patches of grassland or particular desert canyons translate to the level of human beings and to the entire planet. How many strands can we pull out of the web of life—desert bighorn sheep, Sumatran tigers, cutthroat trout, least Bell's vireos—before the whole thing falls apart, taking us with it? We may be about to find out. We face a seriously depleted future or, perhaps, no future at all.

PERSON breaks open a packet of salsa-flavored sunflower seeds and offers me a handful. I accept, wondering what to do with the shells. She and Jorgensen crunch on the seeds and then spit out the shells on the sandy streambed. I'm shocked by this flagrant violation of the "leave only footprints, take only memories" ethic drilled into me by outings with the Sierra Club. But I figure that if the rangers are doing it, why shouldn't I? Compared with the concoction they are spraying on the tamarisk, a few sunflower shells seem like peanuts. I follow their example.

A secondary goal of today's mission is to assess the casualties of the spraying done last fall. How many of the sprayed shrubs died, and how many grew back? How many new seedlings will they find in the canyon? As we continue, the damage report isn't encouraging. Many of the tamarisks are dead, but some—more than the rangers expected—have survived the previous spraying. On that trip, Person and another worker ran out of spray before reaching their target. Now Jorgensen counsels her to conserve her ammo for the mother of all trees. He has trouble following his own advice, though. In one place, new tamarisk seedlings make a carpet like a lawn on the gravel creek bed. Soon, he's spraying even the smallest seedlings. He keeps asking me how much juice he has left.

As we move farther upstream, the canyon narrows. We enter an area of reddish soil; where water runs here, it has the same rust-red color. In places, the banks below the high-water mark are covered with saline deposits. I wonder whether these are deposits from tamarisk. The studies

I've read suggest that only the area near the tree would have a saline crust. Perhaps the trees do well in this canyon because it is already somewhat salty.

As we round a bend in the canyon, we come to a single tamarisk about twenty feet tall, the largest we've seen so far. This one had been sprayed last time, and now it's dead. Buoyed by this victory as well as by the lightened loads they're carrying, the rangers forge ahead. They ignore all the little tamarisks now, their minds set on getting to that last big one. Between them, they have less than a quart of spray left.

Finally, we reach the tree they've been after. Seeing it is a little anticlimactic—it's just one more big salt cedar. The rangers go to work on it, soaking its wide base with the last of the spray. Mission accomplished, Jorgensen lights another cigar, and we start back downstream. Person talks about her plans to drive into San Diego tonight to see *Hello, Dolly!* starring Carol Channing. The heat has sapped my energy, and I just want to go soak my feet in the pool up in Palm Canyon.

"How'd we miss that bastard?" Jorgensen exclaims suddenly. He's pointing to another huge tamarisk up on the stream bank. It's at least as big as the mother of all trees, and it's covered in flowers. With their backpack sprayers empty, there's nothing the rangers can do about it. This one will have to wait for another expedition. By then, it may have seeded out, producing hundreds of new seedlings downstream. Those will have to be sprayed, too.

Jorgensen and Person may have won one battle, but the war seems to go on forever.

THIRD GROVE:
BATTLE FOR
THE BIGHORN

T HE START of the 1997 Fourth of July bighorn sheep count at Anza-Borrego Desert State Park is not auspicious. It's seven o'clock in the morning, and my partner, Carl, and I have just arrived at our count site, a large boulder above Third Grove in Borrego Palm Canyon. The first thing we notice is a scatter of bones and tan hide under a slight overhang of the rock. I find another bone or two a short distance away. By the size of the bones, it's a small animal, and the hide looks like sheep— probably one of this year's lambs. We wonder what got it. Coyotes? A bobcat? Or perhaps one of the mountain lions that seem particularly numerous in these parts recently?

Mark Jorgensen, who organizes the annual sheep count, warned us that most lambs don't survive their first few months of life, falling prey to disease, predators, heat, drought, or a combination thereof. How many have actually survived their first three to five months? This is one of the questions the sheep count seeks to answer, beyond that of the simple trend in the number of sheep. How many lambs are there for every ewe? How many yearlings have survived their first full summer? By keeping track of the age and sex of every sheep we see coming down to drink at this water hole, we can help provide the answers to these questions, and to the ultimate question: are the Peninsular bighorn sheep, now recognized as a distinct subspecies of *Ovis canadensis*, on their way to recovery or moving further toward extinction?

In recent years, the number of sheep spotted at these annual counts has been down, as it has been on helicopter surveys operated by the California Department of Fish and Game (DFG). After the 1996 survey, Jorgensen and others estimated that there were 280 bighorns left in the Peninsular Ranges north of Mexico. This year, the second of two years of little rainfall, Jorgensen expects the count to be down even further. We're not keeping track of dead sheep, but the remains of this lamb are one data point that tends to confirm Jorgensen's suspicion.

Still, we are less dismayed by this finding than we could be. Early yesterday evening, on our way to our count site, we came across a band of eleven or twelve sheep at First Grove—three adult rams with half-curl horns, a yearling ram, several ewes, and two lambs. We didn't bother tallying them precisely because this wasn't our site. Instead, we just observed. Accustomed to the heavy foot traffic to First Grove, they showed no sign of bolting as we drew to within twenty-five yards of the boulder pile where they perched in safety. They did have a curious look about them, as if wondering who were these strange visitors who kept holding odd black instruments up to their eyes. Of course, you can't judge a sheep by its facial expression. Researchers suspect that even though bighorns can seem calm and alert when approached by humans, they may be experiencing great stress.

Most photographs of bighorn sheep show an adult ram, often the Rocky Mountain variety, with a three-quarter or full curl to its horns, a deep chest, and stout haunches, posed on a rock against the sky. Desert bighorns are not as large or as stout, and the ewes are more spindly still, with short, flared horns describing perhaps a quarter circle, elongated faces, and thin legs and necks. The rams appear to be lords of all they survey, but the ewes seem somehow out of place here in the desert environment, too dainty, almost otherworldly. Perhaps because nature photographers have made me accustomed to the appearance of the rams, the ewes have always seemed to me like strange beings.

As we set up our shade tarp and settle in for a long day of scanning the rocky slopes, I'm confident that we'll see more sheep today. Armed with lunch, a gallon of water each, Carl's spotting scope, binoculars, aluminum folding chairs, and spray bottles filled with water to keep us cool, we're all set. Carl, a middle-aged lawyer, has been doing the sheep count for eleven

years now, though he's hardly in shape for summer backpacking in the desert. Struggling up the canyon yesterday, he kept saying, "I don't know why I do this—just for fun, I guess."

He seems to know what he's doing, though, when it comes to searching for sheep. The spot he's picked gives us a broad view up and down the canyon and up a drainage coming in from the north. I rig the shade tarp away from the rock so we can go out and scan the slopes behind us.

At eight o'clock, the sun rises over the eastern canyon wall and pounds its first rays at us. The sun will blast us all morning, but we should have some shade after noon, when the temperature will hit 115 degrees Fahrenheit or so. It's no accident that Jorgensen holds the count at water holes during the hottest time of year—it's the only sure way to know where the sheep will be. The sheep often drink twice daily but can go as long as two days without drinking, if necessary. Counting for three days, we should see most of the sheep that use the creek below us at least once. We're supposed to stay up here, away from the water, from seven in the morning to five in the afternoon. Our best chances of seeing the sheep are in early morning and late afternoon, but we need to scan the hillsides with binoculars or spotting scope virtually all day. We settle down and wait for the sheep.

THE DESERT bighorn, *borrego cimarrón* to the Spanish, is the most visible and popular symbol of wildness in Anza-Borrego Desert State Park and probably in southern California. The park is best known for its spring wildflowers, its most popular attraction, but it was created largely to preserve the bighorn. Not only does it include the animal in its name; it also uses its image in most of its publications.

In the early 1800s, several thousand desert bighorn sheep are thought to have roamed the Peninsular Ranges down to the tip of Baja California. Those numbers declined rapidly on both sides of the border but especially in the United States, mainly as a result of hunting and livestock grazing. The construction of Interstate 8 in the 1960s and poaching in northern Baja California seem to have cut off the U.S. population of Peninsular bighorns from their more numerous relatives south of the border. As recently as 1978, 1,200 bighorns remained in the Peninsular Ranges north of the border. But by 1994, that number had dropped to about 350, with

275 inhabiting Anza-Borrego itself and the remainder spread through the Santa Rosa Mountains north to San Jacinto. By 1996, the total number had declined further, to 280 for the entire range.

The principal causes for the decline through the 1980s seem to be three: loss of habitat, mostly from golf course and housing construction at the lower edge of sheep habitat; fragmentation of habitat by roads and highways; and respiratory diseases the bighorns picked up from domestic sheep and cattle. Normally, only about one-third of bighorn lambs survive their first year, but disease reduced that survival rate to about 10 percent—too few to maintain the species.

In the early 1990s, with bighorn numbers plummeting, biologists at the University of California at Davis, the Bighorn Institute, and the DFG began an intensive research program. The program included radio-collaring more than 100 sheep as well as checking them for disease. From 1993 to 1995, the researchers attempted to observe each radio-collared sheep on the ground at least once each month. The study was renewed in 1998, when 25 additional sheep were collared. Researchers also placed automatic-trip cameras at several water holes to document use.

The study yielded some interesting and surprising results. The animals were heartier and healthier than previously thought. According to Jorgensen, a band of sheep in the Vallecito Mountains near Whale Peak seems never to visit any known water source. He theorizes that these sheep survive on the liquid they get from barrel cacti (they gain access to the pulpy insides by knocking the tops off with their horns). During summer, the sheep move to the cooler elevations of the highest summits, where the temperature seldom exceeds 100 degrees. Even more surprising, respiratory diseases had subsided throughout much of the bighorn's range by the early 1990s. With good rain years and healthy sheep, the population should have rebounded, yet it had declined further. Why? The answer to this question was the most surprising of all.

The transmitters in the sheep's collars were designed to emit a "mortality signal" if the device and its bearer remained stationary for too long. Whenever the researchers picked up a mortality signal, they would do what they call a "walk-in"—hike to the signal's source. Sometimes the collar had simply fallen off the sheep; more often, it came with a dead sheep attached. In 70 percent of the sheep deaths in Anza-Borrego, mountain

lions were the culprits, as demonstrated by paw prints, drag marks, and attempts at covering the carcass. Over the two years of the study, thirty radio-collared sheep were killed by mountain lions. Only one-quarter of the sheep had been collared, so it's likely that more than 100 sheep had been killed in this manner, out of a total population of about 400.

This was brand-new information. Mountain lions had certainly been known to prey on sheep, but at nothing like this level. *The Desert Bighorn,* the bible on the animal, published in 1980, listed mountain lions second to bobcats among the sheep's feline predators. The big cats had been thought to stay in territory with a higher density of game such as deer, not to poach in desert areas, where game is relatively sparse. But by the 1990s, something had changed. California voters had banned sport hunting of the big cats in 1972, and the lion population had increased dramatically since that time. Conflicts between humans and lions had also increased, with two fatal attacks in California in the mid-1990s, several nonfatal attacks, and numerous lion sightings in the suburbs (which before being developed had been backcountry lion habitat, a fact that leads researchers to suggest that habitat loss may have caused the changes in lion behavior and demographics). In recent years, mountain lions have taken up permanent residence in the desert itself, an area where previously they were only visitors. Jorgensen tells me there's a mountain lion living at Middle Willows right now.

Instead of rebounding after respiratory diseases subsided, as the theory of natural regulation would predict, the number of Peninsular bighorns has been kept low by a sudden increase in the number of mountain lions and a change in their eating habits. Jorgensen is careful to point out that the situation is complex, with numerous interrelated factors such as habitat loss, forage and water loss, disease, drought, and predation all interacting to reduce the sheep population. But scientists studying mountain lions and bighorns agree that predation is a significant factor. Ironically, after so much disturbance by humans, it may be the mountain lion that finally does in the bighorn.

In 1998, the U.S. Fish and Wildlife Service listed the Peninsular bighorn as endangered (it was already considered threatened by the state of California). The listing was a sad milestone for the bighorn population, but it puts teeth into efforts to protect the animal's habitat from develop-

ment and road building. It could bring more money from the federal government for bighorn and perhaps mountain lion research, as well as greater cooperation from federal agencies such as the Bureau of Land Management (BLM). The U.S. Fish and Wildlife Service, along with Jorgensen and other bighorn experts, is developing a conservation plan and a precise habitat map that will chart terrain, vegetation, and water sources.

Perhaps all this will turn things around for the bighorn, or maybe it's too late. The Peninsular Ranges, following at least a dozen other mountain ranges in California, could be the next to lose its bighorns, making the mountains one degree more lonely. But this particular population of *borrego* has induced a higher level of human concern. If writer Jack Turner is right in likening wildlife management to invasive medicine, then the Peninsular bighorn has just arrived in the emergency room. Now we'll see what heroic measures will be necessary to save it.

IT'S SUNDAY morning. We've spent three days waiting for the sheep, and so far they've failed to show. Now, with just a few hours left, we're beginning to lose hope. It seems we've examined every rock and cactus and brittlebush on the slopes across from us and up and down the canyon for a mile in either direction. We've spotted numerous "rock sheep" and "cactus sheep," those shapes in the distance that at first glance look like bighorns but turn out to be something else. We've squinted through binoculars and spotting scope for so long that we both have headaches behind the eyes, as well as aching necks and backs from craning our necks into odd positions. But still no sheep.

I'm not convinced that they've left the area—maybe we haven't been looking in the right spots or haven't been looking persistently enough, or maybe neither of us would recognize a sheep at this distance if we saw it. Last year, I spent a day of the sheep count with Esther Rubin, a graduate student from the University of California, Davis, who was studying the bighorns. We saw ten or eleven sheep that day, and Rubin saw every one of them first. After years of scanning distant slopes for bighorns, her eyes had become accustomed to the way a sheep looks when viewed through a spotting scope at distances of as much as a mile. I wish that Rubin and her trained eyes were here with us now.

After two days of blistering heat, I'm beginning to lose enthusiasm for

the whole project. People will tell you that once the thermometer climbs above 100, it all feels the same. They are wrong. I've baked as I've hiked in this oven of a canyon in early June, but now the desert is turned up to broil. During the hottest part of the day, the shade of the palms and alders and cottonwoods below us beckons like Circe. Only an act of will keeps me from descending to the water hole and splashing in.

The first day was the hardest. By now, I imagine I'm getting somewhat adapted. I keep my spritz bottle going most of the day and drink a liter of water mixed with electrolytes every couple of hours. I don't eat much—the heat saps my appetite. Mostly I just sit, moving occasionally to hug the shifting shade, to stretch, or to scan the slopes on the sunny side of the rock.

The best time is the first hour, before the sun rises over the canyon wall at eight o'clock, hitting us like a hammer. In that cool morning light, everything is clearly illuminated—all the rocks look just like rocks, the cacti just like cacti. Then, for an hour after the sun rises, staring at the slopes east of us is useless; all detail dissolves in the glare. Later, with the sun rising higher, the cacti begin imitating sheep—or maybe it's the sun warping our minds.

At five o'clock, when we can finally descend from our perch, even the tepid, algae-clotted water is refreshing as it hits my skin. Pumped through a water filter, it tastes fresh and cool compared with the hot liquid left in my bottle. With only two inches of rain having fallen this year and two and a half last year, the pool is only a couple of feet deep, the lowest Carl has seen it in his years of coming here. So far, Jorgensen seems to be right in his prediction of a low sheep count, at least here at Third Grove.

Despite the heat and the lack of sheep, there are a few rewards for spending time at a desert water hole in July. In the pool itself, I've noticed a form of life I've never seen in cooler months: water beetles diving into the pool and a walking stick, which climbs onto my boot as I pump water. And yesterday, from up at our count site, I heard a bird singing like a meadowlark. The sound was coming from one of the palms, and soon I spotted a yellow-and-black shape flashing among the green fronds. It turned out to be a Scott's oriole, a summer visitor here from Mexico and new to me.

To while away the rest of the time, Carl regales me with stories. He

tells me about clever lawyer tricks he's pulled during lawsuits, about Burns night and drinking Scotch with members of the local House of Scotland. Mostly he tells me about his avocation, drafting a Civil War history based on old journals and letters he's found as part of his lawyering trade. He spends a few hours each day at his office working on it (part of the luxury of having his own practice), though he has little hope of publishing the manuscript.

As Carl continues the story this morning, I take a break from the binoculars. I'll admit it: I'm demoralized now, and I no longer believe that scanning the slopes rock by rock will do any good. I close my eyes for a moment, open them, and look across the canyon. There, perched on a rock out on the edge of the ridge, silhouetted against the sky in the perfect picture-postcard pose, stands a young ram. He's looking right at us. I gesture to Carl, and he sees him, too. Carl trains his spotting scope on the ram and I go back to my binoculars as the ram heads down and across the slope to the right. He seems to be a yearling (about a year and a half old now because the lambs are born around February). Whispering, we compare notes, making sure this really is a ram, given that young males resemble mature ewes.

Peninsular bighorn sheep

The ram pauses to kick at a barrel cactus; then Carl notices that he's staring across the canyon at the slopes above us. I creep out from behind our rock to see what he's looking at. Another ram is walking across the slope above us, heading up-canyon. With half-curl horns, he's a teenager among sheep. Carl climbs to a slightly different spot and sees another one, this time with the three-quarters curl of a mature ram. The two rams continue up the canyon, walking a little faster now, aware of our presence.

The first young ram decides to follow. But he won't go down into the palm grove directly below us. Instead, he angles back to the left, down, and across the slope to a spot where it becomes sheer. This doesn't faze him. He perches on tiny protuberances in the cliff face, stepping nimbly from one to another. At one spot, he leaps down and across ten feet or so, landing with hooves together on a small shelf. Finally, the cliff ends where the side stream comes in, and he has to descend into the grove. We lose sight of him as he heads upstream through the trees to meet his newfound friends. Meanwhile, they pause just before a bend in the canyon, posing on large boulders as if waiting for him. He joins them, and they all disappear around the corner.

That's it—three days of waiting for sheep and about twenty minutes of actually seeing them. We feel fortunate to have seen that band of sheep on our hike in. We continue scanning the slopes for another hour or so, hoping to see these three coming back or maybe others heading up-canyon. But soon, it's one o'clock and time to leave. We pack our remaining gear quickly, douse ourselves in water from the pool, and head out. We hurry from pool to pool, taking long rests in the shade.

Checking with the rangers, we learn that Jorgensen's prediction was right—the count is low this year. Later, however, when all the numbers are in, Jorgensen will report that the lamb-to-ewe ratio is better than expected. Things look bleak for the bighorn, but there is a glimmer of hope.

ON MY first sheep count, in 1996, Esther Rubin picked out a site above Big Spring on a ridge separating two forks of Tubb Canyon, looking down-canyon to the east. In previous years, counters at this site had positioned themselves too close to the spring and been skunked—the spring is so overgrown that sheep no longer use it. Rubin planned to concentrate

on the slopes of the canyon below us, where the terrain was rocky and open, dotted with brittlebush, grasses, barrel cactus, and agave. Everything behind and above us was covered in a thick stand of sugar bush. We were parked just below the line between desert scrub and chaparral.

To Rubin, that line was like a wall the sheep wouldn't cross. "We don't need to waste our time looking up that way," she told me. "That's good mountain lion cover, and the sheep don't usually go in there." In addition to food and water, the sheep need two things: steep, rocky slopes, known as "escape terrain," and open spaces where they can see predators approaching from far off. We spotted fourteen sheep that day—all of them out on the rocky slopes below us. Jorgensen agrees that bighorns won't go into chaparral. The brush has encroached on what used to be sheep habitat, even since 1967, when he began studying bighorns. Then, he saw forty-two sheep in one day at Fourth Grove. "Now I go there and it doesn't even look like sheep habitat," he said. That change is reflected in the annual counts at that site—zero for most of the 1990s and two in 1997.

If you've followed my argument so far, you may already be putting two and two together. The gears of my brain work slower. But over the years since that sheep count, I've begun putting together my own little grand theory, drawing from the area's environmental history as told by Florence Shipek and from Esther Rubin's and Mark Jorgensen's knowledge of sheep behavior. In a nutshell, it is this: One cause of the decline of the bighorn sheep is our own leave-it-alone-and-put-out-the-fires management of these public lands. The Indians used to burn off the chaparral, *creating* habitat for the bighorn as well as for deer and small game. By failing to continue that management, by viewing the chaparral as what should "naturally" be here and trying to preserve it through fire suppression, we have actually reduced sheep habitat, pushing the sheep farther down toward the desert floor and further toward extinction. In some places, the spread of chaparral may have divided two overlapping groups of bighorns, fragmenting the population even more.

An obvious solution is to start carrying out controlled burns of all the chaparral slopes on the desert side of the mountains, in effect reinstating the indigenous land management practices of the area. Jorgensen says that

controlled burning could be one piece of the puzzle in bringing back the bighorn, but it also poses problems. First, of course, is the safety of homes near potential burn sites; controlled burns in this part of the country tend to get quickly out of control. But a greater problem could be unintended consequences for the sheep. Opening up chaparral areas to new growth of grasses and annuals could pull deer into the area and mountain lions along with them, in turn threatening the bighorn. Burning alone could make matters worse for the sheep.

If they were influencing the landscape to increase the numbers of game animals, the Cahuilla and the Kumeyaay must have had similar problems with predators. What was their solution? Lowell John Bean and Florence Shipek agree that both the Cahuilla and the Kumeyaay occasionally, though not often, killed a mountain lion. Like everything else in their physical environment, the mountain lion had a spirit, and it was regarded as a particularly powerful animal. For this reason, there was a general taboo associated with the killing of mountain lions. But there were exceptions if a particular lion seemed to pose a threat to people. When a hunter encountered a mountain lion, he would warn it to go away before it got hurt. Later, the hunter would come back with a hunting party. If the lion was still around, the hunters would kill it. Because mountain lions are powerful animals, only very powerful hunters could kill them, and they gained more power by virtue of the kill.

Jack Turner will hate me for proposing this, but maybe we need to shoot a few mountain lions to save the sheep. Turner believes that we shouldn't look to the Indians for examples of how to treat predators; rather, we should look to the Juwa Bushmen of Africa, who established what he calls a "peaceful covenant" with lions. But the Indians—at least those in southern California—weren't looking for a peaceful covenant with predators. Instead, they saw them as competitors for resources and as potential sources of danger. Fewer lions meant more game and less danger for people. Today, the presence of fewer mountain lions (or the removal of specific lions that prey on sheep) could improve the bighorn's chances for survival.

This is what park personnel and officials of the U.S. Fish and Wildlife Service are considering in their conservation plan for the bighorn sheep.

They are looking at controlled burns and selective killing of mountain lions that are known to prey on bighorns. Existing law allows the California Department of Fish and Game to kill mountain lions that threaten people or livestock. Jorgensen believes that the law should be amended to include threats to an endangered species as cause for selective shooting of mountain lions. Again, he is careful to point out the complexity of the situation. "Some articles you read lead you to think that if we just killed all the lions, everything would be just rosy. But you still have the problems that brought us to this point in the crisis." Still, Jorgensen says that the scientific working group studying the bighorn situation agrees unanimously that removing specific lions would benefit the bighorns.

This is the kind of management of nature that Jack Turner criticizes. It attempts to control an inherently chaotic, complex situation. It's also a Band-Aid approach—the root causes of sheep depopulation and lion overpopulation have to do with domestic sheep grazing and with houses and golf courses and roads sprawling out into the backcountry. We need to fix those problems, the argument goes, instead of mucking around in a natural relationship between predator and prey. If we can't fix those root problems, then we should live with the consequences of our actions and let nature sort itself out. Better to allow the sheep to go extinct wild and free than to subject them and the mountain lions to our control. Unfortunately, this is like an emergency room closing its doors because most of its patients are victims of deeper problems in society.

Proponents of natural regulation might have equally strong objections to shooting one native species to preserve another. We're no longer talking about removing exotic species such as tamarisks and cowbirds or reintroducing locally extinct species such as wolves, the kinds of management that natural regulation supports. Instead, this is "management by interference," the wildlife management equivalent of an emergency room physician calling for a saw and a rib spreader. If the theory of natural regulation is right, then such intervention is usually not needed. Some dramatic event such as a drought or a sudden increase in lion predation can temporarily reduce the number of sheep, but the population should be able to rebound through higher birthrates and survivorship. Only rarely will a species require drastic measures to ensure its recovery. The question is, When will the situation of the Peninsular bighorn reach that dras-

tic state? Has it already happened with their listing as an endangered species, or do we wait for their numbers to plunge further—down to, say, 100? The Peninsular bighorn is in the emergency room, and we're waiting for someone to give informed consent.

IT'S JUNE 1999, and I'm out destroying the wilderness with a group of people that includes Mark Jorgensen, my friend Dave and eleven other volunteers. Our implements of destruction are shovels and McClouds, the latter a combination hoe and rake used in fire fighting. Five of us hack plants out by the roots, cut down into the crumbling granitic rock with the McClouds, and scrape together loose sand and dirt for fill, working to build a level pad for two 2,500-gallon water tanks. Another group shapes a twenty-five- by twenty-five-foot basin uphill from the tanks and covers it with a black Hypalon tarp. Later, we quarry rock from granitic outcrops to weigh down the tarp against the high winds that hit this saddle. When Jorgensen and the other plumbing experts have connected a drain in the tarp to the tanks, which in turn are piped to a galvanized water trough, we've created a watering system for the bighorns on these eastern slopes of Whale Peak. Seven inches of rain will fill the tanks completely, and the sheep will have a year-round water source, as will the bobcats, foxes, ringtails, mule deer, doves, great horned owls, and quail that have been seen using "guzzlers" like this one.

When I began hiking in this desert, I never thought I would end up killing plants and tearing rocks apart. I remember walking down Arroyo Tapiado with a large rock in my hand when a ranger pulled up and admonished me, "All features are protected." We haven't removed anything, but we've certainly stirred it around, disturbing a 100-foot square of desert. A couple of gardeners among us even take the time to transplant a few of the uprooted agaves and cacti to a nearby hillside.

Some would have it that this is now "fake nature." But as we hike back down to our campsite, I have a feeling of accomplishment and satisfaction. Instead of just observing this place and standing in awe of its silent spaces—themselves necessary, vital activities—I've given something back to the land. I've become more a part of it. Dave mentions the same feeling as we walk down the mountain and again repeatedly on the ride home.

"Giving something back" is also the phrase Mark Jorgensen uses to

describe this effort at restoration. The National Park Service and the BLM (of all agencies) have criticized Jorgensen and the state park for this kind of intrusion into nature. "They're purists, as we try to be," Jorgensen says. "But cattle ranching, mining, roads, and campgrounds have taken a terrible toll on wild waters. We see construction of guzzlers, even in wilderness areas, as payback to the wildlife." Dave McCain Spring, three miles north of here, ran dry shortly after it was piped by the McCain family. Before that, it had been an essential water hole for bighorns and other animals. Jorgensen knows of at least five other water sources here in the Vallecito Mountains that have been lost for wildlife. Building guzzlers like these is a piece of the effort to return the bighorn sheep to a more stable population.

The years since the 1997 count have been up and down for the bighorns. The winter of 1997–1998 brought El Niño to southern California, with heavy rains and warm temperatures. The park recorded 11 inches of rain that year, and the number of sheep was back up in the July count. The numbers improved, too, in the biannual DFG helicopter survey, increasing to 335 from the 280 of 1996. The strong lamb-to-ewe ratio observed in 1997, along with a winter of no freezes and good plant growth, meant that more sheep had survived their first year.

Yet El Niño events don't occur every year, and the winter of 1998–1999 was cool and dry. The previous spring, the floor of the Borrego Valley had been carpeted with wildflowers; in the spring of 1999, there were no flowers, and the director of the Palm Springs Desert Museum was alarmed by an unprecedented lack of birds. Despite this mini-drought, the bighorn count in July showed good lambing numbers and good yearling survival, although mountain lion predation persisted. Jorgensen characterized the bighorn population as "holding steady" for the year.

I ask Jorgensen about his gut feeling regarding the bighorn's chances. His answer is bleak. "Big money is going to win out in a lot of mountain ranges in the Southwest, turning habitat into smaller and smaller islands with golf courses, housing development, highways." In the Peninsular Ranges, big money means Palm Springs and the surrounding communities, where a dozen new golf courses are in the works. But can we hold on to the bighorn population here in Anza-Borrego? "I have every hope we can," he tells me. "I've spent thirty years of my life with that hope in mind,

and obviously I hope we can be successful or I wouldn't have spent that much time and energy. We have made some great inroads. We've designated wilderness. We've put water back in numerous places where it was taken away. We've closed vehicle access into valuable sheep habitat. Right now, much of the park is better off than it was twenty-five years ago. In refuges like Anza-Borrego, we are going to be able to hold on to some remnant populations."

How low do the numbers need to be to make shooting of mountain lions necessary? Scientists argue over minimum viable populations and whether natural regulation really works, but Jorgensen doesn't need science or abstract knowledge or even radio collars to know that the sheep will be better off with fewer mountain lions. He's seen it himself. Once, he followed drag marks into the thicket at Middle Willows and watched as a big lion bounded out of the brush and away. In the thicket, he found a freshly killed ram. With only a few hundred of the sheep scattered over 150 miles of the Peninsular Ranges, he doesn't need to see kills like this too often to know that mountain lions are a threat to the sheep. He knows in his gut that the mountain lion could be the last gasp of the Peninsular bighorn.

"Is wildness less important than biodiversity?" Jack Turner asks. I don't believe it's really a question of one versus the other, but if pushed, I would have to answer yes. Wildness, even the kind Turner talks about, is an abstraction, a feeling that we humans (and not even all humans, just some of us) find important. *Biodiversity* may be an abstract word, but it refers to particular animals, particular plants, particular places. We love these particular canyons in Anza-Borrego, with their variety of desert willows, cottonwoods, alders—and, yes, if they didn't take over the whole place, even tamarisks. It is these particular sheep, not an abstract idea of endangered species, that we love and want to save.

In his argument for human influence and against control, Turner made the distinction between human actions that come from "inside" the logic of the land and those that are "external controls." He rejected abstract knowledge of wildness or wildlife in favor of personal, local knowledge. He wrote, "I want to know and care about the grizzly that lives in the canyon above me," rather than grizzlies in general. This reminds me of Mark Jorgensen. He knows and cares about these specific bighorn sheep

living in the canyons above his home in Borrego Springs, and his knowledge comes from more than thirty years of close contact with the landscape.

Underneath Jorgensen's park service bureaucrat facade, underneath the man who can get along with the off-roaders whose sons play Little League with his own sons, beats the heart of a wild-eyed environmental radical. He met Edward Abbey once, and the grand old patriarch of modern environmentalism called him southern California's Hayduke, after the eco-saboteur in Abbey's *Monkey Wrench Gang*. Now, Jorgensen would never tell me this, and I haven't asked him about it, but I can imagine him—if pushed to it, if the sheep got close enough to the edge—taking matters into his own hands. At some point, it may be all he can do to keep from going up Coyote Canyon and shooting a mountain lion or two.

CAMPO:
REIMAGINING
ANCIENT TRADITIONS

A GREAT blue heron flaps its way down Diabold Creek on the Campo Indian Reservation, its gray-blue underside blending with the blue sky above. Across the valley, a meadowlark is singing. Closer at hand, a red-tailed hawk perches on a telephone pole, waiting smugly for a rodent to dart across the open ground below. The valley lies between low, chaparral-covered hills dotted with granitic boulders that shimmer in the warmth of June. In the silence between birdsongs, the land seems to hum like a tuning fork responding to the vibrations of the universe.

At this spot, the creek runs through an overgrazed meadow of scattered sagebrush and short, non-native grasses already dry by this first day of summer. The stream itself lies fifteen feet below steep cutbanks, the result of flooding in the 1990s and a change in stream course caused by mistakes at the tribal sand and gravel operation just a quarter mile upstream. A few tamarisk shrubs cling to the eroded banks. But a short distance downstream, the spot where that heron was headed, the landscape changes. The valley becomes lush with willows, cottonwoods, and dense growths of reeds. Red-winged blackbirds flit about in the vibrant greenery.

Such an oasis seems out of place in the dry San Diego backcountry, so overused by cattle grazing and other abuses. Just five years ago, the creek was little more than a dry ditch that flowed a few weeks out of the year, the result of years of grazing leases that earned the tribe a few thousand dol-

lars per year. Now it's a year-round stream, thanks to the efforts of the reservation's Campo Environmental Protection Agency (CEPA) to restore it to something like its historical condition. The project blended modern technology with traditional Kumeyaay approaches, including a small pond and the kind of small-scale damming and erosion control techniques the Kumeyaay practiced for centuries. As with those earlier practices, the goal of this project is to hold the water on the land.

The water table along Diabold Creek is now rising, and the wetland area is pushing farther upstream each year. Wildlife is returning to the area. David Singleton, tribal planner and my guide for the day, mentions that deer have been spotted in an area from which they had vanished long ago; along the way, we spot raccoon tracks in the mud. The new wetland produces a greater variety of medicinal herbs, basketry materials, and building materials than it did before, providing supplies for Kumeyaay people who follow traditional practices. That may be the ultimate revival of this restoration effort: a piece of Kumeyaay culture.

The traditional rock alignments, those sediment-trapping and water-slowing devices Florence Shipek says the Kumeyaay were using when the Spanish arrived, were one of the main things I wanted to see today. But the restoration has been too successful for my purpose: all of the rock structures have filled in with sediment and become overgrown. Instead of smashing through the reeds to try to find one, Singleton takes me to a new restoration site a couple of miles away on Campo Creek. Here the stream runs clear, with some growth of water plants at its edges, but nothing like the lush growth along the older restoration site on Diabold Creek. We find one of the rock structures, a lining of bluish rock that curves around the base of the steep stream banks. If this "sediment retention structure" works the way its designers say it will, it should help the surrounding area store water and actually raise the water table. Just upstream is an old dam built by the Bureau of Indian Affairs (BIA) in 1943. The reservoir behind it once supplied the tribe's drinking water, but it became silted in. CEPA plans to dredge the pond and raise the dam fifteen feet, creating a lake for recreation and water storage.

One restoration site just downstream from a modern dam, another downstream from a sand-and-gravel plant—this is the kind of balance the tribe has to strike between restoration and economic survival. The tribe

has also considered operating a landfill near the reservation's Mexican boundary as well as a truck stop on Interstate 8. To those with stereotyped views of Indians, such side-by-side efforts may seem ironic. The Kumeyaay, though, are just doing what they've always done: looking for the most appropriate technologies to provide for their needs and manage their resources in a responsible way.

THAT there would still be a tribe of native people clinging to their culture in San Diego's backcountry at the turn of the twenty-first century might have come as a surprise to American observers in the late nineteenth century, to whom the Kumeyaay were a "vanishing people," doomed either to death through slaughter or starvation or to assimilation into white society. Those observers wouldn't recognize the modern Kumeyaay, with their adaptations to modern society. Many have moved to San Diego and other cities, where they blend in with the diverse population. A significant number have stayed on or become affiliated with the reservations, such as the 300 people from various desert and mountain Kumeyaay clans who are now members of the Campo Band of Kumeyaay. In all, there are thirteen Kumeyaay reservations in San Diego County, with a total membership of about 2,000. Yet the Kumeyaay are not wholly assimilated; many have stubbornly clung to the remnants of their culture, despite BIA attempts to force their assimilation into white culture.

"It's just amazing that the people are still here and still fighting and still going strong," says Michael Connolly, a member of the Campo Band and former director of CEPA. The Kumeyaay are proud that they were never officially conquered by the Spanish, Mexicans, or Americans. But surviving on the reservations has never been easy, especially at Campo, the reservation farthest removed from San Diego's urban core. Electricity came to the reservation only in the 1970s. Connolly says that every attempt by the tribe to develop its own resources, from bee farming and other forms of agriculture to the modern plans for a landfill and a truck stop, has been contested by various factions of white society. One battle the Kumeyaay have won, along with other tribes in California, is the right to conduct gambling on their lands. But Campo is too far from an urban center to compete with the three reservations nearer to San Diego that already have casinos.

In their battles to become self-sufficient, the Kumeyaay have had to contend with the persistent myth of the "Digger Indian," that derogatory stereotype that sees California Indians as lazy savages living off the region's "natural" bounty, never developing higher technology or culture. Connolly traces this myth to the takeover of California by the Americans in 1848. "There was this denigration of the Indians in California right from the start, [which held] that they didn't really have a culture or even a language." That denigration had a clear purpose, he says. "The European outlook was that you owned land by improving it. To recognize anything that the Indians had done to improve the land would be to recognize their ownership. So there was this need to not recognize it, or you wouldn't have a justification for taking it." One example is the Indians' use of fire in California, a practice that was suppressed by both Spanish and Americans. "Burning was considered a savage practice; no one even wanted to think the Indians knew what they were doing."

The notion that the Indians don't know what they're doing continues today. When the tribe proposed the landfill on the reservation, owners of surrounding land protested, saying that the project posed a threat to water quality outside the reservation. But beyond raising these environmental concerns, opponents of the landfill resorted to a stereotype of Indians as simple people being manipulated by whites. "There was a lot of racist play," Connolly says. "The argument was, 'We have to help save the Indians because they don't know that this landfill is going to destroy them.'" Connolly was even approached by a white activist who told him, "If you were a technical person you'd know that you can't do this." That activist obviously didn't know that Connolly has worked as an aerospace engineer for companies such as Rohr Industries, Rockwell International, and Northrop.

For white society, with its wealth and corresponding access to distant resources, the not-in-my-backyard syndrome comes easily on an issue such as a landfill siting. For the Campo Band, however, the decision is more stark. With limited resources, the tribe can do little to address problems that have devastated the reservation such as substance abuse, alcoholism, low high school graduation rates, and a lack of recreational facilities. "We can see the results every year of not having the resources," Connolly tells me. "We just recently had four kids who were drinking die

in a head-on collision. You're probably looking at three or four percent of the population under eighteen, just wiped out. So if a facility like a landfill would help address those costs, there's just no question. Would a white community do it? You're damned right!" This is a balancing act that all people go through; the Kumeyaay simply want to be respected for their ability to make such decisions on their own.

This is where the restoration of Diabold and Campo Creeks comes in. With such projects, Connolly hopes to show that his people have always used a kind of technology to shape their environment, confronting directly the Digger Indian myth that still haunts the community. An example Connolly mentions often is the traditional sediment retention structure I saw on Campo Creek. "These structures [*mishay sha-wing* in the Kumeyaay language] are designed to increase the groundwater storage. When you build a structure for a purpose and you accomplish that purpose, that's engineering." Kumeyaay engineering affected more than just individual spots. Connolly believes that his ancestors created a kind of synergy by increasing the groundwater recharge in valley after valley. "When you look at it on a large scale across the Kumeyaay territory," he says, "you're really looking at an engineered system."

That the Kumeyaay not only have engineers such as Connolly in the present but also have had engineers for thousands of years helps to debunk the stereotypes with which the Kumeyaay people have been saddled. "They were engineers, they were scientists, they were people who developed medicines based on the natural properties of the plants," Connolly says. "They understood the relationship between plants and health, and between minerals and health. Whether or not we practice that type of medicine today, just understanding that the people had that kind of knowledge is important for the Kumeyaay people today. It helps them in understanding where they came from culturally, and it helps their self-esteem."

The creek restoration is also important in reviving traditional diet, medicine, and industry because many of the 200 different types of plants and grasses that grow in the wetlands are used for those purposes: willow for building structures, deer grass for making baskets, various herbs for medicinal purposes. Connolly says that the full benefit of the restored wetland has yet to be realized: "It's part of an ongoing process to recover

our traditional practices and to find applications for them in the present day."

Connolly points to the traditional Kumeyaay diet, which has an important modern role in reducing diabetes and obesity, two health problems that have plagued Indian communities. Adapted to a diet of low-sugar grains, nuts, other plant foods, and some game, the Indian metabolism is not geared for modern, high-sugar grains, let alone the processed, sweetened, and fat-laden forms in which those grains often appear. A return to a more traditional diet could improve the health of the community considerably. The problem is that a taste for sweets and fats seems to be part of the human condition; Connolly himself confesses a fondness for Big Mac hamburgers. Still, it's a matter of what one is used to. I had an opportunity to taste *shawii*, a mush or pudding made from acorns. Accustomed to sweeter foods, I found it terribly bland, and my son Joshua turned up his nose the second he put it in his mouth. But Terri Sloane, the woman from the Barona Indian Reservation who made the dish, using her grandmother's recipe, said she craves *shawii*, having eaten it throughout her childhood.

Although the Kumeyaay people of the San Diego region are reviving traditional gathering practices in the mountain and foothill areas of their reservations, so far little is being done in the desert. "There are some of us who would like to expand to explore the whole range from the desert to the coast," Connolly says. "We would like to restore some of the traditions that were associated with all of our historical area. But right now, we're focusing on the chaparral." Terri Sloane gathers acorns in the mountains, but she also goes to the desert for creosote bush, a plant with many medicinal uses. She showed me a bad burn on her hand that she had treated with a creosote salve—it had healed nicely and, she said, more quickly than it might have otherwise.

But gaining access to traditional plants, especially those in parks such as Anza-Borrego Desert State Park or on BLM territory, has not always been easy. I got a mixed response when I asked several Kumeyaay people about access to Anza-Borrego. Clarence Brown, an elder from the Viejas Reservation, near San Diego, told me that his band has an agreement with park officials. Terri Sloane, on the other hand, feels as if she needs to "sneak around" when she gathers creosote. Anza-Borrego does have a

policy that allows native people to gather plant materials for personal use, as long as they fill out a form describing which plants they intend to collect and then receive approval from a ranger. The BLM has a similar program on its lands.

These policies are relatively new and represent a change from the "all features are protected" dictum formerly applied to everyone. One person who is happy with these changes is Jane Dumas, traditional health representative for the San Diego American Indian Health Center and one of the most knowledgeable of the Kumeyaay about medicinal plants. "In the past, I don't think the parks were very aware of the need to allow gathering," she says, but "in the last few years they're more willing to work with the native people. It's good, because we've lost access to our gathering sites, and if we can work with them to preserve the endangered plants, it's better for all of us."

Practices such as gathering fit in with the common perception that the Kumeyaay had little influence on the landscape. What about more intensive traditional practices in the desert? Michael Connolly thinks that the hands-off management policies practiced by many parks aren't necessarily bad—"kind of an experiment in going the other way"—but he wonders whether they lead to monocultures of climax habitat. He would like to see the park apply the same techniques used at Campo, including the use of sediment retention structures, to desert canyons. These techniques could create desert marshlands similar to those that already exist in Coyote Canyon, Carrizo Creek, and San Sebastian Marsh. Connolly believes that this would also create a greater number of microhabitats and transition areas known as ecotones, which are often the areas of greatest biodiversity.

I'M SPEAKING with Michael Connolly just a week after the guzzler-building outing, and it strikes me that the watering system I helped build for the bighorn sheep has a purpose similar to that of the water retention strategies Connolly is describing. But it seems clear that creating—perhaps *reviving* is a better word—wetlands in the desert would have an even greater environmental benefit than the couple of square feet of surface water we made available to sheep and other animals.

When I describe the guzzler to Connolly, he shoots back, "You're creating an outdoor zoo out of the park." This is essentially the same criti-

cism of modern management practices that essayist Jack Turner makes. But whereas Turner wants no human activity in wilderness areas, Connolly makes a qualitative distinction among different kinds of human action. Some human activities can fit in places such as Anza-Borrego without negative effects. This is the same point anthropologist Kat Anderson makes: "When one talks with elders in various tribes today, it becomes clear that there was a realm, pattern, and scale to human use that was suited to wild places."

Viewed in this light, the traditional techniques have some advantages over the modern water guzzler. Most obviously, although they involve the moving of rocks and plants, the traditional techniques use natural, local materials. And instead of replicating a single natural feature—a rock tank, or *tinaja*, in the case of our guzzler—they intensify a whole range of natural processes; they change the habitat type around a stream but then let that new habitat follow its own principles of organization, benefiting an entire range of plant and animal species. The guzzler, on the other hand, focuses on one species and by default supplies water to several other mammals and birds. In that sense, the guzzler represents the reductiveness of modern science, whereas the traditional techniques are holistic. Both approaches are worthwhile, but the traditional techniques are, to me, both less intrusive and more beneficial than the guzzler.

Mark Jorgensen sees it the other way around. He offers a lukewarm response to the idea of using Kumeyaay water management practices in the canyons of Anza-Borrego, pointing out that the park's efforts at removing tamarisk also develop wetland areas, benefiting both plant and animal communities. "We're reluctant to use too much manipulation around a riparian area or potential riparian area," he says. "Our main goal is to undo human impacts, so if there was a place where we thought human impacts dried up a spring, then we would consider some kind of manipulative action."

Before embarking on the kind of manipulation Connolly describes, Jorgensen would also have to see more physical evidence of ancient rock structures in the desert. But it may be that the physical evidence of Kumeyaay management techniques has been lost to us. After 200 years of flash floods and benign neglect, the chances of finding those structures seem slim. But the techniques work, as the restoration project at Campo

suggests, and they are a part of the Kumeyaay oral culture. We'll never know with certainty that these techniques were practiced at any particular site. What we do know is that before the twentieth century, no one ever installed a 2,500-gallon water tank in the desert.

Like many wilderness managers, Jorgensen focuses on half of the equation that has changed these landscapes over the past 200 years: the new effects Europeans have had. Perhaps this will be enough to preserve the present biodiversity of the park. But this view leaves out the other half of the equation, which is the removal of the indigenous human influences on the desert. Without restoration of those influences or an approximation of them, restoration of the desert ecosystem can never be complete. Still, Jorgensen is open to discussion; perhaps as evidence mounts, he and other park managers will begin to see that some human actions are part of the natural processes that shaped, and should continue to shape, this landscape.

A PRECEDENT has already been set for the kind of relationship Michael Connolly would like to have with Anza-Borrego Desert State Park. In February 1999, Death Valley National Park reached an agreement with the Timbisha Shoshone Tribe. Unlike Indians in Glacier and Yosemite National Parks, the Timbisha Shoshone were never pushed completely out of their home range—only relegated to forty acres of sand in the middle of the park. If approved, the agreement would establish a tribal homeland of 7,500 acres, mostly on land owned by the Bureau of Land Management that is adjacent to the park. It would also set aside 300,000 acres of the park itself as the Timbisha Shoshone Natural and Cultural Preservation Area, a place in which the tribe would be allowed to revive traditional practices such as sustainable harvesting of pinyon nuts, clearing of brush from springs, and thinning and pruning of mesquite groves and removal of excess sand from them. Tribe members would also participate in interpreting the area for visitors. Hunting would not be allowed in the preservation area, and no mention is made of the use of fire.

Although the specifics of this agreement have yet to be worked out, it seems a good first step in both aiding the Timbisha Shoshone and returning humans as ecological actors in the landscape. The agreement promises to become a test case for determining what kind of human action is

compatible with wilderness, "fitting the logic of the land," to use Jack Turner's phrase. Tribe members believe that many of the park's plant species have declined without their stewardship, a fact that Don Barry, assistant U.S. secretary of the interior, realized when he spoke with the tribe's president, Pauline Estevez. "She talked about the springs that have disappeared," Barry commented, "and the areas where certain plants are the sweetest, and it became obvious how much the Timbisha were part of the place."

Yet environmentalists are already split over the deal. A battle is brewing over the proposal, a conflict that promises to drive a wedge between advocates of wilderness and advocates of Indian rights. Because they are generally sympathetic to the plight of Indians, many environmentalists have conflicted feelings on the issue. The Toiyabe Chapter of the Sierra Club, for instance, though generally supporting the plan, asked how the proposed manipulations of vegetation would affect wilderness values.

The San Francisco–based Desert Survivors, the same group that opposed the building of cairns in desert wilderness, was more explicit in its opposition to any kind of manipulation, even the gathering of pinyon nuts. Parks, the organization maintained, are for the preservation of natural processes, not for "the furtherance of Indian ways or practices." Quoting the legal definition of wilderness as a place where "man is a visitor who does not remain," the president of Desert Survivors, Steve Tabor, wrote, "Park Wilderness should be allowed to evolve as Wilderness, without the interference of 'management' by either tribal members or Park administration." All these comments presume that the Timbisha Shoshone historically had little effect on their environment. In ecological terms, these people, then, were nonexistent.

In one of the most influential statements of the conservation movement, Aldo Leopold said that the first principle of conservation is to preserve all the parts of what he called "the land mechanism." Environmentalists are rightly concerned with preserving and even restoring some of those parts—grizzlies, wolves, and salmon, to name just the most popular. But another piece is missing in our approach to wilderness preservation: humans. For thousands of years, humans played a significant ecological role in this desert. We may debate the extent and specific nature of their actions, but there is no doubt that they had at least some influence. Until

we understand that influence, we will have only a partial understanding of the "nature" or "wilderness" we are trying to preserve. As one professor of Native American studies is fond of pointing out, "the most unnatural thing you can do is take humans out of nature."

Barry Lopez made a parallel point in an essay about Alaska's Yukon-Charley Rivers National Preserve: "To banish all evidence of ourselves means the wilderness is to that extent contrived. We are not, in fact, aliens; and Yukon-Charley offers a chance to . . . better determine what we mean by 'human disturbance' in such places." Whereas other countries have charted new ground in allowing humans to remain in wilderness and to have an active influence on it, in the United States we have barely begun to examine the question Lopez raised. Death Valley National Park's agreement with the Timbisha Shoshone seems to offer an opportunity to begin exploring that question, and Anza-Borrego Desert State Park could become a second test case.

The opportunity in Anza-Borrego is becoming even more pressing as two management plans are being drafted and submitted for public scrutiny: the U.S. Fish and Wildlife Service's plan for preservation of the bighorn sheep and Anza-Borrego's plan for the newly acquired Sentenac Ciénega, a wetland area on the western edge of the park and a site where the Kumeyaay very likely built one of their dams. The challenge is not only to determine how this specific animal or this specific spot will be treated but also to define a new role for humans in wilderness areas. What historian Mark Spence pointed out about national parks also applies here: "The notion of a usable or inhabitable wilderness would imply that humans might have a place in nature that is something more than a 'visitor not to remain.'" Whether or not the staff of Anza-Borrego will take up this challenge remains to be seen. But in a world of signs reading "Wildlife Habitat—Keep Out," the Anza-Borrego Desert offers a chance to try a new—and also an ancient—way of relating to nature.

WHALE PEAK:
THE WILDERNESS PATH

M ID-OCTOBER. The morning is cool as I begin my journey up Whale Peak, the hulking ridge in the middle of Anza-Borrego Desert State Park. I start in the lower reaches of Smuggler Canyon, a wide, sandy wash filled with creosote bushes and other shrubs still dormant after the hot summer. In a few weeks, winter rains will green them into recognizable individual forms, but now they all look alike—yellowed clumps of dried stems, drained of life. This first mile is always monotonous, a sandy slog to reach the base of the mountain with its variety of pinyon pines, junipers, and manzanitas.

As I trudge toward the mountain, eyes on the wash in front of me, a movement catches my eye. I stop, expecting to see a deer or a rabbit or maybe a coyote bounding away through the creosote. I see nothing. As I continue, I realize that the apparent movement had been created by my own motion through the landscape: a tall ocotillo, foregrounded against a shoulder of the mountain, appears to move as I move. With its arms splayed in the air, it seems as much a desert walker as I am as it appears to pass in front of the golden granitic boulders on the hillside. Eighty years ago, writer J. Smeaton Chase noticed a similar quality in a group of ocotillos, which seemed to gesture at him: "Their skinny arms," he wrote, "moved in the breeze as if signaling of some rare sight that I should come see."

I am reminded of driving with my son Joshua on a partly cloudy, moonlit night when he was three. "Daddy," he said, "the moon is chasing

us." The moon, of course, was keeping its position relative to us but peeking in and out of the clouds as we moved beneath them. But try explaining parallax to a three-year-old. My son's young mind couldn't grasp the abstractions of movement in three dimensions. He experienced it directly, ignoring my fumbling explanation in favor of the evidence of his own senses, which told him that the moon was moving along with us. It had taken me years to learn not to trust my senses but instead to make the mental leap necessary to understand the true movement. But who is to say that Josh's experience wasn't equally real?

We live in a world where we are encouraged to abandon our subjective experience and view the world through the objectivity of science. This is the heart of the Copernican revolution. The sun no longer rises, travels across the sky, and then sets. Instead, we must take a mental vantage point somewhere out in space, where we would see that the earth is actually rotating to reveal and then hide the sun from our view. But we still say that the sun rises, describing our true experience on the ground. And this is just the most common of many examples.

Which brings me back to this ocotillo. I *know* that I am the only one moving here, but I *feel* the ocotillo moving with me. It has a presence that goes past my conscious, thinking mind and makes itself felt through my senses, through direct experience. In *The Spell of the Sensuous*, David Abram argues that the world makes this kind of gesture to us all the time—the sound of the wind, a tree branch waving in the breeze, even the movement of a rock's shadow as the sun travels across the sky. What many derisively call personification is actually the way we experience the world at the most basic level. The world is fundamentally alive, with a presence, a quality of mindfulness—it speaks to us in countless ways. Building on the work of French philosopher Maurice Merleau-Ponty, Abram calls this way of perceiving the world "participation"; desert writer Mary Austin called it "the true movement of experience" and went on to say that what she saw in nature was "mind, conscious mind reacting on mind shaping the world. Mind in the trees and birds and insects, mind in flowers."

Science can tell us much about what is happening in the world; it can explain how processes work and can even make predictions about the future. It can tell us why a diversity of species is important, not just to us but to the overall health of the planet. It can even warn us about what will

happen if we lose too many of those species. But it can't tell us how to feel about that loss. In the end, the fate of the earth will rest with our feelings about the kind of world we want to live in, what Edward Abbey called a "loyalty to the earth" or what Edward O. Wilson calls biophilia. Without that subjective connection to the earth, we might be perfectly happy living in a world of nothing but humans and cows, Bermuda grass and tamarisk trees, rats and cockroaches.

Nor can we look to science for answers to the ultimate question: Why? Why do we exist? Why do the earth and the universe exist? Although many scientists disagree, others such as Stephen Hawking believe they can get it all down to an ultimate formula. We can always respond with "Why?" Why was there a Big Bang, Stephen? These questions are the proper subjects not of science but of philosophy and religion (what we now sometimes call mythology)—and of three-year-olds. I have spent years learning to make abstract leaps of reasoning rather than experiencing the world directly. Now I need to go back and try to experience the world the way Joshua did when he was three and to ask questions like a three-year-old.

AFTER the first mile, the canyon bends east and steepens into a kind of staircase, a portal to the summit of the peak. It's as if I've entered a differ-

Pinyon pine

ent canyon altogether. Boulders litter the canyon slopes, and some have come to rest down here in the watercourse, now only forty or so feet across. The creosote bushes end abruptly and agaves appear on the slopes nearby. These blend with junipers, pinyon pines, scrub oaks, and manzanitas in a confluence of mountain and desert. In most places, different plant communities blur into one another, but here the boundary is as sharp as if a wall separated them.

I come to the first pinyon pine, a sure sign that I'm in high desert. A few of its bristly kindred stand out on the skyline above the canyon, but this is the lowest one on this part of the peak. Probably the extra water concentrated in the canyon allows it to thrive at this relatively low elevation. It's a tall one, maybe thirty feet high, and it grows hard by a large boulder. The rock rises from the dry, sandy bed of the canyon like a shrine placed here for the benefit of passing travelers. It's the size of a small house, one of the thousands or millions of granitic boulders that lie strewn across the canyon slopes.

This arrangement of rock and tree—the angle they make, the juxtaposition of solid rock and brushlike pine branches—reminds me of a Zen garden, one of those careful arrangements of rocks and gravel and trees that seem unarranged, concentrating the presence of nature. I get the same sense of mindful presence here. The tree is spare, like the miniature pines in bonsai designs, and the rock gives the arrangement solidity. Behind them, the canyon slope is a chaos of large and small boulders, cacti, and shrubs, with a pinyon here and there on the skyline. Amid such a jumble, this pairing of rock and tree seems a product of design.

Design? Arrangement? A geologist would explain the positioning and shape of this rock as accidents of the mountain building and erosion that created this landscape. The action of water and gravity cleaves these granitic fragments—offspring of the solid pluton of igneous rock that formed this mountain range—into smaller and smaller pieces. Often, where a boulder has split in two, it forms two perfectly matched sheer faces. In other cases, concave layers will peel away from a boulder's surface in a process called exfoliation. When and why a granitic boulder cleaves or exfoliates has to do with crystalline patterns within the rock—nothing worthy of reverence or awe in its creation, just raw materials being pushed around by impersonal forces.

Yet a feeling of design persists. There's a weight to this particular rock and tree. Mountain chickadees flit in the branches of the pinyon pine. This landscape is alive. But the sense of being in the presence of something sentient goes beyond the living presence of the birds. The rock and tree seem to have an awareness, a being, of their own. I extend my hand and touch the cool solidity of the boulder. Its surface is surprisingly smooth. A fissure runs diagonally across its face—I can almost hear the fracture, sounding through centuries like the crack of a gong struck by a hammer. There is no response, of course, to my touch, but I still have the feeling that something is here, a presence, an . . . I don't know what.

To preindustrial societies, this feeling of a living landscape was part of culture; wherever we've come from, Europe, Africa, Asia, or the Americas of long ago, our cultures once honored this same feeling. For us moderns, it seems like a revelation, a continual surprise, when we encounter nature at this level—and then only if we're listening closely. There may be no logical connection, but for me, this experience always evokes feelings of respect and humility—which is to say, reverence.

As I continue climbing, now and then scrambling over boulders but mostly staying in the narrow, sandy wash, I realize that this desert calls to mind not only Zen gardens but also Asian landscape paintings. Many of these paintings show pilgrims, tiny figures in a vast landscape, making their way toward temples or toward the summits of sacred mountains. That's how I feel, too—a small figure clinging to the flanks of Whale Peak. I'm on my own pilgrimage, or *chao-shan*, as the Chinese call it, paying homage to a mountain. My travels in this desert have revolved around the peak like a spinning prayer wheel, to borrow from another tradition, a collection of journeys circumambulating a sacred mountain. The peak stands isolated from all but one or two lower summits, an island of green juniper and pinyon pine riding the desert sea. Whatever accidents of geology have gone into placing it just here, it now sits at the center of Anza-Borrego's universe. If I'm ever to get to the heart of what this place is, I think, this is where I'll find it.

I reach the top of the canyon, where it opens onto the shoulder of the peak itself. Pinyons, junipers, and manzanitas grow thick, and I need to skirt an occasional cholla or agave. I turn southeast and make my way along the ridge. The term *ridge* is a little deceptive here because this

approach will take me through a series of confusing little valleys descending from the summit like strands of a necklace. They all look alike, and it's easy to get into the wrong one and end up with a steep climb up to the summit. An old Sierra Club leader who has been on this peak dozens of times says he has never been up here without getting temporarily lost.

Someone—or many people, more likely—has been trying to rectify this situation. Here and there, I spot little rock piles, small cairns or "ducks" left by hikers to mark the way. In years past, the ducks were so numerous that they not only spoiled the fun of finding my own route up the peak, ruining the illusion that I was the first person here, but became useless anyway. In recent years, the duck builders seem to have picked one good route up the peak and knocked over the ducks that are off the "path." In some places, an actual path has begun to develop.

I could feel sad about this new human-made trail in a place where just a few years ago only the animals made trails, just as I could regret the fact that far more people visit Whale Peak today than was the case fifteen years ago. (When I first climbed the mountain, in 1987, the summit register went back to the 1960s; now there's a new one every year.) But somehow, the presence of this ducked trail is comforting. I'm reminded of the Chinese pilgrimage societies that helped trekkers on their journeys to sacred summits. A similar community spirit seems to be at work here. And even though visits to this peak have increased, there has been no corresponding increase in such adverse effects as trash, fire rings, and junipers stripped for fuel. The message seems to be "Take care of this place and take care of one another." Preserving, visiting, and caring for this wilderness is a community action and a community value.

We modern hikers surround ourselves with more obtrusive technology than these ducks. Compared with using topographic maps and global positioning systems, following a ducked trail is a relatively traditional way of navigating the landscape. People must have used markers like these for thousands of years. Sometimes markers were also trail shrines, offerings to the spirit of the trail. Chief Francisco Patencio said that Cahuilla hunters removed rocks from trails and piled them on the side to "please the spirits." I no longer knock ducks over, because I might be carelessly destroying a thousand-year-old trail marker.

Besides, this little trace of a path hasn't been "built"; it's been worn in

by use. It snakes mysteriously in and out among the pinyon pines, junipers, and granitic boulders, almost an integral part of the landscape. At one point, it skirts the edge of the drop-off to Vallecito, 3,000 feet below. The feeling of occupying a three-dimensional space is profound; climbing peaks like this changes my perspective, giving a new sense of proportion to the world. Once again, I am reminded of those Asian landscape paintings. I am a tiny part of this landscape, and this thin strand of a path is my link to the summit. If I chose, I could step off the path to explore all the known and unknown places away from the main route. But following the path is like unraveling a story. I want to follow that story to its end.

Is a path in the wilderness a contradiction? Only if I pretend that no one has lived here for thousands of years. But the Kumeyaay visited this summit often enough to leave a deep mortar and scattered potsherds. The path I follow might even be one of their own. And still, wildness persists.

I LIKE writer and environmental activist Rick Bass' simple definition of wilderness: a home for wild animals. To me, this is the most basic of reasons for preserving large tracts of land *relatively* undisturbed by human uses—or perhaps I should say *completely* undisturbed by *modern* human uses. Reenvisioning our concept of nature and wilderness in no way detracts from this primary role of wilderness as a haven of biodiversity. In fact, these reserves are not large enough to prevent a decline in diversity within their boundaries; they need to be expanded and linked, with corridors of open space connecting them.

In an attempt to justify such preservation in human-centered terms, some have argued for wilderness as a source of medicines and other "ecological services." Biologists have argued that wilderness can serve as an "ecological baseline" by which to judge disturbed environments. Even the idea of biophilia can be a selfish notion—we like wild animals, so we will deign to keep them around. But the most basic argument is the ethical one, the argument that other species have an absolute right to exist. It's not a new idea; it's the basic message of the story of Noah's ark.

Ironically, the Wilderness Act's strict definition of wilderness as a place where "the imprint of man's work is substantially unnoticeable" sometimes gets in the way of preserving more land as a home for plants and

animals. Opponents of wilderness cynically rely on this definition when they try to disqualify proposed wilderness areas by bulldozing roads into them. Against this backdrop, many activists believe it is time to enlarge our concept of wilderness, thereby opening more land for protection.

Such a move would help us protect more desert wilderness in southern California, where jeep routes are common in areas otherwise free of modern human influence. The Table Mountain area near Jacumba, for instance, has a complex network of jeep routes over an area of 6,000 acres as well as a half dozen old mines and small quarries. Bob Marshall would roll over in his grave if he knew we were proposing this area as wilderness. Yet a portion of the area is good habitat for bighorn sheep, it is rich in cultural "resources," and it is sacred to the Kumeyaay. Many of us believe that the area deserves the highest protection, similar to that of the state park wilderness surrounding it on three sides, yet we must do backflips to show that it lives up to that strict wilderness ideal.

Still, if wilderness is not a place devoid of people, not a place "untouched by the hand of man," not a place in which we emulate the European explorers, and not a place of absolute freedom and escape from society, there is one element of the wilderness ideal we can salvage: wilderness is a place where we can experience the sacred. For John Muir, the Sierra Nevada was a sacred place, the mountains his cathedrals. My sacred place is the Anza-Borrego Desert, especially Whale Peak.

The Indians, of course, had sacred places. For the Kumeyaay and other groups from Baja California and the Imperial Valley, Cuchama (now known as Tecate Peak) was a place where only the *kuseyaay* could go, and perhaps youths during their initiation rituals. Although no gathering was done at such sacred sites, they were managed with fire. In this view, human influence was compatible with the sacred.

Whale Peak doesn't seem to have been sacred to either the Kumeyaay or the Cahuilla. Unlike Cuchama, no Indian name has been recorded for this peak. This is good—I don't want to disturb the Indians' sacred spots. Too much bad will has already been caused by New Agers performing their ceremonies on Cuchama and at other sites, defacing them spiritually and sometimes physically as well.

Nevertheless, we moderns are badly in need of our own sacred sites. Mary Austin wrote that we newcomers can't truly enter into the heart of

a country until we have adopted—or even made up—myths about its "familiar objects." That seems to be what I'm doing here with Whale Peak. This place serves as a vivid reminder of our connection with the earth, a reminder that there is more here than our own human-centered world. Yet even as wilderness shows us something outside ourselves, the insights we take from it can help us be at home in the world, even in wilderness.

To say that a place is sacred does not necessarily imply a reference to some transcendent reality. Even Henry David Thoreau sometimes rejected transcendentalism: "Is not Nature, rightly read, that of which she is commonly taken to be the symbol merely?" In other words, nature isn't sacred because it points to some transcendent, sacred reality; it is sacred in itself. Gary Snyder likens this to the Buddhist idea of "thusness"; Edward Abbey was after much the same thing when he described Paradise as "the here and now, the actual, tangible, dogmatically real earth on which we stand." The world is sacred because it *is*.

In much of Christian theology, this sense of presence in nature must refer to God on a throne somewhere in the heavens. But the presence I feel all around me in the desert is unfathomable, a riddle without an answer. The desert is like a Zen koan, defying one's sense of logic, tripping the student into enlightenment, a state in which opposites are united. Japanese Buddhist scholar D. T. Suzuki wrote that Zen sweeps aside the dualities of "this or that, reason or faith, man or God . . . as something veiling our insight into the nature of life or reality." To his list of dualities he could have added humans or nature, culture or wilderness.

The experience of the sublime, with its double-edged quality, can also help sweep away these dualities. As I ascend Whale Peak, I have that common experience of being a tiny speck in a vast landscape and simultaneously feeling my consciousness expand to include that landscape. Writer Gregory McNamee has likened this to the Zen experience of satori. There is nothing in this wilderness that is different from me. It's absurd to see humans—or human actions and their effects—as somehow separate from this place. We can certainly do great damage to the earth and the plants and animals that live here, but we are hurting nothing other than ourselves.

Gary Snyder has said that this sense of the sacred is only a beginning.

Dwelling too much on the idea of sacred places means that other places can become "sacrifice zones." For example, I could call Whale Peak sacred and overlook the Ocotillo Wells State Vehicular Recreation Area only fifteen miles away. Sweeping away dualities also means sweeping away these hierarchies of place. Wilderness should inspire us to see that the entire earth is sacred.

I hunger for a sacramental relationship with the land, a place where both the land and my relationship to it can be healed. Barry Lopez has spoken of this need for "respectful human participation in a landscape" and also of a "dignified and honorable relationship with nature." In addition to our modern wilderness preserves, we need a middle ground where we can do good, fulfilling work, a place that we don't just take from but also give back to—a place where instead of being mere visitors seeking natural beauty, we become "plain members" of the natural community, as Aldo Leopold put it.

Many nature writers bemoan the "cancers" of New York and Los Angeles while living a mile outside a small town. Ultimately, this goes back to Thoreau at Walden Pond; we all want to be individuals living alone in nature. But elevating that kind of lifestyle spells doom for any sort of free nature in relatively undeveloped places, such as the Bitterroot Valley in Montana, which is currently being carved into five-acre ranchettes, or the mountains above Palm Springs, where everyone wants to have a house with a view. The result will be the land being subdivided right up to the boundaries of our wilderness areas and national parks.

We shouldn't make Marshal South's mistake and seek to live in sublimity every day. We need to make pilgrimages to sacred places to renew our subjective relationship with the earth. But then we need to take that inspiration back to our cities and suburbs and farms and let it enlighten everything we do. We need to make our cities livable, workable, pleasurable, and less consumptive. We need to find the wildness within urban areas, as we do here in San Diego's undeveloped canyons. Most of all, we need to keep our cities from sprawling out into the countryside.

All this might require us to become involved in issues such as land use planning, zoning, resource economics, and urban design. Ultimately, it might require us to live closer together so there will still be room for wild things. Many thinkers—Paul Hawken, Amory Lovins, and L. Hunter

Lovins in *Natural Capitalism* and Alan Thein Durning in *This Place on Earth*, to name just a few—are beginning to show us how to reshape both our economy and our cities to take nature into account. Yet much of the actual work involved in pursuing these goals—writing letters, attending public hearings, gathering signatures on petitions—is tedious and thankless, which may explain why so few are willing to do it. It's more fun to go sit on a rock in the wilderness.

I REACH the last pitch to the summit, where the trail peters out at the base of a steep, boulder-strewn slope. This is the characteristic "hump" that, at a distance, gives the impression of a breaching whale. The top of the whale is a relatively flat, oblong ridge of a few acres, in the center of which rests an eight-foot boulder marking the highest point. Scrambling to the top of the boulder, above the surrounding pinyon pines, I realize that the sky is the clearest it's been in the ten or so times I've been up here. A storm, followed by a mild Santa Ana wind, has pushed the usual haze out of the Imperial Valley, and I can see eastward into Arizona and southward tantalizingly close to the Gulf of California.

Closer at hand, the familiar landmarks of Anza-Borrego stand out in sharp relief, the ridges brightly lit, the draws deeply shadowed in the slanting sunlight. I turn in a slow 360-degree revolution, marking all the places I've been: Borrego Palm Canyon, Coyote Canyon, Rockhouse Valley, Santa Rosa Mountains, Borrego Badlands, San Sebastian Marsh, Split Mountain, Carrizo Badlands, Coyote Mountains, Carrizo Gorge, Dos Cabezas, Jacumba Peak, Bow Willow Canyon, Vallecito, Agua Caliente Hot Springs, Laguna Mountains, Cuyamaca Peak, Granite Mountain, and, completing the circle, the San Ysidro Mountains. Sitting here in this wilderness, I am encompassed by the stories of each of those places and by my experiences with them, still unfolding. The land has been changing for eons; humans have been changing it for thousands of years. It is this constantly changing mosaic we are called upon to love, not a still life in a museum. Suzuki wrote: "If Nature is to be loved, it must be caught while moving. To seek tranquillity is to kill nature, to stop its pulsation, and to embrace the dead corpse that is left behind."

I sit on the rock and pull out a handful of pinyon nuts I gathered on the way up. Cracking open the shells, I discover that some still contain fresh

seeds. I end up with a dozen or so of them, which I eat one by one. They taste remarkably like the ones I buy in the store. This is a small infraction, perhaps, but still a violation of the dictum "Leave only footprints, take only memories." I could make some intellectual calculations about the number of people who visit this spot each year (perhaps fewer now than when the Kumeyaay lived here), the number of those who indulge a taste for pinyon nuts (probably fewer still), and the adverse effects this action, multiplied, might have on the region's ecology. But I don't. Right now, eating the pinyon nuts is a way of making contact with this place, of making it a part of me. In a small, emblematic way, this is a step toward seeing the desert as part of my home, toward the kind of relationship with the land of which Barry Lopez spoke.

A pair of ravens soars above me and out into space where the shoulder of the mountain drops away. One turns on its back and plummets, the other falling on top of it, and then they straighten out and soar upward again—a twirling dance across the sky. I feel a sense of elation in observing their aerobatics. Why do they engage in this seemingly unnecessary activity? Most likely, the ravens' display is an example of what biologists call play behavior, a sort of catchall phrase for animal activities they don't really understand. There is, after all, much that animals do that we can't explain, that doesn't seem evolutionarily advantageous.

Climber Galen Rowell wrote of seeing a bear on a high summit where there could be no rational (evolutionary) purpose for a bear to be. Likewise, Jack Turner wrote of white pelicans soaring over Wyoming's Grand Teton, even risking the lightning at the edges of great thunderstorms, all the while making an unexplainable clacking sound. Why? Turner said we might as well ask "Why sing cantatas and masses and chorales?" It could be that the ravens do this simply for the love of it, for the sheer ecstasy of aerobatics. There is always something beyond the grip of scientific thought, behavior that can't be explained by logic or economics or even by the demands of survival. "There are more things in heaven and earth, Horatio, / Than are dreamt of in your philosophy." This is where wildness persists.

After the ravens disappear, I turn to the peak's summit register, a collection of small notebooks encased in nested coffee cans. Reading the comments in these mountain journals is great fun; it provides an insight

into the mental states of hypoxic and endorphin-addled hikers. One often finds silly poems and long paeans to the beauty of nature.

Today, I find an entry in which the writer exulted, "God's handy work is awesome!"

Below that, another writer replied: "Yeah, and plate tectonics ain't so bad either."

At the bottom of the page, I add, "God—plate tectonics—they're one and the same."

Chapter 20

EPILOGUE:
EYES IN THE DARK

THE SHEER strangeness of the sound wakes me from a deep sleep. I sit up in my tent, instantly alert. It's like nothing I've heard before: a rasping cough, something like a crow with a bad cold or a frog after a few days in the desert sun. But it's *loud*. It sounds as if it's right outside my tent flap.

I can't see my watch, but it must be an hour or so past midnight. I'm camped alone just above First Grove in Borrego Palm Canyon, Anza-Borrego Desert State Park's most popular attraction and only a mile or two from a large campground. Hiking in yesterday evening, I worried more about getting away from the crowds than avoiding the dangers of wild animals. Yet this spot abuts one of the largest remaining tracts of uninhabited and inaccessible country in southern California. Whatever is out there, I'm sure about one thing—it's not human.

This is the kind of moment when our ancestors must have reached for a firebrand to thrust at those eyes in the night. Now, even a burning palm frond would do. Instead, I reach for my flashlight—and immediately ruin my night vision by illuminating the mesh walls of the tent. To the thing out there, the tent is now glowing from within like a Chinese lantern. I'm not sure what impression this will have on my nocturnal visitor. My mind flashes on a *Far Side* cartoon, the one with the polar bears standing over an igloo, one saying to the other, "I love these things—crunchy on the outside, chewy on the inside."

It must be some kind of bird, I tell myself, with that noise it's making.

I want to find out for sure, so I unzip the tent door and shine the flashlight straight ahead.

Two yellow-green eyes stare back. They're maybe ten yards away from me. They disappear, only to reappear a dozen paces to the right, as rapidly and silently as if they had flown. Again, the rasping noise. Maybe it's an owl, I think hopefully. But I know better. The eyes shine perfectly round in the beam of my flashlight. They squeeze shut with each rasping sound, and I imagine the nose wrinkling up, the fangs bared, a glimpse of pink tongue, hot breath escaping. Then the animal seems to move its head left and right—one eye disappears to the side and then the other. I think I can almost see the outline of its head now, and imagine ears perked and expectant.

For someone being watched by a mountain lion, I'm remarkably calm. All my attention is telescoped into this moment, watching those eyes, alert for any sign of imminent attack. And I am armed with technology, even if it is just one weak flashlight. I cling to this puny defense like the French to the Maginot Line. But I know who is in charge here.

Finding himself in a similar situation, a Cahuilla hunter would warn the mountain lion to go away before it got hurt. I'm praying that the lion will go away without hurting me. Any vague wish I had to see a mountain lion in the wild went out the window the minute I saw those eyes. A lion viewed through binoculars on a distant ridge, sure, even a glimpse of a tawny rear end disappearing into the chaparral, but this is too close for comfort. I feel like prey.

I can't tell how long I spend looking at the lion. It has stopped the rasping now. Gradually, I realize that it's not going to pounce on me, and I decide I want to see something more than eyes. I turn my flashlight off, hoping to catch its outline in the light of the half moon riding over the canyon. But my night vision is shot, so I see only the dim shapes of boulders. The lion blends into them perfectly. I turn the flashlight on again, and the eyes are still there. Finally, they just disappear without a sound. I flash the beam around, hoping to catch sight of the cat moving away, but I see nothing. After a few moments of lighting up the rocks like a Boy Scout on a campout, I zip up the tent, turn off the light, and try to calm down.

Now that the animal is gone, I have time to be afraid. Is it circling the

tent, planning an attack from behind? Exhilaration blends with this fear—my first mountain lion sighting. Some people spend their whole lives in places like this and never see one. I close my eyes and try not to think about all I've read about mountain lions. About how they kill with a bite to the head or the neck. About how, perhaps, just maybe, they sometimes eat their prey while it's still alive. Most of all, I try not to think about Iris Kenna, the fifty-six-year-old woman killed and partly eaten by a mountain lion in the Cuyamaca Mountains in December 1994.

IN THE morning, I find no tracks. The lion must have stayed up in the car-sized boulders surrounding my tent site. They're all tan-colored granitics, perfect for camouflaging mountain lions. Now I sit on the same tan rock where the lion sat watching me. The distance from here to the tent would be one small leap for a mountain lion, and the thin nylon dome looks flimsy and completely ridiculous as protection.

Ordinarily, I love this kind of desert morning—cool air, mellow light touching the rocky slopes high above the canyon, profound quiet. Mornings like this are the reason I keep coming out here. But I feel a little uneasy, as if I'm still being watched. The fear of last night is gone, but it has been replaced with wariness. I take comfort in the light of day and the knowledge that the lion has probably returned to its lair in the hills, waiting for night and another opportunity to hunt.

I could say that the lion was just as scared of me as I was of it, but I don't think that's true. I remember the way it turned its head calmly from side to side as it perched above me on that rock, weighing the situation. In all my desert travels, I've never before had this feeling of confronting another being with an unfathomable will of its own. I've seen thousands of birds, hundreds of jackrabbits and cottontails, now and then a coyote, once or twice a band of bighorn sheep—most of them flying or jumping or running away at the sight of me. Even the one or two rattlesnakes I've come across have slithered away at the first chance.

Last night's encounter shattered my illusion of being the top dog out here. The mountain lion wasn't frightened by my waving flashlight. A little confused by the strange object of the tent, maybe, but still in control of the situation. I knew absolutely that it had a will of its own and that it was confident in exercising it. The Indians called this quality power, but

we have a different word for it: *wild*. It's a slippery word, with about as many meanings as there are people who use it. As historian Roderick Nash has pointed out, it has its roots in the idea of will. To me, a wild animal is one with enough power or will to challenge my feeling of being in control.

As much as we've hunted, poisoned, tagged, collared, and studied mountain lions, they still elude our grasp. As long as we don't cover their remaining territory with houses and shopping malls, they'll still be out there, shocking us out of our complacency when we happen—or are lucky enough—to encounter them.

The same is true of the places we call wilderness. Even though humans influenced these landscapes in the past and continue to influence them in the present, wildness persists. It's only when we dominate a landscape— clear-cutting a forest, "reclaiming" a desert, subdividing valleys and foothills—that wilderness disappears. Even then, as Gary Snyder points out, pockets of wildness exist—peregrine falcons in the concrete canyons of New York, coyotes in Los Angeles, immense numbers of migrating birds at the Salton Sea.

Even though humans have changed the Anza-Borrego Desert's flora and fauna (for better and for worse), there is something timeless here in the bare-boned structure of the landscape, in the particular pattern of mountains and valleys, slot canyons and flat sinks. The shape of the land, revealed more clearly in deserts than anywhere else, hardly seems to

Mountain lion

change over the course of a lifetime if left untouched by bulldozers and earthmovers. At this scale of things, the desert is truly eternal, far older and deeper than I can comprehend. It was this love for the shape of the land—what I might call geophilia—that attracted me in the first place. Even with park ecologists "managing" wildlife, and even if native peoples are allowed once again to "manipulate" plant life on a broad scale, at this level, Anza-Borrego will always be a wilderness.

I PACK up, wash in the cold stream, and head out, hopping over water-polished boulders. The canyon seems somehow more alive than it did yesterday evening. The palms look improbably green and tall in the morning light. I reach the main grove and pick up the tourist trail down to the mouth of the canyon. Now it's only another easy mile back to the parking lot and my car.

But what a difference that mile makes. As close as this spot is to town, and as much as it has been shaped by humans, I know I've been touched by something truly wild.

Notes

CHAPTER 2. *Dos Cabezas: Initiation*

11   *Bioligists now think.* Frank C. Vasek. "Ancient Creosote Rings and Yucca Rings," in *The California Desert: An Introduction to Natural Resources and Man's Impact,* ed. June Latting and Peter G. Rowlands (Riverside, Calif.: June Latting Books, 1995), pp. 83–91.

13   *"They survive in the wild now by having the audacity."* Diana Kappel-Smith, *Desert Time: A Journey through the American Southwest* (Tucson: University of Arizona Press, 1992), pp. 82–83.

14   *"If we can't have places where no man has ever been."* Bill McKibben, *The End of Nature* (New York: Random House, 1989), p. 55.

CHAPTER 4. *Carrizo Badlands: Walking on the Bottom of the Sea*

28   *ʔivaʔa was the motivating power for the entire universe.* Lowell John Bean, *Mukat's People* (Berkeley: University of California Press, 1972), pp. 161–165.

28   *"When the time comes."* Francisco Patencio, *Stories and Legends of the Palm Springs Indians* (Palm Springs, Calif.: Palm Springs Desert Museum, 1943), p. 75.

28   *Geology of the Anza-Borrego region (generally).* Paul Remeika and Lowell Lindsay, *Geology of Anza-Borrego: Edge of Creation* (San Diego: Sunbelt, 1992). This book provided much of the information in this chapter about local geology.

31   *The blocks created a series of steps from the crest.* Patrick L. Abbott, "A Trip through Time in Split Mountain Gorge," brochure (Borrego Springs, Calif.: Anza-Borrego Desert Natural History Association, 1999).

32   *Sometime between 2 and 4 million years ago . . . the river did keep up with the sinking.* Remeika put the date at roughly 2 million years; Harold J. Clifford et al., in *Geology of San Diego County: Legacy of the Land* (San Diego: Sunbelt, 1997), wrote that the damming occurred in "early Pliocene time," or 4–5 million years ago (p. 81). At one time, geologists thought the Gulf of California extended as far north as present-day Palm Springs during this period, but the more recent view is that Anza-Borrego was farther south.

32   *What geologists describe as a "lush, well-watered plain."* Clifford et al., *Geology of San Diego County,* p. 83.

33   *The current uplift . . . began only about 1 or 2 million years ago.* Remeika and Lindsay, *Geology of Anza-Borrego,* pp. 28–29.

33   *What Paul Remeika describes as "four million seasons."* Clifford et al., *Geology of San Diego County,* p. 79.

34   *A graduate student at San Diego State University.* Patrick L. Abbott, personal communication, February 20, 1999.

35   *Ecological life zones (generally).* There are many systems for dividing the diverse habitats and plant associations that make up this landscape, from these generalized life zones to the very detailed and localized "plant series" used by the California Native Plant Society. The system used here is drawn from Bean, *Mukat's People,* which is in turn based on Harvey Monroe Hall and Joseph Grinnell, *Life-Zone Indicators in California* (San Francisco: The Academy, 1919), and it matches quite well the more recent "biotic zones" used by Philip R. Pryde in his *San Diego: An Introduction to the Region* (Dubuque, Iowa: Kendall/Hunt, 1992), pp. 40–46.

CHAPTER 5. *Edge of the World: Creation*

38   *"Coyote called out to the people."* Adapted from Francisco Patencio, *Stories and Legends of the Palm Springs Indians* (Palm Springs, Calif.: Palm Springs Desert Museum, 1943), pp. 19–22, 26. *Mo-Cot* is more often spelled *Mukat,* but I have followed the spellings in Patencio's version for this story.

39   *The marks of Coyote's journey remain in the form of red rock.* Patencio, *Stories and Legends,* p. 26.

40   *"Then there came an awful time."* Ibid., p. 6.

40   *"This power of understanding became less and less."* Ibid., p. x.

41   *The "songlines" of Australia's indigenous people.* Gary Snyder, "Good, Wild, Sacred," pp. 78–96 in *The Practice of the Wild* (San Francisco: North Point Press, 1990), pp. 82–83.

41   *Geologic explanation for red rock (generally).* Paul Remeika and Lowell Lindsay, *Geology of Anza-Borrego: Edge of Creation* (San Diego: Sunbelt, 1992), pp. 64, 131.

41   *Archaeological estimates of human arrival in the New World (generally).* Manfred Knaak, *The Forgotten Artist: Indians of Anza-Borrego and Their Rock Art* (Borrego Springs, Calif.: Anza-Borrego Desert Natural History Association, 1988), p. 6; Shepard Krech III, *The Ecological Indian: Myth and History* (New York: Norton, 1999), p. 35.

42   *Information about the San Dieguito, Pinto Basin, Yuman, and Shoshonean (now referred to as Takic or Uto-Aztecan) cultures (generally).* Diana Lindsay, *Our Historic Desert: The Story of the Anza-Borrego Desert* (San Diego: Copley Books, 1973), pp. 27–28.

42   *Had brought these innovations to the area by at least 1,000 years ago.* Until recently, anthropologists believed that the Uto-Aztecan ancestors of the Cahuilla arrived in southern California between 1,000 and 2,000 years ago (Knaak, *Forgotten Artist,* p. 17). But recent research indicates that the Uto-Aztecans, a group of tribes from the Great Basin of which the Cahuilla are members, may have arrived as much as 5,000 years ago (Eric Slater, "Trail of Shells May Lead to Indians' Past," *Los Angeles Times,* January 19, 1998, p. A3). According to Knaak, Yuman speakers (a group that includes the

Kumeyaay) arrived on the Colorado River about 2,000 years ago, and research conducted in Anza-Borrego Desert State Park suggests occupation by these people about 1,200 years ago (Knaak, *Forgotten Artist*, p. 27).

42 *Cahuilla, Kumeyaay, and Cupeño territories (generally).* Robert F. Heizer, ed., *Handbook of North American Indians,* vol. 8, *California* (Washington, D.C.: Smithsonian Institution Press, 1978).

43 *The Cahuilla alone numbered approximately 10,000.* Lowell John Bean, *Mukat's People* (Berkeley: University of California Press, 1972), p. 77.

43 *A population density of about 4 persons per square mile.* Heizer, *Handbook,* p. 576; Florence Shipek, *Pushed into the Rocks* (Lincoln: University of Nebraska Press, 1986), p. 12.

43 *Within sixty years, the lake had vanished.* Philip J. Wilke and Harry W. Lawton, "Early Observations on the Cultural Geography of the Coachella Valley," in *The Cahuilla Indians of the Colorado Desert: Ethnohistory and Prehistory,* ed. Lowell John Bean (Menlo Park, Calif.: Ballena Press, 1975).

43 *Their population shrank to an estimated 6,000.* Bean, Mukat's People, p. 77.

43 *In Cahuilla stories, Coyote is revered.* Wilke and Lawton, "Early Observations."

44 *Cahuilla plant use (generally).* Bean, *Mukat's People,* pp. 36–67; *Lowell John Bean and Katherine Siva Saubel, Temalpakh: Cahuilla Indian Knowledge and Usage of Plants* (Banning, Calif.: Malki Museum Press, 1972), pp. 19–20; Lowell John Bean, "Cahuilla," in Heizer, *Handbook,* p. 576.

44 *He estimated that 80 percent of the plant foods . . . were within a two- to five-mile walk.* Bean, *Mukat's People,* p. 74.

45 *Kumeyaay living along New River raised corn and melons.* Katherine Luomala, "Tipai-Ipai," in Heizer, *Handbook,* p. 594; Jack D. Forbes, "Indian Horticulture West and Northwest of the Colorado," *Journal of the West* 2, no. 1 (1963).

45 *The Cahuilla's relationships with nonhumans (generally).* Bean and Saubel, *Temalpakh,* p. 15.

46 *The people who oversaw these rituals.* Bean, "Cahuilla," pp. 580–581.

46 *Cahuilla botanical knowledge (generally).* Bean and Saubel, *Temalpakh,* pp. 16, 19.

CHAPTER 6. *Mission Gorge: Fire and Water*

50 *Some archaeologists criticize her work.* The debate seems to reflect a general disagreement between the fields of anthropology and archaeology. The former relies on a more interdisciplinary approach, like Shipek's, that includes slippery evidence such as interviews with "informants." The latter insists on hard evidence dug from the ground or otherwise revealed through techniques such as palynology, the study of pollen traces that can be used to determine the floral composition of ancient habitats. I find the anthropo-

logical account more attractive because it can tell me a story about the life these people lived; archaeology seems to concentrate on pottery and tool types, telling little about the people who used them.

51 *Vizcaíno wrote that he saw "so many columns of smoke on the mainland."* Lowell John Bean and Harry W. Lawton, "Some Explanations for the Rise of Cultural Complexity in Native California," in *Patterns of Indian Burning in California: Ecology and Ethnohistory*, ed. H. T. Lewis (Menlo Park, Calif.: Ballena Press, 1973), p. xix.

51 *"Bay of Smokes."* Ibid.

51 *Governor Arrillaga called attention to "widespread damage . . . from the burning of the fields."* Raymond C. Clar, *California Government and Forestry*, quoted in Stephen J. Pyne, *Fire in America* (Princeton, N.J.: Princeton University Press, 1982), p. 416.

51 *"The gentiles have the custom of burning the brush."* Bean and Lawton, "Some Explanations," p. xix.

52 *The result was an increased diversity of plant and animal life.* Glen Martin, "Keepers of the Oaks," *Discover,* August 1996, p. 48.

52 *Indians doubled the frequency of fires.* Dan Flores, professor of history, University of Montana, personal communication, February 1, 1995.

53 *Indians changed the timing of fires.* H. T. Lewis, *Patterns of Indian Burning in California: Ecology and Ethnohistory* (Menlo Park, Calif.: Ballena Press, 1973), p. 50.

53 *Velásquez saw a column of smoke.* Bean and Lawton, "Some Explanations," p. xvi, note 4. These were probably Pai Pai Indians, closely related to the Kumeyaay. The authors use this mention of "wheat" as an example of agricultural practices spreading west from the Colorado River area, but the guide could also have been using the term *wheat* for the semidomesticated grass the Indians grew.

53 *Orcutt found a far different plant association.* C. R. Orcutt, "Some Native Forage Plants of Southern California," *West American Scientist,* June 1889; "Colorado Desert," *West American Scientist,* October 1890. Both articles are reprinted in Phil Brigandi, *The Livestock Industry in the Anza-Borrego Desert,* report prepared for Anza-Borrego Desert State Park, June 1995.

53 *Desertification (generally).* Manfred Knaak, "Vanished Grasslands," *Sand Paper* (newsletter of the Anza-Borrego Desert Natural History Association), March 1996.

54 *"If you don't factor in changes."* Craig Dremann, personal communication, August 17, 1999.

55 *The Spanish as evil* kuseyaay *(generally).* Florence Shipek, "The Impact of Europeans on Kumeyaay Culture," in *Cabrillo's World* (San Diego: Cabrillo Historical Association, 1986), p. 68.

56 *Father Juan Crespi saw "wild" grapevines.* Bean and Lawton, "Some Explanations."

56   *They raised corn, beans, and squash.* Florence Shipek reported, in a personal communication (March 1, 1998): "Crespi saw what he called a field of common beans on the coast between Ensenada and Tijuana. From the slope above Istaguay (now Sorrento Valley) he saw a field of calabashes, or melons."

57   *Settlers described numerous plants growing in rows.* Florence Shipek, personal communication, March 1, 1998.

58   *"On both sides of the mountains."* Elna S. Bakker, *An Island Called California* (Berkeley: University of California Press, 1971), pp. 259–260.

60   *"The Indian people began digging."* Francisco Patencio, *Stories and Legends of the Palm Springs Indians* (Palm Springs, Calif.: Palm Springs Desert Museum, 1943), p. 58.

60   *"For much, much time the people had an open water ditch."* Ibid., p. 57.

60   *Cave Couts noticed an area.* Cave J. Couts, *Hepah, California! The Journal of Cave Johnson Couts from Monterey, Nuevo Leon, Mexico to Los Angeles . . . 1848–1849,* ed. Henry Dobbins (Tucson: Arizona Pioneers' Historical Society, 1961), p. 82.

61   *"Everybody talks about this always being a desert."* Florence Shipek, oral history interviews conducted by Ruth Held, 1991–1993 (unpublished manuscript in the archives of the San Diego Historical Society).

CHAPTER 7. *First Grove: Gardens in the Wilderness*

63   *There are 142 of these native palm groves.* James W. Cornett, "Indians and the Desert Fan Palm," *Masterkey* 60, no. 4 (1987): 12–17.

64   *Cahuilla Indians burned these groves every four or five years.* Gary Paul Nabhan, *Gathering the Desert* (Tucson: University of Arizona Press, 1985), p. 26.

64   *The U.S. Department of Agriculture rediscovered this technique.* Lowell John Bean and Harry W. Lawton, "A Preliminary Reconstruction of Aboriginal Agricultural Technology among the Cahuilla," *Indian Historian* (1968): 207, reprinted in Lowell John Bean and Katherine Siva Saubel, *Temalpakh: Cahuilla Indian Knowledge and Usage of Plants* (Banning, Calif.: Malki Museum Press, 1972), 197–210.

65   *The people distributed palm seeds from one original tree.* Francisco Patencio, *Stories and Legends of the Palm Springs Indians* (Palm Springs, Calif.: Palm Springs Desert Museum, 1943), p. 101.

65   *One account tells of a grove planted in the 1890s.* Nabhan, *Gathering the Desert,* p. 26; Cornett, "Indians and the Desert Fan Palm," p. 17.

65   *They channeled stream water.* Nabhan, *Gathering the Desert,* p. 31.

65   *This decline continued until 1945.* Cornett, "Indians and the Desert Fan Palm," p. 17.

66   *The pristine myth (generally).* William Denevan, "The Pristine Myth: The Landscape of the Americas in 1492," *Annals of the Association of American Geographers* 82, no. 3 (1992): 369–385.

66   *Kirkpatrick Sale (generally).* Ibid., p. 369.

66   *"The world that existed outside human history."* Bill McKibben, *The End of Nature* (New York: Random House, 1989), p. 52.

67   *Martin's Pleistocene extinction hypothesis (generally).* Paul S. Martin, "Prehistoric Overkill," in *Extinctions: The Search for a Cause* (New Haven: Yale University Press, 1967), pp. 75–120; Shepard Krech III, *The Ecological Indian: Myth and History* (New York: Norton, 1999), pp. 29–44.

67   *The Anasazi (generally).* Krech, *Ecological Indian*, p. 77. Pueblo ceremonies. Dan Flores, personal communication, February 1, 1995.

67   *Population densities and domestication of habitats (generally).* Kat Anderson and Thomas Blackburn, "Introduction: Managing the Domesticated Environment," in *Before the Wilderness: Environmental Management by Native Californians*, ed. Kat Anderson and Thomas Blackburn (Menlo Park, Calif.: Ballena Press, 1993), pp. 16–19.

68   *Burning may even have changed the basic nature of the plants themselves.* Bean and Lawton note that "regular burning by the Indians of the coastal valleys may have exercised a selective influence on the genotypic strains of native grasses" ("Some Explanations," p. xxxi).

68   *Geographer Homer Aschmann suggested.* Homer Aschmann, "The Evolution of a Wild Landscape and Its Persistence in Southern California," *Annals of the Association of American Geographers* 49, no. 3 (1959): 34–57.

69   *"The people no longer use them."* Helen McCarthy, "Managing Oaks and the Acorn Crop," in Anderson and Blackburn, *Before the Wilderness*, p. 225.

71   *"All the wild and lonely places."* Patencio, *Stories and Legends*, p. 72.

71   *A garden gone to seed.* Paraphrasing Kat Anderson, quoted in Glen Martin, "Keepers of the Oaks," *Discover*, August 1996, p. 50.

CHAPTER 8. *Oriflamme Canyon: Bushwhacking with Pedro Fages*

76   *Fages' relations with Serra and with his own soldiers (generally).* Henry R. Wagner, introduction to *Letters of Captain Don Pedro Fages and the Reverend President Fr. Junípero Serra at San Diego, California, in October 1772* (San Francisco: Grabhorn Press, 1936).

76   *He never caught up with the men.* Donald Andrew Nuttall, "Pedro Fages and the Advance of the Northern Frontier of New Spain, 1767–1782" (Ph.D. diss., University of Southern California [University Microfilms #64-13, 532], 1964), p. 367.

77   *Indian encampments have been found.* Hero Eugene Rensch, "Fages' Crossing of the Cuyamacas," *California Historical Society Quarterly* 34, no. 3 (1955).

77   *Fages' brief descriptions of the route.* Fages made only one brief mention of this trip in a note to his diary in early 1772, covering his explorations of a route between Monterey and San Francisco. Theodore E. Treutlein,

"Fages as Explorer, 1769–1772," *California Historical Society Quarterly* 51 (winter 1972): 338–356. He gave a more complete description of the route on a trip in the opposite direction in 1782. Herbert Ingram Priestley, ed., *The Colorado River Campaign, 1781–1782: The Diary of Pedro Fages* (Berkeley: University of California Press, 1913).

78   *It was also part of . . . the Yuma Trail.* Rensch, "Fages' Crossing," p. 205.

79   *"They in like manner indicated to us the road."* Pedro Fages, *A Historical, Political, and Natural Description of California,* trans. Herbert Ingram Priestley (Ramona, Calif.: Ballena Press, 1972), p. 8.

79   *Would ban not only the construction of trails but also the use of ducks.* David Darlington and Paul Rauber, "Just Deserts," *Sierra,* March–April 1998, pp. 64–69.

79   *Steve Roper's attitude toward ducks (generally).* Steve Roper, "High Route Redux," *Backpacker,* August 1997, pp. 44–50.

79   *"The feeling that 'I am the first person here.'"* Ann Zwinger, *Wind in the Rock: The Canyonlands of Southeastern Utah* (Tucson: University of Arizona Press, 1978), p. 155.

80   *"We see signs and hike horse trails."* Jack Turner, "The Abstract Wild," in *On Nature's Terms: Contemporary Voices,* ed. Thomas J. Lyon (College Station: Texas A & M University Press, 1992), p. 96.

80   *"Wake to the sound of absolutely nothing human."* Reed McManus, "Tallying the Taku," *Sierra,* March–April 1998, p. 70.

80   *"To see surroundings unpolluted."* Bill McKibben, *The End of Nature* (New York: Random House, 1989), p. 53.

80   *"That I might have had the joy."* Bob Marshall, quoted in McKibben, *End of Nature,* p. 53.

80   *"There were no musty signs."* Ibid.

81   *Powell and his men found an Indian garden.* John Wesley Powell, *The Exploration of the Colorado River and Its Canyons* (1895; reprint, New York: Dover, 1961), pp. 274–275.

81   *When Montana's Glacier National Park was created.* Mark Spence, "Dispossessing the Wilderness: Yosemite Indians and the National Park Ideal," *Pacific Historical Review* 65 (February 1996): 45; Robert H. Keller and Michael F. Turek, *American Indians and National Parks* (Tucson: University of Arizona Press, 1998), pp. 43–64.

81   *When the monument's managers replaced the Tohono O'odham's techniques.* Kat Anderson and Gary Paul Nabhan, "Gardeners in Eden," *Wilderness,* fall 1991, pp. 27–30.

81   *The Ahwahneechee were evicted.* Rebecca Solnit, *Savage Dreams: A Journey into the Hidden Wars of the American West* (San Francisco: Sierra Club Books, 1994), p. 288; Spence, "Dispossessing the Wilderness," pp. 55–57.

CHAPTER 9. *Box Canyon: Soldiers and Forty-niners*

85   *"I believe we are penned up"* and following quotes. Philip St. George Cooke, *The Conquest of New Mexico and California* (Albuquerque, N.M.: Horn & Wallace, 1964), pp. 187–189.

87   *"With crowbar and pick and ax in hand."* Quoted in Diana Lindsay, *Our Historic Desert: The Story of the Anza-Borrego Desert* (San Diego: Copley Books, 1973), p. 57.

88   *May even have preceded them.* Richard Carrico, "Sociopolitical Aspects of the 1775 Revolt," *Journal of San Diego History* 43 (summer 1997): 145.

88   *Population of Cupeño Indians in Valle de San Jose.* Florence Shipek, *Pushed into the Rocks* (Lincoln: University of Nebraska Press, 1986), p. 8.

88   *The Kumeyaay fared even worse.* Florence Shipek, "The Impact of Europeans on Kumeyaay Culture," in *Cabrillo's World* (San Diego: Cabrillo Historical Association, 1991), p. 71.

88   *"By 1875, European-introduced diseases had reduced the Cahuilla population."* Lowell John Bean, *Mukat's People* (Berkeley: University of California Press, 1972), p. 76.

88   *Other effects on the Indians were more intentional.* Shipek, *Pushed into the Rocks*, p. 23. Shipek calls the forced labor endured by the Indians a "periodic labor tax."

89   *"As he proceeded he found the mustard thicker."* Helen Hunt Jackson, *Ramona: A Story* (1884; reprint, Boston: Little, Brown, 1939), p. 44.

89   *"It is cleared out every year only with great difficulty."* Quoted in John Winterhouse, "Historical Geography of San Diego: Some Aspects of Landscape Change Prior to 1850" (master's thesis, San Diego State University, 1972), p. 184; available in the California Room, San Diego Public Library.

89   *Other introduced species.* Ibid., pp. 181–182.

90   *"The Cahuilla and Kumeyaay . . . escaped Spanish influence."* Shipek, *Pushed into the Rocks*, p. 24.

90   *Indians adopted elements of Spanish agriculture.* Shipek, "Impact of Europeans," pp. 74–75.

90   *The Cahuilla . . . may have begun raising livestock.* Phil Brigandi, *The Livestock Industry in the Anza-Borrego Desert*, report prepared for Anza-Borrego Desert State Park, June 1995, p. 105.

90   *After Pedro Fages' last trip.* Lindsay, *Our Historic Desert*, p. 51.

90   *Santiago Argüello discovered the link.* Ibid., p. 54.

91   *Rancho San Felipe . . . wasn't used for grazing.* Brigandi, *Livestock Industry*, pp. 19–20.

91   *Repeated raids by the Indians kept the Californios near the coast.* Shipek, *Pushed into the Rocks*, p. 21; Shipek, "Impact of Europeans," p. 70. An account of an Indian raid on the Jamul Rancho in 1837 appears in Richard F. Pourade, *The Silver Dons* (San Diego: Union-Tribune, 1963), pp. 29–32.

91 *"The mania that pervades the whole country."* Cave J. Couts, *Hepah, California! The Journal of Cave Johnson Couts from Monterey, Nuevo Leon, Mexico to Los Angeles . . . 1848–1849*, ed. Henry Dobbins (Tucson: Arizona Pioneers' Historical Society, 1961), p. 87.

92 *Arriving at Carrizo Creek, were much astonished.* Cave J. Couts, *From San Diego to the Colorado in 1849: The Journal and Maps of Cave J. Couts* (Los Angeles: A. M. Ellis, 1932), p. 14.

92 *"Of food for them there was none."* Amiel Weeks Whipple, *The Whipple Report: Journal of an Expedition from San Diego, California, to the Rio Colorado, from Sept. 11 to Dec. 11, 1849* (Pasadena, Calif.: Westernlore Books, 1961), p. 39.

92 *"If any are left in Arkansas."* Couts, *From San Diego to the Colorado*, p. 21.

92 *"A perfect Golgotha."* William H. Chamberlin, "From Lewisburg to California in 1849," *New Mexico Historical Review* 20 (July 1945): 245.

93 *"The water, though clear as chrystal."* Ibid., p. 248.

93 *"The stench."* Ibid.

93 *"Few bunches of bear grass."* Ibid., p. 249.

93 *Emory's observations of grass (generally).* W. H. Emory, *Lieutenant Emory Reports* (Albuquerque: University of New Mexico Press, 1951), p. 162.

93 *"Fine green spot of grass."* Chamberlin, "From Lewisburg to California," p. 249.

93 *Benjamin Hayes . . . found short green grass.* Benjamin Ignatius Hayes, "Diary of Journey Overland from Soccoro to Warner's" (unpublished manuscript in the Bancroft Library, University of California, Berkeley). Other portions of the diary were published in Marjorie Tisdale Wolcott, ed., *Pioneer Notes from the Diaries of Judge Benjamin Hayes, 1849–1875* (Los Angeles: private printing), but this portion was inexplicably omitted.

93 *"I was much astonished to find myself here."* Couts, *From San Diego to the Colorado*, pp. 19–20.

94 *"The Indians about speak of it as an old thing."* Ibid.

94 *Some astounding figures.* Brigandi, *Livestock Industry*, pp. 35–40.

94 *Historian Richard Pourade reported.* Richard Pourade, *The Silver Dons* (San Diego: Union-Tribune, 1963), p. 169.

94 *Livestock drives, 1840–1870 (generally).* Brigandi, *Livestock Industry*, pp. 35–40.

95 *Henry Wilson and grass around Carrizo Creek (generally).* James Jasper, "Trail-Breakers and History-Makers of San Diego County" (unpublished manuscript in the archives of the San Diego Historical Society), p. 364.

95 *Indians were also paid to cut galleta grass.* Ella McCain, *Memories of the Early Settlements: Dulzura, Potrero, and Campo* (National City: South Bay Press, 1955), p. 61.

96 *Some ranchers even pastured.* Brigandi, *Livestock Industry*, p. 8.

97   The mountains "had preyed on [the settlers'] minds." Charles Kelly, "Reminis-
     cences" (unpublished manuscript in the California Room, San Diego Pub-
     lic Library, 1900–1924), p. 18.

CHAPTER 10. *Table Mountain: Cowboys and Their Cows*

101 *Peter Larkin and early ranching practices (generally).* Ella McCain, *Memories of
     the Early Settlements: Dulzura, Potrero, and Campo* (National City: South Bay
     Press, 1955), p. 56.

101 *McCain family history (generally).* McCain, *Memories.*

102 *McCains' arrival in San Diego County (generally).* Darrell McCain, inter-
     viewed in Phil Brigandi, *The Livestock Industry in the Anza-Borrego Desert,*
     report prepared for Anza-Borrego Desert State Park, June 1995, p. 70.

103 *"The grass was real high."* Mary Weitz, interviewed in Brigandi, *Livestock
     Industry,* pp. 70–71.

103 *McCains' control of land (generally).* Ibid., pp. 80–86.

103 *"You worked and drove cattle every month of the year."* Ibid., p. 84.

104 *"The old-time cowboys . . . had to endure."* Lester Reed, *Old Time Cattlemen
     and Other Pioneers of the Anza-Borrego Area,* 3rd ed. (Borrego Springs, Calif.:
     Anza-Borrego Desert Natural History Association, 1986), p. 19.

105 *"[Sal] Biles and I are nearing the end."* Ibid., p. 47.

105 *"We found a large gully of water."* Fray Juan Mariner, "Diary of Fray Juan
     Mariner, August 1795," in *Joseph J. Hill, History of Warner's Ranch* (Los
     Angeles: private printing, 1927).

105 *Judge Benjamin Hayes noted.* Marjorie Tisdale Wolcott, ed., *Pioneer Notes
     from the Diaries of Judge Benjamin Hayes, 1849–1875* (Los Angeles: private
     printing, 1929), pp. 49, 51.

106 *Emily Sawday was pessimistic.* Oral history interview with Emily Sawday
     conducted by Edgar F. Hastings, November 21, 1957; in the archives of the
     San Diego Historical Society.

106 *"During the time Mr. Ussery lived there."* McCain, *Memories,* p. 58.

106 *"I remember this country."* Carl Woellwerts, "Tule Jim McCain: Last of the
     Border Mountain Cattlemen," in *Border Country,* ed. Bill Robinson
     (Alhambra, Calif.: Border-Mountain Press, 1976), pp. 21–27.

107 *"The old-timers were not crazy."* Bill Wright, *San Diego Union,* June 10, 1934,
     quoted in Brigandi, *Livestock Industry,* p. 331.

107 *"The real impact on the vegetation."* Brigandi, *Livestock Industry,* p. 330.

107 *Changes in climate in the Southwest (generally).* Thomas R. Van Devender,
     "Desert Grassland History: Changing Climates, Evolution, Biogeography,
     and Community Dynamics," in *The Desert Grassland,* ed. Mitchel P.
     McClaran and Thomas R. Van Devender (Tucson: University of Arizona
     Press, 1995), pp. 92–93; Ronald P. Neilson, "High-Resolution Climatic
     Analysis and Southwest Biogeography," *Science* 232 (April 4, 1986): 32.

108 *Ecologists have concluded that similar fluctuations took place.* Van Devender, "Desert Grassland History," p. 92.

108 *Weather patterns in San Diego County (generally).* Harold C. Fritts, "Tree-Ring Evidence for Climatic Changes in Western North America," *Monthly Weather Review* 93, no. 7 (July 1965): 431. *"Weather data from San Diego County."* John Gaines, *"A Century of Rain in San Diego"* (information from National Weather Service), *San Diego Union,* March 31, 1991.

108 *Although many factors are involved.* Neilson points out that timing of rainfall can determine type of vegetation in Southwest deserts, with summer rainfall favoring desert grasses and winter rainfall favoring shrubs. Neilson, "High-Resolution Climatic Analysis," p. 32.

108 *Grazing acted in concert with climate change.* Ibid.

109 *Decomposed granite . . . particularly susceptible to erosion.* Joseph R. McAuliffe, "Landscape Evolution, Soil Formation, and Arizona's Desert Grasslands," in *The Desert Grassland,* ed. Mitchel P. McClaran and Thomas R. Van Devender (Tucson: University of Arizona Press, 1995), p. 116.

109 *Desert scrub might not shift back to grassland.* Van Devender, "Desert Grassland History," pp. 93, 95.

109 *Orcutt noticed a change in the desert.* C. R. Orcutt, "Some Native Forage Plants of Southern California," *West American Scientist,* June 1889; "Colorado Desert," *West American Scientist,* October 1890, reprinted in Brigandi, *Livestock Industry,* pp. 336–338.

110 *"Now the cattle business is just about finished."* Woellwerts, "Tule Jim McCain," p. 27.

111 *Frederic Clements' climax theory. Summarized in Van Devender (generally),* "Desert Grassland History," p. 85.

111 *Challenges to climax theory (generally).* Ibid.

112 *Changes to Colorado River ecosystems (generally).* Michael E. Long, "The Grand Managed Canyon," *National Geographic* 192, no. 1 (July 1997): 124–134.

112 *Botkin observes that this new thinking seems to "open up a Pandora's box."* Daniel B. Botkin, *Discordant Harmonies: A New Ecology for the Twenty-first Century* (New York: Oxford University Press, 1990), pp. 70, 189.

112 *Worster is even more suspicious of this new movement.* Donald Worster, *The Wealth of Nature: Environmental History and the Ecological Imagination* (New York: Oxford University Press, 1993), pp. 167–169.

CHAPTER 11. *Indian Hill: Homeless*

114 *"A far larger world."* Edward Abbey, *Desert Solitaire* (New York: Ballantine Books, 1968), p. 111.

115 *"The Indians . . . are not kept on their reservation."* Quoted in Phil Brigandi, *The Livestock Industry in the Anza-Borrego Desert,* report prepared for Anza-Borrego Desert State Park, June 1995, p. 71.

115 *"Jack McCain, the blacksmith at Campo."* Ella McCain, *Memories of the Early Settlements: Dulzura, Potrero, and Campo* (National City: South Bay Press, 1955), p. 56.

116 *"Death would come slowly."* Carl Woellwerts, "The Great Jacumba Massacre," unpublished manuscript in the archives of the San Diego Historical Society, Robinson/Jacumba file.

116 *Newcomers' views of Indians (generally).* Florence Shipek, *Pushed into the Rocks* (Lincoln: University of Nebraska Press, 1986), p. 30; Julia Flinn De Frate, *This Was Yesterday* (San Diego: private printing, 1951), pp. 37–39.

116 *"Justice was a concept."* Richard Carrico, *Strangers in a Stolen Land: American Indians in San Diego, 1850–1880* (Newcastle, Calif.: Sierra Oaks, 1987), p. 19.

116 *One mentions the lasting scars.* Woellwerts, "Great Jacumba Massacre."

117 *The Oatman party (generally).* McCain, *Memories,* pp. 72–73.

117 *"Nobody has ever figured out a nice way . . . to take somebody's land."* Quoted in Priit J. Vesilind, "The Sonoran Desert: Anything but Empty," *National Geographic* 186 (September 1994): 51.

117 *Cave Couts as Indian subagent (generally).* Shipek, *Pushed into the Rocks,* p. 29.

117 *Conditions for many Indians remained tolerable.* Ibid., pp. 30–32.

118 *Richard Carrico paints a bleaker picture.* Carrico, *Strangers,* pp. 37–59.

118 *After 1865, conditions worsened.* Shipek, *Pushed into the Rocks,* pp. 31–36.

118 *"He would not come out of his house."* Helen Hunt Jackson, *Ramona: A Story* (1884; reprint, Boston: Little, Brown, 1939), p. 207.

119 *A white man approached.* Ibid., p. 307.

119 *"We lived here, there."* Oral history interview with Julio Ortega conducted by Edgar F. Hastings, 1957; in the archives of the San Diego Historical Society.

119 *History of San Diego County reservations (generally).* Shipek, *Pushed into the Rocks,* pp. 36–37.

119 *Effect of disease on Indians' plant knowledge.* Florence Shipek, "The Impact of Europeans on Kumeyaay Culture," in *Cabrillo's World* (San Diego: Cabrillo Historical Association, 1986), p. 74.

120 *Some Indians simply starved.* Ibid.

120 *Kumeyaay employment.* Ibid., pp. 75–76.

120 *Social problems faced by the Kumeyaay.* Carrico, *Strangers,* pp. 18–32.

120 *Garra uprising (generally).* George Harwood Phillips, *Chiefs and Challengers* (Berkeley: University of California Press, 1975).

120 *"Village sites in Coyote Canyon were abandoned."* Diana Lindsay, *Our Historic Desert: The Story of the Anza-Borrego Desert* (San Diego: Copley Books, 1973), p. 63.

121 *Decimation of the Kumeyaay population (generally).* Shipek, "Impact of Europeans," pp. 71–74.

121 *Creation of reservations (generally).* Shipek, *Pushed into the Rocks,* pp. 39–45;

Charles F. Lummis, "The Exiles of Cupa," *Out West*, May 1902, pp. 465–479.

122 *"You ask us to think what place we like next best."* Lummis, "Exiles," p. 475.

123 *Deaths of elders and children (generally).* Shipek, *Pushed into the Rocks*, pp. 44–45.

123 *"The Warner's Ranch episode is closed."* Charles F. Lummis, "The Sequoyah League," *Out West*, June 1903, pp. 743–745.

123 *Lester Reed commented that Rockhouse was rightfully respected.* Lester Reed, *Old Time Cattlemen and Other Pioneers of the Anza-Borrego Area*, 3rd ed. (Borrego Springs, Calif.: Anza-Borrego Desert Natural History Association, 1986), p. 118.

123 *Some of the ranchers . . . happened to be Indians.* Brigandi, *Livestock Industry*, pp. 105–109.

CHAPTER 12. *Salton Sea: Taming the Desert*

130 *"The one place in all the world."* John C. Van Dyke, *The Desert* (1901; reprint, Layton, Utah: Peregrine Smith Books, 1980), p. 55.

132 *Statistics regarding fish and bird die-offs (generally).* "Salton Sea Fish Deaths in One Day at 7.6 Million," *San Diego Union-Tribune*, August 14, 1999; Eric Niiler, "Sea of Misfortune," *San Diego Union-Tribune*, June 30, 1998, pp. A1, A10; Imperial Valley Community College, "The Salton Sea," available on-line at http://www.imperial.cc.ca.us/birds/saltnsea.htm.

132 *Rocky Mountain Arsenal (generally).* "Album: Unnatural Nature," in *Uncommon Ground: Toward Reinventing Nature*, ed. William Cronon (New York: Norton, 1995), pp. 57–66.

133 *Dr. Oliver Wozencraft (generally).* Mildred De Stanley, *Salton Sea: Yesterday and Today* (Los Angeles: Triumph Press, 1966), p. 17; Lindsay, *Our Historic Desert*, p. 73; George Wharton James, *Wonders of the Colorado Desert* (1906; reprint, Boston: Little, Brown, 1911), p. 354.

133 *William P. Blake . . . noted another problem.* Lloyd Woerner, "The Creation of the Salton Sea: An Engineering Folly," *Journal of the West* 28 (January 1989): 110.

133 *"It is popularly regarded as an empire of hopeless sterility."* Quoted in James, *Wonders of the Colorado Desert*, p. 361.

134 *History of the California Development Company and creation of the Salton Sea (generally).* Woerner, "Creation of the Salton Sea"; James, *Wonders of the Colorado Desert*, pp. 503–518; H. T. Cory, *The Imperial Valley and the Salton Sink* (San Francisco: John J. Newbegin, 1915), pp. 1204–1453; M. J. Dowd, *Historic Salton Sea* (El Centro, Calif.: Imperial Irrigation District, 1960); Daniel MacDougal, *The Salton Sea: A Study of the Geography, the Geology, the Floristics, and the Ecology of a Desert Basin* (Washington, D.C.: Carnegie Institution, 1914); De Stanley, *Salton Sea*, pp. 21–46.

134   *By 1904, more than 8,000 people had settled in the valley.* James, *Wonders of the Colorado Desert*, p. 362.

134   *"Locks, control or headworks there were none."* MacDougal, *Salton Sea: A Study*, p. 592.

134   *Charles Rockwood's actions and reasoning (generally).* Cory, *Imperial Valley and Salton Sink*, pp. 1286–1291.

135   *Effects of flooding and efforts to control the Colorado River (generally).* Woerner, "Creation of the Salton Sea"; Cory, *Imperial Valley and Salton Sink*.

135   *Changes in the depth of the Salton Sea (generally).* Dowd, *Historic Salton Sea*.

135   *Development of fishing and boating industries (generally).* De Stanley, *Salton Sea*, pp. 48–91.

136   *Celebrities at the Salton Sea (generally).* Niiler, "Sea of Misfortune," p. A1.

136   *"The salt may begin to harm the fish as soon as 1970."* Richard D. Pomeroy, quoted in De Stanley, *Salton Sea*, p. 50.

136   *Enough salt . . . to fill a mile-long freight train.* Tom Kirk, executive director, Salton Sea Authority, quoted by Steve LaRue in "In but Not Out," *San Diego Union-Tribune*, July 1, 1998, p. E1.

136   *High salinity, high nutrient levels, and high temperatures.* Bureau of Reclamation, "Salton Sea Restoration Project," available on-line at http://www.lc.usbr.gov/~saltnsea/ssrest.html.

136   *Flooding; selenium warnings (generally).* Niiler, "Sea of Misfortune," p. A10.

137   *Anglers returning to the Salton Sea (generally).* Ed Zieralski, "Maligned Sea Yielding Fish for 'Armpit' Anglers," *San Diego Union-Tribune*, August 1, 1999, p. C8.

137   *A 1999 study brought further good news.* "Salton's Depths Free of Toxins," *San Diego Union-Tribune*, May 24, 1999, p. A3.

137   *"An ecosystem in rapidly failing health."* Milt Friend, lead scientist in the Salton Sea Authority's study of the sea, quoted by Diana Marcum in "7.6 Million Fish Die in a Day at Salton Sea," *Los Angeles Times*, August 12, 1999.

137   *The Salton Sea as a collecting basin (generally).* Dowd, *Historic Salton Sea*.

137   *"The purpose of the sea."* Gary Polakovic, "Farm Runoff: A Challenge," *Riverside Press-Enterprise*, January 5, 1993.

137   *Ken Sturm and Norm Niver on eating Salton Sea fish (generally).* "Fish Kills/Eating Fish," available on-line at http://www.Saltonseainfo.com.

138   *"A Frankenstein created by the blundering of man."* Jim Gogek, "Efforts to Save Salton Sea Are Destined for Failure," *San Diego Union-Tribune*, December 18, 1998.

138   *"An environmental abscess."* Ivan P. Colburn, "Salton Sea Is Dead—Keep It That Way," *Los Angeles Times*, June 18, 1998.

138   *A solution "that only creosote bushes could view with equanimity."* Stuart H.

Hurlbert, "Salton Sea Is Alive and Kicking—Save It" (unpublished letter to the *Los Angeles Times*), available on-line at http://www.sci.sdsu.edu/salton/SaltonSeaHomePage.html.

138   *"I've found an Eden."* Steve Horvitz, "A Bit of Eden" (address to the Salton Sea Symposium), available on-line at http://www.Saltonseainfo.com.

139   *Monarch butterfly seems to prefer the non-native eucalyptus.* Rebecca Slotig-Nolis, *California Report*, National Public Radio, March 22, 1999.

139   *Cathedral Pines in Connecticut.* Michael Pollan, *Second Nature: A Gardener's Education* (New York: Dell, 1991), pp. 209–238.

139   *North Woods of Minnesota.* Daniel B. Botkin, *Discordant Harmonies: A New Ecology for the Twenty-first Century* (New York: Oxford University Press, 1990), pp. 51–71.

140   *One economic study.* Michael Bazdarich, Anderson School of Management, University of California, Riverside, quoted at http://www.Saltonseainfo.com.

141   *Hurricane Kathleen delivered the biggest blow.* Robert M. Hanft, *San Diego and Arizona: The Impossible Railroad* (Glendale, Calif.: Trans-Anglo Books, 1984).

CHAPTER 13. *Seventeen Palms: Our Limits Transgressed*

144   *Chase's description of his journey (generally).* J. Smeaton Chase, *California Desert Trails* (1919; reprint, Palo Alto, Calif.: Tioga, 1987). Unless otherwise noted, all quotes from Chase are from this work, pp. 1, 10, 37, 195, 197, 201, 203, 234, 265, 266, 275, 276, and 325.

148   *"We must be refreshed by the sight."* Henry David Thoreau, *Walden and Resistance to Civil Government*, 2nd ed., Norton Critical Edition Series, ed. William Rossi (New York: Norton, 1992), p. 212.

148   *"The sweepings of the world."* Quoted in Diana Lindsay, *Our Historic Desert: The Story of the Anza-Borrego Desert* (San Diego: Copley Books, 1973), p. 51.

149   *"In sublimity."* John C. Van Dyke, *The Desert* (1901; reprint, Layton, Utah: Peregrine Smith Books, 1980), p. 232.

149   *"The deserts should never be reclaimed."* Ibid., p. 59.

150   *"It would be a tremendous pity."* George Wharton James, *The Wonders of the Colorado Desert* (1906; reprint, Boston: Little, Brown, 1911), p. 353.

150   *The viewpoint of Mary Austin (generally)* Mary Austin, *The Land of Little Rain* (1903), in *Stories from the Country of Lost Borders*, ed. Marjorie Pryse (New Brunswick, N.J.: Rutgers University Press, 1987).

151   *Historians have cast doubt.* Peter Wild and Neil Carmony, "The Trip Not Taken: John C. Van Dyke, Heroic Doer or Armchair Seer?" *Journal of Arizona History* 34, no. 1 (spring 1993): 65–80. Wild has since moved from suspicion to certainty: "Further evidence makes it almost certain that Van Dyke

was a grand hornswoggler—a splendid writer but a hornswoggler none-theless" (personal communication, September 17, 1999).

151 *"A few people are just beginning to catch the idea."* J. Smeaton Chase, *Our Araby: Palm Springs and the Garden of the Sun* (Pasadena, Calif.: Star-News, 1920), p. 25.

152 *Dirt bikers deliberately carved "doughnuts."* Lowell Lindsay and Diana Lindsay, *The Anza-Borrego Desert Region: A Guide to the State Park and the Adjacent Areas,* 2nd ed. (Berkeley, Calif.: Wilderness Press, 1985), p. 162.

153 *"Certain desert areas have a distinctive and subtle charm."* Quoted in Lindsay, *Our Historic Desert,* p. 86.

153 *Creation of Anza-Borrego Desert State Park (generally)* . Ibid., pp. 85–98.

153 *The Table Mountain area . . . was withheld.* Diana Lindsay, personal communication, September 15, 1999.

CHAPTER 14. *Ghost Mountain: Bad Days at Yaquitepec*

156 *"One must have something of the poet."* Marshal South, "Desert Trails," *Desert,* August 1948, p. 21.

156 *"Silence and peace!"* Marshal South, "Desert Refuge," *Saturday Evening Post,* March 11, 1939, p. 36.

157 *"Sanity said that the thing was an impossible dream."* Ibid., p. 119.

157 *"There is nothing soft about Ghost Mountain."* Ibid.

158 *"The toughened muscles."* Ibid., p. 120.

159 *"That gallant infirmity of the soul."* Edward Abbey, *Desert Solitaire* (New York: Ballantine Books, 1968), p. 273.

159 *"Why Everett Ruess kept going."* Ibid., p. 272.

159 *He "forgot caution."* Marshal South, "Desert Diary—March," *Desert,* April 1940.

159 *On a winter visit.* Jeannette De Wyze, "The Hermits of Ghost Mountain," *San Diego Reader,* October 17, 1991.

160 *Jeannette De Wyze dug into the actualities.* Much of the information about the realities of life on Ghost Mountain is from the DeWyze article cited in the previous note.

161 *"Lonely!"* Marshal South, "Desert Diary—January," *Desert,* February 1940.

161 *"He despised the rules."* Randall Henderson, "Just between You and Me," *Desert,* December 1948, p. 46.

162 *"The desert has a way of sapping dreams."* South, "Desert Trails," p. 22.

162 *"Part of a mighty pattern."* Ibid., p. 21.

163 *"The romantic view."* Abbey, *Desert Solitaire,* p. 190.

164 *"Human life is a fleeting thing."* South, "Desert Trails," p. 22.

CHAPTER 15. *Red Rock Canyon: The War on the Desert*

165 *Bombing history (generally).* F. L. Orrell, *Recent Military Operations in the Anza-Borrego Desert State Park* (Borrego Springs, Calif.: Anza-Borrego Desert Natural History Association, 1991).

165 *"On many occasions."* Quoted in Phil Brigandi, *The Livestock Industry in the Anza-Borrego Desert*, report prepared for Anza-Borrego Desert State Park, June 1995, p. 92.

169 *Some 25 to 50 percent of the plant cover has been destroyed.* Confirmed by Mark Jorgensen, associate resource ecologist, Colorado Desert District, personal communication, May 15, 1999.

169 *Diana Lindsay's view of off-roading; ranger's report (generally).* Diana Lindsay, *Our Historic Desert: The Story of the Anza-Borrego Desert* (San Diego: Copley Books, 1973), p. 112.

169 *At a cost of as much as $10,000 per acre.* David Bainbridge, desert restorationist, presentation to the San Diego chapter of the California Native Plant Society.

170 *"An expression of loyalty to the earth."* Edward Abbey, *Desert Solitaire* (New York: Ballantine Books, 1968), p. 190.

170 *"Cutting the bloody cord."* Ibid., p. 177.

CHAPTER 16. *Horse Canyon: Weeding the Wilderness*

178 *Information about tamarisks (generally).* Bernard R. Baum, *The Genus Tamarix* (Jerusalem: Israel Academy of Sciences and Humanities, 1978); Bernard R. Baum, "Introduced and Naturalized Tamarisks in the United States and Canada," *Baileya* 15, no. 1 (1967): 19–25; Bryan T. Brown, Steven W. Carothers, and R. Roy Johnson, "Breeding Range Expansion of Bell's Vireo in Grand Canyon, Arizona," *Condor* 85 (1983): 499–500; Benjamin L. Everitt, "Ecology of Saltcedar—a Plea for Research," *Environmental Geology* 3 (1980): 77–84; Peter Friederici, "The Alien Saltcedar," *American Forests* (January–February 1995): 45–47; William C. Hunter, Robert D. Ohmart, and Bertin W. Anderson, "Use of Exotic Saltcedar (*Tamarix chinensis*) by Birds in Arid Riparian Systems," *Condor* 90 (1988): 113–123; Mark J. Kasprzyk and Gary L. Bryant, *Results of Biological Investigations from the Lower Virgin River Vegetation Management Study* (Denver: U.S. Bureau of Reclamation, 1989); Theodore A. Kerpez and Norman S. Smith, *Saltcedar Control for Wildlife Habitat Improvement in the Southwestern United States*, U.S. Fish and Wildlife Service Research Publication no. 169 (I 49.66:169) (Washington, D.C.: U.S. Fish and Wildlife Service, 1987); John Rodman, "Restoring Nature: Natives and Exotics," in *In the Nature of Things: Language, Politics, and the Environment*, ed. Jane Bennett and William Chaloupka (Minneapolis: University of Minnesota Press, 1993), pp.

139–153; Andy Sudbrock, "Tamarisk Control: Fighting Back," *Restoration and Management Notes* 11, no. 1 (1993): 31–34.

180 *100 acres of native vegetation supported 154 bird species.* B. W. Anderson and R. D. Ohmart, *Wildlife Use and Densities Report for Birds and Mammals in the Lower Colorado River Valley,* report prepared for U.S. Bureau of Reclamation, 1977, cited in Sudbrock, "Tamarisk Control."

180 *The latter point has since been challenged.* Bertin Anderson, "The Case for Salt Cedar," *Restoration and Management Notes* 16, no. 2 (1998): 130–134.

181 *Some researchers reject this idea.* Benjamin L. Everitt argues that tamarisk outcompetes natives only in disturbed conditions, specifically along dammed rivers. Under "natural" conditions, natives should have the advantage.

181 *Bertin Anderson questions earlier tamarisk research.* Anderson, "Case for Salt Cedar."

181 *Cameron Barrows noticed . . . benefits from tamarisk removal.* Cameron Barrows, "The Case for Wholesale Removal," *Restoration and Management Notes* 16, no. 2 (1998): 135–139.

182 *Minute amounts could persist.* Carrie Swadener, "Triclopyr," *Journal of Pesticide Reform* 13, no. 3 (1993): 29–35.

182 *Approval of biological controls; delays due to southwestern willow flycatcher (generally).* Various issues of the *California Native Plant Society Bulletin,* 1998–1999; Michael J. Pitcairn, "Biological Control of Wildland Weeds," *Fremontia* 26, no. 4 (October 1998): 59–64.

182 *Insects wouldn't wipe out all the tamarisk.* Pitcairn, "Biological Control," p. 59.

184 *"The 'preservation as management' tradition."* Jack Turner, "Wildness and the Defense of Nature," in *The Abstract Wild* (Tucson: University of Arizona Press, 1996), p. 124.

184 *"Let whatever habitat we can preserve go back to its own self-order."* Turner, *Abstract Wild,* p. 120.

184 *Wilderness should not be defined by human absence.* Ibid., p. 112.

186 *Those involved with ecological restoration.* John Rodman, "Reflections on Tamarisk Bashing," in *Restoration '89: The New Management Challenge* (Madison, Wis.: Society for Ecological Restoration, 1990).

186 *Humans will survive the . . . waves of extinction.* David Quammen, "Planet of Weeds: Tallying the Losses of Earth's Animals and Plants," *Harper's Magazine,* October 1998, pp. 57–69.

186 *Pioneering work conducted at Cedar Creek Natural History Area.* "Biodiversity: A Productive Way to Grow," *Frontiers: The Electronic Newsletter of the National Science Foundation,* November 1996, available on-line at http://www.nsf.gov/od/lpa/news/publicat/frontier/11-96/11biodiv.htm; William K. Stevens, "In Plant World, Survival Is Rooted in Diversity," *San Diego*

Union-Tribune, October 28, 1998, p. E-5; David Tilman and John A. Downing, "Biodiversity and Stability in Grasslands," *Nature*, January 27, 1994, p. 363.

CHAPTER 17. *Third Grove: Battle for the Bighorn*

190   *Bighorns . . . may be experiencing great stress.* Maureen Zent, "We Say It's Art, But What about Ewe?" *Outside*, June 1999, p. 34.

191   *Peninsular bighorn demography through 1996 (generally).* Mark Jorgensen, associate resource ecologist, Colorado Desert District, personal communication, June 15, 1999.

192   *Principal causes for the decline through the 1980s.* Ibid.; Bob Holmes, "Up against Steep Odds," *National Wildlife*, February–March 1997.

192   *Bighorn sheep population study (generally).* Esther S. Rubin et al., "Distribution and Abundance of Bighorn Sheep in the Peninsular Ranges, California," *Wildlife Society Bulletin* 26, no. 3 (1998): 539–551.

193   *Mountain lions second to bobcats among the sheep's feline predators.* Gale Monson and Lowell Sumner, eds., *The Desert Bighorn: Its Life History, Ecology, and Management* (Tucson: University of Arizona Press, 1980).

193   *Effects of endangered species listing (generally).* Mark Henry and Onell Soto, "Saving the Bighorn: Desert Symbol to Join Endangered Species List," *Riverside Press-Enterprise*, March 13, 1998; Jorgensen, personal communication, June 15, 1999.

198   *Indians and mountain lions (generally).* Kumeyaay: Florence Shipek, personal communication, May 20, 1999. Cahuilla: Lowell John Bean, *Mukat's People* (Berkeley: University of California Press, 1972), pp. 63, 148.

199   *Juwa Bushmen of Africa.* Jack Turner, "Mountain Lions," in *The Abstract Wild* (Tucson: University of Arizona Press, 1996), pp. 49–50.

200   *Natural regulation versus management by interference (generally).* A. R. E. Sinclair, "Natural Regulation of Ecosystems in Protected Areas as Ecological Baselines," *Wildlife Society Bulletin* 26, no. 3 (1998): 399–409; Mark S. Boyce, "Natural Regulation or the Control of Nature?" in *The Greater Yellowstone Ecosystem: Redefining America's Wilderness Heritage*, ed. Robert B. Keiter and Mark S. Boyce (New Haven, Conn.: Yale University Press, 1991), pp. 183–208.

202   *Bighorn numbers, 1997–1999 (generally).* Jorgensen, personal communication.

203   *"I want to know and care about the grizzly."* Jack Turner, "Wildness and the Defense of Nature," in *The Abstract Wild* (Tucson: University of Arizona Press, 1996), p. 118.

CHAPTER 18. *Campo: Reimagining Ancient Traditions*

206 *Now it's a year-round stream.* For more information about the Campo restoration project, see Chet Barfield, "Campo Indians: A Tribe in Resurgence," *San Diego Union-Tribune,* August 11, 1996, B-1; Jessica Maxwell, "The Campo Comes to Life," *Audubon,* May–June 1995, pp. 100–105.

207 *Kumeyaay reservations and membership (generally).* Florence Shipek, *Pushed into the Rocks* (Lincoln: University of Nebraska Press, 1986), pp. 186–191.

207 *Electricity (generally).* David Singleton, Campo tribal planner, personal communication, June 21, 1999.

212 *"When one talks with elders."* Kat Anderson, "Native Californians as Ancient and Contemporary Cultivators," in *Before the Wilderness,* ed. Thomas C. Blackburn and Kat Anderson (Menlo Park, Calif.: Ballena Press, 1993), p. 152.

213 *The Timbisha Shoshone were never pushed completely out of their home range.* Deborah Hastings, "Death Valley Tribe Wins a Future with a Bit of History," *Los Angeles Times,* April 11, 1999 (Bulldog edition).

213 *Death Valley–Timbisha Shoshone agreement (generally).* Bureau of Land Management, "The Timbisha Shoshone Tribal Homeland," available on-line at http://www3.iwvisp.com/blm/report/; Death Valley National Park, "Fact Sheet on Traditional Uses and Cooperative Management," available on-line at http://pigpen.itd.nps.gov/deva/Timbisha_facts.html.

214 *"She talked about the springs."* Quoted in Frank Clifford, "U.S., Death Valley Indians Strike a Unique Land Deal," *Los Angeles Times,* February 25, 1999, p. A20.

214 *Toiyabe Chapter of the Sierra Club.* Rose Strickland, conservation chair, Toiyabe chapter of the Sierra Club, "Death Valley National Park and the Timbisha Tribe," letter to Death Valley National Monument, reprinted in *Desert Report* (newsletter of the Sierra Club California/Nevada Desert Committee), summer 1999, p. 8.

214 *Desert Survivors and the Timbisha Shoshone agreement (generally).* Steve Tabor, "Scoping Comments on the Proposal to Establish a Timbisha Shoshone Tribal Land Base in Death Valley National Park," reprinted in *Survivor,* summer 1999, p. 6.

214 *The first principle of conservation.* Aldo Leopold, *A Sand County Almanac* (1949; reprint, New York: Ballantine Books, 1970), p. 190.

215 *"The most unnatural thing."* Richmond Chloe, personal communication, January 30, 1996.

215 *"To banish all evidence of ourselves."* Barry Lopez, "Yukon-Charley: The Shape of Wilderness," in *Crossing Open Ground* (New York: Vintage Books, 1989), p. 87.

215 *What historian Mark Spence pointed out.* Mark Spence, "Dispossessing the Wilderness: Yosemite Indians and the National Park Ideal," *Pacific Historical Review* 65 (February 1996): 59.

CHAPTER 19. *Whale Peak: The Wilderness Path*

216 *"Their skinny arms."* J. Smeaton Chase, *California Desert Trails* (1919; reprint, Palo Alto, Calif.: Tioga, 1987), p. 247.

217 *Perception as participation (generally).* David Abram, *The Spell of the Sensuous: Perception and Language in a More-than-Human World* (New York: Pantheon Books, 1996).

217 *"Mind, conscious mind."* Mary Austin, unpublished manuscript in the collection of the Huntington Library (HEH AU 363), quoted in John P. O'Grady, "Mary Austin's Gleanings of the Wild," *Pilgrims to the Wild* (Salt Lake City: University of Utah Press, 1993), p. 134.

221 *To "please the spirits."* Francisco Patencio, *Stories and Legends of the Palm Springs Indians* (Palm Springs, Calif.: Palm Springs Desert Museum, 1943), p. 73.

222 *A home for wild animals.* Rick Bass gave this definition of wilderness at a reading during the 1997 conference of the Association for the Study of Literature and Environment, Missoula, Montana.

223 *Many activists believe it is time to enlarge our concept of wilderness.* Timothy Egan, "The Definition of Wilderness Is Increasingly Elusive," *New York Times*, September 12, 1999, late edition, Ideas and Trends section, p. 3.

223 *No gathering was done at such sacred sites.* Florence Shipek, personal communication, March 1, 1998.

223 *Myths about [a country's] "familiar objects."* Mary Austin, quoted in *The Desert Reader*, ed. Peter Wild (Salt Lake City: University of Utah Press, 1991), p. 154.

224 *"Is not Nature, rightly read."* Henry David Thoreau, *A Week on the Concord and Merrimack Rivers* (1849; reprint, New York: Crowell, 1911), p. 478.

224 *Buddhist idea of "thusness."* Gary Snyder, "Blue Mountains Constantly Walking," in *The Practice of the Wild* (San Francisco: North Point Press, 1990), p. 103.

224 *"The here and now."* Edward Abbey, *Desert Solitaire* (New York: Ballantine Books, 1968), p. 190.

224 *Zen sweeps aside the dualities.* D. T. Suzuki, *Zen and Japanese Culture* (New York: Pantheon Books, 1959), p. 361.

224 *Zen experience of satori.* Gregory McNamee, "Spiritual Peaks," *Portland: The University of Portland Magazine*, summer 1997, pp. 14–16.

224 *This sense of the sacred is only a beginning.* Gary Snyder, "Good, Wild, Sacred," in *The Practice of the Wild* (San Francisco: North Point Press, 1990), p. 94. In "Blue Mountains Constantly Walking" (also in *The Practice of the Wild*), Snyder goes further and says that the sacred is "a delusion and an obstruction: it diverts us from seeing what is before our eyes: plain thusness" (p. 103).

225 *"Respectful human participation."* Barry Lopez, "Yukon-Charley: The Shape of Wilderness," in *Crossing Open Ground* (New York: Vintage Books, 1989), p. 91.

225   *"Plain members" of the natural community.* I was reminded of Aldo Leopold's "plain members of a natural community" by Steve Windhager, writing in the winter 1998 issue of *Restoration and Management Notes* p. 128.
226   *"If Nature is to be loved."* Suzuki, *Zen and Japanese Culture*, p. 361.
227   *"Why sing cantatas."* Jack Turner, "The Song of the White Pelican," in *The Abstract Wild* (Tucson: University of Arizona Press, 1996), p. 80.

EPILOGUE: *Eyes in the Dark*
232   *As historian Roderick Nash has pointed out.* Roderick Nash, *Wilderness and the American Mind*, 3rd ed. (New Haven: Yale University Press, 1982), p. 1.

Acknowledgments

In retrospect, writing a book such as this seems to be almost an act of hubris. As much as I feel a sense of ownership for the Anza-Borrego Desert, I am just an occasional, if avid, visitor. The many people who live and work there have a much stronger relationship to the place. Their in-depth knowledge of Anza-Borrego and its surrounding areas has added immeasurably to my own work.

First among these is Mark Jorgensen, associate resource ecologist for Anza-Borrego and eight other state parks in the Colorado Desert. His interest in my project, his generosity with his time and information, and his willingness to take me along on work trips in the park were invaluable. Additional thanks go to Anza-Borrego staff members Fred Jee, Brian Cahill, and Paul Remeika, and to all the volunteer docents at the park visitor center.

Anthropologists Lowell John Bean and Florence Shipek have been unsparing with their time and with their wealth of research on (I should say with) the Cahuilla and the Kumeyaay. Although their approach is sometimes at odds with that of Jorgensen and other resource specialists, my hope is that these two strands of knowledge can be woven into a stronger, more inclusive web.

Without the willingness of many members of the Cahuilla and Kumeyaay peoples to share elements of their cultures, little would be known about their worldview or the ways in which they used and changed the landscape. In the past, these tribe members have included Chief Francisco Patencio of the Palm Springs Cahuilla and Delfina Cuero of the Kumeyaay; today, Katherine Siva Saubel of the Cahuilla and Jane Dumas and Mike Connolly of the Kumeyaay continue that goodwill. In recognition of the debt owed to these storytellers, a portion of the royalties from this book will be donated to Cahuilla and Kumeyaay educational funds.

The primary research of many historians paved the way for this book, especially the works of Diana Lindsay, Phil Brigandi, and Richard Carrico. The staff at the San Diego Historical Society and the San Diego Public Library's California Room were unstinting in digging out materials and suggesting additional avenues of research.

Pat Flanagan and the staff of the San Diego Natural History Museum, who assisted me in deciphering mountain lion vocalizations, and Dr. Patrick Abbott of San Diego State University, who reviewed the geology chapter and made many useful suggestions, have helped make this book more accurate than it otherwise would have been. David Gottfredson and Barton Ward provided companionship on many of my trips to the desert, all the while providing comments and encouragement on this work.

At the University of Montana at Missoula, William Kittredge, Deirdre

McNamer, and Bill Vaughn provided valuable instruction in the art of writing, as did Annick Smith, Terry Tempest Williams, John Daniel, and Robert Clark in university-sponsored writing workshops. Dan Flores, Richmond Clow, and Len Broberg introduced me to environmental history, cultural ecology, and environmental science, and Henry Harrington and Nancy Cook showed me new ways of looking at the landscapes of the West.

Thanks also to Jonathan Cobb of Island Press/Shearwater Books and copyeditor Pat Harris, whose editing and fact-checking made this work both more readable and more accurate. Designer David Bullen and illustrator Joyce A. Powzyk produced a beautiful finished product. Many thanks.

Finally, my deepest gratitude is to Diane Willcox, partner and soulmate, whose support in so many ways has made this work possible.

Index

Abandoned city, the desert as an, 125
Abbey, Edward:
  contemplation, 114
  Glen Canyon, 168
  Jorgensen, Mark, 204
  loyalty to the earth, 172, 218
  mysterious quality of the desert, 15
  paradise, 224
  romanticism, 159, 162
  Van Dyke influenced, 149
Abram, David, 217
"Abstract Wild, The" (Turner), 80
Acacia, catclaw, 11
Africa, desert used to be like East,
  32–33
Agaves, 11, 44, 219
Agriculture, 54–55, 130, 137
  see also Land practices, Indian; Plants;
    Water management, Indian
Agriculture, U.S. Department of, 64
Ahwahneechee Indians, 81
Airplanes, jet, 82–83
Alamo River, 133, 134
Algal blooms, fertilizers and, 136
Anasazi Indians, 67, 79
Anderson, Kat, 67, 68
Animals:
  bears, 227
  chaparral and California gnatcatcher,
    50
  coyotes, 97, 100
  extinctions of large mammals in
    North America, 67
  fish, 131–132, 135–137, 140
  gold rush, California, 93
  horses, 94
  mountain lions, 193, 199–200, 203,
    230–232

  mules, 94
  play behavior, 227
  respect for, Indians showing, 45–46
  sheep, 8, 94–96, 108–109
  see also Bighorn sheep, desert; Birds;
    Livestock
Antonio, Juan, 120
Anza-Borrego Desert/State Park, 3,
  5–8, 152–154
  see also individual subject headings
Apache Indians, 117
Aqueducts, 18
Arenas, Luis, 91
Argüello, Santiago, 90
Arrillaga, Governor, 51
Arroyo Salado, 142–144
Aschmann, Homer, 68
Asian landscape paintings, 220, 222
Assimilation into white culture, Indian,
  207
Austin, Mary, 15, 150–151, 158, 217
Australia's indigenous people, 41

Baja California peninsula, 31, 34
Bajada, 10
Barrel cactus, 36, 175–176
Barrows, Cameron, 181
Bass, Rick, 222
Bautista de Anza, Juan, 48, 76
Bean, Lowell J., 28, 43, 44
Bears, 227
Benson, John, 137
Bighorn Canyon, 15
Bighorn Institute, 192
Bighorn sheep, desert:
  arrival in North America, 182
  counting, 8, 190–191, 194–198, 202
  decline, reasons behind, 192

3/10-17 '01 Sierra Club Trip

CONTENTS

7

Practical Guidelines for

10.   PUBLIC PERFORMANCES AND TRIPS *(cont.)*

Practical Guidelines for

DEVELOPING
THE HIGH SCHOOL BAND

Practical Guidelines for

DEVELOPING INTEREST   1
AND SUPPORT

THE FOUNTAINHEAD–DIRECTOR PHILOSOPHY

An organization eventually is permeated with the personality or character of the individual director. Leadership philosophy, or the approach to daily tasks, greatly affects the degree of success achieved. Some of the more noticeable character traits or manifestations of philosophy that I have observed in successful band directors are:

1. The ability to keep vitality and enthusiasm present in their teaching.

A vivacious personality attracts other active people and together they infuse life into whatever they seek to accomplish. In order to possess this vitality, an individual must maintain an active mind and a healthy body through good diet and sensible rest. We have all heard this "song and dance" since we were youngsters, and it's true! Try a bit of reading of some books like Gaylord Hauser's *Treasury of Secrets* or Bob Cumming's *Stay Young and Vital.*

Couple this vitality with a sort of dedicated salesmanship. We all are salesmen to some degree. We discuss and "sell" our ideas and our goals, or we stagnate. Make your salesmanship grow from a true enjoyment of people: a sincere "soft sell" with missionary zeal, stopping short of becoming obnoxious. *Maintain vitality and sell your goals.*

2. Individual self-discipline and consistently good discipline in teaching.

All successful teachers possess a great deal of tolerance for hard work plus the self-discipline to keep at a task until it is finished. This self-discipline is vital, especially in the realm of adequate class preparation. If you find it difficult to finish tasks alone, enlist the aid of students or assistants. Some individuals can stay with a task longer if it becomes a group effort.

Any group learning must have an atmosphere of order or good group discipline. *I have never seen a good band program that did not have good discipline and sustained hard work at its core.*

3. Teaching techniques congruent with individual personality.

Good teachers are not merely "imitators." By "imitator" I mean someone who simply goes through a routine he has learned without ever stopping to analyze *why* certain techniques yield favorable results. We all learn by both imitation and innovation from infancy on towards maturity. To be effective, ideas that start out "imitative" must mutate to fit individual personality.

4. A high degree of professional dedication.

In order to "pick up" new "imitative"-type ideas, an individual must conscientiously attend professional clinics and workshops where ideas are discussed. At conventions, clinics, etc., there are always good, experienced minds with whom anyone can discuss problems and search for solutions. These events can also be a welcome change of pace, a rededication to excellence, etc.—in short, a "recharging" of the "battery." *Professional participation is the key to professional dedication.*

5. A deep desire for continued musical growth.

A college degree starts, but by no means completes a professional education. I recall hearing a recent college graduate complaining that "he was not taught this in school; he was not taught that" (likely as not this same individual, while in college, complained about all the things that he *did* have to take)—but at any rate, my reply was not very sympathetic. I merely pointed out that *a college diploma is no substitute for individual thought and that a degree starts professional education, but does not complete it.*

I have a vivid picture in my mind of a fine band director (of many years) attending and taking brief notes at a clinic on rehearsal techniques. This individual was well known for his outstanding teaching through the years and was only a few years away from retirement; yet there he was taking time for this clinic, much of the material I'm sure he had heard many times before. He was willing to sit through all the repetition to hear possibly one new idea or approach to a problem. This kind of desire for self-improvement had helped him stay vital and professionally alive through the years.

CREATING STUDENT INTEREST

The key to interest and support of the band program is student interest. If students are interested they interest their parents; their parents spread interest throughout the community; the school administration is affected by community interests; and on it goes ad infinitum. The logical first step in promoting a music program is student interest.

1. Strive to make band activities exciting and enjoyable.

A director attracts the kind of students he expects. If you wish to attract superior students then expect superior effort from the students you have. Word travels fast, and students are attracted to activities that are both constructive and exciting. Talk in a forward positive vein at all times, and be sure that the band's foundation is continuously, firmly anchored in a competent "music fundamentals"-oriented type of teaching. A student must make musical progress if true enjoyment and emotional release are to be experienced in music.

2. Set up a worthwhile, sensible schedule of events.

Remember—performance is the life-blood of a musical organization *unless* you bleed the subject to death. Check over your schedule of events annually and purge those events which are neither vital nor interesting. Few organizations can effectively survive more than one major event per month, and less if there is a big trip or event scheduled for the year. Start your schedule of events with the performances that are traditionally expected (football games, civic parades, concerts, etc.) Wherever possible get the dates of these events and record them on the school calendar early. Check them against possible conflicts with school events (exams, holidays, etc.) and work out obvious problems. Next get a schedule of annual events from your regional or State Music Education Association, discuss these events with your principal and record them on the school calendar. Discuss with your student leaders any other events you feel would be of interest and get the general band's reaction. If the student reaction is not good, drop the idea and try to get some suggestions from your students.

Always first check events through the principal, then record them on the school calendar: otherwise you can easily plan something and then get the props pulled from under you and ill will will abound.

3. Make band activities a vital part of school life.

Many activities that are a part of school life already have the participation of the band as an integral part: football games, pep rallies, assembly programs, etc. If kept in proper perspective, a spring musical or variety show can be a big success. Activities of this type can be expanded to include adults in the community as well.

Music can add interest to subjects from literature to physical education. Select and offer records to: art (background music), history (events commemorated with music), literature (music inspired by the written word), physical education (exercising music), etc. Study a little and offer to teach the sound and acoustics section of physics. Take time to sit down and talk with the coach about how the band can help get the team fired up and ready to play. I once had the opportunity of working with a very successful university basketball coach who worked out his entire warm-up drill to music. Everything was well paced, timed to the second and *rehearsed* to perfection. When this team played the fans came early, cheered the warm-up, and usually saw the team win.

If you have attracted good students to your program, you already are on the inside with school publications. Band students are usually on the staff of newspapers and annuals, and very often are selected as editors of these publications. Frequent discussions with staff members and faculty sponsors will greatly aid publication of band activities.

4. Make the band room an attractive place that students like to visit.

I know of no rules that will guarantee an attractive room but here are a couple of ideas that can usually enhance a music room's appearance. Encourage the art department to sponsor some large wall paintings with a music motif. Many times attractive paintings can be obtained for only the cost of the materials, and the artists are proud to have their work displayed. Either the school shop or a local cabinet maker can make attractive combination trophy cases and picture racks. Picture racks displaying each year's performing groups, outstanding band members, all-state band members, officers, etc. appeal to the student's innate desire to be remembered, and go a long way in encouraging outstanding student accomplishments. Inspection of trophies and photographs is always a popular browsing activity.

Strive to obtain the best in a sound reproduction system. Recording studio type equipment can do wonders toward encouraging listening. Once I was very fortunate in obtaining some fine sound equipment and we set up a music listening period before school each morning. Students from all parts of the school were encouraged to come listen and also to bring their favorite records. Band music, light classics, jazz, and pop music were mixed freely to the pleasure of a large gathering each morning. I generally used the music the students brought as a starting point for expanding their musical tastes. More tips on effective use of the physical plant will be included in the chapter on facilities and program organization.

CREATING PARENT INTEREST

As has been mentioned previously, parents will have a natural interest in activities where their children have interest. Enlisting the aid of parents without allowing them to become a pressure group requires careful planning and a clear understanding from the outset. Here are a few tips that may be of value.

1. "Booster" groups should be regulated by a constitution.

Any club or "booster" group, regardless of title, should be firmly regulated by a constitution that defines their role in the administration of the band. This constitution should be discussed with the principal and any possible hazards eliminated. Any "booster" president who has "visions of grandeur" can be a real pain, if his powers are not clearly defined by organization rules. The only reason for the existence of such groups should be solely for the purpose of fund raising.

2. Outline fund-raising objectives clearly.

Two of the most frequent fund-raising objectives are big trips and new uniform purchases. In addition to these campaigns some programs unfortunately have to depend on "booster" groups for basic operating funds. Continually work for a school-supported budget, based on a fixed amount for each student in the band program. Whenever possible, keep successful fund-raising ideas as annual events and be alert for opportunities to take over concessions, etc. that other school clubs lose.

These two rules should direct fund raising:

A. *Sell only things that give full value for money received,* or B. *Solicit outright contributions for the band.* Anything in between is usually not effective and can create ill will for the band. Poor quality merchandise sold at inflated prices will make lasting enemies and is downright dishonest. When approaching a fund-raising campaign, remember that many people think of their assistance as a contribution, regardless of what you are selling. Why not ask for contributions and get the full amount contributed? Ads in programs, patron lists, etc., are effective ways to solicit contributions, and are in fact much more palatable to many people.

Some of the most effective fund-raising ideas I have seen are: game concessions, football programs, football reserved seat sales, booster stickers, and similar annual events. For outright contributions I have found the patron list to be most effective.

3. Parent assistance in addition to fund raising.

A role that can stimulate parent interest, as well as assist the director, is that of "parent chaperone." Have the parents' club make up a list of chaperones to choose from, or simply let the parent group assign chaperones for each out-of-town event. I have also been fortunate in securing parent assistance from time to time with other helpful projects. Parents can be invaluable with tasks such as uniform assignments and adjustments, band room carpentry and repair, etc. The one element that is vital on such assistance is: let parents be in charge of something rather than expect them to serve as handimen. The band director must be in control of all band activities, but if you cannot delegate authority to responsible, capable parents, then you will not find much parent assistance.

4. Honesty in parent-director relations.

In dealings with parents, individual personality obviously plays a big part. Always try to use "tactful honesty" in discussing a student with his parents. Be fair and courteous.

Give your honest opinion of a situation and explain that it is only an opinion, your opinion. Never argue with a parent when they are irate and be very careful to keep control of your own temper. Be firm in stating your position. Do not retreat if you are correct, but listen and try to understand the parents' position or the situation will soon lead to an explosion. I have seen parents come in ready to fight, ranting like madmen, then leave apologizing for their actions. If you let them "spout off" what is on their mind at the outset then perhaps it will be possible to reason with them. To ward off many misunderstandings, be sure parents are well informed on band requirements, regulations, and policies.

Remember that band can be a very expensive luxury in the eyes of a parent. Keep parents informed well in advance regarding trips or special events. Keep the cost of band participation at a minimum. When a parent seeks your advice regarding an instrument purchase, try to explain that the reputable brands sold at local stores are usually the best buys. There are few if any "bargains" in musical instruments. Appeal to the sense of values of a parent and explain that in musical instruments you usually get what you pay for.

Be sure that all events that occur after school hours (outside rehearsals, trips, etc.)—start and end on schedule. Remember that parents provide a lot of "taxi" service for students and sitting for hours in a car is no fun at all. If the band room does not have a phone, have one installed, even if it is only an extension.

Always try to remember that a parent has interest in the student above interest in the band, while the director's viewpoint naturally must have the band coming first.

BUILDING ADMINISTRATION
AND COMMUNITY SUPPORT

Student and parent interest must provide the backbone of community and school administration support. Any school administration is influenced directly or indirectly by the wishes of the general community. The band director must provide the main thrust in securing community support. Keep in mind that the general public is usually quite naive when it comes to knowledge about the amount of time, talent and money that it takes to operate a band program. Here are some principles and ideas that should help stimulate individual thinking:

1. Use the "pragmatic" approach with public relations.

When you discuss band with anyone, keep their interest in mind. An average downtown merchant usually couldn't care less about the esthetic value of music to a student's individual life. Discuss last year's Christmas parade, or something that is of importance to him. He is business oriented and anything that brings in business to the community or his store interests him. A big selling point with most merchants is: "The band either favorably or unfavorably reflects the community whenever they are appearing (in parades, etc)." A favorable impression by the band creates a favorable impression of the community and will tend to make it attractive in the minds of visitors, manufacturers, etc.

Be interested enough in people to study them and try to analyze what makes them "tick." This is the only way you can ever know how to "sell" band to their natural interests.

2. Work to make band a vital part of community life.

Many community events traditionally call for the services of a band. Never allow yourself or the band to forget that this is one of the reasons that schools first started band programs. Consider reasonable community requests for the services of the band first. If a conflict arises between an "out-of-town" trip and an "in-town" event, perform for the event at home. Avoid playing for one merchant or even one group of merchants. This practice can lead to problems. Keep appearances for the community in general.

Fill the numerous requests for music programs at civic club meetings with small ensembles playing popular styled selections.

The stage band (for large meeting places) and varied trios, quartets, etc., are ideal for these events. Be careful to have some groups that remain intact from year to year because requests also frequently occur during marching season in the fall.

3. Keep the administration and community informed.

Know and respect the administration chain of command. For example, if you must discuss a matter with the school superintendent, go to your principal, get his opinion and approval on the matter first. Any administrator who feels that he is being pressured usually says no!

Keep the principal informed on band activities, but do not become a pest. When you visit the principal's office, have a written list of the matters you wish to discuss. Be well informed on school discipline policies and handle all of your own discipline problems. Keep school business first when visiting the office of an administrator. If you can get to know an administrator socially (golf, parties, etc.) it never hurts; but take care never to "use" these occasions to "push" your band program or you can alienate your administration very quickly.

Be ethical: support the current administration of your school when dealing with students or the general public. *Never* allow yourself or the band to be drawn into school "politics."

Good community press coverage can go a long way in bolstering general community support. It has been my experience that the average band director does not have very much time to devote to "publicity" if he does his job teaching. A good "publicity committee" can be very effective in enlarging and improving press coverage. Keep your committee small and have the duties well defined. Select one band member and one "booster" club member to work with you as the "publicity committee." In consideration of people for this job, keep in mind (1) enthusiasm and flair for reporting, (2) reputation for dependability, and (3) possible news media connections. Encourage all students and parents to report publicity ideas to you. Make complete check lists of all publicity outlets and use them each time there is band publicity information available. Keep a "press" book that records all press releases.

4. Be considerate in association with faculty, staff, and general public.

A band director who does his work well believes deeply in the value of his subject in the life of his students. Therein lies the root of most faculty-relation problems. Always keep in mind: band students usually enjoy and talk about band more than they do other classes. The band receives more publicity than many other school subjects. Also remember that trips and similar events are generally looked upon as exciting diversions by other faculty members.

In order to counteract these natural tendencies, caution students never to brag about band in other classes. Remind them on every trip that classwork missed is work to be made up and not excused. Attend and show interest in the activities of other school departments. Regularly attend faculty meetings and do your share of "extra duties" that are necessary.

Prepare carefully an explanation of the band activities that will take students out of classes during the year; then offer this explanation at one of the early faculty meetings. First discuss the matters with your principal and request that he put the talk early on the faculty meeting agenda. Try an explanation something like the following: "Many of the school-community relations duties naturally fall to the band (parades, civic clubs, etc.). Please understand that these activities mean additional work for the band and myself. Some events will be contests similar to those engaged in by many departments: math, science, forensics, etc. We promise to keep these events to a minimum and I will always remind students to make up any classwork they miss."

Whenever possible use faculty members as chaperones on big trips. This way they can feel a part of the band's activities, see the amount of work involved, and spread the word to other faculty members.

Be ethical: do not discuss other faculty members with students and do not defend students against other teachers.

Be considerate and friendly, never condescending toward school "staff" members (office staff, custodial, etc.) When you must do work after school hours, inform them of this necessity in advance. Give them free concert tickets and encourage band-sponsored gifts for them at appropriate times during the year. Remember—consideration and appreciation are natural human needs.

Make it a practice to write thank you notes to any individual or group that aids the band in any way. Let public appearances of the band speak for themselves: never make apologies or brag about the band. Always speak in terms of the band as an integral part of the community. The band director should take as active a part in civic activities as time and inclination allow.

FACILITIES AND PROGRAM ORGANIZATION   2

THE CURRICULUM

An effective curriculum is the prerequisite for any successful band program. I have seen fine teaching rendered ineffective by a poor schedule. A good band director ·can never take the curriculum for granted, especially where an entire system of elementary, junior, and senior high bands is co-ordinated. Keep in touch with the pulse of the school and current with administration curriculum thinking. If you do not look out for the interests of the band program, who do you think will?

I vividly remember hearing a band director bitterly lamenting how his program had been destroyed because nearly half of the band had been scheduled in such a way that they could not participate in advanced band. This director had never achieved more than mediocre success and his failure to prevent this schedule problem was representative of his operation of the band program.

To help develop and maintain an effective band curriculum, consider the following:

1. Match the music curriculum with the total community environment.

To expect a professional orchestra in a rurally oriented community is sheer folly. I exaggerate, of course, but you see the point. Do not resign yourself to mediocrity, but be realistic

31

with the community needs. In most communities the band program must pave the way in developing a total music curriculum. Vocal music and orchestra are a vital part of the total music curriculum; but in most situations, it is easier to sell the community and school administration on the idea of a band first. It is impossible to formulate curriculum designs for every situation, but a few sample curriculums for representative situations are included on pages 35 through 37.

2. Co-ordinate the band program with the total school curriculum.

This co-ordination requires constant vigilance and effort. Ease in developing an effective teaching schedule is in many ways related to school size. Larger schools that employ both vocal and instrumental teachers, and offer more than one section of all subjects, present fewer schedule problems than do smaller schools that hire one or two music teachers to operate a complete music program.

Since small to medium-sized schools present more problems we will focus our attention on them. Be wary of one-section subjects, especially so-called "college preparatory" classes. To have one of these classes scheduled during the same period as advanced band can be a real headache. Consider the academic interests of the majority of your students, then eliminate potential conflicts before they occur. Develop the understanding and co-operation of your administration first. Other important teachers to keep in touch with are: guidance counselors, coaches, etc. Keep school schedules on file and periodically check on any rumored or proposed changes. Use salesmanship, diplomacy, any trait you possess (short of coercion) in preventing conflicts with your schedule.

For example: if the only section of physics to be offered is the same period as advanced band, good students will be forced to choose between subjects and severe problems can result. If band is offered only during the period that is scheduled for competitive athletics, conflicts are inevitable. Guard against such conflicts; move your own schedule around as a last resort; but do not try to live with "built-in problems." Additional scheduling tips are included in the chapters dealing with elementary, junior, and senior high bands.

3. Effectively pace and utilize teacher time.

The effective use of teacher time depends a great deal on the individual school situation. If there are several music teachers in a school system, then the band director at the senior high should spend some time with program co-ordination and supervision. If the senior high band director teaches his feeder program as well as senior high music subjects, then he must pace and schedule his classes in such a way that he has energy and enthusiasm remaining for each class.

A director in the one-music-teacher situation should constantly strive to add teachers to the music faculty. Remember that before any more music teachers can be hired there must be a sufficient number of students in the music program to justify additional faculty. Do not allow the situation to develop where music teachers must teach non-music subjects against their will. Fill each period with *some* music subject and get enough students for the class to materialize. If you allow vacant periods to occur in your schedule, you will likely be first on the list for chores such as study hall "baby sitting," hall duty, etc. A director will not have the time to recruit additional music students if he is tied down with such chores.

Situations involving more than one on the music faculty involve a different type of problem. Diplomacy and co-operation are vital or the resulting conflicts will leave everyone a loser, especially the students. It is generally most satisfactory where all music teachers are invloved with the total program.

I have known the following situations to work effectively:

A. Two teachers: both teach instrumental beginners in divided classes of woodwinds and brass percussion; each specializes, one teaching the senior high marching band while the other directs the junior high marching band. During concert season the specialities are switched. Other teaching is divided similarly.

B. Two music teachers: one directs junior high band and choral activities while the other teacher has beginning and senior high band.

C. If there are several elementary and junior high directors, it is wise to have all involved with the senior high program in some way. They might direct ensembles, teach privately, etc., but most teachers teach more effectively if they can watch and take pride in their students' continued progress.

D. If the instrumental and vocal departments are separate, engage in cooperative endeavors such as musicals, joint concerts, etc.

Of course, effective use of physical facilities has a great deal to do with the organizing of the teaching schedule.

4. Follow the developmental approach.

Try to pace the total program in such a way that students can see progress from year to year but never feel that they've "done it all." Nothing is worse than the exploitation of music students by their directors. For example, elementary bands that try to emulate junior and senior high bands, junior high bands that try to emulate senior high bands (especially with their schedule of events), and even senior bands that seek to emulate college or professional bands.

Such selfish, short-sighted direction causes students to drop out of the music program all along the line, often with either a biased or unfavorable view of music. I do not mean to be satisfied with mediocre palying at any level, but keep the pace realistic. When students are musically more capable than they were before; when there's work as well as play; when there's a concentration on personal emotional release through music; then they enjoy playing an instrument and have a desire to continue.

Set realistic goals and schedule a reasonable number of annual events for various level groups so that they progress and do more each year without ever feeling like "we've done everything, so why continue?" Remember that present members will be parents of tomorrow's students.

5. Match the curriculum to existing facilities.

This factor is quite important in situations where one music teacher instructs in several schools. In most elementary schools the area used for band instruction is used for other activities during the school day; therefore special arrangements must be made for an instrumental class. Consult with the principals of schools where adjustments must be made before finalizing the total schedule. First work for the times that are nearest your proposed schedule. Try to avoid disrupting individual school schedules; then make necessary total schedule adjustments.

SAMPLE CURRICULUM SCHEDULES

Here are a few schedules I have seen work effectively. The number and length of periods during the day varies somewhat from state to state and school to school. These schedules are based on six 50-minute periods each day.

A. Schedule for a small to medium-sized rurally oriented school system with one band director who also teaches choral activities. See Figure 2-1.

Period	Music Subject
1	Elementary Beginning Band
2	Elementary Beginning or Intermediate Band
Home room or Activity Period	Travel Time
3	Chorus
4	Senior High Band
Lunch	
5	Junior High Band
6	Planning Period

Figure 2-1

In this case, fourth period was chosen for senior band because this period was never "cut" (for assemblies, etc.) The entire school ate during this period so it was an hour and a half in length. Several teachers placed their favorite "college-prep" subjects during the first period because they felt the students were more alert at that time. In addition to this, many students came to school by bus and the buses were frequently late. Sixth period was ruled out because all competitive sports were offered during this period.

B. Schedule for a small to average size town with one "city" senior high school. Two senior high music teachers to cover both vocal and instrumental music plus the related feeder programs. See Figure 2-2.

Period	Music Subjects
Home room or Activity Period	Advanced Band
1	Advanced Band
2	Intermediate or Second Band
3	Beginning Band (High School Chorus)
Lunch	
4	Junior High Band
5	Beginning Band
6	Planning and Individual Help

Figure 2-2

Advanced band was scheduled first period because students were able to get there prior to regular school opening time. This provided time for section rehearsals and individual warm-up and tuning before the full band rehearsal started. Through administrative understanding and cooperation no one-section subjects were offered during the first period. Physical education credit was given for marching band during the first semester. Marching band members were scheduled into second period physical education which allowed two periods for band the first semester. Junior band members ate during the first lunch period which allowed them time to return to the band room for tuning and still have a full hour rehearsal. This schedule worked beautifully due to excellent administrative support.

C. Metropolitan area or "neighborhood city school." Two full time senior high music teachers and two elementary instrumental-vocal teachers. One vocal, one instrumental with separate rehearsal rooms at the senior high. See Figure 2-3.

Period	Instrumental Music Subject
1	Wind Ensemble alternating with Orchestra
2	Large Second Band (Symphonic Instrumentation)
Home Room or Activity Period	Ensembles and Individual Help
3	Cadet Band and Ensembles
Lunch	
4	Music Theory
5	General Music
6	Supervision in Feeder Schools

Figure 2-3

The wind ensemble is a select group of forty-five players. This group meets three days a week—Monday, Wednesday, and Friday; and orchestra meets Tuesday and Thursday. The strings rehearse Monday, Wednesday, and Friday in the choral room. Marching band membership is by audition and meets after school. Membership in the marching band is quite competitive partially because this is the group that participates in the big out-of-town events (marching contests, parades, etc.).

All of these schedules are the result of working toward the best for each individual situation. They might not be applicable neccessarily in other situations but are included with the hope of arousing individual thought.

INSTRUMENTAL REHEARSAL ROOMS

An effective curriculum is very closely related to the facilities available for teaching. Whether the areas that band classes are taught in are makeshift rooms or architect-designed rehearsal halls, it falls to the director to make the best use of everything that is available.

A small struggling school system will not commit money for special buildings unless the community is sold on band first. A large school system can turn a deaf ear to one voice, but rarely to a concerned neighborhood. It therefore falls the lot of any director to start with what he can get and improve it, all the time talking and planning future growth. Here are some ideas on both improving existing facilities and planning for growth.

1. Use do-it-yourself ideas to improve existing facilities.

Personal ingenuity, student help, and school shops can do a great deal in helping improve existing facilities. Start with the rooms that you must use in the feeder schools. If you must teach in a school gym or on an auditorium stage, try to find some sort of storage closet that can be cleaned out and used for instrument and equipment storage (under lock and key). Try to get a piano to be used for accompanying beginning classes and store it nearby. Build storage shelves or lockers in rooms that must be shared.

For large ensemble rehearsal halls, try thinking through the roles of people who will be using the room. Imagine yourself as a student arriving at school with instrument and music each morning. Go to the door the students likely will be hurrying through and you can easily figure out the best place for a music folder rack and instrument storage shelves. Think of these same students as they come from class into band and you can immediately place shelves for the temporary storage of text-books, and provide a place to assemble instruments without leaving the case on the floor. Imagine yourself as a visitor or parent browsing in the bandroom waiting for the director or some student, and you can think of the ideal location for picture racks, trophy cases, etc. This "role" type of thinking can be the idea source for many simple but useful improvements.

Excess sound is a problem in most rehearsal rooms. Old stage curtains or burlap, cleaned and hung along walls, can help control reverberation. Carpet (even factory-second quality) can help the sound and improve the looks of an old room tremendously. If all else fails, enlist student help and paint unsightly rooms. Use the "antiquing" paint technique on battered old filing cabinets, desks, etc. Try to obtain air conditioning to help with room temperature during rehearsals when windows generally must be closed. *Involve students:* they can be a wonderful source of help and ideas, plus the added pride that such work will generate in the care of the "band room."

2. Get maximum use of available space.

Relevant tips for effective use of space are included in each of the chapters dealing with elementary, junior and senior high schools. Some basic tips are: A. Scout around for rooms containing "junk" that could be stored elsewhere. Clean these rooms and use them for storage or individual practice space. B. If the corner of a cafeteria or some similar area must be used for instruction, then get this area partitioned off, even if the partitioned area is small and the partitions moveable. C. Check music and instrument storage space for maximum use of vertical space. All too often, floor space is wasted and vertical space goes unused. Wall racks and shelves can help eliminate this problem. D. If practice rooms are limited or nonexistent, do not overlook the use of music libraries, instrument storage rooms, dressing rooms, etc., for individual practice. Any available area should be utilized for individual practice when rehearsals are not in progress.

3. Work and plan toward new facilities.

The perfect "band room" or music building is a favorite "pipe-dream" of most band directors. It has been my experience that extraordinary facilities do not necessarily extraordinary teaching make, but planning continuing improvements is a part of good administration. In other words, a good teacher has the tendency to teach well in spite of the physical plant, all the while making plans for the future.

Unfortunately, architects and builders tend to be a little negligent in the realm of acoustics. One reason is probably the expense involved in good "sound" treatment. Leave nothing to chance when new music facilities are being planned. Work yourself into the planning and then use every fact you can assimilate to see that the best possible plant is built. Once plans are approved and contracts "let" it is too late to protest "built-in" faults.

A good source of facts and representative plans is the M.E.N.C. book *Music Buildings, Rooms, and Equipment.* This book is available through the national M.E.N.C. offices in Washington, D.C. Most states have minimum "Rules and Regulations" handbooks which can be helpful in insuring adequate facilities.

Here are two of my favorite plans for senior high music buildings. See Figures 2-4 and 2-5.

PERFORMANCE FACILITIES

Other areas of the school are frequently used by the band, especially for public performances. Although these facilities will not generally be the responsibility of the band director, it is to his advantage to be concerned with, and knowledgeable regarding their use.

1. The football stadium.

More people will probably see more performances by the band in the football stadium than anywhere else. Talk frequently with the coach and principal regarding the best use of the stadium. Have a section of seats designated for the band. It is wise to paint the seats in this section a color different from the other stadium seats. Select the color from a shade that is predominant in the band uniform (especially the trouser color). This will help to set this section apart and help in the understanding that these seats are to be for the use of the band. Select a section of the stadium adjoining an exit leading to behind the stands, and near the main cheering section. I have seen good use of separate band bleachers near the end zone. If the band section is a part of the general seating area, construct a banister or border of either wire, chain, or wood around it. Also construct a platform in the front part of this section running the entire width of the band seating area. This platform can be used for conducting and will prevent the problem of the band playing directly into the backs of some spectators. Designate a section for visiting bands also.

Be sure to have knowledge of the location and operation of: all entrances and exits to the stadium and playing field (plus keys to locks), the lighting system, the public address system, etc. This information can be of great value in an emergency or tight situation. Schedule at least one marching rehearsal in the stadium prior to each performance. Check the accuracy of playing field markings used by the band (yard lines, hash marks, etc.). This chore is often assigned to student managers with inaccuracy the frequent result. Since it is unwise to use the stadium for the majority of marching rehearsals, it generally falls to the band director to select and mark off an area for marching practice. This is best done with student help and director supervision, well in advance of the first marching rehearsal. For lasting practice field lines, try mowing the lines closer than the remainder of the field and using athletic field marking paint or burning the lines in with a mixture of kerosene and gasoline.

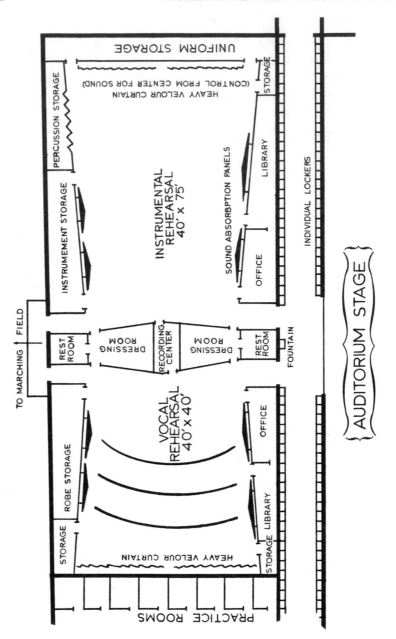

Figure 2-4

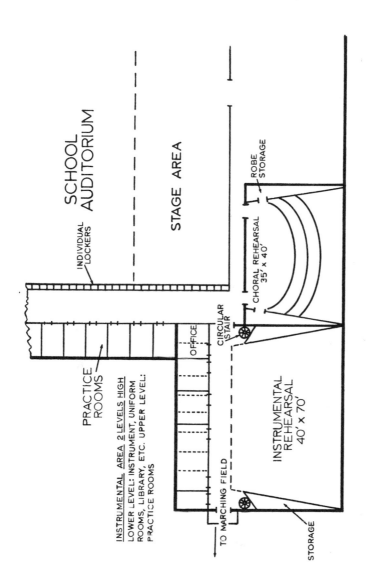

Figure 2-5

2. The auditorium.

The auditorium in most schools is a much-used area. In most communities, the senior high auditorium is used by both the school and the general public. Unfortunately, in some schools it is necessary for the band to use the auditorium for daily rehearsals. In such a situation, be sure to obtain adequate storage space that can be locked.

If there are improvements needed in the auditorium (lighting, sound, curtains, etc.), enlist the aid of other departments that use the auditorium frequently (drama, etc.) Campaign for school-supported improvements, and if this is not fruitful, stage a musical or some similar event with the proceeds going for auditorium or stage improvements.

Use student help in auditorium decoration for concerts, etc. Simple decorations in good taste add to the atmosphere.

A school calendar should be kept in the principal's office regarding the reservation of auditorium use. Be sure to check this calendar before finalizing concert or auditorium rehearsal dates.

3. Gyms, cafeterias, out-of-town performances.

Make it a practice to scout and plan well in advance the use of unfamiliar areas. Spend some time in the room or area to be used. Think through the action of the event and plan for possible circumstances through observation. I have found it wise to go so far as to visit unfamiliar stadiums prior to playing a ball game there. Be sure to scout well in advance so that there is time to make any adjustments that are deemed necessary. Familiarity with performance areas can prove invaluable in making "on the spot" decisions.

INSTRUMENTS AND EQUIPMENT

In addition to a good instruction curriculum plus a suitable building, adequate school-owned instruments and equipment are necessary for a superior band program. These instruments are generally those that are necessary to complete full band instrumentation, but are either too expensive or "specialized" for individual ownership. In order to insure an adequate instrumentation each year, the school system should own the instruments listed in Figure 2-6.

For 55 to 65 Students

VITAL	LUXURY
1 oboe	2 oboes
1 bassoon	2 bassoons
1 alto clarinet	2 alto clarinets
1 bass clarinet	2 bass clarinets
	1 contra-bass clarinet
	1 tenor sax
1 baritone sax	1 baritone sax
2 double horns	4 double horns
2 single F horns	1 bass trombone
2 euphoniums	2 euphoniums
2 sousaphones	2 tubas
2 field snare drums	3 sousaphones
1 bass drum	1 string bass
1 pair medium heavy cymbals	2 field snare drums
minimum traps (triangle,	2 tenor drums
woodblock, maracas, etc.)	1 "scotch" bass drum
2 timpani	1 concert bass drum
1 orchestral bells	1 pair medium heavy cymbals
	1 large suspended cymbal
	1 complete percussion cabinet
	4 timpani
	1 xylophone
	1 marimba
	1 tam-tam (small)

Figure 2-6

The priority to be placed on obtaining these school-owned instruments might run something like:

1. Sousaphone and baritone
2. Drums and necessary percussion

3. Horns and saxes
4. Alto and bass clarinets
5. Timpani
6. Oboes and bassoons
7. Contra-bass clarinet, tubas, and added percussion.

Instrumentation for a larger group would be increased in proportion to this. The additional equipment needed for this group would depend to a certain extent on the level of maturity of the ensemble, as reflected in the difficulty of music played. See Figure 2-7

For 75 to 100 Students

VITAL	LUXURY
1 piccolo	2 piccolos (1 for marching only)
2 oboes	1 E-flat flute
2 bassoons	3 oboes and 1 English horn
1 E-flat soprano clarinet	3 bassoons and 1 contra-bassoon
2 E-flat alto clarinets (or F basset horn)	1 E-flat soprano clarinet
2 B-flat bass clarinets	4 E-flat alto clarinets (or F basset horns)
1 contra-bass clarinet	4 B-flat bass clarinets
1 tenor sax	2 contra clarinets (possibly 1 E-flat and 1 B-flat)
1 baritone sax	1 B-flat soprano sax
3 double horns	1 tenor sax
2 single F horns	1 baritone sax
1 bass trombone	9 cornets
3 euphoniums	2 flugel horns
3 tubas	2 E-flat soprano cornets (for marching use only)
4 sousaphones	8 F alto trumpets*
1 string bass	8 double horns
1 set marching drums	2 bass trombones
1 concert bass drum	4 euphoniums
1 complete percussion cabinet	

Figure 2-7

---

*(for marching use only)

1 pair medium heavy cym-   4 tubas
   bals   2 string basses
1 large suspended cymbals   6 sousaphones
1 set orchestral bells   1 harp (school size)
1 xylophone   1 set marching drums and marching
3 timpani   cymbals, bongos, and suspended
     cymbal
    1 concert bass drum
    1 trap set
    1 complete percussion cabinet
    1 set of chimes
    1 set of orchestral bells
    1 xylophone
    1 "vibes"
    1 marimba
    1 medium large tam-tam
    4 timpani

Figure 2-7 (cont.)

The priority order on these items should be similar to the one listed for smaller groups. "Color" or "speciality" instruments should be added last (according to need).

In addition to instruments, there is a great deal of equipment needed in the operation of a band program. Some of the items needed in most situations are:

For Rehearsal Hall

Chairs (with straight backs to allow comfortable erect posture)
Music stands (metal "desk" type, adjustable)
Music folio racks
Instrument storage racks (roll-away racks for sousaphones and marching drums)
Director podium
Music and office filing cabinets
Director and secretary desks
Bookshelves (library and rehearsal hall storage)
Uniform racks

Sound reproduction and recording equipment
Typewriter, and correspondence filing racks
Duplicator equipment (ditto, etc.)
Bulletin and chalk boards
Trophy cabinets and picture racks
Desks (for class work)

Here are a few suggestions on how to effectively use and maintain instruments and equipment.

1. Keep accurate records in a central location.

The high school band office is usually a good place to keep inventory, instrument card files, etc. Instruments should be checked out with a liability agreement (responsibility for loss, destruction, etc.) to be signed by both parent and student.

2. Charge a maintenance fee for school-owned instruments.

This fee should be used to finance annual major repair, and (as needed) replace school-owned instruments. If possible, it is best to collect this fee in lump sum at the beginning of the school year. Repair made necessary by carelessness should be at the expense of the individual.

3. Inspect instruments regularly.

This inspection should be a part of the student's grade. (See student grading in Chapters 3, 4 and 5). Use student help if possible and insist that needed repairs are made on instruments. This inspection could be each six weeks or as needed during the year.

4. Teach and expect individual student maintenance and repair.

Make preventive maintenance, as well as basic emergency repair, a part of your instrumental teaching. If students are a part of equipment and building maintenance, they tend to take much better care of all facilities.

THE MUSIC LIBRARY

Rounding out the basic necessary music facilities is the music library. Most school music libraries must utilize student help, but it is the director's responsibility to organize, set policies, etc. Here are a few ideas that help to insure that your library will grow rather than need constant replenishment.

1. Set up a complete system of filing.

I prefer a categorical "Library of Congress" type system. Any school librarian can give you the system "basics." This system can be a great assist when building a concert "program order" (see Chapter 10). Even if you do not use a categorical system, at least use a system that relies on a card file rather than some sort of alphabetical order that must be constantly re-shuffled. Keep both a title and composer file with cards containing information such as type of selection, arranger, dates performed, etc.

2. Keep music filed in sturdy folders or filing boxes.

Keep the library neat and preserve music through the use of filing envelopes or filing boxes stored in adequate "legal sized" cabinets. Insist that music be carried in folios rather than carried in cases or loose-leaf.

3. Make music the responsibility of the individual and fine for loss.

In order to help keep music the responsibility of each student, try to provide individual copies of music being prepared. Charge fifty to sixty cents for any parts that are lost or rendered unusable through carelessness, etc.

OFFICE OPERATIONAL PROCEDURES

1. Correspondence and bookkeeping.

An effective way to keep up with these necessary but nonmusical tasks is through the use of student help. More will be said of this matter in the chapter dealing with student help, but suffice it to say that most directors can use assistance in these areas. An understanding and cooperative "business" department in your school can be of great assistance. Often advanced students planning secretary careers can take letters, type, etc. The answer to good correspondence is—make it a policy to reply immediately, while an answer is fresh in your mind; otherwise correspondence falls behind and replies have a tendency to sound stale. It is wise to set aside a short time each day for necessary business correspondence.

Many a headache and problem have come up due to finances—"money!" Many musicians seem to have a definite weakness when it comes to sound business procedures. Enlist the aid of your "accounting" teacher. With a little luck, she might even assign you a student to assist with bookkeeping. At any rate, seek out professional help in keeping simple accurate records. Most states require complete internal school book-keeping and compliance goes "with the territory." Provide clear dated records of fund raising, etc. Dated receipts are the best way of keeping clear quick records. A complete record of income and expenditures is usually kept by the school accountant.

2. Budgets and bids.

If you are to receive a reasonable annual budget, you must demonstrate sound financial management. One of the prerequisites is a realistic budget.

In order to have an adequate budget, try to get a certain amount allotted for each student in the instrumental music program. Twenty to twenty-five dollars per student will maintain and make some progress in most situations. Individual program needs must dictate where the various percentages of the budget should be applied. Reference to the section of this chapter dealing with instruments and equipment can serve as an outline for the priority of purchases.

Figure 2-8 is a sample budget for a program teaching 100 senior high students, 120 junior high students, and 160 elementary students. The budget is based on an allotment of $20.00

per student in junior and senior high and $10.00 per student in elementary levels.

BUDGET $6,000

STUDENT INSTRUMENT FEES $1,500

MUSIC—$1,500
Marching band music—	$250.00
Concert music—	$950.00
Senior high—	$450.00
Junior high—	$350.00
Elementary—	$150.00
Group instruction books—	$150.00
Ensemble music—	$150.00

INSTRUMENTS— $3,550.00
1 Baritone—	$250.00
1 Bass Clarinet—	$400.00
1 Double horn—	$650.00
1 Oboe—	$350.00
1 pair Timpani—	$900.00
Instrument Repair—	$1,000.00

EQUIPMENT— $450.00
20 music stands—	$200.00
2 filing cabinets—	$100.00
1 director podium—	$30.00
20 recordings—	$100.00
5 tapes—	$20.00

UNIFORMS— $1,250.00
10 replacement uniforms—	$1,000.00
100 new pairs of spats—	$250.00

SUPPLIES— $500.00
Paper—	$250.00
Tape, glue, pens, ink, dittos, etc.—	$100.00
Marking paint for marching field—	$50.00
Music folios—	$100.00

MISCELLANEOUS— $250.00
Postage, photographs, annuals, etc.

Figure 2-8

In order to effectively administer a budget, bids should be "let." Many school systems require three sealed competitive bids. I recommend the practice even if it is not required in a school system. Make the bids specific and you invariably save money. This is especially true of big purchases such as instruments, large music orders, etc.

Figure 2-9 is a sample bid form.

CENTRAL HIGH SCHOOL
REQUEST FOR QUOTATIONS

THIS IS NOT AN ORDER. Please furnish us your best quotation on the items listed below. Follow specifications carefully. Bid on each item separately. Do not include federal or state taxes in your bid. We are tax exempt and will furnish exemption certificates with our order. The right is reserved to accept or reject all or any part of your quotation. If your bid is accepted, an order will be sent to you.
Return the original signed in ink, keep the copy for your own records. *Quotations must be received in this office in a sealed envelope on or before* _____ (date) _____

CENTRAL HIGH SCHOOL MUSIC DEPARTMENT

Item Catalog Number	Quantity	Specifications of Article (s)	Unit Price	Amount

Figure 2-9

Also to be included could be required delivery date, shipping costs, terms etc. The quotation sheet, or bid, should have a place at the bottom for an authorization signature.

TEACHING THE ELEMENTARY SCHOOL BAND

3

Elementary bands are the "life blood" of any band program. These groups should provide the solid music fundamentals that enable a student to make consistent progress on an instrument. It takes a great deal of dedication to consistently teach carefully and enthusiastically in the elementary school. Here are a few suggestions to help keep this vital area of teaching interesting and competent.

If you are in a situation where you teach your own beginning students, periodically indicate each year's beginner class progress in the director's manual. This will help insure that you are putting forth consistently good effort with your elementary classes.

If the program involves one or more elementary teachers, make sure that they have some contact with students as they mature. This contact with students may only be section rehearsals, private lessons, etc., but it will help keep teaching more rewarding for the elementary instructors.

Make sure that there is a rate of progress in elementary students that is ambitious but does not "burn the students out." This rate of progress to a certain extent depends on their grade level when they begin. Just make sure that the students are more knowledgeable and capable each week.

In order to have a desire to participate in band, young students must be aware of the band activities. Other enthusiastic band members are the best promotional aid. A few others that I have used with good results are:

1. Instrument demonstrations

These demonstrations are usually done for fairly large groups in an assembly-type situation. It is a good idea for the instructor to be able to play a "pop" or familiar tune on each instrument. If this is impossible, then use good players from the high school band. One of the most successful demonstrations I can remember used a little "dixieland" group. Each student played a short selection and then the entire group "swung" into a lively dixieland number—all of the elementary students wanted to be a part of something like that.

2. Photographs, posters, and displays

Musical instruments and other items associated with music make attractive attention-getting displays. It may be a mannikin in a band uniform or a picture of a popular band player, but seeing and hearing about the band creates interest.

3. "Talent tests" and pre-band instruments

Some elementary band instructors have found "talent tests" to be effective in encouraging some students to take music when the family was not aware that their child might be successful with the study of music. These tests, if used, should never be used to discourage students but to discover students who may have latent talent and encourage them to begin the study of music.

Pre-band instruments may be of some help if they are taught to *entire classes* for the purpose of music notation instruction and familiarization with instruments of the band and orchestra. If used, this instruction should be in the early grades, a year or more before the age that band instrument classes are offered. If taught immediately preceeding instrument classes, many tend to drop out thinking that playing band instruments will only be more of the same. There is a much better chance of keeping students interested with the excitement of a real instrument.

It should be the goal of the senior high band director to see that every student entering high school has had ample opportunity to study instrumental music. Obviously this is much easier to achieve in some situations than others, but strive for this objective nonetheless. If the elementary schools do not feel that this program is needed in their school, then appeal to parents. School administrators are justly influenced by the interest of parents. There are countless individual situations, but perseverance and salesmanship will break down practically any barrier.

THE DEVELOPMENTAL CURRICULUM

The best grade level for starting instrumental beginners is a much-debated question. To a certain extent it depends on school-community activities and the amount of time available in the elementary school. It is best to attract students and have them participating in band before numerous school and community activities lead them astray. If a period of thirty to forty-five minutes daily can be scheduled, I prefer the sixth grade. I must say, however, I have seen examples of successful programs where beginners were started in either fourth, fifth, sixth, or seventh grades. I have also seen many fine players who did not start until high school, but these were exceptions, rather than the rule.

After an active promotional campaign and the collection of beginning band prospect information cards, set up a night for a rental program. Select a night that is relatively free for most parents of the age group you are appealing to. Then contact one or more reputable music dealers who can provide rental-purchase plans. I have used both group, "assembly"-type meetings (with those unable to attend contacted individually) and individual appointments arranged by phone. I prefer the first method, but it is generally best to use the method most effective for the dealers. Advise dealers to include director-preferred extras (good mouthpieces, cleaning kits, folding music stands, method books, etc.) in with the total price, so that no extras will be necessary after the initial purchase. Make sure that every child has an opportunity to participate, even if it means doubling on a school-owned instrument with separate mouthpieces, etc. Begin instruction in classes as soon as several members have instruments.

SCHEDULING ELEMENTARY CLASSES

Remember that often instrumental classes can either be additional trouble for classroom teachers or a welcome break, depending on how well they are scheduled. The ideal way is to have all class members involved with music at the same period. This frees the classroom teacher from "babysitting duties" while only a portion of the class is in music. This "ideal" procedure would require three music teachers and three separate rooms. All students would participate in classes teaching wind and percussion instruments, strings, or general and vocal music. The instrumental teachers could be "roving" teachers and the general and vocal music teacher could be the "public school" music teacher assigned to the faculty of each elementary school. There are some schedule problems that have to be worked out, but the quality of music instruction offered would be well worth the effort required to resolve these problems.

A check list of musical knowledge and performance capabilities should be designated for each elementary grade. This list should be realistic and paced to insure mental and technical readiness for advanced musical literature in the senior high school. I am not selling any method series, but the intelligent, conscientious use of a complete method will insure a solid "developmental" type of instruction program. More thorough recommendations along this line are suggested later in this chapter.

CLASSROOMS AND EQUIPMENT

It is best to have "specialized" rooms for music instruction, but quite often instrumental instruction rooms in elementary schools are areas used for two or more activities. This is logical since it would be extravagant in many ways to have an expensive facility to be used only a relatively short length of time each week.

Some of the more frequently "shared" instruction areas are: auditorium stages, cafeterias, gymnasiums, or some combination rooms that frequently combine two or more of these purposes. As we mentioned in Chapter 2, to get a maximum use of these areas, check first for possible storage areas. Check for closets or similar small rooms that can be locked and have entry into the area where instruction takes place. These rooms are useful even if they must be "scrubbed" out. If no such rooms are accessible, then the next alternative is to build large lockers for storage. In large "shared" areas obtain some type of dividers or folding walls to set this area, aside for music instruction. I have seen good use made of both portable and modular-type rooms.

Regardless of the area that is used for storage and instruction it is necessary to have ample shelving built for both instrument and music storage. One filing cabinet in each instruction-storage area can be quite useful.

Equipment needed in addition to a filing cabinet should be:

A. A sufficient number of chairs and music stands. (Chairs with straight backs, the type that stack rather than fold, encourage better posture; and durable music stands are preferred over the folding variety, which are better suited for individual practice at home.)

B. Some school-owned instruments are needed even in beginning elementary classes; i.e., bass drum, cymbals, pitched percussion instruments (such as bells). For advanced classes add necessary trap and melodic percussion, small tuba, baritone, horn, bass clarinet and other available instruments.

In order to get the best use of teacher time have a "set up" procedure in each elementary school. Make a seating and music stand diagram for each class. The necessary "set up" can be done by students or by custodial staff, but should be done prior to the time the class is to begin. If custodians are used they should be instructed through the school office. Most of the time, selected students are happy to get out of class a few minutes early to "set up" for band. This also gives them some responsibility and they will welcome the chance to contribute to the operational procedures of the school. This sort of procedure must be discussed with the teachers involved and handled in a manner that meets their approval.

With a little salesmanship and tact the elementary instructor can be assured of an area ready for teaching rather than a hurried, irritable, confused scene.

Make the setup in as large a semi-circle as possible in the available area. Make your basic setup for your largest class and have any classes that are smaller sit in the front rows or center section of the area. The semi-circle makes it easier for the instructor to more carefully observe just how each student is playing and makes for more correct instruction.

INSTRUCTION METHODS

It is best to try to schedule classes so that they roughly parallel the maturity of the students. That is, beginner classes first, followed by more advanced classes. This makes it much easier to consistently evaluate student progress.

There are several ways to "group" elementary instrumentalists. As in other areas this is often a logical compromise between what is ideal and what is possible. I have seen very effective elementary instruction using a team of two or three "specialist" instructors teaching simultaneously. This way the class can be divided into woodwinds, brass and percussion. This situation is possible only with large beginner classes and adequate instructional areas available for two or more groups.

In the elementary grades I feel it is best to group classes according to academic grade level. This can help to simplify schedule problems. If it is necessary to have a class where both beginning and intermediate student are together, try to make the most of the situation by using the intermediate students to give assistance in helping the beginners after initial director instruction has been given. This situation is far from ideal but sometimes must be temporarily endured.

A good instruction method series that corresponds to class grouping and beginner age level is very important. For the usual situation where beginners are started during the fourth, fifth, or sixth grade, a series with a reasonable amount of material at the same proficiency level is important. The complete First Division Series by Belwin is a good example. This series has proficiency development that is reasonably slow, plus solos, ensembles, and complete band works all correlated to the level of development. Like materials are identified by corresponding colors. This is by no means the only, or best method available, but it is complete enough to use as a vehicle for explaining a system that insures satisfactory progress. Here is a check list for elementary band achievement:

1. Complete books one and two of the instruction series.
2. Participate in two or more ensembles.
3. Play two elementary solos with piano accompaniment.
4. Be able to demonstrate correct breathing and correct playing position (sitting and standing).
5. Play from memory the following scales: B^b, E^b, A^b, F, C, and G scales plus the chromatic scale encompassing the range covered through book two. (Percussion demonstrate first six rudiments also.)

6. Be able to tune your instrument to the piano. Write, recognize, and sing the intervals M3rd, P5th, and octave.

7. Receive a grade of 100% on a counting test covering combinations of all rythms contained through book two.

8. Receive a grade of 100% on all musical terms used in books one and two.

Strong efforts should be maintained to have each student pass all items on this check list by the time elementary band (6th grade) is completed. This check list should not be used to discourage any student but instead should be used to evaluate where individual weakness or weaknesses in instruction might be.

Here are some methods that might be helpful in achieving these instructional objectives:

1. Students are encouraged (NOT forced) to study four basic instruments: flute, clarinet, cornet, and trombone. If some individual is very certain about the choice of another instrument, they are allowed to study that instrument. Limiting the majority of the class to these instruments simplifies instruction considerably because of fewer instrument idiosyncrasies to explain.

2. Percussion students (would-be "drummers") are also required to take piano. This tends to eliminate the "easy-way-outers" from percussion and insures that there are intelligent musicians in the percussion section, who can read treble and bass clef music when necessary. Melody percussion is played as much as membrane percussion (drums) each class period. Additional percussion alternate on pads.

3. Note values, meter signatures, clefs, and similar basic theory are taught to entire classes as a part of general music, prior to participation in beginning band.

4. Individual instruction (observed by the class) is given as soon as each student obtains an instrument. Correct

instrument assembly and disassembly, correct embouchure and tone production are covered. The student is encouraged to produce steady long tones and shown how to play the first simple melody.

5. As the entire class obtains instruments, long tones as well as correct playing habits are reviewed at the beginning of each class session. It has been my experience that classes maintain a higher motivational level if the class pushes ahead and then goes back to review each exercise where great difficulty is encountered. Periodic repetition with complete instruction is necessary until a satisfactory level of class proficiency is reached.

6. Foot tapping is used and should be minimized (especially extreme use) by the time the students are in the ninth grade. Students who have difficulty in playing and beating time simultaneously also find it difficult to march and play simultaneously later on, unless this tendency is overcome as a beginner.

7. Do not form the habit of orally "counting off" each selection. Stop when there are corrections to be made. Do not merely "plod along." Students will not follow nor correct mistakes unless they are taught to be observant.

8. Make definite assignments each class period. Have students play alone at least once a week. Use the piano frequently to accompany individuals, sections, and the entire class. Even simple chordal improvisation aids in developing harmonic progression awareness. This practice also helps individuals sound better when they play alone. Students should learn to accept individual playing as a regular part of learning an instrument. This practice can help avoid the self-consciousness that frequently occurs with this aspect of instrumental performance as students become more proficient. Tune to the piano periodically. Make sure the piano is kept up to pitch and instruct students to keep instruments

"pulled" to the point where they are usually best
"in-tune."

9. As mentioned earlier, seat the class in a large semi-
circle (if class size and instruction area permit). Make it
a habit to continually watch players for tendencies
toward: bad posture, lack of good breath support,
incorrect embouchures, jaw movement in tonguing,
incorrect band positions, etc.

10. When a fault is observed, wait until the etude is finished, then give corrective advice and play the etude
again while the advice is fresh in the students' minds.
Keep a pencil and write teaching ideas that occur to
you in the director's book. Warnings about frequent
mistakes, alternate fingerings, helpful hints, etc. can
greatly aid effectiveness and continuity in teaching.
Make explanations short, concise and to the point.
Don't scold continuously; use praise when possible;
deal with any discipline problems good naturedly but
promptly and thoroughly.

11. Students in this age group are naturally highly competitive and likely to form "gangs." Use both of these
tendencies to motivate learning. Use competition to
help a student improve his performance, not as an end
in itself. Encourage ensemble playing by groups that
are naturally drawn together.

STUDENT GRADING

Student grading should be an evaluation of four basic
factors:

1. Time spent in individual practice. Pass out practice
sheets with blocks for day of week, amount of practice
and parent signature (see sample in Chapter 5). This is
an honor system that is merely better than a guess.

2. Individual progress. The grade should take into con-

sideration proven progress as well as time spent in practice. This factor can be evaluated through hearing each student alone each week on a required etude.

3. Musical knowledge. Written quizzes covering basic theory, term definitions, fingerings, etc., can help evaluate student progress, and pinpoint areas where additional instructional emphasis should be made.

4. Instrument inspection. Care of the instrument should be stressed (oiling keys and valves, periodic repair checks, etc.), as well as cleanliness (not polishing) with both instrument and case.

Learning for a grade is one of the poorest of all motivations but is a part of the system that students are familiar with in schools.

PUBLIC PERFORMANCES

Some public performances are good motivation for elementary bands. Caution should be used in scheduling and preparing such an appearance. Make sure that students will be capable of good performance, and all the while keeping the "over-all" pacing of public performance in mind. Remember that new musical experiences should be reserved for each musical developmental stage.

Here are some suggested appearances:

1. Christmas concert. This concert could feature both beginning and intermediate groups playing reasonably easy music for the student body, PTA, or some other school group.

2. Annual spring concert. This concert could be a big "festival"-type concert for the general public and featuring all bands in the entire instructional program. I have had success with combined elementary bands of up to 100 players. Classes at each school can be taught the same music, then combined for "mass" rehearsals a few

weeks before the performance. This feat is popular with students and parents alike.

3. Solo and ensemble. Short small ensemble performances for civic and school meetings, general music class demonstrations, etc. can be an incentive for highly motivated students. These ensembles should be "worked up" by the students and heard by the director well before a performance. This fledgling student leadership can provide both encouragement and reward for students. A particularly outstanding individual or ensemble might also be featured on the spring concert.

I do not advocate festival or contest participation at the elementary level. No marching other than a bit of marching fundamentals without instruments (for sixth graders in the spring) is advisable for the elementary level.

Practical Guidelines for

BUILDING THE JUNIOR HIGH SCHOOL BAND   4

Junior high bands should seek to continue the musical development of the individual and foster the important concept of group activity. As mentioned earlier, it is important to have students enrolled in instrumental music before they reach the age where a barrage of school and community activities can confuse and distract them. In order to continue musical development, the junior high program must maintain contact with students by captivating a reasonable portion of their interest and time. In order to achieve this, a schedule of events that is exciting but doesn't burn the student out is important. This is a difficult line to walk but a necessary one. Specific suggestions will be offered in Chapter 10 (Public Performance).

Music fundamentals must be thoroughly taught each day but should be approached by relating them to music being prepared. More activities with solos and ensembles should be developed as well as theory and creative listening enrichment started. To maintain interest, activities should be oriented to give the most enjoyable and rewarding experiences during the present while doing as much as possible to provide progress needed for the future. Remember, the aim should be to create a pleasurable attitude toward music so the talented student doesn't "drop out" before you can discover and help him develop his talent.

For full band, the same procedure as outlined in Chapter 6 (Rehearsals) should be followed, with more variety during the week and possibly a shorter period of time spent each day. Classes should be offered to provide adequate instruction for students who must transfer to other instruments in order to achieve completely instrumentated ensembles. Students should continue to mature through activities that emphasize group effort and dedication rather than selfish ends. Students who respond to the needs of a group, who have the character traits and talents needed for instrument transfers, should be commended and the director should provide assistance in selling the previously owned "elementary band" instrument. Parents respond more favorably to instrument transfers if they realize that a band must have all needed instruments in order to play fine musical literature. Tell them that public school instrumental music is basically to provide a means to experience this great literature and not produce professional musicians. Of course such transfers make adequate school owned "ensemble" instruments a must.

As we mentioned in Chapter 2 (Curriculum), there are numerous community and school situations but one should endeavor to offer the following band opportunities in junior high school:

1. Beginning band and "transfer" class
2. Intermediate band
3. Advanced band
4. Enrichment opportunities through smaller ensembles, music theory, and creative listening
5. Opportunities for private study

THE DEVELOPMENTAL CURRICULUM

The junior high school band curriculum should offer classes that logically follow the elementary band curriculum.

BEGINNING BAND AND "TRANSFER" CLASS

This class should provide another chance for students to start as beginning band members. Students who have been persuaded to change instruments can get the instruction that they need in this class. The ideal time would be the same period as intermediate, or seventh grade band. This way there would be no schedule conflicts and nothing would need be changed in order to add these beginning and "transfer" players to the intermediate band as they were ready. This setup would require two teachers working with the junior high band (also two instruction areas). If such a setup is not possible, then have the students take a class during intermediate band period that would not be too difficult to switch during the year (P.E., etc.). If this class cannot be scheduled this work will have to be done outside the school day or as part of summer band activities.

INTERMEDIATE BAND

If the school situation can allow scheduling an intermediate band and the size of the band can be 30 or more students, then by all means have one. This group should be primarily seventh graders. Instrumentation should be adjusted each year: this insures fairly well-balanced groups throughout the program in the upper grades. This group should work with book three of the instruction series and all materials associated with it. Intermediate band should give a minimum of performances and learn the fundamentals of marching (without instruments) during the spring of their seventh grade year. This format will allow students who change instruments time to adjust without the pressures of performance. Any incorrect playing habits (embouchure, etc.) that have inadvertently developed while in elementary band should be thoroughly corrected. Music theory and creative listening should be incorporated into the rehearsal routine. The music being played can be used as a point of departure for study in these areas (periods of music history, style, etc.).

ADVANCED BAND

This group should be a band with full instrumentation capable of playing grade III and some grade IV music. The fundamentals can be continued through the study of book four of the instruction series and the use of related supplementary materials. Players from the eigth and ninth grades make up this band. A reasonable number of public performances to help keep pride and interest going should be scheduled. Great care should be taken to be sure that more complete performance schedules are reserved for the senior high bands. Familiarization with marching band fundamentals and perhaps participation in a parade or one football half-time show can be a part of junior high band activities. Do not allow more than one junior high marching performance or you will find that people will start to expect the group for everything. Music theory should start to encourage some melody composition and creative listening should deepen into some basic analysis. This will be more fully explained under Instructional Methods. Encourage private study to be started at this stage of development.

SOLOS AND ENSEMBLES

The expansion of solo and ensemble playing should begin in junior high. This "individual" aspect of playing should be stressed more along with the "group" or "community" concept of the band. Solos, section features, and ensembles should be included on public concerts and some participation (particularly in the ninth grade) in solo and ensemble competition festivals should be encouraged. These solos, as well as chamber music, can often be a good incentive for initiating private study. The ninth grade is a good level at which to introduce stage band.

All of the factors listed in Chapter 2 concerning potential schedule conflicts very much apply to junior high school bands. This is especially true where athletics is involved. Students of this age group predominately see themselves as athletic "stars" and if a student must drop band in order to even try out for athletics, you have lost a student from the program, usually forever. Even if the student doesn't make the team, he tries for it and if a big decision has taken place he cannot admit defeat, lose face, and come back to music without being dissatisfied and defeated.

ROOMS AND EQUIPMENT

The curriculum for a good junior high band program demands an adequate rehearsal hall with sufficient storage space for instruments, music, etc., plus some facilities for individual practice during school. In some situations, both junior and senior high groups are able to use the same facilities. There are advantages and disadvantages in such situations which we will not include in this discussion. Suffice it to say that it should be the goal of the director to see that every junior high program has adequate facilities built especially for instrumental music. If it falls your lot to "make do" with some other area until such facilities can be campaigned for and built, then here are a few suggestions. If the room is one large bare room, measure floor space, then divide it up into the areas that are needed, partition it off using "two by fours" and sound-absorbent wallboard. Drapes, carpet (inexpensive grade), false ceiling, etc., can help cut down on sound reverberation and improve looks. Even temporary partitions in a room help designate areas that are vital (separate director office, etc.). Decorate modestly with annual photographs, professional performer photos, charts, etc. Include bulletin boards, chalk boards, etc., in the manner suggested in Chapter 2. Here again, it is important to enlist the aid of students and parents. Nothing fosters pride and care like work in building something.

More equipment and instruments are necessary for the junior high program. The sonority, and "color" instruments that are vital to larger ensembles enter into the picture at this time. First-line instruments are best where possible, but durability is also very important especially for this age level. Refer to the representative list of instruments, both vital and luxury, on page 45. Since many of the instruments will be first encounter situations with students, here are a few suggestions. It might be wise where finances are limited to purchase all woodwind instruments made of resonite instead of Grenardilla wood. This would refer to piccolo, oboe, bassoon, alto, bass and contra-bass clarinets. Resonite does not crack due to temperature and humidity change and is not nearly as expensive. If double horns are too expensive, then purchase single F and B^b horns of equal number and have the "high" horn players use the B^{b}s. Use only three-valve tubas and baritones. The same equipment listed on page 46 will be needed in the junior high program. In most cases the lesser amounts will be adequate. Uniforms can consist of blazers with dark trousers, girls perhaps wearing skirts with the blazers. This uniform is not very expensive, looks good, and is easy to adjust for this "rapid-growth" age group.

Besides the regular rehearsal hall equipment, records, tapes, and excellent quality sound recording-reproduction equipment are needed. Students should be ready to develop a much more mature concept of tone quality and are usually ready to withstand the shock of knowing just how they actually sound. Good records played through good reproduction equipment, plus frequent concert attendance where professional "live" performances can be heard, will do wonders to inspire and develop concept.

INSTRUCTION METHODS

Junior high instrumental instruction should start the trend to rehearsal techniques (as explained in Chapter 6) while retaining the principals of good fundamental teaching. The increased size of playing groups calls for different methods of instruction. The larger the group the more stringent is the need for complete order and the fewer the opportunities for individual attention. As the musician becomes more mature, he should be allowed to do more of what is fundamental in music—"perform." Performance gives a goal to work toward, unless it is so frequent as to become tiresome, tedious, and commonplace.

The teaching of fundamentals, theory, listening, etc., should be related to music being prepared whenever possible. Use music that demonstrates good craftmanship but is popular with the age group you are working with. I'll attempt an example here: select a folk-rock tune in the neo-baroque idiom, arranged by one of the several fine craftsmen that are published periodically. After warming up and tuning, play the selection and capture the interest of the group. Mention a possible performance date to give a time-limit goal and bring to life a slight sense of urgency. Play technical etudes in the keys used during the selection, and emphasize the need for absolute, correct rhythmic values in order to make this number "swing." Play chord studies in the keys used from a book like *Ensemble Drill* by Fussell or *Treasury of Scales* by Smith. Have a fairly easy Bach transcription and use it to explain neo-baroque and baroque ideas of art and their meaning. Play the Bach as written, then play again with a rock beat percussion part and string bass (if possible). Play a recording from the Swingle Singers' *Bach's Greatest Hits* album. Finally play the original selection again with the admonition to observe the musical values that have been demonstrated. Finish; point out spots in need of individual and section attention; mention the performance and the fact that you may select another work that is from the original Baroque era. With a little effort on research and the use of supplementary musical examples throughout the preparation of the selection, this procedure can help educate and enrich through music. With individual mutation and modification this approach can be used on many types of music with the best in the realization of the educational axiom, "We learn by doing." I *do not* guarantee immediate miraculous results, just long-term effective motivation and learning. I *do* guarantee results to be in direct proportion to intelligent director preparation. Once students come to trust your motives and judgment because you care for things that have meaning to them, then they will reciprocate by valuing the things you offer as being of worth.

If the junior high program is large enough to have a complete ninth grade band, then you might wish to introduce marching while playing to them. The introduction of marching while playing to a band is of great importance. There is enough to be said to write a book in itself. We will be as brief as possible and refer to materials that can provide more in-depth study for those who are interested. First it is imperative that players be solid and mature enough in correct playing habits (embouchure, playing position, breath support, etc.) to survive the confusing and demanding exertion encountered while marching and playing simultaneously. Three years of playing plus familiarization with the basic fundamentals of marching while *not* playing should be an absolute minimum. It is of value to have a complete explanatory list of marching fundamentals. These are as important in marching uniformity as basic music fundamentals are in fine playing proficiency. If your school does not have such a booklet of marching fundamentals, then begin to formulate one now. The *Manual of Close Order Drill* by A.R. Casavant is a good example of basic precision drill fundamentals.

Regardless of when marching while playing is introduced, here are some suggestions for combining the two:

1. The first attempt to play while marching should be in a carefully controlled situation designed to retain the maximum amount of precision in the basic step while producing a full, well-supported, resonant sound. The band should be taught to play a dominant-to-tonic chordal progression in any easy key, using an accented quarter note for each of the two chords. The first step is to move forward from a yardline at a moderate tempo accompanied by a drum tap for seven steps (five steps if using 6 to 5). On the eighth step play the dominant chord as the right foot hits the first yardline, and follow

with the tonic chord as the next step is taken with the left foot. The percussion section should accent (possibly with a nine-stroke roll) with the band as these two chords are played. Hold the instruments in playing position during the steps between the chords, so that good posture and proper horn position can be practiced. This type of drill should continue for several yardlines with a halt being executed on the final tonic chord. The objective at this point is to maintain a precise step at a steady tempo with a full sound.

2. The second step uses a whole note pattern based on any easy scale, combined with the basic forward step. The band should step off from a line on the first note of the scale, moving forward four steps for each note of the scale and concentrating on the proper execution of fundamentals. The last note of the scale should be lengthened to five beats so that the halt will be executed with the music "cut off."

3. As soon as the whole note pattern is progressing satisfactorily, change to a half note scale that goes up and down in thirty-two beats (repeat the top note; halt again on count thirty-three). Continue emphasizing the importance of a steady tempo, good posture, good embouchure, a well-supported sound, and precise footwork.

4. The next pattern consists of playing accented quarter note scales in the keys most commonly used on the field. Each scale should be played several times while working on the basic step. The tempo should gradually be increased and different scales combined in sequence as the band becomes adjusted to this pattern. This is one of the most critical points in determining just how precise the marching will be while playing. Spend plenty of time with this fundamental (a short time for several days).

5. The band is now ready to play various rhythmic

patterns while moving down the field. Begin by indicating simple rhythms (i.e. ♩♫♫♩) and have the band
imitate the pattern on each degree of a scale while
executing the basic step. These rhythms should
gradually become more complex, with a few difficult
patterns used from time to time to challenge the group.
Check playing position, posture, and footwork constantly and do not hesitate to return to the previous
quarter-note pattern if any aspect of good playing becomes sloppy.

6. A few of the basic fundamentals should now be combined with scale patterns in order for the band to learn
to execute simple drills while playing. Use fundamentals
such as flanks, rear march, mark time, etc. Devise any
combination of fundamentals up to a total of thirty-two
counts while playing scale patterns and insist that the
group remember the sequences without excessive
repetition of instruction. If the band can develop a
longer span of concentration, the teaching of actual
show routines will be much easier. Cause the students to
listen carefully and think!!!

7. The final step consists of work on basic posture and
stride (both 8 to 5 and 6 to 5) while moving down the
field playing an easy tune (the school song or a march
trio) that has been memorized. As soon as the desired
execution has been attained, simple drill patterns can be
taught and used with the music. When the marching and
playing are executed with the proper style and
precision, the band is ready to proceed in learning an
easy marching routine.

Careful teaching of the above seven steps will allow most
bands to march and play with a high degree of confidence and
precision. Any attempt to move immediately from the basic
drills to a show routine can only lead to frustration or a useless
waste of time. Learning to play with the proper sound and
technique while executing complex drill patterns is one of the

most difficult tasks that faces a band; therefore, it is extremely important that a sufficient amount of rehearsal and planning time be allotted so that these techniques can be mastered.

A reasonable amount of marching should be done in the ninth grade and a minimum amount of performing. When this marching is done and for how long is dependent somewhat on the climate, but in most cases should occur during the early fall or late spring.

As is true at other grade levels, it is necessary for an instrumental teacher to have a fair, systematic method of pacing progress and grading students. Here are some suggestions for student and teacher evaluations:

As with elementary band, use a check list for junior high band achievement.

1. Be able to play all major, minor, and chromatic scales over the entire practical range of your instrument, and be able to write these scales on any given tone. Be able to play all articulations. Percussion students be able to play first 13 rudiments, major scales on mallet instruments and demonstrate knowledge in the playing of timpani, cymbals, wood block, tamborine, and other trap percussion.
2. Read at sight grade II music, demonstrate playing proficiency for grade III music.
3. Receive 100 percent on a test of all musical terms contained through book four of the instruction series.
4. Write an original melody or duet of at least eight measures in length and understand the basic fundamentals of phrasing. Explain basic song and overture forms. Explain melodic contour and other basic melody writing rules.
5. Participate in a minimum of two chamber groups that present public performances. Present a minimum of one solo with accompaniment in public.
6. Demonstrate thorough knowledge of all marching band fundamentals.

Each of these factors should be incorporated into fundamental teaching, and each student should pass all items on the check list by the time junior high band (9th grade) is completed.

STUDENT GRADING

Student grading should consist of four basic factors (as in elementary band):

1. Individual practice time. Charts indicating time practiced daily during the grading period. An honor system signed by parent or director (if practiced at school).
2. Individual progress. Progress as indicated by individual playing during grading period. The playing items on the check list can be checked in this manner.
3. Musical knowledge. Theory, music writing, music terms, and general musical knowledge should be checked each term (progressive accomplishments from the check list).
4. Instrument inspection. Instrument checks, both playing condition and preventive maintenance (cleanliness, lubrication, etc.) each grading period.

It is also possible to initiate a simple form of the merit-demerit system that will be described in Chapter 9. This factor could also enter into student grading or evaluation if so desired.

PUBLIC PERFORMANCE

It is extremely important to "pace" public performance so that the student remains interested but never gets the feeling "I've done everything so why continue." If the junior high band attempts a full schedule of performances, the public will come to expect it and be offended if this practice is not continued.

The best policy is to sit down with your administrator and set a limit of performances that are deemed necessary and not stray far from it. Here is a sample of what has worked for some.

1. *Marching Performances.* One civic parade and playing in the stands at home football games. One simple half-time routine possibly presented also at one of the senior high games. This is plenty of marching familiarization, and leaves the majority of performances and trips for senior high band.

2. *Concerts.* Two concerts a year and perhaps one concert for the student body. Some chamber ensembles might give programs as needed for civic clubs, P.T.A., etc., but this also should be kept within reason.

3. *Festivals.* Competition festivals approached in a constructive, ethical manner can be a worthy goal for a school group with a more professional evaluation than that offered by parents and friends. Solo and ensemble participation should be encouraged but not forced. Work for the best playing that the group is capable of without overemphasis on the rating or "competing" with other bands. I have witnessed groups that put undue emphasis on the rating, at the expense of musical values—*sad!* Concert festivals can also be a good place to hear other bands and make new acquaintances.

4. *Honor Groups and Clinics.* These provide a good opportunity for the exceptional student. Whether the event is regional or local, it can be of value to the individual and arouse the drive to accomplish in other band members. In one system where there was one large senior high school and several smaller junior highs, we had a fine "All-City" Junior High Band. Each of the junior highs was too small to have a fine full-sized symphonic band, so the better students were combined to make up this honor group. The group met once a week, outside school time, in the senior high band room. All the directors, including the senior high director, worked

with the group, and it was a good experience for all
concerned. Both band and instrument instruction clinics
by outstanding teachers are a good opportunity for
students (when not overdone).

THE COMPREHENSIVE 5
SENIOR HIGH SCHOOL
BAND

The senior high should offer each student more diversified musical experiences while keeping the large organization, the "band," as the strong nucleus of the program. It has been the goal of elementary and junior high instruction to motivate and musically educate, but mostly to promote technical proficiency to a point where the reading and performance of fine musical literature is possible. I know of no better way to instill within a student a love for fine music than the insight gained through rehearsal toward satisfying performance. This development is to a large extent dependent upon the manner in which the work is approached, the amount of relevance that is shown the student, plus the length of time and concentration deemed necessary to perform the work well. Love and excitement can turn into lethargy and boredom if you "beat" a selection "to death" with unending repetition and drill. The use of more student leadership should be incorporated into the senior high program. This is of extreme value to both the student and director. Chapter 8 is devoted to the development of this aspect of the band program.

The senior high diversified curriculum should offer opportunities for students who only wish to achieve recreational and social values from band. It should also offer adequate preparation for the student who wishes to prepare for a vocation, or at least an avocation, in music.

Each student should be given opportunity to develop individual talents and interests but the emphasis should be centered in the group or band. Group dedication with a directed purpose is the "community" concept at its best. I once had occasion to be given a testimonial to the importance of this concept and its value to the individual in society. An enthusiastic band "booster" was again taking on extra work with an ambitious fund-raising project. This man had seen three children through the band program and his fourth was a senior in the band at that time. I asked him what purpose could give him the enthusiasm and energy to continue so faithfully for so long. Was it a love of music, a love of young people, or what? He replied that both of these entered into his zeal. He then said that it was more than worth the effort even if his children never played another note after they graduated. The unselfish working together, the guidance of youthful energy in constructive activity made it all more than worthwhile. That testimonial has given me a faith to continue when my work has seemed tired and bleak.

The senior high diversified curriculum should offer participation opportunities in:

1. Marching band
2. Symphonic band
3. Wind ensemble
4. Stage band
5. Theory and music composition
6. Chamber music and solo performance
7. Private study

THE DIVERSIFIED CURRICULUM

The developmental curriculum should prepare the student for full participation in the following activities:

MARCHING BAND

All students should be given the opportunity to try out for marching band. In order to have adequate motivation for this time- and energy-consuming activity, this should be the group that takes the big trips and receives a lion's share of publicity. There are adequate opportunities for such motivation discussed in Chapter 10. One of the best ways to schedule marching band, especially if the band is large, is to schedule everyone in two consecutive periods. This is possible only in large schools that offer several sections of each subject, where marching band also earns physical education credit, and where the administration is very cooperative. I have taught where the entire marching band met only after school and was made up of students from three separate concert groups: it was a fine band.

SYMPHONIC BAND

This group should be the large concert band with efforts made for a complete "symphonic" instrumentation. If the senior high has only fifty to eighty band students this group will be the only large concert ensemble offered. I suggest that one hundred or more students form two or more ensembles. Symphonic band should be instructed in the manner described in Chapter 6 (Rehearsals).

WIND ENSEMBLE

If there are a sufficient number of band students in the senior high program, then some sort of more select group can be offered. This ensemble should consist of a balanced instrumentation of from 40 to 50 of the best players. This group would naturally contain the students who had a vocational interest in music, and could be treated as a college preparatory-type situation. If marching band met for two consecutive periods during the fall, then it would be relatively easy to have the wind ensemble and symphonic band in separate periods "back to back." This would allow challenging and change from group to group without major student schedule changes. I feel that it is important not to have any students playing in both ensembles (unless playing another instrument).

STAGE BAND

Some school systems are able to schedule stage band during the regular school day. This is much more easily done where the school is large and more than one director is involved with the senior high program. Whether it can be scheduled within the school day or must rehearse outside of school time, it is a valuable part of any band program. If approached correctly it can improve musicianship and serve as an exciting outlet for its members. This ensemble can serve as the basic musical unit for musicals, variety shows, and school programs that can be both popular and educational.

THEORY AND MUSIC COMPOSITION

Basic theory and the acquisition of general musical knowledge should still be an integral part of each rehearsal. If at all possible a regular class in theory and composition should be offered in the secondary school music curriculum. This course would naturally be college preparatory oriented, but should be approached from a creative rather than an analytical viewpoint. If it is impossible to schedule this subject during the regular year, then attempt to make it a part of the summer band curriculum (see Chapter 9).

CHAMBER MUSIC AND SOLO PERFORMANCE

If there has been solo performance and small ensemble playing since elementary school band, then the high school student will naturally be motivated to expand these experiences. Solo playing can be tied in with private study and gives an individual (frequently doubling some predominately harmonic part in band) a chance to play more primary melodies. Smaller ensembles, or chamber groups, should be student-rehearsed with director guidance and "polishing" suggestions prior to public performance.

PRIVATE STUDY

Private study should begin during the upper grades in junior high and continue through the "formative" years. This area of instruction is vital for a superior band program year after year. More about the establishment and organization of such a program is covered in Chapter 7.

INSTRUMENTS AND EQUIPMENT

There will be common usage of some facilities and equipment (pianos, recording equipment, etc.) among all areas of instruction (vocal, orchestra, etc.) in the secondary school music department. Since Chapter 2 has dealt with the acquisition of adequate facilities and instrumental equipment, we will now discuss the most efficient use of these facilities. It is important that the band room remain accessible to students, but do not allow it to become a lounge or loitering place. Insist that students enter the music rooms for the purpose of practicing, hearing, and rehearsing music. If this is not strictly adhered to, then many problems are inevitable and the director will find himself in the role of "enforcer" rather than music director. Here are a few student rules to help maintain order:

1. Do not come to the band room without a musical purpose.
2. No food or drink in the band room.
3. No smoking in the band room.
4. Keep cases, music, and books in areas provided for this use.
5. Absolutely no horseplay allowed.
6. Do not use equipment unless authorized to do so.

Use the best enforcement of these rules available—the band students themselves. More will be said about this student leadership in Chapter 8.

Since the band in the senior high does more performing than other groups in the program, naturally more travel and equipment problems are to be expected. The use of student managers (or work-crews), supervised by student officers but organized and instructed by the director, is very necessary. These managers can be motivated by a desire to be a part of the band's activities (trips, social, etc.) They will most likely be non players because of lack of opportunity or talent. Frequently they will be friends of students who are already in the band. The responsibility and respect shown these managers will to a large degree determine their effectiveness. Here are a few tasks they can assist with:

1. Uniforms (issuing and checking in)
2. Daily rehearsal setups (stands, chairs, etc.)
3. Lining off marching practice field
4. Assistance with large instruments and baggage on trips
5. Stage crew for concerts
6. Music library assistance
7. Minor band room equipment repairs and additions (shelves, etc.)

INSTRUCTION METHODS

Marching instruction will be the first task each school year. The chapter on rehearsal atmosphere (Chapter 6) will deal primarily with concert rehearsal procedures, so we give some attention to marching rehearsal techniques in this chapter. Here are a few suggestions for more effective marching rehearsals:

MARCHING INSTRUCTION

1. All commands should be based on a four count system. The Preparatory Command begins on count one followed by a pause on count two. The Command of Execution is given on count three and the maneuver begins on count four. Example:

Counts:	1	2	3	4
Command:	"Right"	Pause	"Face!"	Execute
Command:	"To the Rear"	Pause	"March!"	Execute

2. Commands given to a unit not in motion should be paced in the same tempo as desired for the execution of the movement. A slow command indicates a deliberate slow movement and a fast command indicates a quick snappy movement. For best results, develop a steady cadence of command using a change of speed only to keep the unit alert.

3. The quality and control of the voice is important in developing precision and "snap" when drilling a unit. The commands should be given in a manner that is easily understood. The Preparatory Command begins in a low ascending voice and is followed by a short explosive sound for the Command of Execution.

4. With precision drill fundamentals, commands given to a unit in motion should begin with the Preparatory Command

being given on the left foot followed two counts later by the Command of Execution, also given on the left foot. The maneuver is then executed on the right toe during the next count.

5. The drill instructor should always move with the unit to stay centered so that his voice can be easily heard by the entire formation.

USE OF YARD LINES

1. When standing on a yard line place the arch of the foot on the center of the line.

2. When moving at 8 to 5 the toe is aimed at a point just beyond the line so that the arch of the foot will hit the line as the foot is lowered.

3. When moving at 6 to 5 the heel is aimed at a point just before the line so that the arch of the foot will hit the line as the foot is lowered.

4. When standing in a meshed line (facing both end zones), the arch of the foot must be centered on the line so that the shoulders of the unit will be in line.

5. When turning on a line, the body must stay erect and the head positioned over the line to avoid "tagging." The body must follow the foot over the line if the turn is to be properly executed.

6. Extensive rehearsal of box fours (four steps between flanking maneuvers), and box eights should help to develop the proper use of the feet and body in relation to the yard lines.

POSTURE AND INSTRUMENT CARRIAGE

1. Good posture and proper horn carriage puts the "icing on the cake" and will greatly enhance the appearance of a band. Everyone should be encouraged to stand tall, removing the natural slump in the back. The head is held erect at all times

and every movement should be made with authority and confidence.

2. Once the basic fundamentals have been learned, the unit should be able to move about the field with precision, emphasizing good footwork and correct posture. Any check with the field markings should be made with the eyes only, keeping the head up at all times.

3. A change of direction can be a source of problems in maintaining good posture and carriage. Avoid leaning into the turn with the body or reaching out and tagging the line with the foot as the turn is made. Check horn carriage during turns since this is often a place where sloppiness will occur. (Do not attempt to play during a turn.)

4. A step-off is usually accompanied by leaning forward during the Preparatory Command. This anticipation must be eliminated if the step-off and the first few steps are to be precise.

5. Once the principles of good footwork and posture are understood, the matter of proper horn carriage becomes much easier to teach. Trumpets and trombones should use parallel carriage with the other instruments being carried in a manner that allows "heads-up," and marching without undue strain.

6. Music should not be used on the field while drilling as it will pull the head down, disrupting footwork and posture. If memorization is a problem, use music only in spots where the band is standing still.

7. Good posture and proper carriage are usually the result of careful development of unit pride. A band that plays and marches with authority and confidence in its performance will require a minimum of effort to develop into a superior organization.

GENERAL IDEAS

1. The teaching of fundamentals to a small band (64 members or less) works best from two equal lines facing each

other in open order. Place these lines ten yards apart with the instructor in the middle. A larger band should work in a box or a U-shaped formation in open order so that everyone is in easy seeing and hearing distance. Allow student leaders to work behind the lines so that they will be able to spot errors that are not visible from the front.

2. Use demonstrators to show both the right and the wrong way to execute a maneuver. When criticizing, be impersonal and constructive—this is no time for sarcasm. Slower students will try harder to improve if their efforts are recognized.

3. Assign partners from opposite sides and let one group observe while the other drills. Reverse the procedure and then let the students correct and help each other.

4. Appoint squad leaders and place each student in the approximate place that he will occupy in the marching lineup before the squad drills are taught.

5. Allow the squad leaders to work their squads at least once during each rehearsal. This is a worthwhile change of pace and will help maintain interest during a long rehearsal. The squad leaders can also use this opportunity to gain self-confidence while the unit is learning the fundamentals.

6. Encourage competition from the beginning. A compliment to one group for looking better than another can be the beginning of a type of internal competition that will expand as the unit becomes more proficient in executing fundamentals. Odds can compete against evens; seniors against juniors; boys against girls; etc. . . . Frequent competition builds spirit and is an ideal way to end the rehearsal on a high note!

Twirlers, flag corps, color guards, etc. come under the supervision of the director. It is generally best to have an experienced student in charge of these "supplementary" units. This student should be responsible to and work with the director on the duties each respective unit is to play in the performance. More about the importance and assistance of such student leadership is suggested in Chapter 8. The director should be knowledgeable in all areas of instruction that come under his supervision, such as proper flag usage, twirling fundamentals, construction of routines, etc. If these techniques are not known to the director, he should make efforts to learn them as soon as possible. Until these techniques are acquired, seek out the help of anyone who can help with these areas of instruction. Sometimes other directors in the same system (feed or schools) can be of help and this, of course, helps them to be involved in the high school band more thoroughly.

SOLO PERFORMANCE

Solo performance is a phase of playing very relevant to private instruction if such a program is to be developed within the system. If there is no private instruction program to a reasonable degrce, then here are a few ideas on solo performance. Use an event such as a Solo and Ensemble Festival for a goal. Teach the same solo to groups of four or more players with the "master class" approach. That way several students can be taught within a reasonable amount of time. Assign solos that have recordings available and encourage the student to refer to the recording for phrasing, etc. Along this line I suggest the use of the tapes and recordings (the *Music Minus One* type) for accompanying solos in schools where competent accompanists are hard to come by. A fairly complete record library can be developed if care is taken to preserve what you already have. Duets and a variety of ensembles are available. Director time for individual help is time-consuming but will help to get the ball rolling if no private instruction has been developed. Have students performing solos play them for the band prior to the festival date. This gives others a chance to hear what some are doing, plus it gives the director a chance to teach all some basic aspects of performance manners, performance psychology, etc.

Ensembles or chamber music can also be very personally satisfying and rewarding for individual students. Few "mediums" help develop individual musical competence as well. Here again the school situation to a very large extent determines the manner of approach to this situation. If there are other directors involved with the system, especially elementary instrumental instructors, then ensembles can be a very worthwhile outlet for them, as well as being very fortunate for the students. If the director does most of the teaching throughout the system, then professional help is very limited. The next best approach is through student leadership. Whether the ensemble is a duo of two good friends or a neighborhood quartet, there is a great deal of valuable learning that can take place. Frequently this approach teaches more than others do. Student leaders will soon see that clear understanding is necessary before helping others to understand. They will hear themselves saying many things that they have heard the director say—and understand much better why things are done the way they are. Nothing fosters respect better than understanding (where respect is due). The primary role of the director in such situations will be to help in the selection of music, hear the finished product once or twice (once before the entire band), make suggestions, probably serve as "arbitrator" should *musical* squabbles arise. Other performance possibilities are discussed under "Public Performance" in this chapter.

If there is very little motivation present for solo and ensemble participation, then try placing photographs of each year's participants in picture racks in the band room. In one school system where I taught we had little interest in these activities the first year. Nonetheless I took a photograph of the six who did participate, labeled it, placed it on the wall and put the photo plus names in the school annual. The next year there were thirty participants and we started a modest private instruction program. We again took a photograph and used it in the same manner. From then on we had practically 100 percent participation and a thriving private instruction program. Of course these photos were not the only reason, but the individual need for recognition and even a small bit of immortality can be very strong motivating forces.

STUDENT GRADING

Student grading should consist of evaluation in the following areas (as with elementary and junior high bands):

1. Individual practice time. This should be of the same type as used in elementary and junior high schools.
2. Musical development. As indicated by concert attendance, clinic and private lesson participation, individual playing improvement, solo and ensemble participation, tests on theory and general musical knowledge, etc.
3. Citizenship development. Standing as related to the records kept on the merit-demerit system described in Chapter 8, student leadership, etc.
4. Instrument inspection. Cleaning of instrument and case (not to be confused with "shininess"), playing condition, and necessary accessories.

PUBLIC PERFORMANCES

The senior high band and related music ensembles should be the groups that have the lion's share of performance. Remember "Performance is the life blood of music, *unless* you bleed the subject to death." Since this aspect of the senior high program is so extensive we have devoted Chapter 10 entirely for discussion of the subject. Basic performance events are:

1. Marching—civic parades, football games, patriotic events, etc.
2. Concert—concert series, seasonal concerts, chamber music concerts, recitals, etc.
3. Festivals and contests—marching, concert, solo and ensemble, state, etc.
4. Special events—clinics, honor bands, tours, big trips, etc.

Objectives for performance, financing, procedures, evaluation, and other related aspects are discussed in Chapter 10 (Public Performance).

EFFICIENT AND 6
EFFECTIVE REHEARSALS

THE FOUNDATION:
SETTING WORTHY OBJECTIVES

The attitude of students entering a rehearsal should be one of anticipation and desire to demonstrate personal preparation. All directors want this type of attitude, but what germinates it? What causes it to flourish in some places and wither in others?

As we have indicated with other matters, approach is all important. A clear distinction should be established from the outset regarding "rehearsals" and "practice." For concert band, "rehearsal" should be the word used and should imply prior preparation. This concept should hold true with both students and director. Conversely, "practice" simply means getting together, working and learning to do something as a group. Use the word "practice" only as it applies to individual practice, or work with drill in marching band. The basic purpose of the band period should be rehearsal.

Several basic objectives vital to instrumental performance should be reviewed each band period. Emphasis on the development of correct, solid playing fundamentals should be a part of each rehearsal. Stress should be placed upon facets of playing such as:

1. Maximum control and use of air
2. Individual concept of characteristic tone quality

93

3. Correct embouchure formation

4. Good playing position (posture, hand position, etc.)

5. Alternate fingerings and special problems

All of these and many other factors should be given illustrative attention.

A device I have used effectively utilizes individual students for demonstration. Have a student demonstrate a faulty playing habit that is prevalent among members of a section. Briefly explain the reason this habit is detrimental to good playing technique; then show the group, by demonstration with the selected student, how to correct this problem. As an example, let us say that several members of the clarinet section already have or seem to be slipping into bad embouchure habits; bunched "pumpkin" chins, etc. First explain why this is detrimental to good playing and if possible demonstrate by playing correctly with the chin pointed and flat, then bunched and "biting." The resulting difference in tone quality should be quite convincing. Also point out that a correctly formed embouchure will eventually greatly aid ease in playing.

Next show how faulty embouchures can be corrected by pulling the chin down and tightening the corners of the mouth. Have all of the students check themselves and concentrate on the factors you have mentioned. Watch carefully for players who fail to recognize that they are victims of the playing faults you have mentioned. Then emphasize the importance of correct embouchure for all wind instruments, and comparatively explain how most wind instrument embouchures are quite similar (flat chin, open throat, etc.). Finally, have the entire group play a tone study that is simple enough that all players can concentrate on embouchure formation. Harmonized long-tone scales or simple chorales encompassing the middle tessiturias for most instruments can be quite helpful for this type of concentration. It also is very good to *always* emphasize correct breathing and breath control with such studies. Remember they are all *"wind"* instruments. Similar demonstrations can be devised relevant to other vital fundamentals of instrumental playing.

Of course instrumental instruction opportunities vary from location to location. Some bands may have practically all students taking private lessons, while other bands have few, if any, students studying with private instructors. Regardless of the situation, calling attention to correct playing habits at the beginning of a rehearsal represents sound teaching techniques. If students study privately, you can simply reinforce what private instructors teach them. If they have little or no opportunity to study privately, your explanations are the only exposure they have to correct playing habits.

There are other factors that should be considered in association with instruction of this type. First, the demonstration-lecture must be brief, emphatic and precise. The instructor must demand and get the orderly quiet that is conducive to attention and learning. During this time of the period percussion students should have a room available for work on practice pads with their section leader. This room can help eliminate the discipline problems percussionists often create. In many cases, the problem with percussion players is that they have nothing to do and frequently cannot relate to the type of instrumental instruction you are demonstrating.

Besides emphasis on tone production, a director must encourage and develop ensemble and individual technical proficiency. Unision etudes of a technical nature can be quite useful in this respect. These etudes should be of a type that will capture the interest of the individual student. Simple, familiar melodies with progressively difficult variations are quite good for this purpose. I have found the *Belwin Progressive Studies Book* to be very useful with intermediate students.

Since the band period is the primary contact most members have with music, other musical objectives should be included. Basic musicianship should be emphasized during the first part of the rehearsal so it will be in the mind of the student throughout the rehearsal. Here again, one demonstration can be worth a million words. Let us spotlight the heart and soul of music—the phrase. One successful demonstration I have observed and used explains the phrase in the following manner.

The phrase is a musical sentence. Students will understand readily if you will speak a simple sentence with a variety of inflections and accents on different words; i.e., I am going *TO* town; I *AM* going to town; I am *GOING?* to town; etc. Students can easily grasp how inflection and accent drastically alter the meaning of a sentence, and simply correlate this to the musical sentence—the phrase. Next demonstrate, through singing or playing, several ways of phrasing a passage. Compare musical articulation and notation to vowels, consonants, commas, exclamation points, etc. Finish by explaining how a composer outlines the meaning of his musical sentence with various phrase markings. In ensemble work the conductor is responsible for interpreting and shaping the phrase. In solo work, the individual is the basic interpreter.

Good musicianship also requires basic understanding of theory and general musical knowledge. Most teacher instruction of this sort is effective in short doses tailored to be highly relevant to the music being played. A couple of examples can serve to demonstrate this technique:

1. Relate the overtone principle to characteristic tone quality.
2. Explain form by playing an overture and then describing its original purpose and resulting form.

Theory, history, and general music knowledge will be retained much better when related to the music being prepared.

ACHIEVING GOOD REHEARSAL ATMOSPHERE

In schools, all musical activities generally center around the rehearsal hall. Each director must continually strive to make the rehearsal hall as pleasant and conducive to musical learning as possible. It has been my experience that having students assist in this endeavor is invaluable in creating and maintaining such an atmosphere. Nothing creates pride in something like the work required to produce it. Several factors that aid in creating a good atmosphere are:

1. Keep the basic setup of the rehearsal hall intact. Use front rows or center section for smaller groups.
2. Insist that the band room be used for musical activities only (rehearsing, individual practice, listening, etc.). No loitering should be allowed.
3. Keep the temperature on the comfortably cool side.
4. Decorate sparingly in good taste: trophy cabinets, bulletin boards, musical photographs and paintings, prints, etc.
5. Organize all side rooms for maximum efficiency and keep them orderly (music library with music neatly filed, director's office maintained in a business-like manner, instruments stored in lockers or racks, uniforms in plastic bags and hung neatly, etc.).

Student discipline is quite favorably influenced by a pleasant and orderly room.

A great deal of preparation is also vital to create and maintain good rehearsal atmosphere. Foresight is a must in planning a rehearsal. Many confusing disruptions can be eliminated through the use of intelligent, experienced director thought. Recall previous disruptive rehearsal experiences; then reason out ways to avoid similar occurrences in the future. Here are a few suggestions:

1. Pass out all music *prior* to rehearsal time and make individual music notation corrections at the end of a rehearsal.
2. Make it a policy not to have students or director called from a rehearsal except when absolutely necessary.
3. Have a student in charge of intercepting phone calls, messages to students, visitors, etc.
4. Provide chairs for possible visitors behind the band in some convenient spot.
5. Arrange the band seating so that you take advantage of

the shape of the room. Do not have the students face windows or the clock. (Cover windows in hallway doors.)

Rehearsal methods are affected a great deal by school situations: the length of the rehearsal period, time of the day the rehearsal is held, rural- or urban-oriented school, etc. Here are some illustrative schedule situations and rehearsal procedure suggestions:

Whatever length your period might be, try to allot your time close to the following percentages: 20 percent warm-up and fundamental emphasis, 20 percent theory and general musicianship emphasis, 20 percent sight reading, and 40 percent preparation of music for performance. These percentages might vary a little from day to day. Other systems of percentages can be devised, but this sort of emphasis has always worked extremely well for me.

The time of day in which the rehearsal period occurs is important. If a director is able to create a situation where he can choose the period rehearsals are held, then the following advantages and disadvantages are relevant:

If rehearsals are held first period, students can warm up and tune prior to the start of the rehearsal. They are fresh and alert. In most situations, rehearsals could be started prior to the time school officially begins. There are usually fewer individual absences due to field trips, medical appointments, special assembly programs, etc.

The primary problem encountered with first period rehearsals is getting the students there on time. If school busses are used, they are frequently late and the possibility of starting prior to regular school time is impossible. Parents can be negligent in getting students to school at the time set for rehearsal. Understandably parents are not very sympathetic to a schedule that continually disrupts the family schedule. The problem of oversleeping must be dealt with quite strictly if it is to be held to a minimum.

For schools where an extended lunch period is used, advantages and disadvantages with rehearsal during this period are: certainty of having full rehearsal time each day (since lunch periods are rarely cut for special programs, etc.); in most situations, students can warm up and tune prior to the start of rehearsal; and individual schedule conflicts are less likely to occur.

Most problems are relevant to human nature. When rehearsals are held just before eating, students usually get hungry and anxious for lunch. If you rehearse immediately after lunch, students are full and cannot support as well, and tend to get drowsy after eating.

For rehearsals during the last period of the day, advantages to be considered are: Students will look forward to the rehearsal throughout the day; there is more time for director preparation; and in many cases, rehearsals can be extended past the regular length school day. Problems frequently encountered are: Students are more fatigued; last periods are frequently cut for special programs; and in most schools, athletics are held this period—thus ruling out students participating in both band and athletics.

In urban schools, a variety of musical possibilites are available to students. Students have more free time and cultural opportunities, and live near the school. In rural schools, students frequently respond eagerly to band due to the small number of musical activities. There is more opportunity to unite students and community behind a project in small to medium-sized towns.

In the final analysis, each individual director must weigh the advantages and disadvantages of a situation and work for the best possible schedule. Once the schedule is satisfactory, take care to see that it is maintained in the same fashion.

Discipline—that oft used, oft misunderstood word—is vital to any educational environment. The root word of discipline is disciple. A disciple is one who receives instruction from another; so discipline should simply be an attitude of learning. With any group, especially a band, start with group discipline. Always stress, and strive to mature toward the goal—individual "self-discipline."

Achieving good group discipline requires all these factors:

1. Something worthy to learn (objective)
2. Environment of learning (rehearsal hall atmosphere)
3. Utilizing a system of learning (director preparation)
4. Maintaining a good learning environment (avoiding disruptions)
5. Satisfactory accomplishment (objective achievement)

All this plus a sincere director dedicated to teaching is necessary. Dedication is vital to good discipline, and of all factors discussed, is the one factor that must be innate rather than acquired. A director with such dedication need never mention this philosophy: students invariably sense it because it permeates all he does. Without this dedication, students react accordingly. They can sense a lack of sincere dedication and no amount of convincing glib talk can change the situation. Such propaganda only adds to the hypocrisy of the situation. It is difficult to improve on sincere caring, and being firm and fair.

SUCCESSFUL REHEARSAL PROCEDURES AND TECHNIQUES

Before a band plays a single note, there are many difficulties that must be eliminated through preparation and persuasion. I refer to the size of the ensemble and instrumentation balance. If proper balance has been achieved in "feeder program" bands, this problem is not such a big task.

Most groups play better, sound better, and are more easily taught if they are kept to a reasonable concert-band size. Most marching bands can be as large as the number of qualified players permits.

The size and acoustical possibilities of the rehearsal hall can in many ways restrict the size of an ensemble.

Difficulties in size often arise when a band is too large to reasonably be one unit but is not quite large enough to be two balanced groups. If it is not possible to have two balanced playing groups, a cadet-type band is one possible alternative.

"Ideal" instrumentation is a favorite topic for discussion with many directors; but for the average school situation, it is better and more practical to follow the trends of instrumentation as represented in music publications. The two most frequently used instrumentation groupings would serve a band made up of the number of players listed in Figure 6-1.

FULL BAND	SYMPHONIC BAND
6 Flutes	8 Flutes
2 Oboes	3 or 4 Oboes (English horn)
1 E-flat soprano clarinet (optional)	1 E-flat soprano clarinet
	6 1st B-flat soprano clarinets
4 1st B-flat soprano clarinets	8 2nd B-flat soprano clarinets
6 2nd B-flat soprano clarinets	8 3rd B-flat soprano clarinets
6 3rd B-flat soprano clarinets	4 E-flat alto clarinets
2 E-flat alto clarinets	4 B-flat bass clarinets
2 B-flat bass clarinets	2 Contra-bass clarinets
1 Contra-bass clarinet	3 or 4 Bassoons (contra-bassoon)
2 Bassoons	2 1st E-flat alto saxophones
1 1st E-flat alto saxophone	1 or 2 2nd E-flat alto saxophones
1 2nd E-flat alto saxophone	1 or 2 B-flat tenor saxophones
1 B-flat tenor saxophone	1 E-flat baritone saxophone
1 E-flat baritone saxophone	3 1st B-flat cornets
2 1st B-flat cornets	3 2nd B-flat cornets
2 2nd B-flat cornets	3 3rd B-flat cornets
2 3rd B-flat cornets	2 B-flat trumpets
2 B-flat trumpets	2 1st French horns
1 1st French horn	2 2nd French horns
1 2nd French horn	2 3rd French horns
1 3rd French horn	2 4th French horns
1 4th French horn	3 1st Trombones
2 1st Trombones	2 2nd Trombones
2 2nd Trombones	2 3rd Trombones
2 3rd Trombones	4 Baritones
2 Baritones	5 Tubas
3 Tubas	1 String bass
1 String bass	6 Percussion
5 Percussion	

Figure 6-1

Following this instrumentation insures a balanced ensemble potential plus elimination of the need for the purchase of costly additional parts.

Balancing instrumentation, like other problems, can be solved through intelligent director foresight. Start by projecting your instrumentation as reflected by your feeder program and then make the necessary instrument transfers during the summer program (see Chapter 9). Persuasion should be used in convincing students to transfer instruments. Pick the students with personality traits that would fit the nature of the instrument needed; then appeal to the student's better nature. General salesmanship must be used to convince the student of the need and worth of the change, both to himself and to the band. As was true in junior high band, if large, expensive, and unusual instruments are needed, it is imperative that the band own such instruments.

WARM-UP

Ensemble and individual warm-up should either precede or start every rehearsal. As we discussed in Chapter 2, the situation dictates the procedure to be used. If the schedule allows it, have individual warm-up and tuning during free time before a rehearsal. An electric tuner should be used daily with this method. In most cases, the band must rush in from the previous class. With this sort of situation, a good procedure is as follows:

1. Have students get their instruments and be in their seats before the tardy bell rings.
2. Do not allow playing before director steps onto the podium. Allow preparation for playing only: otherwise chaos reigns.
3. Use an ensemble method book with a good warm-up procedure and ensemble drill. If one is not available, write a warm-up procedure.

The following warm-up is one that will work effectively in such situations:

1. Invigorate the embouchure by having everyone play a sustained pitch in the low tessituria of their instruments. (Low concert F works nicely.) Sustain the pitch for eight counts using good air support. (Do not force the instrument.) Pull the instrument away from the lips eight counts and let stimulated circulation occur.

2. Warm up the embouchure muscles. Use brass lip slurs accompanied by woodwind chords. Go from simple to more complex forms of lip-slur patterns. Emphasize correct use of embouchure and breath.

3. Warm up the muscles of the tongue. Legato tonguing scales in even rhythm patterns works very nicely for this purpose. Go from rhythm patterns that are slow to those as fast as the group can play. Use legato tonguing and emphasize a steady, well-supported stream of air. Staccato tonguing from the outset tends to cause throat constriction.

4. Warm up the hand tendons and muscles with technical scale patterns and etudes. Warm-up ensemble drill can also be used to encourage individual technical proficiency. Start a technical etude at a speed even the weakest players can keep up with. Through several repetitions, gradually accelerate the speed until it is a challenge to even the best players in the group. Stress control and "evenness" of technique. Fingers can move too fast as well as too slow. Individual players will find themselves being carried beyond a speed they thought they could play by the sheer momentum of the group. Continually emphasize individual practice. Players must be kept aware of their own playing problems that are often covered up by the total ensemble sound. Simple tunes with several graduated technical variations are very good for instruction of this type.

Individual tuning is a prerequisite to any serious concentration on intonation improvement. All instruments should be tuned individually with an electronic tuner, such as the "stroble-tuner," periodically throughout the year to keep them fairly well in tune with themselves. Valved instruments should have all valve slides tuned, and woodwinds should have pad height adjustments kept correct with cork or felt bumpers. Tuning to a given pitch individually is quite necessary every day. If rehearsal time can be arranged to permit it, daily individual tuning to an electronic tuner is best. Since most school schedules will not allow a procedure of this type, we will explore methods of group tuning.

Reasonably good results can be obtained by tuning each individual frequently and telling them not to move the tuning very far in either direction. Students can be instructed in the use of an electronic tuner so they can help each other with intonation on their own time. Rehearsal time is too valuable to be spent with individual tuning each day. Let the group check their own pitch by ear. Have the first clarinetist tune to an electronic tuner, then sound the pitch for the band to tune one section at a time.

Another good method of checking pitch is to have the entire band play Bb concert and systematically "cut off" all except one particular section.

When co-ordinated with correct playing emphasis, chorales and harmonized scales are invaluable for improving tone quality, balance, and intonation. The mind can only concentrate on a few things at once. Technical etudes stress technical concentration; sustained etudes stress sound. First must come a concept of good characteristic sound; next, basic knowledge of the playing techniques needed to achieve this sound; and finally, learning to hear one's own sound accurately.

A cappella singing can improve both accurate hearing and correct playing of a wind instrument. Stress singing correctly, well supported with a relaxed, open throat. Of course, adjustment of octaves from instrumental parts to vocal reading is necessary, but the stress on hearing pitches accurately and recognition of intervals is invaluable. Have students sing their part with an open vowel sound and articulate with a consonant wherever a note would be tongued on an instrument. The syllable "la" works very nicely. All students (*including percussion players,* singing from string bass or oboe books) can benefit from this ear training. After singing the parts, have the students try to play them in the same manner they have correctly sung. They will invariably listen more carefully to what they play.

Balance is dependent on the sound the director wants and demands. As mentioned earlier, good recordings, live performances of other ensembles, personal playing experiences, and improving musical taste aid in the development of a good ensemble balance concept.

An instrumental teacher has a lot going for his subject with students. Musical knowledge is not sterile: it is directly applicable. The student is not an observer but a participant. Emphasize this advantage to all students, prospective and present. Of course, adequate director preparation is a must for effectively relating instruction to the music being prepared. Students are quick to see the need for learning where learning has direct application. They respond accordingly.

Relate rhythm patterns, style, interpretation, and general musicianship to the music being prepared. Emphasize the positive to an individual or group—"I think you can do better"—and they will!!

Rhythm and counting in general can be related to sight reading and rhythm pattern problems being encountered in music being prepared. After the group starts responding, expand the study to related areas of music theory.

For style and interpretation, again use singing: even making up words to a phrase sometimes helps. Emphasize emotion in phrasing and the emotional release that can be achieved through fine playing.

HELPFUL SUPPLEMENTARY AIDS

Today more than ever there are many helpful audio and visual aids available to the director, and the market continues to improve every day. One of the most worthwhile investments that can be made is the purchase of good tape and recording reproduction equipment.

A good tape recorder can be extremely useful in the development of individual players, the analysis of rehearsal techniques, and improvement of ensemble musicality. Most directors will be amazed when they tape an entire rehearsal and then play it back, checking how much time is wasted every day. Students can be made aware of their own tonal and technical inadequacies through the use of a tape recorder (after they are proficient enough to stand the shock). Accompaniments for solos, duets and other ensemble "play-along" selections are now available on tape. An ideal situation would be individual practice rooms with tape recorder-record players in each room.

Many promotional type charts showing good playing techniques, fingerings, trills, etc. are available from most instrument companies. When these charts are simply framed they can be instructive, attractive, and durable. A frame of quarter round and glass is very effective, and in most schools can be prepared by students in woodworking shop.

A rich variety of films are available for instructional and illustrative use. Marching band, instrumental demonstration, and general musicianship films are available on a rental basis through state educational agencies. Here again with both recordings and films, relevance to instructional concentration is all important.

Practical Guidelines for

INDIVIDUAL AND   7
SECTION INSTRUCTION

PRIVATE LESSONS

The first requisite of private lessons, like beginning the study of an instrument, is interest. The basic motivational factors are competition and recognition. I do not advocate competition for the sake of competition or at the expense of worthy musical values, but competition is a fact of life, one of the basic laws of nature. When applied intelligently and ethically toward musical ends, competition can help the student and consequently the group. Here are some of the ways competition can be satisfactorily applied:

1. Section leaders
2. Band placement
3. Section order
4. "Honor" groups

Each of these factors plus related items will be discussed under the heading of Competitive Tryouts. The director must be ethical and psychologically wise in handling competition. Musical values should always be stressed. Competition need not be mentioned: it will take care of itself.

In order for competition to be effective there must be some means of recognition that justifies all the time and effort involved in order to achieve. Here are some proven vehicles of individual recognition:

1. "Peer" prestige
2. News media
3. Photograph displays
4. Yearbooks (annuals)

Many a lengthy treatise has been written on the psychological factors involved with individual accomplishment, so I won't add to that. Suffice it to say that if we were all perfectly adjusted we would probably be contented, like cows, and just exist rather than strive to improve. The wise director can help direct individual psychological needs toward worthy goals. The director guides peer or group approval, supported by the factors mentioned, much more than some might realize.

I once took over a program that needed musical incentive (to say the least). There were a good number of students enrolled in the band program but the basic motivation was social rather than musical. As part of my efforts to shift values back to music I began to emphasize All-State Tryouts which were to occur in a month or so. While promoting these tryouts one day, a student who epitomized this social-musical value deficiency suddenly obnoxiously interrupted with "What good is all that All-State stuff anyway?" Normally I make it a policy to never "argue" with any member of a class—but much more was involved in this situation: immediate expulsion would have been interpreted as an "authoritarian"-type cover-up without sufficient reason. I immediately countered with a question, "What good is *any* accomplishment in your opinion?" While he stammered for an answer, I followed with "Accomplishment is necessary for survival, much less satisfaction and progress—if you don't agree, then we have no place for you in this organization. We mean to accomplish something more than an idle waste of time—if you don't value accomplishment then get out and don't come back until you do." If he had said anything else my reply would have been, "One more word and you're out." My anger demonstrated to him and to the group the factors which I believed were of value. Of course it took more than this to shift group values in a more worthwhile direction. Two students who responded with effort and took private instruction were successful in making All-State Alternates. An "artist"-type photo was taken of each student. These photos and complimentary comments were placed in community and school newspapers, the school "annual," and then framed and placed in the band room picture racks we had just installed. The next year twelve students made All-State and three were alternates. Of course the recognition alone did not produce such amazing individual improvement. During the interim a private lesson program had evolved along with total upgrading of ensemble musical standards. Recognition provided incentive; administration provided opportunity; and competent music instruction plus student effort realized the musical improvement that was made.

In order to provide opportunity for students to take private lessons some varied salesmanship and administrative talent must be used. As in other phases of instruction the school-community situation has a great deal to do with the type of program that is set up. Here are some "getting-started" methods that have worked for others:

1. Short lessons during the school day. Ten-minute lessons for each senior high band member once each week. This method can only be implemented where ample director time at the senior high can be scheduled. Students come back during study hall or "free" period. Solos or band music can be used as relevant musical teaching material. This sort of approach should be used to help start outside private study. The better students should be urged to seek more complete private instruction outside the school.

2. Director-taught lessons outside the regular school day. Frequently this is the method that is necessary in order to build a more complete private-instruction program. A solo festival or "honor" band tryouts might provide the short-term goal for such a beginning. Lessons might be scheduled after school or on Saturday. The director might even have to start these lessons

without additional pay; otherwise some might think that this "instruction" was being used only for providing additional director income. Others might look upon the fee as some sort of "bribery" for their student to "get ahead" in regular band. Any private lesson program must develop so that additional teachers become necessary and a lesson-by-fee basis can be solidified. There are many valid advantages to having private lessons taught by the band director, but this of course would eventually limit the number of students taking private lessons, plus drain already scarce director time. Summer band can provide opportunity to initate a private instruction program. Chapter 9 will examine this possibility further.

In most situations, the school music facilities can be used as physical facilities for the private instruction program. If this area proves to be the best (or only) place for such instruction, then make sure that administrative approval is granted first. Use rooms that adjoin the band room for teaching lessons. (Practice rooms, library, office, etc.). This allows students to come in, assemble their instruments, warm up, and leave without disrupting the lessons that are in progress. Other areas that are frequently used are: studios in private homes, music stores, or if you are real lucky, nearby college music instruction.

The best available private instruction should be thoroughly sought after. If teachers must be brought in, then a full schedule of students must be assured (pay in advance), and travel compensation made (booster club, etc.) Here are some possible teacher sources:

1. *Area residents.* Frequently there are members of the community who have fine musical experience and education. Inquire through students, booster club members, local newspapers, etc., and recruit these people for the program. Many will teach well and welcome the opportunity. Be prudent about the validity of their qualifications, how long since they were active, time available, etc.

2. *Active performers.* Most professional musicians supplement their income by teaching privately. This instruction may

be carried on in the school or where the performer resides. If only a few students take lessons from an instructor, it is usually necessary for them to travel to where he operates a studio.

3. *Professional teachers.* This group makes up the best group of potential teachers. They may be faculty members of a nearby or local college, other teachers in the same system (elementary or junior high), or teachers in nearby school systems. These professionals usually do the best job of teaching and will tend to work better with the local band director.

4. *College or university students.* Upper-level students from nearby colleges can be used if no other satisfactory teachers can be found. These students are usually more difficult to contact and are around for only a year or so, but can be very effective teachers in some instances.

If professional teachers are obtained, private instruction credit is frequently possible. Work to get school credit recognition even if it is only "activity" or non academic credit. Lessons with evaluation involved tend to be approached more seriously by both student and instructor. Figure 7-1 is a sample evaluation sheet for weekly lessons.

PRIVATE LESSONS
Wayne Pegram, Instructor

Assignment_____

Solo work in progress_____

EVALUATION OF PROGRESS AND SUGGESTIONS

Tone_____

General Technique_____

_____

Musicality_____

Special areas of emphasis_____

_____

Weekly grade_____

Figure 7-1

In some school systems, private teachers have studios in the music building and some students are allowed to take lessons during "free" periods. This, of course, is an excellent situation. If possible and feasible, it is good for the director to keep musically alive through performing and private teaching of his "major" instrument. This helps with professional interest as well as being inspiring for his students.

COMPETITIVE TRYOUTS

As was mentioned earlier, competition is a natural way of life and is present with students even if it is never mentioned. Caution should be exercised by the director to consistently keep musical values foremost or personal feuds and ill will can multiply. Never should competition be allowed to deteriorate to a level of personalities. Another detrimental factor related to competition is the tendency of the individual to think that once he wins something he has arrived. This can be a big deterrent to individual progress.

There are "tryout" situations that will occur from the beginning of a student's playing career continuing through professional life. These tryouts tend to follow the same basic order and evaluation percentages. Prepared material—demonstrating tone technique, phrasing, general musicianship, etc. and sight reading—demonstrating the quickness of musical perception. Some tryouts that occur during the regular school year might be:

1. *Marching band tryout.* This tryout would be for admission to the organization and could consist of: scales and a technical etude (demonstrating general instrumental proficiency), memorized music (demonstrating desire and ability to memorize), and marching fundamental mastery (demonstrating knowledge and coordination not related to musical values). Section leaders can provide valuable assistance with marching band tryouts.

2. *Grading period tryouts.* These are not really complete tryouts in the fullest sense of the word but evaluations of

individual improvement during the grading period, a "mini" version of music "jury" exams. The fundamental "check-off" lists in Chapters 3 and 4 can provide material for this category.

3. *Band seating placement.* This complete tryout should occur during the latter part of marching season and should be as thorough as time will permit. This tryout will establish initial "chair" order as well as placement in various concert ensembles where more than one concert band is involved. I have found a complete list of all players on each instrument to be convenient and effective in group placement. This list should be kept in the director's office for reference rather than public display. A list I have used consisted of a numerical order, plus the band assigned to each number and the part played. (Figure 7-2). *Example:* (W.E. Indicates Wind Ensemble and SYM., Symphonic Band)

	FLUTES	
W.E. 1st part	1.	
	2.	
W.E. 2nd part	3.	
	4.	
SYM. 1st part	5.	
	6.	
	etc.	

Figure 7-2

This neatly painted chart was covered with glass and names were printed on the glass with black "grease-pencil" to facilitate ease in changing order due to challenging. Figure 7-3 is a sample tryout sheet used in initial tryouts:

4. *Student-initiated challenging.* To provide readjustment in case of incorrect initial tryout evaluation, and to promote continued effort, challenging should be allowed. The student who challenges moves up only one chair at a time. The "challenger" provides the prepared material to the "challenged" individual three days prior to a mutually convenient time. The director and band officers judge the tryout without seeing the players perform. Fundamental material

---

BAND TRYOUT INFORMATION

Name_____ Grade_____

Instrument_____ Part Played Last Year_____

Playing Record:

Tone (40 pts.)_____

Embouchure_____

Mouthpiece Placement_____

Playing Record—Phrasing and Rhythm (20 pts.)

Problems Encountered_____

_____

_____

Sight Reading (40 pts.)

Evident Weakness_____

_____

_____

Recommended Placement_____

Figure 7-3

(sight reading and scales) are selected by the director. The pressure is on the person being challenged but the challenger must "beat" the individual holding the desired chair position. In case of tie the positions remain the same.

5. *"Clinic" or "honor" band tryouts.* These tryouts may be for groups such as: All-State, All-District, etc. If a director encourages such competition he is obligated to see that students who respond are well prepared. Private instruction can help

with prepared material a great deal. Some areas have all players try out on the same selected material (standard repertoire type) and some have students present prepared material of their choice. With sight reading, the best way to improve is to be sure of basic rhythmic and musical understanding, then have the students read everything they can get their hands on. At least one selection a day should be read in full band rehearsals and students can be given various samples that the director receives from publishers, plus obtaining reading material on their own. I always liked to have everyone who was trying out meet as a group and discuss procedures, play prepared material, and sight read. In other words, have a "mock" tryout with musical and psychological tips offered by the band director.

6. *Scholarship auditions.* Many universities and colleges offer scholarships to outstanding performers. I personally feel that this practice is over-emphasized in many cases, but there are some constructive benefits that can be gained from such procedures. The tryouts are usually along the lines as outlined in "honor" band competitive tryouts. For these scholarships, however, student potential and personal (as well as college) needs are frequently given heavy consideration. Factors such as general playing approach, musical background, aural perception ("talent" tests), college placement scores (A.C.T., College Board, etc.), general health, financial situation, etc., are often considered as well as performance. Students should be cautioned to be sure they wish to attend a particular school before signing a scholarship agreement. N.A.S.M. (National Association Schools of Music) ethics forbid schools to offer scholarships to students who have already accepted scholarships elsewhere.

7. *Professional tryouts.* These auditions are as varied as the performance needs of the groups involved (orchestras, jazz or dance bands, military bands, etc.). The same general tryout procedure is customary; however, knowledge of vacancies, etc., make "inside" contacts very advantageous. Professional as well as security references (for military groups) are frequently required.

SECTION REHEARSALS

In addition to private instruction for individual improvement, superior ensemble performance demands regular section rehearsals. Among the many advantages are:

1. Improved understanding. Students will ask questions in smaller groups when they might be embarassed to ask them in full rehearsal.
2. Technical improvement. Sections of works that are difficult can be isolated and explained idiomatically (alternate fingerings, hints, etc.) These sections can be paced to a speed where accuracy is precise and gradually accelerated to performance tempos through repetition. This procedure wastes time in full band rehearsals, but is very helpful in section rehearsal.
3. Tonal improvement. Students will have opportunity to hear and learn through imitation. It is amazing how one outstanding player can influence tonal concept and development through section work. A fine section leader will very favorably influence an entire section over a period of time. Intonation can also be improved greatly when numbers are decreased to the point that the individual begins to hear himself much more clearly.
4. Musical development. This quality is very much correlated to the previous two factors. Technical and tonal proficiency precede demonstration of musical understanding. More detailed phrase emphasis will help the student see the importance of his individual part.
5. Student leadership. Section leaders can provide much assistance with section rehearsals. I have found that a great deal of instruction can be facilitated by having two section rehearsals (in adjoining rooms) scheduled for the same time. This way the director can instruct, then allow the section leader to handle repetitions. We have already mentioned how a good player can favorably

influence a section but also keep in mind how leadership is developed with students. The director should periodically check progress and always be readily available for advice and quick settlement of any "squabble."

6. Notation corrections. Mistakes (that are all too frequent in printed music) can be located and corrected much more efficiently in smaller groups. The director should watch for this possibility, especially during "early" section rehearsals on a selection. The director must be familiar with the parts played by the section involved. This plus study of the condensed score will help the conductor be aware of each section's contribution to the composition. Simplification of individual parts can be effectively handled in section rehearsal.

Section rehearsals should be scheduled in such a way as to insure 100 percent attendance. Attendance should be required (see Chapter 8) and students periodically reminded of the importance of section rehearsals. Try to foster the development of section pride and loyalty. In some school situations it is possible to have section rehearsals during the school day. If there are two or more directors, ample facilities, and band is scheduled as indicated in Chapter 5 (consecutive periods), then frequent section rehearsals are quite feasible. In most cases section rehearsals must be scheduled outside of school time. Whenever section rehearsals are scheduled it is usually best to have them in the music building. In some cases section rehearsal can be scheduled during the regular band period. I do not advocate this procedure, but it might be used in some cases as a last resort.

Here is a suggested procedure for section rehearsal:

1. Prior to the section rehearsal, furnish the section leader with a list of music that you wish to have rehearsed. This list should include the spots to be worked on plus any suggestions that might be of help.

2. The section leader checks roll during preliminary tuning.

3. A warm-up chorale is played (brass also do lip slurs).
4. More precise individual tuning (possible use of electronic tuner).
5. Work on music with the director.
6. Section leader works with "correct" group repetitions.
7. Director checks progress and gives advice for further improvement.
8. Selection for fun (possible section "feature" number) with section leader.

Section rehearsals can provide the nucleus for chamber music, a very important and individually rewarding part of the total program. Chamber music can be worthy recreation and a valuable outlet for self-expression and improvement.

PUBLIC PERFORMANCE

In addition to the recognition of accomplishment through publicity, etc., private instruction and section work need goals to work toward. Solo and ensemble festivals can provide some outlet, but local performance should also enter the picture. Work closely with private teachers in preparing solos that are suitable for civic club performance and also those with band accompaniments suitable for concerts. Try scheduling a concert of chamber music and solos. Student groups receiving "superiors" at festival could be presented in concert. Civic clubs frequently call upon the school music program to provide entertainment for local and regional meetings. Be careful to see that some chamber groups are intact from year to year so requests can also be honored during the fall marching season.

Here are some performance possibilities for solos and chamber music:

1. Solo and ensemble festivals or contests
2. Civic and community clubs
3. Banquets and school meetings (P.T.A., teachers, etc.)

4. Include solos and chamber music in regular band concerts
5. Have a special chamber music concert
6. Talent shows and school assemblies
7. Elementary and junior high instrument demonstrations

DEVELOPING   8
STUDENT LEADERSHIP

Besides the many positive advantages for the development of maturity in students through student leadership, these leaders can provide invaluable assistance to the director (especially in one-director programs). This sort of leadership program is in keeping with the important "community" concept mentioned in Chapter 5. Students who learn to lead and follow whenever necessary have a good basis for joining society as responsible citizens. Parents who understand the philosophy of this leadership are usually quick to encourage participation in the band program. Students will usually accept values embodied in this program while they might shun them when uttered by parents. A good student leadership program should:

1. Embody the principles of good citizenship
2. Aid the director in organizing and carrying on the work of the band
3. Be instrumental in maintaining discipline and the development of "esprit de corps"
4. Have a built-in training program to perpetuate itself.

Students react very favorably to order and system in the operation of the band program. They frequently will complain about the tough rules—the stringent discipline—and then flock right to it. It almost seems as though they have a subconscious craving for an activity that demands the best they have within them. Remember just as the band program attracts the kind of students that it expects to get so does the director receive the kind of help he expects to get.

DEVELOPING LEADERSHIP

The basic concept of leadership, like all other phases of the band program, is an apt representation of the qualities inherent in the director. Like it or not, student leaders will model and relate their actions to you. Here are a few traits that should be kept in mind. A good leader:

1. Believes in and has dedication to his work
2. Works hard to get things done
3. Maintains a positive attitude
4. Shows interest in his students and helps them overcome problems
5. Is as fair and impartial as is humanly possible
6. Is receptive to new ideas and suggestions
7. Admits mistakes without show and strives to correct them
8. Above all, a good leader is a symbol

Admittedly it is not easy to be a symbol. People do not think of leaders (or symbols) as human beings as a rule, and therefore tend to take great "stock" in what they say or (especially) do. The director has many situations (trips, after-school practices, clinics, etc.) where students will open up to him more than to any other adult. This role of counselor is an awesome responsibility. I'm sure that the average director has opportunity to do much more true "counseling" than does the school counselor. The nature of music making itself embodies a closeness, a trust; and so this confidence is natural. The director cannot be so "forbidding" that students avoid him, but neither can he be just "one of the gang." This thin line of difference is a difficult one to walk. When I first started teaching, I was so careful "to do this" and "not to do this" in my personal life and at school, but the longer I teach the more I realize that if you do your job well and are humanly honest with yourself, you're in good shape. Everyone (*especially* students) hates a hypocrite. Here are some suggested guidelines for association with students:

1. Do not lounge, smoke, and joke with students. Conversely, do not maintain a "holier-than-thou" attitude either. Just tend to your business when business is to be done and be friendly when casual attitudes are in order.
2. Restrict yourself to the same rules of conduct that you expect of them (smoking, etc.)
3. Listen fully when a personal problem is presented to you and offer suggestions or advice only when asked.
4. Strictly honor confidences: don't gossip. Giving advice is an awesome responsibility; but if it is given honestly as a personal opinion based upon experience, it is eventually appreciated.

In order to be effective, student leadership should be developed as the beginner develops. Some student leadership can be utilized even in beginning band. Assign a student to be in charge in case the instructor is called out of class. As we have mentioned earlier, use student help in arranging chairs, stands, etc. If music other than individual music is used, use students to pass it out and take it up. Make frequent relevant comments about the responsibility involved with being a band member.

If the intermediate band meets on a regular basis, then student leaders should be elected and appointed (on a proportionately smaller scale).

The junior high bands should use an officer-assistant program very similar to the senior high band. This program should be paced so students know and use student leadership as they mature with it. All along the "developmental" way student leadership should be nurtured and developed on the same level of maturity as is expected in their over-all musicianship.

Students will not know how to lead nor how to follow

other students unless this prevailing attitude is developed along the way. The amount of maturity reflected in responsible student attitude in the senior high is proportionate to the amount of instruction given through the director plus an atmosphere of trust shown to student leaders.

Care must be taken to keep officer qualifications high to discourage undesirable or unqualified officer candidates. Most schools have student leader criteria (grades, citizenship, etc.) to which you can add any requirements relevant to band only. Students must trust and understand that all final decisions rest with the band director and that they are to be co-operative with the band administration.

STUDENT ELECTIONS

Here are some suggestions that I have found to be effective in helping student elections to be fair and generally in keeping with the democratic system.

1. Hold all elections in the spring of the year. Allow at least one grading period for an apprenticeship-type program between newly elected officers and the out-going officers.
2. Be familiar with the qualifications of candidates. I have found it useful to nominate officers a week or more prior to elections in order to fully check qualifications. I have heard it said that campaigning for these offices is not good; but it has been my experience that the candidates who campaign more want the office more and usually do better jobs.
3. As in all full band meetings, officers should be in charge with the director serving in an advisory role. Parliamentary procedure as outlined in Roberts' *Rules of Order* should be followed.
4. Use a constitution (such as outlined in this chapter) and be sure students are familiar with it by using it as a part of acceptance into the band (rookie orientation).

5. Be sure that officers are allowed to exercise the responsibilities outlined in the constitution. There have been times when I have been fearful that the "wrong" person would be elected to a student office, but it has never occurred. If student leaders are expected (and *allowed*) to perform their duties, then other students will elect responsible, qualified officers. If the officers are mere "figureheads" and the director runs the whole show, then students will respond by making elections a joke and selecting the least qualified candidates.

In addition to the school's "required" qualifications, there are some character traits that I feel help to make an effective officer or staff member. Factors such as desire, responsibility, efficiency, other school activities, dedication, etc., all figure heavily in making good leaders.

Section leaders should be selected from the better players in each particular section who also seem to possess the character traits that have been mentioned. In sections involving more than one part (trumpets, clarinets, etc.) it is sometimes advisable to have one or more assistant section leaders. This is especially true during marching season. By using assistants in large sections, you also insure that there will be mature players on each part.

I have noticed that good presidents (like good directors) have tendencies toward "visions of grandeur." I guess it goes with the territory, but it *is* true that a lofty opinion of the office is necessary to respond to the duties that are required.

If officers and staff are to maintain the fortitude that is necessary in the performance of their duties, then there must be sufficient recognition and prestige that goes with the office. First the director must support his officers and staff in the performance of their duties. Make it a policy to back a student leader if they are under fire, especially until you have had a chance to talk about the matter with the student leader involved. There will be some "squabbles," but they will be settled fairly, if good judgment and the band constitution are adhered to. Officer and staff photographs should be placed in newspapers, in school annuals, and displayed in the picture racks in the band room. Credits should be given for programs and other events where the band appears. Some distinguishing medals or insignia can be worn with the band uniform. Recognition along these lines seem to mean a lot to students. In order to keep the director informed and the students knowledgable about what is expected of them, schedule periodic meetings with your officers and staff. If possible, make these meetings a little special by holding them in association with a meal or similar social atmosphere. Meetings of this type might be held in the director's home, a local restaurant, or even a special room or area of the school cafeteria. Both the director and president should prepare an agenda and distribute it to officers a week or more prior to such meetings. The dignity and respect that is acquired in such an atmosphere will tend to carry over into "called" meetings, etc.

If the student leadership program is effectively organized and fairly administered, students will respond and rise to the occasion. I have conducted groups that consistently performed better than I thought possible because of tradition. I have also seen students mature admirably with the tradition of the duties of an office. When students start listing credits in the school year book like—John Doe: band section leader, 3, 4, valedictorian, etc.—then your leadership program has come of age. I was once director of bands in a school that did not allow a student to hold but one major office. The student government president was also elected band president. The student government officers were really only token officers and band president was an active responsibility—he decided to be band president!

BAND CONSTITUTION

Here is an example of a proven, effective band constitution used in a situation that exemplified superb student leadership year after year. With local adjustments according to preference and school situations, it can be used for most programs.

CONSTITUTION FOR THE C.H.S. BAND

The words "Central High School" have acquired an atmosphere of excellence in all fields. Now maintaining one of the finest music programs in the state, the band, as an integral part of this program, must also fulfill these expectations.

In order to maintain as well as improve the excellent qualities which have been characterized by the band in the past, we, the director and the officers, and the members of the C.H.S. Band do write and ratify this constitution assuming the following standards are necessary to insure an attitude of always working and never resting, making the good better, and the better best.

Article I

The motto of the C.H.S. Band shall be as follows: "I will strive to develop the talent I have been given."

The above motto will appear on all outside work turned in to the band.

Article II

The chain of command of the C.H.S. Band is as follows: Director, Officers, Field Commander or Student Conductor, Section Leaders, Assistant Section Leaders, Seniors, Juniors, Sophomores, and Freshmen.

Proper respect for the chain of command will be shown at all times.

Article III

The order of officers of C.H.S. Band will be as follows: President, Vice-President, Recording Secretary, Corresponding Secretary, Treasurer, and elected Representatives from affiliated units.

Section I. Responsibilities

President:

The president is responsible to the Director for the action of the entire band.

He is to preside over the band at all band meetings and assist at every function which the band attends.

The President shall check roll at every band function when such a check is desired and will make announcements when desired.

He will accept public honors, trophies, etc., for the band and represent the band in all student leadership activities.

First Vice-President:

The First Vice-President will carry out all the duties of the President on his absence.

The First Vice-President is responsible to the President for the duties assigned to him.

It shall be the duty of the First Vice-President to provide for the maintenance and care of all band equipment including instruments, music, and uniforms.

All managers shall be responsible to the First Vice-President.

Field Commander:

During any marching performance, the Field Commander shall assume complete and absolute control of the band, being responsible only to the Director.

During the performance of his duty, the Field Commander shall supersede any officer.

The Field Commander will be selected through annual tryout.

Student Conductor:

The Student Conductor assumes the responsibility of the Field Conductor during Concert Season.

The position is appointed by the Director through tryout.

Recording and Corresponding Secretaries:

The Recording Secretary shall be in charge of all merits and demerits. All practice sheets shall be turned in to the Recording Secretary for filing.

The Corresponding Secretary will be in charge of all correspondence of the band. Both secretaries shall work jointly on any records to be kept by the band at the request of the Director. The band secretaries shall be responsible to the President for any duties assigned to them. Secretaries should have a free period for office work.

Treasurer:

All collecting—dues, ticket money, etc.— will be under the direction of the Treasurer.

The Treasurer shall be responsible to the President for any duties assigned to him.

Section 2.

All officers shall have the power to give demerits and merits as they see fit.

Section 3.

Officers (with the exception of the Field Commander and the Student Conductor) are to be elected by a majority vote and shall serve one year except in the case of impeachment.

Section 4.

All band officers are subject to impeachment. Officers can be released from their duties only after 2/3 vote of the band members or direct notification from the Director.

Article IV

Section I. Section Leaders.

Section leaders shall be responsible for roll call in their section. It shall be their duty to maintain order at all times.

A section leader may recommend a demerit or merit for a member of his section to be approved by an officer.

Before any new music is performed in public, each section leader will hear each person individually perform the new music.

Section leaders are appointed by the Director to serve one year unless relieved by the Director.

Section 2.

Head majorette, color-guard captain, and leaders from other affiliated units have the same responsiblities as section leaders.

Section 3. Equipment Managers.

The managerial corps shall be responsible in the performance of all their duties to the Director and to the Vice-President.

They shall be in charge of all equipment; shall assist in

the loading and unloading of instruments; shall assist band members before performance.

Any duty assigned to the managers by the Director or any officer shall be performed at the necessary time.

Section 4. Uniform Managers.

The uniform managers will issue complete uniforms. All complaints or losses with regard to uniforms should be reported to them.

The uniform cabinets will be accessible only to the uniform managers. The uniform managers will be responsible to the Vice-President for the performance of their duties.

Section 5.

Selected members of the managerial corps will form the stage crew for concerts, tours, festivals, and other related activities.

Section 6. Librarians.

The librarians will be in charge of all music. Any loss or need of extra music shall be reported to the librarians.

Only those appointed by the Director shall be allowed in the library.

The librarians will be responsible to the band secretaries for the performance of their duties.

Section 7.

Managers, uniform managers, and librarians are appointed by the Director to serve until relieved.

Article V

Section I.

All school rules will be adhered to by band members.

Section 2.

Every person shall be responsible for his own music.

A fee of $.50 shall be charged for each piece of music lost or destroyed.

Section 3.

A. Instruments are to be properly cleaned, oiled, and kept in good playing condition. Each individual is responsible for all accessories necessary for playing his instrument. Any breakage of equipment will be replaced by the individual responsible for the instrument (including school-owned instruments). Any member of the band who abuses a school-owned instrument in any manner will be immediately expelled from the band.

B. Each member will be expected to practice enough to cut his part. Practice sheets will be given to each individual each six weeks, and his grade will partially be determined by the amount of time spent in individual practice. Each member must attend all section practices and extra band rehearsals. These outside rehearsals will be announced in advance and scheduled at the best time for the majority. Those extra rehearsals will count on extra practice time. Failure to attend these rehearsals will result first in lowering the individual's grade, and expulsion from the band should this continue.

Section 4.

A. After seating order is established (through individual tryout), challenges may be arranged. The person doing the challenging must give three days' notice and the challenge music must be given to the individual being challenged. Challenges for changing bands can be arranged only at the end of a six-week period.

B. All instruments and music must be kept in the places provided for them. Failure to adhere to this rule will cost the offender one demerit.

Section 5.

A. Missing a performance or rehearsal without an acceptable excuse will result in immediate expulsion from the band. Smoking in public while in uniform is not permitted. Chewing gum while playing is not allowed. Disturbance of a rehearsal is not allowed. Each member must be warmed up ready to play at the time of rehearsal.

B. Merits may be earned in the following manner: 1 merit may be given for each hour of outside work for the band. 1 merit for superior inspection on uniform or instrument. 1 merit for attendance at concerts, recitals, etc. (with written report). Merits for outstanding efforts for the band (awarded at will by the Director).

Demerits will be given for the following offenses: 2

demerits for tardiness (plus appropriate comments). 1 demerit for failure to pass inspection (uniform or instrument).

Merits and demerits may be given by the Director, band officers, or section leaders.

An accumulation of 5 demerits without any attempt to work them off will result in expulsion from the band.

Section 6.

All dues, payments, etc., will be due two weeks after notification.

Section 7.

Band members will be subject to inspection any time the unit is to appear in public.

Band members will be subject to instrument inspection upon announcement.

Section 8.

There will be no smoking in the band room, on the field, or anywhere except the place provided by school officials.

There will be no smoking or drinking while in uniform, and chewing gum is not permitted in uniform or during practice.

Section 9.

Any detrimental act which reflects directly on the band shall subject the person to expulsion.

Section 10.

Play only the instrument assigned to or owned by an individual unless special permission is obtained.

There will be no playing of instruments except in the band room or on specific order on the field.

Section 11.

If any part of the uniform is to be worn, the student shall appear in full uniform with the following exceptions: Hat and gloves are not always required; a band sweater may be substituted for the coat.

Section 12.

There will be no eating before the half time at a ball game.

Section 13.

Failure to co-operate with other teachers is considered detrimental to the band.

Section 14.

Two F's in one six-weeks period, or two consecutive F's on a report card will subject a person to a six-week suspension in marching band until the grade is brought up.

Article VI

Section 1.

This constitution must be ratified by a 2/3 vote of the band members before it can take effect.

Section 2.

An amendment of the constitution must be first placed before the Director and officers of the band, and if unanimously approved, it then can be placed before the band, and added if it receives a 2/3 majority.

Some bands traditionally call their officers by other titles such as Captain, First and Second Lieutenants, Drum Major, etc.—more or less in the military tradition. The duties of these officers could roughly correspond to the duties as outlined for President, Vice-President, etc.

There are some other factors that might need adjustment in different situations. The merit-demerit system will work effectively unless it is looked upon with an attitude such as "Well, I've got several merits so now I can 'goof-off' a little and still come out okay." This sort of attitude is best countered with the understanding that truly outstanding individuals contribute *much* above what is required of the average person. Mention to the band frequently that average effort consistently produces average results. Try to instill (through example) a desire to achieve beyond the average. The major advantages of the order and understanding that can be utilized with such a constitution is dependent upon the students through knowledge of the document. Have a band information booklet prepared containing all pertinent information regarding the band. Such a booklet or pamphlet should be neatly printed and distributed to all new band members. A local printer might be persuaded to hold type for such a booklet (in case of changes) and annually print the number you need.

To make this booklet attractive, it might also contain some illustrations or relevant "cartoon"-type drawings at pertinent spots in the information. Such a booklet might contain:

1. Band history and tradition
2. Requirements for membership
3. Band constitution
4. Annual schedule of events
5. School information (Alma Mater, etc.)

Demonstration of knowledge of the contents of this booklet might be a part of the requirements for band membership.

ADDITIONAL ASSISTANTS

In addition to the officers and staff responsibilities as outlined in the constitution, there are other areas in which students can provide valuable assistance. Some of these duties might be categorized in the following manner:

Office Assistants. These students (young ladies are nice) might be provided or selected through the business education department in your school. In some cases "on-the-job" training credit and personal recommendations can help as incentive. These students may or may not be members of the band but to be effective they should come to feel a part of the total band program. Their duties could include:

1. Answering the telephone
2. Greeting visitors
3. Accepting messages (for director or students)
4. Typing and correspondence assistance
5. Other clerical assistance.

There should be one assistant (only) each period of the day.

Concert Assistance. For most concert appearances and

other related band events it is necessary to secure responsible, personable individuals to sell and "take up" tickets and serve as ushers (passing out programs, etc.) Qualified individuals for these tasks may be selected from any non playing members of the band organization: managers, office assistants (if not required to play instruments); possibly girls from the majorette squad or flag corps can fill these necessary roles. Frequently members of booster or parent clubs can be of assistance in selling tickets, etc.

Publicity—Advertising. If there are band members who have some degree of specialized talents along this line or have valuable connections through parents or friends, then enlist their aid and place them in a position on the band staff. Try to establish a regular column relevant to music and the band's activities in local and school newspapers. When special events such as concerts, musicals, etc. occur, use the help of all who can make posters, and form committees to handle various media of communication:

1. Publications (newspapers, etc.)
2. Radio and television
3. School and store marquees
4. Posters and signs
5. Handbills and letters.

The major responsibility still rests with the band director but valuable assistance can be provided by band members. Student leadership is also very necessary in fund-raising campaigns and ticket sales. It is a good idea to learn from the professionals in this area—groups such as magazine subscription companies and large candy companies. They divide students into teams, give pep talks and put great emphasis on team leaders and outstanding individual salesmanship. The same sort of approach can be effectively used in any fund-raising campaign. What is needed is organization to make use of the leadership potential present in all groups.

Student leaders can also be of great value during trips and events away from home: more will be said about this in Chapter 10.

SUMMER INSTRUCTION PROGRAMS 9

Most of the better band programs also include instruction offered during the summer. There are several advantages to such programs and, of course, some problems to be overcome. Some of the advantages and opportunities are:

1. year-round director salary
2. continued contact with students
3. students improve technical and reading proficiency
4. more individual attention is possible
5. greater flexibility with enrichment subjects
6. adjustment of instrumentation for coming year
7. marching band readiness (majorette and field commander classes)
8. band tryouts and uniforms fitted
9. fund raising and other activities.

The biggest problems and conflicts that normally must be overcome include:

1. student summer jobs
2. family vacations and camps
3. summer school schedule and conflicting recreational activities.

These conflicts can be overcome with the flexibility of the schedule that we will discuss later in this chapter.

There are several methods of financing the summer band program. As in other areas where various methods are used there are advantages and disadvantages present in each. Here are some of the options:

1. School board twelve-month employment. This has the advantage of guaranteed income and makes possible classes that are small and highly specialized. The disadvantages are that parents do not pay directly and therefore do not hesitate to pull students out for any reason at any time. It also has a tendency to fail to encourage the initiative of the director (I also support merit pay).
2. Employment through summer recreation activities. This has the same advantages and disadvantages of school-supported salary. Frequently the pay is less and there may be some strings attached, such as civic parades, etc.
3. Student tuition payment. I have had the best success with this plan. Both parents and students tend to treat the summer program with more respect when they pay directly. There are fewer absences and a high quality of instruction is expected. Unless the program is very small or the area is very "low-income," I recommend this approach.

THE CURRICULUM

The curriculum should be designed to have enough flexibility to allow maximum participation regardless of other student summer activities. I have used similar curriculums, on a tuition basis, with 98% to 100% participation. In some communities it is possible to organize a municipal band and present a few concerts (the outdoor type). This sort of activity is not usually possible during the regular school year but is a wonderful opportunity to gain support through civic participation.

The curriculum's basic approach should be oriented toward recreational concepts with the intent of maintaining and improving over-all playing proficiency. The summer also offers good opportunities to start beginners without the usual academic pressures of the regular school year. Beginners should not be recruited from the grade level where they will have opportunity to start during the regular school year. This tends to weaken beginning band participation and can upset the balanced developmental curriculum that has been established.

The success and enrollment of the summer instruction program is largely dependent on timing and advertising. Send letters to *parents* six to eight weeks prior to the end of the regular academic year. Collect names and addresses of all students who will be entering the senior high in schools where there is more than one elementary director. I suggest sending the letters by mail. The added assurance of the parent receiving the information plus the attention given mailed information is well worth the expense. Figure 9-1 is an example of a letter to parents:

SUMMER INSTRUMENTAL INSTRUCTION

Dear_____,

Again this summer we are pleased to be able to offer your children worthwhile musical activities. Our curriculum is organized to assist students in achieving as much musical advancement as they wish, plus providing the best type of recreational activities. Students can make amazing musical improvement during the summer through this instruction, partially because of the additional practice time available without the academic pressures of the regular school year.

Our curriculum offerings this summer will include:

Full Band Rehearsals
Beginning Instrumental Classes
Intermediate Instrumental Classes
Advanced Instrumental Classes
Music Enrichment

Figure 9-1

(The schedule for these classes can also be included as appears on the Weekly Schedule chart, Figure 9-2.)

We hope your child will be able to participate along with the other band students so his improvement will continue along with theirs. The tuition fee for this accredited instruction is less than $1.00 per hour of instruction for a six-week period. The following options are offered:

(prices listed considered minimum)
Beginning Band—$15.00
Full Program(technique classes, full band, enrichment) —$25.00
Half Program (technique classes, full band)—$15.00
Full Band only—$6.00

Our schedule is designed to offer the ultimate in individualized instruction and flexibility. Lessons missed because of trips, camps, or out of town visits may be made up during the times scheduled on Fridays so that every student can receive equal instruction. We hope you take advantage of this opportunity for your children. If you desire additional information please contact me at _____(phone number)_____. Please fill out the enclosed form and send it with your check on or before _____. Thanking you for your interest and cooperation, I remain

Sincerely,

Director of Bands

Figure 9-1 (cont.)

A form can be included that includes relevant information: (Figure 9-3)

Such a letter (as with other information in this book) should be altered to fit individual situations and personal style but is offered here as an example of a letter that has worked very favorably. The replies to reasons "unable to participate" should be used to make any possible modifications needed in

WEEKLY SCHEDULE

Monday	Tuesday	Wednesday	Thursday	Friday	Times
Beg. Band	Beg. Band	Beg. Band	Beg. Band	Beg. Band	8:00 a.m.
Inter. W.W.	Adv. W.W.	Inter. W.W.	Adv. W.W.	Make-up Lessons	9:00 a.m.
Inter. Brass	Adv. Brass	Inter. Brass	Adv. Brass	Make-up Lessons	10:00 a.m.
Inter. Perc.	Adv. Perc.	Inter. Perc.	Adv. Perc.	Make-up Lessons	11:00 a.m.
Music Enr.	Music Enr.	Music Enr.	Music Enr.	Make-up	1:00 p.m.
Full Band	Combined Adv. Class		Combined Adv. Class		7:00 p.m.

Figure 9-2

the schedule. If finances are truly a problem with some student, check with school officials. If no student financial assistance is available (civic clubs, etc.), try having the student do band work (repair, filing, etc.) for you in lieu of tuition. This program should be started as soon as regular summer school gets underway. Make sure that all students with whom you have contact, return the "Summer Instruction" form before exams begin. In addition to the letter to parents, seek out any students mentioned by band members plus students who move into the community. Also advertise through all local media (newspapers, etc.).

The curriculum should be adjusted so that students in regular summer school can also participate in instrument classes. Many fine students now take enrichment courses in other areas through summer school. Work with the school administration in resolving any potential conflicts. Night classes as well as full band are scheduled in such a way that students who have daily jobs can still participate. Try to pick the night that is most free from other activities involving band members, then settle on it so it will come to be set aside in the community as "band practice night." Most conflicts can be resolved if a student has sincere interest in participation. This schedule (with the inclusion of "make-up lessons") should not deter students from enrolling if family vacations or camps take them out of town two or even three weeks. If more than half of the time will be missed, encourage the student to participate while in town and prorate the tuition accordingly. It is wise to encourage students to also participate in intensive summer camps such as are offered in many areas as "National" or "Regional" music camps plus the camps held on various college or university campuses. These camps can provide superb musical instruction, often at bargain prices.

SUMMER INSTRUMENT INSTRUCTION
_____(Date of Instruction Period)

Please check option selected:

_____Beginning Band ($15.00)

_____Full Program ($25.00)

_____Half Program ($15.00)

_____Full Band only ($6.00)

_____I will be unable to participate in summer band.

Reason_____

If unable to participate, please state reason (Participate, please)

_____

Make checks payable to_____(director or school)_____

Name of Student_____

Address_____

Phone_____

Figure 9-3

INSTRUCTION METHODS

The diversity of instruction can be as varied as the community situation. The examples given here have been successfully used in one-director (plus student assistants) situations. The variety of specialties and available faculty, number of students enrolled, method of financing, and general economic level of the community all greatly influence the diversity and intensity of the program offered. I do favor a program that is more recreational in style, otherwise you can "burn students out" (just as in any other phase of the total program) so that they are "stale" when the busiest season starts in the fall! The following methods are recommended for one director with this purpose in mind.

Beginning Band. Should be restricted to older students (grades 7-9) who have somehow been missed in regular curriculum offerings. Students who agree to transfer instruments for balancing instrumentation should be in this class and possibly be awarded free (or reduced) tuition. The program would have to be (of necessity) quite intensive so as to prepare a student for the level to be entered at the start of school. This would require above-average intelligence and desire, strict attendance and hopefully some previous musical experience or demonstration of talent.

Intermediate Classes. All students who sign up for instrument classes should be assigned to intermediate or advanced level. These classes should be taught in the "master class" method or like a mass private lesson of sorts. The number studying each instrument, available rooms for teaching, and the number of faculty will all greatly influence the material used for study and the amount of individual instruction possible. Classes should at least be divided into woodwinds, brass, and percussion.

Advanced Classes. The better players should be grouped into these classes. The general type of instruction methods and class organization should be similar to that of the intermediate classes; but, of course, the materials used for study will be more advanced and of a more specialized nature. Advanced technique classes should also be offered during the evening hours for those students who wish to study but have daytime jobs. These classes will usually be small enough that a reasonable amount of individual attention can be given.

Music Enrichment. This class can offer a good degree of "specialized" musical knowledge. It can be of particular use to students who plan careers in music. Basic music theory, music composition, notation, transposition, ear training, music history, and form (through records), and also basic conducting can be incorporated into such a course. This type of summer instruction can be especially helpful in situations where such courses cannot be offered during the regular school year.

Full Band. Everyone in the music program should participate in this group. This should at least keep everybody together and in touch with what's going on, and help keep their playing proficiency from deteriorating. The approach should be mostly recreational with light "pop"-type music, and plenty of reading of new, more challenging music. There should be some emphasis on fundamentals and students should be helped in preparation for tryouts and pre-school marching activities. All fundamentals used as a part of playing tryouts for marching band should be reviewed during summer band.

ADDITIONAL PROGRAMS

There are other related summer activities that can be combined with the over-all summer instruction program. Here are a few possibilities:

Majorette Twirling and Field Commander Lessons. The summer is an ideal time for instruction of this sort. Classes should be taught by the best-qualified instructors available. If no other qualified instructors can be found such classes might be taught by an outstanding majorette or drum major from a nearby college or even the senior high specialists themselves.

Fees should be in keeping with the other instruction fees in the program.

Fund Raising. There are several opportunities for fund raising during the summer and some bands prefer this season for such activities. Some fund-raising activities such as car washes, "slave" sales, etc., are well suited for the summer season. If funds are needed for trips during the fall, with this objective in mind, fund raising will have more urgency and consequently more success.

Band Tryouts. Marching band tryouts should be started during the summer. Section leaders can be of considerable assistance in tryouts involving large numbers. If the band is not very large, perhaps both section leaders and director can conduct the tryouts. Such tryouts should demonstrate three capabilities:

1. Knowledge of instrument (scales, etc.)
2. Music memorization (school songs, etc.)
3. Marching ability (marching fundamentals)

Social Activities. Some form of social activities such as picnics, dances, etc., can be scheduled near the end or soon after the summer instruction session is over. Frequently these "socials" can be organized by the band booster club. They can be a big boost to morale that can carry into the fall season.

Marching Camp. A marching band camp can be of value in most situations. Some of the advantages are:

1. Uninterrupted concentration on marching preparation.
2. Prepares the band early for the start of marching season.
3. Solidifies the band through new friendships.
4. Provides enjoyable change of scene.

The marching camps I have been associated with have been very successful in achieving their purpose and were very enjoyable to the students. Some of the problems that must be overcomy include:

1. Selection of site
2. Recruiting competent staff

3. Providing financing

4. Achieving maximum attendance

If such a camp is not deemed necessary, it would be futile to waste time, energy, and money on such a venture. If marching practice held at school prior to the opening of school has not produced the results that you had hoped for, perhaps such a camp can then be of benefit.

Start looking for and securing a site early in the year. State park "group camps," early season 4-H and other club-type camps are a good place to start. Some bands hold their marching camps on the campus of an area college offering adequate facilities. After selecting and securing a site and establishing the dates of the camp, then begin looking for a competent staff. Be most careful in selecting a good dietitian because food is extremely important. Many things can go wrong in a camp (rain, sore muscles, etc.); but if the food is good, other ills are soon forgotten. The dietitian should handle all aspects of food buying, hiring helpers, etc. The camp enrollment number and the amount available to spend on food should be given to the dietitian. In selecting all staff members (chaperones, etc.) be careful to select those who truly enjoy young people. A sour apple can really be a pain to everyone.

Some financing might be provided by the band booster club, but the majority of the funds must usually come from the students. Keep the cost as low as possible without operating an unsuccessful camp. If some student cannot afford camp then perhaps some civic club or local business can provide assistance.

In order to achieve maximum attendance set the date and make it known to parents as soon as possible each spring (state parks reserve camp sites early in the year). If this is done, and students understand the importance of maximum attendance, then there will be very few conflicts arising (vacations, etc.) A week or two prior to the opening of school is usually the best time for such a camp. Schedule a week or so between the summer instruction classes and marching band camp.

Figure 9-4 is a sample letter to parents concerning marching band camp:

CENTRAL HIGH SCHOOL BAND

—————————————

————————— , 19————

Dear Band Parents:

The time for the annual Central High School Band Camp is drawing near. This camp will open August ____ (on Sunday afternoon) and run for 6 days, ending on August _____ (on Saturday afternoon). Our camp last year was a very satisfactory undertaking, and again this year depends on you parents for its success. This camp will be held at

————————————————————.

Enclosed is a daily schedule of camp activities. Swimming will be permitted only during supervised periods. Permission *will not* be granted to leave camp. Counselors will assist in the operation of the camp, and I will secure a large number of parent chaperones before the camp deadline. Every precaution will be taken to insure your child's well-being; but, of course, the school or management cannot assume complete responsibility. I will be happy to discuss any phase of the camp with any of you who wish to learn more about some part of its operations. I am sure you would not like to send your children with us for a week if you were anxious or disturbed about any of the camp's activities.

Please impress upon your children, as I shall, that for their pleasure and the success of the camp, all rules of safety and conduct, which will be outlined to them, *must be strictly* followed. I feel every student in the marching band is reliable and capable of conducting himself properly on all band functions, since that is one of the requirements for membership. However, in case I have over-estimated someone, any infraction of the rules will result in the student concerned being sent back home_____ by bus, the parents being notified of this action by phone.

The staff of the camp will consist of _____, dietitian; _____ chaperone; and registered nurse; (other staff); myself; and my wife. There will also be counselors who

Figure 9-4

were seniors in the band last year. They are ——————,
——————————, ——————————, ——————————, and
——————————————. Also during the week there will be
other visiting band directors who will assist in some of the
instruction. I plan to secure at least———parent chaperones
for the camp.

I sincerely hope that no events will occur this summer
which will prevent anyone from attending this camp, since
maximum attendance is necessary for maximum results. The
fee, which again will be ————————, is for food and food
preparation, close to the amount you would have to spend for
food even if the child stayed home. This meal fee is the only
expense, since the Band Parents' Club pays for the camp rental
and transportation. Only money for incidental purposes need
be brought.

TRANSPORTATION: We will have one school bus going
to and returning from camp. There will be one truck for
carrying large instruments and equipment. Since we will be
carrying ———————— students, ———————— counselors, ————————
chaperones, and a staff of————————,which totals to————————
persons, it will be necessary for several parents to take and
pick up thier children. Perhaps this can be done by one family
taking 2 or 3 children to camp and another picking them up as
has been done in the past. Each person will be responsible for
all of his personal and musical equipment. Please make an
effort to get your child to camp by car.

DEPARTURE TIMES: ————————————————————
——————————————————————————————————
——————————————————————————————————

HOW TO GET THERE: ————————————————————
——————————————————————————————————
——————————————————————————————————
——————————————————————————————————

PARENTS AND ALUMNI OF THE BAND will be
welcomed as visitors, but band members *will not* be excused
from camp routine nor allowed *to leave camp premises.* There

Figure 9-4 (cont.)

are a few overnight facilities available for visitors at the camp if you have your own bedroll, etc.

CLOTHING: Clothing for all occasions—completely casual, such as shorts, blue jeans, levis, etc. No dress clothes, please. *Bermuda* shorts or jeans are required for marching: no short shorts please. Be sure to include 2 pairs of comfortable shoes for marching, a warm jacket (cool nights very common), a rain coat, sun cap, and swim suit. No laundry facilities except as you might improvise.

WHAT TO BRING: Bed linens, 2 blankets, pillow, towels, wash clothes, toilet articles, 2 pencils, paper and instrument in good condition with plenty of oil, reeds, etc. for it. If so desired, bring—camera, games, flashlight, stationery and postage, portable radio, heaters, or other stunt night and cabin equipment.

*MAILING ADDRESS DURING CAMP:*_____

_____

HEALTH STATEMENT: Written by family doctor (basically an examination for any communicable diseases or physical defects that would limit their camp activities) to be turned in with camp application. This statement may be returned if you need it for anything else.

PLEASE SIGN THE STATEMENT BELOW AND RETURN TO ME WITH THE MEAL FEE AND HEALTH STATEMENT BY _____. KEEP THIS LETTER FOR REFERENCE.

Sincerely,

Director of Bands
Central High School

Phone:_____
Address:_____

—————————————————————————————————————

STATEMENT
(To be returned)

_____, 19____

I have read the letter concerning the Central High School Band Camp to be held at _____, August _____, 19____,

Figure 9-4 (cont.)

and give my consent for _____ to attend.
This relieves the band camp and faculty of legal responsibility.

                                    _____
                                    Signature of parent or guardian

Check List
_____Health Statement
_____Camp meal fee
Checks payable to: Central High Band Camp
                   Check One:
                   My child will go to and return from
                   camp by car_____
                   My child will need bus transportation
                   _____

                   Other arrangements_____

_____

Figure 9-4 (cont.)

The secret of successful camps (as well as trips) is to keep
students occupied with constructive activity a majority of the
time. Here is a sample camp schedule and a few basic rules.

DAILY SCHEDULE
Central High Band Camp
(All times on daylight savings time)
  7:00 A.M. . . . . Reveille
  7:20 A.M.* . . . . Physical fitness on marching field
  7:40 A.M. Breakfast
  8:10 A.M. . . . . Prepare for inspection
  8:30 A.M. . . . Assemble for morning drill (cabins will
                              be inspected during drill)
  9:30 A.M. . . . . .10-minute water break
 10:30 A.M. . . . . Recreation (no boating *except in the
                                            morning)*
 12:00 noon* . . . . Lunch
 12:30 P.M. Rest Hour
  1:30 P.M.* . . . . Music rehearsal
  2:30 P.M. . . . Break for sectional rehearsal (optional full
                                      band continued)
  3:30 P.M. . . . . Recreation (no boats)
  4:30 P.M.* . . . . Supper
  5:30 P.M.* . . . . Fall in for evening drill (with instruments)

7:15 P.M.	Report to quarters—free time
8:00 P.M.*	Evening recreation
10:00 P.M.	Report to cabins
10:10 P.M.	Cabin checks
10:20 P.M.	Cabin devotional
10:30 P.M.	LIGHTS OUT—*COMPLETE SILENCE*
10:35 P.M.	Taps

---

*Bugle will sound 5 minutes ahead of time

CAMP RULES

1. All boating to be done on morning recreation time. Boats must have life preservers worn by each person in the boat.
2. No noise after lights out (this means noise that would disturb other cabins: talking quietly allowed). Punishment: 15 minutes double-time marching and 15 minutes attention. Constant trouble-makers will be sent home.
3. No alchoholic beverages or drug abuse of any type tolerated. Punishment: Offender sent home immediately, dismissed from marching band.
4. No smoking inside the cabins. Smoke outside if you want, but not in the cabins. Same punishment as noise after lights out.
5. No one around waterfront after lights out. Offenders will be sent home.
6. Anyone late for any event—two laps around camp area road. If there is a second offense—stand at attention entire rest hour.
7. Swimmers must stay within designated area and comply with all swimming regulations or stay out of the waterfront area.

To conclude a marching camp, a short marching demonstration (or show) for parents and visitors at the morning the camp closes works nicely. This also gives the students a short-term goal to work toward during the week. The ultimate goal of a camp should be uniform mastery of marching fundamentals by the band, plus the learning of a football show or two.

Practical Guidelines for

PUBLIC PERFORMANCES 10
AND TRIPS

PERFORMANCE OBJECTIVES

Public performance should be an outgrowth of a quality music education program. If this policy is conscientiously followed, public performances will be paced just as wisely as other aspects of the program. Remember our statement "public performance is the lifeblood of music—unless you bleed the subject to death." Among the many interrelated objectives that performance should seek are:

1. Enlightenment through entertainment of your audience.
2. Encouragement of quality "programming" and quality performance.
3. Providing a goal for relevant teaching.
4. Promoting love and appreciation of music through artistic emotional release.
5. Presenting performances that emphasize enchantment rather than endurance.
6. Offering viable proof of the significance of music education.
7. Promoting continued interest and enthusiasm for music.

Needless to say this list could go on as far as the individual can imagine, with such axioms as: individual poise and self-esteem; service to school, community, and country; worthwhile leisure time; out-of-town trips favorably projecting the image of the town; etc., ad infinitum. All of these lofty phrases can be very true, but keep in mind that all you have to do to stop them "cold-in-their-tracks," to negate every positive axiom, is— perform badly!

For this reason public performance must be paced for the entire program and each separate organization as well. At every stage of development and during every day of the year there should be something to look forward to, or else frustrating "stagnation" can set in. For this reason a director must formulate an interesting, active, educational, but not exhaustive annual schedule of events. This schedule should be followed as closely as possible year after year, with exchanges and adjustments in the schedule that are deemed necessary.

PERFORMANCE SCHEDULES

Well before the heat of the fall begins, set aside some time to formulate a framework or criteria for decisions regarding public performances. Use a calendar of events from the previous year as a basis for beginning. Consider options in the light of criteria something like:

1. contribution to school and community
2. possible music education inherent in preparation
3. enjoyment and emotional release for band
4. tradition and prestige of the band
5. professional growth afforded

Next prepare an outline of monthly events. If the system is taught by one director, make a "schedule of events" outline for every group. If the director is also a supervisor of several instructors, then he should formulate such a schedule of events for the groups he conducts and make recommendations for the entire program. Such an outline might be:

PUBLIC PERFORMANCES

Beginning Band: Two, possibly three performances a year of the concert type. These might include one or two simple tunes on a school Christmas concert, another appearance for P.T.A. or student body, and a combined band appearance with other area schools in the spring festival.

Advanced Elementary Band: Same performance schedule as beginning band with the possible addition of some solo or ensemble appearances for civic club or school club meetings. These elementary concerts should be shared with the beginning band. The advanced elementary band will naturally perform selections of increased difficulty.

Intermediate Band: Since there will be some instrument changes and adjustments, this group should not perform in public before approximately mid-year. Performances could include a portion of a Christmas concert, a portion of a mid-winter concert, and participation in a spring festival or combined concert. Solo and ensemble appearances on a limited basis.

Junior High Band: Performances will be more diversified to include:

SUMMER—Participation in summer instruction program

FALL—marching band limited activity (for 9th grade band), "in the stands" playing for home football games, possibly one simple football halftime show, one civic parade and a visit to a marching festival.

WINTER—combined-type Christmas concert, one late winter independent concert, a P.T.A. or student body concert.

SPRING—concert competition festival participation, and a spring combined concert. Solos and ensembles should continue; stage band should be introduced; and ninth graders urged to participate in clinics, honor bands, and solo and ensemble competitions.

Senior High Band: The senior high band should offer a relatively complete schedule of public performances. In order to effectively perform at these varied events it takes considerable planning and organization if the student's time is not to be infringed upon (an unfortunately frequent occurrence). This annual schedule could include:

> SUMMER—summer instruction program, one summer concert (unless there is a municipal band also), marching band camp (or pre-school marching).
>
> FALL—football shows at home and two away games, necessary civic parades, marching festivals and contests (two well-spaced appearances should suffice), possible use of solos or chamber music for civic or school clubs.
>
> WINTER—combined Christmas concert, All-Region and All-State band tryouts, winter concert (or start of concert series), solo and ensemble festival, chamber music concert.
>
> SPRING—area (state) concert competition festivals, school concerts or concert tour, All-State band, combined spring concert, possible graduation participation.

All performances should be discussed well in advance with the school administration (principal)—then dates cleared and recorded on the school activity calendar. Be especially careful in the justification of events that will cause students to miss regular classes. Remember—accept requests in order of importance to school, community, profession, and fun or prestige. All events should be handled in such a way as to derive whatever education and interest values that can be achieved.

The dates of community, state, and professional events are quite varied from locale to locale. This factor has the tendency to influence the performance schedule of the band considerably.

Here are a few additional performance ideas that may be worked in with good effect:

Area Music Festivals: The scope of such events depends on the intent of the performance. They can range from a region or city "Honor Band" to a single complete band program with all phases of instruction (and all students) being represented in performance. There are certain merits to all approaches but we will concern ourselves here with the local school system. Two good seasons for such area music festivals are Christmas and late spring. If not properly organized and limited to a few selections from each group (with a minimum of stage changes) such events can easily turn into musical (?) marathons. With a couple of selections from each group most of the positive advantages can be realized without the possible devastation of your audience occurring.

Concert Series: With a very fine senior high band or in larger situations where two or more concert bands may be involved, there is a good opportunity for a concert series. A few approaches such as theme-type concerts might be tried. Concerts might be made up of:

1. original band literature
2. band transcriptions
3. Broadway musicals
4. pops concerts
5. international favorites
6. featured soloists
7. chamber music concert

There can be considerable good music education opportunities in preparing study plans for such concerts, then having the concerts be a natural outgrowth of your teaching.

Musical Show: There are very fine musicals written for high school age students now. These musicals can be the co-operative work of several specialist instructors (speech, vocal, etc.), or can be put on entirely by the band director. If a good understanding with confident, well-adjusted instructors is developed at the outset of such a venture, then all will be bright and fair. If such a working agreement is not possible then "there's trouble ahead." I have found in most cases musicals written for this age group are better received than are "watered-down"

Broadway musicals. I must admit that I have seen some good Broadway-type musicals performed also, but they are by far the exception rather than the rule, and do not usually justify the amount of preparation time required.

Variety Shows: Variety or talent shows have a great deal of popularity especially when they are expanded to include the entire student body. The stage band can serve as the basic musical unit for the accompaniments and features. A format of available talent can be designed similar to any of the popular television variety shows. Frequently the great disadvantage is the amount of work (arranging, rehearsing "raw" talent, etc.) that is required. If a director's talents and inclination lead him in this direction, however, these shows can become very popular annual events.

Exchange Concerts: Many bands have found that exchange concerts offer a means of enjoyable musical events. These trips can even be developed into short annual tours that are not extremely expensive. Most are arranged by directors who seek out similar music programs in not too distant areas and then propose an exchange concert. Expenses are held to a minimum since students stay in the homes of the "exchange" students. The major expense is transportation. Such trips must be handled very tactfully, with full school administrative approval; but students tend to enjoy meeting new friends and come to eagerly look forward to such events.

PERFORMANCE PREPARATION

There are many more roles inherent in the title of band director than most people ever realize. Almost in order the basics are: organizer-teacher-conductor. A good musician with a good teaching personality and a flair for conducting can be a flop as a "director" unless he knows or learns how to organize. I have seen some very good organizers who were not very good musicians or conductors who were quite "competent" as directors"; however, their work tends to reach a plateau of high mediocrity and level off. They don't completely "flop"; most keep their jobs and hopefully improve their musicianship.

A systematic method of arranging concerts will work for most directors. Since no one can keep everything in his head and still have thinking power left for teaching, I suggest making check-off lists and dutifully using them. We will take the major performance categories and recommend some systematic manner of approach.

Marching Shows: As in all basic categories of performance consider the reasons for, and the conditions of the performance. This season of the year is one of the busiest, and how it "comes off" is largely dependent on student preparation with marching and playing fundamentals, and how well the shows are designed and taught. That's common sense, isn't it—yet how many bands really do this? Competent teaching is necessary all through the lower grades as we have described at length in this book. The pre-school marching, either at camp or at home, serves as a refresher course and final check on fundamentals, and then the shows begin. Most football shows can be categorized as:

1. Pageantry
2. Military or precision drill
3. Feature or variety show type

1. *Pageantry.* Many high school bands make a mistake imitating large university bands and their pageantry-type shows. Most H.S. stadiums do not afford the spectator anything like the same viewing perspective of the field. Outside of block-type numerals and letters, most formations (even good ones in a high school stadium) are dependent upon the P.A. announcer for identification.

2. *Military or precision drill.* Few bands can learn and master more than one complete show of marching drill a year. It is my opinion that the average football fan wants more variety than this.

3. *Feature or variety show-type half-times* are usually popular at home but what about marching festivals and contests? What to do?! Take the relevant best from each and artistically

combine, that's what. Use a definite formula or format and add a drill each show until you have your marching festival show complete and have presented three shows that have all contained new, entertaining material. It takes considerable planning and foresight but it's worth it. Here's basically how such a procedure can work:

FIRST SHOW

ENTRANCE (precision drill—learned during pre-school marching—use all year.)
PRESENTATION (can be presentation of colors, field commander salute or announcements)
FEATURE FORMATION (form a concert formation using drill techniques, feature majorettes, drill team, various sections, soloists, trios, etc.)

If so desired, concert formation can be inverted to the opposite of field and features presented there also. The formation of the block-type school letters and possibly the school Alma Mater could top off a pleasing show.

SECOND SHOW

ENTRANCE (same entrance polished more)
PRESENTATION (same with possibly a fanfare added)
CENTER DRILL (a flashy or "show-off"-type drill added to go with the first two segments of the complete drill show being developed)
FEATURE FORMATION (a concert formation similar to the first show, but with different feature selection)

Again this feature or concert-type formation could be inverted and features played to the opposite side of the field (only if needed).

THIRD SHOW

ENTRANCE (same, but improved)
PRESENTATION (same, but improved)
CENTER DRILL (same, but improved)
CONCERT (same feature formation, new selection played)
EXIT (final drill can be sideline or end-zone exit)

A show suitable for marching festival or contest would now be complete. The feature-type formation could be used as a "staging" formation from which simple pageantry-type formations could be formed to add to impact a selection, present homecoming court, etc. For the final shows of the year, the band could again return to more "features" for variety as the weather becomes less suitable for marching.

If you do not have a system of marching fundamentals, get A.R. Cassavants' first book, aptly entitled *Precision Drill,* and use personal innovations and preference from there. Marching shows can be quickly taught either orally or by charting (depending on size of group) if a complete system of marching fundamentals is utilized.

For purposes of unity and timing, a good music line-up for each show should be formulated. Prepare these music line-ups well in advance of marching season. Keep the time of the shows between five and seven minutes. Figure the time from the tempo (M.M. 120 is two beats per second, etc.) multiplied by the number of beats in the selection; i.e., 64 beats at M.M. 120 = 32 seconds performance time. Allow time for announcements, etc. A good music line-up has continuity, contrast (or change of pace), and a climax. To achieve this, consider each tune from the standpoint of dramatic and emotional impact, identity (school, patriotic, tradition, etc.), key change (especially between tunes), predominate style, purpose, unusual effects, and difficulty (endurance, etc.) Study music line-ups that impress you and try to analyze why they are good. As was mentioned for concerts, a thematic approach can be a good source of ideas—tunes from a popular musical, a patriotic show, songs from across the sea, etc. Some groups have good success with a similar music line-up from year to year, based again on the format-type approach with new tunes filling old purposes and improvements being made in older arrangements.

After figuring your music "line-up" start to search for the arrangements you want. Try to find good published arrangements (more good arrangements are appearing all the time) and if none are available, then try to get an arrangement done for you (if you are unable to arrange or re-score your own music try to learn. Ralph Muchler has a good book entitled *How To Arrange for Marching and Pep Bands*. There are also good books to help you get started.) Be careful to secure permission due to copyright laws. Most publishers do not object if:

1. there is no available arrangement
2. you do not seek personal gain from the arrangement

Many tunes are in the realm of "common domain" *but be sure*—it can be sticky!

Civic Parades: Even though there is not nearly as much emphasis on street parades today as there once was, they are nonetheless very important. Many people will form their opinion of the band on the impression presented in parades. Here are a few suggestions for parade marching:

1. Use 30-inch (military step) stride (or 6 to 5 yard marching).
2. Emphasize rank and file alignment (use right guides).
3. Use diagonals to check spacing.
4. Use military signals and maneuvers (column movements, etc.)
5. Play one (possibly two) medium length selections, with only short drum cadence interlude where there are concentrations of people (no one hears you play more

than once in a parade). For sparse spectator areas include longer drum interludes.

6. Memorize music.
7. Maintain strict discipline in carriage and demeanor at all times.

Street parade competition routines should be approached in the same manner as football shows but on a more limited scale (like a "mini" half-time show).

Public Concerts: Concerts, like other performances, should be the natural result of good preparation, good teaching, and finishing touches: in short, the outgrowth of good music education. After all this work it is important to have a good audience that has an enjoyable time because of your performance. All of us know this, but few plan effectively enough to bring together all details and produce a sterling performance.

Music: Please keep the connotation *"public"* in mind. This important word indicates that we should use our musical taste to select music that will allow every member of the audience to really enjoy at least one selection. It is very important that the music be of a quality that can be enjoyed by both conductor and student *plus* offering something worth teaching; but do not overlook the general audience. All too often musicians tend to do things to impress each other rather than enlighten and entertain their audiences. Just as every rehearsal should have both concentrated serious moments and lighter, even humorous moments—so should a concert. Consider these factors in the selection of music:

1. *Format.* The over-all program should reflect unity (or continuity), contrast (or variety), and climax (dramatic, emotional, or brilliant virtuosity). There are many means (and media) of balancing and using these elements, but all artistic endeavor must work with them to some degree.

2. *Inherent teaching opportunities.* Frequently music should be selected primarily for the aesthetic value it has. That is why I disagree with people who get "arty" about bands

within the framework of music education. Use only music written for band and you eliminate centuries of fine music. I feel there is no sacrilege inherent in band transcriptions. It is true that in some cases compositions can lose flavor in transcription, but only a few cases exist where *all* the works of a composer are unsuitable. (Consider the number of contemporary composers who have the same composition available for orchestra, band, and frequently even condensations for piano.)

3. *Feature and showmanship potential.* Selections that feature soloists or sections tend to inspire increased interest and improvement. Consider possible lighting, staging, and novelty effects that can be coordinated with a particular selection. Most selections in this category tend to be light, "flashy," or humorous.

4. *Technical and endurance demands.* Do not make the mistake of scheduling too many difficult selections, and then ending up performing all of them in a mediocre to poor fashion. Use only two (no more than three) selections of the grade of difficulty you plan to play at contest. It is ulcer time when you rehearse separate numbers daily and try them all in order a week before the concert, only to find the group "wasted" with two numbers to go.

5. *Weight and effect of each selection.* People use funny terms to describe music. For example, they say heavy or light music (serious or trivial), dark or bright, (somber or gay), etc. All of us have a general common body of more or less conditioned responses to different "types" of music. These should influence the program order according to how we wish to arrange artistic elements we mentioned in number 1.

Program Order: The number of participating groups (one or more), the mediums represented (vocal, orchestra, band, etc.), the general "taste" of the audience, the occasion, length of concert, the auditorium, etc.—all of these affect program order. Without attempting to touch on all possibilities, here is my favored program design:

NATIONAL ANTHEM—(somewhat dependent on the occasion: presentation of colors can be incorporated).

STIRRING "ROUSER"—(a march, fanfare, or grand march)

WORTHY "HEAVY"—(overture, fine transcription, or major work for band)

EFFERVESCENT—(virtuoso solo, ensemble feature, or novelty)

LEAVE-EM-LONGING—(brilliant original, or selection written for the dance)

INTERMISSION—(10 to 15 minutes in length)

SHOCKING "GRABBER"—(fast march, impressive virtuoso-type selection)

CHANGE OF PACE—(tone poem, "heavy" solo, or ensemble)

AMERICAN "THEATRIC"—(selections from theatre, movies, pop music, etc.)

CLINCHING "HEAVY"—(overture with stirring finale, dramatic work for band)

ENCORE—(light classic, stirring march, good "pop" tune)

For concerts involving several groups consider these factors:

1. Order of appearance according to ability and experience of groups (weakest to strongest)
2. contrast in groups (vocal, instrumental, etc.)
3. use as much uniformity of set-up as possible (have stage set up for largest group)
4. work for unity and variety in musical selections (as in any other concert)
5. no intermission should be necessary (time between stage changes will be sufficient—be efficient!)
6. consider a combined finale-type selection for the climax ending of the program.

Publicity—Management: There are so many small details involved in concerts, musicals, and other events that it is wise to make a "check-off" list, and secure as much responsible assistance as is deemed necessary. Assistance for preparation could include:

1. Publicity committee
2. Ticket committee
3. Decoration committee
4. Correspondence committee

Assistance in presenting the concert should include:

1. "Set-up" crew
2. "Lighting" crew
3. "Sound" crew
4. Ticket takers
5. Ushers
6. Clean-up committee

In concerts where more than one group is invloved, there might need to be an adult assistant or student leader to sit with each group to insure proper concert conduct (elementary bands). Student assistants who normally assist in tuning with an electronic tuner should be on duty well before the time for warm-up for the concert.

SAMPLE CONCERT CHECK LIST

Six Weeks Before Concert
Music Selections Decided _____   Programs Ordered_____
Tickets Ordered_____   Committees Set_____

Four Weeks Before Concert
Check with Publicity Committee on:
Posters_____   News Releases to:
Bulletin Boards_____   Radio_____
Newspaper Articles_____   Television_____
Check with Ticket Committee on:
Handing Out Tickets   Ticket Sales Downtown___
    To Students_____
Ticket Sales in School Office_____

Two Weeks Before Concert
Have Committees:

Mail Complimentary Tickets_____   Take Photos for Paper_____
Distribute Posters_____   Send Final News Releases_____

Check Details with Crews and Individuals on:

Set-up_____   Sound (Recording)
Tuning_____   Curtain Cues_____
Lighting_____   Decoration_____

One Week Before Concert

Pick Up Programs_____   Distribute Concert Details _
Finalize Ticket Sales   (for participating students)
Final News Releases_____   Rehearse in Auditorium_____
Contact Photographer_____

Night Before Concert
Dress Rehearsal_____
Programs to Head Usher_____
Final Check With:

Set-Up Crew_____   Curtain Cues_____
Lighting_____   Sound_____
   (recording check at dress
   rehearsal)

The information given to students should include:

1. Time to warm up and tune
2. Uniform to be worn
3. What to do with cases (if necessary)
4. Exit and entrance points (if necessary)
5. Auditorium seating area (if necessary)

As many rehearsals as possible in the performance auditorium (or gym) should be held. The director should check balance and general effect while the band is conducted by the student conductor. Complete instructions on staging, acknowledgement of applause, etc. should be included as in performance.

It is very important to the director that sufficient assistants be informed and on the job to avoid disruptive problems right before a performance.

Competition—Festivals: Many professional band and

orchestra directors' associations sponsor festivals for marching, solo and ensemble, and concert performance. These are generally held for elementary, junior, and senior high levels. Such events are sometimes sponsored by civic associations and colleges or universities. Whatever the event, before entering, check the following:

1. What are the requirements of this event?
2. What are the standards of performance in the class where your group will compete?
3. Approximately how will your group rate in this competition?
4. Is the group ready for this competition, and what are the possible advantages and disadvantages?

Each director must decide what to do in a given situation, but I have always found more to be gained from competition than lost. We will not delve into the pros and cons of such events here—suffice it to say that most detrimental factors are generally due to the inept or unethical approach that directors can take toward such an event. The attitude and approach of a director predetermines the positive or negative effect on his students.

Marching: Some discussion regarding preparation for marching festivals has already been given. The contest routine should be presented in public at least once before the festival. If inspection is a part of the festival, then check the following:

INSPECTION SHEET

I.   Uniforms
      A. Coats
         1. proper fit
         2. cleaned and pressed
         3. in good repair with all buttons and accessories
      B. Trousers
         1. proper length
         2. cleaned and pressed
         3. in good repair

C. Hats or Shakos
    1. worn straight
    2. clean visor and strap
    3. in good repair

D. Accessories (belts, gloves, socks, cords, medals, etc.)
    1. properly worn
    2. cleaned and polished
    3. in good repair

II.   Instruments
    A. Woodwinds
        1. pads, corks, and springs in good condition
        2. cleaned and oiled
        3. reed, ligature, and mouthpiece in good condition
    B. Brass
        1. cleaned and oiled
        2. valves and slides in good working condition
        3. mouthpiece in good condition
        4. corks, felts, and springs in good condition
        5. all major dents removed
    C. Percussion
        1. tension screws lubricated
        2. clean heads in good condition and properly tuned.
        3. chrome and pearl cleaned and polished
        4. proper sticks in good condition
        5. clean straps

III.   Personal Appearance
    A. no jewelry
    B. minimum amount of make-up
    C. neat haircuts (girls put hair above collar)
    D. clean nails
    E. good shave for boys

IV.   General Information
    A. know instrument brand and serial number
    B. know transposition and range of instrument
    C. present instrument in a military manner
    D. respond to questions in a military manner
    E. do not move the eyes or head while being inspected

Concert: Here again, a big part of preparing for a concert festival is the same as preparing for a concert and should be approached in the same manner. Of course the criteria for performance are much more intense. Special attention must be given to sight reading preparation but most other factors are the same. Here are some of the considerations that are particularly relevant:

1. Select music carefully well in advance. Select music to enhance the group. Emphasize strong sections and cover any weakness as much as possible.

2. Study the adjudicator's sheet to be used in the festival. As soon as selections are played well enough to record them, study tapes and make evaluations in each category. Invite associates to make similar criticisms: they may notice things you have come to ignore.

3. Use all rehearsal techniques that are recommended for correcting any difficulties noted. Many of these are included in Chapter 6.

4. As a last resort, rescore and simplify parts that are not being played well. Rewrite parts for stronger instruments that sound similar (think of how instruments that sound similar are often cued). Simplify runs and especially difficult technical passages.

5. Cut out players who present intonation and balance problems in delicate "transparent" passages. Sometimes it is unrealistic to expect several young players to be able to play a particular "exposed" pitch in tune. One can frequently do the job better.

6. Appearance and behavior are very important factors. Remember that adjudicators are just human beings with specialized talents and training. The same factors that favorably affect others will also affect them.

Solo and Ensemble: Most of the preparation for solo and ensemble festivals should be done through private and section instruction. If such instruction is not available, some of the methods suggested in Chapter 5 may be of help until a private lesson program is established. It is helpful to have soloists and the various ensembles perform before the band prior to participating in these events. This gives them the advantage of performing under pressure and making possible relevant discussion concerning their presentation.

PERFORMANCE PSYCHOLOGY

What are the factors that cause some individuals to perform better than they usually play and others to simply go to pieces?   I suppose that few people can really pinpoint the exact causes, but here are a few tips that have been of use in helping both individuals and groups.

FOR INDIVIDUAL PERFORMANCE:

1. Consider performance a normal part of learning an instrument. If you will note we have recommended solo playing from the beginning level on.

2. Explain that all performers have a certain degree of nervousness before performances. The good performers learn to use this energy in helping them play even better.

3. Explain that the time to worry is well before the performance, when it will do some good. Concern should initiate practice, and once you are sure you have left no "stone unturned" in preparing for a performance don't worry about it—it won't do any good. Frequently, nervous players are ill-prepared players.

4. Reassure students who need it; prod those who need that. (Every student has individual problems and achievements all his own: that's part of the joy and challenge of teaching).

FOR GROUP PERFORMANCE:

Many of the same factors discussed concerning individuals also apply to groups as well. Groups, however, tend to be more influenced by the actions and attitudes of the director. If the director is confident and well prepared, the group tends to be the same. Here are a few tips on achieving the best from a group in performance:

1. Act out all the actions to be taken by a group prior to the performance. The same type of "role" thinking we discussed in Chapter 2 can be of use in keeping "cool" when potentially upsetting situations occur just before a performance (getting lost, locked doors, etc.)
2. Allow enough time so as not to be rushed, but delays that cause "draggy" boredom should be avoided.
3. At festivals, do most of your listening after your performance. Groups tend to overrate others and berate themselves into a shaky lack of confidence.
4. A short prayer before performance (in private) is a great settling influence with some groups.
5. Often a funny remark or even some "corny" joke can help relax a group just before a performance. They are often desperately searching for something to break the tension.

BAND TRIPS

Whether the trip is a short one to an "away" football game or a big national event, there are many factors to consider:

1. Transportation
2. Meals
3. Financing
4. Equipment
5. Housing (overnight trips only)

6. Rules and supervision
7. Legal responsibility

Transportation: For most events, buses furnished by a reputable company seem to be the best bet. All transportation is expensive. To get the best prices, competitive bids are the thing.

Meals: Food must of necessity be the responsibility of the individual. Ample funds in Travelers' Cheques or similar "safe" currency should be taken by each student.

Financing: Total cost of a big trip should be figured, then divided by the number of students going. All fund raising should be prorated against this individual cost so that each does his fair share or pays the difference. This method entails considerable record keeping, but it is necessary and it works.

Equipment: A complete check-list of all necessary equipment should be compiled by the director and managers and used on all trips.

Housing: Should be very near the major activity area of the event you are attending. Of course the best accomodations for the most reasonable cost should be the goal.

Rules: Here are a few rules that may be relevant:

1. Two students should share a suitcase due to limited space available on the buses.
2. Casual clothing in good taste is allowed en route.
3. Do not change buses.
4. Limited clothing on hangers may be hung in the rear of the bus.
5. Property managers will be in charge of loading and unloading plus handling heavy equipment.
6. Each band member is responsible for his instrument and luggage.
7. Each student must tag all personal and musical equipment.

Supervision: Student officers and parent chaperones

should provide supervision with the director retaining final decision-making authority.

Legal Responsibility: A release similar to the one listed in Figure 10-1 should be filled out and turned in by each student:

LEGAL RELEASE

To Return With Money For Trip

I have read the letter concerning the Central High School Band's Orange Bowl Trip to Miami from December 27, 19_____ to January 4, 19_____, and agree to abide by all rules and suggestions made by persons in charge of this trip.

Signed_____
                        Student

I have read the letter concerning the Central High School Band's Orange Bowl Trip to Miami from December 27, 19_____ to January 4, 19_____, and give my consent for _____ to participate. This hereby relieves Central High School, its faculty, and the chaperones of all legal responsibility.

Signed_____
                        Parent or guardian

Medical Information:

Last tetanus booster given_____
                                              (date)

Blood type_____
Any allergies that student is known to have:

_____

Any reaction to penicillin or sulfa drugs or other medications:

_____

Who to contact in case of any emergency:

_____   _____
name   phone

Figure 10-1

All student officers and related committees should work on the planning and successful organization of big trips. The director, as in other matters, is in charge with final decisions, etc.

Figure 10-2 is the complete itinerary of a very worthwhile and successful trip. This schedule is representative of the planning that is necessary for such an event.

The bus company reserved the places to eat en route; we traveled express. Housing was obtained relatively inexpensively in dormitories on the campus of Miami Military Academy.

ITINERARY AND DAILY SCHEDULE
FOR C. H. S. BAND ORANGE BOWL TRIP

December 27

Load buses at high school band room	11:00 a.m. (CST)
Leave Murfreesboro	12:30 p.m. (CST)
Rest stop in Chattanooga	3:45 p.m. EST)
Evening meal in Atlanta (EST time here on)	6:30 p.m.
Arrive in Macon	9:45 p.m.

December 28

Rest stop in Waycross	1:30 a.m.
Breakfast in Daytona	5:00 a.m.
Cape Kennedy Tour	8:00 a.m.
Noon meal in Orlando	11:15 a.m.
Arrive in Cypress Gardens	1:30 p.m.
Arrive Miami Military Academy	7:30 p.m.
Evening meal in Miami	8:00 p.m.
Room check and lights out	10:00 p.m.

December 29

Reveille	7:00 a.m.
Breakfast	7:30 a.m.
Marching rehearsal for Jr. Orange Bowl Parade	9:00 a.m.
(room inspection during marching rehearsal each day)	
Change into uniforms for parade	10:30 a.m.
Light lunch	11:00 a.m.

Figure 10-2

Leave for parade in Coral Gables	12:00 noon
Back to Academy	3:00 p.m.
Room check and lights out	10:00 p.m.

December 30

Reveille	7:00 a.m.
Breakfast	7:30 a.m.
Rehearse for King Orange Parade	8:30 a.m.
Leave for Greyline Tour (lunch may be obtained on tour)	9:45 a.m.
Back to Academy	6:30 p.m.
Evening meal	7:00 p.m.
Room check and lights out	11:00 p.m.

December 31

Reveille	8:00 a.m.
Breakfast	8:30 a.m.
Final rehearsal for King Orange Parade	9:30 a.m.
Free time (shopping, sightseeing, lunch)	10:30 a.m.
Be back at Academy	2:30 p.m.
Dress for King Orange Parade	3:00 p.m.
Evening meal (light food)	3:30 p.m.
Leave for King Orange Parade	4:45 p.m.
Parade forms	5:30 p.m.
Back at Academy	9:30 p.m.
New Years eve party for group	10:00 p.m.
Room check and lights out	1:00 a.m.

January 1

Reveille	8:30 a.m.
Breakfast	9:30 a.m.
Church services	10:30 a.m.
Noon meal	12:00 noon

Afternoon free for tours (Museum of Science, Museum of Art, Miami Wax Museum, Garden of Our Lord, etc.)

Evening meal	6:00 p.m.
Assemble at Bayfront Park Bandshell	7:30 p.m.
Program—"Sunday Evening Under the Stars"	

Figure 10-2 (cont.)

Back to Academy	9:00 p.m.
Room check and lights out	10:00 p.m.

January 2

Reveille	7:30 a.m.
Breakfast	8:00 a.m.
Leave for day at Crandon Park (beach and zoo)	9:30 a.m.
Back to Academy	4:00 p.m.
Evening meal	4:45 p.m.
Leave for Orange Bowl Classic	6:00 p.m.
Back to Academy	10:30 p.m.
Room check and lights out	11:00 p.m.

January 3

Reveille	8:00 a.m.
Breakfast	9:00 a.m.
Pack and load buses	10:30 a.m.
Leave Miami	12:00 noon
Arrive at Fort Lauderdale—lunch	12:30 p.m.
Evening meal in Orlando	6:30 p.m.
Rest stop at Valdosta	12:30 a.m.

January 4

Arrive in Macon	4:00 a.m.
Rest stop in Atlanta	5:30 a.m.
Breakfast in Chattanooga	8:45 a.m.
ARRIVE IN MURFREESBORO	11:30 a.m. (CST)

Figure 10-2 (cont.)

If the "pacing plus preparation" that is outlined in this book is followed, then combined with the talent that is in every school, performance can be a tremendously satisfying experience. Without the exhilaration that can come from fine performance, music is lacklustre for both performer and audience. Once your students experience the satisfied fatigue that comes from full, sustained effort yielding the attainment of a worthy goal, they are a long way down the road of a rewarding life.

CONCLUSION

In this book, we have outlined procedures and practices that have achieved many of the personal and performance goals our profession embodies. The ideas we have offered come from a variety of experiences and innumerable fine teachers. Essentially, every personality is a melting pot of ideas and values acquired from associates and personal, innovative ideas that come from the great unknown. Many of the charts and outlines are intended as material to be referred to year after year. We sincerely hope you find the book useful and thought-provoking.

INDEX

INDEX

D

E

G

H

I

M

Q

R

W